Making the Most of Marriage

ACC SOCIOLOGY SERIES

John F. Cuber, *editor*

Alfred C. Clarke, *associate editor*

APPLETON-CENTURY-CROFTS

Educational Division

MEREDITH CORPORATION

New York

Making the Most of Marriage

PAUL H. LANDIS

Washington State University

FOURTH EDITION

Preface

This revision continues, with somewhat greater emphasis, to deal with the underlying factors which predetermine success or failure in marriage: developmental psychological and sociological factors which affect one's capacity to love; role conceptions, which have become so important in the adjustment of male and female; psychosexual orientation, from the initial process of sex identification to the sex drives of male and female as factors in the marriage bond.

There is somewhat greater emphasis, too, on the initial processes of socialization and of love deprivation as they affect personality and ability to realize a secure relationship in marriage. Somewhat less attention is given to dating, with which college students have already had considerable experience. Emphasis is placed, rather, on marriage problems: sexual adjustment, handling finances, parenthood, child training, marriage failure, and post-divorce adjustment as it affects mates and their children. Because of a relative lack of significance to college students and space limitations, the chapter on the later phases of the life cycle and that dealing with the unmarried adult have been omitted.

The tone remains that of optimistic realism. The aim is to be frank, objective, research-oriented, problem-conscious, and helpful to students. Treatment of subject matter is designed to be functional, rather than theoretical and conceptual, to help students understand themselves and the opposite sex and their mutual involvement—the source of much of their concern and of many of the problems of which they are most aware.

The autobiographical outline for self-analysis, which so many students have found helpful, some even therapeutic, is retained in the Appendix, as also are citations to books of readings in the chapter bibliographies. These readings make possible study of a wide range of topics and points of view. Audio-visual suggestions are in the Teacher's Manual rather than the text.

Since the previous edition, discussion with several colleagues has been particularly helpful: Dr. Victor A. Christopherson, Chairman of the Department of Child Development and Family Relations at the University of Arizona; Carol L. Stone, Lecturer in Family Life in the School of Home Economics at the University of Washington; and Professors Sophia Derbyshire and Charles Hoeppner, who teach the marriage problems course at Orange Coast College in California and who prepared the Study Guide which accompanies this edition.

To my wife Bes, I am indebted for insightful help at all stages of the revision.

P.H.L

Contents

III   THE PREFACE TO
MATE CHOICE

IV   MATE CHOICE

V   MARRIAGE ADJUSTMENT

VI   PARENTHOOD

VII   MARRIAGE PROBLEMS

1

INTRODUCTION

1

Marriage Has Improved

A philosophy teacher gifted with both optimism and realism told his class, "If you wish to worship the past, don't study history too closely." This bit of advice is particularly timely in the area of marriage and the family where the trend has been toward a more complete development of the individual person, a deeper understanding, and a closer, more harmonious relationship between husbands and wives, parents and children. Although it is primarily by psychological standards that improvement is measured, progress is also evidenced in the duration of marriage and increased privacy and greater material comforts surrounding the married pair and their offspring.

The Lasting Quality of Marriage

Pessimism of young people about marriage is in considerable part engendered by our much-advertised divorce rate. It makes many feel that marriage is a highly risky venture. Divorce is a measure of failure, yet the fact remains that the average marriage lasts longer today than ever before. Divorce has replaced premature death as a factor in terminating marriages, but fewer are terminated early than at any time in history.

Paul H. Jacobson's monumental study, *American Marriage and Divorce* (see Figure 10, p. 141, and Table 70, p. 142, New York: Rinehart & Co., 1959) shows that in 1890, 33 marriages per 1,000 were terminated annually, now the number is 29 (see Figure 1–1). At that time 30 of the 33 broken homes were due to death of husband or wife, only 3 to divorce. Of the 29 broken annually now, acording to data of National Center for Health Statistics, about 10 will be broken by divorce, 19 by death.

Now at age 20, young people can look forward to approximately 55 years of life. White persons in their first marriage in 1900 could expect about 30 years of married life before a mate died, now a couple can

FIGURE 1–1   NUMBER OF MARRIAGES BROKEN PER 1,000 ANNUALLY. Source: Table B, "Divorce Statistics Analysis, United States, 1963," National Center for Health Statistics, Series 21, No. 13, Washington, D. C., October, 1967. Data for 1890, Paul H. Jacobson, *American Marriage and Divorce.*

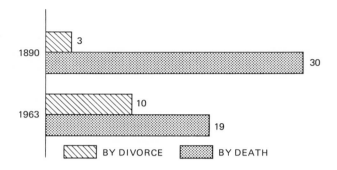

The average marriage lasts longer than it did in 1890 because of the decreasing death rate. In 1890, 33 marriages per thousand were terminated annually; in 1963, 29. Life expectancy permitted 30 years of married life in 1900 compared to 45 years today.

expect about 45 years.[1] The chances of a golden wedding anniversary, taking only the death rate into account, are twice as great as in 1900. The chances will be even greater for those now in college.

Our present divorce rate, about 2.3 per 1,000 marriages per year compared with 4.3 in 1946,[2] has remained fairly constant for several years since reaching an all-time high in the post World War II period. Parke and Glick think[3] it will probably decline with the increase in affluence of the lower socioeconomic layers of our society. The rapid decline in poverty, a stated national objective, should also bring greater marriage stability. Another factor in the probable decline in divorce is the falling rate of teenage marriages (see Chapter 16 for data). These marriages and poverty have been the two most important social factors in the nation's high divorce rate.

Marriage lasts so long today that the Roys propose[4] that we allow couples to have marriages of fifteen years each with perhaps a five-year

[1] "Married Couples Living to Advanced Ages," *Statistical Bulletin,* 49:9–11, June, 1968. See also "Survival and the Life Cycle," *Statistical Bulletin,* 47:5–7. September, 1966.

[2] There may well be a temporary flurry of divorces when the Viet Nam war ends. The return of men long absent from wives and families brings this aftermath. The refined divorce rate (rate based only on women of marriageable age) is already showing an increase. See *Monthly Vital Statistics: Divorce Statistics, 1966,* Vol. 17, No. 10 Supplement, January 6, 1969.

[3] Robert Parke, Jr., and Paul C. Glick, "Prospective Changes in Marriage and the Family," *Journal of Marriage and Family Living* 29:249–256, May, 1967.

[4] Rustum and Della Roy, *Honest Sex* (New York: New Library, 1968).

single break between marriages. Margaret Mead believes that the "totally monogamous marriage" for a lifetime is untenable in view of contemporary longevity, but testifies that the idea persists among the young.[5] They want marriage to be "forever."

Part of our divorce rate today must be attributed to the greater length of life. We speak of menopause divorces—which take place in midlife— when psychological stress is not unusual for women and when husbands and wives both may feel a letdown as they find life together without purpose after children leave the home. Few pairs lived to go through the middle-aged slump together at the beginning of the century. One was already in the graveyard, usually the wife who had died in childbirth or been worn out by too frequent pregnancy for which she had no effective control, and the husband had already taken a young bride. Even then, of course, there was the occasional sturdy woman who lived to marry a succession of husbands, having survived the first or subsequent husbands.

Divorce in middle age, after children are reared, is certainly a brighter prospect than death, but couples now have the alternative of twenty to thirty years more of married life together. In spite of learned theorizing to the effect that little social damage is done if couples choose to divorce and freshen up their future with a new mate, more readjust to a home without children and live together to share the joys of seeing grandchildren grow to maturity and marry, carrying the family line into the third generation. The majority of couples complete these long modern marriages still enjoying a great deal of happiness in each other's companionship.

The Equalitarian Trend

The status of women and children in most cultures has been that of inferiors, sometimes even property. One of the great achievements of this century has been the elevation in the position of women and children in the American family. The stern patriarch has been eliminated and with his passing, the rule of fear based on punishment has disappeared from the average family. Women and men share as equals to an increasing extent.

"The Pill" age, using this concept broadly to embrace all forms of contraception, has arrived and may well mark the final and most significant step in the emancipation of women.

Freedom from the penalty of unwanted pregnancy produces genuine equality in the sense that sexual activity brings no greater biological

[5] "Margaret Mead's Sound Insights into the Furor over Shifting American Morals," *Life* 65:30–34, August 25, 1968.

consequences to the female than to the male. It is almost impossible to envision the full psychological, social, moral, and economic consequences of the removal of this threat to women's freedom of action, and to the mutuality made possible in the physical union of marriage.

American women have been freed from the belief that reproduction is their primary function. They can be individuals in a sense they never could have been before. The population explosion has given them the moral right to make use of the new birth control technology. Limiting children in numbers and scheduling their appearance during a brief portion of the life span—the twenties—leaves them some fifty years of life after childbearing is over. Not least of the developments has been the weakening of the authority of the Catholic Church in this area, liberating millions from the guilt of disobedience and giving many communicants the courage to use effective means of family spacing and limitation.

Security For Children

Although youth think of marriage in terms of their own happiness and fulfillment, its ultimate purpose is the well-being of children. Marriage now gives children greater assurance of security, in terms of marriage lasting, than ever before. Today few children are orphaned (see Figure 1–2). The man who marries at age 23 has 88 chances in 100 of seeing his last child marry. The girl who marries at 21 has a 94 in 100 chance of living to see the marriage of her youngest child.[6] Death rarely leaves children orphaned during their younger years. Divorce may, but as we have seen, the overall risk of broken homes is far lower than ever before.

The average family has less than half the funerals it had in 1890. Most couples never experience death in their families, even of the parents, until their own children are married. In most cases both parents live until their children are grown. Even if there is a divorce, the one denied custody still usually has some influence in helping support and train the child. Unlike death, divorce does not terminate parental influence. (There are a few cases when it would be better eliminated, if the child is kept under tension by parental visiting, but this is the exception.)

The threat to children from premature death has been drastically reduced. The deaths which do occur are usually the result of accident. The marriage is spared the fearful economic and emotional cost of having to sire many children in order to rear a few to maturity.

---

[6] "Survival and the Life Cycle," *Statistical Bulletin,* 47:5–7, Metropolitan Life Insurance Co., September, 1966.

FIGURE 1–2   PERCENTAGE OF ALL CHILDREN WHO WERE ORPHANS IN THE UNITED STATES, 1920 and 1958.* Source: Health Information Foundation. Data by L. O. Shuddle, **Social Security Bulletin.**

* Jan. 1, 1958. All basic data for both years are estimated and refer to population under age 18.

Marriage and family are safer today than ever before. Most couples live to see their children reach maturity, thus removing from the more favored populations of the world much of the age-old anxiety of untimely death of a mate and parent. The probability of a golden wedding anniversary has doubled if the couple remains together until death parts them.

Divorce often gives children first consideration. Some conscientious couples divorce for the sake of their children. They can see that their own conflicts are robbing their children of peace. Tragic as divorce can be for the child, in many cases it is the better alternative, and children do find happiness many times in the remarriage which follows. Stepparent relationships are not as unpleasant as fiction has presented them to be. (Divorce and remarriage as they relate to children are discussed in Chapter 30.)

Marriage Opportunity

During this century, those who wish to marry had an increased opportunity to do so. As a result of the great economic developments making early self-support possible, the chance comes earlier in life (see Figure 1–3).

FIGURE 1–3 EARLIER MARRIAGE AND LATER WIDOWHOOD FOR WOMEN. Source: U.S. Department of Labor, Women's Bureau, **American Women,** Report of the President's Commission on the Status of Women, Washington, D. C., 1963, Chart 3, p. 6.

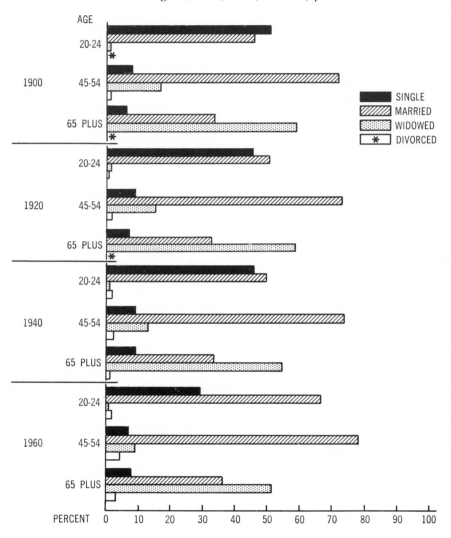

Early marriage and long duration of marriage are characteristic of our day. This trend gives the average couple a longer life together than at any other time in our history.

The typical groom of 1890 was just over 26 years of age at the time of his first marriage, the typical bride 22. Today the typical groom is just over 23 and the bride just past 20.5. In 1890, the average age difference between bride and groom was over 4 years, now it is about 2.5 years (see Figure 1–4).

FIGURE 1–4 MEDIAN AGE FOR MARRIAGE. Source: U.S. Department of Commerce, Bureau of the Census, "Population Characteristics," Series P–20, No. 122, March 22, 1963, Table C.

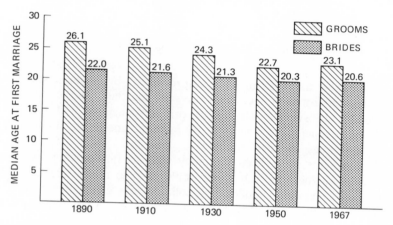

Note that the difference in age of bride and groom is also less than formerly —4 years in 1890 compared with 2.5 in 1967. Marriage age is decreasing throughout the world, but the average is higher—24 years for women, 27 for men—than in the United States (**Demographic Yearbook, UN).**

Compare the prospects life offers young people in the United States, where economic circumstances and customs permit early marriage, with Ireland, where economic hardship and religious taboos against birth control cause more than a third of the women and almost two-thirds of the men to delay marriage past thirty years of age. Many there must postpone marriage until they have passed the childbearing age.[7]

In 1960 the U.S. census showed that only 7.2 percent of males had never married by age 45–49, 6.5 percent of females. In 1965, 64 percent of all women 55–64 were married and living with a husband (first or subsequent). According to predictions this figure will be 72 percent by 1980. Of women now 65 to 74 years of age, only 64 percent were married

[7] William J. Goode, *World Revolution and Family Patterns* (New York: Free Press of Glencoe, 1963). The disadvantage of too early marriage, particularly marriages under age 20, are discussed in Ch. 16.

at age 25, now 93 percent of women age 25 are married; for men the figures are 42 percent and 72 percent respectively.[8]

In the United States, about 94 percent of all women are or have been married by the end of the childbearing age.[9] This is the highest record in American history. Except for the sick and badly crippled, the deformed, the emotionallly warped, and the mentally defective, almost everyone has an opportunity to marry. Even the handicapped often marry, thanks to social security, to routine machine-powered jobs, and to labor-saving devices in the home.

The Marriage-Family Environment

It is not popular today to measure improvement by material standards, and yet the environmental circumstances of marriage and family living are important to success. Degree of privacy, quantity and quality of environmental space, and adequacy of material goods are influential in the lives of couples and their children.

Improvements have been so many and so far-reaching in impact on marriage and the family that one would have to review the most vital aspects of the technology and welfare policy of our civilization to encompass them. Since this is not possible or desirable, only a few improvements can be mentioned.

Broad social and economic programs of state, federal, and voluntary organizations have come to the aid of couples, particularly in child care and development. Some critics resent the invasion of bureaucracy into family life, as well as the concept of the "welfare state" programs but the rapidity of social change has made such programs necessary and advantageous to the family. A great burden is lifted from parents and the growth of children is facilitated.

School lunch programs, school medical examinations, and accident insurance have been great boons to the health of children, particularly those of the lower socioeconomic classes. Innovations in teaching mathematics, spelling, reading, and the sciences, and the use of computer techniques have brought such progress in learning as to make parental help with homework difficult, in many instances impossible. But the intellectual growth of the child is greatly enhanced.

In many aspects of life, the couple of today can expect to have the assistance and guidance of experts for their child's health and education from Head Start, through nursery school, and on through college and

[8] Parke and Glick, *op. cit.*

[9] U.S. Department of Commerce, Bureau of the Census. "Population Characteristics," Series P–20, No. 122, March 22, 1963, Table 1, p. 9.

university. Inexpensive paperbacks of the best professional quality on child rearing, the television "Children's Doctor," women's magazines, medical columns, and features on parent-child relations all come to the mother's aid. Parents may have to struggle to keep up with the latest innovations in the area of child training but can delegate much more of the care of their child to school, clinic, and specialists in other agencies, even at the expense of spending a great deal of time transporting and waiting for children.[10] But the child profits and the parent gains in seeing the child develop at a rate and in ways they could not have realized for him.

The later years of marriage, too, show improvement in living conditions. Pensions, Social Security, Medicare and other such benefits, along with increasing earned abundance on the part of more of the elderly have permitted them to maintain separate households. Since 1960 nearly one-third of new households have been one-person households,[11] and the proportion of one-person households increases with age. With Social Security and Medicare the elderly are able to live outside the families of their children and to maintain their independence. Their wish of "not having to live with our children" is realized. Increasing mobility and affluence have at the same time made visiting possible.

Not the least of these benefits has been the removal of the burden of caring for their parents from the younger generation during their child-rearing period and also feelings of guilt for their neglect.

The dream of "a place of our own" is realized by young and old alike here more than in any other Western nation.[12] The separate dwelling has done much to alleviate the in-law problem and the grandparent problem. It gives the couple and their children the privacy they want to pursue individual growth. Dependence on the large family has been replaced by various forms of social insurance and social security. Burdens of ancestry and of relatives, still present in most cultures of the world, have been lifted from the modern American family.

Many even have a separate house and yard, although apartment dwelling must increase because of the high cost of land and increased crowding due to population growth. Even so, home ownership climbed from 33 million in 1960 to 37 million in 1967.

[10] Otto Pollak, "The Outlook for the American Family," *Journal of Marriage and Family Living* 29:193–205, February, 1967.

[11] John C. Belcher, "The One-Person Household: A Consequence of the Isolated Nuclear Family," *Journal of Marriage and Family Living* 29:534–540.

[12] In January 1969, *Reader's Digest* reported the remarkable progress in Soviet housing, but also stressed the poor quality of the housing, and the great current shortage. Even with this progress, 40 percent of Moscow citizens still live in "communal flats" where they share kitchen and toilet facilities. Three or more family members live in two small rooms. Divorced persons may still have to live together with a blanket hung between beds. These are standards which would be judged far down in the poverty level in the United States. Although Soviet housing shortage represents the extreme, apartments are in chronic short supply in many European countries, making it difficult for the young to marry and live separate from relatives.

During the 20 years from 1947 to 1967, the percent of married couples living with relatives declined from 7 percent to 1.6 percent.[13] Since an important factor in the romantic marriage and the nuclear family is "a place of our own," where couples can maintain privacy, the housing trend is significant to our kind of marriage and family.

Our Problem Consciousness

As a people, we make much of our problems, and in so doing sometimes exaggerate them. Having cast aside tradition, we pursue elusive goals and entertain lofty hopes and dreams, often too romantic, and beyond reach. This is especially true of marriage. Long ago we ceased to believe that fate ruled our destiny, and began to seek remedies for our problems.

Almost every woman's magazine and some magazines written for the more general public carry articles that outline and suggest help for some critical marriage problem. Divorce statistics are much quoted and the pro and con of the sex revolution is considered.

An outsider to our culture, particularly one from the more institutionalized, custom-controlled, Asiatic cultures, where marriage adjustment is not an accepted concept and where it is never discussed, might well think our marriage institution is but the ruins of some earlier state of equilibrium. Safe and relatively unchallenged by change, the joint family system of these cultures is based on the secure foundations of centuries of custom. Little wonder that they see in our nuclear marriage-family system, where so much is left to the individual choice and so little to ancestral heritage, little pattern at all.

Recognizing that problems exist is the first step toward improvement. Traditional family systems will never improve until they become problem-conscious. They are fate oriented, believing that what has been must always be. The fact that our society exhibits concern for the welfare of husbands and wives, parents and children, represents a vast leap forward. The numerous minor miseries of the pair and their children have become social concerns.

Failure Often Reflects High Hopes

If the view that couples aspire to more in marriage than they did in earlier generations is accepted then it is easy to believe (1) that the successful

[13] Marital Status and Family Status: March 1967, "Population Characteristics," Series P–20, No. 170, February 23, 1968, United States Census, p. 1.

realize more satisfaction in marriage than did their ancestors and (2) that many suffer defeat because they expect marriage to bring more in the way of happiness than is possible.

By the same logic, it is understandable too, that failure is more likely to lead to decisive action than in earlier generations. There is little doubt that many divorces today result from overly idealistic expectations for marriage. Many expect the impossible. As English novelist Somerset Maugham has said, the American wife expects to find in her husband "a perfection English women only hope to find in their butlers." And what perfection in romantic attraction, home management, and social competence American men expect of their wives! It is doubtful that marriage has ever been asked to pass such a high test.

If a culture makes happiness the goal of marriage, it must grant the right of divorce to those who fail in its attainment. Only by this means can they be freed to seek fulfillment in another marriage, or to return to the single state. The right of divorce is important in the new system of marriage values. It recognizes two facts: first, human judgment is fallible in mate choice, and second, those who fall in love may also fall out of love.

Divorce is doubly serious when it represents the failure of high aspirations, but is not more tragic than living together in bitter conflict and frustration. In an earlier day, when a more stoic marriage philosophy prevailed, personal clashes may well have brought less torture than now when marriage values are different.

Divorce and its meaning in the modern scheme of values are discussed in Chapter 30. It is enough here to say that divorce is a recognized adjustment device in the modern marriage-family system—the ultimate, desperate, but sometimes necessary one. Divorce is, in fact, a part of all marriage-family institutions, historic and contemporary. In ours, its causes are related to our new marriage values.

Our much-used reason for divorce, "mental cruelty," is indicative that marriage is no longer judged in terms of traditional value, but by the quality of the interpersonal relationship involved. Marriage is a dynamic interrelationship of two individuals with personal destinies.

Margaret Mead has suggested that we try to make all relationships too intense today, even in marriage.[14] Too much is demanded, and we despair too easily. She believes America does not even accept the fact of divorce yet, we are so loyal to the monogamous ideal. Children are disturbed and women feel abandoned and hurt if a marriage fails even after twenty years. Yet most couples historically did not live together that long before death. The ideal of a lifelong union, she suggests, was fine when vigorous men buried a succession of three wives and when sturdy wives survived a succession of husbands.

[14] "Margaret Mead's Sound Insights into the Furor over Shifting American Morals," *Life* 65:30–34, August 25, 1968.

It is a remarkable testimony to our monogamous ideal that marriage is still looked upon as a lifetime partnership.

Shortcomings of Marriage

With all its remodeling, even with the claim of improvement in the quality and durability of the relationship, marriage is not the answer to the personal needs of everyone. Too many people marry who have no capacity to meet its demands. Much of the failure of marriage is chargeable to a relatively small group, some of whom try and try again. They inflict hardship on mates who would have been successful in marriage with other partners.

Marriage may be much too popular in our society. Many enter it before they are ready for the inherent responsibilities, and many have unrealistically high romantic and/or sexual expectations. They expect too intense a relationship, not realizing that life cannot be lived on the plane of the great romance.

And the family, with all its material comforts, often fails to meet the needs of children, of wives, of husbands. Many influences from without the family circle impinge upon it and strain its relationships. And it is inevitable that with their independence and self-sufficiency, many of the elderly will suffer loneliness and neglect.

There is in the picture the forgotten poor, for whom basic needs are never met, among whom birth control is inadequate, and for whom crowding and lack of privacy is chronic.

Marriage is not paradise in the United States, it is just better than man has been accustomed to. It fulfills deep social and personal needs, perhaps more fully than ever before, and the family is more lasting, seeing more children through to maturity before the death of either parent.

Problems

1. The chapter develops the thesis that marriage has improved. Many do not agree with this view. Present evidence to support arguments on both sides of the question.
2. Explain the longer duration of marriage today, even with the higher divorce rate.
3. Comment on the importance of separate residence as a factor in marriage and family life.
4. Discuss the qualities of marriage which make it more meaningful than other relationships.

5. Can you state objections to the ease with which many marry today compared to earlier times. Is it a handicap or asset?
6. Do you think the increasing closeness in age of couples today compared with, for example, the difference in 1890, is an advantage?
7. Is it a sound philosophical principle that failure often represents the frustration of hopes that were too high at the beginning? Apply your answer to marriage today.
8. Do you believe that everyone who marries for money, property, or economic security is to be condemned? Why or why not?
9. Discuss shortcomings of modern marriage and family life.

Selected References

Articles in Books of Readings

Cavan, Ruth S., *Marriage and the Family in the Modern World: A Book of Readings*, third edition (New York: Thomas Y. Crowell Co., 1969).
Burgess, Ernest W., "The Changing American Family," Reading 3.
Gans, Herbert J., "Family Life of Italian Americans," Reading 5.
Hosterler, John A., "The Family System of the Amish," Reading 6.
Lewis, Oscar, "The Culture of Poverty," Reading 7.
Cavan, Ruth S., "Stages of the Family Life Cycle," Reading 13.
Nimkoff, Meyer F., "The American Family," Reading 2.
Morioka, Kyomi, "Life Cycle Patterns in Japan, China, and the United States," Reading 14.
Christensen, Harold T., *Handbook of Marriage and the Family* (Chicago: Rand McNally, 1964).
Cavan, Ruth Shonle, "Subcultural Variations and Mobility," Ch. 14.
Landis, Judson T., and Landis, Mary G., *Readings in Marriage and the Family* (Englewood Cliffs, N. J.: Prentice-Hall, Inc., 1952).
Mead, Margaret, "The Contemporary American Family as an Anthropologist Sees It," pp. 1–9.
Sirjamaki, John, "Cultural Configurations in the American Family," pp. 9–17.
Rodman, Hyman, *Marriage, Family and Society* (New York: Random House, 1965).
Reiss, Paul J., "Extended Kinship Relationships in American Society," Reading 18.
Burgess, Ernest W., Locke, Harvey J., and Thomes, Mary Margaret, "The Companionship Family," Reading 21.
Rodman, Hyman, "Talcott Parsons' View of the Changing American Family," Reading 22.
Sussman, Marvin B., *Sourcebook in Marriage and the Family*, third edition (Boston: Houghton Mifflin, 1968).
Sirjamaki, John, "Cultural Configurations in the American Family," Reading 8.
Furstenberg, Frank F., Jr., "Industrialization and the American Family," Reading 12.
Parke, Robert, Jr. and Glick, Paul C., "Prospective Changes in Marriage and the Family," Reading 13.
Vincent, Clark E., *Readings in Marriage Counseling* (New York: Thomas Y. Crowell Co., 1957).

Nimkoff, M. F., "The Family in the United States," pp. 2–12.
Winch, Robert F. and Goodman, Louis Wolf, *Selected Studies in Marriage and the Family*, third edition (New York: Holt, Rinehart and Winston, 1968).
Adams, Richard N., "An Inquiry into the Nature of the Family," pp. 44–57.

General References

Goode, William J., *World Revolution and Family Patterns* (New York: Free Press, 1963).
Kirkpatrick, Clifford, *The Family as Process and Institution*, second edition (New York: The Ronald Press Co., 1963).
Neugarten, B. L. and Weinstein, K. K., "Changing American Grandparents," *Journal of Marriage and the Family*, 26:199–204, May, 1964.
Ogburn, W. F. and Nimkoff, M. F., *Technology and the Changing Family*, (Boston: Houghton Mifflin Co., 1955).
Parke, Robert, Jr. and Glick, Paul C., "Prospective Changes in Marriage and the Family," *Journal of Marriage and the Family*, 29:249–256, February, 1967.
Pollak, Otto, "The Outlook for the American Family," *Journal of Marriage and the Family*, 29:193–205, February, 1967.
Stephens, William N., *The Family in Cross-Cultural Perspective* (New York: Holt, Rinehart and Winston, 1963).

2

Values and Goals
of Marriage

Marriage is a universal institution designed to provide a stable pair relationship, to assure the rearing of the helpless child, provide status, and
transmit wealth. These common prerequisites of human survival are the
institution's reason for existence, but they do not encompass all values and
goals of marriage. These are added by the various cultures. To appraise
marriage, to understand its significance, even to grasp the reason for its
failure, one must study it within its cultural context, for cultures provide
the framework of human social aspirations.

The very personal nature of the modern couple's hopes for marriage
in our society is illustrated by Strauss' study of 173 engaged or newly
married men and 200 women with a check list of 26 needs they had hoped
to find fulfilled in their pair relationship. Here are the 15 items most often
checked:[1]

	Men (percent)	Women (percent)
[1] *Wish someone to:*		
love me	36	54
confide in me	31	42
show me affection	21	38
respect my ideals	26	26
appreciate what I wish to achieve	28	24
understand my moods	23	28
help me make important decisions	15	33

[1] Anselm Strauss, "A Study of Three Psychological Factors Affecting Choice of
a Mate," Ph.D. Thesis, University of Chicago, 1945, cited in E. W. Burgess and Paul
Wallin, *Engagement and Marriage* (Philadelphia: J. B. Lippincott Co., 1953), p. 203.

stimulate my ambition	27	21
look up to	16	29
give me self-confidence	20	24
stand back of me in difficulty	16	26
appreciate me just as I am	20	21
admire my ability	19	20
make me feel I count for something	21	17
relieve my loneliness	19	19

It will be seen that in general a higher proportion of women than of men listed needs fulfilled, particularly those in the area of love, affection, confidence, and understanding. This is an indication of a greater sense of dependence in women than in men on the marriage for love, security, and intimacy. More men than women want marriage to stimulate their ambition, indicating their need for ego support.

Institution to Companionship

Some years ago Burgess and Locke used the "institution to companionship" terms to describe the characteristic trend of American marriage-family system.[2] Their conceptualization has been quite generally accepted by sociologists. It designates the radical transition from conceiving of marriage and family in terms of customary formal arrangements and traditional values to conceiving of them in terms of personal relationships and values.

Both the old and new systems have many names, depending on their expression in various periods of history and depending on the particular aspect of the marriage-family system being stressed.

In the broadest sense, the institutional family system includes all systems in which the institution is given priority over individual inclinations and wishes. The *joint family* system of Asia and the *affiliated* family system of Latin America represent the extremes in submerging the wishes of the individual in the traditional family system. The elders dominate mate choice, provide the joint residence, and provide a joint economic security. The large family is governed by the patriarch.

The farm family of our recent past demanded less of the individual, included fewer relatives, and gave more freedom; but even so, the family

[2] Ernest W. Burgess, Harvey J. Locke, and Mary Margaret Thomes, *The Family: From Institution to Companionship*, third edition (New York: American Book Co., 1963).

and its traditions were the beginning and the end of marriage. Personal whims were not of first consideration.

Asians, viewing our current urban industrial marriage-family system, describe our marriage as the "love marriage." It is significant and surprising to them that mate choice would be left to youth, rather than being in the hands of elders, and that love rather than social status and wealth should guide mate choice.

Sociologists focusing on this aspect of our marriage system call it the romantic marriage type. This concept of marriage stresses the individual's supreme right to love and be loved in a romantic, sexual sense. This is considered the essence of happiness.

In a broader framework, sociologists use the term *nuclear* family to describe the new independent family unit, consisting of the pair and their offspring.[3] This family system has reached its most ideal form in the United States, with its high standard of living and high level of personal income. There is no need for the pooling of family funds as in the joint family, or even the pooling of family effort as in the rural economy of an earlier day. Personal insurance programs, company fringe benefits, and government security provisions liberate the individual and the pair from the economic bonds of kinship. The separate living arrangement provides the setting for the nuclear unit.

In fact, the separate abode is considered a prerequisite to independence. The pair is free to work out their relationship unhampered by close-living in-laws and rear their children with minimum interference from parents and other kinfolk.

The stress on interpersonal relationships in marriage and family has led to the current emphasis on companionship as a major test of mate relationships. The institution is of secondary importance, romance is the lure by which mates are drawn together, but the quality of the relationship which binds it together, if it is to be durable, is companionability. Those who not only love, but who also have enough common characteristics and interests to share each other's life as companions are the ones who are destined for the happy, durable marriage.

In a 1967 study of 581 couples, at least one of whom had taken a course in marriage at the University of California, under Judson T. Landis, ability to "communicate with each other" was most universally associated with marriage in the minds of the subjects.[4] Love, meeting each other's emotional needs and satisfactory sex relations were also mentioned by most couples. But almost every pair mentioned the importance of communication.

[3] In some literature, the term *conjugal* is used with much the same meaning as *nuclear* and *consanguine* to refer to the larger family group.

[4] See Judson T. Landis and Mary G. Landis, *Building a Successful Marriage*, fifth edition (Englewood Cliffs, N. J.: Prentice-Hall, Inc., 1968) Table 2, p. 10.

This communication need may be a more significant item in marital happiness for the college group than for those of less education. The college group may well talk more than those who are not college-educated and than those involved in occupations where physical rather than communicative interaction is basic. But it is most certain that communication is essential to success.

Judson T. Landis also found that peaceful discussion of problems with the spouse was a way of reacting to crises employed by 69 percent of successful couples, but by only 35 percent of a group receiving counseling because they were in marital difficulty. Peaceful discussion had been used by only 45 percent of divorced persons studied.[5]

The meaning of any goal is relevant to the culture in which the family functions. It is within the framework of urban industrial culture that the goals of marriage must be appreciated.

Companionship As a Goal

In the United States, a man builds a house in which to spend his old age, and he sells it before the roof is on; he plants a garden and rents it just as the trees are coming into bearing; he brings a field into tillage and leaves other men to gather the crops; he embraces a profession and gives it up; he settles in a place, which he soon afterwards leaves to carry his changeable longings elsewhere.

DE TOCQUEVILLE, *Democracy in America,* 1831

Each year 35 to 40 million Americans change their residence—for some it will mean a switch to a new house or apartment close by; for others, across the continent, or even an international move. The U.S. Census shows that only 35 percent of the heads of families in the nation are living in the place of their birth. Of those aged 30, 60 percent have already moved from the place of their birth. One family in five is living over a thousand miles from the place of the head's birth. Five million families a year move across state lines. In western states more than half of family heads were born elsewhere. College graduates are twice as likely to move as grade school educated persons.[6]

"Mobility insecurity" affects couples, small children, teen-agers, and grandparents not tough enough to take it. The stability that place gives to

[5] *Ibid,* Table 2, p. 296.

[6] For Census study of mobility see U. S. Department of Commerce, Bureau of Census, "Mobility of Population of the United States, March, 1959 to 1960," Series P–20, No. 113, January 2, 1962; see also their "Population Characteristics," Series P–20, No. 156, December 9, 1966, and Series P–23, No. 16, January, 1966.

children and adolescents is lost with mobility. Young couples must learn to adapt to new attitudes and standards in attempting to meet the expectations of new groups in new social climates. The elderly must accept the loss of authority and respect as their wisdom and experience are eclipsed by new generations moving not only horizontally but also vertically, gaining the experience so necessary for survival in the competitive struggle with their peers.

Mobility, and consequent anonymity, affect the typical American, particularly the urban dweller. Migration takes him, in the course of a lifetime, far from the intimate circle of his birth. This has created in the human spirit a longing for a close emotional tie such as those who lived in a world of kin and neighbors never knew. The joint family system, the close tribal unit, the integrated primary group neighborhood give the individual continuous social support. He never bears his burdens alone. His crises are shared from cradle to grave, giving his emotional life a sure anchor. He need not demand a close love-life or the compatible association of a mate in marriage in order to guarantee a full social and emotional life.

The loneliness of the great city, its social isolation for the stranger, creates in the mind of man a sense of isolation and futility that has driven many persons to suicide, and others to the companionship of dogs, cats, parrots, and even to the companionship of silent, nondemonstrative pets or objects—fish, turtles, and flowers. Those most deprived of companionship even talk to these silent, unresponsive companions to hear their own voice and keep in touch with the flow of language which makes man social. A filling station operator in a neighborhood gas station recognized this problem when he said, "People come here to have someone to tell their problems to." Many a bartender feels that his place serves the same social need.

Little wonder that marriage has had to take on new meaning and that almost everyone seeks marriage today and seeks it early. The family home is a launching platform into the competitive world outside. As young people grow older and sense more keenly the impersonal character of the adult experience of our time, they understand more deeply the need to establish a close tie—one that will guarantee them not only companionship but sociability itself—stable, tangible, and ever-present sociability.

More than forty years ago, Harvey Zorbaugh described life in the "Furnished Rooms" section of Chicago, where young people from farms and small Middle West towns landed on their arrival in the city in quest of fame and fortune.[7] Here, where the turnover of residents was very rapid and anonymity characteristic of social life, many of the couples living together as married were not married at all. Excuses given were that they

[7] Harvey Zorbaugh, *The Gold Coast in the Slum* (Chicago: University of Chicago Press, 1929).

wanted to have, "someone to come home to," "someone to talk to," "someone to tell my troubles to."

Morals cannot always stand the test of the great loneliness and the feeling of being cut off from social life. Marriage is modern man's best arrangement for avoiding the solitariness of adulthood. Marriage is the institution which provides for permanent companionship. A mobile society provides no other source of enduring companionship.

Those who find marriage so miserable that they cannot endure it and seek a way out in divorce, do not survive the single state long in our society. Very soon they seek another mate, some even return to the former mate to make another try. The widowed too seek another mate in our day, when to be outside the fold of marriage is to be lonely in a sense that people are not lonely in societies with deeper ties in family and locality groups. As will be shown by data in Chapter 30, the divorced are more likely to marry than are the single; the widowed also are more likely to marry than are the single of comparable age.

The need for the companionship of a marriage partner in the industrial world cannot be written off as a spurious value. In terms of a different kind of society, it may be an unnecessary value, but not in terms of the world in which modern urban industrial man must live his life.

The human being, to remain human, needs someone with whom he can interact on a continuing basis, expressing his deepest joys and fears, plans and failures, hopes and needs. The more that is known about human nature through the study of psychology and sociology, through clinical experience, even from an understanding of suicide—lonely man's last desperate resort—the more clearly it is understood that the human being who can talk frankly and freely with a confidant travels life's journey most safely.

Those who lack companionship and who have no direct way of expressing their hopes, fears, anxieties, and longing to another human being are in danger of losing their sense of personal direction, of meaning, and of rationality. Normality is determined by the opportunity one is given for constant, meaningful communication with other persons.

A rural couple celebrating their seventy-second wedding anniversary was asked how they had managed a successful marriage. The wife's answer to the question was, "We did little fussin'. We said little. Mostly we just set."

This may not be too unrepresentative of many rural marriages of yesterday. But today's couple has much greater need to communicate with each other—to fuss, to do, and above all, to talk. A marriage of silence and sitting would fall far short of success in terms of meeting the modern person's needs.

FIGURE 2-1   HIGHER MORTALITY OF UNMARRIED OVER PERSONS EVER MARRIED—BY SEX AND AGE (20 AND OVER) UNITED STATES, 1963.*

MALE   FEMALE

1963

* Adjusted to 1940 standard.

Marriage is related to health and longevity. Better conditions of living, more to live for, a full expression of basic wishes all undoubtedly are factors in the greater longevity of married persons, even though biological selectivity may also operate. United Nations' data show that marriage is related to longevity everywhere, not just in the United States **(Demographic Yearbook, UN).**

The democratic marriage creates an atmosphere of confidence and trust in which free communication on a person-to-person level is continuously possible. Even law courts preserve this confidence by refusing to require a person to testify against his spouse. Only the companionable couple can attain a really confidential level of expression, and only they realize the most from the marriage relationship.

One of the best indices of the effect of social isolation and a sense of anonymity on personality is the suicide rate. Data for a 3-year period, 1949–1951, indicate that the married are by far the least likely to suicide. Of white males, only 21 per 100,000 of those married committed suicide, compared to 80 of those divorced, 76 of those widowed, and 44 of those single. Comparable rates for the white female are 19 for divorced, 13 for widowed, 8 for the single, and 7 for the married. This is striking evidence that marriage is an insurance factor, as far as the individual's hold on his own life and the future is concerned—a vital hedge against anonymity[8] (see Figure 2–1).

Happiness As a Goal

In the United States 150 years ago happiness was not the primary concern of marriage. A person was more likely to pick a mate for qualities that wore well and to be concerned about the practical aspects of the marriage. But people also worked 14 to 16 hours a day in order to make a living. They struggled for the conquest of a frontier. Life was rigorous. A puritanical attitude toward all levity still carried over in the culture. Life was serious and the stake was survival itself. Pleasure seeking as such was condemned, and condemned no less in marriage than in all other aspects of life.

In our culture abundance of good and leisure have become the lot of the majority, and life moves in terms of a different set of values. With the increase of luxury and leisure, moderns have come to look upon happiness as a desirable goal not only for marriage but for all of life. Recreation and pleasure are considered man's just due; they are even considered rejuvenating and worthwhile—the proper rewards of work and of earned leisure.

In terms of such contemporary values, who is to say that this goal of marriage happiness is a spurious one? Most students of American marriage prefer to accept the contemporary values and hold not only that happiness in marriage is a worthy goal, but also that it represents a new and higher level of human aspiration than earlier generations dared hold.

The fact that youth can make happiness the first demand of marriage testifies to the luxury enjoyed today, both in material blessings and spiritual values. On the material side, the human spirit has been freed from the overwhelming burden of incessant work and duty. On the spiritual side, modern concepts of well-being provide a culture in which man dares dream that he can be happy. It is logical that marriage is placed at the center of this dream.

It is doubtful that humanity has ever sought a goal in marriage so difficult to realize and yet so worthy of realization as "happiness." One must grant the psychological necessity of many people compromising

---

[8] Metropolitan Life Insurance Company, "Mortality Lowest in Married Population," *Statistical Bulletin*, 38:5, February, 1957.

the ideal with the demands of reality in everyday living as man and wife, but even so, about three couples in four live out their life span without completely shattering this dream. One cannot claim that all who remain loyal to their marriage pledge fully realize happiness. But many studies[9] that have measured the happiness of married couples show that about two marriages in three are either happy or very happy.

Some critics challenge such research, saying one cannot depend on people's ratings of their own happiness or success. But some studies have used not only self-ratings, but have had friends rate the marriage too. Self-ratings and rating by others agree.[10] This suggests that a couple knows whether or not the marriage is happy, and that the great majority of marriages that survive actually realize happiness. A few generations ago no one would have thought of asking couples whether or not their marriages were happy.

Even legal grounds for divorce today indicate how seriously the value "happiness" is accepted in the culture as the standard for marriage success. Many divorces are granted for "mental cruelty," an intangible quality but one which well expresses the opposite of happiness. The Mosaic Law recognized no such treatment for dissolving marriage, nor did our nation's customs and laws of 1890. The philosophy of marriage has changed to the point where even the law recognizes that marriage is a dynamic interrelationship of two individuals with personal destinies and must produce happiness or fail.

At the beginning of the century, few farm couples who were considered successful in their family life manifested any affection. Some of them battled and nagged at each other chronically. The community did not worry about these marriages breaking up. The couple had land, children, and the respect of neighbors and relatives. No one expected that they would run to a lawyer simply because they did not like each other. In the good religious neighborhood, few couples acted as though they did like each other, but they had enough mutual activities to keep them occupied and interdependent. They had a farm to operate and children to raise; this was all they demanded of marriage.

Perhaps part of the impression they gave was the customary reserve of farm folks of the day in expressing affection. There was a reticence among all but the teen-age group about admitting in public any interest in the opposite sex. Even the teen-agers were shy about it.

Nowadays, the male admits quite openly that there is no creature on earth quite so interesting to him as woman. The once-reserved female

---

[9] E. W. Burgess and Leonard S. Cottrell, *Predicting Success or Failure in Marriage* (Englewood Cliffs, N. J.: Prentice-Hall, Inc., 1939); Lewis M. Terman and others, *Psychological Factors in Marital Happiness* (New York: McGraw-Hill Book Co., 1938) are the best of these studies; see also Landis and Landis, *op cit.*, Table 2, p. 109.

[10] Burgess and Cottrell, *op, cit.*, Ch. 3.

now lets her own sex know quite frankly that the opposite sex interests her, and likely as not she acknowledges this interest to the male.

Well within the memory of some of our older citizens, boys and girls were kept on separate playgrounds for fear they would discover that there was a natural fascination of the sexes for each other. Now, from early teen-age up, young people are taught to seek happiness with each other. The relationship of male and female has become the most important one in life.

Love As a Value

A few years ago a group of practicing psychologists were guests at a ministers' institute at which ministers and psychologists gave papers in turn. After three of each had spoken, it was very apparent that the psychologists were making a better case for love as a key to personality than were the ministers. There has been much recent writing of psychiatrists and clinical psychologists in which the love theme is as prominent as in the New Testament.

That love has a therapeutic effect, few can doubt today. That it is the key factor in making man's life complete and worthwhile, few question.

If this is true of mankind in general, in an industrial society love of a mate must be recognized as a supreme value for so many aspects of life have become competitive that much social experience is the very antithesis of love. The human being of our time and place on earth must find a love focus that is dependable and sure. In such a world, the "love marriage" is not merely a nice arrangement, it is a necessity.

A human being is in a dismal state indeed when he begins to feel that there is no one in the world who cares deeply about him or about whom he cares very much. A person's life is most meaningful when it means a great deal to some other person or persons. This need for unqualified love is fulfilled in the normal childhood home by the parent-child relationship.

The love of a member of the opposite sex comes gradually to replace the affection parents expressed in so many forms during childhood. This affection is not the one-sided affair parental love often is. Parents often give, expecting nothing in return. Mature love involves not only the feeling of being cared for by others, but even more important, of caring for others. It means not only wanting others to feel deeply about oneself, but also feeling a personal responsibility for their happiness.

It is through an understanding marriage that one can be most fully assured of an enduring love in adulthood. The husband-wife relationship becomes for the adult the most important outlet for affection. Here, as in all human relationships, affection is found by being affectionate. The Strauss study shows women are more hopeful of fulfilling this need in marriage than are men.[11]

There are other kinds of close comradeship, but our society recognizes none as full, close, and complete as the marriage tie. It brings emotional security. If the marriage meets this need, it provides a place to relax and feel free from competition and assault. It is a refuge from trouble and a hiding place in a world that often brings rough treatment. Those with a normal childhood have been trained for this kind of inner security by their childhood-parental relationship. It is easy for them to find the psychological counterpart of parental affection in marriage.

Those who have not been permitted to form a close emotional attachment to parents in childhood often find it difficult to realize emotional security in marriage. But if a sense of security can be realized at all, through any human relationship, marriage is designed to bring and maintain it. One without emotional security always feels that he has a flank exposed to the enemy, that he lacks defense against his own misgivings and fears. Failure to realize emotional security is failure indeed.

Complete realization of love does much to put ego-striving in its proper place. The love-starved personality often works itself out in inordinate ambition, intolerable vanity, unreasonable demands for the service and respect of others. The personality that has found itself in a secure emotional relationship is mellowed and matured. The ego takes a more subdued place in the scheme of living and other people are given a larger place. It is in this sense that love, with the inherent sense of emotional security it brings, is not only the savior of the world but of the marriage relationship. It is the antidote for belligerence, conquest, conflict, competition, and self-seeking.

The late Willard Waller,[12] observed that spouses going through the alienation process leading up to divorce develop overwhelming egos. The security and fullness of love is vanishing and in its place the ego emerges and makes overwhelming demands. The ego-subduing love element of marriage must, in the process of divorce, be replaced by compensatory ego fictions. The mate must be blamed and the self, justified. The wife who has never written a line declares she is going to write a best seller. The husband of modest wealth or ability is going to become a financier or inventor. Grandiose purposes and plans represent the struggle of the personality to fill the void left by the loss of emotional security in the marriage.

With women particularly, the sense of belonging emotionally is associated with the desire to have and to give to children. The desire for motherhood, which may be in large part socially cultivated, is a normal

[11] *Op. cit.*

[12] Willard Waller, *The Old Love and the New* (New York: Horace Liveright Co., 1929).

yearning of woman as she reaches the years of maturity. She desires the full life which motherhood promises. In motherhood she sees the closest kind of human relationship and sees in it also a chance to contribute to her own future happiness and security in having children who belong to her, and to whom she belongs. Many young couples also share this feeling to the extent that it becomes a major aspiration in their lives together.

Many, of course, cannot visualize family life this clearly in advance of marriage. Men generally have to be taught to be parents. Couples who seriously undertake parenthood in faith and confidence, however, do develop a deep sense of emotional security from it and thus enrich their marriage. The total family becomes the area of emotional expression and unity. The marriage relationship itself is strengthened by the extension of the bonds of affection to include children and by the joint aspirations which parents hold for them in planning their development.

In a world that too often seems filled with pessimism and gloom, children give the couple a vital stake in the future. One who senses the world of childhood and its simple hopes has difficulty being pessimistic about the future or about man's and his own high destiny. Although these realities are often only vaguely sensed in early youth, they are a part of the reality which makes marriage and family the basic institution of mankind and one which, when a substantial part of its goals are realized, promises the fulfillment of the greatest possible range of emotional needs.

Ego Support

Harold Summers, president of the guild of London hairdressers, declared, "modern women no longer require love—what they want and constantly seek is reassurance."[13] Man's craving for recognition of his personal worth is a perpetual hunger. As has been suggested in the preceding section, love and a deep sense of belonging do much to feed the ego and put it in its proper place, but do not annihilate it. The Strauss study indicated that men, more than do women, hope for ego support in marriage.[14]

Social changes have radically modified the ways of satisfying ego needs. In generations past a man was known to many people in many ways. The village shoemaker was not just a shoemaker to his acquaintances—he had a name, a past, a reputation and a family connection by which he was identified. He might be thought of, for example, as gentle and honest, a good father, a steady citizen and a devout churchman, a

[13] Press release on hairdressers' convention.
[14] *Op. cit.*

practical joker and an all-around good fellow. Acquaintances judged him not only as a shoemaker but also as a person and a neighbor. Today the man behind the counter at the local shoe-repair excites little interest in his many patrons. They are not concerned about his personal life or interests. They only want to know if he can fix shoes.

But man does not fit well into this impersonal and indifferent atmosphere that he has created for himself. He is no more an insensitive robot than he was in the past. The neighborhood shoe-repair man has interests, values, hobbies, abilities, and opinions about which he needs to feel proud, but who even knows of them? If he is fortunate, his wife does. From her he receives the praise, the encouragement, the constant reassurance that reminds him that he is after all an individual, that he is someone special —apart from the mass—that he is a "somebody" rather than a "nobody." This description of life does not fit all people even today, yet modern living provides relatively few with recognition in abundance. Those who make a big splash probably get more publicity and acclaim than they did in the past. With urbanization and increased vocational specialization, however, the majority of individuals are likely to feel like strangers even among their acquaintances. Without a feeling of significance, of amounting to something, many forms of personality distortion develop because the human ego must have satisfaction. Marriage today is one of the most certain ways to fulfill the need to feel significant.

Marriage must above all things help both man and wife meet the need for status and recognition. Even when there are many other channels through which ego satisfaction can be realized—and there are, particularly for the male, and for the female who can continue a career along with marriage—most persons today are very dependent on marriage for a share of their ego satisfaction.

If marriage and homemaking are a major part of her life, the demands of the wife on the spouse for ego satisfaction through her relationship with him will be great. In dating, the successful male succeeds in making a woman feel that she is the most important creature in the world because she is a woman. He makes her feel that she is beautiful, wise, comfortable to be with, understanding—that she in fact embodies all that makes life beautiful and worthwhile. If homemaking and wifehood are to be her primary role after marriage, he must continue not only to express such sentiments but to actually hold them if she is to be content and feel significant.

Because this goal is so difficult to achieve in modern marriage, the wife often feels compelled to seek outside activities as means of acquiring status and recognition. Very often she must do so or succumb to feelings of inferiority and uselessness, particularly if she has been in the limelight prior to the marriage.

If a work outlet is blocked for the wife whose ego is suffering in marriage, she is likely to unwittingly turn her frustration toward tearing down her husband's achievements. By criticizing, ignoring, or belittling his satisfaction in his own achievements, or in other ways working out her feeling of defeat she tries to draw her husband down to her own level. This is particularly true if the love bond has also weakened.

Finally, both men and women want in their mate someone who will command the approval and respect of others—parents, relatives, friends, colleagues at work, even strangers. And just as important, both want a mate who will bring credit, not shame and embarrassment. A proper mate draws social approval to the spouse and lends dignity and worth to the marriage motive.

An Approved Sexual Outlet

Marriage is our society's only sanctioned outlet for the sex drive. Religion and custom sanction the joining of man and wife in the flesh as normal, natural, and moral. Sex is a value not only with biological meaning, but also with emotional content.

Sex needs are real physical needs. Their mutual expression in marriage is one of the elements in the fulfillment of one's need for feeling successful, safe, and whole. In this sense of bringing personal unity, sex needs are psychological as well as physical and organic. The romantic marriage integrates the psychological and physical aspects of sex and makes them inseparable. It is in this sense that mates must be able to satisfy each other. Neither prudes nor the unconventional, who use sex merely for excitement, adventure, or for domination, can meet the sexual requirements of marriage.

The periodicity of sex hunger, the frequency with which this need must be met by release in sexual contact varies from individual to individual. But the need is there and can be completely satisfied in American society in no other way as satisfactorily as in the constancy of the marriage relationship. Once marriage is entered into it becomes the habitual way of bringing relief, pleasure, relaxation, comfort, and closeness to the marriage relationship.

Only in marriage does sex become a responsible act, involving for the woman the possibility of motherhood with the obligations and joys which this entails. Thus in marriage she too can participate in the sex act without feeling that she is risking the future of the child who may be born. For the man it carries the responsibilities of parenthood, with the age-long requirement that the male care for and support the female and her young, an arrangement that is as old as human history and probably predates mankind.[15]

Sex as a factor leading to marriage is probably a much more important and conscious factor for the male than the female. At least this is so if one is considering sex as physical appetite. Even those women who cannot accept sex as a pleasure generally look upon it as a means to marital security and ultimately to parenthood.

Studies of contemporary mores suggest that for several reasons, the married pair is capable of realizing more in this area than in any previous period of history: (1) Fear of unwanted pregnancy has been reduced. The spacing of children is approaching the level of a practical science. The sexual union is now an act of pleasure, release, and mutual satisfaction, which it could never be in an atmosphere of fear and anxiety about an unwanted pregnancy. (2) Psychological impediments to mutual sharing have been greatly reduced. The taboo-ridden female, taught to be passive, felt it was a sin and she was ashamed to be sexually assertive. The young wife of today, if she is fortunate in having been given adequate sex education, looks forward to the sexual life of marriage. She views this as a form of close sharing, of appropriate sensual delight. Rather than merely catering to the male, she is an active and responsive partner. This is the ideal. (In Chapters 22 and 23 we shall indicate how difficult its realization is.)

The lowered fertility rate—confining childbearing to a short span, usually less than 10 years—and the increasing length of marriage make possible a sharing of sex life for a period of 40 years or more in the average marriage. The new ability to control conception, Mead suggests,[16] makes more frequent copulation, and with more partners, less relevant as a social issue. Certainly this is true in terms of the less likely conception of and birth of an unwanted child.

Social Compulsions to Marry

There are still many social compulsions to marry. One of the most important is the realization, as one leaves the parental home, that the only way one may feel complete again is by establishing a family of one's own. Only by establishing a home can a person enjoy again the pattern of living he himself experienced or longed for as a child. Only thus can life seem fully proper and adequate; only thus can he find again the intimacy, warmth, and sharing that are so much a part of the satisfactions of the socialized human being.

[15] Margaret Mead, *Male and Female* (New York: William Morrow & Co., Inc., 1949).

[16] Margaret Mead's Sound Insights into the Furor over Shifting American Morals," *Life*, 65:30–34, August 25, 1968.

As has been so vividly pointed out by Levy and Munroe, one's drive to marriage begins in childhood in his own home.[17] "Marriage begins in infancy," they say. "People who have learned about family loves and hates, rivalry and cooperation in their parents' homes carry these lessons into their own homes. The most perfect system fails if it does not meet the expectations formed in childhood."

Women undoubtedly feel greater social and emotional pressure to marry than do men since their upbringing is much more family-oriented. Then, too, marriage is still looked upon as their most important evidence of having attained adulthood through the competitive means of mate seeking.

Another powerful pressure to marry today is the general social expectation that, particularly in recreational affairs, people will participate in pairs rather than as individuals. In the earlier agrarian economy, all age groups associated in social life, but this is rarely so in urban industrial society where all social groups are stratified by age and where pairs are the normal unit of association in adulthood. One reason the older adolescent feels a little out of place is that it is expected that he will attend any private function with a member of the opposite sex. This is more true of women than of men, since it is assumed that a woman will have an escort in her attendance at public and private functions.

The extent to which a person of a given age feels social pressure to marry depends a great deal on the kind of community in which he lives. The college girl of twenty with two years of school remaining will sense no social pressure to marry, rather will sense considerable pressure of parental and peer group opinion not to marry. The girl of eighteen who has left high school for a job may sense great pressure to marry.

Then, too, the social prestige of marriage in some communities is very great. In those rural communities where large numbers of young people marry in or immediately out of high school, great social pressure is exerted on girls to marry early and on parents to see them married. To be able to acquire the status of marriage and begin homemaking and childbearing is one of the higher values of the community.

A countertrend may well be emerging. Owing to the population explosion, commentators on the social scene are becoming bolder in expressing views to the effect that it would be better if fewer persons married. In large cities singles' clubs and apartment houses for singles have multiplied. There is an increasing attempt to fill the time of the single person and to cater to his needs. These ventures are profit motivated, but the fact that they prove profitable may be an indication of a move toward the single life as a satisfactory state. It is possible, however, that these institutions are still primarily places to find a suitable marriage partner.

[17] John Levy and Ruth Munroe, *The Happy Family* (New York: Alfred A. Knopf, Inc., 1938), p. 5.

Negative Motivations for Marriage

The positive aspects of the motivation to marry have been stressed, for it is assumed that these are the most compelling, yet motivations are rarely unmixed. Many marry in part, or perhaps chiefly, with an avoidance motive. To cover pregnancy is one of the motives in our culture, perhaps for 10 to 25 percent of the population.[18] In this classification are to be found many of the teen-age marriages. Marriage may have been in the thoughts of one or the other or of both but the actual precipitating event was the pregnancy.

Many youths reach the decision to marry when they find the situation at home increasingly unbearable. They want greater freedom than they can have under the parental roof. They hope to find it in marriage. This probably explains in part why young people from large families and underprivileged families so often marry young. Crowded conditions of the parental home, the constant conflict with brothers, sisters and parents, the rather authoritarian patterns that of necessity prevail in such homes lead young people to choose early marriage as the better of two alternatives.[19] Margaret Mead cites this as a problem of the nuclear family— two women cannot get along under one roof.[20]

Some young people marry from a sense of loneliness which has developed because of neglect or lack of affection during childhood in the parental home. They are insecure souls fleeing loneliness and seeking warmth, closeness, and affection that will shield them from the anxieties and fears of a world in which they have always felt exposed to fear, anxiety, and unearned guilt. Marriage for them is often a mistake, for these feelings are exaggerated as frequently as they are cured by a youthful marriage. Often they become too demanding and monopolistic of the mate and thus invite marital failure.

Some marry to cover a feeling of sex guilt. Their sex drives or acquired sex appetites, or habits, have become a constant source of guilt and anxiety. They seek marriage primarily as a sexual outlet—to sanctify desires which have plagued them from the time of earliest adolescence,

[18] Harold T. Christensen and Hanna H. Meissner, "Studies in Child Spacing III—Premarital Pregnancy as a Factor in Divorce," *American Sociological Review*, 18:641–644, December, 1953; see also Harold T. Christensen, "Child Spacing via Record Linkage: New Data Plus a Summing Up of Earlier Reports," *Marriage and Family Living*, 25:272–280, August, 1963.

[19] The author's studies indicate that all these generalizations tend to be true of the large family. See his *Teenage Adjustments in Large and Small Families*, Bulletin No. 549, April, 1954; *The Broken Home and Teenage Adjustments*, Bulletin No. 542, April, 1953, both of the Washington Agricultural Experiment Station, Pullman, Washington; see also Carol L. Stone and Paul H. Landis, "An Approach to Authority Patterns in Parent-Teenage Relationships," *Rural Sociology*, 18:233–242, September, 1953.

[20] *Op. cit.*

sometimes even before. Some such individuals have been haunted by a sense of guilt over masturbation or other types of sexual exercise which are harmless in and of themselves, but which have proved to be harmful because of feelings of deep anxiety induced by teachings to the contrary. Others feel keenly guilty because their sexual desires, even their sensuous thoughts, seem to conflict with the teachings of their parents or the church. Others hasten into marriage to cover feelings of guilt and fear involved in a sexual relationship already begun with the future spouse.

Some marry primarily for spite, or self-justification. The loneliness, the rancor, the bitterness of a breakup are buried in a new, drastic plunge into the risky security of a hasty marriage.

Today many remarry to cure an intolerable loneliness following divorce or widowhood. They seek also to find the satisfactions which they once had and lost, or never found in a previous marriage. This statement refers to the one in five marriages which are contracted by persons who have been widowed or divorced.

It is said that some people marry for pity. One finds this the theme of an occasional novel, so one must suspect that it happens in real life. The individual marries another in order to save him from some real or imagined fate, perhaps nothing more than the fate of failure to achieve marriage. One finds it hard to account for the marriage of the physically normal to the severely handicapped in terms of a motive other than that of pity, or some altruistic motive.

Probably every motive of which human beings are capable enters into one marriage or another: escape, fortune, prestige, economic security or status seeking. Both man's negative and positive drives affect almost every decision he makes. Although one cannot say that it is wrong to marry for any of these motives, one must recognize the weakness of a marriage based on some of these motivations.

Needs Thwarted by Marriage

Very fundamental needs are fulfilled in marriage as in no other human relationship, yet marriage drastically interferes with other needs. The need to be loved, for example, often runs counter to the need for self-realization and ego satisfaction.

Certain hostilities inevitably develop when the demands of love become so great that they thwart one's desire to attain economic or vocational status and success. The shelter of marriage, which makes one feel secure, may at times interfere strongly with one's desire to be free of ties and obligations, to be foot-loose, so to speak, to venture and experiment and seek new experience. The need to be reassured and comforted is all-important at times, but at other times, when one feels more sure of one-self, a sense of self-sufficiency takes precedence. Independence replaces the need for a refuge. At such times one is ashamed of former weakness and does not want to be reminded of it.

So the changing needs manifest themselves from day to day in the up-and-down fluctuations of moods and the adversities of the world in which we live and work. Marriage is, therefore, a constantly shifting pattern, ever new and in a certain sense never fully adequate for balancing the human being's dual need for oneness and for personal freedom. There are numerous mainsprings to behavior and motivation, not all of them conscious, but all of them purposeful in terms of meeting the individual's particular needs at a particular time.

Often the marriage is called upon to fulfill needs that have been thwarted in outside activities. The husband who comes home feeling uncertain or unsuccessful in his work may be in need of consolation and reassurance. The mate in this case is expected to rally to the occasion when perhaps she has even greater need for reassurance herself. Yet the husband's reactions are not irrational. They are purposeful in terms of his monetary needs, even though contradictory to the self-sufficient man he may have appeared to be in the morning when he left home. The wife may have greater difficulty in accepting him as the humble child, needing comfort and strength, than as the strong man she respects and honors.

Needs are not always rational and often cannot be expressed in words, but the human organism always moves in response to them, even though they are quite contradictory from one time to another. Marriage is, therefore, a moving equilibrium in which two personalities work to find fulfillment of each other's needs, with love the overall bond helping to compensate for the inevitable clashes.

Marriage is as potentially capable of creating deep hostilities, animosities, and frictions as it is of giving happiness and mutual satisfaction. Because of the high aspirations that center in it and the close intimate demands that are made upon personality in the marriage institution, hostile tendencies are always latent in it. When they come to the surface, they can be of the most violent nature.

It is for this reason that marriage, designed to meet more human needs than is any other institution, is also capable of producing more misery, human suffering, and personal torture than any other relationship developed by man. The pair relationship has throughout history been laden with tragedy where failure has replaced success and where defeat has replaced hope. The tragedies of married life have been the favorite themes of drama and fiction, ranking second only to love itself. This kind of plot is always fascinating, for every person can as readily identify himself with this phase of the marriage relationship, as with the comedy and glory of marriage.

Of all murders committed in the United States, 38 percent are within the family.[21] The family, being the closest of all relationships, is capable of "failure, hostility and destructiveness. They are as much a part of the family system and relationships among members as success, love, and solidarity are."[22]

It would be inappropriate, therefore, to close this chapter without this word of caution. Marriage at a distance often looks much less problem-free than it is, particularly to the young, who in the throes of happy romance lose sight of the realities of life. Marriage is not a one-way street to happiness, and the pronunciation of a marriage ceremony is no guarantee that personal needs will be met. Only as marriage is entered into seriously and with the full understanding of one's own characteristics and those of the person he marries, can one venture safely and expect to realize in substantial measure the fulfillment of personality needs.

As this book develops, an attempt will be made at numerous points to differentiate between types of persons and types of background that hold high promise of success in marriage, and also to point out those types of persons and backgrounds that show comparatively little promise of success. So far, social science has no positive answers but the indications from research are superior to folklore which has been the only guide for past generations.

Problems

1. The modern marriage is usually expected "to meet the individual's needs for love and emotional security, status, recognition, companionship, and sex." Marriage is also sought for negative reasons—as a means of escaping certain undesirable circumstances. These needs vary in importance from one person to another, depending upon his personality and background.

   Analyze your own personality needs as best you can. Which of their various items—love, emotional security, status, recognition, companionship, sex, or negative motives—do you think will rank first in determining whom you marry? As you analyze your development why do you feel this one need is of first importance in your life?

2. Among your various personality needs, are there some which you would expect to satisfy in relationships outside of marriage? Discuss possibilities of need fulfillment through such avenues as job, friends, children, church,

[21] *Family Life,* Vol. 28, 1968.

[22] Alice S. Rossi, "Transitions to Parenthood," *Journal of Marriage and Family Living,* 30:26–39, February, 1968.

parents, brothers and sisters, hobbies, community activities, girls (or boys) you've previously dated, pets, etc.

3. *Research exercise:* Prepare a list of expectations concerning your marriage (kind of relationship expected, kind of needs to be satisfied, kind of family life planned, number of children expected, and level of living expected).

   To ensure frankness, lists should preferably be anonymous with sex of respondent indicated on the sheet. Tabulate and discuss results. Compare tabulations of men and women separately.

   What do results show with regard to marriage values in this generation? Do men and women seek substantially the same goals? Far different ones? If different, are they complementary rather than contradictory? Appraise the various answers given from the standpoint of their being (*a*) practical, (*b*) realistic, (*c*) consistent with the expectations of the average community.

4. *Sociodrama:* A young woman is talking with her happily married sister, seeking help in deciding whether or not she should accept the marriage proposal of the night before. Her sister tries to help her decide by asking a number of questions based on contemporary values in mate selection. Their grandmother enters and adds her advice, which is largely based on the criteria of her own youth.

5. Define "anonymity." Briefly indicate why it is so characteristic of many sectors of society today and show how it affects marriage and family life.

6. Once a modern couple have married do you consider that each is obligated to "love, honor, and obey" the other for a lifetime? Explain.

7. Read the following statement and select one of the four conclusions below which you feel best describes a realistic philosophy of marriage. Explain your choice briefly. If you believe that there is a fifth alternative, state it and defend it.

   It has been said that "when you don't expect anything of your marriage you can't be disappointed." Do you believe that couples would be happier in the long run if they:

   a. Expected nothing of marriage but a working arrangement for the purpose of raising a family?

   b. Expected to fulfill most of their needs other than for sexual satisfactions in relationships outside of marriage?

   c. Continued to expect complete need fulfillment, as most do today, but worked harder at attaining their goal?

   d. Tempered their expectations with an understanding of the limitations of all human beings and all human relationships?

8. Have you known persons to marry for motives you would consider with suspicion? Did they succeed?

9. Have you known persons whom you considered unmarriageable? What was the basis for your conviction?

10. *Sociodrama:* A friendless young woman marries to escape her lonely world. Her husband is a popular, out-going person whose need for companionship is satisfied by his friends and work associates. He thinks of a wife primarily in terms of her role as a housekeeper.

    Act out a situation or conversation in which the expectations of each are pictured. If possible have the husband and wife reach a new understanding of one another as a result of the conversation.

Selected References

Articles in Books of Readings

Cavan, Ruth Shonle, *Marriage and the Family in the Modern World: A Book of Readings*, third edition (New York: Thomas Y. Crowell Co., 1969).
  Goode, William J., "The Family as an Element in Social Structure," Reading 1.
  Edwards, John N., "The Future of the Family Revisited," Reading 4.
Haimowitz, Morris L. and Haimowitz, Natalie, *Human Development: Selected Readings* (New York: Thomas Y. Crowell Co., 1966).
  "What Kind of People Do We Want?," p. 1.
Landis, Judson T., and Landis, Mary G., *Readings in Marriage and the Family* (Englewood Cliffs, N. J.: Prentice-Hall, Inc., 1952).
  Ogburn, William F., "The Changing Functions of the Family," pp. 18–21.
  Landis, Paul H., "The Changing Family," pp. 27–31.
Sussman, Marvin B., *Sourcebook in Marriage and the Family*, third edition (Boston: Houghton Mifflin Co., 1968).
  Sussman, Marvin B., "The Isolated Nuclear Family: Fact or Fiction?", Reading 11.
  Population Bulletin, "Boom Babies Come of Age: The American Family at the Crossroads," Reading 14.
Winch, Robert F. and Goodman, Louis Wolf, *Selected Readings in Marriage and the Family*, revised edition (New York: Holt, Rinehart and Winston, 1968).
  Nimkoff, M. F. and Middleton, Russell, "Types of Family and Types of Economy," pp. 35–43.
  Ogburn, William F., "The Changing Functions of the Family," pp. 58–63.
  Goode, William F., "The Role of the Family in Industrialization," pp. 64–69.
  Winch, Robert F., and Blumberg, Rae L., "Societal Complexity and Familial Organization," pp. 70–92.
  Glick, Paul C. and Parke, Robert Jr., "New Approaches in Studying the Life Cycle of the Family," pp. 166–176.

2

MALE AND FEMALE: PREDISPOSITIONS AND ROLES

3

Male and Female: Biology

Each of the thousands of cells in the human body have 46 chromosomes except the egg and sperm cells. They have only 23. The chromosomes of the female egg cell are all alike and are called X chromosomes. The sperm cells of the male carry either 23 chromosomes or 22 X and 1 Y chomosome. It is this Y chromosome that accounts for the male's beginning.[1] If a sperm with the Y chromosome fertilizes the egg cell the male results.

Nature provides in the male a ratio of about 60 Y sperm to each 40 X sperm, so that more male conceptions take place. In some marriages, however, all children are females, in others all males. It is now known that some males produce almost no Y chomosomes, others almost no X. One family had produced no males for five generations. A young man in this family was found to have 96 percent X chromosome sperm. Y sperm are small, round headed and move more rapidly than the X carrying sperm, which are larger and long headed. The reason some families run to males and some to females is that these ratios are probably hereditary.

This is the biological beginning, but biology alone is not a guarantee that the individual produced will be classified psychologically, or sociologically in the sex class which the chromosomes foretold. The making of a male and of a female is a process involving hereditary determinants, glandular activity (including hormonal balance), and social conditioning to assure proper role identification by self and others. If either the biological or sociological sequences fail, a misfit individual results.

[1] A recent genetic development is the discovery that some males have, instead of a simple XY chromosome makeup, an XYY or even an $XYYY$ composition. Preliminary study suggests that prison populations have a relatively high ratio of the excess Y group. This may revive theories of the "born criminal type" made popular by Lombroso. The XYY seem to be tall and thin, highly excitable, given to uncontrollable violence. The extra Y chromosome has already become a legal issue in court procedures involving trial of criminals with the extra Y characteristic. No such behavioral characteristics have been associated with extra X chromosomes in the female.

Genetic Classification

External genitalia are critical in sex identification. The doctor and parents are dependent upon them for the immediate classification of the newborn child into one or the other sex category. The first question of all concerned is certain to be, "Is it a boy or girl?" It would hardly be appropriate for the doctor to reply, "I do not know," yet in a small proportion of cases he cannot know, the child being a hermaphrodite.

The term comes from the Greek word meaning half man, half woman, child of the gods Hermes and Aphrodite. When external genitalia are not clearly definable confusion in sex classification takes place. Currently in hospital births, doubts are allayed by a microscopic examination of bucal cells scraped from the mouth. Every cell in the male is male and in females, female.

The hermaphrodite is of one sex by gene determination. However since hormonal balance is not realized because of inherited malformations or parental injury, particular sex characteristics fail to develop.[2] Failure to realize anatomical development may be in external sex organs, internal, or both. A few hermaphrodites produce both egg and sperm cells, but there is no known case where a human being has been capable of being both mother and father.

Each embryo starts with the rudiments of sex glands in the form of genital ridges. The chromosome makeup determines which will go forward in the development of the embryo, male or female. The actual development seems to be controlled by the hormones produced by the primitive gonad (undifferentiated glands) and later, it is believed, by other hormones of the adrenal cortex. If the primitive gonads develop a liberal amount of male hormones (testosterone and androsterone), the direction of development is toward maleness; if they produce a sparse amount, toward femaleness. Research seems to suggest that all embryos could develop in the direction of femaleness if it were not for the secretion of the testes which lead embryos toward masculine development.[3]

Adult males and females carry in their genitalia marks of the opposite sex. The male carries a seam down the underside of his penis and across his scrotum which could have opened, during the embryonic stage, into the labia of the female's vulva. The female carries rudiments of the penis—the bud-like clitoris, which contains the same kind of nerve plexis as the male glans penis. Both sexes produce the same hormones but in different quantities. Even after adult development, if the hormonal

[2] Howard W. Jones, Jr. and William Wallis Scott, *Hermaphroditism, Genital Anomalies, and Related Endocrine Disorders* (Baltimore: The Williams & Wilkins Co., 1958).

[3] *Ibid.*

balance is disturbed, modifications in the somatic structure may occur. Some women at menopause, when male sex hormones are excessive, and the imbalance is not medically corrected, tend to develop mustaches and beards. When a male is castrated the production of sex hormones is reduced and the male may develop a disposition often identified with the female in our society.

After birth, rearing must be in the appropriate sex category or the individual will not be able to function in the social group, even though biologically complete for his genital sex group. In the past, where gender classification was made at birth on the basis of external genitalia, physicians had to make an on-the-spot decision which determined sex rearing. This sometimes led to an error in sex rearing.

The Critical Period in Sex "Imprinting"

Wrong sex classification is not unalterable during the first two years of life.[4] In fact, experience shows that the sex category of a child can be changed with little disturbance until he is two and a half years of age. Psychologists refer to certain ages in the psychological development of the individual as "critical periods." Apparently the critical period for internalizing his sex category comes prior to age two and a half: a time when he is learning language and beginning to take an interest in play with his own group. Any attempt to shift the child from one sex category to the other after this age is accompanied by increasingly severe disturbances. By age six, sex identity is for all practical purposes irreversible.

"As gender role and identity become fully differentiated, they become permanently indelible and imprinted, and subsequently, irreversible and powerful in influencing behavior as if innately preordained. . . . The evidence from hermaphroditic cases of sex assignment is that the critical period of gender imprinting is in early childhood, beginning with the onset of the mastery of language. The die is cast, pretty well, by the age of six, after which major realignment of gender role and identity is rare."[5]

Subculture Rearing

Subculture rearing can apparently alter the sex psychology of any individual so much that it will be difficult for him to assume the behavior

[4] J. P. Scott, "Critical Periods in Behavioral Development," *Science*, 138:949–958, 1962.

[5] John Money, "Developmental Differentiation of Feminity and Masculinity Compared," in Seymour M. Farber and Roger H. L. Wilson (eds.), *The Potential of Woman* (New York: McGraw-Hill Book Co., 1963), pp. 51–65.

suited to his biological constitution. The sociological process of role indoctrination is a process so smoothly handled that it seems automatic. So effective are the means by which the male and female internalize attitudes, behavior, and expectations of their sex that subculture identification becomes practically irreversible.

A girl who is brought up as a boy and treated as a boy, no matter what her genetic and hormonal structure, comes to think of herself as a boy, to act as a boy, and will, if allowed to develop very long in this direction, find it almost impossible to ever develop the appropriate attitudes. The same is true of the boy reared as a female. Many individuals have inappropriate gender identification in much or in part of their psychological orientation, even when the family and other social groups handling them fully intended that they would identify themselves psychologically and sociologically with their own sex.

Gender Identity—A Delicate Balance

The sex a person feels himself to be may be opposite to his anatomy. Herein lies the responsibility of the family for helping the child internalize the correct conception of his gender. The preceding brief summary indicated that interacting biological, parental, and subcultural forces enter into the making of a male or female, and that the achievement of sex identity is an intricate process involving all these factors.

The well-balanced, biologically distinct male or female is produced by heredity and proper glandular functioning during the interuterine period of development. Right sex classification is determined by those who place the child in one sex category or the other. Gender self-identification is a product of the sex roles played by the individual and these roles, when wrongly typed, need not fit glandular makeup of the developed male or female.

The individual must be so handled that he will internalize his gender as a prerequisite of assuming the roles of the subculture of his own sex. Otherwise an individual with all male characteristics may have the psychological constitution and sexual proclivities of the female. Gender identification is likely to follow the sex rearing of the individual, no matter what his biological sex, but if it does not conform to his sex, conflict is certain to result. It is also possible that his erotic dreams, fantasies, and practices will conform to his biological sex, even when he is reared in the wrong sex group, inducing further conflict.

Hormonal composition alone will not overcome wrong sex rearing. Role training is made easy only if one is trained from the beginning for roles in the subculture he will occupy. The general deportment of male and female, as they are shaped in their respective subcultures, takes deep roots from the standpoint of social obligation and social expectation.

In this sophisticated age of international athletic competition, those with mistaken sex identity are routinely eliminated through the chromosome test. It is not considered fair that individuals, who are typed by this final test as genetically male, but who have always considered themselves and behaved as females, be allowed to compete with women.

Since marriage involves the interrelationships of male and female in their biological constitution, their psychological orientation, and their role conceptions, each of these areas will be explored as a basis for understanding both the preface to marriage and adjustment during marriage.

It is now believed that homosexuality is a psychosocial development and not a biochemical or hormonal one. Failure in gender identification manifests itself in many degrees of divergence, from transvestism (desire to dress like the opposite sex) to different degrees of latent and overt homosexuality. Even overt homosexuality varies in degree from the desire for a sex partner of one's own sex as an element of sexual variety, to an attraction to one's own sex exclusively.[6]

Gender confusion, when it takes the form of homosexuality, becomes a serious problem in societies such as ours, which expect clear-cut identity with one's own sex and the appropriate sex behavior.

A study of 300 homosexuals by the New York Mattachine Society, a group of homosexuals, showed that only six answered "yes" to the question "If you had a son, would you want him to be a homosexual?"[7]

Homosexuality is a development of the parental home. It is the product of certain types of relationships that exist between parent and child, and between husbands and wives. A nine-year study of homosexual males by Dr. Bieber, Associate Clinical Professor of Psychiatry at New York Medical College, concludes that the roots of homosexuality are in disturbed situations in the early family relationship. In almost every case he found "a close-binding intimate" mother and/or a hostile, detached, or unrespected father, or other parental abberations. In a majority of cases he found the father hostile to the child. He concludes that a warmly supportive, constructive father neutralizes the effect of "seductive, close-binding" attempts of the mother.[8]

The recent study of the Wydens[9] stresses the importance of developing the child's sense of masculinity or femininity between the ages of three

[6] See such works as Frank S. Caprio, *Female Homosexuality* (New York: Citadel Press, 1954); Donald Webster Cory, *Homosexuality: A Cross-Cultural Approach* (New York: Julian Press, Inc., 1956). See also Peter and Barbara Wyden, *Growing up Straight* (New York: Stein and Day, 1968).

[7] *Family Life* 28:1, August, 1968. See also Peter and Barbara Wyden, *op. cit.*

[8] Summary by Robert C. Doty in *The New York Times*, Western edition, December 27, 1963.

[9] *Op. cit.*

and ten. With boys and girls this is largely a matter of normal relationships with parents and setting a good example. The development of the homosexual daughter seems to be produced by the presence of a feared and puritanical father who secretly shows a sexual interest in the daughter, much like the close-binding mother in the case of the male child.

Dr. Harvey E. Kaye and associates made an intensive study[10] of 24 homosexual women and found in their background fathers who were "puritanical and explosive." Daughters feared them, although not from physical abuse. The fathers were overly possessive, interested in the daughter physically, and both mothers and fathers tended to discourage their daughters' development as adults.

Other environmental conditions may contribute to homosexuality, but it is generally considered impossible for a homosexual to be produced in a warmly loving home of sensible parents who are themselves sexually adjusted.

The Wydens suggest[11] that the following factors are important in addition to setting a good example for the child:

1. Breast feeding if possible, although the affection accompanying feeding may be the important factor.
2. Unemotional toilet training. Enemas and rectal suppositories should be used only if medically necessary.
3. Separate sleeping room away from the parent after the first year, or even sooner. The child should never be taken into the parents' bed.
4. Parents should not become excited about the child's masturbation.
5. Children should have plenty of contact with other children.
6. Children should be helped to feel free to discuss sex.
7. Boys should get into competitive activities, but not where they are sure to fail.
8. The child should know that he is loved without being smothered.
9. He should be made proud and happy with his own sex and comfortable with members of his own sex.

Biological Rhythms and Sequences

The female   The sexual life of the female moves through complex changes which have no counterpart in the male. As pointed out by Margaret Mead, "Coming to terms with the rhythms of woman's life means coming to terms with life itself."[12] The imperatives of the body are her

[10] *Archives of General Psychiatry* reported in *Family Life* news notes.
[11] *Op. cit.*
[12] Margaret Mead, *Male and Female* (New York: William Morrow & Co., Inc., 1949).

most pressing realities: they cannot be ignored, and must be reckoned with by society and by the marriage partner as well as by the woman herself.

The major developments are, first, the arrival of puberty with the event of menstruation—the primary sex-life rhythm; second, defloration, on first intercourse,[13] third, pregnancy, with its disturbance of body function and social habits;[14] fourth, childbirth—an event of great biological and sociological moment; fifth, lactation, which has both physiological and psychological effects;[15] and sixth, menopause, or the change of life, which marks the cessation of ovulation, menstruation, and fertility, and which is accompanied by glandular changes and, often, strong emotional reactions.

Defloration, pregnancy, lactation, and the menopause will be discussed later. The most significant of the biological events, in terms of adjustment during a large portion of adult life, is menstruation. This marks puberty, beginning suddenly and continuing more or less without interruption, except when pregnancy takes place, for a period of thirty-five to forty years.

The physiological process itself has often been made a great impediment to woman. Many cultures have declared this a period of uncleanness and surrounded it with taboos. Numerous restrictions have been imposed, not only on physical activities, but also on social intercourse. Ashley-Montagu, anthropologist, has listed some of the common menstrual prohibitions and beliefs on which they are based.[16] Menstruating women cause flowers to wilt and wither, preserves of every sort to spoil, dough to fail to rise, seeds to become sterile, meat to decompose. In Europe women are excluded from many occupations on this account. They are not allowed to work in French perfumeries when menstruating, to pick mushrooms in commercial growing places, to tend silk worms. Rhine women are barred from handling vessels in which wine is to be fermented. They are also excluded from sugar factories.

He believes that there is some scientific basis for these prohibitions, arising from observation of the effects on living plants. Sweat secretions at this time do kill or damage certain kinds of living tissue. In some cultures anything menstruating women touch must be purified by religious ceremonials. They may be entirely barred from religious participation during menstruation, and among some primitives must even live apart during this period.

Fewer concessions to the menstrual period are made now in our cul-

[13] Considered in Ch. 12.

[14] The subject of Ch. 26.

[15] Discussed in Ch. 26.

[16] M. F. Ashley-Montagu, *Anthropology and Human Nature* (Boston: Porter Sargeant, Publishers, 1957).

ture than formerly although it is still referred to as "the curse," and more rarely as the "sick time." The use of modern sanitary protections, the daily bath, and higher standards of personal hygiene have removed "uncleanness." Modern drugs and the stress on physical activity for women have removed the taboo on activity. For a few women it remains a critically painful period.

Menstruation is an inescapable fact of women's life from about age thirteen to age forty-nine, month in and month out, with its moods, its discomfort, its requirements for special sanitary precautions, its limits on contacts with the male. No matter what her time cycle, menstruation is part of her life, and any cessation of it is a matter of concern. If she has been involved sexually, either before marriage, in marriage, or after widowhood, cessation may be due to pregnancy. The cessation may also be due to factors of health or emotional strain, but even so the suspicion of pregnancy is likely to be present.

The male   The male's sexual development and decline is a gradual thing without marked periods of change.[17] Prior to puberty his capacity to reproduce gradually develops. Maturation of sexual capacity comes at puberty accompanied by rather marked body changes. From early adolescence on, his sexual drive gradually declines but rarely disappears until well beyond age sixty, often not until the eighties, or in certain cases not until death in extreme old age. Some men when in their 90's have sired children. Men's decline is a gradual aging process which seems to affect the whole organism rather than sex characteristics as such. Nature spares women the strenuous toil of reproduction in old age. The male need not be spared. His role is primarily economic and he is often more able to provide for children after fifty than before.

There is no physical damage to the male from first sexual intercourse

---

[17] Although the above statements are true of the general stages in the development of male and female, a more detailed tracing shows that the development of sexual maturity is not as climactic in either male or female as these obvious stages indicate. The concept "adolescent sterility" has come into the scientific literature in recent years primarily because of research among primitive peoples and among animals. It is evident that the boy is capable of semen ejaculations before ripe spermatozoa are produced. Menstruation begins in the girl also before ovaries are fully developed, and ova are often produced before the womb is sufficiently well developed to carry a fetus.

It has become particularly evident, from the study of primitive peoples, that among those who permit free sex play prior to marriage, pregnancy is not frequent during the early years of adolescence. In many such tribes, sex play continues uninterrupted until the girl does become pregnant and thus attests to her readiness for marriage and parenthood. In these societies it is evident that fertility rarely comes with the beginning of menstruation. Maximum fertility in the female probably is not reached until the early twenties. For a brief, nontechnical statement on this subject, see Therese Benedek, "Some Problems of Motherhood," in A. M. Krich (ed.), *Women: The Variety and Meaning of their Sexual Experience* (New York: Dell Publishing Co., Inc., 1956), Ch. 7.

to mark the end of his virginity, and he has no physical responsibility for offspring other than the act of copulation itself. Copulation is an end in itself rather than a beginning, as for the female. Society places on him the responsibility for the care of the female and her helpless offspring, but this is a social obligation, not a part of nature.

The male is spared the stress which may characterize the female menopause. The decline of potency and fertility in the male is a life-long process once full maturation is reached prior to twenty years of age.

The Development of Appetites and Drives

In this field it is most difficult to separate biology from cultural conditioning. No man or woman is permitted to grow up as designed by nature. From earliest infancy, personality is subject to the molding influences of culture. Manifest drives and appetites are certain in most instances to reflect some degree of modification of biological forces by education.

Glandular factors   Biological forces in and of themselves are, however, decisive factors in the shaping of the male and female personality. The profound effect of the sex glands and their hormone secretions on the male personality, particularly on such traits as aggressiveness and courage is illustrated throughout the animal kingdom by marked change in psychology, as well as in physical build, of the animal which has had the gonads (testes) removed. The potentially courageous, sinewy, heavy-necked bull, when castrated as a calf, becomes a fat, placid, soft-tissued steer. A similar transformation is seen in the castrated rooster. Instead of a crowing cock, the capon becomes a tender-meated passive-dispositioned fowl much like the hen in temperament and tenderness of flesh.

A comparable change takes place in the human male when he is castrated at a prepubertal age. Such males (eunuchs) become pliant in disposition, fail to develop masculine secondary characteristics such as beard and body hair, become soft and girl-like in voice and flabby in muscle. Such males lose most of their interest in the opposite sex and become entirely different in psychological makeup from normal males.

Many cultures in the past have, and some still do, make much of this transformation in the male. One of the most cruel aspects of African slavery was the castration by the Arab captors of large numbers of boys to become servants in the harems of the Arab world. The crudity of the operation lead to a very high death rate. The Byzantine State based its vitality as an empire in part on the practice of the extensive employment of eunuchs in key government and military positions. Great numbers of boys were castrated for state positions. Eunuchs had no ambitious sons to place in office and could, unmotivated by nepotism, be objective in administration.[18] In the temples of Judaism, eunuchs were used because they could possess a purity of mind unmatched by males controlled by normal glandular pressures. Eunuchs are the entertainers today at christenings and other special occasions in Pakistan.

The removal of both ovaries in the young female produces marked changes also. The modified female, both among animals and human beings, tends to become more masculine in appearance and characteristics, indicating that these glands and their hormone secretions have a decisive effect upon the development of the female. Some women at menopause, with the decrease of female hormones, take on certain masculine characteristics such as facial hair growth and deepening of the voice. In such instances there seems to be an increase in the secretion of male hormones that are always present in the female.

The sex glands with their hormonal secretions, in fact, affect the growth of the body and account for many differences in height, weight, and tissue formation of male and female.

There is undoubtedly a biological basis for man's urge to pursue and woman's passivity. Certainly these traits are widely observed among most creatures in nature. Even so, culture can blunt the male's ardor if tradition so dictates.[19] Where sexual intimacy in childhood and adolescence is a part of the culture pattern, frigidity and impotence will be rare. If too great taboos are built about sex, both male and female may lack interest. The Manus tribe, for example, looks upon seminal discharge as a form of excretion and treats it with repugnance and shame.[20] The birth rate in this tribe is extremely low and the tribe is on the way to extinction.

Psychosexual development   The rate of psychosexual development differs for male and female. Sex interest for the male is at its height in the teens. Masturbation and other sexual expressions are nearly universal for the young male.[21] Often the teen-age girl has little or no localized sexual desire and she is much less likely to masturbate.[22] Female sex interest reaches its height near the age of thirty, long after sex sensation has been localized by sexual activity. The teen-age girl is interested in being cuddled

[18] Herbert J. Muller, *The Loom of History* (New York: Harper & Row, Publishers, 1958), pp. 337–338.

[19] Margaret Mead, "Potency and Receptivity," in Krich, *op. cit.*, Ch. 4. Money stresses the fact that the male sex urge is hormonally regulated. *Loc. cit.*

[20] For an excellent discussion of the effect of culture patterns on sex patterns, see Margaret Mead, "Potency and Receptivity," in Krich, *op. cit.*, Ch. 4.

[21]Alfred C. Kinsey and others, *Sexual Behavior in the Human Female* (Philadelphia: W. B. Saunders Co., 1953), p. 126.

[22] Kinsey and his co-workers found in their studies of thousands of males and females that at age 22, 40 percent of females had never experienced a sexual orgasm, whereas 80 percent of the boys had experienced an orgasm by 15 years of age, and 98 percent by 18 years of age.

but in most cases is not interested in erotic expression as such. Of course, the range of difference in psychosexual interest in both male and female varies from individual to individual. Some mature in sexual interest earlier than others. Some have very weak sex drives; others are often overwhelmed by them.

It is in the consequences of the sex act that one of the most important sex differences inheres. Women house the embryo and nurse the child. As anthropologist Margaret Mead has stated, "Men have to learn to want to be fathers. Girls are committed in every cell of their bodies," for the mother role. Sexual intercourse for both man and woman is a matter of a few minutes, but for the man those few minutes end. For the woman, they are "laden with commitments before and commitments afterward."[23]

Coitus is the most intimate and private human activity, yet in its consequences it is of great public importance. This is particularly true for women. From early adolescence and throughout adulthood, women are much more concerned with their bodies and their personal appearance than are most men. It is their biological function to attract the male and bind him to the responsibilities of parenthood. Men are much more concerned with affairs and activities external to themselves than with their own bodies and feelings. These are, in part, matters of conditioning in American culture, but probably not entirely so.

Cultural adaptations to biology   One of the most penetrating analyses of organic differences between male and female as factors in their respective sexual training and behavior is that by Frank K. Shuttleworth.[24] The essence of Shuttleworth's view is that male and female are conditioned differently sexually because they are so different in their biosexual makeup. Differences in conditioning begin in infancy and continue through childhood and adolescence. At least five biosexual differences lead to the differences in conditioning.

First, the female is a childbearer and has the mammary equipment for nursing. This Shuttleworth states as a fact, but he does not elaborate on the significance of it.

Second, the male has the greater height, weight, and physical prowess, which Shuttleworth feels most societies make a great deal of. He believes that sex aggressiveness is part of the total pattern of the male's superiority in physical build and energy.

Third, the male sex organ is the erectile penis, which, being external, is exposed from earliest childhood to stimulation from bedding, clothes, and later from self-manipulation. The male infant has frequent erections. These continue throughout childhood and friction brings gratifying re-

[23] Margaret Mead, "Introduction," in Krich, *op. cit.*
[24] Frank K. Shuttleworth, "A Biosocial and Developmental Theory of Male and Female Sexuality," *Marriage and Family Living*, 21:163–170, May, 1959.

sponse. Thus, there is a profound difference between the baby boy and the baby girl, as well as between the male and female child and adolescent. The boy is aware of this organ and of the sensation which it brings. He develops genital responsiveness very early and cultivates it through maturity.

Female children have no such awareness, because of the different formation of the sex organs themselves. The first sexual arousal of the male comes early; Kinsey suspects between the ages of six and eight.[25] The first sexual arousal in the female comes later, usually between eight and thirteen.[26]

In later childhood, masturbation begins. It usually is learned from other boys; but if it is not, the boy learns it by himself. Girls do not masturbate in nearly as high a proportion of cases; and when they learn, it is often from boys, rarely from other girls. Very few learn from self-discovery.

Nature has prepared the male for instant readiness. His desires are easily aroused by a wide range of psychic stimulation. This is nature's way of preparing him for the sex act, for his part in reproduction depends upon his readiness to take the initiative when the opportunity is offered.[27] To fail to be able to respond to opportunity is one of the greatest threats to his masculinity.

The Kinsey[28] researchers find, for example, that although male and female are alike in their ability to experience sensation of an erotic nature in various parts of the body and that there is no difference in the time male and female require to reach orgasm, once the sex act has begun, there are striking differences in the kind of psychological stimuli to which the two sexes respond and, therefore, in psychological preparation for the sex act.

They studied men's and women's reactions to a list of psychological phenomena: seeing the body of the other sex, seeing the other's sex organs, viewing one's own body, erotic art, motion pictures, etc. In all, thirty-three different types of psychological stimuli were presented and the male was found to respond to twenty-nine of the thirty-three items more fully and more quickly than did the female. In one they were equal. The only three items to which the female responded more readily were motion pictures,

---

[25] Alfred C. Kinsey and others, *Sexual Behavior in the Human Male* (Philadelphia: W. B. Saunders Co., 1948).

[26] Alfred C. Kinsey and others, *Sexual Behavior in the Human Female, op. cit.*

[27] *Ibid.* Numerous studies have indicated that the male is much more aggressive in sexual matters than the female. For an excellent summary of studies dealing with the premarital period for both high school and college groups, see the summary made by Warren Breed, "Sex, Class and Socialization in Dating," *Marriage and Family Living*, 18:137–144, May, 1956.

[28] Alfred C. Kinsey and others, *Sexual Behavior in the Human Female, op. cit.*, pp. 687–689.

reading romantic literature, and being bitten. Differences on these three items were not great.

The male's erotic dreams are usually accompanied by sexual fantasies concerning untried situations. The female can also have erotic dreams that end in orgasm, but they usually involve the recall of experience. Some women can have orgasm by imagining situations, men rarely can.

The male progresses in sexual development by learning more effective ways of erotic stimulation, until he eventually reaches the ultimate satisfaction of sexual intercourse. His sex life begins in the nonerotic masturbation at ages three to five. It recedes, and then reaches another peak at six or seven years of age when it again subsides. Responsiveness to sex talk reaches its peak in boys of ten to eleven years of age, and then this interest declines. Homosexual responsiveness reaches its crest at around twelve. Masturbation reaches its peak at about fifteen, after which come responsiveness to female nudity, day-dreaming, dancing, and so on. Nocturnal dreams seem to increase up to the late teens or early twenties. Petting experiences are more common in the twenties. And finally, of course, the male experiences the more perfect means of sexual arousal and orgasm that comes from sexual intercourse.

By contrast, Shuttleworth finds that the sexual development of the female is a slow gradual learning process, encouraged by the male. Most of what women know about practice in the area of sex is taught them by men. In many tribes, initiation of girls to sex experience is by older men, men experienced in the arts of stimulation.

Fourth, there is a major biological difference in orgastic response. In males it is an inherent reaction; with females it is not. Males are more often rewarded than are females. In nature there is nothing in female reproductive physiology that requires an orgasm. The ancestors of the male who cannot reach an orgasm are long since extinct, since to reach an orgasm is a part of the reproductive act with the male. Shuttleworth believes that few females in the animal world respond to orgasm—that there are probably human females who are biologically incapable of orgasm. Universally, males respond to an orgasm in very much the same way. It is a part of their natural response. The variation in females is from none to multiple orgasms.

Fifth, seminal fluid is a biological factor which affects the differences in sexuality of male and female. Shuttleworth presents extensive evidence, recalculating some of the Kinsey data for various groups of males and females, to show that one of the major reasons for the male's constant and persistent sexuality is the buildup of sexual fluids. The method for stimulating the discharge will vary by social class, by education, by religion, and other environmental factors, but the regularity of the discharge is more or less constant throughout all social groups, by age level. The frequency of discharge will depend on the particular male. It may be in the form of a nocturnal emission; it may be induced by masturbation, by homosexual contacts, petting, or by heterosexual intercourse. But the regularity of the male seminal discharge is an incontrovertible fact. Whether the man is married or unmarried these discharges take place. Shuttleworth presents strong evidence to the effect that the frequency of the outlet for the male is governed by the production of seminal fluids and not by sociocultural factors. Religion seems to be one of the most effective sublimating factors, for there are actually fewer total outlets among the religious than the nonreligious. The nonreligious less often find an outlet in nocturnal dreams than the religious.

Shuttleworth does not feel that the five factors discussed are the only biological ones which may be of importance in male and female differences in sex behavior. He does present a very strong case for the fact that some of them are of great importance in understanding the difference in the sexual development and sexual expression of males and females.

Confirming evidence of male persistent sexuality is found in studies of male sex activity. The Kinsey research group reports that men who are divorced continue to have about the same number of sexual outlets as during marriage, and most of the outlets involve heterosexual coitus.[29] Goode finds that although the folk conception of a divorced woman is that she is a "loose woman," divorced women may cease sexual activity altogether and most are much less active sexually than they were in marriage.[30]

Female Receptivity

The rhythm of sexuality throughout nature is pretty much determined by the female and her seasons, although in some species the male's sex interest and potency are also seasonal. Her seasons, in turn, are determined by the period of ovulation and the consequent flow of hormones and genital secretions which increase her excitation and attract and excite the male, challenging him to win or overpower her. His is normally the problem of pursuit.

In human beings, where the sex act, because of romantic connotations, becomes conditioned by psychological and esthetic considerations, biological rhythms are for the most part lost and sex stimulation becomes associated with tenderness, wooing, caressing erotic areas of the body, and other such types of excitation which operate the autonomic nervous system.[31]

[29] Alfred C. Kinsey and others, *Sexual Behavior in the Human Male* (Philadelphia: W. B. Saunders Co., 1948), pp. 294–296.
[30] William J. Goode, *After Divorce* (New York: Free Press of Glencoe, Inc., 1956).
[31] For a discussion of the estrus period (period of receptivity) see Ch. 22.

Among humans, the woman may become an active, rather than merely a passive, participant in the sexual act. The pattern will vary according to the culture. Even so, the female is generally the less active partner in initiating as well as in performing the sex act. Many cultures have depreciated her sexuality by various psychological and physiological means. The Victorian philosophy, to which our culture is heir, illustrates the psychological; clitoridectomy and infibulation are examples of physiological means.[32]

Woman's role in the performance of the sex act could be much easier than that of the male, for she can be a passive partner and accomplish what nature intends for her. All she has to do is avoid blocking the male's advance and make herself so attractive that she will interest the male and assure his readiness to perform the act of fertilization when social circumstances make this appropriate.

The female learns to value many other rewards apart from sex, and modifies any natural period of receptivity she has by these other rewards. All that receptivity requires is relaxation of her body. She needs none of the readiness which must be sustained by the male. She can easily fit into the sex pattern of the culture by compliance, "balancing the mood of the moment against the mood of tomorrow, and fitting her receptivity into the whole pattern of a relationship."[33]

For most women, the physical act of sex is an inadequate expression of love. Woman demands a much broader sense of completion, since sex for her involves a range of feminine roles, the climax of which is motherhood. From early childhood she is taught the risks of coitus. She knows the penalty of an ill-advised relationship.[34] She develops a modesty based on fear of what sex can cost her unless she behaves wisely and confines it to the type of relationship with the male that gives her maximum security. Often she even carries this reserve over into marriage, for the ceremony does not have the magic power to remove many of her built-in inhibitions.

The fending off of the male's advances has been in part a reaction of the female to a fear of pregnancy. This has been no less true in marriage than outside marriage. Family standard of living, as well as the advance of civilization itself in terms of improvement in conditions of life, is dependent on the control of her fertility. She is much more aware of this

---

[32] *Clitoridectomy* involves cutting off the labia and clitoris at the time of puberty. It is practiced among a group of Australians and by many groups in Egypt and the Upper Nile.

Infibulation involves sewing up the entrance to the vagina. It is opened in part by the husband at the time of marriage, and fully just before childbirth, then partially closed again after childbirth. See Ashley-Montagu's, *The Natural Superiority of Women* (New York: Macmillan Co., 1953).

[33] Mead, in Krich, *op. cit.*, p. 16.

[34] *Ibid.*

problem than is the male, who becomes lost in the momentary satisfaction of the sex act itself. It is women the world over who must limit offspring, who destroy unborn infants, who practice infanticide if custom or personal wishes so dictate; and it is women who pioneer the family limitation movements by crusading for and adopting practices of birth control.

The female has much greater tolerance both for sexual excess and for sexual deprivation than does the male. In general, she has coitus more under volitional control. Havelock Ellis long ago observed the tolerance of women for sexual excesses.[35] Kinsey has shown their greater variability compared to the male in sexual activity, and has also indicated that many married women do not suffer from the sudden termination of a regular sex life.[36] The male does.

Male Potency

Sexual potency is the key to masculinity in most cultures. Destroy it and the male's confidence and assurance is lost. The male's satisfaction is derived from activity; the female's from receptivity. The male is easily distracted from one erotic object to another; the female is not. He devotes a great deal of energy to sexual pursuit and performance. In nature, and to a more covert extent in human society, this leads to roaming, aggression, assertiveness, and the defense of territorial rights and sexual property. The glandularly impelled differences even show up in the higher death rate of male children from accident (see Chapter 4).

Margaret Mead has pointed out that a civilization that goes too far in denying the male sexual spontaneity will destroy itself, since the male's performance is dependent on his spontaneity.[37] Female ardor is unimportant in race survival, provided she will yield to the male's advances for the sake of motherhood.

The Practical Problems of Sex Drives

Basic differences in potency and receptivity are one of the troublesome aspects of dating relationships. The female adolescent can rarely fully understand the male. Surveys of high school girls indicate that they consider

[35] Havelock Ellis, *Man and Woman: A Study of Secondary Sexual Characteristics*, fifth edition (New York: Charles Scribner's Sons, 1915).

[36] Alfred C. Kinsey and others, *Sexual Behavior in the Human Female, op. cit.*

[37] Margaret Mead, *Male and Female* (New York: William Morrow & Co., Inc., 1949).

him "sex-driven." This may be a shocking discovery but there is a natural basis for it. The college male is no different.

The male identifies his sex drive with localized glandular tensions. Culture teaches him to sublimate and control, yet he constantly seeks more satisfactory sexual outlets. To elevate sexual attraction to the level of romantic love, the goal of our marriage system, requires the suppression and sublimation of the male's physical desires.

The female without sexual experience, by contrast, is less likely to be aware of localized sexual tensions. She tends to be romantic by nature, her love impulses being more diffused and less identified with sex drives.

Much misunderstanding between the sexes in dating is due to the fact that they do not comprehend or accept the differences in the way they view the natural sequence of steps following sex attraction. For women, there are generally three steps: (1) friendship, (2) respect and love, and (3) sexual intercourse.[38] Most men can skip the first steps. A man is attracted to a "sexy" woman physically even though he does not respect her otherwise. A woman may be sexually attracted to a man by physical qualities but more likely senses sexual attraction after she respects him and is to some extent in love with him.

With a woman, friendships grow into love relationships. Men often claim "love at first sight." When lightly claimed, this is a man's approach for sexual exploitation without love being involved at all. When serious, some authorities believe that love at first sight, without previous friendship having been established, is indicative of a pathological state—"symptomatic of profound disorder in the love life."[39]

The female is more cautious in yielding to sex attraction at each step, since at the end of the consummated love relationship, for her there is always the risk of pregnancy, with the biological and social obligations which this entails. This is why the female generally requires a permanent relationship before yielding completely to the sexual demands of the male.

In conclusion, male and female anatomical sex differences appear during embryonic growth. Genetic potential, in terms of masculinity and femininity, and even in terms of the sexual object toward which the person will gravitate, do not inevitably unfold. In normal, loving family life, yes; in family life that is badly twisted in emotional climate and emotional objectives, it will not do so. If parents fail to give the child the correct role training, the chromosomal trend can be altered, and the individual be incorrectly oriented in his sex identity and sexual behavior.

Glandular and hormone developments at puberty bring with them other marked sex-differentiating characteristics. These unique attributes

[38] This observation was made by Ralph Eckert in lectures in The University of California Family Life Education Workshop in 1949.

[39] Willard Waller and Reuben Hill, *The Family* (New York: Holt, Rinehart and Winston, Inc., 1951), p. 200.

of male and female, although often greatly modified by culture, still affect male and female emotional and social growth decisively.

The softer flesh and more gentle disposition of the female, her different emotional and social reactions are, in part, attributable to the role for which nature has designed her—that of caring for and nursing the young. So also the more aggressive disposition of the male is, in part, glandularly induced. Culture may either thwart or encourage these tendencies. The differences in certain psychological and psychosexual responses of male and female also relate to the part each plays in nature. The male is gifted with sexual preparedness. For the female, in cultures where the source of life is known, readiness usually involves some foresight with regard to the social consequences of the act.

Male and female are biological complements to each other, each being equally important to the process of reproduction and yet far different in specific capacities and functions. The female is handicapped by the menstrual cycle, by the burden of carrying the young, and by all the responsibilities which center around these functions. The male bears none of these burdens, but in most cultures he has to bear the economic burden of supporting the female and her helpless young.

One can make too much of biological differences in male and female, as history indicates so clearly. In the relationships of men and women today, social roles are probably more decisive in the success of dating and marriage.

Problems

1. Do you think that this chapter gives too much weight to biological factors in male-female development? Explain.
2. Do you feel that women still suffer discrimination in our culture because of their so-called infirmities?
3. Discuss the importance of male-female biological differences in drives as they bear on marriage relationships.
4. *Research exercise:* Poll members of the class or some other student group on (a) color preferences, (b) favorite recreation, (c) favorite hobby (other items may be added). Tabulate results for men and women separately. Analyze, discuss and point up significance of findings.

    Are innate or conditioned factors involved? What differences are probably attributable to peculiarities of American culture? How do certain differences bear on the relationships between men and women?
5. Custom is still somewhat opposed to women in certain positions: high governmental posts, the ministry, executive positions in business, campaigning for office, practicing law, etc. (a) Tell why the customs came into being. (b) Describe assets or liabilities women possess for these activities.
6. Do you think anxiety about being homosexual is a common feeling among college students?

Selected References

Articles in Books of Readings

Cavan, Ruth S., *Marriage and the Family in the Modern World: A Book of Readings*, third edition (New York: Thomas Y. Crowell Co., 1969).
Symonds, Percival M., "Difference in Attitude Toward Love and Sex," Reading 17.
Deutscher, Irwin, "Socialization for Postparental Life," Reading 42.
Krich, A. M. (ed.), *Women: The Variety and Meaning of their Sexual Experience* (New York: Dell Publishing Co., Inc., 1954).
Mead, Margaret, "Introduction," pp. 9–24.
Mead, Margaret, "Potency and Receptivity," pp. 111–135.

General References

Ashley-Montagu, M. F., *The Natural Superiority of Women* (New York: The Macmillan Co., 1968).
Crawley, Lawrence Q., and others, *Reproduction, Sex and Preparation for Marriage* (Englewood Cliffs, N.J.: Prentice-Hall, Inc., 1964), Ch. 1.
Farris, Edmund J., *Human Ovulation and Fertility* (Philadelphia: J. B. Lippincott Co., 1956).
Jay, Phyllis C., "The Female Primate," pp. 3–13; Maccoby, Eleanor E., "Woman's Intellect," pp. 24–39; Overstreet, Edmund W., "Biological Make-up of Woman," pp. 13–23; "Research on the Nature of Woman" (Panel Discussion), pp. 40–50; all in Seymour M. Farber and Roger H. L. Wilson (eds.) *The Potential of Woman* (New York: McGraw-Hill Book Co., 1963).
McCandless, F. D., "Emotional Problems of the Climacteric," *Clinical Obstetrics and Gynecology*, 7:489, 1964.
Mead, Margaret, *Male and Female* (New York: William Morrow & Co., Inc., 1949).
Rubin, Isadore, "The Sexless Older Years—A Socially Harmful Stereotype," *The Annals*, 376:86–95, March, 1968.
Rutherford, Robert N., M.D., "The Climacteric Years in the Woman, Man and the Family," in Richard H. Klemer, *Counseling in Marital and Sexual Problems* (Baltimore: The Williams and Wilkins Co., 1965).
Shuttleworth, Frank K., "A Biosocial and Developmental Theory of Male and Female Sexuality," *Marriage and Family Living*, 21:163–170, May, 1959.

4

Male and Female:
Physique and Emotions

It is easy to take for granted the superiorities of the male and the inferiorities of the female in our culture where the male has almost always been the favored sex. Science now probes more deeply to try to learn what men and women are capable of—physically, psychologically, tempermentally. It is not always possible to detach innate factors from those grafted on by male and female subcultures, but complete isolation of these factors would serve only a theoretical purpose, not the functional one which is the concern of this book.

Physical Strength and Stamina

Although the female is less muscular than the male and falls short in tests of physical strength, she is more durable and has greater resistance to fatigue. She can stand more suffering and go longer without sleep. At every age of life from birth to old age, the death rate of the male exceeds that of the females (see Figures 4–1 and 4–2). Even prenatal deaths of males exceed those of females, more males being stillborn. Nature offsets this in part by a sex ratio at birth which, in most countries, runs from about 105 to 106 male births to each 100 female births (105.7 in the United States). The higher general mortality rate and war together explain why men are in the minority in all of the older nations and why with the cessation of immigration from other lands (long-distance migrations are always dominated by males) they have, since the early 1940s, become so in the United States.[1]

---

[1] For a comprehensive discussion of this topic, see Paul H. Landis, *Population Problems: A Cultural Interpretation*, second edition (New York: American Book Co., 1954), Ch. 4.

FIGURE 4–1   DEATH RATES OF MALES AND FEMALES—PER 1,000 MID-YEAR POPULATION—BY AGE, UNITED STATES, 1967. Source: **Vital Statistics Report,** Vol. 17, No. 12, Supplement, March 25, 1969, U.S. Public Health Service, Table 7, p. 9.

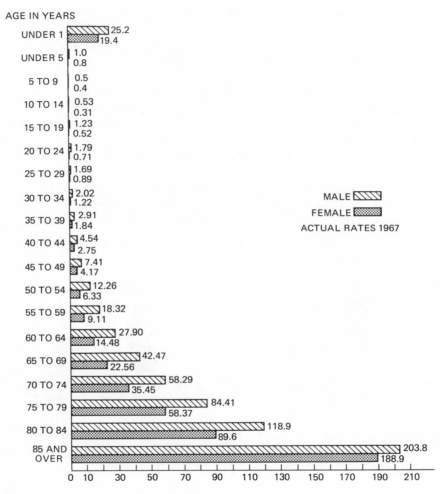

At all age periods the male death rate far exceeds that of the female. During the teens and early twenties it is more than twice as high. It is almost twice as high in the years 50 to 70.

Women's operative rate runs 46 per thousand compared to 38 per thousand for men. Rates run about the same for the common ailments like the removal of the tonsils, adenoids, and appendix. Surgery on the genital organs is four times as frequent on women as men, but hernia operations are five times as frequent on men as on women.[2] Coronary thrombosis almost always involves the male. Vital statistics data show that during the years 25 to 44 the death rate of men from diseases of the heart runs 63 per 100,000 and for women only 18. Between ages 45 to 64, the rate for men is 647, for women only 216. A hospital study of the frequency of 365 diseases found that 245 of them almost always occurred in men.

The sex hormone, estrogen, gives the female protection against many diseases. After menopause, when this hormone decreases, her disease rate goes up.

Women have minor illnesses more often than men. Before the days of psychosomatic medicine these were known as "female complaints." But women survive them. They do have a much more complicated glandular makeup to reckon with than do men. Much can go wrong with the female urogenital mechanism because it is so complex. In advanced

FIGURE 4-2   WIDOWED MEN AND WOMEN. Source: U.S. Department of Commerce, Bureau of the Census, "Marital Status of the Population: 1960," **Supplemental Reports,** PC(SI)–39, December 28, 1962.

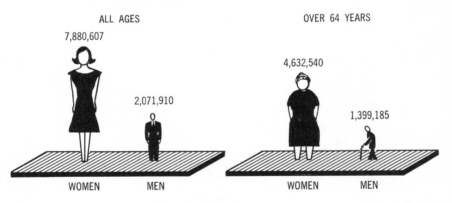

Sex ratio of widows and of the widowed 65 years and over. At all ages females are greatly in the majority. Much of the difference is explained by the higher death rate of the male.

societies, where diagnosis and treatment prolong life, many women have difficulty in connection with menstruation or childbirth, and some undergo operations involving some part of the reproductive mechanism. Males rarely have difficulty in this part of their anatomy except for the enlargement of the prostate gland in later life. No doubt another reason for

[2] Data reported by Dr. Morris Fishbein of the American Medical Association in "Medical News of the Month," *McCall's,* September, 1960, p. 66.

women's most frequent complaints is that they get more of a hearing in social intercourse—their operations certainly bring more social acclaim than do those of men. Men, at least in American culture, get no credit for their frailties. Women are getting less credit for them than in an earlier day when their role in society was a more passive one.

FIGURE 4-3   INCREASE IN AVERAGE LIFE SPAN. Source: Irving Fisher, U.S. Public Health Service and U.S. Department of Commerce, Bureau of the Census. 1975 projection by the Metropolitan Life Insurance Company.

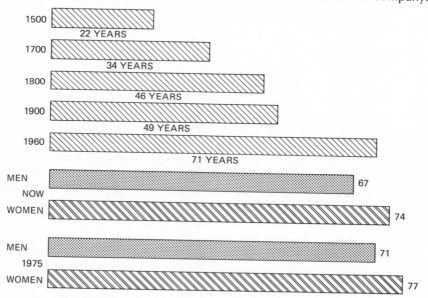

The increase of average length of life in 450 years. The child-rearing span is but a fraction, enabling a mother to begin a new career during the "empty-nest" period of family life.

Even so, the differential in length of life is increasing. Today girls can expect to live 4 years longer than boys—73.8 compared to 70.1 years.[3] In 1926, white males in the United States averaged 57 years, a difference of 2.6 years.[4] By 1975, the Social Security Administration predicts a life span of 71 years for males, 77 years for females (see Figure 4-3).

Women's greater longevity may be in part due to the fact that they

[3] *Monthly Vital Statistics Report,* Final, 1966, Vol. 16, No. 12, Supplement, March 12, 1968.

[4] Metropolitan Life Insurance Company, "Sex Differences in Mortality Increasing," *Statistical Bulletin,* 58:1–4, September, 1957.

visit doctors more, even aside from calls related to childbirth, and that they are able to take better care of themselves, not so often being under the pressure of a scheduled job as are men.[5]

In our culture, men are more definitely committed to the work world than are women. A man's ego satisfaction is found there; he measures his success by the achievements of work and by the advancements in his work position. The warning to the aspiring executive sometimes given is "promotions can kill you." This is indicative of the high pressure which may be inherent in great success in the work world.

The extent to which men are committed to the work world, particularly to heavy manual labor, is partly a matter of culture, rather than biology. In peasant economies and primitive cultures, women often are thought to be as fit for hard labor as men; in some, even more fit. Ethel M. Alpert reports that she was advised in Central Africa that: "Everybody knows that men are not suited to heavy work, that women are stronger and better workers. Men drink too much and do not eat enough to keep up their strength; they are more tense and travel about too much to develop the habits and the muscles needed for sustained work on farms."[6]

Woman is physically awkward, by man's standards. But man is thinking of the way he throws a baseball. If a graceful man were forced to unfasten a back-zippered garment, as women often must, he would soon learn how awkward he is. The male reaches over his shoulders to skin off a sweater; the female, around her ribs. He pulls his gloves on from the front; she, from the back of her hands. He doubles his fingernails into his upturned palm to look at them; she turns her palms down and straightens her fingers to look at the fingernails. He strikes a match toward him; she, away from her. He carries books hooked in a hanging hand. She cradles them on her stomach. He is hinged for certain movements; she, for others.[7] Different, but unequal only if one prefers one style of movement to the other.

In our day when many industrial jobs take nimble fingers, employers have long since learned that many women have physical skills unequaled by many men. Employers sometimes pay women less than men, but this is a survival of custom rather than a denial of equality in ability to produce.

[5] For a discussion of various aspects of this problem see a statement by George Bugbee, President, Health Information Foundation, 6:6, December, 1957.

[6] Ethel M. Albert, "The Roles of Women: Questions of Values," in Seymour H. Farber and Roger H. L. Wilson (eds.), *The Potential of Women* (New York: McGraw-Hill Book Co., 1963), pp. 105–115.

[7] For photographs of these various actions, see Leslie Lieber, "Double Standard in Actions!" *This Week*, March 14, 1954, pp. 14–15.

Historical Performance

The male's greatest claim to superior natural endowment over the female is the record of history. The chronicle of humanity's long past is studded almost exclusively with the accomplishments of the male. Even those women who achieved enduring fame generally did so by influencing the activities of men rather than by achievements of their own. Yet history shows that now and then a women has demonstrated superior accomplishment.

What the worshipers of precedent forgot in making historical comparisons of male-female accomplishment is that it is no less a product of opportunity than of genetic inheritance. Few cultures have allowed the female to assume what they considered a creative role; practically all cultures have placed the male in this role. The infrequent references to women in history probably proves little except that women in most cultures have been excluded from all but the subservient or domestic activities of the group.

Psychological Differences

Among the first comparative scientific studies of male and female were those of the anthropologists and psychologists which compared brain weight, reaction time, and sensory acuity of the sexes. The brain-weight test favored the male—more grams of brain, therefore more brain capacity. By such simple logic was the die cast in favor of male superiority.

It remained for the intelligence test, and the competitive situations provided by coeducation to correct this error. The notion that men have superior innate ability as a gift of nature seems so absurd now that few would even attempt to argue the case, yet the proof on which the modern notion of equal ability of the sexes rests is little more than fifty years old. It is not surprising that many still act as though they did not believe women were equal in mental ability to men.

In certain sensory abilities there are slight differences between the sexes. Women, at least as trained in our culture, are generally better coordinated in speech. They rarely stutter. Men inherit a sensory defect, color blindness, which women carry in the genes, but pass on in body characteristics chiefly to the male.

Watts finds that the male tends to "spotlight" knowledge, whereas women tend to "floodlight" it. The female senses a variety of things simultaneously.[8] He finds that our culture tends to specialize in and reward the spotlight kind of performance.

In nursery school, boys quarrel more than girls and are more aggressive.[9] The male takes chances more often. Among males 15 to 24 years of age 60 percent of the deaths are accidental, among females of the same ages only 35 percent.[10] Deaths from falling are twice as high among males as females during childhood.[11] Throughout life, the male accidental death rate far exceeds the female (see Table 4–1).

Table 4–1   Accidents in the Male and Female Death Rates, 1962

Percentage of Accidental Deaths

Age Group (years)	Male	Female
1–4	31.3	22.7
5–14	23.4	9.9
15–24	90.2	21.0
25–44	65.4	16.5
45–54	78.8	27.0

Source: Adapted from *Statistical Bulletin*, Metropolitan Life Insurance Co., November, 1964, p. 6. (Data are for the white population only.)

Margaret Mead believes that the work cycle of the female in most cultures tends to be adapted to the rhythm of her biological nature.[12] Not all cultures do adapt their work cycle to the natural rhythms of the female, that is, to the rhythm of the monthly cycle and the cycle of pregnancy, nursing, and so on, although it is more convenient if they do so. Man is under no limitations of this kind.

She finds evidence that the man tends to work by spurts of great effort, and that the activity-rest pattern of the male may be related to his endocrine system. Women tend to work at a more constant pace, although Mead cites cultures in which women also work at a spurt-rest cycle. Women have greater capacity for monotonous, repetitive work and bear up under it with less psychological expense.

In the area of interests there are measurable evidences of significant psychological differences between male and female.

Eleanor E. Maccoby, Stanford University psychologist, reports that

[8] Alan Watts "The Woman in Man," in Farber and Wilson, *op. cit.*, pp. 79–86.
[9] Darrell K. Adams in Yvonne Brackbill (ed.), *Infancy and Early Childhood* (New York: Free Press of Glencoe, 1967), p. 404.
[10] "Accidents of the High School and College Ages," *Statistical Bulletin*, 47:6–8, November, 1966.
[11] "Fatal and Nonfatal Accidents," *Statistical Bulletin*, 49:7–8, October, 1968.
[12] Margaret Mead, *Male and Female* (New York: William Morrow and Co., Inc., 1949), Ch. 8.

girls early develop greater interest in people than boys do and are more concerned about what people think of them. They are more conforming and more influenced by the opinions of others.[13]

Years earlier other Stanford psychologists, after months of study in this field, and after covering more than forty of the best researches made by scientists in different fields, reported:

Women are consistently more intimate and personal than men. They are strongly interested in persons and spend more time and thought on people and personalities than men do. Excellent studies of young children show that girls very early are more interested in relationships with others, while boys are more interested in material things.[14]

This gives a scientific basis for women's greater tendency to gossip and men's greater interest in material gain.

Studies made by eavesdropping show that women talk mostly about personal things—other people, their friends, themselves, or their feelings and loves; men more often talk about activities—politics, business matters, sports, their sexual exploits, and their accomplishments.

Dr. Theodor Reik, Director of the New York Society for Psychoanalytical Psychology, has observed that a woman is rarely separated from her husband or lover in her thoughts and emotions, even when at work. They do not like impersonal work; they want to be working for someone —husband, boss, child, community, or they may want to impress a man through their work. Men are always trying to produce an effect; they want to change the world. For the woman the nicest words are, "I love you," for the man, "I am proud of you."[15]

Research on college dating shows that the bright coed will often deliberately "act dumb" to keep from outdoing her less brilliant date. Of course, a part of this is a woman's sense of the practical in human relations. In this, as in so many of her relationships with the male she must masquerade.

A woman will express herself in terms of how she felt on a certain occasion; a man, in terms of what he said, did, or at least thought. Characteristic female reactions might be "I was embarrassed to death," or "I could have died, I was so humiliated." But in talking about a similar situation, the man boasts, "I told the guy to shut up or I'd knock his teeth down his throat."

If the conversation turns to generalized traits of human nature—like selfishness, greed, obstreperousness, or goodness, for that matter, the woman immediately says to herself, and maybe to others, too, "Am I like

[13] Farber and Wilson, *op. cit.*, pp. 24–39.

[14] Winifred Johnson and Lewis M. Terman, "Some Highlights in the Literature of Psychology of Sex Differences Published Since 1920," *Journal of Psychology*, 9:327 ff., 1940.

[15] Theodor Reik, *Sex in Man and Woman* (New York: Farrar, Straus & Co., Inc., 1960).

that?" She personalizes generalizations about people. A man shifts the generalization to someone else who fits the picture. It never occurs to him that he might be that way himself.

Women are more frequent readers of fiction, for they identify themselves with characters and situations much more readily and completely than do men. If asked to criticize a bit of fiction, a woman appraises situations in terms of how she has acted or thinks she would act under similar circumstances. A man is more likely to rationalize his criticism in terms of principles and universals rather than his own experience.

A man must always be careful in making any criticism of women in the presence of wife or sweetheart for she immediately feels that his abstract criticism is really meant for her. A man, on the other hand, may fail to get the point when a woman's criticism, aimed at "men," is really meant for him. Likely as not he recognizes that men are that way, but is equally sure that he does not share these imperfections of his sex. His ego is too well fortified to be punctured by so dull a weapon.

A male, in meeting others, tries to influence them by his conversation and behavior. The female is more often interested in making an impression by her appearance.

Women are seldom as direct in stating what they think as are men. For instance, if a man doesn't like what another does, he is likely to tell him so. A woman is more likely to tell someone other than the offender, thus approaching the issue indirectly. Of course, she hopes her remarks will eventually get around to the right party without her receiving the blame for them.

Men are more inclined to be competitive, to outdo others, to achieve success and fortune. Women are more interested in getting along with people, although this pattern is changing because of coeducation and women's work experience.

Emotional Differences

Romantic inclinations   There is little doubt that the inhibiting of sexual impulses has much to do with romantic feeling. In American culture, at least, perhaps in most cultures of the world, women have more cultural inhibitions imposed upon them in the matter of sexual expression than do men. This explains in part why women are much more romantic in temperament and outlook, why their sex impulses more often take on the character of fantasy, daydreaming, and other forms of covert erotic expression which are in themselves often more satisfying than the physical sexual experience.

This tends to enrich a woman's erotic life and bring to her a more diffused sexual sensation than that of the male, who approaches sex more directly. It has been proposed by some psychologists that such a diffused development of sexuality may actually, in the case of some women, interfere with physical expression of love or make the physical expression seem much less important when experienced than is the enriched sexual fantasy. Eroticism may more readily, in the case of women, also lead to a degree of narcissism, or self-love, which expresses itself in adoration of the body, excessive pride in personal appearance, and general self-absorption as a substitute for sexual love.

It is possible that the female finds it easier to develop masochistic traits than does the male. The male is the active, aggressive partner in the sexual relationship. The female by nature is the passive partner, and these psychological traits may more readily be converted into a masochistic self-torture, which carried to an extreme becomes a perversion. A masochistic personality tends to develop if the father is cruel with the girls or employs overly stern discipline and physical punishment (see Chapter 6). The tendency of the female to psychologically identify with the male and feel herself a part of him and his activities, which is a natural part of so many cultures, creates a psychological climate which makes it easier for her to develop a martyr complex than it is for the male.

Deutsch has suggested that women who commit suicide because of the breakup of a love affair often do so, not because they are suffering from a loss of the love object, but because of narcissistic injury to their ego.[16]

The connection between woman's sexual and emotional life is quite different from that of the male. Nature has provided him with an insistent and easily aroused sexual desire, and it may be quite emotion-free in the larger connotation. He is vulnerable if his readiness fails him. The woman's problem is that of attracting the male she wants as a mate. Her role is that of surrender but surrender has a price, she wants coitus identified with love.

When cultures choose to make the female highly aggressive, as among the Zuni Indians, stories of fear of the wedding night are about grooms, not brides. In polygynous cultures of the world the universal quest is for an aphrodisiac to bolster the male's prowess in sexual performance.

The premenstrual syndrome   The emotional life of the female must be reckoned with in part because of her biological rhythms, which may be reflected in moods. The temperament cycle of the female tends to affect her energy and sociability during the twenty-eight day menstrual

[16] Helene Deutsch, *The Psychology of Women, a Psycho-analytical Interpretation* (New York: Grune & Stratton, Inc., 1944), p. 198.

cycle. The first peak energy period is shortly after the menstrual flow, the second is near the mid-period at about the time of ovulation, and the third is just before the onset of the menstrual flow, when there is a rise is basal metabolism rate. Each of these energy periods are found to be associated with secretions from the ovaries which are evidenced by increased work performance of women.[17] Generally speaking, during the rebuilding of the uterine wall following menstruation, there is a period of great activity, vitality, and sociability. This is known as the estrogen phase of the menstrual cycle. It is climaxed by a slight rise in temperature near the time the ovum is released. After ovulation, the progesterone-phase begins and the woman is more likely to be moody and suffer some tension. Her tensions increase as the time of menstruation approaches, although just before menstruation there is an upturn in physical energy due to a rise in the basal metabolism rate.[18]

Tension may express itself in various moods and in various antisocial reactions. Some women become depressed prior to menstruation, a few so much as to be almost suicidal. Others become overtly hostile. Some of the most violent conflicts between mothers and teen-age daughters come at the premenstrual period of the daughter, when she becomes unmanageable and uncooperative. Roommates, husbands, and friends need to come to understand this transitory behavior. The more mature woman who is well adjusted readily brings herself under control, but even so, she may need an unusually sympathetic husband at times previous to menstruation.

The subject of premenstrual tensions has received much study by gynecologists, internists, and psychiatrists, since they have been concerned with the "premenstrual syndrome." The majority of women have some elements of the syndrome.[19]

Morton found 80 percent of 249 women prisoners had elements of the premenstrual syndrome.[20] Eichner found 70 percent of nurses had symptoms.[21] Several other studies show 30 to 75 percent. Pennington found 95 percent of 1,000 high school and college students had symptoms.[22] Proportions showing symptoms depend on symptoms described by interviewers.

Most symptoms appear in the premenstrual week; some women have emotional symptoms at the beginning of menstruation, a few at the mid-menstrual period, and a few past the midpoint. Early in the new menstrual

[17] Edmund J. Farris, *Human Ovulation and Fertility* (Philadelphia: J. B. Lippincott Co., 1956).

[18] *Ibid.*

[19] Irwin N. Perr, "Medical, Psychiatric, and Legal Aspects of Premenstrual Tension," *American Journal of Psychiatry*, 115:211–219, September, 1958.

[20] *Ibid.*

[21] E. Eichner, "Premenstrual Tension Syndrome," an address reported in Perr, *op. cit.*

[22] V. M. Pennington, *Journal of American Medical Association*, June, 1957.

phase relief from tension comes to most, although some experience physical and emotional stress in the first quarter of menstruation.[23]

W. R. Cooke[24] reported that most crimes of a group studied in Paris were committed during the premenstrual period. J. H. Morton and colleagues report that at New York State Farm for women prisoners 62 percent of crimes of violence occurred during the premenstrual week, 17 percent during menstruation.[25]

The most common theory is that premenstrual tension is due to low progesterone and to high levels of unantagonized estrogen. The estrogen-progesterone ratio seems to be most disturbed at this time in those with symptoms. The premenstrual syndrome is more severe in women with neurotic constitutions.[26] It is also more severe, Cook found, among women who have a fear of becoming pregnant.

Frequency of symptoms as reported in several studies dealing with the premenstrual period are seen in Table 4-2. Note that headache is the most common experience reported by various groups. Fatigue, depression, and irritability are often reported, as is swelling and tenderness of breasts.

Although sex desires of women tend to be weak during the period of menstruation, the sex content of dreams is highest according to studies of undergraduate women by Ethel Swanson at the University of Wyoming.

Temperament   Because of women's biological constitution, as well as by unique cultural conditioning, there may be truth in the folk conception that the female is more highly keyed, more sensitive, and more gifted with those emotions which lead to protective behavior of the infant and child. Women may be more intuitive. They no doubt are less ego-centered, live less in bold and courageous action than does the male in most cultures. They may be vain, but not as ruthlessly ambitious as the male.

Crying remains a part of the female subculture. It is strictly taboo for the adult male of American culture (this is not so of the Latin cultures, where crying as an expression of joy or sorrow is much more acceptable). The American male is not as stoical as the native Indian but he is very stoical compared to the female when it comes to expressing emotions.

These subtle emotional differences are the theme of many works of fiction and of some scientific literature. These supposed traits, and many like them, may be myth or reality, but it is known that a feeling of need

[23] Judson T. Landis' study gives attention to all four quarters, rather than the fourth only. Most studies have been concerned with the premenstrual phase. See Table 4-1 for source.

[24] W. R. Cooke, *American Journal of Obstetrics and Gynecology*, 49:457, 1945.

[25] J. H. Morton, *American Journal of Obstetrics and Gynecology*, 65:1182, 1953.

[26] The probable effect of the menstrual cycle on sexual desire is discussed in Ch. 24.

Table 4–2 Symptoms Found in the Premenstrual Syndrome

	Greene and Dalton†	Rees‡	Eichner and Waltner§	Eichner and Waltner#	Landis¶
	Patients (%)	Patients (%)	Normal Subjects (%)	Patients (%)	181 College Girls (%)
Headache	69.5	63	—	—	33
Nausea	29.7	37	—	—	10
Lethargy (fatigue)	13.1	63	59	—	44
Rheumatism	16.7	—	—	—	—
Vertigo (dizziness)	10.6	—	—	—	—
Depression	6.0	80	62	—	48
Irritability	6.0	100	51	—	43
Edema (congestion)	6.0	73	32	72	—
Rhinorrhea (excessive mucous secretions from nose)	7.2	—	—	—	—
Mastalgia (swelling or tenderness of breasts)	2.4	63	69	—	44
Tension	—	100	—	—	—
Emotional liability (inability to concentrate, etc.)	—	—	—	56	39
Anxiety	—	73	—	—	36
Insommia	—	40	—	—	—
Pruritus (itching and skin eruptions)	—	40	—	—	58
Marked thirst	—	20	—	—	—
Physical discomfort (chills, cramps, etc.)	—	—	—	58	23

Adapted from Irwin N. Perr, "Medical, Psychiatric, and Legal Aspects of Premenstrual Tensions," *American Journal of Psychiatry*, 115:211–219. September, 1958, with additions.

† R. Greene and K. Dalton: *British Medical Journal*, 1:1007, 1953.

‡ L. Rees: *British Medical Journal*, 1:1014, 1953.

§ E. Eichner and C. Waltner: *Medical Times*, 83:771, August, 1955.

E. Eichner, "Premenstrual Tension Syndrome," Presentation at N.Y.S. Academy of General Practice, October, 1957.

¶ Judson T. Landis, "Physical and Mental-Emotional Changes Accompanying the Menstrual Cycle," *Research Studies of the State College of Washington*, 25:155–162, June, 1957.

for security, emotional and economic, is very strong in women of our culture. Whether innate or learned, or a combination of both, is not known.

Stanford psychologists[27] found that women are more temperamental, for the female glandular system is much more complicated than is that of the male. Women are given to up-and-down moods during the monthly cycle of glandular functioning and during pregnancy. Their moods exceed the temperamental deviations of the male. Women are also more given to tears than are men. These traits are, in part, culturally determined, of course. Cry, they do, but when emotional problems must be faced, women have more toughness than do men. During World War II, they stood the strain of air raids better than men.

Built-in shockproofing   Although women have more emotional problems, or at least are more aware of their problems, it is men who most often get ulcers. Even during the teen years, girls are much more aware of problems and tensions in the parental home and in their social relationships generally than are boys.[28] Tradition holds that women fret and

Table 4–3   Suicide Deaths and Suicide Death Rate—by Sex, Color, and Means of Suicide, United States, 1960–1962

| *Means of Injury* | *White* | | *Nonwhite* | |
	Males	*Females*	*Males*	*Females*
Suicide—Total				
Average annual number	13,812	4,458	745	218
Rate per 100,000	17.5	5.5	9.1	2.4
Percent	100.0	100.0	100.0	100.0
Poisoning	19.3	40.7	10.6	24.0
Hanging and strangulation	16.8	15.5	17.0	17.0
Firearms and explosives	54.7	25.3	52.7	25.9
Other	9.2	18.5	19.7	33.1

Source: Metropolitan Life Insurance Company, *Statistical Bulletin*, 45:8–9, July, 1964. Data from reports of U. S. Division of Vital Statistics.

Observe that three times as many males as females commit suicide among whites; almost four times as many males as females commit suicide among nonwhites, where the suicide rates is much lower than it is for whites. Women, however, attempt suicide more often. Do you see a possible explanation for the sex difference in success of means used? Are there other reasons?

[27] Winifred Johnson and Lewis M. Terman, "Some Highlights in the Literature of Psychological Sex Differences Published Since 1920," *Journal of Psychology*, 9:327 ff., 1940.

[28] See, for example, Table 10 in Paul H. Landis and Carol L. Stone, *The Relationship of Parental Authority to Teenage Adjustment* (Pullman, Wash.: Washington Agricultural Experiment Station, 1952), Bulletin No. 538.

worry more than men throughout life, but only about a third as many of them take their anxiety seriously enough to commit suicide.

Even so, far more women than men attempt suicide in the United States (see Table 4–3). Whether they do not have the courage to do it effectively, use the wrong tools, or for some other reasons of a more subtle nature fail, is a matter of speculation.[29] It is very probable that many do not seriously wish to kill themselves. They may use suicide as an attention-getting device, to spite someone, to get publicity, or for other such reasons, and plan the act, perhaps subconsciously, so they will be discovered before it is fatal.[30]

Autocide accounts for much unreported suicide today. Although such deaths are reported as accidental, they are in fact suicide by automobile. This means is probably used more by males than females.

Men and women fall victim to nervous breakdowns and mental illness in about equal numbers, but women are more likely to respond to psychological treatment and to recover.[31] It seems very probable that men, being disciplined in ignoring pain and discomfort, and being taught to be tough, neglect nervous problems longer than women do and reach the clinician after the disease is much further advanced. Women express their feelings more than men; therefore, men may get in a much worse emotional state before they or others recognize it.[32] Our culture denies men the safety valve of tears, tantrums, and other such releases permitted to women.

Male and female differences in temperament, emotions, and physical strength and stamina are not all a matter of folk myth. Some differences do exist and they are important to man and wife relationships. In some respects women are the stronger sex, in others, men. Their strengths and weaknesses may complement each other, but cultures do not always take advantages of differences in defining male and female roles. In the area of emotional differences, the female biological constitution may be a major factor.

[29] Women, rather than using firearms, usually use poison or overdoses of drugs which in prescribed quantities are not dangerous. Lack of familiarity with firearms is a factor, but also their desire not to disfigure themselves for the funeral. These and many other aspects of suicide are discussed in Paul H. Landis, *Social Problems: Unfulfilled Welfare Aspirations of Nation and World* (Philadelphia: J. B. Lippincott Co., 1959), Ch. 10.

[30] Being more social than men, they are more likely to be discovered by a roommate or friend, in case of slow-acting methods of suicide.

[31] Amram Scheinfeld, *Women and Men* (New York: Harcourt, Brace & Co., 1943).

[32] The male has more emotional instability at ten than at any other age. The male generally is the stoical sex according to Carle C. Zimmerman and Lucius F. Cervantes, *Marriage and the Family* (Chicago: Henry Regnery Co., 1956).

Problems

1. Discuss the proposition, "Custom, rather than native endowment, is probably responsible for the fact that men hold more positions of authority in our society."
2. Women are frequently credited with having a greater capacity for "spiritual love" than do men. Explain the probable basis for this belief. Do you think it is justified?
3. Do you believe men and women differ in any or all the following traits: mental superiority, reasoning ability, emotional stability, quick thinking, sense of humor, ability with figures, practical common sense, sensitivity, sympathy, efficiency in work, submissiveness, stubborness? Those who believe in differences should offer proof for their views. Note whether each sex always considers the opposite sex deficient.
4. Philip Wylie has written a book entitled *The Disappearance* in which he alternately describes our country suddenly left peopled only by women, and then, only by men. He speculates about governmental changes, social changes, even changes in war and international behavior.
   Make your own statement on such a world as you visualize it.
5. Is it true that studies have proven that there are practically no native differences between men and women other than those of anatomy? Explain and illustrate.
6. For what reason have women traditionally been referred to as the "weaker sex"? Upon what grounds might it accurately be said that women are the "stronger sex"? Read Ashley-Montagu below for a point of view.
7. Do you think women stand the stresses of family life better than men?

Selected References

Articles in Books of Readings

Cavan, Ruth Shonle, *Marriage and the Family in the Modern World: A Book of Readings*, third edition (New York: Thomas Y. Crowell Co., 1969).
    Greenberg, Selig, "Why Women Live Longer than Men," Reading 15.
Krich, A. M. (ed.) *Men: The Variety and Meaning of their Sexual Experience* (New York: Dell Publishing Co., 1954).
    Deutsch, Helene, "Prepuberty in Woman," pp. 71–75.

General References

Ashley-Montagu, M. F., *The Natural Superiority of Women* (New York: Macmillan Co., 1968).
Kaufman, Sherwin A., M.D., *The Ageless Woman: Menopause, Hormones, and the Quest for Youth* (Englewood Cliffs, N. J.: Prentice-Hall, Inc., 1967).

Landis, Judson T., "Physical and Mental-Emotional Changes Accompanying the Menstrual Cycle," *Research Studies of the State College of Washington,* 25:155–162, June, 1957, p. 160.

Mead, Margaret, *Male and Female* (New York: William Morrow & Co., Inc., 1949).

Neugarten, B. L. and Kraines, R. J., "Menopausal Symptoms in Women of Various Ages," *Psychosomatic Medicine,* 27:266 ff., 1965.

Overstreet, Edmund W., "Biological Make-up of Woman," in Seymour M. Farber, and Roger H. L. Wilson (eds.), *The Potential of Woman* (New York: McGraw-Hill Book Co., 1963), pp. 13–23.

Perr, Irwin N., "Medical, Psychiatric, and Legal Aspects of Premenstrual Tension," *American Journal of Psychiatry,* 115:211–219, September, 1958.

Perr, Irwin N., "Sex Differences in Mortality Increasing," *Statistical Bulletin,* 58:4, September, 1957.

5

Sex Identification

We live in a time when there is confusion about sex identity. Fear is expressed that we are creating a "unisex." Women are dressing more like men, and men are adopting long hair styles, cosmetics, bright colors, and behavior once considered feminine. The college campus harbors anxiety about homosexuality, both men and women restrain contacts with their own sex for fear of being considered homosexual.

Still every individual must, if he is to feel at home in our society, clearly and consciously identify with his sex group.

Sex Assignment

Cultures do amazing things to human beings by virtue of sex assignment. What is appropriate for the female in one culture may be strictly masculine in another culture, and vice versa. Granted clear-cut biological differentiation, the male and female are cultural products and a great deal of socialization is required to form the appropriate male and female personality. In every known society, male and female subcultures are different, and an individual growing up in one subculture is never quite at home in the other, no matter what the biological sex category is. The boy becomes a man by participating in the male subculture and imitating males; the girl becomes a woman by living in the female subculture and imitating females.

It is only when the training process goes astray that its striking significance is made apparent, and often it does go astray, for in spite of the best efforts of society to condition the female toward female attitudes and expectations and the male toward masculine patterns, many failures result.

On the genital level, failure to develop sex identification leads, as we have seen, to homosexuality. On the social level, such failure produces women who identify primarily with the male role, have male interests, and feel frustrated in living by the female life patterns; and it produces males whose social training has been such that they identify in their secret wishes and often in their external behavior with the opposite sex.

The Genital Stage of Sex Identification

Very early in childhood the striking fact of genital sex differences impresses itself upon the child. How early this comes depends greatly on whether or not the children are allowed to see each other/or parents nude. If so, within the first two or three years of life, consciousness of male-female genital differences dawns on the child. It is possible that the significance becomes apparent to the girl at an earlier age and presents a greater challenge to her, leading to questions and a need for explanation. The small child lives in an environment of absorbing mysteries which challenge his investigation. By investigating, he learns. Body differences are such a mystery. It is a fortunate child whose parents, recognizing the critical but at the same time random and incidental character of the child's interest, allow free and unemotional exploration.

Probably few parents—or, for that matter, few adults—are capable of objectivity in this area. Children sheltered in infancy from the knowledge of sex differences may become aware of body structure only after starting school. Many modern nursery schools do not segregate the sexes for toilet use. Teachers of young children have themselves been taught the great importance of handling the innumerable curiosities of their small charges with naturalness, honesty, and without shock. The teachers can help the "delayed learner" to catch up, but the school situation, no matter how enlightened, cannot adequately substitute for enlightened parents.

Freudian psychologists have emphasized *penis envy* as a factor in female inferiority. This presumably develops when the young girl first observes that the young male has an external organ which she lacks. This makes her feel deficient and is the beginning of her feeling of inferiority to the male. In more severe cases penis envy leads to what is described as *genital trauma*. This in turn, according to the Freudian view, tends to build up female passivity in the sexual relationship. Whether this is a bit of imaginative fiction or fact has been long debated, and skeptics increase with the years.

Deutsch points out that young children envy anything the other child possesses and that penis envy, therefore, is normal and more or less inevitable.[1] She points out that many girls claim they once had a penis and

[1] Helene Deutsch, *The Psychology of Women, a Psycho-analytical Interpretation* (New York: Grune & Stratton, Inc., 1944), pp. 234 ff.

lost it. Other young girls, seeing a boy's penis, may try to take it away from him. Penis envy, therefore, is the same kind of envy that arises from the possession by another of any kind of property.

It is possible that the girl feels something is lacking in her body when she first becomes aware of the male difference. Whether or not her awareness develops psychological significance depends largely on the way in which it is treated. If parents explain frankly and honestly and without any sense of shock, "Yes, a boy does have more on the outside, but you have much more in the inside. You can be a mother. A boy never can," she is usually able to accept the difference without being psychologically scarred. A fact of life has been established that takes on no more significance than difference of hair color or any other physical trait. If the parents are shocked at this query or shocked when the girl, first observing the male organ, touches it and asks questions, if they hush her and shame her, the difference may become of vital psychological significance.

It is possible, too, that the necessary differences in toilet training of the boy and girl may have a psychological impact on sex identification. The girl may envy the boy's standing position in urination. The expanding use of standing facilities for both sexes, as is evidenced in some modern schools as well as in other public buildings, may well mark the beginning of a decline of cultural difference here. Other cultures—those in Asia, for example—have long experience in identical toilet posture for the sexes.

Finally, one may well question whether observing the sex organs is for the child any more surprising, or shocking, or any more a part of awareness of sex identification than observing the length of hair on the head or observing the mother's breasts. The adult who registers shock in connection with the child's observation of genital differences assumes that the child is equally shocked. Of course, if the child's first knowledge of genital differences comes from observing another child, then the problem is unique in that the child of the opposite sex shows no other differences in physical form.

The Oedipus Complex

Freud saw sex identification as a deeply complex, incestuous struggle. He coined the term *Oedipus complex* to describe it, taking the name from a famous Greek myth. The infant Oedipus was exposed to die in the ancient Greek fashion of disposing of a child who did not appear to be strong at birth. A shepherd found the boy and adopted him. He grew to manhood and became king of a state rival to that of his father. Later, he conquered his father's kingdom and killed his father, not knowing it was his father. Becoming king on his father's throne, he married the queen mother, his own mother, and had four children by her. Eventually the truth became known. His mother-wife killed herself and Oedipus tore out his own eyes in guilt.

Freud used this Greek myth to symbolize what he thought was the love attachment between mother and son, an attachment which the child, when he reaches the age of social insight, has to fight and destroy within himself.

The *Electra complex*, based on another Greek myth—the story of Electra's love for her father—involves the same mechanism of love and guilt in the relationship between daughter and father.

Freud carried these concepts over into the theory of "parent image" in heterosexual love. The male and female child, he held, are attracted to the person who represents the parent of the opposite sex—the boy to the image of his mother, the girl to the image of her father.

To begin with, both sexes love the mother because she satisfies their needs. They resent the father because he is regarded as a rival for the mother's affections. The development of the male Oedipus complex begins with the boy's incestuous craving for the mother and his growing resentment toward the father which brings him into conflict with his parents, especially the father. He imagines that his dominant rival is going to harm him, and his fears may actually be confirmed by threats from a resentful and punitive father. He is afraid that his jealous father will remove his genital organs because they are the source of his lustful feelings. Fear of castration or, as Freud called it, *castration anxiety,* induces a repression of the sexual desire for the mother and hostility toward the father. Castration anxiety also helps to bring about an identification of the boy with his father. By identifying with the father, the boy also gains some vicarious satisfaction for his sexual impulses toward the mother. At the same time, his dangerous erotic feeling for the mother is converted into harmless tender affection for her.

The sequence of events in the development and dissolution of the female Oedipus complex (the Electra complex) is more involved. According to Freud, when the girl discovers that a boy possesses a protruding sex organ and she has only a cavity, she can have varying reactions of disappointment. It is a traumatic discovery for her and has several important consequences. She holds her mother responsible for her castrated condition and transfers her love to the father because he has the valued organ which she aspires to share with him. However, her love for the father, and for other men as well, is mixed with a feeling of envy because they possess something she lacks. Penis envy is the female counterpart of castration anxiety, and collectively they are called the *castration complex*. She imagines that she has lost something valuable, whereas the boy is afraid he is going to lose it.

Unlike the boy's Oedipus complex, which is repressed or otherwise changed by castration anxiety, the girl's Oedipus complex tends to persist although it undergoes some modification due to the realistic barriers that prevent her from gratifying her sexual desire for the father. But it does not fall under the strong repression that the boy's does. These differences in the nature of the Oedipus and castration complexes are the basis for many psychological differences between the sexes.

These Freudian conceptions of the complexities of sex identification may or may not have a basis in reality, but to read intelligently one must understand them, for these conceptions are a part of the heritage of psychoanalytic theory. Although they have been widely propagated and have influenced much writing in the field of child development, they are as far from scientific verification as when first propounded.

Social Pressures in Sex Identification

The social pressures to insure proper sex identification actually begin prenatally. First of all, males and females are labeled with different names. These names are usually tentatively selected before the birth of the child. Second, a layette is planned with a difference of color for boy and girl. Thus, the social stamp of approval is put on sex identification from the outset.

If the child of two or three does not begin definitely to move toward identification with his own sex, parents make deliberate attempts to push him in that direction. The boy interested in dolls, dressing-up, and other feminine interests is cautiously pushed toward cowboy gunplay and other masculine pastimes. To encourage him, the parents buy a special costume or toys for masculine activities.

Similarly, the girl who is too absorbed in masculine types of play is steered toward feminine interests, encouraged to imitate her mother, provided with dolls and equipment for baby care so that she can practice the accustomed roles of motherhood. With the girl, however, more latitude is permitted than with the boy. Her tomboy interests are of less concern to parents than are the pursuits of feminine interests by the boy.

Usually, by the age of four, often earlier, the affection a child feels toward members of both sexes is strongly colored by his own identification with one sex. A boy feels tender love and dependence upon his mother, but if he has lived around a domineering and demanding father, he may also treat his mother with what he considers proper male condescension. He feels a strong attachment to members of his own sex but is careful to display his feelings only in a very masculine manner. From about eight to twelve or fourteen years of age he thinks of girls as sissies— and in his attempt to be the complete man, scorns not only the activities and ways of women, but women themselves. He teases and fights his sister and her friends.

This period of rebellion against the opposite sex makes identification with his own sex more complete. It does not, however, kill interest in the opposite sex. The very fact that the sexes wish to fight and tease each other indicates that the interest is still there, even though at this period, negatively defined.

The instances of going steady among preadolescents has little to do with any real affection. The eight- or ten-year-old girl (or boy) who admits to being in love generally does so in order to further imitate grown-up behavior. Any strong attachment felt by a child of this age toward members of the opposite sex is more likely to be directed toward an adult—a girl may have a strong romantic interest in the rock and roll singer, a movie star the age of her father, a teacher, or her own father. The general rule is, however, that until late childhood or early adolescence, the strongest attraction is to members of one's own sex.

The Adolescent's Preoccupation with His Body

The growing boy takes increasing interest in the penis and the satisfaction which results from its manipulation. In spite of certain prohibitions, fears, and a sense of guilt that may center around it, the penis becomes a source of great sensous enjoyment and a symbol of manhood.

This development is so important in the life of the male that Freud saw masturbation guilt being converted in the mind of the adolescent boy to a *castration fear*. This castration fear, Freud felt, reflects the high evaluation the boy is beginning to place upon his genital organs. This presumed fear, which has no scientific basis, Freud defined as the *phallic phase* in the boy's sexual development.

Much of the adolescent male's preoccupation with role identification at this period has to do with physical prowess in all areas: capacity for sexual expression (usually through masturbation), testing muscles in games of skill, flexing muscles and comparing them with pals, testing himself in feats of daring, torture, or endurance. He has come to see maleness as physical toughness and endurance.

In rural culture, male and female subcultures are so completely differentiated by division of work that special channels for male development are not needed. The boy works and hunts with his father and thus avoids the world of women. In urbanized society, where the boy has no contact with his father's work, and is often exposed to mother's activities, sports are used to build male identity. They may become the consuming passion of the boy from Little League through college.

Attention to the physical prowess of the male was even observed by the Harlows in their studies of monkeys. They find that the young male often initiates rough-and-tumble play and more often engages in copulatory play, indicating that these inclinations in the human male may have a strong natural base.[2]

The female becomes preoccupied with her person and its care during the period of adolescence, since with the maturing of sexual functions her body becomes her stock in trade in mate seeking and in realizing the deepest interest of human life, that of childbearing. This interest in the body is not narcissistic in character; it is a normal interest which accompanies social awakening and interest in the opposite sex.

The technique of attraction is, of course, greatly stimulated by those cultural values which encourage attractiveness and display and by the informal training in the art of being alluring. Cosmetics culture has been until recently largely female: scents, style, powders and paints are much more her speciality than a male's speciality. Here again Harlow finds a parallel in the behavior of monkeys, where the play of the young females involves a great deal of mutual grooming. Even throughout her adult life, the next most time-consuming activity of the female monkey after motherhood is mutually relaxed grooming.[3]

That culture plays a profound part in developing feminine techniques, for example, is definitely shown in regional comparisons within the United States. Historically, the Southern girl was trained well in the art of flirtation. In the Far West, where women were scarce and men competed for them, the development of these characteristics was at a minimum. In fact, women could be independent and unconcerned and still succeed in attracting a man. The culture of the West, therefore, neglected the development of the mate-attracting traits in the female.

It is during adolescence that direction in sex-role identification becomes most pronounced. With the coming of puberty, the society insists on greater separateness, greater role identification with one's own sex. Most societies have provided rites of passage designed to impress deeply upon the young adolescent his maleness or femaleness. The male in primitive societies may be put through torturous initiation ceremonies to test his capacity for suffering. When he has demonstrated by suffering that he is worthy to be a man, he is accepted as such. Girls in these cultures are

[2] Harry F. and Margaret I. Harlow, "Social Deprivation in Monkeys," *Scientific Amercian*, pp. 137–146, November, 1962. Also Harry Harlow, "The Nature of Love," *American Psychologist*, 13:673–685, 1958.

[3] Phyllis C. Jay, "The Female Primate," in Seymour M. Farber and Roger H. L. Wilson (eds.), *The Potential of Woman* (New York: McGraw-Hill Book Co., 1963), pp. 3–12.

often isolated for the initiation rites of puberty. They may be taught about sex, marriage, and the roles of womanhood. This period may involve sex initiation and modifications in hair or dress, even body multilations. For example, among the Kikuyu of East Africa, there is circumcision for the male and clitoridectomy (the cutting off of the clitoris) for the female. In some tribes sex initiation may involve the splitting of a labia for the girl. It may also involve, for both male and female, extensive scarification of the body, modification of hair style, and other such ritualistic procedures.

In modern society less attention is given to initiation rites. In certain social circles, debutante balls are in order; in the school program, there is often a break between junior high and senior high school at this period, but sex identification by elaborate ceremony scarcely exists.

There are, however, at this stage some marked psychological transitions symbolic of sex identification of the period. Some psychologists feel that all adolescents at this time become homosexual in their attachments, with many homosexual activities actually being engaged in.[4] On the emotional level one observes evidences of such behavior; the close pal relation of boys with boys and girls with girls, the small intensely loyal clique groups and other such phenomena are near universal. The constant association between these pals, their lengthy conversations on the telephone when absent from each other, their frequent desire to spend nights together are indicative of the deeply emotional loyalties which are characteristic of this period.

With girls custom permits a considerable amount of physical expression without casting suspicion of homosexuality; putting arms around each other and hugging and kissing each other are common behavior. For boys, such overt expressions are less common, but there is the close intimate palship and sometimes mutual masturbation and other sex activities.

The psychology of this transition seems to be that of the young person, becoming emancipated from the emotional ties of childhood, tends to cast his parents aside, except at times when he feels abandoned by friends. He seeks a love orientation outside the immediate family. The transition toward attachment to members of the opposite sex seems to be too great for the average adolescent, so he transfers intense, extra-familial loyalty to his own sex and only gradually does he emerge from this period into true heterosexual relationships. Some never get beyond the homosexual stage. Their love life becomes fixated there. Those who move into heterosexual love eventually move into marriage and complete the full cycle of sex identification by taking on the roles of father and mother.

[4] Ralph Eckert, *Sex Attitudes in the Home* (New York: Association Press, 1957).

Formal Training for the Male Role

At the turn of the century a majority of men, particularly in urban occupations, spent most of their waking hours away from home. Twelve- and fourteen-hour working days were not uncommon. Men had little if any time to spend with wives and children. As a result parenthood required of men little preparation. Today a seven- or eight-hour working day and a five-day work-week are standard practice. The future holds promise of even more free time. Males find themselves in the wife's domain for long weekends, and sharing evening hours. Many feel awkward and out of place; some feel guilty about not helping but embarrassed at the very thought of domestic tasks. All too many are bored and completely unprepared to enjoy this new opportunity for sharing in family life.

E. E. LeMasters has shown that for most young fathers, fatherhood is a crisis of real significance, partly because the male has little conception of what it involves.[5] Other studies have indicated that marriage is more disillusioning for the male than the female, because the male is untrained in the responsibilities he is undertaking. Child expert, Dr. Benjamin Spock, has commented on the lack of training of the young male for the parenthood role and the need for it.[6] It has been found that where boys are allowed to indicate subjects in which they are interested, without fear of shame from peers, they place study of marriage and interpersonal relationships high on the list.[7]

Some college males still have difficulty in accepting women as their full equals. Their feelings are comparable to those of the late Richard Neuberger, United States Senator from Oregon, who admitted that when his wife was elected to the same legislative body, he accepted her for the first time as an equal and came to respect her as a person of real competence, rather than as "just" a wife, a companion, and the mother of his children. An important bill was before the house and Mrs. Neuberger was to speak on it. He confessed taking her aside and coaching her carefully in what to say. She was new in the legislature; he knew all the ropes, or so he thought. His wife thanked him generously, but having ideas of her own, she prepared her own talk. It proved to be more effective than the attack he had planned.

One of the traditional aspects of male role preparation has been the

[5] E. E. LeMasters, "Parenthood as a Crisis," *Marriage and Family Living,* 19:352–355, 1957. This research has been further verified by Everett D. Dyer, "Parenthood as Crisis: A Re-study," *Marriage and Family Living,* 25:196–201, May, 1963.

[6] In an *Associated Press Release,* New York, October 15, 1958.

[7] A group of teen-age boys, when asked what interests they would most like to consider in discussion groups, listed dating, courtship, and marriage above other interests like hobbies, current events, etc.

conditioning in the direction of sex exploration. Some fathers in the older generation encouraged boys to visit a prostitute as a proper initiation to sex life. Even now some boys visit prostitutes in their early teens as a way of proving their manhood. Often they do so on dares, usually in groups, since none of the boys really intends to go, and sometimes older boys take younger boys.

From his study of a small number of cases, Kirkendall believes that it is a male group experience through which the boys are trying to achieve a group purpose.[8] It results often from trying to prove that they are grown-up, daring, and worldly-wise. Curiosity about how a prostitute operates is also a factor. For the most part, the sex experience is unsatisfactory. Because of fear they are often unable to carry out the sex act.

In an earlier day, when the male sexual role was one of conquest and dominance, when the wife was supposed to be passive, this kind of training may have had some place. Today, in the setting of the romantic marriage bond, where mutuality is the goal of marriage adjustment, such training is inappropriate. Fortunately, the prostitute is no longer sought as a teacher by many young males.

Even though the criticism directed at the training of the American male for adult family roles is deserved, it is only fair to state that his role preparation for family life is much more adequate than given the male in many other cultures. For example, it is doubtful that the British male ever feels really at home in the family in the sense that the American male does. His training is for administrative duty. His discipline in the boys' school, often away from home, is under the stern master. It is designed to make him immune to many of the personal sentiments, interests, and pleasures of our culture. As an adult, he will probably feel more at home in the office, the club, the army, and the pub than in the domestic scene.

Formal Training for the Female Role

When the domestic role was the only culturally predestined one, the forming of personality in women was clear-cut. A woman knew her place and her roles and was trained for them. Only the rebellious and unconventional felt thwarted because roles were so completely institutionalized. Here is a comment, made a century and a half ago, on the direction the education of women should take.

The profession of ladies, to which the bent of their instruction should be turned, is that of daughters, wives, mothers, and mistresses of families. They should be therefore trained with a view to these several conditions, and be furnished with

8 Lester A. Kirkendall, "Why Teen-age Boys Visit Prostitutes." A paper before the 1959 meeting of the Pacific Northwest Conference on Family Relations, Seattle, Washington.

a stock of ideas, and principles, and qualifications and habits, ready to be applied and appropriated as occasion arises . . . An early habitual restraint is peculiarly important to the future character and happiness of women. They should, when very young, be inured to contradictions . . . They should be led to distrust their own judgment; they should learn not to murmur at expostulation; but should be accustomed to expect and endure opposition. It is a lesson with which the world will not fail to furnish them . . . It is of the last importance to their happiness in life that they should early acquire a submissive temper and a forebearing spirit.[9]

One cannot deny that the role of the woman who chooses to marry and devote herself, for a period of twenty years or more to homemaking is vastly different from the roles of the woman who will spend all her active years in a career role similar to that of the male. The difference involves attitudes and values as well as roles. After her years of competition with men in school and at work, many an intelligent and ambitious woman has found the role of wife and mother most frustrating. Many of the most competent and competitive women have found themselves ill-prepared psychologically and emotionally for the maternal role, and even awkward in its routine demands.

The conflict of her two roles is one of the most serious dilemmas in the life of modern woman and of modern education. The problem has been of great concern to educators who believe that women must be prepared both psychologically and technologically to assume both roles.[10]

Education must give more attention to qualifying women for the parenthood role. LeMasters' study showed that young mothers had no conception of what they were getting into with their first child.[11] For them, parenthood constituted a real crisis and demands many attitude changes that women trained to anticipate the role of motherhood would have found less drastic. Such a situation is uncalled for in a culture which takes up so much of a young person's time in training him, presumably, to meet life's situations. (For a discussion of problems of adjusting to parenthood, see Chapter 27.)

Mature Sex Roles

For those in whom the process of identification with their own sex-group roles has been adequate, moving into adult roles is relatively easy.

[9] Hanna Moore, *Strictures on the Modern System of Female Education* (Boston: J. Loring, 1883), Vol. I, pp. 61, 8–182.

[10] For a good statement of the dilemma and possible solution, see Lynn White, Jr., *Educating Our Daughters* (New York: Harper & Bros., 1950); see also Terry Ferrer, "Rosemary Park: New President of Barnard," *Saturday Review*, April 20, 1963, pp. 66–68.

[11] E. E. LeMasters, "Parenthood as a Crisis," *Marriage and Family Living*, 19:352–355, 1957.

These roles are motherhood for the woman and fatherhood for the man.

Motherhood, Margaret Mead[12] found, requires very little encouragement from civilization. Fatherhood, on the other hand, is a social invention and requires a lot of cultural conditioning. It consists, essentially, in the tie between male and female based on the economic arrangement of the male providing for the female and her young. Among primates, to some extent, the male shares in the protection of the young, but only among human beings does the male share food with the female and her young as a consistent practice. This is a practice found in all cultures. Although the female may do much of the actual raising of the food, men do the things that are considered to be most essential to the economic survival of the group.

Since the dawn of history this practice has marked the relationship between man and woman. Margaret Mead[13] believes that the marriage system predates the knowledge that there is a relationship between the sex act and offspring. The marriage system may be closely related to the willingness of the female to grant sex favors in return for food and protection. "In every known human society," she finds, men learn as they grow up that to be a full member of society they must "provide food for some female and her young."[14] However, this does not necessarily mean that a man cares for a wife—he may have to care for his sister instead.

She points out that in all societies there are some tramps, ne'er-do-wells, and recluses who refuse to accept the burden of fatherhood. There are also culturally accepted ways in which a man may avoid the social obligation. He may join the priesthood, or monastic orders, or the Buddhist priesthood in Burma, or join the army or navy. For women, on the other hand, motherhood is so natural that only complicated social arrangements can break it down entirely.[15] Only the Catholic Church has been able to do so on a large scale, with the chastity requirement for its nuns. It is interesting to observe that both priests and nuns are rebelling in great numbers and dropping out to marry.

Margaret Mead also points out that under certain conditions society may raise the status of the single woman so high that women will strangle their children with their own hands. She also points out that illegitimacy may be such a shame in the culture that women resort to abortion or give their children away secretly. But there are the rare exceptions to the general rule of a mother nurturing and protecting her child.

In conclusion, sex itself is physical, but becoming a male or female in behavior and aspirations is a complicated social process. It moves so

[12]Margaret Mead, *Male and Female* (New York: William Morrow & Co., Inc., 1949).

[13] *Ibid.*

[14] *Ibid.*

[15] *Ibid.*

smoothly in the average case that little attention is given to formal training, yet failure of the individual to learn the role behavior of his own sex is failure indeed.

Problems

1. Are you aware of any of the training that entered into your conception of your sex role?
2. What do you think of Freud's views in the area of sex identification?
3. Do you willingly and naturally accept most of the roles assigned your sex in our culture?
4. Contrast male and female adolescent interests.
5. Do you agree that the key male role in our society is that of provider for women and children?
6. Contrast two cultures in their shaping of males or females: British, German, American, Latin, or take cases from Margaret Mead, *Male and Female*.
7. Compare developmental play of male and female monkeys.
8. Appraise the "unisex" trend among youth.

Selected References

Articles in Books of Readings

Winch, Robert F., and Goodman, Louis W., *Selected Studies in Marriage and the Family*, third edition (New York: Holt, Rinehart and Winston, Inc., 1968).
  Brim, Orville G., Jr., "Family Structure and Sex Role Learning by Children: A Further Analysis of Helen Koch's Data," pp. 325–336.
  Barry, Herbert III, and others. "A Cross-Cultural Survey of Some Sex Differences in Socialization," pp. 318–324.
  Lynn, David B., "The Process of Learning Parental and Sex-Role Identification," pp. 281-287.

General References

Barclay, A., and Cusumano, D. R., "Father Absence, Cross-Sex Identity, and Field-Department Behavior in Male Adolescents," *Child Development*, 38: 243–501, March, 1967.
Churchill, Wainwright, *Homosexual Behavior Among Males* (New York: Hawthorn Books, 1967).
Coser, Rose Laub, *The Family: Its Structure and Functions* (New York: St Martin's Press, 1964).
Crawley, Lawrence Q., and others, *Reproduction, Sex and Preparation for Marriage* (Englewood Cliffs, N. J.: Prentice-Hall, Inc., 1964), Ch. 3.

Eckert, Ralph, *Sex Attitudes in the Home* (New York: Association Press, 1957).

Gershman, H., "Reflections of the Nature of Homosexuality," *American Journal of Psychoanalysis*, 26:46–62, 1966.

Green, Richard, and Money, John, *Transsexualism and Sex Reassignment* (Baltimore, Md.: Johns Hopkins Press, 1969).

Harlow, Harry, "The Nature of Love," *American Psychologist*, 13:673–685, 1958.

Jay, Phyllis C., "The Female Primate," in Seymour M. Farber and Roger H. L. Wilson (eds.), *The Potential of Woman* (New York: McGraw-Hill Book Co., 1963), pp. 3–12.

Money, John, *Sex Errors of the Body* (Baltimore, Md.: Johns Hopkins Press, 1969).

Schreiber, F. R., "Female Homosexuals," *Science Digest*, 60:13–14, October, 1966.

Scott, J. P., "Critical Periods in Behavioral Development," *Science*, 138:949–958, November 30, 1962.

Willis, Stanley E., M.D., *Understanding and Counseling the Male Homosexual* (Boston: Little, Brown, 1967).

Zuk, G. H., "Sex—Appropriate Behavior in Adolescence," *Journal of Genetic Psychology*, 93: 15–32, September, 1958.

6

Female Roles
in Transition

"Thus the whole education of women ought to be relative to men. To please them, to be useful to them, to make themselves loved and honored by them, to educate them when young, to care for them when grown, to counsel them, to console them, and to make life agreeable and sweet to them—these are the duties of women at all times and what should be taught them from infancy."[1]

In most cultures the female is the more sheltered and therefore has more roles denied her. She can be raped and can conceive. These experiences can drastically change her life and that of her family. Society is affected since it may have to bear the economic and social burden the male ordinarily carries.

One can certainly attribute too much to biology, but viewing women's roles in terms of our cultural history, it appears that many limitations on female roles had their origin in this need for sheltering the female. It is probable that there is still a lurking fear of her being violated sexually in the new areas of freedom grudgingly given. The most extreme example in our culture has been protection of the white woman from the Negro male by devices of segregation.

A second important factor is that the male has never liked to be in a position of direct competition with the female. He resents and fears her sexual initiative since he needs to feel that there are many things he can do better than women can. The way to prove his superiority is to keep women from trying. He is typically less willing to admit women to new roles than women are to enter them.

But women have been assuming new roles for many years and seem to have protected themselves quite well. New role achievements still do not come easily, and there is always a price to pay for new freedoms— added responsibilities for choice and tensions that come with alternatives.

[1] Jean-Jacques Rousseau, *Emile*, Translated by William H. Payne (New York: Appleton-Century-Crofts, 1896), p. 263.

Life Planning

Men have always had to plan. Marriage was women's lot and there were few contrary expectations. "The ever-widening variety of occupations now opening for them makes more comprehensive planning a requirement for satisfactory living."[2] Women now have love, work, and marriage, if they are not to drift, they must learn to deal with the future.

The lifetime alternation between roles "inside" and "outside" the home, and the identification of self in new orientations is the essence of the role problem of modern woman.[3] Some never move "inside" and some never move "outside." However most assume both roles more or less successfully, but not without stress. During their lifetime most women have to make the transition rather completely from one role to the other and back again and must accept themselves in the roles chosen for the particular stage in the life cycle in which they are functioning.

In school she is the equal of the male, competing with him in the classroom and sharing with him in extracurricular activities. She moves into the work world as a temporary worker to remain there until children come. For most, motherhood brings a radical change. She retires temporarily from the work to become submerged in the lives of husband and small children. The ego-satisfying roles are lost, competitive achievements are abandoned.

But motherhood is also a temporary period. Childbearing is confined to a span of half a dozen years. Perhaps soon, perhaps not for fifteen to twenty years, she moves back into the work world where she will stay until retirement age forces her back to the home. She is "only a wife" again. This state is terminated in widowhood in the later years.

The problem of woman's roles in this day in history is that they are not and cannot be structured by tradition, and yet no culture can shed the persistent past, which so often affects the emotions and even the overt behavior of the individual.

Maximum flexibility is required if she is to retain her identity. And facility in learning the skills for the role shifts, and for self acceptance in adopting them, are a necessary part of her adaptation to marriage and family. Victor L. Christopherson,[4] addressing the annual meeting of the Arizona Home Economics Association, visualized the lifetime training task faced by teachers of women thus: "We must plan for the entire life cycle, from infancy through the gerontological stage . . ."

[2] Gladys E. Harbeson, *Choice and Challenge in the American Woman* (Cambridge, Mass.: Schenkman Publishing Co., Inc., 1967), XV–XVI.

[3] Helena Znaniecki Lopata, "The Life Cycle of the Social Role of the Housewife," *Sociology and Social Research*, 51:5–22, October, 1966.

[4] "Women in Modern Society," *Journal of Home Economics*, 57:99–102, 1965.

Roles in Historical Perspective

Throughout much of history, in many cultures female infants have been unwanted. This is so today in much of the world. The male child, it has been assumed, brings advantages to his family; the female, disadvantages. Female infanticide as a way of reducing girls in the family has been common. For a wife to bear sons is to be honorable in the eyes of the husband and his relatives and to rise in status in the community. Having daughters only, in some societies, is sufficient grounds for divorce.

Even American culture is not completely free from the traditional preference for a male child. A study of 380 university students revealed a strong preference for the male child, both among the male and female students.[5] Asked if they would prefer a boy or girl if they had only one child, 92 percent of the male students and 66 percent of the female students, making a total of more than three-fourths of both sexes, would prefer a boy. The results were not quite so extreme in expressing a preference that the first child be a male, yet almost 62 percent of the men and 59 percent of the women expressed preference for a boy. Only 4 percent of the males and 6 percent of the females preferred a girl first. The rest of the group expressed no preference. The Jewish students showed a greater preference for a male child as the first child than other religious groups. Almost as great a number of Catholics indicated a preference for a male child. Fewer Protestant students stressed a desire for a male child as the first child.

The authors of the study raise the question of whether there is as much equalitarian philosophy in American life as we usually hold, when even the college population shows little evidence of accepting the girl on the same basis as the boy. The authors also speculate as to whether or not we can expect couples to treat the male and female children equally under such a value system. They also question what might happen when it becomes possible to control the sex of the child.

For the first time, the sex of the child can be predicted with 100 percent accuracy by tapping fetal water and examining the cells. The cells of a female fetus contain a chromatin mass not found in the male fetus. It is now possible to know the sex in time to have an abortion if the wrong sex is found in the fetus. In rabbits, researchers have already succeeded in controlling sex with 100 percent accuracy, and with techniques that could in time be applied to human beings.[6] This may be in the distant

[5] Simon Dinitz, Russell R. Dynez, and Alfred C. Clarke, "Preferences for Male or Female Children: Traditional or Affectional?" *Marriage and Family Living*, 16:128–130, May, 1954.

[6] "Genetics," *Time*, June 7, 1968, p. 98.

future, but it is interesting to speculate how couples will handle the choice when offered.

The subservience of the female to the male, the denial to her of common rights and privileges, her lack of place in the esteem of both men and women, and even of children, has been and is so commonplace that only violent social revolution can revise her status in any particular social order. In many cultures it is still appropriate for her to be the hod carrier, the water carrier, and the tiller of the field, in addition to her domestic tasks and her function as mother.

Much stress is placed on the freedom gained by American women, yet evidence of prejudice survives. For example, a recent Gallup poll compared prejudice against women in the political area with religious discriminations.

Would you vote for a qualified:	Yes (percent)
Catholic	84
Jew	77
Woman (of men 58) (of women 51)	55

Foley observed that women hold very few key places in either elective or appointive offices in government. This is only partly because of a lack of interest.[7]

American Woman—The Symbol of Freedom

Even with these limitations, the American woman has become the symbol of the new woman of our day throughout the world, thanks to the wide advertising of her freedom, her attractiveness, and her daring as displayed by Hollywood. Most Scandinavian women have more sex equality than women of the United States, but it is less well advertised and in certain respects perhaps less accepted by the male there than are woman's rights and prerogatives in the United States.[8]

[7] Paul Foley, "Whatever Happened to Women's Rights," *Atlantic*, 243:63–65, March, 1964.

[8] *Social Sweden* (Stockholm: Social Welfare Board, 1953). See also Birgitta Linner, *Sex and Society in Sweden* (New York: Swedish Information Service, 1966). Bruce Gould, Editor of the *Ladies Home Journal*, is reported to have concluded after a visit to England, "In England I would rather be a man, a horse, or a dog, or a woman, in that order. In America, I think the order would be reversed."

The influence of Hollywood and the world travel of American women are certainly factors in the world-wide revolution in the role and status of women in our day. In all but the most isolated regions of the globe, their struggle for liberations is not only challenging old social structures, but is also bringing modifications in marriage patterns, child rearing, political systems, work roles, and standards of living.[9] Take for example, Africa, the last great continent to feel the immense impact of urban industrial civilization and its attendant patterns. In East Africa women have always been chattels by Western standards. They are sold by their fathers to prospective husbands for the standard medium of exchange, cattle or goats. Thousands of one-time bush families are now residents of great modern cities where they have cash incomes. The men now buy their wives with cash, sometimes on the installment plan. If they are delinquent in their payments, the father repossesses the daughter for resale. As the woman moves into the urban labor market she wonders why she should any longer be sold and bought by father and husband. She can earn her living and be independent of both. If she losses her job, sex can be sold in the marketplace, with more choice involved than in the customary marriage.[10]

In the Moslem world, where purdah and the harem have secluded women and protected men from the competition of women, the shackles of centuries are being broken—violently in some places, gradually in others, but here as everywhere in Moslem culture is the beginning of the revolution in sex statuses.[11] The tent of purdah goes, then the confining harem (walled-in home in which wife and older daughters stay isolated from men outside the immediate family), and soon the courageous and privileged few are on the public platform and in the halls of state. In India, where motherhood has been part of the symbol of woman's inequality, and where her status has been won by bearing sons, the shackles are falling off. Some of the most modern-minded Indian delegates to the United Nations and some of the most progressive members of the Indian Parliament are women. They are among the most aggressive leaders in challenging women's age-old subservience to the automatic operation of the laws of human fertility. Planned parenthood is state policy in India, as it is not in the United States or European countries.

Even in the conservative Latin American culture of Puerto Rico, Hill reports change in mate-seeking practices which would indicate a change in sex roles.[12] The American ideal of free mate choice is being accepted increasingly by the new generation, but parents, who have been accus-

[9] United Nations, *Report on the World Social Situation, Part II* (New York: United Nations, 1957).

[10] *Ibid.*

[11] Dorothy Fahs Beck, "The Changing Moslem Family in the Middle East," *Marriage and Family Living*, 19:340–347, 1957.

[12] Reuben Hill, "Courtship in Puerto Rico: An Institution in Transition," *Marriage and Family Living*, 17:26–35, February, 1955.

tomed to the institutional system of choosing mates for children, still hold the veto power over the young people's choice.

The sweeping changes in sex roles and in the relationships of men and women around the world constitute one of the great revolutions of our day. American women, being directly and indirectly responsible for this in considerable part, have achieved a level of equality which, though inadequate still, seems liberal indeed compared to that found in much of the world. What has been the price? Will others have to pay it?[13] What has she yet to realize? Where have her attainments put her in her relationship with men? with children? in her own conception of herself?

The New Feminism

As this goes to press there are rumblings of a new feminism which may set the world right for women. ("The New Feminism: Revolt Against Sexism," *Time*, November 21, 1969, pp. 53–56.) As yet largely unorganized, the movement is a revolt against "sexism," and takes many of its cues from the racial revolt. In fact, many of its more radical activists are dropouts from the racial and students revolts in which they feel they were considered a sex pool for the males rather than as equals promoting their respective causes.

The women meet in "rap sessions" to discuss their disillusionment and deepen their awareness of the indignities which have been heaped upon them. They burn brassieres, lingerie, false eyelashes, and steno pads—symbols of their oppression. Some are in a violent mood and are learning karate.

They oppose the male's use of the woman's body, the viewing of sex as a commodity, "Miss America" contests, *Playboy*, and consider death from illegal abortion "execution by the state." On the positive side, they demand courses in women's legal rights and in the history of women's successes, and seek other developments which will increase women's self-esteem.

Betty Friedan, author of *The Feminine Mystique*, founded a less radical movement called the National Organization for Women (NOW) which draws heavily from the professions, especially teaching, and seeks pragmatic objectives such as more day-care centers for the children of working mothers.

If this rebellion gains momentum, as some believe it will, it can have more far-reaching effects than the black revolution. At stake are the rights

---

[13] This problem cannot be handled adequately here. For a more adequate treatment see Paul H. Landis, *Social Problems: Unfulfilled Welfare Aspirations in Nation and World* (Philadelphia: J. B. Lippincott Co., 1959), Ch. 15. Other aspects of the problem of sex roles have also been covered in Paul H. Landis, *Social Control*, revised edition (Philadelphia: J. B. Lippincott Co., 1956), Ch. 9, and Paul H. Landis, *Introductory Sociology* (New York: The Ronald Press Co., 1958), Ch. 17.

and status of 51 percent of the population, not 11 percent as in the case of the Negro, and the situations have long had many parallels. As Gunnar Myrdal, the Swedish economist, noted in his classic study of the American race problem, *An American Dilemma*, both Negroes and women suffer from the same prejudices and discrimination.

The Culture-Concept Approach

The relationships of men and women are culturally defined. Since the development of the "culture concept" in sociology and its use in interpreting behavior over the past forty years, it has become apparent that a culture can create almost anything in the way of social relationships. The customary behavior of men and women of one culture may be contradicted by their customary behavior in another. Manners and morals are relative to the cultural history of the group. Informed people no longer assume that behavior of men and women is dictated by "nature" as it was once thought to be. Culture is the final umpire of appropriate behavior.

Rainwater's study[14] suggests that customary roles now are different between couples of social classes in the United States. The upper-middle class is most likely to share role relationships, while the lower class tends to segregate roles rather strictly. The intermediate classes fall between these extremes.

Role-Status Orientation

Another sociological concept of great importance in understanding the relationships of men and women is "social structure." Briefly, the social structure is the framework of statuses characterizing any given social system. Social structures, like manners and morals, differ from one group to another. Roles that bring high status in one social structure may bring a much different rating in another.

In all social structures certain social statuses are ascribed to large groups. The status of the female in the broadest sense is in this category, as are several of her more specific statuses, such as, for example, the single girl, the virgin, the young married woman, the mother, the grandmother. These are all statuses which are usually ascribed by custom within any given social structure.

Likewise, the male has certain statuses which are more or less universal within his group and are ascribed to all men, regardless of their

[14] Lee Rainwater, *Family Design: Marital Sexuality, Family Size, and Contraception* (Chicago: Aldine Publishing Co., 1965), pp. 28–60.

particular achievements; the baby, the boy, the teenager, the young male, the father, the grandfather.

In advanced societies, social structures become extremely intricate. In open-class societies, like our own, so many statuses are achieved rather than ascribed by custom, as in caste social structures, that the complexities of social status are almost beyond the comprehension of an outsider. In a society with many achieved statuses, the complex variety of roles performed by each sex, the overlapping roles of male and female, and other such problems are always present. It is with the complexity of these achieved roles that we are particularly concerned as we try to analyze the relationship of men and women in contemporary American culture.

Customary Roles vs.
Expected Roles of Women

Customary roles are learned largely from the family. It is through the attitudes, expectations, and habits formed in the family that a young person gets his basic training in role attitudes and role expectations, both for his own sex and for the opposite sex. In our time these customary roles are often in direct contradiction to the expected roles of the peer group.

The peer group is for the most part oriented toward new attitudes and new expectations for both sexes. The high school and university experience of today's youth has probably been the main influence in the creation of new role expectations in America. The interaction of boys and girls in school situations, where they function for the most part as equals, has tended, in the course of three generations, to break down much of the customary role expectations of the past. From this teen-group culture has emerged a new concept of equality such as feminists of an earlier day could never have conceived. More and more young men and women are participating in similar kinds of recreation, intellectual endeavors, and even in similar vices. Here, in playing up to the role expectations of their peers, they tend to part company with the role expectations of the family group.

It is at this point that much of the conflict between the generations has come.[15] Parents of the succeeding generations have seen their daughters moving into types of role behavior foreign to their concept of "young lady." They have registered shock as the daughter has taken on new role behavior considered appropriate for her in the urban industrial community. To many parents, her informality of dress, her companionship

[15] The U. S. passed the crisis in this area prior to World War II. Japan is the best example of this revolution since World War II.

with the male, her ignoring of the impediments of female biology have been symbols not merely of an emancipated generation, but of a wayward generation.

Learned Perspectives on Women's Roles

There are three major perspectives on the place of women in society and the significance of their roles. Adler believed that women carry an inferiority complex in relationship to the male. According to this view, there is a secret wish in women to have been born men. Adler,[16] a Viennese psychoanalyst, in developing the concept of inferiority feelings, identified power with masculinity and weakness with femininity. Inferiority was created with unmanliness of femininity, the compensation for which he called the *masculine protest*. Overcompensation, he believed, is indulged in by both men and women when they feel inadequate and inferior. He may well have reflected a traditional masculine bias. However, his views have been a part of the intellectual culture for some years.

Margaret Mead[17] and Ashley-Montague[18] both view women's roles as superior. Mead believes men do also. No man can ever attain the sense of reality which his childhood conception of the role of motherhood has given him. Men must, therefore, be given work roles, and the culture defines these roles as superior to fortify his ego and make him think that his life is worthwhile. Only in this manner can he gain a sense of "irreversible achievement" which his childhood knowledge has taught him women have by motherhood. Only as men can be allowed to surpass women in some work sphere can they be made to feel important.

Cultures, on the other hand, have to work very hard to make women want anything more than motherhood to make life full for them. Most societies, in fact, find in motherhood the model for the mystic, the artist, and the saint.

Montagu stresses not only the physical superiority of women but also their moral and spiritual supremacy. He visualizes a better world to the extent that masculine virtues disappear and feminine values and dispositions take over family, state and international affairs.

Betty Friedan, in the best seller, *The Feminine Mystique,* revived the masculine superiority position, but saw a way for women today to become "self-fulfilled" by entering a "fourth dimension." In her view the house-

[16] *Individual Psychology of Alfred Adler,* edited and annotated by Heinz L. Ansbacher and Rowena R. Ansbacher (New York: Basic Books, Inc., Publishers, 1956).

[17] Margaret Mead, *Male and Female* (New York: William Morrow & Co., Inc., 1949).

[18] M. F. Ashley-Montagu, *The Natural Superiority of Women* (New York: Lancer Books, Inc., 1953).

wife role is servile, helping others to perform the more vital and stimulating ones outside. She believes that women, to live with the fullest significance and the greatest sense of fulfillment, must take on the added dimension of outside achievement. Perhaps she voices the appraisal of women's roles as seen by a certain group of professional women.

With the more ambitious and perhaps more talented women, there is some drive toward fulfillment in roles of distinguished achievement. In order to be happy, they want and need to cultivate their special aptitudes. But the great mass of women, even the college educated women, want a family, are interested in human relations, and want to take their place in the community, but have no intention of entering into ego-serving conquests in a fourth dimension. Their orientation is toward rearing capable children, helping achieve financial goals for the family, becoming a better person for the sake of their families, being useful in the community, rather than winning personal laurels.

The desire for a fourth dimension finds very little expression among the thousands of student autobiographies which have passed through the writer's hands during the last fifteen years of teaching the marriage course. At the outset of teaching in this area, he felt quite sure that many college women had dreams of vocational conquest, and had a need to feel productive in the creative sense.

If college women do have such aspirations, they develop after marriage. College women do not claim them. This situation may well change drastically should the new feminism capture a large following.

Role Conflicts

Young women with children visualize greater happiness when they can pursue roles outside the home. But women who are involved in work outside the home think in terms of the time they "can return home where they belong" and "always wanted to be."[19]

In the life of each sensitive woman today, there is likely to be a great deal of confusion in her concept of her role due to her exposure to conflicting value systems. Part of her concept of what her role ought to be is internalized in the parental home. Yet, in the early adolescent years, the pressure of the peer group has supreme meaning to her. If she cannot measure up with this group, she has lost her closest and most vital tie, binding her to her generation. Therefore, she is likely to play roles consistent with peer group expectations. This, in turn, often brings her into

[19] Helena Znaniecki Lopata, "The Life Cycle of the Social Role of the Housewife," *Sociology and Social Research*, 51:5–22, October, 1966.

open conflict with her parents, and she is forced to rationalize her concept of how a girl "ought to behave" and how she must behave to get along in her group.

Her role concept is extended as she becomes acquainted with male friends and dates and later moves into betrothal and marriage. Often she finds that her husband's concept of the female role fails to coincide with any of her previous concepts; neither that of her parents, her peers, or that which she has personally evolved through conflict and compromise. She often finds herself resisting role concepts that her husband gathered in his own family from observing his own mother or sisters, or from association with other young women during the dating period. Since any woman, to have a successful marriage, must try to reproduce in her personality some semblance of her husband's image of what a woman should be, she must yet again try to recast her values, her philosophy, and her behavior to fit new role concepts.

Children often cannot reconcile the various activities of their mother with the concept of motherhood they see represented in the homes of some of their own playmates. Although most married women work at some time during their marriage, and the work role seems to be a well-established practice, a study[20] of eighth- and twelfth-grade children showed that boys were more often opposed to their future wives working than the girls were opposed to working.

If those close to a wife and mother do not see eye to eye with her regarding her own role expectations, she will probably internalize their standards to some extent. As a consequence, she may feel considerable guilt and anxiety and build within herself the feeling that she is neglecting her children, her husband, or her household duties. Yet, at the same time she must, to satisfy herself, continue to play her roles in the larger world, for she knows from previous experience that if she drops these roles she is less than the person she must be to retain her self-respect and to feel herself productive, useful, and significant.

It may well be that the mother-in-law will have a part in the wife's role conflict, particularly if the girl crosses class lines where role expectations are different. This influence may come in the form of direct criticism from the mother-in-law or through her husband who wants her to be like his mother. Many a wife is forced, in facing the realities of marriage adjustment, to modify her behavior for no better reason than that it must fit her husband's concept, or his mother's concept, of what her role as a wife should be.

Finally, in the broader circles of the community, she must face new roles defined in the particular segment of the community where she is active. In industry, appropriate role conceptions are demanded. They

---

[20] Raymond Payne, "Adolescent's Attitudes toward the Working Wife," *Marriage and Family Living*, 18:345–348, November, 1956.

FIGURE 6–1 EVERY THIRD WORKER IS A WOMAN. Source: U.S. Department of Labor, Women's Bureau, **American Women,** Report of the President's Commission on the Status of Women, Washington, D. C., 1963, Chart 10, p. 28.

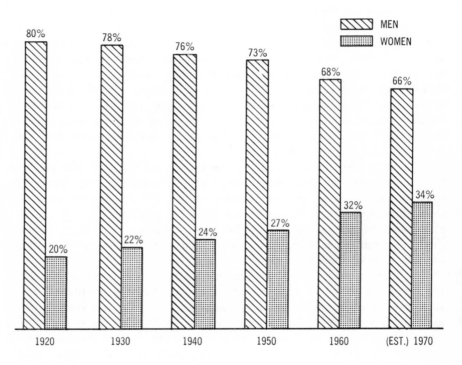

Of the new roles for women, none is more important than the work role which takes them outside the home and family circle. Increasingly women have entered the field of profitable employment. This modern trend brings with it both new freedom and new responsibility.

represent not only work-role situations, but also interest-group activities of which she must become a part (see Figure 6–1).

There is always, of course, the ultimate dilemma. "What do I do if I do not get a chance to marry at all?" A college girl expressed it in this way, "I have a double set of life goals; one set is for if I get married, the other if I remain single."

Marya Mannes in a discussion panel on the roles of modern woman commented, "I believe whatever decisions one makes, one pays for. Therefore, there is such a thing as complete acceptance of choice but no such thing as finite and complete fulfillment. We make a mistake in thinking, Will I be happy if I do this or that? We cannot be entirely happy all the time, and conflict, in a creative woman, often makes for pain and difficulty along with its joys. We must accept a degree of unhappiness, which I think is a natural condition of man."[21]

This analysis of the female dilemma may seem pessimistic. It is not so intended, nor is it intended to suggest that we return to the former customary roles for women. Women could not go back to their former position, even if it were more satisfying, which it most probably would not be. The modern industrial world has left no place for the kind of secure, family-absorbed woman of previous generations. Today women, as well as men, must function as individuals and, through performing significant roles outside the family, achieve their own distinct social status.

Woman still faces many of the discriminations long common to her sex. In wages and in occupational rank, she is still generally subservient to the male. In dating and in marital choice, the initiative is still his. In sex matters her unequal status is most blatantly obvious. The siring of a child out of wedlock by the male brings little personal or social guilt. The conception of a child by an unmarried female is still looked upon as one of the most serious of moral offenses. Society gives the woman and the child little protection or sympathy. The double standard obviously remains at the point where it hurts most.

Women are not now considered an inferior group, looked down upon by men, treated as subjects, humored, and used, as once they were, but at times men still like to think of women in the traditional way. Many men want their wives to be ornaments and clinging vines, even those men who expect their wives to support them. They miss the honor and respect that were once considered their inherent right. Today the male must earn these from his wife and children as well as from his male associates. In most cases, however, men are becoming aware of the more-than-compensating advantages that equality has brought. They want the strength, support, intelligent direction, advice, and companionship that only this modern woman can provide.

The threat to the male ego has been great and many men still cannot take it. Yet the trend is in the direction of greater equality in sex roles, and both men and women are growing in their understanding of each other under the new philosophy.

Once the successful wife was often a shrewd student of the male personality, for most of her wishes had to be realized by manipulating him indirectly. By indirection and subtlety she acquired whatever prestige and advantage she held in the household and in the pair relationship. Today, women need be much less subtle. They approach men on a different level.

[21]Marya Mannes, "The Problem of Creative Women," in Seymour M. Farber and Roger H. L. Wilson (eds.), *The Potential of Woman* (New York: McGraw-Hill Book Co., 1963), pp. 153–154.

The Female Life Cycle in Role Adjustments

The customary roles defined for a particular group may ease the transition through various phases of the life cycle, or make them unnecessarily difficult. It appears that in the United States the culture has tended to create difficult periods of adjustments for the female. The first critical stage comes when she moves from her adolescent beauty in the late teens into mature womanhood. This transition has been analyzed by Sirjamaki, who sees the woman's highest point in status in the United States at the college-age period.[22] Then, as never again, she is the center of attraction—the envied coed, the beauty queen, spending her time in dressing-up, dating, and dancing. In this, our culture contrasts decidedly with most other cultures in which the highest status role for women is motherhood. Supreme ego gratification prior to assuming mature roles may well leave a young woman feeling let down as she takes over mature roles.

Where the girl reaches her climax in social status prior to marriage, as in our culture, the marriage is often blamed for the eclipse in popularity which would have come in any case with increasing age and more limited social circulation. For the popular college girl, particularly, the quiet and unspectacular role of housewife is a striking and often unsatisfactory contrast. The ego suffers and she may feel rebellious against the limitations family and motherhood have imposed upon her. Many neuroses originate here. Popular articles lead one to believe that the campus beauty queen does not often prove to be the contented, happy, satisfied housewife. It must be recognized, however, that few reach the beauty queen level of ego satisfaction in the teens.

American culture defines the male peak role much more realistically. He does not achieve his maximum point of recognition and respect until he is somewhere in his thirties and has won it by social placement through occupational achievement and by home and family.

The status peak for both sexes, when contrasted with other societies comes strikingly early. Elsewhere, it is more usual for the aged—regarded, to use A. G. Keller's phrase, as "repositories of wisdom"—to be most revered of all age groups. Where elders are so revered, they have a secure place in the bosom of their families. Where their wisdom is regarded as the outmoded folk wisdom of yesterday, they frequently must spend their last years outside the family in loneliness.

Finally, the "empty nest" crisis for the devoted mother marks the beginning of her loneliness. With the loss of her children, her most vital

[22] John Sirjamaki, "Cultural Configurations in The American Family," *American Journal of Sociology*, 53:464–470, 1948.

role of her mid-years goes. Grandmothers are suspect in our culture if they interfere with the relationships of husbands and wives or if they so much as hint how young Johnny should be brought up. The loss of work at retirement sends the aging male and female into eclipse. No longer can they manipulate others or expect to be respected for their know-how. Youth in a technological age soon outstrips the wisdom of experience.

For the aging woman, roles shrink so much after widowhood that she considers herself fortunate to maintain her own household and takes pride in self-maintenance.

The Statistical Picture of Woman's Life Cycle

Analysis of census data by Paul G. Glick makes possible the charting of the life cycle of the average marriage, thus indicating the role shifts that will occur in the life of the average woman.

The pair stage is fairly short for most couples. They are inclined to begin their family early. This may be changing, with the current emphasis on restricting birth. Even so, once childbearing begins, the span is likely to be short.

In the modern family of from one to three children, childbearing will likely be over in five to eight years after the date of marriage. Statistically speaking, according to Census data, in the average United States marriage childbearing is over by age twenty-nine. This short period, when small children keep the mother more or less restricted to the home with a rigid domestic routine, is such a distinct break from the freedom of girlhood which preceded it that it requires considerable adjustment. For the woman who planned to work after marriage, it is also a trying period; this is the period when it is most essential that she give her full attention to babies.

The wife may console herself with the fact that it is a five- to eight-year period for her rather than a twenty-five year period as it was formerly. If she can adjust to the rigid routine it imposes, it may be one of the happiest periods of her life. It should be, for no period is more deterministic in the personality formation of the child. Her happiness with her child, as well as her full emotional acceptance of the mother role, is basic.

If the average wife finds domestic life less than fully satisfying she may, after her children are well along in school, reenter the work world herself, at least on a part-time basis. If she has hobbies or club interests, she will probably spend an increasing amount of time in them. The husband too may begin again the cultivation of old or new interests that do not involve his children. This will help prepare both parents for the next stage, the "empty nest," or more technically, the postparental period. The

FIGURE 6–2   ROLE CHANGES OF WOMEN DURING LIFE CYCLE (FAMILY
WITH THREE CHILDREN).

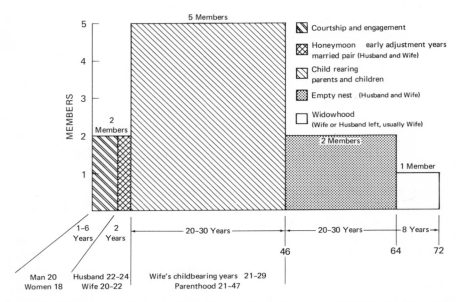

Childbearing for most wives ends by the 29th year. Child rearing is over by about age 47, requiring only about a third of the life cycle of modern women. As the life span increases, the time after the responsibilities of parenthood have terminated may well become almost half of an average lifetime. Reentry into the working world, often after retraining, is one choice now open.

children leave home and the couple is again alone. The final stage is widowhood, for rarely do both members die at the same time.

Marriage, for most couples, passes so rapidly and naturally from one of these stages to another that the problems or pleasures shift before they realize it. In Figure 6–2, the various stages of the typical four or five-member family of today are shown. It is assumed that the family is unbroken by divorce or death until the years when death normally takes one member of the pair, usually the husband, since women live longer and the husband is usually the older.

Glick's calculation of the life cycle for the average family for 1950 shows the median age for husband and wife at marriage is 22.8 years. The last child comes at 28.8 years, making the childbearing period only 6 years. Marriage of the last child comes at age 50; death of one spouse at 64; death of the other spouse at 72.[23]

[23] Paul C. Glick, "The Life Cycle of the Family," *Marriage and Family Living*, 17:3–9, February, 1955.

FIGURE 6–3   PROFILE OF WOMEN WORKERS. Source: **Work in the Lives of Married Women** (New York: Columbia University Press, 1958).

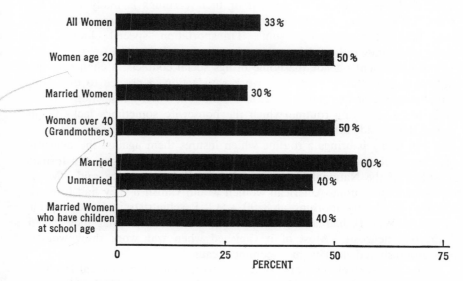

It will be seen that as high a proportion of women over 40 are working as of women age 20. Even of women with children of school age, 40 percent work.

Emancipation by Work Roles

No doubt the most influential factor in the emancipation of women, aside from education, has been their entry into the work world. Two wars produced the manpower shortages which drew women into the labor market. Once there, they stayed, and by staying, brought about revolutionary changes in home administration, in the male-female relationship, and the role conception.

Work roles are of profound significance to role interaction of husbands and wives today. Women work not only prior to marriage, but early in the marriage, and then typically enter the labor market again after a period of childbearing. Childbearing is over for most at about the age of 28. When the mother is 34, the youngest child is in school, so the mother enters the labor market again. A third of all married women work and they are still working as grandmothers. Half of the group of married women over 40 are working. In fact, as many grandmothers are working as are teen-agers (see Figure 6–3).

For the most part, married women do not work for economic reasons primarily, but rather to fulfill other wishes which homemaking leaves unsatisfied. As much as 40 percent of their earnings is likely to go for taxes.[24] If there are dependent children, the cost of child care and household help takes substantial sums. Transportation, special clothes, and other incidentals reduce the margin of profit (see Table 6–1).

Employment outside the home brings social contacts, a chance to use skills and capabilities, a sense of work satisfaction, a chance to dress up, a real need for beauty parlor care, and numerous other satisfactions. Work gives life a satisfying routine which the housewife sometimes lacks in an age of household technology, and it also brings status and independence.[25]

For many it brings a routine which insures them against the neurosis of a purposeless existence. Dr. Nadina Kavinoky, gynecologist and former president of the National Council on Family Relations, once said, "Much of the neurosis among American women would vanish if they had to leave for the office every morning at 8:00 A.M." Psychiatrists in London prior to World War II had a large case load afflicted with what they called "suburban neurosis." Most of it vanished when war work drew women into group-shared activity in a common cause.

One can scarcely conceive of all the social and psychological implications of the developing work role of American women. It has brought them great freedom, for only those able to earn and support themselves can have any real freedom of choice. Marriage is optional now, as is divorce, for the threat of dependency in the absence of male support has been greatly reduced.

A common difficulty created by women's entrance into the work world is its psychological effect upon some husbands. When wives become seriously interested in their own jobs they are thrown into competition with their husbands on two counts: (1) their husbands feel they are losing their wives' love and devotion and (2) they fear their wives may beat them at their own game. Few men of an earlier generation could stand this kind of competition,[26] men are becoming accustomed to it today, although it is particularly difficult for the American male to maintain his self-respect while being outdistanced by his wife. The attitude that a man who cannot support his wife adequately is a failure has disappeared with the rising level of aspirations and family living standards. But some husbands fear, and others actually sense, the development in their wives of assertive, individualistic, aggressive traits (see Figure 6–4).

---

[24] For a comprehensive view in this area see the report of a Columbia University Symposium, *Work in the Lives of Married Women* (New York: Columbia University Press, 1958).

[25] *Ibid.*

[26] The above points are discussed in John Levy and Ruth Munroe, *The Happy Family* (New York: Alfred A. Knopf, Inc., 1938).

Table 6–1   Gross Versus Net Income of Working Women

Couple	Husband's Income after Taxes	$5,000 4,245	Wife's Income Tax Costs†	$3,900 845 850
			Net	$2,205
Husband and Wife with one Child	Husband's Income after Taxes	$5,000 4,365	Wife's Income Tax Costs† Maid or Nursery School	$3,900 833 850 1,250
			Net	967
Couple	Husband's Income after Taxes	$15,000 12,095	Wife's Income Tax Costs†	$3,900 1,265 850
			Net	1,785
Husband and Wife with one Child	Husband's Income after Taxes	$12,000 9,965	Wife's Income Tax Costs† Maid or Nursery School	$3,900 1,137 850 1,250
			Net	633
Couple	Husband's Income after Taxes	$35,000 25,304	Wife's Income Taxes Costs†	$10,000 5,181 3,000
			Net	1,819

Source: "Does It Really Pay for the Wife to Work," analysis by U. S. News and World Report, 42:154–158, March 15, 1957.

† Transportation, lunches, clothes, laundry, dry cleaning, beauty shop. Costs are considered conservative and allow for no more eating out as a couple than before.

On the positive side, the work role of women has increased their insight into a man's life and problems. There is some evidence that successful work experience prior to marriage is favorable to success in marriage.[27] No doubt the insight gained into work roles is a factor. The

[27] Ernest W. Burgess and Leonard S. Cottrell, *Predicting Success or Failure in Marriage* (Englewood Cliffs, N. J.: Prentice-Hall, Inc., 1939), pp. 398–401.

FIGURE 6–4   PERCENTAGE OF WORKING WOMEN WHO ARE MARRIED.
Source: U.S. Department of Labor, Women's Bureau, **American Women,**
Report of the President's Commission on the Status of Women, Washington,
D. C., 1963, Chart 11, p. 29.

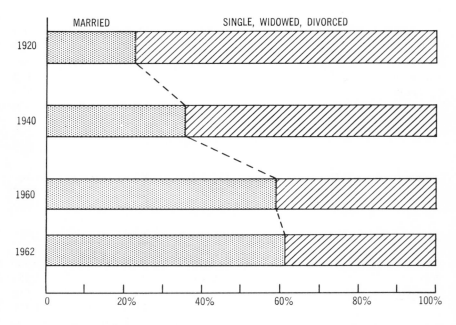

During the venturesome early days of women in the working world it was
the unmarried career women who sought profitable employment. Today
over 60 percent of the female working force is married. Then, the career
versus marriage dilemma was one for the unmarried girl. Now, working out
a marriage in which roles of homemaking and working are synchronized
is a lifelong problem for an increasing number of women.

new work roles have increased woman's incentive to acquire an education,
with the privileges and breadth of experience which this brings. Competition in the classroom has increased men's respect for women and their
capabilities as even their competition in the work world could not have
done.

Male prejudice against women's activities outside the home has decreased, although one must grant that each new venture of women has
been marked by initial sneers and vulgar suspicions. Although this country
has not permitted women to fight alongside men, as some nations did when
involved in World War II, women were taken into the armed forces for
special duties in offices and hospitals.

For this venture, they were not accorded the same patriotic respect
as service men, or credited with a motive of sincerity. It was assumed by

many that the only women who joined were those of questionable character seeking male association. Certainly in many quarters their morals were questioned and their characters suspected. So it has always been when women have ventured beyond the accustomed roles of the social order. Virginia Gildersleeve, speaking of the Waves, said, "If the Navy could possibly have used dogs, ducks, or monkeys, certainly the older admirals would probably have preferred them to women."

FIGURE 6–5   PERCENTAGE OF WORKING WIVES BASED ON HUSBAND'S INCOME. Source: "Special Labor Force Report No. 94," U.S. Department of Labor, Table J, p. A–15.

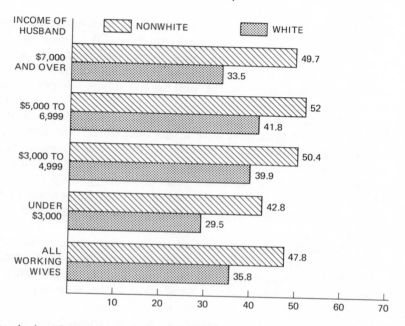

Data deal with marriages in which the husband is present. A much higher percentage of nonwhite wives are in the labor force than of white wives. There are fewest in the labor market when the husband earns the least.

Contrary to what one might expect, the wide-scale entry of women into the world of work served as an incentive rather than a barrier to early marriage. As the work world opened to younger women, regardless of their marital status, the economic handicap to early marriage was largely removed. By the careful use of contraception and by both working, young people may marry immediately after high school or college. They will have a struggle economically, and the chance of marriage success is relatively low. Some may even, in fact, marry and continue in school, each working part time and during summer vacations, or if the wife seeks no further schooling, she works and sees her husband through college or graduate school. (This topic is discussed in Chapter 16).

The highest proportion of working women whose husbands are living with them, is found in the middle-income brackets, white and nonwhite, rather than among the very poor and the affluent (see Figure 6–5). At all levels, there are more nonwhite and white women working whose husbands are living with them.

In all these respects, therefore, the entry of women into the work world has been an incentive to early marriage, and to marriage in general. Once again, as in an agrarian society, a wife can be an economic asset rather than an economic liability.

The major occupational field for women today is clerical (see Figure 6–6). (In 1947 the main occupational outlet was the "operatives"— mostly manufacturing.) Service work (protective services, waitresses, cooks, etc.) ranks second in women's occupations. Operatives are now third and the professions rank fourth. Of the professional group, 40 percent are teachers and 23 percent nurses.[28]

In March, 1967, 39.7 percent of all married women living with their husbands in the same household were in the labor force. The percentage of those in the labor force was greatest among those with the most education and smallest among those with the least education. For example, in March, 1963, of those with less than 5 years of schooling, 20 percent were in the labor force; of those with grade school training, 27 percent; of the high school trained, 35 percent; of the college graduates, 50 percent[29] (see Figure 6–7).

Although more single and married women are working than ever before, the fact remains that women favor marriage more than careers. This is clearly demonstrated in a study by Lemar T. Empey at Washington State University, where he found that 8 out of 10 college women preferred marriage to a career, if it came to an alternate choice; only 8 percent actually preferred a career; the remainder were uncertain.[30] The sample dealt with over 1,000 high school girls and over 400 undergraduate women at Washington State University.

Significantly, in this study Empey found that high school girls are more likely to look upon work as a pleasant activity than are boys. The differences, however, were slight. Approximately three-fourths of each group looked upon the work world as a pleasant one.

---

[28] "Special Labor Force Report," No. 40. Reprinted from *Monthly Labor Review*, Reprint No. 2433, February, 1964.

[29] *Ibid.*

[30] Lemar T. Empey, "Role Expectations of Young Women Regarding Marriage and a Career," *Marriage and Family Living*, 20:152–155, May, 1958.

FIGURE 6–6   MAJOR OCCUPATIONS OF EMPLOYED MARRIED WOMEN, HUSBAND PRESENT, APRIL, 1947 and MARCH, 1967. Source: "Special Labor Force Report No. 94," U.S. Department of Labor, Table E, p. A–4.

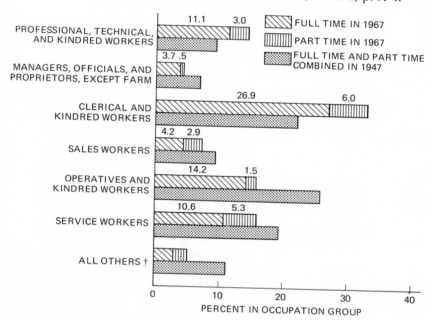

† Includes craftsmen, farmers, and laborers.

The Career Dilemma

The career dilemma is largely history. When feminism was at its height, women then were demanding a new status in the work world and daring souls, defying all tradition, achieved it. They usually did so at the cost of marriage. At that time, less than half of the graduates of women's colleges married, as did less than three-fourths of the women graduates of the coeducational college. Marriage for a woman was assumed to be a waste of college training.

With college education becoming more nearly universal, these attitudes have changed decidedly. The college woman must still weigh the alternatives in deciding whether to marry, and what to do about a career. It is known that each year's delay reduces the probability of a woman's marrying (see Figure 16–4). It is also known that college women in general have greater difficulty in marrying than do noncollege women. A special table (Table 6–2) developed by the Bureau of Labor Statistics shows the marital status of women ages 35 to 44, by education.

Male and Female: Predispositions and Roles

FIGURE 6-7 RELATIONSHIP OF EDUCATION AND EARNING POWER. Source: U.S. Department of Labor, Women's Bureau, **American Women,** Report of the President's Commission on the Status of Women, Washington, D. C., 1963, Chart 20, p. 68.

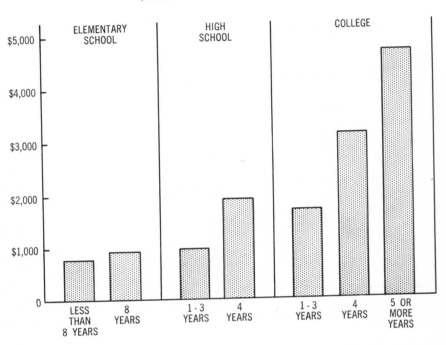

(MEDIAN INCOME OF WOMEN, 1961)

Education is an economic elevator for women as it is for men. (For income of men by schooling see Figure 25–1.)

Women with the greatest amount of education show the lowest marriage rate. Paul Popenoe, founder of the American Institute of Family Relations in Los Angeles, who has counseled many spinsters in the high educational brackets, warns the college woman that she should not neglect the development of her romantic interests. Most men are not interested in the college degree itself but in the warmth and humanness of the girls they marry.[31] He also believes that men still want wives who will bolster their egos rather than detract from them. He feels that the competitive woman is not particularly attractive to the American male.

[31] Paul Popenoe, "Where Are the Marriageable Men?" *Social Forces*, 14:257–262, December, 1935.

Table 6–2   Educational Attainment of Women 35 to 44 Years Old—
By Marital Status, March, 1962 (Numbers in Thousands)

| Years of School Completed | Marital Status | | | |
	Total	Single	Married (husband present)	Other	Percentage ever married
Elementary school					
less than 5	399	37	263	99	90.7
5 to 7	829	36	631	162	95.7
8	1,326	57	1,086	183	95.7
High school					
1 to 3	2,463	88	2,042	333	96.4
4	5,160	238	4,495	427	95.4
College					
1 to 3	1,314	56	1,134	124	95.7
4	903	100	741	62	88.9

Prepared by U. S. Department of Labor, Bureau of Labor Statistics, September, 1964.

A college girl in her autobiography, senses a trend in her own personality development unfavorable to marriage. She writes:

I have enjoyed college tremendously ever since I arrived. I can literally feel myself changing, and I honestly believe the changes are all for the better. I'm neater and much more considerate since I share a dorm room, rather than having a room of my own. I've got a quicker, clearer mind, and much more self-assurance since I've been subjected to the brisk discussions of many of my classes.

Still, in the back of my mind there is a growing uncertainty as to what all this will mean in my future. Even today, after only a few months of college, I know that I would be less acceptable to most fellows as a wife than when I first came. I'm too opinionated, too independent and ambitious. I have the terrible feeling that after four years I could never play the part of the self-effacing, hero-worshipping wife that most men want.

There may be some carry-over of tradition in the resistance of men to the intellectual woman, and certainly there is much injustice in it. But there is some evidence that those who drive hardest toward a career, and who become most motivated along vocational lines, are not particularly marriageable persons.[32] Such women may be quite content without marriage and should not let the usual values that prevail among women interfere with their becoming the creative persons they should be. There are, no doubt, some women for whom marriage should be secondary in our culture. Certainly, the generations can be replaced without all women participating in childbearing. It would be unfortunate, however, if a large portion of the inherently talented and capable should fail to replace themselves in the next generations.

To college women, the choice of career or marriage often comes, not as a major theoretical decision, but as a personal choice whether or not they should accept a good opportunity to marry before finishing college.

There is no one answer to this question. Some women are more strongly motivated than others toward academic and vocational achievement, and they could not possibly find happiness in terminating college for marriage. For them, marriage would represent more an end than a beginning. Others, in spite of parental pressure, should at this point marry, even though it costs them their college degree. Ruth Reed, in her book *The Single Woman*, has shown that the reason some single women missed marriage was that either they or their parents placed too high a value on finishing college. Looking back on their decision, they have regretted that they did not marry, for no other satisfactory proposal for marriage came.

The woman who wishes to marry must consider that after college graduation there are comparatively few opportunities to meet marriageable men on an intimate and long-time basis. However the choice need not be "either, or" for marriage need not represent the termination of a girl's opportunity for schooling.

Whether a girl continues her college education or terminates a college course prior to graduation seems to be in part a matter of social class background, according to Christensen.[33] The girl from the more privileged home is inclined to rate marriage above graduation, if the right opportunity comes along; whereas the girl from a family that is fighting its way up the social scale is more likely to finish her college education, even at the risk of losing a marriage opportunity.

It is increasingly possible for women to have both career and marriage. Children must have affection and care, but this does not mean that

[32] Evelyn Ellis, "Social-Psychological Correlates of Upward Social Mobility Among Unmarried Career Women," *American Sociological Review*, 17:558–563, October, 1952.

[33] Harold T. Christensen and Marilynn Swihart, "Postgraduation Role Preferences of Senior Women in College, *Marriage and Family Living*, 18:52–57, February, 1956.

the able and talented mother must spend all her time with the children. With help in the home she often can carry on her career with only short interruptions. Moreover, she can often start her career before marriage, have it during marriage before children come, and with the increased length of life continue it after the children are in school, even if she drops out completely during the period when her children are small. The small family of today—two or three children born close together—takes up only a short span of the mother's life.

A change of attitudes in this area will go a long way toward correcting frustrations in marriage centering around problems of parenthood. Confinment of the mother to the care of the young child is the most trying, particularly for the college woman whose life pattern is changed with the coming of the first child. Many roles are set aside in favor of those centering on the demands of the child. Orientation is definitely inside the home for a time.[34]

The child is a definite threat to the individualistic roles, goals, and ambitions of the educated wife. Childbearing tends to isolate her from her role as an independent woman. In a sense, childbearing itself becomes a concession to biological forces which automatically limit her chances of realizing the social and economic goals she has been conditioned to desire.

In all previous societies, children were an inevitable part of marriage. To fortify woman's role as childbearer a whole series of precepts was built up about a mother's duty and obligation to her children. Children fitted into this conception of life organization. If there were too many, one accepted them as the gift of an all-wise Providence. Today, it is not uncommon for women to bear children whom they actually do not love.

Modern Woman's Failure

Women seem to be quite as vocal as men in pointing to areas where modern woman has failed in role-status attainments. Margaret Mead, in lectures to college audiences, has criticized American women because they no longer want to be wives, but only mothers.[35] European women, she points out, want to be wives. She feels that American culture is caught in an "extreme reproductive cycle," which may be a threat to national survival. Men have been drawn very much into the inner circle of caring for children. Early dating, early mating, early parenthood threatens in-

[34] Lopata, op. cit.

[35] Student Marriages: Good or Bad," U. S. News and World Report, June 6, 1960.

dividual development. She points to the verdict of history, suggesting that no civilization has survived which allowed men to get "too close to children." They must be free to venture, to explore, to invent.

The "extreme reproductive cycle" may be over. The birth rate is dropping and women's values may be changing.

We have more young people in school, and more women college graduates per capita than any nation on earth, yet the proportion of women entering the professions and other creative work endeavors is much less than a generation ago. The National Manpower Commission concludes that only one in 300 women capable of earning a Ph.D. gets one. Only 12.6 percent of all Ph.D. degrees are granted to women today compared to 15 percent in the 1920s. *Time* reports (November 21, 1969, p. 54) that in the past 10 years women have lost 50 seats in state legislatures. There is one woman in the U.S. Senate, and there are only 10 Congresswomen. There were 17 Congresswomen in 1960.

Packard finds[36] only 16 percent of Ph.D. degrees and 24 percent of masters degrees at the University of Chicago Department of Sociology given to women during the period 1960–65. At the University of Pennsylvania Graduate School of Fine Arts, women make up only 7 percent of the enrollment in architecture and 40 percent in Fine Arts.

Today young women are more ready than ever to take jobs, yet few want to risk marriage and family for career aims like medicine.[37]

The contrast is often made between our output of trained women in medicine and that of countries with far fewer proportions of women privileged by the opportunity of college and university training. The Soviet Union is heavily staffed with women doctors,[38] some 75 percent being women compared to 7 percent in the United States. A third of their engineers are women, 1 percent of ours. There 35 percent of Soviet higher education staffs are women, even biological and chemical sciences employing many women. However, we should consider that Soviet woman do not usually advance to higher ranks, and that four-fifths of the female labor force is involved in physical labor, primarily agriculture.

Some critics say that the American college woman is afflicted by what has been called the "marriage blackout," by which is meant that a young woman's vision stops at the point of marriage. Here she loses sight of herself "as an individual human being."[39] Part of the reason is that she is still

---

[36] Vance Packard, *The Sexual Wilderness* (New York: David McKay Company, Inc., 1968), p. 103.

[37] David Riesman, "Permissiveness and Sex Roles," *Marriage and Family Living*, 21:211–217, August, 1959.

[38] Harbeson, *op. cit.*, also, Paul Foley, "Whatever Happened to Women's Rights?," *Atlantic*, 243:63–65, March, 1964.

[39] *Ibid.*

clinging to the false idea that she must choose between marriage and career.

Women are stampeded into marriage here, Foley believes, more than in any other enlightened society, by the social stigma which attaches to the unmarried. The motto becomes, "Marry as early as possible without appearing to be frantic, and try for the best prospect of suburban prosperity and security."[40]

There is increasing opinion among critics that women should "perfect themselves as human beings," that this is the only road to happiness and often is the surest way to a really successful life and marriage.

Marya Mannes, discussing the problems of creative women, comments, "The United States is plunged into an orgy of domesticity and childbearing."[41] Britain, Scandinavia, and Russia, by contrast, are pushing more and more women into intellectual attainments. She feels that in the United States there are "hidden pursuaders . . . cultural forces telling a woman it is unladylike to use her mind."

While Mannes presumes that women throughout history have found their fulfillment in motherhood, she asks whether many women in our society with its alternatives would not have been happier and had a greater sense of fulfillment as doctors, mathematicians, etc. She feels that our culture should recognize that procreation is a luxury today, not a necessity for all. She believes that mass media must recognize that many women are not satisfied with domestic roles, and that we must no longer stifle the creativity of the girl of great capacity by making her feel that creativity is unfeminine. She says that "the identity of women as human beings is as essential to them as their identity as wife and mother."

Betty Friedan has perhaps received more attention for her views than any contemporary writer and lecturer—whether permanent or passing, it is too early to know.[42] She feels women have slid back from the feminist achievements of an earlier day and become involved in the "feminine mystique," which identifies fulfillment with motherhood. As a result, she finds them unhappy and disenchanted.

Friedan feels that the talented woman must make a genuine commitment, not just to a job for a job's sake, not just to community busywork, but to a job she can take seriously as part of a life plan, "work in which she can grow as part of society."

Rosemary Park, Barnard President, believes that the woman's college is still necessary for women today, for it is so difficult for a woman to

[40] *Ibid.*

[41] Marya Mannes, "The Problems of Creative Women," in Farber and Wilson, *op. cit.*, pp. 116–130.

[42] Betty Friedan, *The Feminine Mystique* (New York: Dell Publishing Co., Inc., 1963).

develop a "sense of independent individuality." In the background of a girl's mind lurks the traditional thought "that someone will take care of her, that some man will come along and give the answer."[43]

"Most of you," Park says, "will probably live to be 100. If you want to keep from being a stuffy old bore for forty years, that is, between sixty and 100, then you've got to learn something now. . . . To be young and feminine at sixteen is no achievement. To be a respected person at sixty is."

This long-run failure of women is often expressed in both learned opinion and in research findings. Too early and too complete commitment to motherhood without an awareness of the long-term perspective of life is often tragic to marriage, to parenthood, and to every following phase of the life cycle. Only the purposeful individual can survive happily the later phases of the life cycle in our day of increasing longevity.[44]

Finally, we know that the woman who has enthusiastic interests in work and creativity is not handicapped for marriage or parenthood. Those with a purpose other than marriage make good in marriage and family life. Long ago Burgess and Cottrell found a high correlation between educational achievement and marriage success (see Table 6–3).[45] Contemporary studies show that women who prior to marriage and childbearing were "most taken up and bound to their jobs are the ones who are most enthusiastic and committed as mothers when they do have children."[46]

Table 6–3   Marriage Adjustment Scores at Different Educational Levels

| | Marital Adjustment Score | | | |
Wife's Educational Level	Very Low	Low	High	Very High
Graduate work	0.0	4.6	38.7	56.5
College	9.2	18.9	22.9	48.9
High school	14.4	16.3	32.2	37.1
Grades only	33.3	25.9	25.9	14.8

Source: Ernest W. Burgess and Leonard S. Cottrell, *Predicting Success or Failure in Marriage* (Englewood Cliffs, N. J.: Prentice-Hall, Inc., 1939), p. 271.

[43] Terry Ferrer, "Rosemary Park: New President of Barnard," *Saturday Review*, April 20, 1963, pp. 66–68.

[44] Several papers in Farber and Wilson, *op. cit.*, discuss this problem; see also Lawrence E. Dennis (ed.), *Education and a Woman's Life,* Proceedings of the Itasca Conference on the Continuing Education of Women, American Council on Education, Washington, D. C., 1963.

[45] Burgess and Cottrell, *op. cit.*

[46] Eleanor E. Maccoby in a discussion, in Farber and Wilson, *op. cit.*, p. 45.

Serious commitment to intellectual pursuits, to a profession or other career may well be indicative of prospective success in marriage and parenthood. Psychologists describe this process as "feeding from one facility to another."

Problems

1. Outline the lifetime shifts characteristic of women's roles in our culture today.
2. Men: Present your views on the proposition below which you are willing to defend:
   a. "I would rather marry an 'old fashioned' girl because . . ."
   b. "The 'modern' girl, in my opinion, makes a more ideal wife because . . ."
3. Women: Present your views on the proposition below which you can conscientiously defend:
   a. "The men of yesterday were a different and better breed than their modern counterparts. I would rather marry the kind of man who lived about _____ than a modern man because . . ."
   b. "Men have changed but mostly for the better. I'd prefer to marry a 'modern' man because . . ."
4. Discuss the implications of points of view expressed in activities 2 and 3. Do you think a young person's view on these alternative questions reflects primarily (a) his upbringing, (b) his experience with the opposite sex, or (c) other factors.
5. Describe several areas in which the line of demarcation between male and female roles seems to be disappearing.
6. Can you name roles that are still primarily one-sex roles?
7. Which sex seems to be changing the most in terms of traditional roles? What do you think accounts for this situation? Do you approve?
8. In what occupations and activities will you find women who have moved further away from the traditional female role?
9. In what occupations and activities will you find men who are most determined to live up to the traditional concept of the "masculine role?" In what occupations and activities is one most likely to find men who have adopted some traditionally feminine interests and activities?
10. Do you think that the differences in the social roles of the male and female will continue to diminish? Explain.
11. Briefly describe the situation to which the author referred in speaking of "the modern dilemma" in male-female social roles.
12. What is meant by the expression "women's career dilemma?" In what way may it be said that the dilemma is a less serious one today than it was a generation or so ago?

Selected References

Articles in Books of Readings

Cavan, Ruth S., *Marriage and the Family in the Modern World: A Book of Readings*, third edition (New York: Thomas Y. Crowell Co., 1969).
  Herzog, Elizabeth, "Children of Working Mothers," Reading 58.
Landis, Judson T., and Landis, Mary G., *Readings in Marriage and the Family* (Englewood Cliffs, N. J.: Prentice-Hall, Inc., 1952).
  Sirjamaki, John, "Cultural Configurations in the American Family," pp. 9–17.
  Komarovsky, Mirra, "Cultural Contradictions and Sex Roles," pp. 375–383.
  Wallin, Paul, "Cultural Contradictions and Sex Roles: A Repeat Study," pp. 384–386.
  Kirpatrick, Clifford, "Inconsistency in Marriage Roles and Marriage Conflict," pp. 386–392.
Sussman, Marvin B., *Sourcebook in Marriage and the Family*, third edition (Boston: Houghton Mifflin Co., 1968).
  Rainwater, Lee, and others, "The Inner Life and Outer World of the Workingman's Wife," pp. 180–193. Reading 20.
  Sirjamaki, John, "Cultural Configurations in The American Family," Reading 8.
  Komarovsky, Mirra, "Functional Analysis of Sex Roles," Reading 30.
Winch, Robert F., and Goodman, Louis Wolf, *Selected Studies in Marriage and the Family*, third edition (New York: Holt, Rinehart and Winston, Inc., 1968).
  Sugimoto, Etsu Inagaki, "Old Love and New," pp. 451–452.
  Whyte, William H., Jr., "The Wife Problem," pp. 177–189.
  Komarovsky, Mirra, "Cultural Contradictions and Sex Roles," pp. 189–195.

General References

Amgrist, Shirley S., "Role Conception as a Predictor of Adult Female Roles," *Sociology and Social Research*, 50:488–489, 1966.
Ashley-Montagu, M. F., *The Natural Superiority of Women* (New York: The Macmillan Co., 1968).
Axelson, Leland J., "The Marital Adjustment and Marital Role Definitions of Husbands of Working and Non-working Wives," *Marriage and Family Living*, 25:189–195, May, 1963.
Bernard, Jessie, "The Status of Women in Modern Patterns of Culture," *The Annals*, 375:3–14, January, 1968.
Bird, Caroline, *Born Female: The High Cost of Keeping Women Down* (New York: David McKay, Inc., 1968).
Blood, Robert O., Jr., "Long-Range Causes and Consequences of the Employment of Married Woman," *Journal of Marriage and the Family*, 27:43–47, February, 1965.
Cussler, Margaret, *The Woman Executive* (New York: Harcourt, Brace & World, Inc., 1958).

Farber, Seymour M., and Wilson, Roger H. L. (eds.), *The Potential of Woman* (New York: McGraw-Hill Book Co., 1963). This is a symposium. See particularly Part Three, "The Roles of Woman."

Foote, Nelson N., "New Roles for Men and Women," *Marriage and Family Living*, 23:325–329, November, 1961.

Hoffman, Lois Wladis, "Effects of the Employment of Mothers on Parental Power Relations and the Division of Household Tasks," *Marriage and Family Living*, 22:27–35, February, 1960.

Kammeyer, Kenneth, "The Feminine Role: An Analysis in Attitude Consistency," *Marriage and Family Living*, 26:295–305, August, 1964.

Kammeyer, Kenneth, "Sibling Position and the Feminine Role," *Journal of Marriage and the Family*, 29:494–499, August, 1967.

Katelman, Doris K., and Barnett, Larry D., "Work Orientations of Urban, Middle-class Married Women," *Journal of Marriage and the Family*, 30:80–88, February, 1968.

Kirkpatrick, Clifford, *The Family as Process and Institution*, second edition (New York: The Ronald Press Co., 1963), Chs. 7–17.

Mead, Margaret, *Male and Female* (New York: William Morrow & Co., Inc., 1949), Ch. 2.

Myers, George C., "Labor Force Participation of Suburban Mothers," *Marriage and Family Living*, 26:306–311, August, 1964.

Nye, F. Ivan, and Hoffman, Lois Wladis (eds.), *The Employed Mother in America* (Chicago: Rand McNally & Co., 1963).

Riesman, David, "Permissiveness and Sex Roles," *Marriage and Family Living*, 12:211–217, August, 1959.

Scheinfeld, Amram, *Women and Men* (New York: Harcourt, Brace and Co., Inc., 1943).

7

Male Roles
in Transition

Masculinity and femininity are in essence the typing of role patterns for each sex. All cultures have conceptions of what male and female must be like to fit adult life expectations. To be masculine in American culture has meant physical courage and sexual aggressiveness. We have not stressed physical courage to the extent some militaristic cultures have, or as much as traditional Masai culture of East Africa, where manhood was marked by killing a lion with an iron spear. In the area of sexual aggression, we disapprove of whistling at or pinching the girl on the street, as Latin cultures do, but the "girl-watcher" theme is a popular one.

Masculinity is associated with the appearance of physical strength and atheltic skill, and, with sexual prowess in the mind of the male himself. Female aggressive orientation in the area of sex has for the first time in American history placed the male on trial in the area of sexual performance. No longer merely passive, she measures his masculinity by his ability to satisfy her sexual needs. However, since the male measures his masculinity very much in terms of sexual potency, many a man has received a severe blow to his masculinity.

As women become more aggressive sexually, no longer accepting the timing of the sex act as an exclusive male prerogative, the male must meet the challenge or face humiliation and retreat into impotency. The definition of his sex role is not likely to change in terms of what is expected of him or of what he expects of himself. Psychiatrists have seen their case load of impotent males rise.

Males are confused about what women expect of them in the way of dominance, as in many other areas. Most women seem to want a strong man to lead them, and to lean on when they feel weak, but they will accept none of the domination that used to be the husband's prerogative. The line between weakness and dominance is a thin one indeed, and a man can risk his standing with women by being either too weak or overbearing.

124

Penalties of Deficient Male Role Performance

Deficiencies in female role performance, particularly that of mother, and their effects on children, have been studied and discussed. Perhaps inadequacies in male role performance have been neglected, particularly regarding their consequences in the personality formation of children.

Dr. Tess Forrest of the William Allan White Foundation claims that the father, in not taking his proper role, is a factor in manic-depressive psychoses and alcoholism.[1] Dr. Julian Bergas of St. Justine Hospital in Montreal finds "paternal deprivation and deficiency in father-daughter relationships" a factor in the background of a high proportion of attempted suicides in adolescent girls.

Child clinics and juvenile court personnel have long recognized that seldom is a child in court if his father is decent, kind, and responsible. Psychiatrists at Walter Reed Army Hospital find that boys whose fathers failed to take their proper role tend to exaggerate masculine behavior to cover their femininity and even have dreams and fantasies of a feminine quality. Those who couldn't accept their fathers, couldn't choose a career.[2]

It may well be that in an age of rapid male role changes, the disturbance of masculine roles has been far more serious than has been realized and that some of the role problems exhibited by wives and mothers reflect failure on the part of their fathers to adjust to the new requirements of marriage and parenthood.[3]

We have discussed the father's influence in the development of homosexuality in both male and female in Chapter 3.

The Complementary Goal
of Male-Female Performance

In any social structure there must be some complementation and coordination in male-female roles. Therefore, we must assume that the shift in women's roles in America has involved a radical change in men's roles. To the extent that women have gained privilege, men have had to change attitudes and expectations or suffer considerable loss of self-esteem. Woman's crusade for equality with men strikes at the core of the male's ego strength, the tradition of inherent masculine superiority. When woman

[1] Reported in *Family Life,* 28:6, November, 1968.

[2] *Ibid.*

[3] Judson T. Landis, "A Re-Examination of the Role of the Father as an Index of Family Integration," *Marriage and Family Living,* 24:124–128, May, 1962.

assumes that she can play any role which man can play, he must either accept that premise, fight it and retain his dominance, or reach some kind of workable compromise.

As young people attend classes together, date, go steady, and reach different degrees of commitment toward each other, there is evidence that young women affect career choices of the male. The image of science, medicine, and the military as vocations is affected very much by feminine appraisals.[4] There is a growing disdain for technology because of its application to the pursuit of war. This is not solely a female reaction, but in this as all areas of vocational choice, girls' appraisals carry weight with males of the peer group.

Young women now hope to avoid the postponements required by studies like medicine, with years of training, support by the wife, night duty, and in internships. Girls are increasingly inclined to evaluate male roles in terms of their effect on domestic life and their views may be crucial in forming the attitudes of those with whom they go steady.

This is not to pass judgment on the desirability or undesirability of this tendency, but to point out its existence in high school and college culture. As we have seen, Margaret Mead looks[5] upon it with some suspicion in warning college audiences, "No society has survived which permits men to get close to babies," one sex must be enough removed to take the risks of war and outer space.

Conflicting Expectations in Male Role Behavior

The male has maintained throughout the centuries a pattern of more nearly uniform role behavior than has the female. Yet he has not escaped, in this age, the pressure to conform to new roles. Modifications of behavior, which have been strenuous, embarrassing, and sometimes disastrous to him have been necessary. No doubt the male would have preferred to remain in his traditional role as patriarch of his family, master of his household, and guardian of the family property. This role, so long given community support and so long unchallenged, has had to be sacrificed in part to the newer values of the equalitarian marriage and the democratic household.

The wife has, often in spite of his protests, moved into the work world. He has thus had to share the provider role. He has also had to give up his position as custodian of family wealth as the wife has come to share

[4] David Riesman, "Permissiveness and Sex Roles," *Marriage and Family Living*, 21:211–217, August, 1959.

[5] Margaret Mead and Rhoda Metraux, "Image of the Scientist among High-School Students: A Pilot Study," *Science*, 126–384–390, August 30, 1957.

in the spending. Lynn White, Jr., former President of Mill's College, declares that many young husbands who not many years ago would have been ashamed of their wives working, now boast about the economic prowess of the little woman. He points out that this represents a definite mutation of the male's ego.[6]

The husband has come to recognize his wife's equality and sometimes her superiority as she has become more educated and more aggressive in community affairs. With her increased knowledge of child training and psychology she has educated him in the belief that children have rights equal to his own and that the fullest development of the child's personality is achieved, not by authoritarian methods, but by the counseling, developmental approach.

The big deficiency in men's training, White says, is their lack of preparation for the role of parenthood and family life. Women are much more adequately prepared. Men's training ignores this reality of their adulthood.

The Domesticated Male

In the broadest sense, the American male is more domesticated than in any previous period of American history. On the frontier, the masculine virtues were valued far above refinements. The strength of a man's arm and his physical performance in field and forest had survival value, and because they did, such qualities were rated highly in the culture. The virtues of brute strength and accomplishment have always been rated highly where man is pitted against nature. These values still survive, particularly in the logging and mill towns of our West, and to some extent in all of rural America.

In direct contrast to these traditionally masculine values are the so-called effeminate characteristics of the urban male today. Some attribute the increasing effeminacy of the male to childhood training. Because of the long daily absence of the father from the suburban home, the training of the child is left largely to the mother. Added to this has been the decrease of the number of male teachers in grade schools with the consequence that the training of the child in the formative years in the schoolroom has usually been carried out by women. Those who criticize this trend feel that the effeminate development of the male personality makes for softness and is a disadvantage to national survival.

The writer believes that there is a trend toward more effeminate character development of the male. The maternal supervision of home and schoolroom may be important factors. Perhaps even more important, how-

---

[6] Lynn White, Jr., "The Changing Context of Women's Education," *Marriage and Family Living,* 17:293, November, 1955.

ever, is the shift in dominant values in the American culture itself. Human brawn, generally speaking, has long since been replaced by horsepower, kilowatt power, and machine and atomic power. Today, a refinement of perception, a delicacy of touch, and a fine coordination are generally of more value than the strong hand, arm, or back. The brute strength of the frontier is no longer worshiped because it is no longer needed. Development along different lines would seem, therefore, to be more appropriate to the life men live now.

Masculinity Appraised

Ashley-Montagu has no fear of the effeminization of the male. He believes that the culturally induced, so-called masculine qualities of "self-assertiveness, aggressiveness, and bluntness" are not the qualities that build the kind of world we want. He sees love, sympathy, compassion, and the "desire to conserve," predominantly feminine qualities as our culture rates them, as the key virtues in human survival. He attributes the failure of humanity to achieve greater happiness to the fact that women have been denied the opportunity for "active participation in the government of human affairs."[7]

He would also so organize the work world as to permit men greater time for fatherhood, reducing the work day of fathers with young children to four hours a day with no pay cut and supplementing income with family allowances to help with the economic burden of child care.[8]

Swedish women are beginning to demand some of the goals which Montagu sets forth. They ask that men be freed from demanding work roles so they can participate more fully in domestic life. According to an Associated Press release, Swedish wives want husbands to be free from work more often to cook dinner, do the washing, take the children to the dentist, and in other ways share the chores of homemaking and parenthood. This would require shorter work hours and educating the man to be more domestically oriented in his activities. They want husbands to have leaves of absence with pay so they can spend more time in the home while the children are young. (In Sweden, 70 percent of women have jobs.)

Masculine values in the United States have changed profoundly. In an earlier day all of the arts and all things domestic were defined as effeminate and shunned by the male. The boy talented in music could

---

[7] M. F. Ashley-Montagu, *Education and Human Relations* (New York: Grove Press, Inc., 1958), p. 170.

[8] *Ibid.*, Ch. 10. Family allowances are paid the mother for each child by most industrial states. See Ch. 31 for a discussion of family allowances.

expect the scorn of his father, maybe even of his mother, and certainly of other boys and adults of the community, if he indulged this talent. As vocations, all of the arts—drama, sculpture, painting, even writing and scholarship—were looked upon as effeminate. Few males aspired in these directions. No boy dared dream of these kinds of accomplishments and expect to be accepted in his neighborhood.

Thomas Wolfe, one of the greatest of the American novelists, who grew up in Asheville, North Carolina, describes in his book, *Look Homeward, Angel*, the disappointment he was to his parents and to his father, particularly, when he chose to write. His father thought his gifted son should go into law.

Many boys hesitate, even now, to indulge their desire to cook. That activity, perhaps especially in rural cultures, has traditionally been effeminate. In urban life, the arts are more often considered as natural to the masculine temperament as to the feminine. In radio, stage, and screen, in sculpture, writing, and music, and also in cooking, the doors are as open to men as to women, and the roles are as readily accepted by men as by women.

With the entrance of women into numerous vocations, it is not impossible for the male and female roles to be reversed in the field of parenthood itself. There are a few families in which the mother is a driving, ambitious person, and in which the father has actually taken over the maternal role insofar as his becoming the emotional center of the household is concerned. In such cases, the father actually mothers the children, giving them the affection and intimate attention which children require. While these instances are rare and perhaps not yet fully approved by the culture, they do represent the extreme to which the male role has been and can be modified in our day.

The twentieth-century democratization of the American home has played a significant part in refashioning the domestic role of men. This new pattern of family life encourages the maximum involvement of the father and husband in family affairs. Thus not only do modern wives demand greater involvement on the part of their husbands and modern occupations allow time for this greater domestic involvement, but, most important of all, the modern male actually seeks this involvement for his own satisfaction.

When marriage and family relationships are based upon companionship rather than upon economic considerations and rigidly patterned institutional roles, the male is found to seek the company of his wife and children more than in the past. The husband who, for example, bathes the children while his wife washes the evening dishes, does so not only out of a sense of obligation or because of his wife's insistence. He enjoys this opportunity to play with his youngsters and to feel that he is contributing to their daily care and development. By reducing the number of his wife's after-dinner tasks he also insures their maximum number of hours together as a couple.

An occasional cartoon still feaures the aproned, bedraggled, domesticated husband, but such cartoons are becoming fewer and less popular. The apron, the dustpan, the dishcloth, and diaper pins are symbols of his new domesticity, it is true; but today we are coming to realize that they may also be symbols of a deeper and more satisfying family life than men have ever had before.

Even the child-training function, traditionally considered a female one, is shared by the male today. Johannis' study of father roles with an urban sample taken in Tampa, Florida, shows this strikingly (Table 7–1).

The first three items may always have been largely in the male's hands in the rural society which is the American heritage. If so, these data indicate that they have carried over into urban life. But fathers share the responsibilities of training in many other phases of behavior, as these data show.[9]

Strain in Contemporary Male Roles

Helen Hacker[10] sees that the masculine role has been greatly modified by the new role demands of the female, and somewhat to the male's disadvantage. She finds, first, that many of the role demands of an earlier period still exist and may have been increased by the numerous status pressures now centering around the traditional role of bread winner. Second, she feels that the male may suffer from feelings of inadequacy because of the uncertainty and ambiguity of his role expectations. She finds that he is particularly confused about his own masculinity. It is sometimes hard to know what is masculine today, and what kinds of masculinity will be accepted. Finally, she finds that there are problems in adapting male roles to the new freedoms and responsibilities of women.

Hacker feels that man's status as a lover has been challenged. Man's evaluation of himself from time immemorial has been supported by his dominance in the sex act. Historically this has been an almost unilateral male expression. Today his sex prowess is being determined more and more by his ability to evoke a full sexual response from the female. The new sexual emancipation of women has in a definite way been a threat to this key aspect of his masculinity. She believes male ego adequacy is dependent on sexual success. The female's is not. A woman can have

[9] *Ibid.*
[10] Helen Meyer Hacker, "The New Burdens of Masculinity," *Marriage and Family Living,* 19:227–233, August, 1957.

Table 7–1   Percent of 202 Middle-Class and 341 Lower-Class Fathers
in Tampa, Florida, Who Usually Assume or Share Child-Training
Functions Listed

Task	Middle-Class Fathers (percent)	Lower-Class Fathers (percent)
1. Teach the children right from wrong and how the family expects them to behave	82	79
2. Teach the children facts, skills, and how to do things	80	75
3. Punish the children when they do something wrong	76	76
4. Tell the children what time to come in at night	73	70
5. See that the children have fun	68	67
6. Help the children choose what they will do when they finish school	65	58
7. See that the children have good table manners	50	47
8. See that the children go to bed on time	40	49
9. See that the children do their homework	44	40
10. Help the children with their schoolwork	49	35
11. Care for the children when they are sick	35	38
12. See that the children get to school or work on time	32	25
13. Get the children up on time in the morning	28	20
14. See that the children eat the right foods	19	19
15. See that the children wear the right clothes	3	7
16. See that the children get washed and dressed	5	5

Source: Theodore B. Johannis, Jr.,   based on data presented in a paper before the Research
Section, National Council on Family Relations, Oakland, California, July 9, 1954.

status and not live up to any of the standards of femininity. A man
cannot be a man without living up to standards of masculinity. A woman
can be unfeminine and still be important as a person. To use Hacker's
phraseology, "there is a neuter category for women, but not for men." She

sees increasing homosexuality as part of the flight of men from the stigma of their inadequate relationship with women.

She sees the male's position in society being challenged in many subtle ways. Women are concerned with survival; men with honor, but man's honor in many areas is now subject to question.

Unique Male Roles

There is little doubt that the strong, domineering, aggressive, pugnacious male of frontier days has been modified, just as the gentle, passive, submissive female has become a character of yesteryear. Yet there is little doubt that men are still trained to be more worldly, more materialistic, and more success-minded. Men still seem to be more politically and community oriented than women and to find less support in religion and virtue. Although their interests in domestic tasks and activities have greatly increased, and they are more aware of the psychological and social needs of their children, they are still less gentle in disposition, less family-centered, and certainly less domestically oriented than are women.

Strength, courage, the ignoring of minor infirmities, are still values of the male subculture, not the significant values they were and are in agrarian culture, but still genuine values. Men still rate themselves and each other more in terms of efficiency, competence, material success, and prowess in sports and in sex than in terms of beauty, refinement, virtue, and goodness. It is probable that the average man still rates leisure below work, and luxury below the tools of productivity.

It appears also that woman expects many of these traits in man even though she has encroached on all his prerogatives. Many women still want the male to be strong when the test comes; many wish at times to feel dependent. They want to be treated as an equal; they do not wish to be dominated ruthlessly, pushed around, made subservient and made to feel lower in status, but, if college class discussions are indicative of female attitudes, they still admire and feel more safe with a strong male. If these assumptions are correct, men still have to display some of the traditional elements of courage and roughness to meet the expectation of the female subculture.

These expectations of masculinity have not spared the male a certain amount of conflict and anxiety. In a strictly male-dominated culture he did not have to be careful in drawing the line in his dominance. If he overstepped, the woman was not likely to challenge him. Today, even those elements of masculinity approved by the female must be displayed with discretion. How masculine he must be in order to win and hold her depends on the particular woman and her conception of the male's place in the family relationship. He risks being the offender in the delicate balance of role relationships, but she is more likely to be the one to take issue and to decide when he has overstepped his bounds. Women take the initiative in most of the divorce actions today.[11]

Even the timing of the sex act itself, traditionally controlled by the male, has to some extent been taken out of his control in modern culture. The female who was trained to a passive role in the marriage bed and taught that to be assertive was to be vulgar never put him on trial. Today, the female may also take the initiative in the sexual relationship, and she may properly recognize her needs as the equivalent of his own. He is often put on trial and may be found wanting.

Role Sharing

Prior to any marriage, the average young woman is likely to display considerably more interest in performing joint roles on a sharing basis than she will be willing or able to continue after the marriage is concluded. The great emphasis on companionship, today a value which serious couples rate above love as a basis for mate choice,[12] has led the young woman to go all out in being a pal in the man's world. She has adopted the short haircut and donned slacks; she goes hiking, hunting, skiing, hot-rodding, and fishing. Many of her clothes have become more utilitarian, less delicate, and less alluring. She has adopted the male's manner of speech, even his strong language. (A part of the shock of protest movements of the late 1960s, as far as police and public were concerned, was what might be called the "creative cussing" by girls. It was as filthy, vile, barnyardy and sacreligeous as the vocabularly of the old-time lumberjack living in isolation from female subculture.) She may sometimes share his broad humor; she patronizes the tavern; she smokes. Her liberties in the area of sublimated sex behavior are very broad, catering to males' recognized sex needs.

In her youth the gun, fishing rod, skis, golf clubs, and other paraphernalia of the rugged outdoor type are indicative to the male that she shows the same eagerness for speed, blood, and gore as he. She has become a worker beside him and is perhaps more likely than he to lay by a nest egg for establishing a home. Thus she proves to him that she is a real companion and that this companionship is likely to cost him nothing. He retains the traditional statuses; enjoys the traditional recreational forms, and she is a real pal to him, undemanding, enthusiastic, making him feel that life is complete.

[11] Discussed with support of data in Ch. 30.
[12] Ernest Burgess and Paul Wallin, *Engagement and Marriage* (Philadelphia: J. B. Lippincott Co., 1953).

It would be unfair to claim that all of this is part of the deceptive technique of the female in winning her man. Many modern young women thoroughly enjoy these activities, but many who participate in them do so as part of the necessary game for capturing the kind of male they want. After marriage, however, the requirements of home and family will most likely make this type of mutual role participation difficult, if not impossible, except on rare occasions. Then the male finds that he must seek other companionship, usually of his own sex. At the same time he will find himself drawn more tightly in to the inner circle of the family. The role demands of the female, so unapparent prior to marriage, may become very great. Whether they are greater where the palship has been established prior to marriage is a matter of speculation. Certainly much of the after-marriage palship must be in relation to domestic activities, yard- and home-centered.

The male may find also that most of his pal relationships, rather than being in the field, on the golf course, or in a boat, are at social functions, church, PTA, and other institutionalized relationships which are more carefully structured, and which may or may not be pleasing to him, depending on his own inclinations. Many males who have been very much outdoor oriented, or sports oriented, once they are married become oriented toward domestic activities and family-centered institutional activities to a point they never dreamed possible. If they make the adjustment readily, there may be a definite gain to the family. If they make this transition with resentment, feeling they have sacrificed their roles and liberties as men, or feel they have been denied the right to function in the male sub-culture, it may create issues that are quite disastrous to the marriage.[13] The same thing may apply to a woman who feels she has been denied her right to work, or other role activities.

The adjustments required after marriage are undoubtedly related to the degree of honest understanding that couples have of their expectations in these areas.

This analysis is presented, not as a criticism of women or in justification of men, but rather as an effort to clarify premarital role expectations that may not always be understood by either husband or wife.

The Strain of Harmonizing Roles

The strain put upon a wife in meeting role expectations of her husband and his family, in adapting to the demands of his work schedule, in

[13] Charles W. Hobart, "Disillusionment in Marriage and Romanticism," *Marriage and Family Living*, 20:156–162, May, 1958.

moving to the location of his work, and so on, are the most severe adjustments made. Women bear the brunt of marriage adjustment. But there is a case for the male's problem which seems to be of increasing significance. The crux lies in his taking a wife from the college, school, or work situation in which she has established roles and statuses which are precious to her, and which she may in one way or another project on him. With most women today, entering marriage from either the work or school situation has become a near universal situation.

To make the problem concrete and illustrate how the role shift of the female impinges on the man marrying her, we take the situation of the boss who marries his secretary. In the office, her role as secretary has been well defined. He gives her orders, makes the decisions. She does his secretarial work, buys small items from petty cash, keeps a list of his appointments and reminds him when they come due. She controls the coming of persons for interviews and conferences. She is his confidante in many important business decisions. Then they marry. Is he still her boss or does he now become her equal? Who is to give the orders? Who decides the coming of guests? Who handles the money?

What about the role changes of the boss? He has been used to pressing the buzzer or switching on the intercom and having a woman appear to do all his office chores. She has been a pleasant person, always neatly dressed and properly made up in the appropriate cosmetics. She has treated all his business as confidential. She has been willing to stay overtime and sacrifice her own interests for his at times when work was pressing. He has learned to shift all routine to her, to depend on her for his memory work.

Now he is her husband rather than her boss. There is no buzzer or intercom. He makes his own telephone calls and shares the home work by answering some of the calls coming into the home. He shares money matters with his wife, and likely as not is expected to help her with the home chores and baby care. Most often than not, she rather than he makes the social engagements in which they will spend their leisure time. In the office he says without fear of contradiction: "Tell them I'm not in. It's too nice a day not to be on the golf course." Does he tell her that at home now and go unchallenged?

This example shows how marriage roles differ from many other roles in everyday life, and how impossible it is today to handle roles of husbands and wives by custom. They have to be worked out by each couple for themselves. A good secretary may or may not be a good wife, and a good boss may be a wretched husband—will be if he tries to demand of a wife the same kind of loyalty, obedience, and sacrifice he expects of a private secretary. Secretaries like to work for the big boss who manipulates men, materials and money on a large scale, but wives don't like to be manipulated.

Protected Male Domains

When cigarette smoking was first becoming common among women, an anthropologist predicted that cigarette smoking would soon become a strictly feminine pastime; that once the female took up the practice, it would no longer be appropriate for men to smoke cigarettes. He was basing his judgment on the tendency of all cultures to assign certain practices to one sex or the other. He apparently failed to take into account either that the cigarette habit is very hard to break or that we are approaching a time when men do not resent encroachment on their cherished prerogatives; for men have not given up the smoking of cigarettes with the growth in cigarette smoking by women.

When women can take over men's vices and men still do not drop them, does any protected reserve of male prerogative remain? LeMasters contends that there is still a tavern society that is basically the male world, that there are male organizations that constitute the male-club society from which the female is excluded; some athletic clubs, some luncheon clubs, some hunting clubs are a unique part of this male society.[14]

Expense-account society is a male world which women, and particularly wives, rarely share. A survey by the Dartnell Corporation shows that the typical top-layer businessman travels some 30,000 miles on 19 trips, with 54 days away from home per year. Louis Harris and Associates estimate than 86 of every 100 airline trips are business trips. The corporation bill may run as high as four million for travel; many companies have a bill running a million or more dollars.[15]

While there are men who really hate travel, and some who refuse jobs with extensive travel, these jobs do carry status. Travel itself is a status symbol. Many who enjoy it, picture its dismal aspects to their wives, telling them of the boredom and loss of sleep. To the home-bound wife the romance of it, the adventure, the breadth of experience, may inspire envy. Often too, it is the basis of suspicion and distrust as she reads of the call-girl society. Few companies are willing or able to pay the cost of travel for the wife, and even if they could, the wife with young children is not free to join her husband in the expense-account world.

Much of the business world is a male society. There is undoubtedly

[14] E. E. LeMasters, *Modern Courtship and Marriage* (New York: The Macmillan Co., 1957).

[15] For a discussion of this male world see *This Week*, May, 1964, pp. 14–16. For an earlier study see William H. Whyte, Jr., "The Wives of Management," *Fortune*, 44:86 ff., October, 1951; and his "Corporation and the Wife," *Fortune*, 44:109 ff., November, 1951.

much in the world of the man that most women do not and do not want to understand. The operation of the stock and commodity markets, the phenomenon of inflation, or the significance of interest, are matters much less likely to concern her than the male. There is also a world of mechanics, with the torsion bars, the gear ratio, and a thousand other details of mechanical precision that are primarily male interests. It is not that women do not have the capacity to understand these refinements of technology, merely that their interests are more likely to be devoted to other matters.

Bossard has pointed out that sex distinctions are apparent in the very vocabulary that survives in the male and female subculture.[16] The male uses a language of stronger terms, while the female uses her own more gentle adjectives. For example, the adjective "lovely" is used extensively by women, rarely by men. The stock phrases of men and women differ, as well as the subjects they discuss. The child grows up learning the appropriate phraseology of his subculture.

In conclusion, the male's once lofty position has not gone unchallenged in this day of approaching sex equality. His authority, his sexual prerogatives, his favored roles have all been challenged, and he has gradually become domesticated as the male of the frontier could never have been. He is as a consequence more closely drawn into the intimate family circle.

Problems

1. Do you feel that men in America are becoming more effeminate? Is this equally true of all sections, or is it an urban phenomenon? Is it as true of one region as another?
2. If you consider that men are becoming more effeminate, how do you explain this and what are some of the risks, if any?
3. Do you agree that at times most women want their man to be the strong commanding type whom they can look up to?
4. Occasionally one sees a very strong female type married to a very flexible and spineless male. Do you think there is a tendency for the stronger female to seek the weaker male in marriage?
5. "Momism" is sometimes referred to as a curse of American society. Appraise this view.
6. Do you agree that there is considerable confusion in male roles today? Illustrate.

[16] James H. S. Bossard, "Private World of Man and Women," *Family Life,* 18:1–3, October, 1955.

Selected References

Articles in Books of Readings

Krich, A. M., (ed.), *Men: The Variety and Meaning of Their Sexual Experience* (New York: Dell Publishing Co., Inc., 1954).
    Benedek, Therese, "The Meaning of Fatherhood," Ch. 7.
Sussman, Marvin B., *Sourcebook in Marriage and the Family*, third edition (Boston: Houghton Mifflin Co., 1968).
    Komarovsky, Mirra, "Functional Analysis of Sex Roles," Reading 30.
Winch, Robert F., and others, *Selected Studies in Marriage and the Family*, revised edition (New York: Holt, Rinehart and Winston, Inc., 1962).
    Whyte, William H., Jr., "The Wife Problem," pp. 177–188.

General References

Ashley-Montagu, M. F., *Education and Human Relations* (New York: Grove Press, Inc., 1958).
Benson, Leonard, *Fatherhood: A Sociological Perspective*, (New York: Random House, 1968).
Farber, Seymour M., and Wilson, Roger H. L. (eds.), *The Potential of Woman* (New York: McGraw-Hill Book Co., 1963). This is a symposium. Part Five deals with "The Male Revolt."
Foote, Nelson N., "New Roles for Men and Women," *Marriage and Family Living*, 23:325–329, November, 1961.
Hacker, Helen Meyer, "The New Burdens of Masculinity," *Marriage and Family Living*, 12:227–233, August, 1957.
Hoffman, Lois Wladis, "Effects of the Employment of Mothers on the Power Relations and the Division of Household Tasks," *Marriage and Family Living*, 22:27–35, February, 1960.
Klein, Ted, *The Father's Book* (New York: William Morrow & Co., 1968).
Landis, Judson T., "A Re-examination of the Role of the Father as an Index of Family Integration," *Marriage and Family Living*, 24:122–128, May, 1962.
Lynn, David B., "The Husband-Father Role in the Family," *Marriage and Family Living*, 23:295–296, August, 1961.
Riesman, David, "Permissiveness and Sex Roles," *Marriage and Family Living*, 12:211–217, August, 1959.
Spock, Benjamin, M.D., "What a Father's Role Should be," *Redbook*, February, 1967, pp. 202–215.

8

Unsolved Role Relationships

The cultural approach to social life leaves little room for biological determinism in the area of social behavior. While nature may better prepare men for some roles and women for others, most roles can be reversed by culture. Margaret Mead, for example, in her anthropological studies of sex and temperament among the primitive Mundugumor and Tchambuli women, found that the men were the submissive, fearful, nervous ones; the women the virile, agressive, domineering sex.[1] In their training from childhood, boys and girls were taught to play roles which are the opposite of the sex roles of our culture and most other cultures, indicating that personality traits of men and women have grown, in part at least, out of the roles which society expects each sex to play.

We must assume that men and women will continue to work out their role relationships through the process of social interaction with no appeal to innate predisposition or cultural tradition. A new age demands new patterns of behavior.

The Ego Struggle in Role Conflict

Perhaps the greatest ego struggle in the relationships of husbands and wives, growing out of the new roles of women, lies in the area of work. Prior to marriage, girls become fond of having a pay check of their own; they learn to spend in ways which men consider unimportant. The superiority of the male role has been primarily in his ability to earn and to control spending. His status is threatened when he can no longer control income— and he no longer can do so if the wife has money of her own. This became

[1] Margaret Mead, *Sex and Temperament in Three Primitive Societies* (New York: McGraw-Hill Book Co., 1935), p. 119.

139

apparent in Great Britain when the family allowance was introduced. The lower-class male had always dominated by virtue of the pay check. When the family allowance was introduced, payments were made to the wife directly in order to help guarantee that children's needs would be met first. These lower-class women began to assert themselves in new ways, to demand greater independence, and to make it clear to their husbands that they no longer ruled the roost unchallenged.[2]

One must recognize that in some relationships between husbands and wives, role reversal provides mutual insight. But if rivalry results, there is a serious threat to the marriage relationship. Margaret Mead is convinced that the male's ego strength has largely depended upon his position as supporter of the family, and that therefore cultures have defined certain work roles as of first importance and have denied to women the right to perform them.[3]

The Power Struggle

Blood and Hamblin have studied the effect of the wife's working on the power structure of the American family.[4] Although they found evidence of her greater feeling of equality because of her work, the working wife seems to have little more effect on the power structure as evidenced in decision-making than does the nonworking wife. It was found that 45 percent of the working wives' suggestions in the home were adopted compared to 43 percent of those of the nonworking wives. The median amount of housework performed by husbands whose wives worked was 25 percent, while the husbands of nonworking wives performed 15 percent. Working wives wanted their husbands to do more housework, and the researchers believed that work sharing was a matter of cooperation rather than a shift in roles involving the power structure of the marriage.

Perhaps the most striking finding of this study is the great degree of equalitarian behavior in both decision-making roles and work roles. It may well be that the power struggle has passed for the average American family. If so, this means that wives as well as husbands are recognizing that responsibility is inseparable from power. Wives as well as husbands must fact the consequences of their decisions. Equality, in other words, has its price. There may well be in many marriages, also, the knowledge that to misuse power is to threaten the love relationship, perhaps the marriage itself.

[2] So marriage counselors in London advised the study group led by the author.

[3] Margaret Mead, *Male and Female* (New York: William Morrow & Co., Inc., 1949).

[4] Robert O. Blood, Jr., and Robert L. Hamblin, "The Effect of the Wife's Employment on the Family Power Structure," *Social Forces*, 36:247–252, May, 1958.

If the power struggle has ceased in the more privileged classes in the United States, it has not done so in most cultures of the world. The power struggle for equalitarian roles is only in its beginning. The right to work and to spend are key issues, as they have been in the evolution of equalitarian roles in this country.

Environmental Pressures

Lynn White, whose experiences as president of Mills College—a woman's college in California—makes his views significant, states that the suburb has created a new type of family life which is neither rural nor urban as it relates to men's and women's roles. This new family is definitely white-collar and leisurized. Both inside and outside the home, there is convergence of interest of the male and female. Husbands have been brought into the home as never before, and women have been drawn out into the work world in order to make marriage possible and family life more satisfactory in terms of material possessions.

The work world now embraces many jobs which do not require brute strength and which women can satisfactorily perform. The shortened workday permits the husband to enter family life in a way that has never been possible before. Men and women dress and act more alike; White believes they actually feel more alike.

The "crucible" of this new alchemy is the suburban home which represents the key both to living and recreation. White cites *Sunset Magazine* as indicative of this new suburban trend. This magazine is devoted to home and outside yard activities, and White concludes that "men and women are turning to marriage and larger families, to the home and its industries, to counteract the loneliness of this age."

With this new type of role interchange, White feels that the big problem of education is not women's education but men's. He feels that authorities in men's colleges still work under the assumption that men are going to live celibate lives. Men students may feel a need for orientation toward family life. When Radcliffe girls were offered a course in child psychology at Harvard, more men than women enrolled. Whether this was a genuine interest in child psychology or in meeting Radcliffe girls one does not know.

Ashley-Montagu, seeing the development of love in children as the great challenge both to parenthood and to teaching, feels that we should stop teaching women as though they were going to be men, proceed on the assumption that they are going to be mothers, and train all women first of all for motherhood. This is the way to the improvement of humanity.

The second phase of their training should be in the direction of "social participation" so that they will not be "second-class or third rate men," or an inferior group, but complete persons with rights, privileges, and obligations in the community. Being a good mother and wife, he sees, as the greatest service a woman can perform in her society. When the raising of children is largely completed, she then has many useful years ahead in which to contribute creatively to other activities.[5]

With the leisure and material comfort that modern life has brought to the family. White feels the big problem now is not one of staying alive, but of wanting to live. This he feels calls for emphasis on things of the spirit so that the modern family will not be destroyed by idleness and boredom.[6]

Role Conflicts Inevitable

The values of the female subculture today are very much in conflict. The residual values of an earlier age persist in the home training of a girl, yet the school curriculum, especially the college curriculum, treats the girl much the same as it treats the man insofar as goal expectations are concerned. The possible exception is the curriculum in home economics. Moreover, there is little, if any, direct training of the male in role expectations with regard to the female. The man may expect of his wife the same role behavior as his mother practiced. In fact, this will probably be the strongest conditioning element in his upbringing, as far as attitudes toward the roles of his wife are concerned. Yet, in marriage neither husband nor wife may be able to follow their own concept of what their role should be. The force of circumstances bears very heavily on roles in urban industrial society. Here a high standard of living, high pressure of advertising, and the needs of a comfortable home often compel a type of role behavior on the part of the woman, particularly in the work world, which is foreign both to her and her husband's expectations.

One sees this among college couples. Consider, for example, one young couple who came from a fairly high standard of living and had two children while in college. In order to maintain what they considered a decent way of life, the wife had to obtain a job. Without her husband's knowledge, she became a "carhop" in a local drive-in establishment. When the husband found out he was so embarrassed at the threat to their status that he tried to get her to quit. Failing in this, he went to the manager of the establishment and asked him to fire his wife. It was some weeks

[5] M. F. Ashley-Montagu, *Education and Human Relations* (New York: Grove Press, Inc., 1958), see especially Ch. 10.

[6] Lynn White, Jr., "The Changing Context of Women's Education," *Marriage and Family Living*, 17:291–295, November, 1955.

before his wife found out that her husband had tried to get her fired. She was very much upset. Her comment was, "What if I had been fired, and not known the real reason." It created a rift which will heal only with the passage of time.

Among college wives one sees many contradictions between role expectations and the actual roles circumstances demand. Couples put up with this situation with the rationalization that "when we are done with college we'll really live!"

A description of one of the worst cases of "couple conflict" that has come to the writer's attention is quoted here because it represents many aspects of the interaction between husband and wife involving differing role concepts, differences of equality, and differences even in the feelings of romance—the husband using his college contacts to sharpen his appreciation of the opposite sex.

> I have found many problems as a result of my working. I do feel intellectually on a lower level than my husband. There is no time to read and study things of interest to me that would help me. Although this may not bother some people it does bother me a great deal. Our social life is nil. No time, always studying. We have few friends and they are in my husband's field only. I object to this greatly and would like to join University Dames where there is a cross section, so to speak, of various fields, but my hubsand just wants me to be intereted in Veterinarians' Wives, a very narrow group. No time for just relaxing, knitting, sewing, etc., unless housework suffers and my husband objects to that most strongly. Insecurity. I sometimes feel my husband could have just married me to help him through school.
>
> Working poses another problem. It tires me so that when I have to go home and work some more (housework) it's enough to drive me out of my mind. Rush, rush all the time. I'm nervous and cranky as a result and give my husband a very bad time.
>
> Another problem—there is not as much time for personal appearance as there was before we were married and my husband does so appreciate the opposite sex and how much more attractive they (women students) are.[7]

Role conflict may lie in the fact that the wife actually wants to go to school and regrets the fact that she is married and working for the purpose of making it possible for her husband to finish his education. She may feel that her work life actually decreases her attractiveness and holding power over her husband. She recognizes the chief place of the husband as a breadwinner, but has a very difficult time sublimating her own desire for an education. Often entering into these feelings is a fear that the husband will outgrow her or find someone more attractive.

Other wives resent the fact that, while they work constantly, the husband does not help adequately with the housework or even assume the amount of financial responsibility which he should. Perry pointed out, after

---

[7] I am indebted for this example to Mr. Joe Perry, who interviewed a group of working girls on the campus of Washington State University as a part of a seminar project.

personal interviews with 18 working wives, that college couples tend to subordinate many goals to that of finishing school and live in the hope that most of their role conflicts will disappear once they are out of school.[8] While he admits schooling often aggravates role conflicts, creating difficulties which might not appear under other circumstances, Perry feels couples may be too optimistic about a change in role conflicts and role expectations after school.

The writer suspects that the worst role conflicts in husband-wife relations are to be found among couples both of whom have already obtained a college degree. Robert Coughland, writing on "The Changing Roles in Modern Marriage" for *Life* magazine, describes what he found in the suburbs as the "suburban syndrome."[9] Here the wife who worked before marriage, or who was otherwise very active, finds her married life one of boredom. She has been educated and conditioned toward a stimulating type of work and intellectual activity which carries prestige and ego satisfaction. She marries and finds herself in the psychologically degrading position of being "just a housewife." Coughland feels that many intelligent married couples confined to a small home or apartment with children needing constant care and with little money for servants or luxuries, face the problem of a morbid wife whose emotional condition may actually be bordering on depression.

London psychiatrists, prior to World War II had a heavy case load of what came to be termed "suburban neurosis." The bombings and war brought the chance for wives to work for money or in the social services. Women then felt themselves a part of current world and the case load in this category was reduced to near zero.

This experience is contrary to the assumption long-held by sociologists that the working wife had more problems than the nonworking wife. It appears now, however, in certain levels of American society at least, or perhaps rather on certain levels of education, that the nonworking wife shows just as many problems, mostly of a psychological nature, as does the working wife.[10] This leaves out of the discussion the problems of the children of working mothers. At this point our interest is in role conflicts of husbands and wives rather than in problems of children, which will be handled elsewhere.

One of the best descriptions of role behavior of the wife in the highly complex and stratified structure of the large industrial community

[8] *Ibid.*

[9] *Life*, Vol. 47, December 24, 1956.

[10] See, for example, Harvey J. Locke and Muriel Mackeprang, "Marital Adjustment and the Employed Wife," *American Journal of Sociology*, 54:556–558, May, 1949; see also, Ivan Nye, "Employment Status of Mothers and Marital Conflict, Permanence, and Happiness," *Social Problems*, 6:260–267, Winter, 1959; see also F. Ivan Nye and Lois Wladis Hoffman (eds.), *The Employed Mother in America* (Chicago: Rand McNally & Co., 1963).

is given by sociologist Whyte, in *Fortune* magazine. Whyte analyzed this role behavior and its relationship to the status hierarchy in the industrial community. The good executive wife, according to Whyte[11] is not a fixer, meddler, climber, or one who pushes a husband around, but rather a stabilizer who makes the home a place where the lonely and the over-worked executive may relax. At the same time, she must be a gregarious social operator and be able to put people at ease. Several unwritten rules apply to her conduct. She (1) doesn't talk shop or gossip with the girls, (2) doesn't invite superiors in rank until after they have made the first bid, (3) keeps away from the office, (4) avoids getting chummy with wives of men her husband may soon pass in the climb, (5) isn't disagreeable to company people she meets—you never know . . ., (6) is attractive, (7) is a phone pal of her husband's secretary, (8) never gets tight at a company party, (9) isn't too good. She keeps up with the Joneses, but doesn't try too obvi-ously get ahead. Getting ahead must be timed exquisitely in connection with her husband's advancement.

It is pointed out that if the husband moves up faster than his age group, the wife is almost forced to move into a higher-class residential community, because he so completely controls the destiny of the lives and families of her former intimates that she no longer feels at home with them or they with her.

Family possessions are a symbol of rank. One does not get a grand piano until one "is ready for it" in terms of the husband's place in the managerial hierarchy. Automobiles, particularly, are symbols of one's place in the system. One moves cautiously from one model to the next higher, leaving the luxury cars for the president and members of the board.

Whyte finds that the corporation does not object to a climbing executive getting a divorce, apparently assuming that he will choose a new wife more sympathetic to his position, work, and new status in the corporation hierarchy.

The Unsolved Sex-Ratio Problem

The problem of failure to marry in many communities is a matter of uneven sex ratio. The situation in this country is not as serious as in most Euro-pean countries. In Germany, France, and Russia, for example, there are millions of women with no chance of marriage. In those countries war casualties have been such that there are insufficient men of marriageable age in the population.

[11] William H. Whyte, Jr., "The Wives of Management," *Fortune*, 44:86, Oc-tober, 1951; and his "Corporation and the Wife," *Fortune*, 44:109, November, 1951.

In the mid-1940s the United States for the first time became a nation with a low male sex ratio. Previously there had been more males than females in the population. This situation will become more critical in the years ahead if we continue to bar immigrants from our shores, for in any normal population women tend to outnumber men because of their greater length of life. Age differential of men and women in marriage also exaggerates the unfavorable sex ratio. The average male is two years older than his bride. With each year of age death eliminates some from the marriage market.

Seldom, in a world of wars and migrations, are sex ratios even. Uneven sex ratios call for modifications in behavior to increase bargaining power of the surplus sex. Table 8–1 shows the recent trend in sex ratio by age. The great excess of females is in the older age bracket, because of the higher death rate of the male. But the data show males falling below the 100 level even in the early marriageable ages. The sex ratio is more uneven for nonwhites than for whites, there being a greater shortage of males. For example, in the age group 15 to 24, July 1, 1963, there were 99.2 white males per 100 females, among nonwhites there were only 95.4 males per 100 females. In the age group 25 to 44, the white ratio was 96.8

Table 8–1   Sex Ratio of White and Negro By Age, 1950 & 1968
(Males Per 100 Females By Age)

Age	1950	1968
White		
Under 15	104.2	104.3
15–24	101.0	103.3
25–44	97.8	98.8
45–64	99.9	92.6
65 & over	89.2	74.4
Negro		
Under 15	100.4	100.5
15–24	90.7	98.9
25–44	89.0	88.3
45–64	99.9	86.2
65 & over	91.3	77.7

Source: "Estimates of Population of the United States by Age, Race, and Sex: July 1, 1968," *Current Population Reports*, Series P. 25, No. 416, February 17, 1969. Table 5, p. 17.

males per 100 females, for nonwhite 87.1 per 100.[12] The sex ratio of the Negro population is very uneven and is getting worse (see Table 8–1).

The Population Reference Bureau, working with census data for the year 1967 indicated that of young people of the post World War II baby boom of marriageable age, girls in the 19 to 20 age group numbered 3.6 million, but males of the group most likely to marry then, ages 21 to 22, numbered only 2.8 million, an excess of 800,000 females. Parke and Glick recognize this "marriage squeeze" but also point out that men are not being pressured into early marriage by it.[13] If girls are trying to bring about earlier marriages, they are not succeeding. Younger men are warding off marriage more successfully than 20 years ago.

These figures, of course, exaggerate the shortage. Many women do marry their own age, where the supply of males is greater. But many will have to delay marriage, probably eventually marrying a divorced man or widower.

Migration greatly exaggerates sex-ratio differences in particular localities. Farm and small-town girls flock to the cities in higher proportions than do young men. This leaves both farm and small-town areas short of women of marriageable age, with the situation being more pronounced in the farm and ranch areas. Large urban areas tend to have a great excess of marriage age. The extent of the unbalance depends on the dominant occupational character of the city. Washington, D.C., with its large population of young government clerical and office workers, has a great excess of unmarried women of marriageable age. A few heavy-industry cities of the Great Lake area are dominantly male in population. Most metropolitan communities have a considerable excess of females in the marriageable ages because of work opportunities and social attractiveness; in large cities there are, per 100, ten to twelve more women than men in the most marriageable ages. And within the city there are barriers to the intermingling of single men and women. Women tend to congregate in the residential apartments of the white-collar and professional classes; men in the heavy-industry sections. The two worlds seldom meet, and when they do, they often find their differences too great to make for compatibility.

In most large cities the better residential apartment areas are crowded with young bachelor women who have little chance of meeting marriageable men. At the same time, there are many young men in the industrial sections with poorer housing who have little contact with eligible young women. These men do not appear particularly attractive to white-collar girls who are able to earn a good wage as secretary or office worker and share expenses in a beautiful apartment house with another bachelor girl. Many girls prefer their life of bachelorhood to settling for a husband who

[12] U. S. Department of Commerce, Bureau of the Census, Series P–25, No. 276.
[13] Robert Parke, Jr. and Paul G. Glick, "Prospective Changes in Marriage and the Family," *Journal of Marriage and Family Living*, 29:249–256, May, 1967.

represents a different level of living and of aspiration from their own.

The isolation of the sexes in war is another unavoidable factor. It has greatest impact on the generation of girls the same age as the military men being separated from civilian life. If long removed, when they return these men often marry someone considerably younger rather than one of their own age group. The man in his late twenties usually marries someone about five years younger than himself, whereas, had he married in his early twenties, he would probably have married someone not more than two years younger than himself.

Once a woman becomes established in a white-collar job, she is, for the most part, in a one-sex world. The principal professional positions available to women are teaching, nursing, library work, welfare, charity, and religious work. In none of these, with the possible exception of nursing —and nurses are preponderantly in the older age group—is there much contact with males. In business and industry, her chances are probably somewhat better.

With the decrease in their bargaining power, a certain proportion of women tend to become more aggressive in mate seeking. They become more willing to use sex as a bargaining device in attracting and holding the male, and in trying to secure a favorable marriage. The uneven sex ratio is also a threat to the stability of marriage.

No doubt the uneven sex ratio has tended to develop greater aggressiveness on the part of the average urban female than existed in the more chivalrous rural culture of another day, in which women were taught to be modest and meek and to play the passive role in their relationships with the opposite sex. Of course, there have always been women who assumed the role of the aggressor in mate seeking, where the occasion seemed to demand it. We must also grant that the majority of women, even today in urban areas, still play a passive role.

The increase in the illegitimate birth rate in this country (see Chapter 18 for data) is suggestive that women are, in certain instances at least, using sex as a bargaining resource for marriage, particularly women in urban areas where illegitimacy rates are highest. In this respect, they may be approaching, by degree, standards of women in Northern Europe and Scandinavia where births out of wedlocks run as high as 10 percent of all births.

If the sex-ratio situation should become critical, it is very probable that the more individualistic American women would come to demand artificial insemination, with the rights of motherhood out of wedlock being accorded full respectability. At present, it would seem that this day is some years ahead.

In Europe, after both world wars, polygamy was considered as a theoretical solution for the millions of women without prospects of marriage and legitimate motherhood. The uneven sex ratio undoubtedly had an effect on the morals of women, as evidenced by the easy shift to respectable out-of-wedlock motherhood so widespread during the Hitler regime.[14]

Equal Pay and Equal Advancement

It has been pointed out that most women who have reached the top have failed in traditional feminine roles.[15] They are, in the majority of cases, single or divorced. Others have married very late or are in their second marriage with a man who accepts their ambition.

The problem, of course, runs deeper than male discrimination against women in places of authority. Male and female subcultures designate certain roles for men and others for women. Legislation and even opportunity do not quickly erase these subculture patterns, which are the essence of social arrangements. The executive role is unfeminine in the traditional subculture of the female. Both men and women accept this as part of their value system and have difficulty in rising above it.

With the "brain drain" creating shortages in many areas, England, for example, it may well be that female ability will come to be sought increasingly, even for the higher levels of administration.

The Civil Rights Acts of 1964 was a big step forward in guaranteeing equal pay for equal work, regardless of race, creed, or *sex*. It also provided for equal opportunity in job training, promotions, fringe benefits and so on, but as a *Life* editorial points out,[16] in the labor force, one-third of which is women, they are still often paid less than men for equivalent work, and are discriminated against in raises and promotions. Of 9,000 top-ranked civil service jobs, only 1.7 percent are filled by women. In 1968, men's incomes averaged around $7,800, women's only $4,550. The low wages paid women is particularly significant when one considers that 36 percent of the nation's poor families are headed by women.

Harvard Business Review abandoned a study of executive careers for women, concluding, "the barriers are so great that there is scarcely anything to study."[17]

In 1968, a group of women brought a case into the courts under the Civil Rights Act of 1964, claiming that newspapers discriminated in running

[14] Margaret Mead reports "It is said that the sex ratio in Germany after World War I may have been one of the factors which defeated the Weimar Republic and gave rise to the Nazi Party. Jobs were given to the older man. This left young men unable to compete with older men for women's favors." Margaret Mead, *Male and Female* (New York: William Morrow & Co., Inc., 1949), p. 151.

[15] Marilyn Mercer, "Is there Room at the Top?", *Saturday Evening Post*, July 27, 1968, pp. 17 ff.

[16] *Life* editorial, "Unsexing the Classified," December 6, 1968, p. 48.

[17] *Ibid.*

help wanted ads under separate Male and Female headings. They described it as "Jane Crow" advertising, and accused those who tolerate it as "Aunt Toms."

This may well become women's best wedge to economic equality. Although, as *Time* pointed out (November 21, 1969, p. 54), "sex" was added to the Civil Rights Act partly as a joke by Congressman Howard W. Smith of Virginia, then 81, and drew a good deal of laughter from the House. It passed and some 7,500 complaints have so far been filed on behalf of women with the Equal Employment Opportunity Commission.

An interesting and significant adaptation of business to the needs and talents of women is Manpower, Inc., Kelley Services, and several smaller organizations with a similar purpose, that of training and placing women in temporary and part-time positions (see Table 8–2). Commenting on these training programs and the need for them, *Fortune* says of Manpower:[18]

It holds frequent clinics in department stores, complete with fashion shows, to persuade housewives to go back to work. "The women are full of all sorts of anxiety," says William Gallagher, vice president for service operations. "Will they be up to the job after so many years at home? Will they be able to compete with younger women? We try to reassure them."

For women to have equal opportunity for employment, the culture must take into consideration the fact of motherhood and its penalties. Before this can be a reality, various adjustments must be made in social institutions. This has been done in Sweden and some of the other Scandinavian countries by various devices—stopping work and receiving half pay some weeks before confinement, and continuing this throughout confinement and for a period of weeks afterward. The reduction in pay is offset by some sort of birth allowance. This birth allowance may be in cash, or, as in Sweden, the layette and various other items for the child may be provided. This latter arrangement presupposes that the state will pay some sort of family wage or family allowance and thus take into account the economic load of another child. In Sweden, as in most democratic countries of the world except our own, this is done by a family allowance which is paid by the government for each child from birth to sixteen years of age. Ordinarily this allowance is paid to the mother. In some countries, Canada for one, it is paid monthly—$6 to $8 per child, depending on age, from birth to age sixteen. In other countries, the allowance is paid on a quarterly basis.

There must be assurance for a mother that when her confinement is over, her job will be waiting. Mothers have this assurance in Sweden and in the other Scandinavian countries. There must also be some sort of com-

[18] Irvin Ross, "For Rent: Secretaries, Salesmen, Physicists, and Human Guinea Pigs," *Fortune,* October, 1968, pp. 164 ff.

munity system of medical care. This may take the form of state medicine, maternity insurance, or general insurance for medical-hospital care. Only in this way can serious economic anxieties be removed from the field of childbirth for the working mother.

Table 8–2   Offices and Income of the Top National "Temporaries"

	Annual volume† (millions)	Offices
Manpower, Inc. (Milwaukee)	$157.2	581
Kelly Services, Inc. (Detroit)	62.9	287
The Olsten Corp. (New York)	25.2	113
Western Girl, Inc. (San Francisco)	15 *	137
Employers Overload Co. (Minneapolis)	15 *	81
AGS Services Corp. (New York)	7.2	80
Labor Pool of America, Inc. (Oak Brook, Ill.)	7	38
Victor Temporaries (division of Victor Comptometer, Chicago)	5.8	80
Staff Builders, Inc. (New York)	4.2	47
Dot Girls (division of Dictaphone, Rye, N. Y.)	4 *	34

†Latest fiscal year   *Estimated

Source: Irvin Ross, "For Rent: Secretaries, Salesmen, Physicists, and Human Guinea Pigs" *Fortune*, October, 1968, p. 244.

Equal opportunity, not only for the mother but for any couple with children, can be assured only by some sort of public recognition of the costs of child rearing. The family allowance is one form of assistance. There are others.

Throughout much of Europe and Scandinavia, priority in public housing quarters and in cooperative housing units is based on a point system which takes into consideration the number of children in the family. In some countries, private homes for families with children are exempt from taxation for a long period of years after construction. These measures take into account the economic responsibilities of childbearing in a competitive economy where wages and salaries are the prevailing means of support. Only by such devices can the married worker have children without being penalized economically.

To summarize, in competitive industrial societies there can be no economic equality except as parenthood is taken into account by some sort

FIGURE 8–1   RELATIONSHIP OF CHILDREN AND INCOME. Source: "Consumer Income," **Current Population Reports,** Series P–60, No. 53, December 28, 1967, Table 5, p. 26.

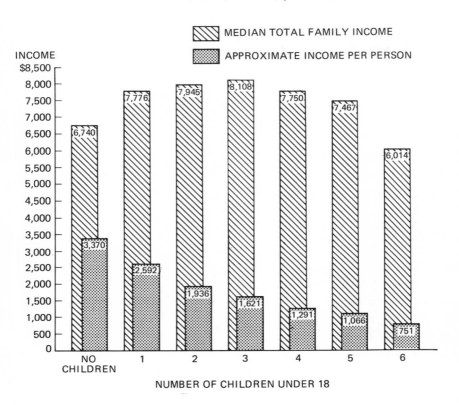

Couples without children have an average per capita income of $3,614. Add a child and that average drops to $2,391 per capita. Add six children and it drops to $736 per capita.

of allowance for children, and as supplemental institutions shift the load of child care from the individual worker to the social group.

In the United States, for example, we have the very difficult situation of couples trying to rear families on incomes that are the same as those of childless people. The childless people may live in luxury, but the couple with children may live in relative poverty. This has been demonstrated again and again. The Census data in the accompanying chart gives the picture as of 1967 in the United States (Figure 8–1).

It is certainly clear that the more children there are in a family, the smaller are the pieces into which the economic pie is cut. Labor leaders in the United States have fought a family allowance such as practically all industrialized countries now have. They want to see the wages of every worker raised to the point where families with children will have enough. The theory is commendable but illogical, for regardless of how high the level of living, those with small families or no children can still indulge in luxuries which the large family cannot aspire to. The situation of gross inequality would still prevail.[19]

Freeing the Mother from Subservience to the Child's Needs

For those mothers of young children who work, either from economic necessity or for psychological good health, industrial society has made too few concessions. In the large family system, warmth and loving care are not dependent on the mother alone, as in the nuclear family. The nannie system is a passing institution. Yet the young child must have constant care and love.

In order to free the working mother from those demands and still make it possible for her to have children, numerous adjustments are required in our culture. We have, through the nursery school and kindergarten, freed part of the mother's time. During the war we made ambitious beginnings with nurseries for child care. In the nation today 2,700,000 children need day-care centers but there are centers for only 530,000. As indicated, this is an area of need for which Friedan's organization NOW is seeking a solution.

Again one can cite Sweden and Denmark as countries which have provided at least some of the social institutions that help emancipate the working mother from the child. In these countries large apartment[20] houses, some exclusively for working couples or for unmarried mothers, with home service for the care of children and for the care of living quarters is provided. Some of these housing projects are cooperative; some are privately supported. For low-income groups the services are subsidized by the state or municipality—even the building itself is subsidized.

These housing units have nurseries which are open from six in the morning till eight at night. Here young children are given the best care by trained nurses and yet may spend the night with their families. For every age group these units have summer play schools, after-school play schools, and provisions for an after-school snack, homework study, workrooms,

[19] Few, if any, family allowance schemes or other subsidies in any nation are sufficient to completely equalize the burden of people having children with that of people having no children. The financial demands of parenthood are probably more nearly met in France than any other country.

[20] *Social Sweden* (Stockholm: Social Welfare Board, 1953).

shops, sewing rooms, kitchens, libraries, art rooms, recreation rooms. Each group through the teens can be occupied creatively and under supervision until the mother and father return from work. In this way children are given constant care by professionals during the period when mothers and fathers are required to work.

That these institutions are effective in helping to socialize the child and in making him feel a part of the social system is evidenced by the fact that in Copenhagen, for example, a city of a million people, there are only a dozen or so court cases dealing with juvenile delinquents in a year's time. These compare with the thousands of cases that appear before the juvenile courts in the average American metropolitan community.

To have genuine sex equality, it must be generally recognized that motherhood is a worthwhile activity and an end in itself entirely apart from other work. This requires that the mother have help available through the community, help which will permit her to obtain some freedom from the home, perhaps an annual vacation whether she can afford it or not, and other benefits.

In Sweden, couples who cannot afford baby-sitters may turn their children over to professionals without expense to themselves and with small expense to others, for an evening a week. Mothers who need it are given at municipal expense a two-week holiday completely apart from husband and children. The children are usually sent to camps.

While these measures are helpful in relieving mothers from the constant strain of caring for young children, their psychological importance probably far exceeds their physical benefit. These measures recognize that homemaking and motherhood are vocations of social importance, and grant them the same social status as other vocations.

Even freeing mothers from work during a longer period before the child is born may become socially desirable. Several studies, particularly in Great Britain, show that the success of a pregnancy drops significantly when women work during pregnancy. Census data indicate that in 1963 one-third of all births in our nation were to women working during part of their pregnancy.[21]

Must Role Differences Persist?

Even with the very decided trend toward merging of male and female roles and personalities during a half century, the significance of sex roles is still of vast importance. Our abhorrence of homosexuality and our inhumanity toward the homosexual are indicative of how important we consider the dividing line between the sexes. A man born with, or trained into, exces-

[21] See *Family Life*, Vol. 28, December, 1968.

sively effeminate traits has a rough time in our culture, as does the very masculinely inclined female.

The case of the effeminate American youth who submitted to months of painful surgery at the hands of a Danish physician in order to change his sex role attracted worldwide attention and interest. It was of no less interest in the United States than in countries where the gulf separating the sexes is far wider. Tragic, indeed, is the person who for some reason cannot fit the male-female subculture patterns of his culture.

The division of labor between men and women and the work roles of husband and wife vary greatly from society to society, but everywhere boys are brought up to know that they are expected to help provide for a woman and her children as part of their adult role.

This conditioning in itself affects personality patterns of male and female as they train for and take up their respective roles, and is a fact of life that cannot be fully evaded even in our machine age. As long as the institution of the family persists as society's approved relationship for conceiving and rearing children, it is likely that work roles and to some extent domestic and social roles will tend to differ between the sexes. If, however, state institutions continue to develop around child rearing—taking the child at an early age and keeping him for longer periods of time—distinctions between the roles of husband and wife can be expected to grow less clear. And if the educated woman and her husband can accept parenthood as a temporary but highly rewarding role, much role conflict may be avoided.

Some Major Cultural Modifications Needed

The longevity of modern woman, combined with the fact that childbearing and child rearing are limited to so short a span of her life, creates problems of life-long adjustments. Millions of women become grandmothers by age 45.[22] Even before that age their major task of rearing children has been completed, and the school and other community institutions have taken over most of the load. Large numbers must move into the work world or feel that their lives are filled with frustrated uselessness and boredom.

Many have lost contact with the work world during the child-rearing period, yet they constitute a skill reserve of immense dimensions. Often they can, by very brief retraining programs, enter the work world, or enter it on a higher level than if such training were impossible. Often women who had specialties in college or in the work world prior to childbearing, have, due to their experience as mothers, developed new interests or

[22] Nelson N. Foote, "New Roles for Men and Women," *Marriage and Family Living*, 23:325–329, November, 1961.

FIGURE 8–2   PERCENTAGE OF WORKING WOMEN OVER 45 IS RISING.
Source: U.S. Department of Labor, Women's Bureau, **American Women,**
Report of the President's Commission on the Status of Women, Washington,
D. C., 1963, Chart 4, p. 11.

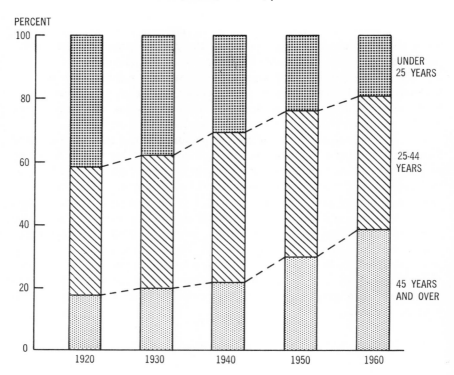

The increase in the number of older women who work reflects a great need
for effective retraining programs for housewives finished with child rearing
who still have many years to give to workworld activities.

values and wish the kind of training which will help them move in the
direction of these new interests.

A survey[23] of 15-year alumnae, showed that after this span of years
following graduation, a third were employed and five out of six were
either seeking positions or thinking of doing so. Many wanted to go into
teaching, having learned as mothers how great the need for better teachers
is. Many of those with teaching aspirations had not considered becoming

[23] Esther Peterson, "The Impact of Education," in Seymour M. Farber and
Roger H. L. Wilson (eds.), *The Potential of Woman* (New York: McGraw-Hill Book
Co., 1963), pp. 188–198.

teachers when they were in college. Many were interested in preschool teaching, feeling that a great need for competence exists at that level of teaching.

It is apparent that many of these women at mid-life are anxious to go in the direction of acute social need, provided that the opportunity for training and for work are open to them. It may be assumed that there would not only be a social gain if short courses for retraining would make the fulfillment of their aspirations possible, but that these women would get greater psychological and financial reward by being upgraded in their work. It is not expecting too much to hope that as happy, creatively useful persons they would also be better wives.

It may well be that propaganda campaigns aimed at employers, calling their attention to this competent reserve of labor, will be needed. It has been estimated that in the labor force of 1970, 56 million will be men, 29 million, women. In this labor force, 10 million will be professional persons as compared to only 7.5 million in 1960 (see Figure 8–2).

It is apparent that in the training of all women from the beginning we need a program that will feature "flexibility and adjustment to change." The life cycle is becoming quite definitely marked by a series of steps which most women will follow:

1. coeducational schooling
2. a brief work-world experience
3. home and family
4. return to work world (preferably after a short retraining course)
5. retirement and return to domesticity
6. widowhood

In conclusion, the great complexity of social roles is the dominant aspect of relationships between the sexes in modern times. That numerous problems are involved in this complexity of roles, and in the lack of precise definition of roles, is self-evident. This situation is indirectly at the base of most marriage problems.

On the other hand, the very fact that men and women are highly individualistic in the development of their personalities and are capable of so many diverse roles—most of them interchangeable between the sexes —has provided a basis for a new level of understanding, communication, and companionability. The marriage which can cast aside the traditional concept of role differences holds promise of an equality such as marriages of an earlier generation never achieved. In marriage today, there can be a genuine sharing in nearly every aspect of life. This makes marriage itself a far richer experience than was possible under the old regime, and makes parenthood a shared joy such as it probably rarely was in the patriarchal family.

Modern woman's life involves a series of major role shifts in the course of a lifetime. If the latter half of her life is to be fulfilling and useful, she must be broadly trained in youth, and then after the brief period of child rearing, return to the work world or to other meaningful activities, this often after a period of brush-up in school or of retraining to enter occupational activities that are different from those she aspired to while in school.

Problems

1. *Sociodrama:* A husband has just come home from work, tired, hungry, and in need of a little sympathy after a difficult and frustrating day. He finds no dinner, an untidy house and a wife who has spent her afternoon electioneering for a friend. The husband's first line is an angry one:

   "What kind of a wife are you? Women didn't used to be like this!"

   The wife answers indignantly:

   "You're right; times have changed and so have women!"

   Go on from there to show how confusion and disagreement in role behavior can be at the bottom of marital conflict.

2. *Research exercise:* Poll a student group on the following (other questions dealing with roles may be added if desired); (a) favorite work, (b) greatest ambition, (c) what I want to be at age 50. Tabulate and analyze results by sex. Are marked differences apparent in the roles of men and women? Do they reflect cultural conditioning or biological inclination primarily? If differences appear in life patterns of men and women, do they seem to be supplementary rather than contradictory? What implications do they suggest for the relationships between men and women of this generation?

3. It is sometimes asserted that the more choices we have, the more problems we have. If this is true would you say that the young woman of today has greater or fewer problems than young women of the past?

4. List several choices a young unmarried woman might consider that were never open to women of several generations past.

5. Think about the merging that has already taken place and is taking place in male-female roles. Now do a little speculative thinking about the future if this merging continues. Elaborate on such topics as the following:

   a. "The man of the future . . ."

   b. "The woman of the future . . ."

   c. "The marriage of the future . . ."

6. If you feel that there is a need for greater sex equality in the United States, prepare a program fulfilling this need. Your program should include any institutions or legislation which could help to bring about the desired reforms.

Selected References

Articles in Books of Readings

Cavan, Ruth Shonle, *Marriage and the Family in a Modern World: A Book of Readings*, third edition (New York: Thomas Y. Crowell Co., 1969).

American Institute of Family Relations, "The Private Worlds of Men and Women," Reading 16.

Vincent, Clark E., "Helping the College Woman Choose Her Role," Reading, 36.

Goode, William J., *Readings in the Family and Society* (Englewood Cliffs, N. J.: Prentice-Hall, Inc., 1964).

Heer, David M., "Dominance and the Working Wife," pp. 115–123.

Rodman, Hyman, *Marriage, Family and Society* (New York: Random House, 1965).

Ehrmann, Winston W., "Being in Love, Going Steady, and Sexual Intimacy," Reading 1.

Komarovsky, Mirra, "Cultural Contradictions in Sex Roles," Reading 2.

Sussman, Marvin B., *Sourcebook in Marriage and the Family*, third edition (Boston: Houghton Mifflin Co., 1968).

Rainwater, Lee, and others, "The Inner Life and Outer World of the Workingman's Wife," Reading 20.

Hoffman, Lois Wladis, "The Effect of Maternal Employment on the Child," Reading 40.

General References

Ballweg, John A., "Resolution of Conjugal Role Adjustment After Retirement," *Journal of Marriage and the Family*, 29:277–281, May, 1967.

Bird, Caroline, *Born Female: The High Cost of Keeping Women Down* (New York: David McKay, Inc., 1968).

Blood, Robert O., Jr., and Hamblin, Robert L., "The Effect of the Wife's Employment on the Family Power Structure," *Social Forces*, 36:247–252, May, 1958.

Dennis, Lawrence E. (ed.), *Education and a Woman's Life*, Proceedings of the Itasca Conference on the Continuing Education of Women, American Council on Education, Washington, D. C., 1963.

Dinitz, Simon, Dynez, Russell R., and Clarke, Alfred C., "Preferences for Male or Female Children: Traditional or Affectional?" *Marriage and Family Living*, 23:325–329, November, 1961.

Foote, Nelson, N., "New Roles for Men and Women," *Marriage and Family Living*, 23:325–329, November, 1961.

Glenn, Hortense M. and Walters, James, "Feminine Stress in the 20th Century," *Journal of Home Economics*, 58:703–707, November, 1966.

Haavio-Mannila, Elina, "Some Consequences of Women's Emancipation," *Journal of Marriage and the Family*, 31:123–133, February, 1969.

Hafstrom, Jeanne L. and Dunsing, Marilyn M., "A Comparison of Economic Choices of One-Earner and Two-Earner Families," *Journal of Marriage and the Family*, 27:403–409, August, 1965.

Harbeson, Gladys E., *Choice and Challenge for the American Women* (Cambridge, Mass.: Schenkman Publishing Co., 1967).

Hobart, Charles W. and Klousner, William J., "Some Social Interactional Correlates Marital Role Disagreement and Marital Adjustment," *Marriage and Family Living*, 21:256–263, August, 1959.

Hunt, Morton M., "The Direction of Feminine Evolution," pp. 255–272, in Farber, Seymour M., and Wilson, Roger H. L. (eds.), *The Potential of Woman* (New York: McGraw-Hill Book Co., 1963).

Kammeyer, Kenneth, "The Feminine Role: An Analysis in Attitude Consistency," *Marriage and Family Living*, 26:295–305, August, 1964.

Kirkpatrick, Clifford, *The Family*, second edition (New York: The Ronald Press Co., 1963), Chs. 7, 17.

LeMasters, E. E., "Parenthood as a Crisis," *Marriage and Family Living*, 19:352–355, November, 1957.

3

THE PREFACE
TO MATE CHOICE

9

Foundations of Love

Love seems to be triggered by a very simple mechanism at its outset, the mechanism of physical warmth and comfort. Food is incidental to this comfort: the child is usually held next to the warm body of the mother when given food. Studies by Harry F. Harlow, President of the American Psychological Association, leave little doubt that it is the warm, comfort-giving, body-to-body contact that actually triggers the emotion of love, and with it the feeling of security and safety.[1]

He experimented with newborn monkeys, providing an unheated wire mother for one group and an electric-light-bulb-heated, cloth-covered, sponge-rubber mother for another—a mother soft, warm, and tender. Each substitute mother performed the nursing function. The contact with the heated-cloth mother proved to be the one that built the affectional response. This also proved to be the contact to which the young monkeys fled when fear-producing stimuli were introduced. The older the monkeys became, the more they fled to this warm substitute mother for comfort. Evidence of some psychosomatic development was indicated where monkeys had only the wire substitute mother.

Harlow concludes that the main factor in the emotional development is the infant-mother body contact, rather than the nursing contact as such.

Built-in Security Through Mother Love

The length of these warm contacts and their certainty probably has much to do with the feeling of security which the person has as he faces the

[1] Harry F. Harlow, "The Nature of Love," *The American Psychologist,* 13:673–685, December, 1958.

colder situations life brings. Anthropologists and psychologists have commented on the great security of children reared under certain types of child-rearing practices.

Here is LeBarre's appraisal of child rearing among American Indians and the resultant effect on personality:

There was an old army man in the 1890's, James Mooney, who was involved in the Sioux wars—The Battle of Wounded Knee and Custer's Last Stand—who from a lifetime of experience with various Indian tribes, came to the kind of understanding that I think is essential to the issue.

"The Sioux," he says, "are direct and manly, the Cheyenne high-spirited and keenly sensitive, the Arapaho generous and accommodating, the Comanche practical and businesslike."

And the reason clearly is that the Sioux, the Cheyenne, the Arapaho, and the Comanche have different ways of bringing up their children. . . .

In the most primitive groups, because of their pediatric backwardness and lack of Frigidaires, a child is ignorantly suckled a minimum of two or three years—and, worst of all, he is fed whenever he is hungry, in a hopelessly unscheduled fashion! (Some American Indians are permitted an occasional visit to the breast even up to the age of five.) Is the dignity, the inexpungable security, the settled self-judgment and self-possession of such American Indians a surprise to us, then? I have known American Indians whom the threat of the atomic bomb itself would not disorganize; upon knowing the worst of all imaginable situations, they would continue to adjust to them. I know one American Indian who conducted himself through the terrors of a modern war with a really distinguished aplomb. We would mistakenly call it courage—for him it was something to be taken for granted like his own manhood; he simply lacked these reservoirs of neurotic anxiety which flood us in stress situations. He lacked the culturally defined guilts that would lead him irrationally to anticipate punishment; he had not experienced the frustrations and hence did not have the hostilities to project and to be persecuted by as neurotic fears; he had not had his childhood ego systematically attacked and traumatized so that he had any doubt of his ability to cope with any current situation. . . .

The really serious thing is the kinds of human being we make, and the ways in which we go about making them. The child, we say easily, is the father of the individual man. But more than that, in the larger sense, the child is the father of all future mankind.[2]

With the infant, it is not long before the warmth of body contact becomes associated with other stimuli that broaden the base of love—the voice, the smile, the caress by the mother are all a part of the broadening process. Then comes play with the mother and other members of the family—the father, sister, brother, grandparent, and others. Others enter into this circle as the infant develops the ability to smile and thus respond to attention. The association of safety and well-being with the mother gradually spreads out to include "people." At this early stage in his development the child is already learning that love and happiness are associated

[2] Weston LeBarre, "Wanted: A Pattern for Modern Man," *Mental Hygiene,* 33:2–8, April, 1949.

with the interdependence of individuals. He is developing a physical concept of love. For him, there is nothing complex in the manifestation of affection—it amounts to nothing more than physical comfort, gentle voices, and warm caresses.

The Heartbeat and Security

The rhythmic sound of the mother's heartbeat seems to be a factor in the emotional security of the infant, apparently helping to allay its fear of abandonment. Dr. Lee Salk, clinical psychologist, found that infants in a nursery with recorded heartbeats transmitted to them cried less and showed greater depth and regularity in breathing and less restlessness than the control group.[3]

With the infant, ease of feeding and depth of sleep are the evidences of security. Dr. Salk found that babies who had trouble getting to sleep were helped by the recorded heartbeat. In the experimental group exposed to the heartbeat, 70 percent gained weight. In the control group not exposed to it, only 33 percent gained weight on the same amount of milk. Salk has developed a mechanical heartbeat which is used in hospital nurseries.

Separation Anxiety

Studies of animal psychology have shown that young creatures develop impressions that have a lasting effect on their subsequent behavior. This fixing of the impression is called imprinting. The time span during which it takes place in a given creature is brief. With the duckling, the tendency to follow an object, be it a hen, a box, or a human being, begins at thirteen to sixteen hours after hatching and ends when it is about twenty-four hours old. With puppies, the imprinting period is somewhere during the time span of three and a half weeks to thirteen weeks. It is at the imprinting period that association of creatures with human beings makes them identify life-long with human beings. Once the imprinting attachments are formed, fear of strangers normally develops. Thus fear of the unknown becomes a counterpart of the close tie.

With the human infant, tie to the mother is firmly fixed by five or six months. Previous to that time most children do not differentiate between mother and others. They need the close warm tie, the comfort giving, the cuddling but do not suffer severe separation anxiety and fear

[3] Paul Popenoe, "Close to the Mother's Heart," *Family Life,* 21:1–2, May, 1961.

FIGURE 9–1 DEVELOPMENTAL RATES OF INFANTS IN NURSERY AND IN FOUNDLING HOME. Source: René A. Spitz, "The Role of Ecological Factors in Emotional Development in Infancy," **Child Development,** 20:145–155, 1949.

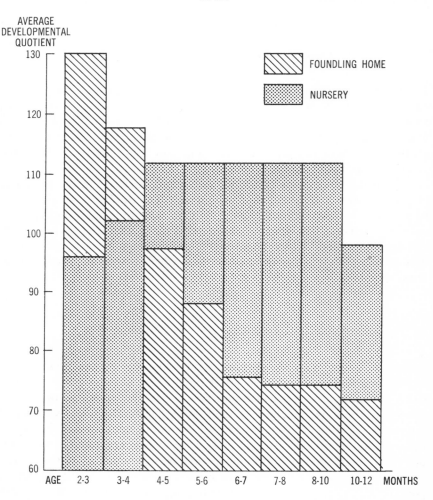

A comparison of development of 239 children in a nursery home (mothers present) with 91 children in an orphan home (mothers absent after the first three months and nurses overworked). Observe that the orphaned children developed even better than the nursery children during the months their mothers were present; after that, development was at a proportionately decreasing rate. The absence of emotional interchange with a mother or mother substitute was the critical factor.

of others. It is after five or six months that separation anxiety is severe and it will last until the child is around three years of age. Until then he needs her as an ever-present companion (see Figure 9–1).

John Bowlby believes the anxiety problem at this stage in development arises from the child's inability to grasp time. To him "a short time may seem like an eternity."[4] After about age three the child begins to learn to maintain a relationship with her for short periods during her absence. By age four or five he can usually tolerate absence for a few days under favorable conditions. By seven or eight he can accept absences for longer periods of time with less strain.

Studies[5] of monkeys and of apes indicate that after a period of constant association with the mother, the infant begins to stray by gradual steps until he becomes acquainted with others of his age. The mother in time tends to push him away, encouraging his attachment and association with peers.

This is the normal situation with human beings. After the close mother-child attachment stage, the range of love bonds extends to father, brothers, and sisters and eventually to peers, with the ultimate step that of moving away from adults as a primary attachment and to closer attachments with peers.

Love Deprivation

Sociologists have long been interested in the study of "feral men," the product of isolated rearing, some with animals, some shut in cellars and attics away from human contact. These reports range from myth to fairly well substantiated accounts. Introductory texts cite them as evidence of the importance of social contact to human development.[6] Other studies have focused on retarded socialization due to loss of senses, particularly hearing. Sociologists, psychologists, and child specialists have also observed the tendency of orphanages of the traditional type to produce

[4] John Bowlby, "The Nature of the Child's Tie to his Mother," *International Journal of Psychoanalysis,* 39:350–373, 1958. Also in "Child Care and the Growth of Love," No. 7 in *The Anatomy of Love,* A. M. Krich (ed.), Dell Paperback LC141. See also Aase Gruda Skard, "Maternal Deprivation: The Research and its Implications," *Journal of Marriage and Family Living,* 27:333–343, August, 1965.

[5] Harry F. and Margaret K. Harlow, "Social Deprivation in Monkeys," *Scientific American,* November, 1962, pp. 137–146. Also appears as Article 28 in Haimowitz and Haimowitz, *Human Development,* second edition (New York: Thomas Y. Crowell Co., 1966).

[6] The most famous of these is Casper Hauser. For a study of this case and many others, see any introductory sociology text. Some of these are presented in Paul H. Landis, *Introductory Sociology* (New York: The Ronald Press Co., 1958), pp. 138–139.

children lacking important aspects of socialization and prone to delinquency.

More precise studies were begun during the 1930s by John Bowlby in England.[7] Independent studies in other parts of the western world have added to our knowledge of the effects of social deprivation. These studies have revealed that an undue proportion of delinquents come from orphanages. Also children from emotionally deprived backgrounds tend to be unfeeling, aggressive, violent, and are difficult to help. They show little capacity to relate positively to others. Their feelings are shallow, they lack capacity to respond to or establish close attachments with others, even though some of the children give boisterous shows of affection. Some of the socially deprived children are pathologically withdrawn.

Separations by war can cause emotional starvation resulting in the emotionally withdrawn and isolated child. The phenomenon was widely observed in England during World War II with the evacuation of London and separation of young children from their families. On the continent during the occupation, parents were deported and their children shifted to foster homes—often from one such home to another.

Love deprivation can take place in the home for a lack of mothering, or from mothering by a cold or neurotic type. It may appear due to extreme conflict in the relationship of parents. It may be avoided even in institutions if a mother-type long-term contact with a mother-substitute is present during the years of primary socialization. The important point is that to become a creature capable of love and closeness with others, the child must have been loved.

The child is soon able to evaluate the quality of the relationships about him. As Benedek has stated:[8]

> "It does not take long for the child to begin to know what are the actions for which the mother will like him and those which will increase the expressions of her love—thus enhancing his security—and he also will soon realize what are the actions which bring about punishment, that is, a reduction of love and thus a reduction of his basic security . . ."

Studies of affectionless persons indicate that they have experienced a lack of affection during the period of primary socialization due to parental absence, parental neglect, mobility that disturbed family situation, or other factors which denied them affectionate relationships. The most serious period is apparently the last half of the first year, but denial is serious until the child is beyond three years of age.[9]

[7] For an excellent summary of studies see John Bowlby, "Child Care and the Growth of Love," Article 25 in *Human Development*. Morris L. Haimowitz and Natalie R. Haimowitz, second edition (New York: Thomas Y. Crowell Co., 1966).

[8] Therese Benedek, "The Psychodynamics of Love," No. 8 in *The Anatomy of Love*, A. M. Krich (ed.), (New York: Dell Publishing Co., 1960).

[9] For a good summary of research in this area see Aase Gruda Skard, *op. cit.* See also John Bowlby, *op. cit.*

Here is a summary of a filmed study by Dr. René A. Spitz, an American psychiatrist, of children in a South American orphan home who were almost completely denied love and close human association:

Foundling Home was an excellent institution from the standpoint of hygiene. The food was varied, adequate, and carefully prepared; no person whose clothes and hands were not sterilized could approach the babies. A well-trained staff of physicians and many consulting specialists checked daily on the infants' health. This institution harbored babies from birth to the sixth year. Up to the fourth month the infants 'in this institution developed well, even better than the average of a family child. The average baby up to four months in this institution was a month ahead of its age level.

From the fourth month on, however, this picture changed radically. The developmental level of these children dropped more and more until at the end of the first year the average child of Foundling Home was alarmingly retarded. A 12-months-old child in Foundling Home showed the picture of an 8-months-old child.

What happened to bring about this change in the developmental picture of the 69 children in Foundling Home, without any exceptions? All the conditions of hygiene were identical for younger and older children. There was only one factor which had changed. The presence of the mother. The practice in Foundling Home was that mothers brought in their children at birth and stayed with them until the end of their fifth month. They took care of them and breasted them. After this time the mothers had to leave the institution. Trained nurses took over the care of the children. However, the financial provisions of the institution provided only one nurse for 12-15 children. Therefore infants in Foundling Home from their fifth month on had only a twelfth or a fifteenth part of a mother. Their emotional interchange with human beings was drastically reduced, their response to it was drastic deterioration.

Unfortunately the limited duration of my stay in the country in which the institution was situated did not permit me to follow these children after their first year. An assistant I trained during my stay was entrusted with the follow-up. Although these data seem superficial they are revealing.

The most striking result of this study was that 27 children of those observed originally had died. This is really an alarming figure considering the utmost precautions which were taken in regard to hygiene. It seems that in spite of good food and meticulous medical care these children had too little energy left to resist minor and major ailments.

Besides the 27 children who died, some other children could not be accounted for, as they were adopted, placed in other institutions or simply lost from sight. My assistant had only the opportunity to observe 21 children who ranged from 2½–4¼ years. These children were all undersized and under-weight. Only 3 of these 21 children had the normal weight of a 2-year-old and only 2 attained the length normal at this age. Their mental performance was no better. Of these 21 children, of whom the youngest was 2½ years old, only 5 could walk unassisted, only one had a vocabulary of a dozen words and only one, a 4½-year-old, used sentences. On the other hand, 8 of these 21 children could neither stand nor walk, 6 could not talk at all and 11 were limited to the use of 2 words. Even this superficial sketch reveals these children as ranging from mental debility to idiocy.

Psychotherapeutic intervention was tried in a few cases by other investigators to abolish or at least to mitigate the consequences of such early institutional care. The result was nil. The damage inflicted to the children's systems seems irreversible.

This tragic consequence of deprivation of the mother represents not only a theoretical challenge to the scientist who investigates the dynamics of early childhood, but also an important challenge to anyone concerned with the future of a nation, with the future of the world. . . .

Presence or absence of the mother is the to be or not to be for the development of the baby. If a society wants to guarantee the health of its young generation and with that its own survival it has to guarantee an average amount of motherly love to the average child.[10]

This is a striking picture of the meaning of love. Its denial presents in this instance a stark picture of the destruction of personality, and in many instances of life itself.

The mother is the key person with whom all love experience begins. As Spitz[11] concluded from his research with infants, "During the first year of life it is the mother, or her substitute, who transmits literally every experience to the infant. Consequently, barring starvation, disease or actual physical injury, no other factor is capable of so influencing the child's development in every field as its relations to its mother."

The reporting of extreme physical deterioration has been challenged in Spitz' study. The basis for this challenge was the discovery that this particular area of South America is deficient in certain soil elements necessary for producing foods adequate from a dietary standpoint. However, his work is widely confirmed as to emotional deprivation as a factor in mental and social growth.

Yet Spitz was not entirely wrong in his inferences regarding physical results of emotional deprivation. Pediatricians have recently coined the term "deprivation dwarfism"[12] to describe stunted growth for which they find no cause other than unhappy home conditions. They suggest the child be placed in a situation of tender care, where such emotionally starved children would experience a spurt of growth. If returned to the same cold emotional situation of the home, growth slows down. The typical situations producing deprivation dwarfism in complete families are alcoholism, sexual incompatibility of parents, illness, beating of the child, unwanted pregnancy, unemployment with accompanying unhappiness and conflict. Stunting may begin as early as two years of age in such homes.[13]

[10] René A. Spitz, "The Importance of Mother-Child Relationship During the First Year of Life," published by the Washington Society for Mental Hygiene and the Graduate School of Social Work, University of Washington (Seattle, 1947). Based on a series of film lectures presented in Seattle, June 15–17, 1947.

[11] René A. Spitz, "The Role of Ecological Factors in Emotional Development in Infancy," *Child Development*, 20:145–155, 1949.

[12] "Deprivation Dwarfism," *Time*, February 7, 1969, p. 39.

[13] It is not known why emotional factors so drastically affect growth. Various hypotheses are advanced: happy conditions may slow down the closing of cranial

The Point of No Return

It remains to be determined how long social deprivation and lack of love can continue during the critical period of the child's socialization before recovery becomes impossible. The Harlows' studies show that monkeys isolated for six months are irreversibly socially and sexually inadequate, but that sixty to ninety days is not too long to expect recovery under favorable conditions of socialization.[14] They point out that this latter period would be equivalent to six month's isolation for the human infant. They suggest that up to a year of age the situation with the child might be remedial, since the child has little social awareness until he is six months of age. He may retain emotional scars, but will recover. By two years of age, the child may have reached the point of no return. Their tentative conclusion is not entirely based on the assumption that children react like monkeys, but on a knowledge of researches with deprived children.

The answer is not an easy one. Monkeys were kept under rigidly controlled conditions—children rarely are. Interaction with other children, a kindly neighbor or relative, even pets, may in part fill the gap for many emotionally deprived children. Time is no doubt an important factor, for the critical period is a time span, but a child's isolation is seldom complete, nor is the denial of the human touch and affection ever totally lacking.

On the other hand, any degree of neglect may mean that the child will be a step or more short of being the loving human being he could have been with adequate human relationships.

Tragic Results from Emotional Crippling

The more psychologists, sociologists, and biologists study the human personality, the more apparent it becomes that any severe denial of love is costly, particularly where this denial is by the mother. Those denied must find substitutes if they are to reach any practical degree of social adjustment.

The sexually delinquent girl, the homosexual individual, the juvenile

---

sutures; the pituitary gland which controls growth may be affected drastically by the emotional climate of the home; the digestive processes may be so affected as to limit the absorption of food. *Ibid.*

[14] Harry F. Harlow and Margaret K. Harlow, "Social Deprivation in Monkeys," Article 28 in Haimowitz and Haimowitz, *Human Development*, second edition (New York: Thomas Y. Crowell Co., 1966).

delinquent, the insecure individual who is a likely candidate for the mental institution or for suicide, the potential alcoholic, and the drug addict, the poor marriage risks—the majority of these types are persons who have been afflicted by a denial of love. The degree of denial is in a general way related to the seriousness of their deficiency in social relationships. Many of their errant ventures are in a quest of love, or are compensations to gain recognition and ego satisfaction to balance their lack of love.

Research shows that the home atmosphere, the relationship of parents to each other and to the child is the key factor in juvenile delinquency. A long-time study of delinquent children, following them into adult life, indicates that where the home situation is lacking in warmth and harmony, community efforts, social-work programs, and counseling show little results in improvement. Denial of love as a disciplinary device seems to help produce a personality prone to suicide.[15]

But if this is the true story of human growth, how do so many survive who seem to have been greatly denied love? Fortunately there are parent substitutes in many families and social groups outside the immediate family. Many a child has found love in the close tie with the motherly parent of a peer. Others have found it in an older brother or sister. In primary groups there are neighbors, relatives, and grandparents, whose capacity to love is often very great indeed. In the growing years beyond childhood, buddies, or army associates may have great emotional meaning. Pets are very demonstrative of affection, dogs particularly and horses, even cats to a degree and with the small child, the warm blanket is a comforting substitute when there is a feeling of denied love.

In the teaching of marriage courses, it has been the practice of the writer to require autobiographies of the students based on the outline which appears in the appendix. Every semester in every class there are papers from those who clearly recognize in themselves an impaired capacity to love. Their experience can be classified into two types: (1) impairment because of a lack of affection between child and parents, usually the mother—their lack results from emotional rejection, the child's capacity to love not having been developed, causing much hostility in the personality—and (2) a denial due to folk cultures—in these cases young people come from families, usually immigrant families or stern rural families, in which the tradition of covering up affection is strongly

[15] William McCord, *Origins of Crime* (New York: Columbia University Press, 1959). This is a report of the Cambridge-Somerville Youth Study begun in the early 1930's with 650 boys—a delinquent group of 325 and a matched control group. The one was subject to all the reform efforts which money and social-work knowledge could provide. Reform for the most part failed utterly, yet it was probably the most intensive and costly ever attempted in this country. For an analysis of the relationship between love frustration, guilt, and suicide see Andrew F. Henry and James F. Short, *Suicide and Homicide* (Glencoe, Ill.: Free Press, 1954).

ingrained. In these families there is often deep loyalty between family members, but there is no affectional expression of this loyalty, and therefore young people feel crippled in not being able to express affection overtly.

Slocum, studying 2,500 high school upperclassmen in Washington state, asked about the affectional patterns in their immediate family. Of the boys, 23 percent classed their families as unaffectionate; of the girls, 30 percent. Girls apparently are more aware of the emotional climate than are boys. At the other extreme, 27 percent of the boys and 33 percent of the girls classified their families as affectionate. The remaining group said that their families were sometimes affectionate, sometimes not.[16]

The Father in Love Development

The broadening of the range of love is brought about in part by the father and his contacts with the growing child. In this the mother has a part in encouraging sharing of the child, his comfort giving (like that inherent in bathing and changing the diapers), and his play with the father. Thus the mother helps provide the opportunities for emotional growth which will not come if she monopolizes the child. The child becomes accustomed to the larger physique, the rougher touch, the deeper voice of the male.

If the father remains a stranger or primarily a disciplinarian in the minds of his children it is easy to understand why boys may develop distorted concepts of the role of the male in family and society, and undesirable attitudes about the relationship of man and wife.

Judson T. Landis,[17] studying family patterns, finds closeness to the father predictive of positive family values. The Cambridge-Somerville youth study showed poor relationships of fathers to boys to be highly predictive of criminality.[18] "Warm fathers and passive fathers produced very few criminals. Parental absence, cruelty, or neglect, however, tended to produce criminals in the majority of boys."

We have already discussed the role of the weak father in the development of homosexuality in the male child, and of the too physically interested father in the development of homosexuality in the girl (Chapter 3).

A girl who has lived under a harsh or brutal father may not be able to respect and love a kind man. She may actually be capable of loving only

[16] Walter L. Slocum, *Family Culture Patterns and Adolescent Behavior* (Pullman, Wash.: Washington Agricultural Experiment Station, October, 1963), Bulletin No. 648.

[17] Judson T. Landis, "A Re-examination of the Role of the Father as an Index of Family Integration," *Marriage and Family Living,* 24:122–128, May, 1962.

[18] McCord, *op. cit.*

a brutal man and may love him most deeply after he has given her a beating. The love life of a person can actually be so formed. The book and film, *The Quiet Man,* depicted well how such a process of conditioning is elevated to the level of custom in a locality of Ireland.

Psychological studies of "critical periods" in development orientation of young animals show that "imprinting" during critical periods need not be accomplished by pleasant association; the only requirement is that the time be right in the cycle of development of the individual and that the emotional association be strong. During the imprinting period, hunger, fear, pain, and loneliness are effective just as are love, comfort, food, and other pleasant stimuli. Whatever the stimulus, it becomes self-enforcing after the critical period is past, and in time becomes irreversible. Scott, commenting on the implications of this research for human beings, states that this may explain why neglected children, often have "strong affection for cruel and abusive parents."[19]

One may speculate a step further and guess that children who develop such a love orientation beyond the irreverisble point could love only an abusive mate. Observation of human cultures leads one to believe that the female is more easily turned in the direction of a masochistic orientation of love than is the male.

Girls are also affected in their ability to relate to other males by the role their father plays. Attitudes can vary from love to hatred and defiance, depending on the relationship established. Whether or not a girl can love the opposite sex is very much affected by her concept of how men act as determined by her relationship with her father. A father has it in his power to develop in the daughter the capacity to love or to hate his sex.

Childhood Love Acquires New Dimensions

During the first two or three years of life, the child understands and expresses love almost exclusively in terms of physical manifestations. At this stage in the development of the capacity for love, the parents' attitude toward the infant's bodily eliminations is considered by some authorities to be critical.[20] If his physical eliminations lead to disgust or to punishment on

[19] J. P. Scott, "Critical Periods in Behavioral Development," *Science,* 138:949–958, November 30, 1962.

[20] See Erik H. Erickson, *Childhood and Society* (New York: W. W. Norton and Co., Inc., 1950) for a full discussion of problems in this area of child development. To many such Freudian views seem fanciful. Freud believed that the child passes through a series of dynamically differentiated stages during the first five years of life which are decisive for the formation of personality. The *oral stage* is the first stage of development and lasts for about a year, during which time the mouth is the principal region of dynamic activity. The *anal stage* follows, during the second year when toilet training is usually initiated. During this period the child has his first decisive

the part of the mother, it is believed that the capacity to love may be damaged. Bowel and bladder voiding should be accepted with praise on the part of the mother, as it is the first experience of the child in giving. Its control should be left until later and should never be treated authoritarianly. The more love and affection denied the small child, the more likely that voluntary control of bowel and bladder will be delayed far into childhood.

As the child grows, his range of association widens and so also do the stimuli which evoke the love response. He watches the play of his brothers and sisters and their friends; gradually, he takes part in their play himself. He begins to include giggles, laughter, loud but happy voices, rough treatment, and occasional bruises in his concept of affection interaction. He learns that the funny-faced frown and the playful spank of his mother are just as loving as her kiss or gentle hug, but in a different way. He is learning of companionship, a nonphysical kind of love.

Less is known about the ultimate effect of the rough-and-tumble play of childhood on love development in humans than in monkeys. Harlow's studies[21] show clearly that if monkeys are denied such play with their age mates, they never develop normal adult sex and parental patterns. In childhood the male monkey more often initiates play than does the female, and he is the aggressor in rough-and-tumble play. As age increases, his activity often takes the form of copulatory play. The female's role is more persistently in the direction of grooming playmates.

Placed in individual cages, with no chance for play with age mates, monkeys in the experimental situation fail to develop normal sexual patterns upon maturity. Neither sex is able to master the copulatory act even under the tutelage of an experienced mate. A few of the females did become pregnant with experienced males, but proved very inept mothers, as likely to crush and kill their babies as to pick them up gently. Similar defects from isolated rearing were observed with young chimpanzees. These defects in sexual and parental behavior do not appear if the monkeys are allowed spontaneous play for at least twenty minutes per day.

One cannot assume that the same defects in personality result with the human child, but Money[22] has raised the question as to whether suppression of play, particularly childhood sexual play, among children may adversely affect sexual development in adulthood.[23]

---

experience with the external regulation of an impulse. He has to learn to postpone the pleasure that comes from relieving his anal tensions. Depending upon the particular method of toilet training used by the mother and her feelings concerning defecation, the consequences of this training, according to the fanciful Freudian view, may have far-reaching effects upon the formation of specific traits and values such as stinginess or generosity.

[21] Harlow and Harlow, *op. cit.*

[22] John Money, "Developmental Differentiation of Feminity and Masculinity Compared," in Farber and Wilson, *op. cit.*, pp. 51–65.

[23] Some sexual play takes place in the experience of most children even in our

We do know that in the case of the human child, only-child rearing is a definite liability to normal love development. The only child has more dating problems, less often feels secure in dating relationships, less often marries, and when he marries is less often successful than are sibling-reared children. How much of these love deficiencies are the product of lack of contact with age mates and how much a product of other factors in the only-child situation is unknown.[24] In many only-child families sufficient contact with other children is no doubt provided to offset serious damage.

From the time a child is able to toddle alone across the lawn toward a neighbor or a group of children at play, the wise parent has stepped aside and let the youngster begin the development of new relationships. Encouraging him in the formation of friendship throughout childhood and adolescence; helping him develop loyalties to his friends as well as to his family; understanding that as he forms closer ties outside the family, the family ties themselves are bound to loosen—all are important ways in which normal parents help their youngster in the normal process of emotional growth.

The love and companionship of infancy and childhood have a bearing on the love given and sought in marriage.[25] A childhood barren of these important experiences in affection does little to prepare individuals for marriage and family happiness in later years. When a child is born unwanted or grows up in a family that has no time or inclination to love and play with him, his attitude toward people is likely to be suspicious, overly demanding, or one of fear and utter dependence. He has difficulty in dating and in building the attitudes, relationships, and ties that lead to an affectional relationship. In the worst cases, he finds it impossible to do so.

When these first experiences in love have been happy ones, the infant develops into a child who can easily accept new people—first pals and grown-up friends, then teachers, scoutmasters, and complete strangers. He looks upon the world with trust because he has no cause to fear it. The exact importance of the early months of life to later happiness has never been accurately appraised, but all of the evidence indicates that a child born into a loving devoted family goes into marriage with a better chance for happiness than a child whose first steps were taken in an impersonal, unloving world. In most families, certainly in the ideal family, love is given as easily as companionship and as naturally as food, clothing, and shelter. It is not something which a child must demand or even earn. It is his

---

inhibited culture. See William R. Reevy, "Child Sexuality," *Encyclopedia of Sexual Behavior* (New York: Hawthorn Books, Inc., 1961).

[24] More attention to the only-child problem and to bibliography on this subject is given in Ch. 29.

[25] Ian D. Suttie, in *The Origins of Love and Hate* (New York: Julian Press, Inc., 1952) has stressed the need for companionship rather than sex as the basic element in love.

birthright. This is why most human beings develop with considerable capacity to love and be loved.

Direction Is Needed

Brothers and sisters, parents, teachers, friends, and even casual acquaintances all play an important part in helping or hindering an individual in the growth of his capacity to love. Older brothers and sisters as well as friends and acquaintances of both sexes are frequently responsible for the attitudes and behavior a young person develops toward the opposite sex. A boy whose older brother, or whose pals, brag of their sexual conquests is apt to develop attitudes of exploitation toward female companions. Tenderness, respect, and selflessness—characteristics commonly associated with the concept "true love"—are neither natural nor inevitable in themselves. There is much in the upbringing of the average male to make him less than he ought to be as a lover. Usually, a girl, by imposing restraint and requiring affection, teaches him to love intimately, if as an adult he is to love in a true sense at all.

A child who, by formal or informal learning, has picked up attitudes of disrespect or condescension toward the opposite sex, cannot be expected to make an about-face when the time comes for his own engagement and marriage. Conditioned attitudes, whether good or bad, are deep-grained and pervasive. They affect one's capacity to love and be loved.

Developments at Puberty

The physiological changes of puberty make interest in the opposite sex take on new dimensions. But most young people do not immediately become interested in the game of pursuit. In fact, the transfer of the primary core of love from parents to a member of the opposite sex seems to be too great to be made in one step. Close attachment to a member or members of their own sex is usual for both adolescent boys and girls. This transition stage is sometimes referred to as the homosexual stage. At a later time the young person begins to show an increased interest in age mates of the opposite sex. This occurs somewhat earlier among girls than among boys, but even within one sex the age of budding interest in the opposite sex varies considerably.

Actually, there is no way of knowing how much of the awakening is due to physical maturation and how much is a consequence of social customs. Both operate. Young people begin dating early or later, as their community dictates. The conformity of the young teenager to the customs and expectations of his group suggests that the part nature plays in determining when love begins is only one aspect of the total situation.

Regardless of the basic motivations for this transfer of affection from one sex to the other, the transition does take place in all but a small minority of young people. When it does, most adolescents are able to move on with relative ease into heterosexual love. When there is a fixation of interest on the parents or on a member of one's own sex, the development of heterosexual interests is blocked.

Human parents are not always as intelligent as monkeys in knowing when to release the child. The Harlows found that this mother rejection was essential to the development of normal sexual behavior.[26] The young had to have the rough and tumble play of their own age group. Anyone who has observed domestic and wild animals has observed the rejection pattern. With seasonally breeding animals, like deer, the male often aids in the rejection process by fighting off the young. Human parents sometimes bind their children to them too long.

The growth of affection in the adolescent in the contemporary family is made possible by cooperation, fairness of discipline, and democratic management of the family.[27] The father, particularly, seems to have much to do with the adolescent girl's attitude toward the opposite sex and her capacity to love in a normal way. The father in a very real sense becomes for her a symbol of men.[28]

Problems of Transfer of Love Objects

Even when a younger person is eager to and completely capable of a growing interest and attraction to the opposite sex, problems frequently arise to complicate the process. Some young people, because of acquired attitudes, have been habituated to depreciating the opposite sex and find it difficult to reverse themselves. After all, it is hard to admit, even to oneself, that the little girl who only yesterday was scorned, now seems both beautiful and interesting.

Some adolescents have grown up in such a tightly knit family circle that they find it new and awkward to form relationships with other young people.

[26] *Op. cit.*

[27] Walter L. Slocum and Carol L. Stone, "Factors Associated with Family Affectional Patterns," *The Coordinator,* 7:21–23, December, 1958.

[28] Ralph Eckert, *Sex Attitudes in the Home* (New York: Association Press, 1956).

At this stage in emotional growth one of the most common stumbling blocks is raised, not by the young people themselves, but by one or both of their parents. Well-meaning fathers and mothers, in their attempts to protect their children, frequently stand in the way of the normal development of their sons and daughters. In some instances they set up rules and regulations around social life and dating that make normal interaction with the opposite sex virtually impossible. In other cases they use ridicule, shame, or an appeal to family loyalty and affection to hold their teen-agers back. In either case, they only complicate and delay a process which must begin before normal heterosexual love can be cultivated.

Some parents meet this period in their teen-agers' lives awkwardly because they have exaggerated notions of the dangers involved; others, because they know too little about the part they can and should play in helping their youngsters safely to the next stage. Some parents get panicky because they are made suddenly aware of broad areas in child training that they never bothered with; they are uncertain of what the results of their neglect will be. In some instances the parents are thus awakened to the fact that their child or children are almost grown. They think ahead to the years of loneliness that await them when the children are gone, and they hope that by delaying the social development they can hold them back for a little while longer.

Parents who set up harsh or unnecessary restrictions at this point seldom accomplish the results they desire. The youngster whom they hope to hold is more often driven to open rebellion. The parent-child ties, instead of being strengthened, are often irreparably broken by the youngster in anger and disgust. This may drive the child to seek love desperately, often through sex experience.

At this point the wise parents realize that in order to keep their children—their love, respect, obedience—they must give a greater measure of freedom and self-direction. This is a time when counsel may be welcomed by the younger person, but dictates and commands are despised.

The mature parent ceases directing the life of the young person and gives him experience in making his own decisions and suffering the consequences of his own mistakes. He even stands by at times and sees his teen-ager take risks which may not be safe. This is a part of the unbringing of children in our time when a great deal of independence and self-reliance is required of them as they grow into adulthood. Unwise and experimental love affairs may be a part of this venturing in a quest to replace the lost affection for parents.

During adolescence, young people normally grow progressively more independent of parents and home. Most of their waking hours are spent in the outside world. Most of their favorite activities and keenest interests are shared with age mates. Their life becomes almost completely absorbed in the teen group. Their need to feel loved and to love in return is as strong as ever, yet custom and circumstances are carrying them even farther from the parents. One of the most common phrases by which the girl expresses her attitude toward her mother is, "Oh, but you wouldn't understand." Boys are less likely to say it, but they feel this way also. Their confidant is their close friend, and not adults.

As the strong childhood attachment to his parents weakens, the teen-ager revolts against his parents and may consider the family old-fashioned. He finds it necessary to defy the traditions of the parents and start life on his own, with different aspirations and more distant goals than his parents ever dreamed of having. This is a necessary step in attaining freedom from the emotional attachments of the family. While parents sometimes look with alarm and fear at the spirit of rebellion which often character-izes the teenager, the wise parent will look upon this with favor as long as it doesn't get completely out of bounds. This rebellion increases his need for a strong attachment to the teen group and intensifies his need for love of the opposite sex to replace the strong parental love that no longer seems appropriate.

The young person who cannot go through this period of revolt is seldom able to break his ties with the parental home and establish a home of his own. To fail to make this break is to remain so attached to parents that marriage becomes difficult, if not impossible. When the adolescent emerges from this stage of rebellion, his childhood affection and devotion to his parents, his blind worship of them as the only people in his life, is gradually replaced by mature respect and affection. He looks on them, then, as equals rather than as authoritarian superiors.

Once family ties begin to weaken—as they must and should—they can never be completely restored. The older adolescent in college or on a job may feel an ever-growing need for the kind of love he used to feel at home, but if he is healthy and growing in maturity, he realizes that he must seek it elsewhere and not attempt to return to the past. He begins to see marriage as the chief means for satisfying this need.

It may well be that only after marriage will the child be sufficiently mature to view life as an adult. Then the parents are seen in a different light. The young person begins to see that the parents were not as far out of step as he thought.

Problems

1. Describe briefly the reaction of your own parents to your early ventures in love. Did they seem eager or reluctant to help you transfer your affec-

tions outside the family circle? What effect did their reactions or expressed attitudes have on you?

2. Develop a comprehensive definition of love.
3. Suppose that you are a parent keenly aware of the loathing most people feel toward homosexuals. You observe that your twelve-year-old daughter is very much attracted to another girl in the neighborhood, carries her picture in her wallet, talks about her, imitates her, and prefers her company to that of any other person. As a parent would you:
   a. Forbid her to associate with the girl?
   b. Arrange for a medical examination?
   c. Seek psychiatric aid?
   d. Try to interest her in dating boys?
   e. Encourage the relationship?
   f. Warn her about the dangers of the relationship?
   g. Recognize it as a transient phase of development?
4. Explain your choice of alternatives in terms of the material presented in the chapter.
5. Which alternative represents the worst possible course you could follow? Why?
6. *Sociodrama:* A man and woman visit a family relations counselor and explain that, try as they may to make their home a joyful place and themselves interesting, their adolescent children (aged 15 and 17) seem bored with them and eager to be out with their friends most of the time.
   Present the drama so that it emphasizes the attitudes of the parents as well as the explanation and advice given by the counselor.
7. The "movie magazine" craze is often thought of as a normal part of an adolescent girl's development toward mature love. Do you consider this belief justified on the basis of the facts presented in this chapter? What is it about these magazines that appeals?
8. Upon what grounds is it often argued that the first few years of life greatly affect the success or failure of many marriages?
9. State your views on each of the following propositions:
   a. Custom has provided that marriage should occur sometime during an age period of 18 to 22 because this is the time when the emotion called love begins to manifest itself.
   b. The most unselfish appearing lovers (those who willingly suffer in order that their mates can be happy) may be shown to be fundamentally selfish.
   c. Nature has devised a scheme whereby individuals grow normally from one stage of love to the next. It is therefore undesirable for the school or parent to interfere with the affectional development of the youngster.
10. Select and defend one alternative. Children brought up in orphanages:
    a. Are probably incapable of adjusting to marriage since they have not known parental love.
    b. Are likely to be unusually successful in adjusting to marriage because it provides them with an intimate realtionship such as they have not previously known.
    c. Will probably have a more difficult time adjusting to marriage than children from a happy home.

Selected References

Articles in Books of Readings

Cavan, Ruth Shonle, *Marriage and the Family in the Modern World: A Book of Readings*, third edition (New York: Thomas Y. Crowell Co., 1969).
  Prescott, Daniel A., "Role of Love in Human Development," Reading 24.
  Symonds, Percival M., "Expression of Love," Reading 25.
Christensen, Harold T., *Handbook of Marriage and the Family* (Chicago: Rand McNally & Co., 1964).
  Dager, Edward Z., "Socialization and Personality Development," Ch. 18.
Coser, Rose Laub, *The Family: Its Structure and Functions* (New York: St Martin's Press, 1964).
  Goode, William, "The Theoretical Importance of Love," pp. 202–219.
  Spitz, René A., "Hospitalism," pp. 399–425.
  Davis, Kingsley, "Isolated Children," pp. 394–398.
Christensen, Harold T., *Handbook of Marriage and the Family* (Chicago: Rand McNally & Co., 1964).
  Dager, Edward Z., "Socialization and Personality Development," Ch. 18.
Goode, William J., *Readings on the Family and Society* (Englewood Cliffs, N. J.: Prentice-Hall, Inc., 1964).
  Carpenter, C. R., "Social Relations of the Gibbon," pp. 2–6.
  Harlow, Harry F., and Harlow, Margaret K., "Social Deprivation in Monkeys," pp. 7–10.
Haimowitz, Morris L. and Haimowitz, Natalie R., *Human Development: Selected Readings*, second edition (New York: Thomas Y. Crowell Co., 1966).
  Haimowitz, Natalie R. "Development Patterns: Birth to Five Years," Reading 18.
  Hess, Eckhard H., "Imprinting," Reading 21.
  Bowlby, John, "Child Care and the Growth or Love," Reading 25.
  Prugh, Dane G. and Harlow, Robert G., " 'Masked Deprivation' in Infants and Young Children," Reading 26.
  Harlow, Harry F., "The Nature of Love," Reading 27.
  Harlow, Harry F., and Harlow, Margaret K., "Social Deprivation in Monkeys," Reading 29.
Winch, Robert F., and Goodman, Louis W., *Selected Studies in Marriage and the Family*, third edition (New York: Holt, Rinehart and Winston, 1968).
  Skard, Aase Gruda, "Maternal Deprivation: The Research and Its Implications," pp. 266–280.

General References

Blanton, Smiley, *Love or Perish* (New York: Simon and Schuster, Inc., 1955).
Bloom, Martin, "Toward a Developmental Concept of Love," *Journal of Human Relations*, Second Quarter: 246–261, 1967.
Crawley, Lawrence Q., and others, *Reproduction, Sex and Preparation for Marriage* (Englewood Cliffs, N. J., 1964), Ch. 3.

Daniels, Anna K., *Five Kinds of Love for Mature Women* (Englewood Cliffs, N. J.: Prentice-Hall, Inc., 1953).

Harlow, Harry F., "The Nature of Love," *The American Psychologist*, 13:673–685, December, 1968.

Harlow, Harry F., "The Heterosexual Affectional System in Monkeys," *American Psychologist*, 17:1–9, January, 1962.

Harlow, Harry F. and Margaret K. "Social Deprivation in Monkeys," *Scientific American*, pp. 137–146, November, 1962.

Mead, Margaret, *Male and Female* (New York: William Morrow & Co., Inc., 1949).

Orlansky, H., "Infant Care and Personality," *Psychological Bulletin*, 463:1–48, 1949).

Scott, J. P., "Critical Periods in Behavioral Development," *Science*, 138:949–958, November 30, 1962.

Skard, Aase Gruda, "Maternal Deprivation: The Research and Its Implications," *Journal of Marriage and Family Living*, 27:333–343, August, 1965.

Wintour, Eleanor, "Bringing up Children: The American vs. The British Way," *Harper's*, 229:58–63, August, 1964.

10

Romantic Love

Man's love is of man's life a thing apart,
'Tis woman's whole existence; man may range
The court, camp, church, the vessel, and the mart,
Sword, gown, gain, glory, offer in exchange
Pride, fame, ambition, to fill up his heart,
And few there are whom these cannot estrange;
Men have all these resources, we but one,
To love again, and be again undone.

Lord Byron

Kephart, studying 1,079 white college students, reports[1] that although females have more romantic experiences, they are less controlled by romance than is the male. They are matrimonially directed and as they grow older reject romantic experience in favor of more rational values.

In the United States, romantic love is one of the major concerns of the teen years, and interest in it does not cease with the twentieth birthday. Throughout most of the Asiatic world, on the other hand, romance is not considered a significant part of relationships between men and women. This has been true since ancient times. Sensuous desire is known and looked upon as a kind of human madness.[2] People in many cultures have considered romantic love a sign of weakness and have ridiculed the person who yielded to it, others have glorified it in poetry, fiction, movies, and in adolescent experience.

Since our culture has staked so much on romantic love, each individual of necessity does so. He acquires his values as naturally as though these values were in the nature of things, and meant to be. But love is a trait that must be cultivated in human nature, and the patterns of

[1] William M. Kephart, "Some Correlates of Romantic Love," *Journal of Marriage and Family Living,* 29:470–474, August, 1967.

[2] Oswald Schwarz, in A. M. Krich (ed.), *Women: The Variety and Meaning of Their Sexual Experience* (New York: Dell Publishing Co., Inc., 1954), p. 290.

romantic love, too, are formed by custom. Even the key points of allure are culturally defined. Whether this be the trim ankle or the hidden ear lobe depends on what culture has defined as romantic.

Sex Attraction

Romantic love begins in sex attraction. The list of additional elements which may enter into the love of man and woman is endless. The happiest love affairs are those including such qualities as respect, admiration, the desire to please, to protect, to share, and to assist. Many other qualities may characterize a relationship. Sympathy, even pity, is occasionally an important part of love. The desire to dominate or to be dominated is also common. The desire to have children may be uppermost, or the desire to have money, status, adventure, or security.

In a sense, one has no right to condemn any of these motives or elements in love. When they are sincere, they represent nothing more than the manifestations of an individual's personality needs. The only thing that can justifiably be said against the more selfish motives is that they less often produce mutually satisfying love affairs and seldom lead, in themselves, to successful marriages.

Numerous writers have described components of sexual love in various language—the language of poets, of scientists, of philosophers, of lovers. Like life itself, love is most difficult to put into words.

The great English philosopher, Herbert Spencer, in his *Principles of Psychology,* classified love of man and woman for each other into nine distinct elements as follows:

1. physical sex impulses
2. feeling for beauty
3. affection
4. admiration and respect
5. desire for approbation
6. self-esteem
7. proprietary feeling
8. extended liberty of action from the absence of personal barriers
9. exaltation of the sympathies

Sexual Desire As a Factor in Romantic Love

Walter R. Stokes, M.D., marriage counselor, has said, "The only sound motive for a happy marriage is being overwhelmingly in love on a frankly sexual basis, centering about physical desire."[3] Had Dr. Stokes stopped at that point many an infatuated young couple would have had excellent argument for combating paternal opposition to a youthful marriage. But Stokes went on to add that fundamental though sex is, "there is much more to a good marriage."

Sex alone is hunger—raw animal appetite. Love is a combination of sexual desire with all the other impulses that go into the highest type of association between the sexes. Love is a synthesis of friendship, tenderness, self-surrender, altruism, kindness, loyalty, self-sacrifice, and, in fact, of all the finer traits of human nature combined with the feeling of sexual need.

In sexual desire, the ego motive is dominant, the desire to conquer and force to surrender, or to be conquered and to surrender. The physical appetite is animal; love is social in the finest sense. Sex need is the basis for reproduction; it is Nature's way of assuring that passion will lead to fertility and from fertility to the reproduction of the species. Physical desire is concerned with no more distant goal than this.

Love is social, humanized, institutionalized, and becomes the basis in one way or another for almost every activity of the human being. It is, in fact, the basis for society. Love is sexual desire idealized, controlled, and made to conform to social living. Physical appetite is self-centered. Love is other-centered. Physical appetite is craving for an intimate sharing with another.

The most significant aspect of sexual love is that it becomes socially purposeful as it is harnessed and directed by culture. Sexual need is the biological motive for marriage. As love expands in the personality, it brings with it a sense of shared obligation to the mate and to offspring. This provides the social basis for the loyalty of marriage and for the permanence of family life as expressed in the care of dependent children.

An exceptional few rush into marriage with little more than an overwhelming desire for one another and, years later, are still in love. Motion pictures and popular fiction would have us believe that the experience of these few is very common. Part of it is; most of it is not. Many people do marry, particularly during wars, solely on the basis of sexual attraction, but these marriages are seldom successful over a period of time. Either new and more lasting reasons for love are soon discovered or the marriage falls apart. Men and women are so constituted biologically that, demanding though their sexual desires are, they are quickly satisfied. Once an individual has obtained sexual satisfaction, his partner must be much more than beautiful or desirable to hold his continued interest. The existence of strong sexual attraction does not diminish the importance of shared interests, values, and expectations. Neither does it guarantee their existence.

[3] Quoted by A. K. Davis in *Coronet*.

While love may not be blind, it is most certainly often blinding. The man or woman who mistakes physical attraction for complete love frequently does so because of a sincere, though inaccurate, conception of what a complete love is like.

Romance and Physical Restraint

Romantic love at its best is a game of double make believe, and it flourishes best at a distance. The term romance comes from the French word *roman,* which meant a novel or play set in the provincial style of southern France. The idea of romance was spread by the twelfth-century troubadours as a "remote love," separated by great distance and obstacles, which precluded its consummation. This left the imagination free to enlarge upon it, nourishing it to a "happy reciprocal passion."[4]

It has always flourished most where there are great obstacles, or intervening circumstances to hinder its consummation: feudal restrictions, caste, Christian law, an existing marriage, for example. It is scarcely to be found in cultures permitting sexual freedom.

If this analysis is correct, romantic love will be expected to diminish in our culture to the extent that sex becomes unrestrained. It may well already have diminished with the increasing physical contact in dating, even though this contact usually stops short of coitus.

The Psychological Advantages of Romance

Havelock Ellis defined romantic love as the synthesis of sex and friendship. The female is so constituted that, unless conditioned otherwise, sexual attraction, respect, and deep friendship tend to give her a love feeling that is diffused throughout her body, something far more than a localized sexual need. With the male, sex attraction tends to create localized sensations which are no more diffuse and meaningful than a desire for the sex act itself. In the male, sex is specific, local, glandular. The synthesis of sex attraction through love and friendship, where it involves restraint of sex expression in the form of coitus over a period of time, seems to have the effect of diffusing love feeling much more widely in the male, sublimating sex desire, sanctifying it, making it a thing of supreme importance in the personality, preparing the male for the ultimate unifying of the pair in the sex act when marriage is consummated.

[4] Denis de Rougemont, "The Crisis of the Modern Couple," No. 6 in *The Anatomy of Love,* A. M. Krich (ed.), (New York: Dell Publishing Co., Inc., 1960).

It is a sound psychological principle that the more interpersonal love becomes, the more a matter of mutual interest and sharing, the more sublimated in character, the more it grows in personality. A tribe of Plains Indians discovered this to their great satisfaction. The young bride was wooed for weeks after marriage before the sex act was consummated. Warriors often talked with nostalgia of the first weeks of marriage when they would lie awake all night "quietly talking to their young wives."[5] Some tribes developed the chastity-blanket as an encouragement to restraint, and perhaps as a way of birth control. Couples were expected to seek the pierced blanket from the chief, since sexual intercourse required use of the blanket. Other cultures use the locked chastity belt, with parents retaining the key.[6]

Ernest Van den Haag, analyzing the cultural prerequisites to the growth of romantic love concludes:

> When sexual objects are easily and guiltlessly accessible, in a society that does not object to promiscuity, romantic love seldom prospers. For example, in imperial Rome it was rare and in Tahiti, unknown. And love is unlikely to arouse the heart of someone brought up in a harem, where the idea of uniqueness has a hard time. Love flowers best in a monogamous environment morally opposed to unrestrained sex, and interested in cultivating individual experience. . . .[7]

If there is any truth in this view, the restrained dating relationship and the restrained engagement which stop sex activity prior to consummation would seem to be the logical preparation for the romantic type of marriage-family system developed in our culture. It is significant that, to date, studies show that chastity prior to marriage is the best preparation for successful marriage. The subtle psychological factors discussed above may well be important here.

The Course of Love

The idea that one "falls" in love is widespread. This concept of American culture probably carries over from the day when love was looked upon as something instinctive and inevitable, something that swept one off his feet against his wishes and carried him into a blind and blissful state from

[5] Margaret Mead, *Male and Female* (New York: William Morrow & Co., Inc., 1949).

[6] Bernard Farber, *Family: Organization and Interaction* (San Francisco: Chandler Publishing Co., 1964), p. 97.

[7] Ernest Van den Haag, "Love and Marriage," in Rose Laub Coser (ed.), *The Family: Its Structure and Functions* (New York: St. Martin's Press, Inc., 1964), pp. 192–202.

which there was no return. The more informed young person of today recognizes this as an idea which has little likeness to the more durable relationships of modern life.

While a person may suddenly be swept off his feet once in his lifetime, most individuals are more wary the second time and control their emotions until they are surely channeled toward a person who has the traits, attitudes, and life aspirations which make the relationship appear to be safe.

The idea that love is a fate from which one cannot escape is held by comparatively few informed young people and by none of those who have had variety in dating experience. Such persons know that an enduring love must be something that is cultivated, and that the soil in which it is grown must be appropriate. It usually begins with friendship which continues until respect and admiration develop. Only then may the emotions be given free play.

Ralph Eckert, teacher and counselor, has stressed the view that a young person should expect to grow in love, putting aside the notion of falling in love as a phenomenon of immaturity.[8]

Love is rarely an unmixed emotion. One tends to resist its involvement. It is an up-and-down affair in most pair relationships. In fact, it is often very complicated. It is not always a thing of excitement and discovery. It is certainly not always a thing of novelty. There are long periods when the thrill is absent and life takes on prosaic routines. Love becomes what people make it by constant interchange through communication and contact of personalities with each other.

Love does not stand still, neither does it continue on the same level nor at the same intensity for a lifetime, but this does not mean that all loves are destined to die. The normal course of love may be compared to a wave. The successful loves surge upward; the unsuccessful affairs fall away. Regardless of their ultimate outcome, most loves begin alike with a strong attraction involving physical awareness between the partners. This initial attraction may characterize the couple's first meeting or it may come after months or even years of casual contact. In either case, no real heterosexual love may be said to exist until some feeling of sexual attraction has been aroused.

From this point on, the affair may move to a quick conclusion or develop very slowly. In instances where physical attraction alone unites a couple, the spiral generally begins a rather early downward course. The highest point of love in such an affair is either at the beginning or soon after. With increased knowledge of one another, the attraction lessens and the interest subsides.

Unfortunately, many marriages take place before the course of the

[8] Ralph G. Eckert in lectures at the University of California at Los Angeles, Summer Workshop in Family Life Education, 1948.

spiral has been revealed. In other instances, couples decide to marry in spite of the fact that they are each aware of a slackening interest in one another. One disillusioned young bride described the logic of such a marriage in this way:[9]

> Ken and I were madly in love for about three months. We were together almost constantly and found it difficult to keep from getting too involved physically. We necked quite a bit, I guess you'd say, but both of us wanted to avoid doing anything wrong.
>
> When we began to quarrel and disagree and get on one another's nerves, we thought it was probably due to the fact that we both were constantly restraining ourselves. We decided that if we would hurry up and get married all of our tensions would be relieved and we could easily save our dying friendship.
>
> That's what we did and for the first two months everything was grand. Now we've discovered that the quarrels we had amounted to more than we thought they did. Marriage is no solution to an affair that is dying.

Other affairs begin with an immediate, upward spiral. Initially, they may grow very rapidly. As the couple discover more and more reasons for loving one another, the love itself grows in intensity. If the affair continues into a happy marriage, their love may continue its upward spiral for a lifetime, although seldom if ever at its initial pace. When the first few years of mutual discovery have passed, the love spiral develops more slowly. Each event or situation that brings the couple together, or gives them a new understanding or appreciation of the other, causes their love to grow, but new events and new insights are likely to decrease in number as the years pass by.

Love can only grow with increased acquaintance, but at any point in this process of "getting acquainted," what one person learns about the other may cause him to cease to love.

Tests of Love

Bergler[10] has catalogued eight characteristics of love as follows:

1. subjective feelings of happiness
2. self-torture
3. overvaluation of the love object
4. undervaluation of reality
5. exclusiveness
6. psychic dependence on the love object
7. sentimental behavior
8. predominance of fantasy

[9] From a student autobiography in the author's collection.
[10] Edmund Bergler, *Unhappy Marriage and Divorce* (New York: International Universities Press, 1946), p. 5 ff.

Popenoe,[11] founder and now president of the American Institute of Family Relations, has listed five factors that characterize the well-rounded attitude toward love:

1. biological impulse leading to sex attraction
2. tenderness and affection
3. comradeship
4. a developing desire for children
5. a desire for economic interdependence

Biological impulse, tenderness, and affection may come early in an affair; but real comradeship, the desire for a family, and economic interdependence generally develop only as a result of long and mutually satisfying acquaintance.

Popenoe has also devised a scorecard test that he has found "goes a long way toward determining whether the basic and most essential elements of real love are present." The scorecard is designed as a series of questions one should ask concerning the other person. The questions may easily be reworded to apply to oneself, however, and they are equally effective in revealing the intensity and maturity of one's own state of affections:

1. He seems to take pride in you and wants to show you off, to introduce you to his friends and relatives.
2. He tries, when you are in a group with him, consistently but inconspicuously to put you in a favorable light.
3. His plans seem to keep organizing themselves around you as well as around his own personal ambitions.
4. He seems to defer to your judgment and give full weight to your views.
5. He is eager to share his experiences with you.
6. He shows respect and consideration for your family and friends.
7. He seems eager for your success and fulfillment of your own plans and ambitions.
8. He seems to find intellectual as well as emotional stimulus in association with you.
9. He acts as though he really wants to love you—that he is not doing so against his better judgment.
10. He gives you to understand that he wants children.

Analyzing their love affairs in terms of factors such as Popenoe suggests in these questions will convince many young people that, exciting though their loves may be, not all affairs can or should lead in the direction of marriage. Love relationships that are terminated short of marriage need not be looked upon as unfortunate experiences nor as failures. Since each new relationship can contribute something to the personal development of both parties, we might even safely say it is fortunate that few first loves are so successful as to be last loves.

[11] Paul Popenoe, *Marriage, Before and After* (New York: Funk & Wagnalls Co., Inc., 1953), Ch. 3.

The Cycle of the Unsuccessful Love Affair

Most events that enter man's experience have their ups and downs. All are familiar with the business cycle, with its booms and depressions. Even one's mood has ups and downs.

Love affairs also move in a cycle. The pace will differ from person to person, and with the same person in different affairs. Kirkpatrick and Caplow[12] plotted the cycle of love affairs with a group of University of Minnesota students. The 455 students (141 men and 314 women) were given a sheet of graphs and asked to check the one which pictured best the progress of their emotions during the courtship period. They were given four additional graphs to check which indicated the trend of their feelings after breaking up. In case none of these graphs fitted his case, the student was asked to draw a chart which did (see Figure 10–1).

The group plotted their total 582 love affairs by this means. Most students followed the steady up-and-down pattern, with no radical fluctuations; that is, the love rose to a climax, from which it fell in an uninterrupted line. Only a few went through a whole series of ups and downs. A gradual rise to the point of love, followed after a longer or shorter period of time by a steady decline would seem to be the pattern for most couples who fail to continue in love.

On breaking up, some couples (15 percent) rise to a new height of idealized love (Graph A) after which decline takes place. (Historically, many inexperienced lovers failed to return to earth, if one is to take fiction and biography seriously. The idealized love and phantom lover continued to live on, making interest in further loves impossible. Most college young people seem to be able to avoid this.)

Graph B is a pattern of complete indifference after the breakup. Over half of these college loves ended this way. Graph C is a pattern in which indifference turns to positive dislike (10–13 percent ended so). Graph D is a pattern of repeated, but gradually weakening flare-ups of love (15 percent of students checked this pattern). In all, 90 percent of these student love affairs terminated in what the researcher considered a normal pattern. In a later chapter, breaking of the engagement and its consequences will carry the study of this aspect of the love experience further.

The writer has collected data in graph form of several thousand love affairs of college students over the past fifteen years. They follow patterns

---

[12] Clifford Kirkpatrick and Theodore Caplow, "Emotional Trends in the Courtship Experience of College Students as Expressed by Graphs, with some Observations on Methodological Implications," *American Sociological Review*, 5:619–626, October, 1945.

FIGURE 10–1 EMOTIONAL PATTERNS IN BROKEN LOVE AFFAIRS OF COLLEGE STUDENTS. Source: Clifford Kirkpatrick and Theodore Caplow, "Emotional Trends in the Courtship Experience of College Students as Expressed by Graphs, with Some Observations on Methodological Implications," **American Sociological Review,** 5:619–626, October, 1945.

Graphs presented to students to represent patterns of their broken love affairs. Percentages indicate proportion of men (M) and women (W) selecting each graph. The regular graphs (left column 1–5) were selected by most students. Most often selected was number 1—attraction to a period of love, followed by a gradual cooling off to indifference. About 15 percent followed the up-and-down fluctuations represented in the cyclical charts (second column I–III). Less than 20 percent selected the irregular patterns of charts in column three (X–Z). The graphs in the column at the right represent their ways of getting over a love affair. Well over half picked B to represent their experience—one of indifference. Of both men and women, 15 percent experienced an after flare-up of love, as in graph A; about the same proportion, the hot and cold fluctuations of D. A few experienced a strong dislike of the former lover, as in C.

similar to the typical ones described in the chart. Occasionally one finds a relationship in which the initial contact is one of hostility, rather than attraction. "I couldn't stand him when I was introduced to him. I thought he was the most obnoxious, egotistical person I had ever met." But later the miracle of attraction takes place, then love, and in some cases even marriage.

The Control of Romantic Love

Most cultures have distrusted romantic love. Where the institutional family structure is in existence, romance tends to create many awkward relationships. In the institutional family system, marriages are for social status, for guaranteeing the family inheritance, and improving economic status. People with this conception of marriage cannot let romantic love interfere with parental arrangement. Therefore, they tend to laugh at romantic love or consider it shameful and transmit this idea in the culture.

After marriage, romantic love is distrusted in the joint family. Through romantic love, parents lose first place in their children's affection. In patri-local family systems, where the husband brings the wife into the family home, the mother and sister try to outdo the wife in holding the son's and brother's affections and attention.

Most cultures also put numerous impediments in the way of romantic love prior to marriage. They may require marriage between relatives, usually cousins. They may employ child betrothal, often bringing the engaged into the home as a servant long before the marriage is consummated. They may limit betrothal to persons in a certain social position or class. Segregation of the sexes, precluding secret romances among the young; the veil, the harem; selection of mates by parents or other elders; stressing the value of chastity before marriage; and many other such devices have been and are a part of folk cultures, one important purpose being to control the romantic impulse and keep it from disturbing customary arrangements.[13]

While we have come to recognize romantic love as a legitimate basis for mate selection, we have had to face the reality that romantic love is not enough. One of the chief advantages of marriage courses has been to help young people discount romantic love as an independent value and force them to check it against some of the realities of human experience.

---

[13] For an excellent analysis of this problem see William J. Goode, "The Theoretical Importance of Love," *American Sociological Review*, 24:38–47, February, 1959. Also reprinted in Rose Laub Coser, *The Family: Its Structure and Functions* (New York: St. Martin's Press, Inc., 1964), pp. 202–219.

Research in the field of marriage and the family has concentrated largely on the problem of trying to determine the kind of background factors and social-emotional traits which help or hinder success in marriage. By presenting young people with this factually derived information, which, although tentative, far exceeds folklore in authority, teen-agers are helped to temper romantic expectations with realistic ones. It is not unusual for such teaching to break up existing romances, and to cause young people to appraise future relationships in other than romantic terms. The marriage counseling clinic is another device that has emerged in answer to the needs of our modern urban-industrial culture in which total strangers often meet and date. These clinics are available for helping young people critically appraise each other before marriage. The inquiring couple usually faces a battery of tests that evaluate their emotional, background, and personality factors. The clinician then tries to give them some objective awarness as to their likelihood of success or failure in marriage.

Those who study marriage and the family have learned to consider romance as only one of various prerequisites for mate selection. They realize that some of the most fabulous romances end in the most tragic marriages. The film *This Charming Couple* presents a wonderful romance. The man is a dreamer, an interesting classroom lecturer, a bohemian by disposition. He is sophisticated, profligate, his economic values are unrealistic. The girl in the pair is the systematic, thrifty, conventional secretary whose life must be ordered according to plan, whose future must be made economically secure and framed in a familiar niche of people with familiar patterns. The romance is out of this world. Their very differences fascinate the couple and make their moments together moments of supreme joy. Their marriage, however, is tragic, for they have no basis whatever for a life of similar habits, expectations, and plans.

Many a romance between the American GI and the foreign girl reaches a romantic peak which is impossible for couples of similar backgrounds. The girl's spoken accent is sexually attractive to the man and charms him, but, making a marriage with one of vastly different cultural background is quite a different matter from romance. Romance often flourishes brilliantly across racial lines. Many persons have a deep sexual affinity for members of a race of a different skin color. Their hearts flutter, their imaginations run rampant, they feel a compelling sexual urge— being drawn to the member of the contrasting race with an almost hypnotic fascination. This is ground for wonderful romance, not necessarily for a successful marriage.

One might go on with examples to show that romance is not enough, nevertheless, marriage without some romance would be dull indeed. Older cultures have recognized this for centuries and have often reserved romance for the mistress, not for the wife, thus ensuring family stability.

Wifehood and motherhood are recognized as institutions, not merely as flighty emotional experiences. They are symbolic of the persistent, systematic, demanding routine aspect of life.

In trying to combine romance and marriage in the marriage-family system, Americans have made some gains, but these can be had only as realities of married life are projected into romance.

Romantic Love as a Basis for Marriage

One of the exciting and yet dangerous aspects of the romantic love situation is the influence of what psychologists characterize as "halo effect" —assessing of personality entirely in terms of some particular trait. Given one or several attractive traits, the personality is wholly accepted on the basis of these traits. Or, conversely, given one or several unattractive traits, the personality is wholly rejected on the basis of these traits.

Halo effect operates in the love relationship more than in any other social relationship. Sex attraction and the appeal of certain superficially valuable "dating skills" provide a brilliant halo that obscures all other personal qualities. They symbolize to the attracted partner the ultimate of everything that is desirable. If the love is not pursued to the point where the halo can be penetrated, permitting a reasonable appraisal of the romanticized one's true capacities, the risk is great indeed. This is a hazard of marriages that occur without an adequate period of acquaintance. Disillusionment following marriage is an inevitable consequence of marriages that have occurred in the glow of the halo effect.

Margaret Mead, with the comprehensive view of the anthropologist, sees the American concept of romance as a factor in marriage instability.[14] After marriage, in our culture, even casual flirtation is considered a threat. In cultures where marriage is a permanent institutional relationship, however, as in Europe, flirtations and even heated extramarital affairs are not serious threats to the marriage. In our marriage system romance is put to the test after marriage as well as before.

Even if Mead is right in assuming that our romantic marriage leads to too much temperature-taking after marriage, the essential elements of the romantic mate-choice system are likely to continue in our way of life—with, perhaps, some tempering by other values.

Actually, it appears that romance, as a method of mate selection, is on the wane in the United States, although much on the increase in some

[14] Margaret Mead, *Male and Female* (New York: William Morrow & Co., Inc., 1949), pp. 64–65.

other countries. In Japan, where for centuries mate selection has been by proxy and go-betweens, romantic love matches are greatly on the increase, and there, where society is in transition between old and new philosophies of marriage, a Supreme Court Justice has estimated that marriages made by parents and go-betweens end in divorce four to five times as often as "love matches."[15]

Sociologists Burgess and Wallin, studying 1,000 engaged couples in the United States, express the belief that romantic love is on the decline in the United States as a major factor in mate choice, and that an increased emphasis on companionship and compatibility are in evidence.[16] They find that 12 percent of men and 15 percent of women even go so far as to think that it is all right to marry a person when not in love with him.[17]

One suspects that a reason for the emergence of this view is the emphasis upon romance and thrill seeking during the dating period. Many young people learn during this period that highly excited romance is often a temporary thing, so that when they settle down to selecting a mate, they are more interested in the enduring qualities that can survive in a day-to-day relationship. This means ability to get along together in social and recreational life; ability to make plans together for children, family, and for an economic future.

There probably is more realism in mate seeking today, at least among the more intelligent groups of the population, than there was a generation ago. Of course, professors in the field of marriage and family like to think that they have played a part in this, in that for more than two decades the emphasis in marriage education through books, magazine articles, and lectures has stressed the desirability of realism. But one must grant that if professors thought love was all that mattered, there would be no reason for their writing books and articles on marriage or teaching about marriage. Nature would handle the job of mating and marriage.

Problems

1. Draw curves of your various love affairs. What kind of up-and-down pattern do they show? Are they all similar in trend? Do all move at the same speed?

[15] For a current study of Japanese marriages as compared to ours, see Robert O. Blood, *Love Match and Arranged Marriage: A Tokyo-Detroit Comparison.* (New York: Macmillan Co., 1967).

[16] Ernest W. Burgess and Paul Wallin, *Engagement and Marriage* (Philadelphia: J. B. Lippincott Co., 1953), p. vii.

[17] *Ibid.,* pp. 393–395.

Can you mark the relationship or act that brought about the termination of former love affairs?

2. As a group project, devise what you believe to be an adequate test of love. With one person at the blackboard as recorder, have members of the class suggest behavior, attitudes, etc., which an individual should expect of himself or his loved one before concluding "this is love." For example:

    a. "I am physically attracted to him or her."

    b. "I am proud to have my family and friends meet him or her."

3. Make three criticisms of the dating customs of your campus or community. Briefly describe how these shortcomings could best be remedied by individual or community action.

4. Have the class divide into sections for an informal discussion concerning the most desirable function of dating. Have one group support dating as "preparation for marriage"; have the other defend dating as "a form of amusement." At the end of the discussion decide as a group whether the two interpretations seem irreconcilable or not.

5. Do library research on the dating or mate-choice customs of other countries and report.

6. Pick the three items which rate highest with you. In asking for or accepting a date I am most interested in someone who:

    a. Is good looking.

    b. Is popular among individuals of my sex.

    c. Is courteous.

    d. "Rates high" on campus or in the community.

    e. Is modest and unassuming.

    f. Shares my religious and cultural background.

    g. Would live up to my parents' standards.

    h. Enjoys a good time and isn't too prudish.

    What does your choice suggest with regard to (a) your background? (b) the kind of marriage you are likely to have? Does the consensus of male and female students differ? If so, discuss the significance of this fact.

7. The dean of women in a small coeducational college described the following situation to a gathering of the dormitory house-mothers. She did so in order to get their suggestions for improving the situation. Read her description and consider possible action that could be taken:

    "Girls on our campus outnumber boys almost two to one. Competition among the young women for the available dates is intense and of an alarming character. Girls from the finest homes seem to lose all of their respect for propriety, modesty, and fair play; those who do not, are left dateless.

    "The mode of dress on the campus is changing from that of traditional college simplicity to one of open suggestiveness. Drinking and petting are becoming the rule instead of the exception on off-campus dates. Girls are willing to risk open criticism and poor grades by cutting class in order to keep coke dates with the fellows.

    "Girls who came to our college seriously concerned about an education seem to have lost their heads in this mad scramble for male attention.

    "One's first inclination is to 'crack down.' We have seen that done on many campuses. I came here to speak to you, hoping that we might avoid this by immediate action of a more positive and constructive nature."

Selected References

Articles in Books of Readings

Cavan, Ruth Shonle, *Marriage and the Family in the Modern World: A Book of Readings*, third edition (New York: Thomas Y. Crowell Co., 1961).

Reiss, Ira L., "Heterosexual Love Relationships," Reading 26.

Christensen, Harold T., *Handbook of Marriage and the Family* (Chicago: Rand McNally & Co., 1964).

Burchinal, Lee G., "The Premarital Dyad and Love Involvement," Ch. 16.

Coser, Rose Laub, *The Family: Its Structure and Functions* (New York: St. Martin's Press, Inc., 1964).

Goode, William J., "The Theoretical Importance of Love," pp. 202–219.

Krich, A. M. (ed.) *Women: The Variety and Meaning of their Sexual Experience* (New York: Dell Publishing Co., Inc., 1954).

Schwarz, Oswald, "On Love," pp. 286–311.

Landis, Judson T., and Landis, March G., *Readings in Marriage and the Family* (Englewood Cliffs, N. J.: Prentice-Hall, Inc., 1952).

Kirkpatrick, Clifford, and Caplow, Theodore, "Courtship in a Group of Minnesota Students," pp. 79–90.

Trusal, Andrew G., and Merrill, Francis E., "The Family and Romantic Love," pp. 108–113.

Winch, Robert F., and Goodman, Louis Wolf, *Selected Studies in Marriage and the Family*, revised edition (New York: Holt, Rinehart and Winston, Inc., 1962).

Goode, William J., "The Theoretical Importance of Love," pp. 468–480.

General References

Burgess, Ernest W., and Wallin, Paul, *Engagement and Marriage* (Philadelphia: J. B. Lippincott Co., 1953), Ch. 7.

Goode, William J., "The Theoretical Importance of Love," *American Sociological Review,* 24:38–47, February, 1959.

Goodenough, Ruth, "Dating and Security," *Understanding the Child,* 26:59–60, January, 1957.

Kirkpatrick, Clifford, and Caplow, Theodore, "Emotional Trends in the Courtship Experience of College Students as Expressed by Graphs, with Some Observations on Methodological Implications," *American Sociological Review,* 5:619–626, October, 1945.

11

Dating

Dating is an American invention, and one of the more diffusable patterns of our civilization. It is being borrowed widely wherever American films and other influences are to be found. The older generations abroad mistrust it; the young like it. So it is spreading rapidly in countries like Japan, our most conscious imitator, and to a lesser extent in other parts of the world.

Whether we are doing the world an injustice in providing such a pattern only history will tell. Certainly it is a daring thing to trust mate choice to the impulse of youth. In mate choice society risks its most cherished values—family status, which is a precious social heritage; its property, for property is transmitted through family inheritance; family name, which is its method of biological survival through the centuries. These values have, in most societies, been jealously guarded. Historically, it was assumed they could not be trusted to the judgment of youth, certainly not to youth guided by the elusive quality we call romance. Elders have thought it necessary to arrange marriages of their young people, and have in most cultures created devices of isolation and taboo designed to make romance impossible prior to the wedding night, when couples meet face to face and are alone for the first time.

The American frontier was certainly responsible for banishing caste lines. A man on the frontier came to be measured by his performance; woman, by her ability to hold her own in meeting the challenge of an untamed environment. The tradition of established English and European society offered few status patterns that assured survival in frontier culture. A person survived or perished by his wits and endurance. His status was achieved, not prescribed by the social position of his ancestors. Geneologies tended to be forgotten and mates chosen on the basis of performance rather than social position. And in a nation of abundant resources, the need to pass on an inheritance was minimized as compared with cultures where generations of family effort were required to accumulate any property at all.

A direct contrast is seen in India and Pakistan, where parent-arranged marriages have been the pattern for centuries. A Ph.D. candidate at Washington State University explained that his degree would be worth $3,000 to him in a marriage bargain when he returned to Pakistan. An Indian seeking the Ph.D. said his would be worth even more to his family in bargaining for a wife.[1]

Here are advertisements clipped from the "Matrimonial" column of a New Delhi metropolitan newspaper. These are young people for the most part whose relatives have died, and who have no one to negotiate for them, but some are liberated young people who assert their right of mate choice. Note that status, education, and/or earning capacities are included in qualifications:

An Advanced Beautiful, Educated, well-versed, Maharashtrian girl 21 and engineer 25, invite confidential details from similar cultured parties, view matrimony. . . .

Gujarati Double Graduate Respectable Bania youth doing business invites correspondence from beautiful, cultured girls or their parents, view matrimony. . . .

Wanted A Youngman Of Liberal views, educated and well settled in life for a highly accomplished and cultured girl of 23 B.A. (Hons.) : only daughter of a Gazetted Officer, belonging to Maharashtrian, Brahmin community, holding high position outside Bombay State. . . .

To the influence of the frontier as a factor in breaking class barriers and institutionalized marriage forms we must add the growth of urban industrial culture and of a mobile population—all developments that have made dating a necessary innovation in mate choice. In a society in which young people leave the family nest to go to college or to seek their future in a distant state or city, parents and other elders are in no position to choose for their young people.

Add to this the rapid upward climb made possible in a land of opportunity, where education and occupational achievement tend to raise the new generation above their parents in schooling and vocational level, and one has a situation in which the new generation distrusts the elder's

---

[1] The "dower" is a form of marriage insurance for the wife in cultures where there is no insurance of other types. See J. Henry Korson, "Dower and Social Class in an Urban Moslem Community, *Journal of Marriage and Family Living*, 29:527–533, August, 1967.

Here are typical bride prices in various cultures: *Baskir* (in Asiatic Russia), high: 3,000 rubles, low: One cartload of wood; *Uganda*, high: 100 goats and 16 cows, low: 6 steel sewing needles; *Shastika* (Indian tribe), 12 ponies; *Fiji*, One whale's tooth; *Kenya*, high: One motor scooter, low: Five cows; *Eskimos*, One steel file or hammer.

ability to choose and in which the elders often as not feel incompetent to do so. The elders sense that their sons and daughters have already outdistanced them in knowledge, even if not in the practical judgment that comes with age.

These are some of the cultural and social factors that have led to the pattern of dating in our society, a pattern of increasing interest. Young people are dating earlier and the proportion of the teen group dating seems to be increasing. Also, dating is increasingly accepted by adults.

Youth, influenced by movies, becomes skilled in the technique of lovemaking. The automobile has provided privacy—a quality lacking in most other cultures—for only here in America can many teen-agers have a car to use. Dating has become an important pastime of the adolescent years—an experience of thrills, hurts, confidences, and betrayals—through which the age group becomes seasoned in experience with the opposite sex.

Because of the dating pattern of mate choice and the romantic emphasis of teen-age social life, love (in this narrow sense) has become a national problem. It is certainly one of the greatest personal problems of high school and college social life. The girl's counselor at both levels of schooling spends much of her time listening to the woes of the brokenhearted. Many a long session involving high school or college teen-age peers is spent in analyzing "love" mates and "love" experiences. The relationships between men and women are the primary concern of the girl previous to marriage, and not a minor concern of men, although certainly girls major in this concern more than do men.

From "Keeping Company" to Dating

Dating as it is now known was not a part of the accepted pattern of life. In the horse-and-buggy days, "keeping company" was standard practice. Taking a girl home from church was almost the equivalent of being pinned or engaged today. The reason was that everyone knew everyone else, their families, their reputations, their economic status, their character. When young people "walked out" together, they already knew a great deal about one another. Intentions could be and were more or less serious from the beginning. A boy and girl seen together more than once were assumed to be "courting." The community so regarded them, as did competing young men or women.

Dating is a social engagement between two people for the sake of the date itself, and without marital intentions.

Dating—a Step in Psychological Weaning

Ceremonial rites (rites of passage) marking the transition from child-hood, or adolescence, to manhood have been extensively practiced among primitive peoples. Such initiations for boys often take the form of ordeals testing a youth's capacity to suffer. In many societies the period of puberty is spent in isolation from parents in special shelters or camps. In these bachelor quarters the boys are initiated into the roles and phi-losophies of adulthood in their community, and are taught their new relationship to women, to work, and to children. Girls in similar camps are in the custody of wise old women who teach them what it means to grow up and become mothers and administrators of tribal house-holds.

There are no such formal rites in America culture unless coming-out parties, mixed social gatherings, dances, and such could qualify. These functions unquestionably help to push young people out of the family nest. More significant, however, is the sanction of informal dating relationships which permit the growth of heterosexual attach-ments.

The roots of emotional life are in the family. They remain there throughout childhood, the parents and siblings being the natural center of emotional attachment. During adolescence there must be a gradual shift of this attachment from the family focus to members of the opposite sex. The ultimate attainment of emotional maturity depends in large part, as was suggested in an earlier chapter, upon the effectiveness with which the adolescent succeeds in making this transfer of his deeper emo-tional attachments to a member of the opposite sex. Those who fail to make the transfer and who remain permanently "tied to the mother's apron strings," fail to achieve the kind of emotional maturity that is necessary for establishing a new, independent family.

Dating is not necessary to this weaning process, but it does seem to provide a normal and natural shift to heterosexual emotional align-ment outside the family.

Dating, with its close personal ties, is a factor in developing the psy-chosexual nature of the individual, particularly today when concrete expressions of emotion are expected. Kissing and necking when they express genuine emotion, become overt steps in a young person's emo-tional transfer from the family circle. The stimulation such contacts provide often represents a desirable preliminary to the growth of natural heterosexual interests. The way is paved for a normal responsive ap-proach to members of the opposite sex. Without dating, the young person lacks this experience and is to that extent retarded in emotional development.

Dating has evolved as the natural and logical product of the anonymity, urbanization, individualism, secularization, and the emancipation of young women from chaperonage that has gradually come to characterize American society. As the nation's population shifted from farms and small towns to large cities, the earlier customs defining boy-girl relations broke down. Courtship patterns of the past were built around a relationship involving two people who had known one another more or less intimately for years—usually since childhood. There are today few city residents who have known their neighbors and friends very long.

While many of the transplanted families tried to maintain what they considered the "high standards" of their rural past, this usually meant isolation and loneliness for the young people of the family. After all, a girl in a large city who was forbidden to go out with anyone she had not known for years, usually found that, in effect, this meant she did not go out at all.

Traditions of mate seeking were not so ingrained and sacrosanct as to withstand the numerous contacts of teen-agers in the modern city. Gradually, the rules and regulations in most families relaxed, and newly acquainted young men and women began building together new codes of behavior and new concepts of right and wrong to govern their associations with one another. Somehow they had to get acquainted, and, since conditions did not allow for the growth of familiarity through inevitable day-to-day relationships, a more casual type of initial relationship was demanded. Thus dating—a means of getting better acquainted, of looking one another over, and of indicating interest but with no strings attached —has gradually become the rule.

The family has ceased to be the center of life for the young person. Dating received a further impetus as high schools and colleges brought together increasingly large groups of young people of the same age. The daily association of young people in curricular and extracurricular activities in coeducational high schools and colleges made dating the central activity of social life for this age period, and hence, also, the key to much of happiness or disappointment.

It is possible for a person to date through high school and/or college without ever having any serious intention to select a mate. Although potentially any date may develop to the point of serious interest, dating as such is now a part of the normal social activity of young people. By dating, they size up members of the opposite sex and extend their close acquaintance with them long before they have any intention of choosing a partner for marriage. It is in this setting, nonetheless, that romantic love has become exaggerated out of all normal proportions, as viewed historically and as viewed by most other peoples in the world.

Opposition to Dating

European college women have a low opinion of American dating. One finds the same attitude among foreign students here, at least until they become used to the customs of American college campuses.

They think American young people must be a promiscuous lot since they date so freely, kiss, and engage in other forms of physical intimacy after only casual acquaintance. The Europeans expect these contacts only after a considerable period of "walking out" and often only with the person whom they expect to marry. They see dating as a strenuous competitive game in which the American girl is trying to secure as many men as possible at the same time. This, they suppose, is her only way to become popular. They assume that such a girl has to resort to all kinds of tricks to keep the male coming back for more dates. While she is doing this, she isn't sure of her relationship with any one man. European women feel that such a relationship is too uncertain to be interesting.[2]

The European male, from his observations of love making in American movies, and from his noting the sex emphasis of advertising and love stories in American magazines, is quite sure that the American female is ready, on the most casual acquaintance, to participate in full sexual relationships with any male she finds attractive. In America, one hundred years ago, this close association of the sexes sanctioned in dating circles today was reserved for the final stages of going together or for marriage itself.

But it has not been the superficial observer alone who has challenged dating. Those who have made a study of marriage and the family have attacked it on scientific grounds.

The late Willard Waller[3] observed American dating as a competitive game, engaged in primarily for status, rather than serving any useful function in the mate-selection process. He found that on the college campus it means thrill seeking and adventure. He saw dating as a game of trying to win favors without becoming involved emotionally oneself: with men and women trying to associate on an intimate basis, without either one breaking down and losing control. He felt the least emotionally involved member manipulated the situation, with the most involved being the likely victim of exploitation. The male has his line, and the female her wiles. Each tries to win the other without being won. He observed that the man

[2] For a scathing criticism of American women, and particularly of coeds, by a French woman who spent three years in high school and college teaching in the United States see Christie Rieuf, "Praying Mantises," *Atlas*, 1:40–45, April, 1961.

[3] See Willard Waller, "The Dating and Rating Complex," *American Sociological Review*, 2:727–734, 1937. His theories are also discussed in Willard Waller and Reuben Hill, *The Family*, revised edition (New York: Holt, Rinehart and Winston, Inc., 1951).

who rated highest on the campus had plenty of money, a car, good clothes, and fraternity membership. The experienced college man was one with a "good line," smooth manners, good appearance, and the ability to dance well. With the girls, the keynote was "nothing succeeds like success." Women who rated best were those who managed to be seen at the right place with the most popular men. However, an appearance of propriety with respect to drinking and unconventional behavior was also important. Waller felt that students "extend themselves enormously" in order to meet the qualifications of the campus standards for dating according to these varied and yet fairly well understood norms.

Waller saw in these values much that is contradictory to success in marriage. He felt that these spurious considerations tended to distract a student's attention from the kind of values that contribute most to lasting marital success. The whole dating pattern, he believed, was built upon competition and materialistic display—two values that have only a negative association with happiness and adjustment in marriage.

He held that this dating-rating game has no relationship to serious mate seeking, and he felt that the entire activity tends to indicate a decay of the moral structure centering around family behavior; that the objective is largely one of physiological sensation and tension relief. He believed that dating, with its necking and petting, should be regarded as a game rather than as having any serious relationship to courtship. He also felt that the risk of emotional injury resulting from dating is great. He believed that when a person shifts from casual dating to the serious matter of courtship, an entirely new set of values and behavior patterns are required; that, in fact, there is a distinct break between the one type of experience and the other.

Even though he considered that many of the dating practices have no positive relationship to marriage, and may actually detract from marriageability, he did grant that, in some cases, courtship does follow. However, he felt that the thrill-seeking experiences of dating were better training for future thrill seeking than for marriage. He believed that dating developed the habit of dalliance, that is, of deliberately stalling the development of any close emotional relationship which might lead to courtship and marriage.

Sociologists have taught the Waller theories for more than thirty years, have discussed them, and have subjected them to research. The controversy still goes on and evidence increases.

An extensive study by Burgess and Wallin of dating practices among students in three Midwestern and two Western coeducational colleges found that dating involves considerable rating on the college campus.[4] They feel that the acceptance or rejection of a date is definitely related to

[4] Ernest W. Burgess and Paul Wallin, *Engagement and Marriage* (Philadelphia: J. B. Lippincott Co., 1953).

the status aspect of the situation. Dating being regarded as an event, with no direct relationship to marriage, it can be treated entirely as a matter of gaining status, if a person so desires to use it. These authors find that fraternities, sororities, and other organizations play a decided part in dating on the college campus, and that their social events require or encourage dating. Jessie Bernard has described fraternities and sororities in coeducational schools as "in large part dating and courting institutions."[5]

Rogers and Havens, at Iowa State, find that status enters decidedly into dating.[6] Eleven undergraduate judges rated major residence groups as to prestige. Data show that prestige classes entered into all phases of mate selection from casual dating up to mate choice itself. Students date, become pinned, become engaged, and marry within their own prestige class. They conclude further that, "Waller's hypothesis that prestige rating governs casual campus dating but not more serious mate selection is not substantiated to any great degree by present findings. Instead, these findings indicate that students follow prestige lines at all stages in the mate-selection process."

McCormick and Sundal of Wisconsin University find that, in general, fraternity men tend to marry sorority women.[7] The above researchers find that in these intimate groups on the campus, rating takes place, too. A fraternity man, for example, is generally given a higher rating than a nonfraternity man; sorority girls rate higher than nonsorority girls. Different statuses may be assigned to different fraternal groups, as to different offices or positions on the campus. This rating affects personal relationships in that a couple often is as much aware of the impression they are going to make on others as they are of the impression they are going to make upon each other. Campus queens and similar competitive contests based upon feminine beauty or feminine form enter into this rating complex.

This study, however, found no basis for the theory that dating develops a habitual pattern of dalliance—that is, putting off close relationships with the view to deferring marriage. It showed no evidence that men and women in their dating relationships try purposely to avoid the growth of emotional bonds which might lead to love and marriage.[8] There was no consistent tendency for an individual's later dating relationships to be longer or closer than his earlier ones. In fact, if anything, some of the earlier relationships for men tended to be longer than some of the later ones. Women seemed to report the opposite, later relation-

[5] Jessie Bernard, *American Community Behavior* (New York: The Dryden Press, Inc., 1949), p. 394.

[6] Everett M. Rogers and A. Eugene Havens, "Prestige Rating and Mate Selection on a College Campus," *Marriage and Family Living,* 22:55–59, February, 1960.

[7] T. C. McCormick and A. P. Sundal, "Age at Marriage and Mate Selection," *American Sociological Review,* 16:37–48, February, 1951.

[8] *Ibid.*

ships tending to be somewhat more permanent. In over a fourth of their early dating relationships, both men and women had discussed the possibility of marriage.

Herman[9] believes he finds some evidence that there is dalliance in the dating pattern on college campuses. While many couples are oriented toward marriage in their heavy dating, others are definitely dalliant in their attitudes.

Dating is dalliance to the extent that it is uncommitted association. There is no obligation to repeat the date, or to give the slightest consideration to marriage. What is done on a date is without future irrevocable commitments. The dating continues only so long as each finds it interesting and each other's behavior satisfactory. Moreover the very attitude of putting off serious commitments may develop a habit of dalliance which is hard to overcome. As a college senior age 26 said, "I have put off being serious so long for the sake of my education, now that I am ready for marriage, I can't overcome the habit of looking for faults and magnifying them in prospective mates."

A study of young men and women at Pomona College sought to learn the reasons why these students did not become seriously interested in the young man or woman they dated.[10] The three reasons most often given by 300 young women who had dated more than 1,100 young men were that the men: (1) were self-centered, (2) were weak, dependent, or had no ambition, (3) represented cultural and family differences.

A hundred young men gave the following as their three most important reasons for not becoming seriously interested in any of the over 350 young women whom they had dated: (1) the women were shallow, weak, or the clinging-vine type, (2) they were self-centered, or (3) they represented cultural and family differences.

Robert O. Blood,[11] sociologist at the University of Michigan, made the Waller rating hypothesis the subject of a special study, using a group of University of Michigan students. He also made comparisons of his findings with data from two other institutions. He found very little support for the Waller thesis. Although students were found to be aware of most of the items in the Waller thesis, such as fancy clothes, fraternity-sorority membership, a "good line," great popularity, money, and so on, they rated them much lower than many other factors in their dating behavior and in their evaluation of dating partners. Blood found that "more than half of Waller's items failed to be chosen by a majority of Michigan

---

[9] Robert D. Herman, "The Going Steady Complex: A Re-examination," *Marriage and Family Living*, 27:36–40, February, 1955.

[10] Ray E. Baber, *Marriage and Family*, revised edition (New York: McGraw-Hill Book Co., 1953), pp. 130–133.

[11] Robert O. Blood, Jr., "A Re-test of Waller's Rating Complex," *Marriage and Family Living*, 17:141–147, February, 1955.

students and, therefore, do not constitute norms for this campus as a whole in 1953."

He finds little support for Waller's idea that a student has to change to an entirely different type of behavior when he shifts from casual dating to serious dating.

Riesman[12] sees campus life less oriented toward rating and dating than to seeking relationships "more profound and sincere. There is more desire to share, less desire to impress. There is less desire to dazzle members of one's own sex and more to come to some sort of humane terms with the opposite sex."

No doubt a major factor in the decline of the college "rating" system is the product of profound changes in values in American youth culture. The college population has long since ceased to be upper class or even upper middle class. The base of selection has broadened to include the lower middle class and even a sprinkling of the lower class as scholarships have been made more numerous. Competence rather than pedigree tends to be the criterion of worth as both high school and college students become more serious about scholastic matters. Competition for college entrance, and for survival once enrolled, has tended to develop seriousness of purpose in the student. The decline in the prestige of fraternity houses, along with the stress on integration, have brought added pressure in the direction of equalitarian values. They carry less snob appeal than in earlier generations. In many quarters, their value system has been made suspect. Some campuses have dared to ask the question of whether or not such class-conscious groups should be permitted in a democratic social order, and some campuses have already outlawed them.

The Values in Contemporary Campus Dating

Blood has tried to arrive at the values which college people hold uppermost in their evaluating of a date. A group of 95 men and 134 women, a cross-sectional sample of the undergraduate students at the University of Michigan was presented with a check list of 37 items pertaining to dating values.[13] They were asked to check values for both casual dates and for serious dates. Table 11–1 lists the six items that were selected by almost all men and women students for both casual and serious dates.

[12] David Riesman, "Permissiveness and Sex Roles," *Journal of Marriage and Family Living,* 21:211–217, August, 1959.

[13] This summary and the tables are taken from a mimeographed report presented by Robert O. Blood before the Groves Conference on Marriage and the Family, at Purdue University, April 30, 1954. See his "Uniformities and Diversities in Campus Dating Preferences," *Marriage and Family Living,* 18:37–45, February, 1956.

Table 11–1   Items Selected with Substantially Unanimous Approval
of University of Michigan Students as Elements in the Campus Rating
Complex for Both Sexes and as Qualities Preferred in Casual and
Serious Dates

Item	*Percent of Respondents Choosing Item*		*Personal Preferences*	
	Campus Rating Complex			
	for women	for men	casual dates	serious dates
1. Is pleasant and cheerful	100.0	97.8	97.9	99.4
2. Has a sense of humor	91.6	97.8	96.8	98.7
3. Is a good sport	93.7	97.8	94.5	98.9
4. Is natural	93.7	96.3	95.5	100.0
5. Is considerate	95.8	99.3	96.6	100.0
6. Is neat in appearance	100.0	97.8	98.2	99.4

Blood doubts that, in the light of this evidence, Waller's contention
that casual dating is unfavorably related to mate selection is valid; in
fact, he doubts that it has any application to contemporary college students.

In November, 1950, The *Purdue Opinion Poll for Young People*
studied 8,000 high school students scattered throughout the United States.
While conditions will vary in different localities, this is the best picture
at present on just how high school young people rate various traits in
dating. They checked the following seven traits as of first importance in
making or accepting a date.[14]

1. is physically and mentally fit
2. is dependable, can be trusted
3. takes pride in personal appearance and manners
4. is clean in speech and action
5. has pleasant disposition and sense of humor
6. is considerate of me and others
7. acts his own age, is not childish

Both boys and girls were pretty well agreed that these are the things
that count most in a date. There is little evidence here of rating being of
major importance among the younger set.

A study of unmarried students in the University of Colorado showed
the traits these young people rated highest in characterizing a good mate.
Both men and women rated companionability as the most important

[14] The findings reported here are from Harold T. Christensen's analysis of a
stratified sample of 2,500 cases drawn from the above sample and published in his
"Dating Behavior as Evaluated by High School Students," *American Journal of Sociology,* 57:580–586, May, 1952.

characteristic of a good date and a good mate. Men and women differed somewhat in certain values. Men rated physical appearance fairly high, whereas women rated social graces higher than looks.[15]

Defense of Dating

Most sociologists contend that dating is a necessary and important part of the mate-selection process in modern society. They believe that it fulfills the function of sexual selection; that it is a normal stimulus to maturation; and finally, that it involves a chain of "allure and pursuit, by means of which the prospective mates are ultimately carried on toward biological union."[16]

It is quite logical to believe that some kind of dating is necessary to the development of the judgment and pair interaction that is at the root of real objectivity in mate selection. Since few people can marry a play-mate from the old home town, dating is the modern way of bringing this gap. It is the only way of bringing potential mates, their pasts and their values, under scrutiny before any serious intentions are declared.

Those who have dated more than one person have a chance to compare and to learn some of the usual behavior patterns of members of the opposite sex. They learn to distinguish between personalities that seem to promise a durable compatibility and those which obviously do not. Dating is an exploratory experience. It no doubt contributes to the development of the ability to feel at ease with the opposite sex and the love play sanctioned in dating may well be an important factor in the development of a normal heterosexual orientation in the psychosexual area.

In the United States, where nearly all young people have so many superficial and transient contacts, there is no other way to get acquainted with members of the opposite sex and to discover their ways of acting and thinking. If marriages are to be based on compatibility, young people must learn to size up members of the opposite sex in all aspects of their personalities.

In most circles today, therefore, it is considered desirable that young people "circulate," rather than "go steady" from the beginning, until they find a relationships that will satisfy both their temperamental and intellectual tastes. It is even considered that some variety of dating experience is favorable to ultimate mate choice. The girl who is considered desirable

---

[15] Eleanor Smith and J. H. Greenberg Monane, "Courtship Values in a Youth Sample," *American Sociological Review,* 18:635–640, December, 1953.

[16] Niles Carpenter, "Courtship Practice in Contemporary Social Change in America," *The Annals of the American Academy of Political and Social Sciences,* 160:38–44, 1932, presents a representative statement of this view.

as a date by a number of fellows is presumed to be the one most likely to be sought after in marriage. Dating experience teaches that there is no "one and only" by predestination. After normal experience in dating, the average young person comes to recognize that at the same time there are many other individuals with whom he could not possibly be happy, and with whom he could live happily. He may even discover that the more normal and adjustable he is, the greater the range of persons whom he could marry and with whom he could be content.

Steady dating early in college can reduce social life and limit social contacts. It may develop a desire to marry quickly at the cost of other goals. This is not to deny that those who have gone steady may gain more insight into what marriage is like, and may actually be helped to prepare for it sooner, but it does not dispose of economic and educational considerations that an early marriage may bring.[17]

Early steady dating may limit the horizon of both members of the pair, and to their later regret. This problem was mentioned as a factor in dating in Chapter 7. Boys may be very much influenced in career choice and educational direction by a marriage-oriented girl who is too limited in her vision of the future as it affects his preparation for a profession. The cost may in the end be great in terms of level of living and life satisfactions for the couple and their family. The male may limit the girl's vocational horizon too. She may adjust her ambitions downward, compromising them for an early marriage. The boy may actually encourage her in so doing. Later both may regret their short-sighted perspective.

A Reappraisal of Dating

In summarizing what they observed about college dating, Burgess and Wallin conclude that the good-night kiss is usually reserved for the second or third date, necking for a later stage—often when going steady or when pinned. Petting is reserved for engagement, and sexual intercourse for marriage. The study finds the coed usually primarily responsible for holding this flexible rule. The college male, while he has respect for these standards, especially in the one he hopes to marry, is quite willing to violate them at almost all stages in the sequence. He is inclined to be interested in sexual satisfaction as an end in itself, and can readily divorce it from affection as such.

Burgess and Wallin conclude that dating has become a highly individuated phenomenon and an area in which a personal sense of responsibility determines what is or is not done. They find dating to be one of the

---

[17] *Ibid.* See also Riesman, *op. cit.*

few remaining areas where American life is characterized by "unbridled competition and individualism."[18] Though dating may appear to be democratic, actually a large number of young people are excluded from it; and on a college campus, particularly, it takes on many aspects of status seeking, superficiality, and social immaturity.

After this rather lengthy review of fact, theory, and opinion concerning dating, it is necessary to reappraise this social institution of American culture and to arrive at a tentative answer as to whether dating is merely a new game for young people—an activity to be enjoyed for its own sake—or whether it is a social invention having some important relationship to mate selection and marriage in the modern world. Certainly it is an interesting game, one of the most interesting of the teen years. The evidence points to the fact that dating also serves an important purpose in preparing the way for mate choice and marriage.

First, dating offers a means whereby modern youths may form intimate friendships with members of the opposite sex. In the relatively impersonal climate of today's city, male-female relations of a companionship nature are not easy to initiate outside of the dating relationship. The urban world is not like the small town or rural community of the past where the number of one's friends was limited only by the size of one's town, and where friendships with all were the result of having grown up together from childhood. Today, dating has become the substitute for many of yesterday's inevitable and informal contacts.

Second, dating serves the very necessary function of preparing young people for marriage. It does this in several ways: (1) It provides opportunities for youth to meet and develop a closer acquaintance with a number of potential mates. (2) It allows young people to study character and personality types which will help them in judging the potential compatibility of their final choice. (3) By bringing couples together under a variety of circumstances, it provides actual experience for each in adjusting to and getting along with members of the opposite sex.

Third, dating seems actually to contribute to the personality development of the individuals involved. Dating is a highly competitive activity, and one in which most young people want desperately to succeed. While some youths may turn to compensative behavior—elaborate spending, conspicuous dress, or sex play—the majority rely upon the cultivation of their own personalities to insure dating success. Dating may thus be thought of as an intense type of motivation for self-improvement—a type of motivation seldom provided in the family, by the school, or even in relationships with one's own sex. Many young people begin to see the importance of being a fine person, rather than merely expecting somehow to find the right mate.

[18] Burgess and Wallin, *op. cit.*, pp. 121–126.

Finally, dating makes an important contribution to the general ideological maturation of the individual. During the course of the average period of attraction in which two people will date one another there are many opportunities for more or less serious discussions of ideas, ideals, and expectations. As a matter of fact, it is only as a result of such discussions that most dating relationships finally break up or reach a point of real seriousness. By talking over their values, their convictions, their life plans, young people come to see just how much they do or do not have to offer one another. The desirable outcome of these discussions is not so much what one young person learns about the other, but what each one learns about himself. Through discussions of this type, young people come face to face, perhaps for the first time, with their own lifetime accumulation of attitudes, values, and ideals. In voicing them, defending them, comparing them, they learn many things about themselves and hereby achieve ideological integration. By providing for the crystallization of his values, dating helps a young person to develop a coherent and conscious philosophy of life.

The dating pattern is becoming widely diffused in industrial cultures of Europe and Japan. Male students from most countries who attend our universities participate and express pleasure in dating, even though the system is foreign to their culture.[19]

Awkward as this dating business may seem to outsiders, it appears to be the only method open to a highly individualistic society. It gives young people more moral responsibility. It burdens them with the momentous choice of a life partner; yet this is a choice which young people in an individualistic society such as ours prefer to retain.

The Nondater

In any competitive activity, some must lose. Dating is competitive: failure here is real failure. The girl's self image is especially threatened, since she is the one who must do the attracting.

In the statistical situation many cannot win. Boys are not ready for dating as soon as girls, either in terms of physiological readiness or interest. They face the economic burden, which is particularly limiting during the early teens, and throughout all the years of dependence on parents.

There is considerable evidence that young people from more privileged homes, where opportunity for social growth generally exists, are the ones who tend to date earlier, to date a greater number of persons, and

[19] Robert O. Blood, "The Experience of Foreign Students in Dating American Women," *Journal of Marriage and Family Living*, 24:241–248, August, 1962.

tend to avoid extensive steady dating. They also tend to defer marriage longer for the sake of education.[20]

Early dating and going steady is found to be typical of those who are American in heritage, above average in education, and from small families of relatively high socioeconomic status. They play the field. Late dating is more typical of those of foreign heritage, with less education, and from large families. They go steady soon after dating begins.

Judson T. Landis,[21] studying 3,000 college students, related their dating history in junior high, high school, and college to happiness of the parents' marriage. Those from happy homes formed friendships more readily in early adolescence, developed more active and confident dating patterns, had a more favorable self-evaluation of their personalities, and had greater confidence in their likelihood of making a successful marriage.

The *Purdue Opinion Poll for Young People* showed that almost half of the high school boys and 39 percent of the girls in their sample of 8,000 had rarely or never dated (Figure 11–1). This included, of course, the whole age range from freshman to senior year. A study of college people[22] showed that 31 percent of the men and 20 percent of the women had not yet begun dating at age seventeen.

Here then is a statistical picture of the nondating group. If this were all a matter of personal choice, the statistics might have little significance. However, the girl who fails to obtain dates and, later, proposals of marriage, suffers one of the unfortunate by-products of our highly romantic conception of marriage. She is likely to feel that she has lost out in the most important competition of a woman's world, and she will probably feel defeated and frustrated. Although this is primarily a woman's problem, some men also are crowded out in the competitive process.

Winch has tried to appraise the factors that relate to dating behavior.[23] This study showed that a favorable attitude on the part of parents helped to determine early dating; that young men and women of higher socioeconomic status tended to date more than those of low status; that better-looking men and women dated more persons and more frequently than those who were less attractive. Appearance and money may be almost as important to the dating behavior of the younger adolescent boy as to the girl.

---

[20] See Samuel H. Lowrie, "Early and Late Dating: Some Conditions Associated with Time," *Marriage and Family Living*, 23:284–291, August, 1961; also *Purdue Opinion Poll for Young People*, 15:4a, February, 1956.

[21] Judson T. Landis, "Dating Maturation of Children from Happy and Unhappy Marriages," *Marriage and Family Living*, 25:351–353, August, 1963.

[22] Ernest W. Burgess and Paul Wallin, *Engagement and Marriage* (Philadelphia: J. B. Lippincott Co., 1953), p. 119.

[23] R. F. Winch, "Interrelations Between Certain Social Background and Parent-Son Factors in a Study of Courtship Among College Men," *American Sociological Review*, 11:333 ff., 1946; also R. F. Winch, "Courtship of College Women," *American Journal of Sociology*, 55:269–278, 1949.

FIGURE 11-1   STUDENT DATING. Source: Ernest W. Burgess and Paul Wallin, **Engagement and Marriage** (Philadelphia: J. B. Lippincott Co., 1953). Reproduced by permission of the publisher.

HIGH SCHOOL STUDENTS (seldom date)

BOYS   48%

GIRLS   39%

                                                    PICTOGRAPH CORPORATION

COLLEGE STUDENTS* (did not begin dating by age 17)

MEN   31%

WOMEN   20%

                                                    PICTOGRAPH CORPORATION

* 1,223 college students.

Dating is a highly selective institution.

Comparative Personality Ratings of Daters and Nondaters

Since preoccupation with dating and its related activities is unquestionably characteristic of today's adolescent world, one might logically expect to find those who do not date seriously deficient in personality development and in general adjustment.

Yet Nimkoff and Wood's study of dating and courtship among Bucknell University students found only a slight relationship between dating and social and emotional adjustment. In fact, those who did not date had almost as high adjustment scores on the *Bell Adjustment Inventory* as did those who dated.[24]

There was a slight but significant difference in personality. Those who never dated were more retiring and had some tendency toward emotional maladjustment. The best adjustment was found among those who started going steady during the senior high school years. Excessive dating was related to only moderate emotional adjustment, and was also related to social aggressiveness. This study, of course, does not answer the question whether dating itself is conducive to adjustment or whether people merely feel maladjusted because they do not date.

A study of the dating habits of 500 students in coeducational colleges showed that very early pairing off may be a serious emotional handicap.[25] This study showed that those who started going steady in grade school or in junior high school were in great danger of having emotional maladjustments later than were those who deferred going steady until senior high school or college, when marriage could be seriously considered. Of course, there is no way of knowing whether this going steady at an early age is cause or effect. The maladjustment may already be there, and the early steady emotional attachment may be an expression of it, rather than the reverse.

Burgess and Wallin's study of college students[26] found that those who did not date suffered slightly from defects in personality, that they sometimes were less well adjusted emotionally, and sometimes exhibited a lack of skill in social relations. On the other hand, students often do not date because of preoccupation with other interests, sometimes athletic, sometimes intellectual. It was found that those who willingly forgo dating usually find more or less satisfactory compensation for this lack in their own personalities.

This study found girls were more aware of the positive effect of dating on their personality development than are boys. Since girls take the passive role in dating, success in dating tends to replace an inferiority feeling with self-assurance. Self-image is improved in both sexes. Both tend to feel that dating has a bearing on ability to size up prospective mates in terms of temperament, interests, ideals, and general compatibility. On the negative side, students felt that dating is a competitive game and that

[24] Meyer F. Nimkoff and Arthur L. Wood, "Courtship and Personality," *American Journal of Sociology,* 53:263–269, 1948.

[25] *Ibid.*

[26] Ernest W. Burgess and Paul Wallin, *Engagement and Marriage* (Philadelphia: J. B. Lippincott Co., 1953), pp. 121–126 ff.

those who most need dating from the standpoint of personality development are largely excluded.

There is a tendency toward superficiality in dating relationships which may result in a selfish, highly competitive, aggressive type of boy-girl relationship. Such a relationship ignores many human qualities and kindnesses that perhaps are less often apparent in those who play this game than in those who are excluded from it. The girl who cannot date is left out of many, if not most, of the important activities of the campus. This is cruel and in many cases extremely unjust, since there is as much character and ability among those who do not date as among those who do. The nondaters frequently lack only the more superficial qualities that are so important in obtaining college dates.

In the case of the girl, particularly, being without dates intensifies her feeling of inferiority. This experience of being left out seems to be cumulative, in that if a girl does not get started dating early in her college career, it likely means that her chances decline progressively with each year in college. Soon she will begin to doubt her social competence and ask herself chronically, "What's wrong with me?"

Improving Dating

Burgess and Wallin conclude that since dating is young people's own invention, they must find the cure for its problems, and suggest an increase in activities in which boys and girls can associate together in groups rather than as pairs. They see hope, particularly, in group gatherings where young people having specialized interests will be drawn together.[27]

The importance of this suggestion is confirmed by Kirkpatrick and Caplow's study at the University of Minnesota.[28] Fifty percent of college students there felt that opportunities to meet members of the opposite sex were inadequate. Almost three-fourths of college men felt that when they did meet girls, they were of the wrong kind.

Computer dating has become a highly commercialized adaptation of the "lonely heart's club" approach to the problems of anonymity of the large metropolitan community. The questionnaires which must be filled out are often thorough and reveal personality traits and attitudes, others tend toward the superficial. The price range for computer matching is very wide and there is no connection between cost and quality. It is not surprising that many are disappointed in the results, but they may be ex-

[27] *Ibid.*

[28] See Clifford Kirkpatrick and Theodore Caplow, "Courtship in a Group of Minnesota Students," *American Sociological Review*, 51:114–123, 1945.

pecting too much. They may have experienced the same disappointment with random dates met in other situations. Computer dating does bring people with similar interests and backgrounds together. No doubt it succeeds in finding satisfactory mates for some people.

On the campus, students may wish to use the computer service to meet someone new for one particular occasion. It is effective in this case, but could be more so if students did not enter false information about themselves. This is often true of boys who are curious to see what kind of companion they will have for the evening. No scientific instrument can be useful when treated as a joke.

Social scientists do feel that a well-designed instrument can be helpful in bringing persons together who could make a good team in marriage. No instrument can reveal all the idiosyncrasies that are discovered by actually knowing a person; in and of itself, no instrument is sufficient to choose one a mate. Some college administrators are using computer selection of dormitory roommates with much better results than chance matching.[29]

Karl Wallace, with his wife as associate, began a service to provide research data for a doctor's thesis. After graduation, he ran a dating service as a vocation. His results have been published in the book, *Love is More than Luck*.[30]

Wallace found that most of those who registered were in an older-age group. The sex ratio of registrants was dominantly male, particularly in the younger-age group. Wallace's registrants were almost four men to one woman in the age group under 35. In the group above 55, there were more women than men. Of his first 6,023 clients, 10 percent married. A follow-up study of 320 couples after marriage found them much happier than average.

For the lonely in our impersonal society of the great cities, legitimate means of contact and introduction, such as that by Wallace, should be developed. Many countries give such services social approval. We have cited the matrimonial ads of daily newspapers in India (see p. 201). For more than one hundred years, England has published *The Matrimonial Post and Fashionable Marriage Advertiser* where a person may announce the type of mate he seeks and lists his or her own personal characteristics.[31]

In summary, it has been observed that dating is not merely a game, as some authorities have claimed, but a necessary outcome of our age.

---

[29] "Computerized Companions," *Time,* October 4, 1968.

[30] The Karl Wallace Foundation has a history of a reliable scientific approach in the operation of an Introduction Service. (270 S. Alexandria Ave., Los Angeles) See also the analytical report on his work in Karl Wallace, "An Experiment in Scientific Matchmaking," *Marriage and Family Living,* 21:342–348, November, 1959.

[31] Joseph K. Folsum, "British Family Welfare," *Marriage and Family Living,* 7:25, 1945.

One cannot deny that dating has its status aspect,[32] but human beings enter into few social relationships that are completely free of this.

Those who are inclined to discount dating solely on its rating aspects will do well to remember that courtship in the more staid period of an earlier day had its rating aspects, too. Marrying for connections, for dowries, for a share in the quarter section of land down the road, are as old as human nature. In many cultures rating is still a very much institutionalized part of the mate-selection-marriage pattern, and is given precedence over young people's romantic inclinations.

Dating is a necessary development in the mate-selection process in a mobile society. With the casual contacts brought about by the mobility of an urban-industrial society, comparative strangers meet and associate under varying circumstances. Dating has become a means of getting acquainted. It can be and often is conducive to social development and psychological and emotional emancipation from the parental family. It provides a liberal education in the appraisal of and adjustment to members of the opposite sex.

Many improvements are needed to extend this experience to greater numbers of young people and to check some of the more vicious competitive aspects of dating practice.

Problems

1. We have emphasized that there is no "one and only" and that a successful marriage is primarily a matter of mutual adjustment. Therefore, dating to find the "right mate" is a valuable preface to mate selection. Do you agree with this view?
2. Discuss the pro and con of the proposition: "Where competition for dates is intense but the group's codes of dating behavior are high, the competition may actually be a constructive force in personality development."
3. Discuss the Waller thesis on dating and present research evidence to support or refute it.
4. Poll the class on the five traits they most desire in a date. Tabulate the results and compare responses of men and women. Do the standards held by the group appear to be spurious and superficial or genuine and durable? Do preferred traits mentioned seem to be of the kind on which a sound mate choice could be made? Are the values of men or women more sound?
5. Discuss the extent to which girls on your campus feel they must play the role of temptress or coquette in dating. What effect does this have on their personal adjustment? The views of both men and women should be sought on this problem.

[32] Another approach to the status aspects of dating has been that of the social class theorists who are interested in the extent to which lines of social stratifications are held. This is quite a different problem. August B. Hollingshead, for example, has shown that dating is usually within the same social class. See his *Elmtown's Youth* (New York: John Wiley & Sons, Inc., 1949), pp. 211 ff.

6. Do you consider the girl or fellow of college age who dates a great number of persons, but refuses to go steady, emotionally unstable and in need of personal counseling? Discuss the pros and cons of this question.
7. Is petting considered necessary or at least desirable for successful dating on your campus?

Selected References

Articles in Books of Readings

Cavan, Ruth S., *Marriage and the Family in the Modern World: A Book of Readings* (New York: Thomas Y. Crowell Co., 1969).
  Reiss, Ira L., "Social Class and Campus Dating," Reading 18.
  Scott, John F., "The American College Sorority: Its Role in Class and Ethnic Endogamy," Reading 20.
  Skipper, James K., Jr., and Nass, Gilbert, "Dating Behavior: A Framework for Analysis and an Illustration," Reading 21.
Christensen, Harold T., *Handbook of Marriage and the Family* (Chicago: Rand McNally & Co., 1964).
  Burchinal, Lee G., "The Premarital Dyad and Love Involvement," Ch. 16.
Landis, Judson T., and Landis, Mary G., *Readings in Marriage and the Family* (Englewood Cliffs, N. J.: Prentice-Hall, Inc., 1952).
  Waller, Willard, "The Rating and Dating Complex," pp. 60–65.
Sussman, Marvin, B., *Sourcebook in Marriage and the Family*, third edition (Boston: Houghton Mifflin Co., 1968).
  Skipper, James K., Jr., and Nass, Gilbert, "Dating Behavior: A Framework for Analysis and an Illustration," Reading 23.
Winch, Robert F., and Goodman, Louis W., *Selected Studies In Marriage and the Family*, third edition (New York: Holt, Rinehart and Winston, Inc., 1962).
  Winch, Robert F., "The Function of Dating in Middle-Class America," pp. 505–507.
  Hollingshead, August B., "Dating in Elmtown," pp. 507–510.
  Scott, John Finley, "Sororities and the Husband Game," pp. 507–510.

General References

Ashley-Montagu, M. F. *The Natural Superiority of Women* (New York: The Macmillan Co., 1968).
Blood, Robert O., Jr., "International Dating Experiences of American Woman Students," *Marriage and Family Living*, 24:129–136, May, 1962.
Blood, Robert O., Jr., "Uniformities and Diversities in Campus Dating Preferences," *Marriage and Family Living*, 18:37–45, February, 1956.
Breed, Warren, "Sex Class and Socialization in Dating," *Marriage and Family Living*, 18:137–144, May, 1956.
Burgess, Ernest W., and Wallin, Paul, *Engagement and Marriage* (Philadelphia: J. B. Lippincott Co., 1953), Ch. 3.
Coombs, Robert H., and Kenkel, William F., "Sex Differences in Dating Aspirations and Satisfaction With Computer Arranged Partners," *Journal of Marriage and the Family*, 28:62–66, February, 1966.

Coombs Robert H., "Value Consensus and Partner Satisfaction Among Dating Couples," *Journal of Marriage and the Family*, 28:166–173, May, 1966.

Duvall, Evelyn M., and Hill, Reuben, *Being Married* (New York: Association Press, 1960), Chs. 7, 8.

Kirkpatrick, Clifford, *The Family as Process and Institution*, second edition (New York: The Ronald Press Co., 1963), Ch. 12.

Landis, Judson T., "Dating Maturation from Happy and Unhappy Homes," *Marriage and Family Living*, 25:351–353, August, 1963.

Linner, Birgitta, *Sex and Society and Sweden* (New York: Pantheon, 1967).

McDaniel, Clyde, Jr., "Dating Roles and Reasons for Dating," *Journal of Marriage and the Family*, 31:97–107, February, 1969.

Mead, Margaret, *Male and Female* (New York: William Morrow & Co., Inc., 1949), Ch. 9.

Myers, George C., "Labor Force Participation of Suburban Mothers," *Marriage and Family Living*, 26:306–311, August, 1964.

Nye, F. Ivan, and Hoffman, Lois Wladis (eds.), *The Employed Mother in America* (Chicago: Rand McNally & Co., 1963).

Papanek, Mariam L., "Authority and Sex Roles in the Family," *Journal of Marriage and the Family*, 31:88–96, February, 1969.

Podell, Lawrence, "Sex and Role Conflict," *Journal of Marriage and the Family*, 28:163–165, May, 1966.

Rallings, Elisha M., "Family Situations of Married and Never-Married Males," *Journal of Marriage and the Family*, 28:485–490, November, 1966.

Reiss, Ira L., "Social Class and Campus Dating," *Social Problems*, 1965, pp. 193–205.

Schob, Fred, "Some Attitudes of the Male Undergraduate Concerning the Female Undergraduate," *Journal of Home Economics*, 58:204, March, 1966.

Tallman, Irving, "Working-Class Wives in Suburbia: Fulfillment or Crisis?" *Journal of Marriage and the Family*, 31:65–72, February, 1969.

U.S. Department of Labor, Women's Bureau, *American Women,* Report of the President's Commission on the Status of Women, Washington, D.C., 1963.

Williamson, Robert C., "Dating, Courtship and the Ideal Mate: Some Relevant Subcultural Variables," *Family Life Coordinator*, 14:137–143, October, 1965.

Waller, Willard, "The Dating and Rating Complex," *American Sociological Review*, 2:727–734, 1937.

12

Sex Roles and
Sex Codes in Dating

It is not possible for the male and female to play the game of dating by the same sex rules. Biological differences have been discussed. Even more important is the difference in the subcultural values of male and female as instilled from childhood. They cannot play by the same rules, as they do not view the outcome with equal objectivity.

Roles Played in Dating

The American dating pattern is one in which favors are exchanged between the sexes. Although it is not a strictly commodity-oriented activity, there is something of this element present in dating in that values are exchanged. The man invests money and time. He expects sex pleasure in return. It is a matter of degree as to how much sex pleasure is expected and how much is given. Some men look upon every date as an opportunity for sexual conquest, and boast of success to male peers. Research suggests that an increasing number, perhaps the best adjusted, are more interested in confining their sexual life to close relationships, as most young women are inclined to want to do.

Probably the greatest parental concern, where daughters are involved, is sex conduct in dating. As the girl gets older, this proves to be the area of greatest conflict between mother and daughter. In a college sample, Bell and Buerkle found this true in the relationship of mothers with daughters age twenty and older.[1] Mother-daughter views clash as do their ideals of conduct.

The part each sex plays in dating and the way the other sex reacts to the role played determines the nature of the game, its interest and outcome.

[1] Robert R. Bell and Jack V. Buerkle, "Mother and Daughter Attitudes to Premarital Sex Behavior," *Marriage and Family Living*, 23:390–393, November, 1961.

The *Purdue Opinion Poll for Young People* previously cited[2] throws considerable light on sex roles in dating in the early teen period. Girls felt that boys are usually more careless and thoughtless, uninhibited, disrespectful, sex-driven, and loud. Boys criticized girls for being "less natural and more touchy, money-minded, unresponsive, childish, and flighty."

When it came to placing blame for lack of success in dating, boys were much more likely to blame the girls than themselves or other boys. Girls were more likely to think that some other girl was a competitor, thus hindering the success of the date.

Male Initiative

Both boys and girls of the high school group confessed that they very often feel "shy, self-conscious, or ill-at-ease" when dating. This is probably why almost half the boys and a little more than a fourth of the girls thought girls should take more initiative in making dates. This question and some other important questions of the poll are shown below:

Do you believe that:	Percentage Answering Yes	
	Boys	*Girls*
It would be a good thing if girls could be as free as boys in asking for dates?	48	27
It would be a good thing if girls would pay half the expenses of dates?	29	21
It is all right for a couple to kiss on the first date?	51	33
Intimate petting should be delayed until after marriage?	31	66
Sexual immorality is more wrong for girls than for boys?	27	36

As one looks this list over, he sees reasons why young people often differ as to what should be done on a date. In asking for a date, and in money matters, the boys are much more willing to have the girls share equally with them than the girls are to do it. In matters of intimate relations, the girls claim stricter standards than do the boys.

Viewing roles in dating at the college level, college men and women

[2] A. J. Drucker, Harold T. Christensen, and H. H. Remmers, "Some Background Factors in Socio-Sexual Modernism," *Marriage and Family Living*, 14:334–337, November, 1952.

approach dating from different perspectives.[3] The college man looks upon dating as a form of entertainment by which he postpones marriage until he is established in a career. The college woman is interested in dating as a means of securing a partner from the freshman year on. Men who do not date avoid it because they are not interested in it. Women who fail to date ordinarily have no opportunity to date. Women rarely choose not to date; men do choose not to date.

If girls were to pay their way in casual dating, it is likely they would feel less obligated to yield to sexual pressures of the male; there would be less of a bargaining relationship involving exchange of obligation.

In college situations, dating often centers around particular activities, and may not lead to a romantic relationship. College dating also involves certain codes that are more or less standardized on the campus, in addition to whatever personal codes the individual may have. Such group codes offer considerable moral protection to the girl in the dating of relative strangers on the college campus.

The chief problem in dating is the sex problem. Anything from a goodnight kiss to necking, light and heavy petting, or in some cases even sexual intercourse may be involved. Men take the aggressive role; women appraise it in terms of whether or not it is accompanied by affection. The girl is more likely to "draw the line" than the boy. Girls are more interested in the moral reputation of the men they date than are boys in the moral reputation of the girls they date. Fear of acquiring a bad reputation acts as a factor in sexual restraint on the girl's part.

The distinction in sex roles in dating, however, is beginning to disappear, with women taking more initiative and encouraging "Dutch treat"—even at times paying the expense of the recreation. Women enter into planning the date more than formerly, too. Possibly there is also a relaxing of the double standard of morality. If this is so it is because women's codes are relaxing. All these points are debated issues. One study which compares dating practices through three generations, finds no evidence of any change in the matter of men paying the bills and giving most of the gifts.[4] In Scandinavian cultures the practice is one of sharing costs.[5] Class discussion suggests that sharing in the United States comes only when the couple have dated a great deal and know each other well. Perhaps the male ego is too vulnerable in the earlier stages of dating.

In sexual matters, it is still assumed that the male will be the aggressor and that the female will set the standards. The usual, and perhaps

[3] Ernest W. Burgess and Paul Wallin, *Engagement and Marriage* (Philadelphia: J. B. Lippincott Co., 1953), pp. 63–109.

[4] Marvin R. Koller, "Some Changes in Courtship Behavior in Three Generations of Ohio Women," *American Sociological Review*, 16:366–370, 1951.

[5] William Simenson and Gilbert Geis, "Courtship Patterns of Norwegian Students and American University Students," *Marriage and Family Living*, 18:334–338, November, 1956.

natural tendency of the male, is to see how far the female will go. The girl is more restrained because she fears society's unsympathetic condemnation of premarital pregnancy, and because of her awareness of her role as a potential mother.

Some people believe that the male's tendency to take sexual initiative, and the female's role of being seductive and alluring, rather than aggressive, have their roots in biological evolution.[6] These characteristic male-female traits are in evidence in many animal species. Those who hold this theory believe that the female is unnatural when she tries to assume initiative, and becomes aggressive. They believe such a woman hinders her cause in dating and marriage.

Male-female roles are still definitely typed in American culture and affect the reaction of the sexes to particular approaches. In large cities where the sex ratio, from the standpoint of mate choice, is greatly in the male's favor, the female not only has become more aggressive, but is expected to be. In rural areas, where men are in the majority and where the traditional attitudes toward the female still persist, the aggressiveness of the urban female would be spurned.

Physical Contact in Dating Success

In dating, the question of how far to go in physical contact is a matter of considerable importance to women. Playing the passive role in dating as they do by custom, having dates represents for them a kind of competitive achievement. Being able to hold the interest of the male is a constant problem. Sex plays a part in this.

Waller[7] believed that girls in competitive situations, particularly where males are in the minority, have to compromise on sexual morality in order to keep the male from breaking up the relationship.

At the University of Minnesota,[8] 141 young men and 258 young women were asked this question: "Did you give in on important moral or theoretical issues for fear of losing him or her?" Of the women 81 percent denied ever having done so; 16 percent said they did occasionally and only 3 percent said they often did. Two-thirds of the men said they never did; 28 percent said, occasionally; 4.5 percent, often.

Girls who indulge in close forms of physical intimacy rationalize that only if they do so can they have dates. Girls holding the opposite view,

---

[6] See, for example, Paul Popenoe, "Mate Selection," *American Sociological Review*, 2:635–643, 1937.

[7] Willard Waller, "The Dating and Rating Complex," *American Sociological Review*, 2:727–734, 1937.

[8] Clifford Kirkpatrick and Theodore Caplow, "Courtship in a Group of Minnesota Students," *American Journal of Sociology*, 51:114–125, 1945.

however, seem to be correct. Studies of attitudes on college campuses over many years show that most college students do not believe moral compromise necessary for popularity. One may be sure that many students are speaking from experience.

A study of the attitudes of 364 students at Cornell in 1941 showed 94 percent did not consider that "a girl must pet on dates to be popular." In 1947, 2,000 students at Michigan State were asked the same question, and in 1952, 450 students at the University of California. At Michigan State, 77 percent of the men and 94 percent of the women said, "No." At California, 82 percent of the men and 92 percent of the women said, "No." Very few at any school answered, "Yes." A number were undecided.[9]

LeMasters[10] is skeptical of such research. He believes girls reply in the negative, for to reply otherwise would reflect on their confidence in their other charms. Also the "no" reply fits the mores better. Boys also say "no"—otherwise it would appear they cannot rise above sexual conquest in their dating relationships. Men want girls with sex appeal. LeMasters believes it is the unusual girl who can be popular without the use of such devices of sex attraction.

Zetterberg,[11] discusses what he calls the "secret rank" or "erotic rank," which is the measure of ability to induce a "state of emotional overcomeness among persons of the opposite sex." He feels that this erotic ranking enters into the rating-dating complex and other aspects of courtship. The rating matter is visible, the erotic hierarchy tends to be secret. High status in various activities may be considered with erotic rank by the opposite sex. If sex relations take place, it will be with surrender where erotic rank is high. (There may, obviously, be sex relations where there is no emotional surrender.)

Although most young people state that petting is not a factor in holding a member of the opposite sex, it is common practice, as are other forms of intimate sexual contact. This is due partly to social sanctions, and partly to cultivated interest in sexual excitement. One suspects, too, that it is an indication of an effort on the part of many girls to prove to themselves that they are adequate, neither frigid nor homosexual.

So much is made of sex in contemporary culture, and the average male's drives are so specific and intense, that many girls feel inadequate. They fear their lack of specific sexual feelings and want to play a compensating part, not knowing that most women in their teens have little or

---

[9] These studies, the first by Rockwood and Ford, the others by Judson T. Landis, are graphically summarized in Judson T. Landis and Mary Landis, *Building a Successful Marriage,* third edition (Englewood Cliffs, N. J.: Prentice-Hall, Inc., 1958), pp. 85–90.

[10] E. E. LeMasters, *Modern Courtship and Marriage* (New York: The Macmillan Co., 1958), pp. 192–193.

[11] Hans L. Zetterberg, "The Secret Ranking," *Journal of Marriage and Family Living,* 28:134–142, May, 1966.

no recognizable sexual desire. The nature of woman's sex drive is discussed more fully later (Chapters 22 and 23).

There is much current literature about "sex on the college campus." Pressure for interdormitory visiting on some campuses has added fuel to their suspicions of the breakdown of sexual morality. There is no doubt that young people are more aggressive in wanting sex left in their own personal control, unregulated by administrative authority. There is an increase in premarital sexual intercourse as confidence in birth control increases.

Ehrmann's extensive study of college behavior, with particular attention to sex behavior, finds that physical contact in dating tends to go through certain stages with increasing degrees of intimacy. The male usually initiates; the female usually determines the limits. The male with extensive dating experience tends to be the one with most experiences in erotic behavior. For the "female, sexual expression is primarily and profoundly related to being in love and to going steady."[12]

Technically virginity is the norm of the middle more educated classes. It is less so for the lower social classes and lower educational group. Data of the Kinsey research team[13] strongly suggest that necking, petting, and masturbation are sublimating devices, primarily of the middle-class group, which help this group to delay coitus and marriage for the attainment of goals realizable through a college education.[14] Girls enforce the limitations on sex, which stop short of coitus, but the middle-class male believes in this standard, too, since he expects conformity to it of the girl he becomes serious about. Even heavy petting seems to be primarily a substitute for sexual intercourse, rather than a stimulus to it.[15] It permits sexual excitement of a high degree without defloration.

The significance of defloration in our society is largely cultural, for the biological process is, in the case of most women, a minor incident. In most instances the hymen is very easily broken.

Our culture, like many others, makes the hymen a symbol of virtue and judges morality by its presence or absence. This means that defloration under unapproved circumstances can be a major crisis in the life of a woman. In some cultures, the absence of the hymen is taken as absolute evidence that the girl has lost her virginity through sexual inter-

---

[12] Winston Ehrmann, *Premarital Dating Behavior* (New York: Henry Holt and Company, 1959).

[13] Alfred C. Kinsey and others, *Sexual Behavior in the Human Male* (Philadelphia: W. B. Saunders Co., 1948), pp. 343 ff. Alfred C. Kinsey and others, *Sexual Behavior in the Human Female* (Philadelphia: W. B. Saunders Co., 1953), pp. 233–234; see also Margaret Mead, *Male and Female* (New York: William Morrow & Co., Inc., 1949), pp. 209–291; also Eugene J. Kanin and David H. Howard, "Postmarital Consequences of Premarital Sex Adjustments," *American Sociological Review,* 23:556–562, October, 1948.

[14] *Ibid.*

[15] So the Kinsey group data suggest.

course. In such cultures it is a major tragedy, often of lifelong importance, for no man will think of marrying the woman who is not a virgin. This philosophy has been very prominent for the upper classes in Latin cultures, in Pakistan, India, and in many other societies as well as in some primitive tribes.

In Egypt and Arabia the ballane woman checked the upper-class bride before the wedding to see if the hymen had been ruptured. Other cultures have intentionally terminated virginity before marriage with defloration rites. These involved sexual relationships with a person other than the husband—often one or more older, experienced men. In some cultures even incest taboos are suspended for the defloration rites.

A broken hymen is not necessarily proof of loss of virginity. Some girls have practically no hymen at birth. In others it has been injured in infancy and early childhood, so that practically no hymen remains. The hymen may be accidentally broken by the very athletic girl in various play activity; it may be destroyed through masturbation; it is stretched or broken by internal medical treatment and by routine monthly use of tampons. In some environments, however, presence or absence of the hymen is still of great social significance.

Physiological and Psychological Reaction to Petting

After long petting sessions, many young people report negative physiological and psychological reactions. Shipman's study[16] of 400 college students shows that 40 percent of the males suffered pain in the testicles, about one-fifth experienced nervous reactions, and about one-fifth developed negative feelings toward the girl partner. Of the girls, about 38 percent experienced tension and 18 percent developed negative reactions toward the male partner.

Male and Female Conceptions of Sex in Dating

Kirkendall has stressed[17] the fact that the girl miscontrues the man's concept of sex. She lures him by various devices of sex attraction and in doing so arouses him sexually. If possible he involves her in sexual intercourse. If she yields, she thinks it is the beginning of affection and a lasting relationship. Often she gets "contempt and abandonment."

[16] Gordon Shipman, "The Psychodynamics of Sex Education," *The Family Co-ordinator,* 7:3–12, January, 1968.
[17] Lester A. Kirkendall, "Understanding Premarital Sex Problems," in *Sex in the Adolescent Years* (New York: Association Press, 1965), Chs. 24 and 25.

If she pushes for a steady dating relationship, the boy is likely to fight back. This is particularly likely if pregnancy results, so she is left without emotional support or loyalty.

If the girl suggests engagement, the boy may take advantage of the situation to press for sexual intercourse, even when he has no intention of continuing a steady relationship. It is his opportunity, for she may have reached the point where she is willing to yield to any of his wishes.

If intercourse takes place, the boy may drop her. He is then likely to tell his friends, who try to date her with the express purpose of enter— ing into a sexual relationship with no serious romantic interest at all.

Kirkendall says the phrase "lost respect for her" is used very loosely by boys, and that it ofen means he never did have any respect for her. All he ever wanted was sexual intercourse. Having achieved that goal, and the excitement of the physical act, disgust comes to the surface.

Disgust, he finds, is often intensified when his friends make lewd remarks about the girl, and make the relationship the butt of their jokes and teasing. Often he brings it on himself by making boast's of his conquests.

Kirkendall finds, too, that the male's disgust is triggered if the girl is too willing. The male's interest often ends with the girl who ceases to be coy and resisting. When the challenge of seduction is gone so is the male's interest; it may cease even more quickly with the aggressive, seductive girl.

Other areas of misconception, he finds, involve the girl's use of dirty language, often offensive to the male, even though he uses it. The girl who becomes quite free with intercourse may provoke in the boy friend a fear that she is so interested in sex that she will not be his exclusively.

Once sexual intercourse has taken place, a girl may begin to pressure the boy for engagement and marriage, because the girl who enters into a sexual relationship is usually the insecure type. But the thought of marriage is frightening to the male and grounds for terminating the relationship.

It is quite evident from various research samples, that only in cases where both are deeply involved emotionally does sex mean the same to male and female. In general, the boy is interested in sex for itself. The girl believes that as a person she means something to the boy. It is more difficult for her to imagine that he would be interested in sex if he did not care for her. Admittedly, she may realize at times that she is rationalizing for giving in to his wishes, or using sex in an attempt to win the affection she wants from him and is not sure she has.

Where there is genuine and deep emotional commitment on the part of both, the situation may be more nearly played by the same rules, but this time rarely comes during dating as such.

Riesman[18] feels that sexual intercourse with campus couples occurs

[18] David Riesman, "Permissiveness and Sex Roles," *Marriage and Family Living,* 21:211–217, August, 1959.

less often from desire of men to present trophies of their vanity than to "secure themselves against the anxiety that they may not be truly and deeply loved, or capable of love."

If this is true, the situation is more nearly equal than off campus, or, than it has existed historically.

Balance in Dating Interactions

Cultivating emotional responsiveness while maintaining standards of morality is the chief problem of modern dating. Many primitive societies permit unrestrained sex play previous to marriage. Other cultures condone or even encourage pregnancy before marriage. In these cultures, the female becomes a more desirable mate if she can show her suitors that she is capable of pregnancy.

American culture still places a high value on chastity. Most young men who initiate sexual relations with their dates prefer to marry girls who have never compromised their own standards. At the same time, those young women who participate in intimate premarital relations seldom do so as a matter of principle or preference. More likely, they succumb to momentary excitement, or they yield to men they respect, or they have a mistaken notion of "what a girl must do to hold her man." Few do so because of an overwhelming desire.

In our society the whole business of boy-girl relations is complicated for some young people by this contradiction between values and behavior. The girl or boy who gets off to a good start in interpersonal relations, who has an outgoing personality, who makes friends easily and shares many interests and activities with age mates is seldom faced by the problem. The unsuccessful boy or girl, on the other hand—the one who wants friends but doesn't know how to make them, who wants dates but feels that he or she has little to offer—generally stumbles into this dilemma at one time or another. The problem is not just "what others will think," but also what the promiscuous individual thinks of himself. An individual cannot long live happily believing one way and behaving in another way.

With emotionally insecure young people, the love-sex element in dating is particularly risky. Having no deep anchor in parental love, the dating game becomes a substitute for the love these young people missed as children.

But even the emotionally secure youth today runs a considerable risk of becoming prematurely involved in an emotionally exaggerated relationship. The intense loneliness and uncertainty produced by living in a highly mobile, ever-changing group, drives many young people to desperate lengths to find a sense of permanency. In our chaotic modern world, it is inevitable that some adolescents will reach out to members of the opposite sex for the security and sense of belonging that emotional involvement seems to promise. Some of the most striking examples of this are to be noted among soldiers, who, in times of war, quite seriously propose marriage to girls whom they have known for as little as half a day, or for only an evening.

In novel circumstances and situations of psychosocial isolation, deep affection for a member of the opposite sex is likely to be used as a device for restoring self-assurance, and for protecting oneself against the apparent hostility and coldness of the world. For such an individual, love comes to stand for success in social adjustments.[19]

In the long run, certain attitudes on the part of the male or female do more than anything else to insure the success or failure of their dating relationship. The double standard in sex matters is a relatively insignificant factor, for example, as compared to the more general attitude of the individual toward members of the opposite sex.

Many men still cannot genuinely accept women as equals. This is bound to affect their behavior in dating situations. It is also true that many women do not as yet accept themselves as the equals of men. Some intelligent women feel that in order to succeed on a date they must play down their intelligence and competence, lest they overshadow the male ego and in that way threaten his loyalty to them. There is no doubt some carryover in the male of the days of chivalry. Some want the female to be a clinging vine. The male likes to be admired and to have his ego flattered. Some college girls actually do play down their intelligence, skills, and competence as persons, in their dating relationships.[20]

It is doubtful that such tactics, however, can in the long run win or hold a man. Almost any man, in the final analysis, respects a woman for being what she is, without pretense. Trying to hide one's interests, temperament, and abilities can later bring trouble and misunderstanding.

Paul Popenoe, marriage counselor and founder of the American Institute of Family Relations in Los Angeles, reproduced in his newspaper column a letter from a girl who said, "I'm getting tired of acting inferior to my dates in order to hold them."

Popenoe's reply was "They're probably getting more tired of it than you are."

The dating situation is one of changing sex roles, and in an area of

[19] For a discussion of some of these psychological problems see Karen Horney, *The Neurotic Personality of Our Time* (New York: W. W. Norton & Co., Inc., 1937), pp. 286–287; also J. K. Folsom, *The Family and Democratic Society,* revised edition (New York: John Wiley & Sons, Inc., 1948).

[20] Paul Wallin, "Cultural Contradictions and Sex Roles: A Repeat Study," *American Sociological Review,* 15:288–293, 1950.

locally defined—often campus-defined—custom. Although certain sex roles in dating are fairly well-defined, all are subject to challenge.

Sex Practices in Casual and Serious Dating

One of the great complications of dating—and perhaps this is the fascination of it—is that men and women approach their dates not only with different conceptions of what their roles should be, but also with different conceptions of what the opposite sex expects their role to be. Nowhere is this more evident than in the area of sex behavior. Blood's students at the University of Michigan were asked to indicate from a check list their perceptions of what the opposite sex expected of a date. They were also asked to check their own ideas of traits a good date should possess.[21]

In Table 12–1, the left-hand column shows the percentage of women checking a particular item as their idea of what men want when they take a woman out on a casual date. In the right-hand column appear college men's actual preferences. Most college women think popularity with the opposite sex is an essential. Little more than half the men think so. About

Table 12–1 Significant Discrepancies between the Female Rating Complex at the University of Michigan as Perceived by Women Students and the Actual Dating Preferences of Men Students*

Female Characteristic	Percentage of Respondents Choosing Item	
	Women's Perceptions	Men's Casual Dating Preferences
1. Is popular with the opposite sex	86.6	54.7
2. Has a car or access to a car	2.2	11.6
3. Doesn't have a reputation for necking	62.3	29.7
4. Doesn't have a reputation for petting	68.9	38.9
5. Is willing to pet on occasion	29.1	58.9
6. Is willing to join in a group	97.0	82.1
7. Is a well-rounded person	91.8	81.1
8. Is a good listener	97.0	87.4

* Differences between percentages are considered statistically significant when the probability of their occurring by chance in a sample of this size is not greater than .05.

[21] Robert O. Blood, Jr., "Uniformities and Diversities in Campus Dating Preferences," *Marriage and the Family*, 18:37–45, February, 1956.

two-thirds of the women are inclined to think that reputation concerning physical contacts (questions 3, 4, 5) has a decided bearing on being a desirable date. Men are much less particular about a woman's reputation on these matters than women think.

The following table (Table 12–2) reverses the situation and men show what they think women want in a date (left column). The right column shows what women actually want. Men rate a car much more highly than women, as they do also fraternity membership, activities, money, clothes, visits to popular places, skill in dancing, and looks. Here again differences in sex codes of men and women are in striking contrast, with women discounting a man for the kind of sex behavior men think women expect of them. It is little wonder that the sex problem has become the most critical one in modern dating relationships. It must continue to be so as long as attitudes of men and women are so far apart.

Table 12–2   Significant Discrepancies between the Male Rating Complex at the University of Michigan as Perceived by Women Students and the Actual Dating Preferences of Man Students

| | Percentage of Respondents Choosing Item | |
Male Characteristic	Men's Perceptions	Women's Casual Dating-Preferences
1. Is popular with the opposite sex	77.9	61.2
2. Has a car or access to a car	57.9	11.2
3. Doesn't have a reputation for necking	44.2	70.9
4. Doesn't have a reputation for petting	50.0	78.4
5. Is willing to pet on occasion	53.3	8.2
6. Is willing to neck on occasion	74.7	34.3
7. Is affectionate	77.7	54.5
8. Belongs to a fraternity	50.5	11.9
9. Is prominent in activities	49.5	17.2
10. Has plenty of money	34.7	6.7
11. Has plenty of clothes	20.0	4.5
12. Has polished manners	81.1	68.7
13. Dates popular students only	12.6	3.7
14. Goes to popular places	77.9	38.8
15. Knows how to dance well	76.6	49.3
16. Is good looking	86.2	61.2
17. Is willing to drink socially	50.0	32.8
18. Is natural	90.5	98.5

It is often stated that young people's attitudes toward intimate contacts during dating depends on whether or not the relationship has reached the serious and steady stage of going together. Strong support is found for this view in the responses of University of Michigan students. Men, as tradition holds, impose much higher sex behavior standards on the girl they are seriously interested in than on the girl they take on a casual date. Here are the men's responses to two key questions dealing with sexual contacts in dating:

	Prefer on casual dates (percent)	Prefer on serious dates (percent)
Doesn't have a reputation for petting	39	75
Doesn't have a reputation for necking	35	67

Almost twice as many men prefer the woman who is free with intimate behavior on casual dates as prefer the woman who is free with intimate behavior on serious dates.

Most women, by contrast, want their intimate contacts confined to serious dates. Here are college women's responses to two key questions:

	Prefer on casual dates (percent)	Prefer on serious dates (percent)
Is willing to neck on occasion	34	68
Is willing to pet on occasion	8	32

Hewitt,[22] also, finds that young people are much more selective about a marriage partner than they are about a date. Things they consider crucial in the selecting of a marriage partner, they consider as relatively unimportant concerning the date. For marriage they want companionability, which requires a mate who is well-mannered, emotionally mature, affectionate, thrifty, and who has a sense of humor.

Hewitt's study of young men and women at Ball State Teacher's College shows also that men and women have rather serious misconceptions regarding what the other sex wants in certain areas.[23] In the areas of physical attractiveness, being affectionate, and sexual conventionality, there is considerable disagreement in what men and women want in future mates. In traits like having a car, men enormously overrate what

[22] Lester E. Hewitt, "Student Perception of Traits Desired in Themselves as Dating and Marriage Partners," *Marriage and Family Living,* 20:344–349, November, 1958.

[23] *Ibid.*

they think women want. In the matter of sexual conventionality men very much underrate what women want, since women are great sticklers for convention. In the area of ambition and being sensible about money, both men and women rate these traits as very important for themselves but underrate them in the opposite sex. On the matter of rating socially, both men and women depreciate this trait for themselves but are unable to give the other sex credit for not thinking it important.

The Male Line

The sexually aggressive male has numerous techniques for turning the date into a sexually complete experience. The physical technique of love-making may be no more important than the verbalized attempts in achieving his goal. The girl must not only know where to draw the line, in terms of point of termination of necking or petting activities, but also must know what weight to give to words in terms of their motivations as persuasive techniques. Here briefly are some of the verbal tactics employed in sexual exploitation:

Technique	*Verbalization*
The domineering or threatening	"Do you think I'll spend my time and money and not . . ."
Big shot	"I've got plenty of girls who will."
Love at first sight	"No girl has ever affected me as you do."
Pity	"I'm so tense."
Injured	"But you've led me on, and now, . . ."
Shame	"Don't you have any feelings?"
Abnormal	"You're a cold cucumber."
Logic	"It's good experience, etc, . . ."
Universality	"Kinsey found . . ."
Authority	"Kirkendall believes . . ."
Restrained, calculating	No love-making, until girl breaks, then move in for the kill.

"We Do Not Sign Contracts!"

If the girl, prior to consenting to sexual intercourse, were to ask, "Are you willing to enter into a contract to support me and our child, whether we marry or not, should I become pregnant?" the atmosphere would quickly cool and some realistic consideration be brought to bear.

Professor Sophia Derbyshire of Orange Coast College says she has asked young men in her class how many would enter into such a contract and has received a universal negative; the girls seemed a little shocked by male reactions to this question.

Society has only one protective contract in the sex relationship, the marriage license. The girl who settles for less in a society as mobile as ours isn't using very good sense. This is true no matter how persuasive the argument about safety of birth control methods, the safe period, and other such considerations. The fact is that an increasing proportion of girls do get pregnant out of wedlock, about three times as many as thirty years ago when ignorance of birth control was more common and when methods were less effective.

A girl who is pregnant in her teens and decides to see the pregnancy through and care for the child, must immediately write off most of her life plans. She drops out of school, or may be unable to obtain and hold a regular job. She is likely to marry from necessity rather than choice, and someone who can give her little if any security. Had she not taken the risk she could have had many choices in life which by this one event are closed to her.[24]

Had she waited she could have saved parents much anguish and changes in their plans, for in most instances they are drawn into the situation, having to house and support the mother and child.

The Venereal Disease Consideration

Students of marriage call attention to the risks of premarital sexual intercourse, knowing quite well that fear of unwanted consequences is not the most effective control. The negative incentives are important in total awareness and the degree of sex ignorance in our culture is such that they need to be stressed.

The reasons, however, that most persons refrain from sexual relationships during dating are moral, esthetic, and futuristic considerations. They want to feel that they have not compromised themselves. This is much more likely to be a female than a male attitude, because of the different moral upbringing of the female and greater concern about a secure marriage relationship in the near future.

Although venereal disease has about disappeared as a fear in casual dating relationships, its disappearance is premature. Venereal disease is

---

[24] Arthur A. Campbell, "The Role of Family Planning in the Reduction of Poverty," *Journal of Marriage and Family Living,* 30:236–245, May, 1968.

very much on the increase, particularly among younger teen-agers. The number of new cases reported to the United States Public Health Service Communicable Disease Center has risen from a low of 6,400 in 1956 to 25,000 to 30,000 a year. Most cases are in the 15–24 year-old group. Venereal diseases have been reported in the middle- and upper-class social layers recently, not merely in the lower classes.

Venereal diseases spread from person to person almost exclusively by sexual intercourse, one infected person often spreading the disease to many others. Teen-age boys sometimes, on a dare or to prove themselves manly, go to a prostitute. Most prostitutes sooner or later acquire venereal disease. They are never safe. The pick-up girl or sexually promiscuous girl runs the same risk of contracting the disease and in turn may pass it on to a great number of males, as the infected prostitute does.

Syphilis is the most destructive of diseases, having been called the great killer of the human race. It is a great crippler as well, yet all the medical knowledge and skills are at hand for its complete eradication. President Kennedy set the year 1972 as the date when it would vanish from the nation. President Johnson reaffirmed that goal. It is paramount that doctors cooperate with the U.S. Public Health Service in reporting infected persons, and that all those who suspect they have the disease report to a reliable physician rather than depending upon unreliable "cures."

About twenty nine days after sexual contact a cancer-like sore appears at the point of infection. There may also be body rash, sore throat, headache, or other symptoms. The disease may quickly go underground but the destructive germs continue to multiply in the bloodstream. Later it will reappear, often imitating other diseases. It may cause blindness, heart trouble, crippling or general paresis, a mental disease caused by the destruction of tissue of the central nervous system. Early detection by examination even on suspicion of the disease is the only safe course. Detection is by the Wasserman Test, such as is required in the premarital medical examination in most all the states.

Gonorrhea is by far the most common venereal disease, and it has more apparent symptoms, particularly in the male. Both sexes develop a puslike discharge and burning during urination. Gonorrhea is a frequent cause of sterility in that it may close the egg and sperm ducts. A byproduct has been *blennorrhea*, blindness caused at the birth of an infant. A routine dropping of a silver nitrate into the eyes of the child has eliminated this cause of blindness.

Early treatment by reliable medical practitioners offers a remedy for both venereal diseases that is sure and relatively inexpensive, provided the infected person seeks help promptly. Negligence, using self-administered drugs, or going to quacks for treatment gives the disease a chance to do great damage, and eventually cure may be difficult or impossible.

A serious deterrent to treatment in many states is the law that an under-age person may not be treated without parental consent. The secretive nature of the ailment keeps many young people from seeking treatment. Much venereal disease, therefore, runs beyond the period of effective treatment and the infected person may spread it to many others.

There is no permanent immunity to either disease, and having the disease does not build immunity. Repeated infection is possible.

Crab lice, a flat louse which gathers in the pubic hair, is another plague of the unsanitary conditions of promiscuous intercourse.

Sexual Aggressiveness and Personality

Although dating is not always mate-choice oriented, it may eventually become so. The question as to whether sexual aggressiveness is associated with qualities that are likely to fit well in marriage is one which has not been studied thoroughly.

Kanin[25] finds sexually aggressive males most successful in obtaining sexual relations, but also finds them sexually frustrated and dissatisfied. He feels that peer-group associations with males of similar aggressiveness is a factor in their feeling of frustration, in that erotic expectations exceed accomplishment.

Dana L. Farnsworth, director of Harvard University Health Services, reports that nonconformists in sexuality are more given to depression, emotional conflict, and loss of self-esteem than others.

Riesman[26] believes a new fear may lead some to sexual quests—the fear that they may be homosexual. This fear "haunts the campuses." Males are particularly fearful in their contacts with teachers and male friends and may seek out heterosexual relationships to assure themselves.

No doubt the extent to which sexual quests represent variations from the norm in personal adjustment depends on their motivation. The above suggests that this is an area of very complex motivation. Female motivations are equally complex, and often much different.

Drinking and Sex

Drinking is one of the problems of modern dating. A comprehensive study[27] of the drinking habits of 5,000 American college women and 10,000

[25] Eugene J. Kanin, "An Examination of Sexual Aggression as a Response to Sexual Frustration," *Journal of Marriage and Family Living,* 29:428–433, August, 1967. *Family Life,* news note.

[26] David Riesman, "Permissiveness and Sex Roles," *Marriage and Family Living,* 21:211–217, August, 1959.

[27] The study is published as one of the Yale Center of Alcohol Studies publica-

American college men in 27 colleges scattered throughout the country indicates very clearly that college is not to be blamed for the drinking habits of very many young men and women. An overwhelming majority of college young people who use liquor, used it before they came to college. It was a pattern in their homes; it was imbedded in the customs of their families. The study shows that those who drink tend to associate with each other. It shows that drinking increases with the amount of income; almost as much excess drinking results from the use of beer as from stronger liquors. Comparatively few college men or women drink to the point of becoming drunk.

In clarifying the effect of drinking on dates, this study is inconclusive. While the authors recognize the folk belief that alcohol stimulates sex activity, breaks down inhibitions, and facilitates intimate contact in dating, they find that there is a counteracting tendency also; that young men who are tempted to drink to excess often restrain themselves for fear that they will be involved in violence, and that young women who may drink to excess often restrain themselves sexually for fear of the pregnancy and reputation risks involved. They find that few students attribute school problems, encounters with law, accidents, or social difficulties to their drinking. Six percent of the students who drink, however, already show tendencies toward alcoholism.

The study shows that 17 percent of men and 10 percent of women have considerable anxiety about their drinking, apparently fearing its consequences. For the most part, this group was made up of the heavy drinkers. The study also shows that drinking has greatly increased in recent generations.

Rather than alcohol being a stimulant, the authors of the study, after a review of medical research, conclude that it has a depressant effect, bringing loss of sensitivity, reducing speed of reaction, and tending to cause loss of control. They find also that it tends to reduce discrimination.

Drugs and Sex

Drugs have invaded the grade and high schools and the college campus. This brings a new series of problems into dating behavior and mate choice. Drugs are used as a way of releasing inhibitions, of relaxation and escape in much the same way as alcohol. For those who become victims, the ultimate consequences to personality, to marriage and to family life, are as bad as or worse than alcoholism.

---

tions, and is by Robert Straus and Selden D. Bacon, *Drinking in College* (New Haven: Yale University Press, 1953).

The effect of drugs on genetic material and on the fetus is as yet unknown. It will no doubt depend on the particular drug or drugs used and may depend on the quantity. There is evidence that LSD particularly is destructive to fetal development. (This problem is discussed in Chapter 16.) Research suggests that it destroys chromosomes, much as the fatal blood disease, leukemia. It is likely that drugs expose the girl to greater risk of pregnancy. A reason for the use of drugs with sex, given by young people, is that the drugs make coitus more enjoyable. This may reflect primarily a release from inhibitions. In part it may be the disorienting and illusory effect of chemically-induced reaction to the drugs themselves.

Problems

1. *Research exercise:* Poll the class with the following brief questionnaire (other questions may be added if desired). Indicate your sex but do not give your name.
   a. I have on occasion drunk while on a date.————yes
   ————no
   b. I did so—because I enjoy drinking————.
   —because I wanted to fit in with the others————.
   c. I believe drinking among students on the campus is—common————.
   d. I believe a girl who won't "neck" a little on a casual date is too prudish.
   ————yes
   ————no
   e. My feeling is "you're only young once," so if you can have some sexual thrills without running much of a risk I say go ahead.————yes
   f. I would resist heavy petting because I know it would
   —displease my parents————.
   —be unfair to my future mate————.
   —leave me with less self-respect————.
   —soon "get around"and spoil my reputation————.
   Compare results for men and women. Discuss the significance of findings to marriage and family life.
2. The following statement was made by a popular college senior who, by the way, did not drink. Analyze it and discuss its merits:
   "The reason so many of us get in trouble about drinking is that drinking is always associated in our minds with 'being adult' but 'moderation' is a virtue we cannot understand. I believe that if drinking were permitted during adolescence as is smoking, it would soon lose its mysterious appeal. Girls who want to should be able to learn to prepare a decent cocktail in college as well as a full-course dinner. Fellows who want to drink on their date should have access to decent cocktail lounges where moderation and propriety are the rule; this would make secretive drinking unnecessary and unexciting."
3. A college sophomore girl is urging her friend to accept a double date with a fellow who has a reputation for drinking and petting. Present both arguments, as each girl sees them, in a convincing manner.

4. Discuss dating regulations on your campus. Are they:
   a. Reasonable?
   b. Too lax?
   c. Outmoded?
   d. Overly authoritarian?
5. When young people of high school or college age begin to drink on dates or in mixed groups of their age mates, do you consider that they are trying to make a bid for status in their group's eyes, or to imitate Hollywood, or what are they trying to do?
6. The male animal in most species, and in most human societies, is the aggressor in male-female relationships. Do you consider that it would be against nature's design, and therefore undesirable, to encourage female initiative in dating and courtship behavior, or is this merely a matter of modifying customs? Discuss.

Selected References

Articles in Books of Readings

Cavan, Ruth S., *Marriage and the Family in the Modern World: A Book of Readings*, third edition (New York: Thomas Y. Crowell Co., 1969).

Hall, Marian D., "Understanding the Adolescent Sex Behavior," Reading 28.

Reiss, Ira L., "Sexual Codes in Teen-Age Culture," Reading 29.

Birdwhistell, Miriam, "Adolescents and the Pill Culture," Reading 30.

Herzog, Elizabeth, "Unmarried Mothers: Some Questions to be Answered and Some Answers to be Questioned," Reading 31.

Vincent, Clark E., "Unmarried Fathers," Reading 32.

Christensen, Harold T., *Handbook of Marriage and the Family* (Chicago: Rand McNally & Co., 1964).

Ehrmann, Winston, "Marital and Nonmarital Sexual Behavior," Ch. 15.

Landis, Judson T., and Landis, Mary G., *Readings in Marriage and the Family* (Englewood Cliffs, N. J.: Prentice-Hall, Inc., 1952).

Murdock, George P., "Sexual Behavior, What Is Acceptable? A Comparative Anthropological Approach," pp. 403–408.

Woodward, Luther E., "Viewpoint of the Mental Hygienist," pp. 408–412.

Kirkendall, Lester A., "Sound Attitudes Toward Sex," pp. 419–427.

Rodman, Hyman, *Marriage, Family and Society* (New York: Random House, 1965).

Riesman, David, "Permissiveness and Sex Roles," Reading 3.

Sussman, Marvin B., *Sourcebook in Marriage and the Family*, third edition (Boston: Houghton Mifflin Co., 1968).

Ehrmann, Winston W., "Premarital Dating Behavior," Reading 24.

Reiss, Ira L., "Social Class and Premarital Sexual Permissiveness: A Reexamination," Reading 25.

Vincent, Clark E., *Readings in Marriage Counseling* (New York: Thomas Y. Crowell Co., 1957).

Kirkendall, Lester A., "A Viewpoint on the Premarital Sex Problem," pp. 117–126.

General References

Bell, Robert R., and Buerkle, Jack V., "Mother and Daughter Attitudes to Premarital Sexual Behavior," *Marriage and Family Living*, 23:390–392, November, 1961.

Birdwhistell, Miriam, "Adolescents and the Pill Culture," *The Family Coordinator*, 12:27–32, January, 1968.

Broderick, Carlfred and Bernard, Jessie (eds.) *The Individual, Sex, and Society* (Baltimore, Md.: The Johns Hopkins Press, 1969).

Burgess, Ernest W., and Wallin, Paul, *Engagement and Marriage* (Philadelphia: J. B. Lippincott Co., 1953), Chs. 4, 11, 12.

Christensen, Harold T., "Scandanavian and American Sex Norms: Some Comparisons with Sociological Implications," *Journal of Social Issues*, 22:60–75, April, 1966.

Clark, Le Mon, M. D., and Rubin, Isadore, *150 Sex Questions and Answers* (New York: Health Publications, 1960).

Cohen, Sidney, *The Drug Dilemma* (New York: McGraw Hill Paperback Series In Health Education, 1969).

Croog, S. H., and Teele, J. E., "Religious Identity and Church Attendance of Sons of Religious Intermarriages," *American Sociological Review*, 32:93–103, February, 1967.

Dedman, Jean, "The Relationship Between Religious Attitude and Attitude Toward Premarital Sex Relations," *Marriage and Family Living*, 21:171–176, March, 1959.

Drucker, A. J., Christensen, Harold T., and Remmers, H. H., "Some Background Factors in Socio-Sexual Modernism," *Marriage and Family Living*, 14:334–337, November, 1952.

Duvall, Evelyn Millis, *Why Wait Till Marriage* (New York: Association Press, 1965).

Ehrmann, Winston, *Premarital Dating Behavior* (New York: Henry Holt and Co., 1959).

Furstenberg, Frank, Jr., Gordis, Leon and Markowitz, Milton, "Birth Control, Knowledge and Attitudes Among Unmarried Adolescents: a Preliminary Report," *Journal of Marriage and the Family*, 31:34–42, February, 1969.

Griden, Robert E., and Schmitt, Sue S., "Coeds and Contraceptive Information," *Journal of Marriage and the Family*, 28:471–479, November, 1966.

Kanin, Eugene J., and Howard, David H., "Postmarital Consequences of Premarital Sex Adjustment," *American Sociological Review*, 23:556–562, October, 1948.

Kinsey, Alfred C., and others, *Sexual Behavior of the Human Female* (Philadelphia: W. B. Saunders Co., 1953).

Kirkendall, Lester A., and Libby, Roger W., "Interpersonal Relationships—Crux of the Sexual Renaissance," *Journal of Social Issues*, 22:45–49, April, 1966.

Kirkpatrick, Clifford, *The Family As Process and Institution*, second edition (New York: The Ronald Press Co., 1963), Ch. 14.

Manley, F., "Toward A Syphilis Vaccine," *Science News*, 92:356, October 7, 1967.

McBroom, P., "VD Menace Alarming," *Science News*, 90:402, November 12, 1966.

Poffenberger, Thomas, and others, "Premarital Sexual Behavior: A Symposium," *Marriage and Family Living*, 24:254–278, August, 1962.

Pope, Hallowell and Knudsen, Dean D., "Premarital Sexual Norms, The Family and Social Change," *Journal of Marriage and the Family*, 27:314–323, August, 1965.

Rainwater, Lee, "Some Aspects of Lower Class Sexual Behavior," *Journal of Social Issues*, 22:96–108, 1966.

Reiss, Ira, "Contraceptive Information and Sexual Morality," *Journal of Sex Research*, 2:51–57, April, 1966.

Robinson, Ira E., King, Karl, Dudley, Charles J., and Clune, Francis J. "Change in Sexual Behavior and Attitudes of College Students," *The Family Coordinator*, 17:119–123, April, 1968.

Shipman, Gordon, "The Psychodynamics of Sex Education," *The Family Coordinator*, 17.3–12, January, 1968.

Smigel, Erwin O., and Seiden, Rita, "The Decline and Fall of the Double Standard," *The Annals*, 376:6–17, March, 1968.

Spock, Benjamin, M.D., "Too Much Sex Too Soon," *Redbook*, 130:26, January, 1968.

Straus, Robert, and Bacon, Selden D., *Drinking in College* (New Haven: Yale University Press, 1953).

Terkelsen, Helen E., *I'm Going to Have a Baby and I'm Not Married* (Philadelphia: Fortress Press, 1968).

Vincent, Clark E., "The Pregnant Single College Girl," *Journal of the American College Health Association*, May, 1967, Special Issue.

Vincent, Clark E., *Unmarried Mothers* (New York: Macmillan Co., 1969).

Walker, Brooks R., *The New Immorality* (New York: Doubleday & Co., 1968).

4

MATE CHOICE

13

Limits on Mate Choice

Finding a future spouse by our love-method may look easy to one unfamiliar with the American cultural pattern. It is not. Each person must relate himself closely with another during a period of trial and error. Few dates produce a person who meets the test for a prospective mate. Karl Wallace reviewed studies in this field over a period of twenty-five years.[1] Few men and women meet and become acquainted with more than three or four persons whom they consider suitable mates; rarely do women receive more than two or three proposals of marriage. The conclusion of even those who have dated very widely is that there are few persons in one's dating experience who could be considered really eligible.

From the background of these previous studies and from his own experience in operating a dating service, Wallace concludes that the problem of finding a suitable mate is most serious for the American middle class. This is because their moral code eliminates many of the methods of meeting mates used by the lower class and because they are more demanding in mate choice. He lists nine factors that limit their mate choice:

1. Conservative attitudes toward methods of meeting mates. They tend to taboo efforts to meet suitable persons, "wait for the right person to come along." Wallace finds that marriages more often result from the type of secondary contacts tabooed by the middle classes than in approved contacts—bars, night clubs and so on.

2. The cultural emphasis on beauty and sex. These values are especially prominent in the values of the male. They hinder many in finding a suitable mate.

3. The unbalanced sex ratio in various localities

[1] Karl Wallace, "Factors Hindering Mate Selection," *Social Forces,* 44:317–329, May–June, 1960.

4. Social stratification and segmentation. Class, race, and religious differences act as barriers.

5. Urbanization. Its complexities make the finding of a suitable mate extremely difficult because of isolation and anonymity.

6. Sex differences in attitudes and expectations which make it difficult to meet on common ground.

7. Our competitive courtship system which tends to award the aggressive, dominant, and ambitious type and to bypass the quiet, reserved, unsocial person.

8. The widowed and divorced, of whom there are thirteen million, encounter special problems.

9. Hereditary differences in glandular activity, I.Q., in health and energy, in height, weight, etc., not to mention disfiguring defects. For example, the woman who is 5 feet 10 inches tall will be excluded from the eligible list of 90 percent of the men she meets.[2]

This list of hindrances suggests that the practical problem of meeting a suitable mate is not solved merely by meeting or by dating a number of people at random.

The principle of "preferential mating" has operated[3] throughout history. Incest taboos usually bar kinsmen, although in some cultures certain kinfolk are eligible. Brother and sister marriages were the rule for certain royalty in Hawaii, Egypt, and among the Incas. Cousin marriages are not unknown in the United States and have been common in the Arab world.

Many cultures have added taboos, sacred restrictions, endogamous-exogamous rules, parental obstacles, sororal laws, rigid barriers of rank or caste, in addition to factors of age, race, religion, or nationality.

Even though few persons are ineligible by law or custom in our society, choice is still limited by virtue of the individual's own attitudes and values instilled largely by his own family. He finds few persons of the opposite sex whom he would care to marry. If divorce statistics are indicative, he may in the end choose the wrong person.

It would be fortunate indeed if some genius could develop a color chart or statistical device by which couples who find their dating becoming

---

[2] How severe extreme problems of height can be for a girl is illustrated by the case of a 6-foot 1-inch Ontario, Canada, girl who had her legs shortened by three inches. This required three operations and a total stay of six months in the hospital. Before the operation she said, "Boys would flee after a single dance," and "I felt like a freak!" "Now I can at last have happiness, marriage, and children—all the things every girl dreams of—now that men no longer have to look up to me." "Medicine Today," *Ladies Home Journal*, October, 1968, p. 55.

[3] Linton C. Freeman, "Marriage without Love: Mate-selection in Non-Western Societies," in Robert F. Winch, Robert McGinnis, and Herbert R. Barringer, *Selected Studies in Marriage and the Family* (New York: Holt, Rinehart and Winston, Inc., 1962), pp. 439–455; also Russell Middleton, "A Deviant Case: Brother-Sister and Father-Daughter Marriage in Ancient Egypt," in Rose Laub Coser, *The Family: Its Structure and Functions* (New York: St. Martin's Press, Inc., 1964), pp. 92–94.

serious would know at once whether or not they were suited to pursue each other into the pleasant but painful depths of romantic involvement.

In this area, women's insight is greater than men's. A study of marriage failures showed 70 percent of the husbands whose marriages failed felt very confident in advance that the marriage would succeed; only 48 percent of the wives.[4] Even the girl's family and her best friends are better prophets than the boy's family and his best friends.[5]

Scientific Effort to Assist in Mate Choice

As early as the 1930s, sociologists set out to direct mate choice toward success. Ernest W. Burgess and Leonard S. Cottrell did the research[6] which laid the foundation for the first marriage prediction scale. This scale has been perfected by others and similar scales have been developed. Norms have gradually been built. The scales are not as reliable yet, as for instance, American College Entrance Examination, which predicts college performance, but the ACE test is built on norms of hundreds of thousands.[7]

Sociologists believe that marriage can as accurately be predicted as college performance, job performance, and any other area of social behavior by the building of norms by which persons and pairs can be measured. Most marriage clinics, like guidance and vocational placement clinics, now use some kind of measuring devices which give couples a tentative profile of their temperaments and personalities, and interpret findings as

[4] Ernest W. Burgess and Paul Wallin, *Engagement and Marriage* (Philadelphia: J. B. Lippincott Co., 1953), p. 563.

[5] *Ibid.*, pp. 565–566.

[6] *Ibid.*

[7] Clifford Adams in his book *How to Pick a Mate* (New York: E. P. Dutton & Co., Inc., 1946), published a list of traits on which both men and women should check themselves; also other traits by which a couple could match their personalities by totaling up the score. Many of his traits are from the Burgess-Cottrell *Marriage Prediction Scale,* which itself was a tentative measurement device for predicting marriage adjustment. For many years Dr. Paul Popenoe and his colleagues in the American Institute of Family Relations in Los Angeles have used Roswell Johnson's *Temperament Test* as a means of helping a person to understand himself and as a guide to his marriageability. Both Adams and Popenoe report very favorable results from the use of these instruments, supplemented by premarital counseling and medical advice. How much of their success in guidance is due to the measurement devices and how much to the intangible aspects of the counseling experience is unknown. Burgess and Cottrell, as a consequence of their pioneer research, *Predicting Success or Failure in Marriage* (Englewood Cliffs, N. J.: Prentice-Hall, Inc., 1939), developed a marriage prediction scale which has had wide usage in various modified forms. Karl Wallace, a Ph.D. in Sociology, has attempted to put dating on a scientific basis with his Introduction Service (The Karl Wallace Foundation, 270 South Alexandria, Los Angeles). He uses punch cards and statistically matches persons for introduction. See his book, *Love is More Than Luck* (New York: Wilfred Funk, Inc., 1957).

they relate to marriageability. These tests, along with personal guidance, and medical examinations are used to appraise likelihood of success. These are standard procedures for those who seek such guidance. The body of research knowledge still accumulates and will provide a better guide for the future.

Not all persons are marriageable. Many persons—and these cause much difficulty—are marginal in marriageability. Unfortunately, datability and marriageability are not synonymous. A person may seem very interesting on a short-time acquaintance, but become intolerable as a long-time companion. On the other hand, many people who have little or no opportunity to date are very marriageable persons. So the winnowing process goes on, not always logically, and certainly with much error in judgment, as the rate of marriage failures shows.

In movie-made romance, impulse is assumed to be a safe and infallible guide. Few intelligent young people, particularly those who have had some variety in steady dating, can believe in impulse as a safe guide. They know from experience that one must be alert to the long-term values in the man-woman relationship. Unless they get completely carried away, young couples know that differences in ideas and values, aspirations and life goals are basic in determining the success or failure of marriage.

On college campuses, young people are very much aware of these long-term values when they begin to face the serious business of mate selection. For example, a group of students were asked to rate eighteen factors in order of importance in mate selection. Both men and women put "dependable character" first. They rated emotional stability and maturity second. Pleasing disposition was rated third. Mutual love and attraction was fourth on the list, showing that this group was well aware that love is not all that matters. Here are some other traits in the order in which they were listed: good health, desire for home and children, refinement, neatness, ambition and industriousness, good cook and housekeeper, chastity, education and general intelligence, sociability, similar religious background, good looks, similar educational background, favorable social status or rating, good financial prospects, similar political background.[8]

Engaged men and women rate compatibility and common interests much higher as factors conducive to success in marriage than either love or sex as such.[9]

During the last thirty years, sociologists and psychologists have directed a great deal of research to the problem of sorting out the marriageable and unmarriageable on the basis of personality traits, social background, developmental history, parental relationships, and other such

[8] Reuben Hill, "Campus Values in Mate Selection," *Journal of Home Economics,* 37:557 ff., November, 1945.
[9] Ernest W. Burgess and Paul Wallin, *Engagement and Marriage* (Philadelphia: J. B. Lippincott Co., 1953), p. 412.

factors. This research has also called attention to the problem of matching —that is, of learning what kinds of people can safely marry. For example, is there anything to the notion that like backgrounds, like temperaments, like religion are desirable? Or is variety truly the spice of life?

Since experience is the only safe guide, research has attempted to bring together the experiences of hundreds of persons who, successfully or otherwise, have run the gauntlet of mate selection. Although the experiences of a multitude could never give an infallible answer to anyone, they can at least clarify the nature of the mate-selecting problem.

Is There an Ideal Mate?

In the dreamy days of adolescent romance young people are likely to feel that their love is heaven sent, that they were created for each other. The idea that there is somewhere in the universe a "one and only" for everyone is deeply rooted in fiction and tradition. Probably due to the dating custom, this idea is fast losing ground.

A more practical view is that the loving, well-adjusted person can marry any one of a number of people and be happy, whereas the maladjusted, unhappy person can be successfully married to no one.[10] This view emphasizes the thought that one needs to be the "right" person. It agrees with marriage counselors and students of marriage who know that one finds in marriage much of what he takes into it. Ceremony has no magic power to make people over. Happy and successful persons make successful marriages.

While the view that no one is predestined for any specific member of the opposite sex is generally accepted today, young people nonetheless have some concept of the traits and qualities they want their mate to have. A study of college young people shows[11] that almost a third of the men and almost a fourth of the women are very conscious of the characteristics of their ideal mate. Almost equal numbers have a vague consciousness of such ideals. Very, very few are entirely without any awareness of what their ideal mate should be like.

Research has attempted to define the ideal mate in terms of general background. Here are the ten factors in the background of a person which will tell most about his marriageability.[12]

[10] Proposed in lectures by Ralph Eckert, who has had many years of experience working with young people in high schools and colleges.

[11] Ernest W. Burgess and Paul Wallin, *Engagement and Marriage* (Philadelphia: J. B. Lippincott Co., 1953), p. 188.

[12] Lewis M. Terman and others, *Psychological Factors in Marital Happiness* (New York: McGraw-Hill Book Co., 1938), pp. 366–367. This study analyzed the background factors in the happiness and unhappiness of 792 married couples.

1. superior happiness of parents
2. childhood happiness
3. lack of conflict with mother
4. home discipline that was firm, not harsh
5. strong attachment to mother
6. strong attachment to father
7. lack of conflict with father
8. parental frankness about matters of sex
9. infrequency and mildness of childhood punishment
10. premarital attitude toward sex that was free from disgust or aversion

Any person who possesses all ten of these is a much better than average risk in marriage.

It will be seen at a glance that all of these important background factors indicating favorable marriage prospects have to do with interpersonal relationship in early home life, with the example the parents have provided, and with the attitudes and training they have passed along to their children. Of all the factors listed, happiness of parents' marriage and one's own childhood happiness are most deterministic. This was indicated not only by the research cited above but is further confirmed by several additional studies.[13] Few children from unhappy homes make happy marriages.

Marriage happiness runs in families; so does unhappiness and divorce. One judge of a divorce court, addressing an audience, felt this so strongly that he said, "I sometimes think divorce is hereditary." Heredity, of course, is not the primary cause of the problem. The vital factor is rather the pattern of adjustment set in the home. But marital unhappiness and divorce do, nonetheless, run in families. Parents who are happy, well mated, and who settle problems together, set a pattern of relationships children learn and carry into their own homes. Families characterized by constant bickering between parents and brothers and sisters also set a pattern that children are likely to imitate in their associations with each other and carry over into their relationship as husbands or wives. Families which are unhappy, in which husband and wife are dissatisfied with each other, in which there is pessimism and gloom, pass these traits on in the habits and attitudes of their children. This, in turn, complicates the job young people face in establishing and maintaining a happy home and a desirable place for rearing their own offspring.

Close relationships between child and parent are shown to be favor-

---

[13] Ernest W. Burgess and Leonard S. Cottrell, *Predicting Success or Failure in Marriage* (Englewood Cliffs, N. J.: Prentice-Hall, Inc., 1939), pp. 101 ff. Deals with 526 marriages. Paul Popenoe and Donna Wicks, "Marital Happiness in Two Generations," *Mental Hygiene*, 21:218–223, 1937. Deals with 4,000 marriages. Judson T. Landis has found that divorce tends to run in families. For a summary of data see Ch. 30.

able to marriage.[14] Yet a boy may not fall in love with a girl without a feeling of guilt about forsaking his mother. There are the girls who can't possibly leave home because father and mother need them. Too strong family attachments take on the character of fixation and make marriage impossible. This is one of the most important reasons why otherwise normal people do not marry. Good relationships with parents must be within the normal range of emotional attachment, which means that the young person, when the time comes for mate choice, must be capable of making the chosen member of the opposite sex the first person in his affections.

Theories of Mate Choice

Sociologists and psychologists have propounded various theories of mate choice, some dealing with more obvious environmental factors, others with subtle and largely unconscious forces in the personality.

Value theory   Robert H. Coombs has expounded a "value theory" of mate choice which he feels incorporates most other theories, or at least explains the factors which make them a reality. Briefly, he holds that each person possesses a value system which consciously or unconsciously guides him in mate selection.[15]

Propinquity theory   Considerable study has centered around the idea of propinquity as a major factor in mate choice. The theory originally was applied to those living in the same general neighborhood. Some would now include those who go to school or work together. This theory states that people must and usually do meet each other by some form of daily association—same neighborhood, school, church, or office. To stress propinquity and engage in extensive proof, as has been so often done, would seem to be an elaboration of the obvious.

Parental image theory   Freudian in origin, this theory holds that the child tends to develop a deep affection for the parent of the opposite sex: boy for his mother, girl for her father. In certain instances, the tie may be between a brother and sister or other sibling. In the mate chosen the youth

---

[14] This was shown, not only by Terman and others, but also by Burgess and Cottrell, *op. cit.*, pp. 341–349.

[15] Robert H. Coombs, "A Value Theory of Mate Selection," *Family Life Coordinator*, 10:51–54, July, 1961; also Robert H. Coombs, "Reinforcement of Values in the Parental Home is a Factor in Mate Selection," *Marriage and Family Living*, 24:155–157, May, 1962.

sees the image of this childhood attachment. This puts mate choice largely on a level below consciousness.

The theory has not been well substantiated. To accept it at face value would be to make the study of mate choice largely meaningless, for it would remove choice largely from the voluntary level, assigning it to the predestination of childhood parental attachments.

Coombs concludes that since the parents are the agents of socialization, the parents and child hold similar values. This becomes a basis for choice of a mate who has characteristics and values similar to those of the parents. Strauss[16] finds little similarity per se, but he concludes that parents do influence choice in that if the child has shared meaningful relationships with parent, he wishes to find similar traits in the mate; if hostile relationships with parents have persisted, he seeks different traits in the mate.

Complementary needs theory   The theory of complementary needs has been propounded by Winch and given some testing, but it lacks objective support. It assumes that the individual seeks out a mate to complement his own personality.

All students of the family accept the view that wish fulfillment is the strongest motive for marriage. Folk knowledge too takes this for granted. But Winch introduced the theory to explain why a particular person picks the mate he does. He holds that "in mate selection the need-pattern of each spouse will be complementary rather than similar to the need-pattern of the other spouse."[17] It is as though the mate is chosen to fill out weaknesses of one's own personality. In these psychological needs, opposites tend to attract, thus complementing the self.

Although this theory is a challenging one, and Winch found some support for it with a small sample, other researchers have failed to confirm it. In fact, the preponderance of evidence to date leads to the conclusion that the theory has no foundation.[18] Quite to the contrary, couples want to satisfy similar needs in each other.[19]

Homogamy theory   This theory is concerned with whether or not a

---

[16] Anselm Strauss, "The Influence of Parent-Image upon Marital Choice," *"American Sociological Review,* 11:554–559, October, 1946.

[17] Robert F. Winch, *Mate Selection: A Study of Complementary Needs* (New York: Harper & Row, Publishers, 1958).

[18] Charles E. Bowerman and Barbara R. Day, "A Test of the Theory of Complementary Needs as Applied to Couples during Courtship," *American Sociological Review,* 21:602–605, 1956; also James A. Shellenberg and Lawrence S. Bee, "A Reexamination of the Theory of Complementary Needs in Mate Selection," *Marriage and Family Living,* 22:227–232, 1960.

[19] See data from Anselm Strauss' Ph.D. thesis in this area, summarized in E. W. Burgess, Harvey J. Locke, and Mary Margaret Thomas, *The Family,* third edition (New York: American Book Co., 1963), p. 261.

person in mate seeking chooses one with similar or different (heterogamous) economic, racial, religious characteristics. In general, we know that like marries like, particularly in general social characteristics, and that the more homogamous pair succeeds most often in marriage. Similarity in church background, education, economic background, social class,[20] age, race, moral and religious background is important. Even the divorced and the widowed tend to marry their kind.[21] It is in this general area that most fruitful sociological research has centered.

"Ideal mate" theory   This last theory assumes that the individual has some more or less tangible idea of the perfect mate for him. Coombs would hold that one's conception of an ideal mate for oneself is within the framework of one's value constructs.

Personality Factors in Mate Selection

A person with dating experience learns that some personalities clash, while others supplement each other, creating a feeling of completeness. The "battle of the sexes" is a frequently heard phrase and has some meaning, yet antagonism cannot be the rule of successful pair relationships. Some couples may profit from a flare-up once in a while. In temperament and disposition couples need not be alike, but they must supplement each other, giving a sense of need fulfillment.

It has even been found[22] that the extrovert may successfully marry the introvert, but this does not mean that all extroverts will be satisfied with introverts as mates. More often the socially active marry others with the same interests. One person may find a sense of security and the satisfaction of emotional needs in a person of like temperament; another may find his own personality filled out by someone quite his opposite in temperament.

One person may need a mate to lean upon while another needs to feel that he or she is the tower of strength in any relationship. One person needs the center of the stage and wants to marry an admirer rather than

---

[20] See, for example, August B. Hollingshead, *Elmtown's Youth* (New York: John Wiley & Sons, Inc., 1949), p. 211.

[21] Charles E. Bowerman, "Assortative Mating by Previous Marital Status, Seattle, 1939–1946," *American Sociological Review*, 18:170–177, April, 1953; also T. C. McCormick and A. P. Sundal, "Age at Marriage and Mate Selection," *American Sociological Review*, 16:37–48, February, 1951. Jerold S. Heiss and Michael Gordon, "Need Patterns and Mutual Satisfaction of Dating and Engaged Couples," *Marriage and Family Living*, 26:337–338, August, 1964.

[22] Terman and others, *op. cit.*, pp. 125 ff.

a competitor; another feels more secure when he or she can stay in the background and bask in the mate's accomplishments.

Most men, in persistent traditional patterns, prefer to be the strong member of the household. Probably most women like them to be. Women of dependent disposition must marry this kind of man in order to be happy. The sensitive, insecure, cautious man may need a maternal type generous with comfort and sympathy. This man will often marry a woman considerably older than himself. A high-strung person may need a placid mate, or he may want one with whom to race through life. Two strong-willed persons may date, but may have so many clashes of will that the relationship ends short of marriage. If they marry, one or both will have to learn to give ground, and they may still agree to disagree in certain compartments of their lives. The chances are they may be happier with more yielding partners, although even here rules are hard to make.

Personality tests help some people in understanding themselves and their prospective mate. Counselors' advice, based on test results, is often even more helpful. There is, however, no substitute for an extended period of going steady, followed by an engagement of at least six months, to test compatibility of personality types in real-life situations. In the early days of going steady, couples are on their good behavior. It is only after long acquaintance that the mask is laid aside and the real self begins to show. When this stage is reached, the serious couple will know if they antagonize or complement each other. The adjustment that results will be symptomatic of future marriage relationships.

Background Factors

The approach to wise mate choice by studying specific personality traits has not been particularly rewarding. Various personality and temperament traits considered in constellation, as is done with tests in premarital counseling services, can be very indicative of one person's marriageability and the likelihood of a pair's success in marriage. But they take careful administration by experts and even more careful interpretation.

Students of marriage have found that the most critical sociological factors in determining success are what may be called general cultural background factors. Marriage requires the blending of two ways of life, as represented by two families, into a common way of life. A marriage is, in a very real sense, a continuation of family patterns already existent in the personalities of the couple themselves.

Chapters 14 and 15 focus attention on broad sociocultural factors as they affect marriage.

Problems

1. Recently the Master of Ceremonies of a radio quiz show asked a female participant how she met her husband. She answered, "I was brought up very strictly and although I dated a number of young men, none of them ever lived up to my high standards. I was thirty-two and on vacation in New York when I finally met the right one. It was just as I knew it would be. A friend introduced me to this fellow and after one date we were sure that we were meant for each other. We got married immediately and we haven't been unhappy for a moment since then." "How long ago was that?" the Master of Ceremonies asked in amazement. "Last month," the woman replied. "We're on our honeymoon."

   In your opinion is this woman one of the rare few to find her ideal mate? Was there anything in her statement to suggest that the future may be less rosy?

2. In the light of evidence in the chapter studied, would you say similarity of background is generally more significant in marriage success than similarity of temperament? Discuss.

3. Try to type men and women whom you feel should never get married.

4. After hearing the following statement from a young bride-to-be, a marriage counselor urged the young couple to either postpone their marriage for a while or else to consider continued counseling after the marriage should take place. Read the statement and decide whether or not the counselor's requests seem justified. What do you think were his reasons for urging a delay?

   "I think I'll make Ted a pretty good wife because I'm not sloppy and unstrung like so many girls I know. I like to get up at exactly 6:45. In fact, I always get up then. It upsets me until I'm almost ill if I have to stay in bed later for some reason.

   "The first think I do is make my bed. That takes about twelve minutes, because I like it perfect. If I see a wrinkle or a crooked sheet it bothers me all morning. Then I wash my hands and face and scrub my fingernails with a disinfectant soap.

   "There won't be any germs in our house! I rinse the plates and cups off too and I rub each spoon and fork with a clean napkin. I'm just that way with everything. It takes all my time but it pays off. I'm healthy and strong and I'm determined to keep my Ted healthy too."

5. Do you think most young couples fear what a premarital counseling session in a marriage clinic would reveal about themselves? Should they?

Selected References

Articles in Books of Readings

Goode, William J., *Readings on the Family and Society* (Englewood Cliffs, N. J.: Prentice-Hall, Inc., 1964).

   Kerckhoff, Alan C., and Davis, Keith E., "Value Consensus and Need Complementarity in Mate Selection," pp. 83–89.

Landis, Judson T., and Landis, Mary G., *Readings in Marriage and the Family* (Englewood Cliffs, N. J.: Prentice-Hall, Inc., 1952).

Strauss, Anselm, "The Influence of Parent-Images upon Marital Choice," pp. 99–106.

Rodman, Hyman, *Marriage, Family and Society* (New York: Random House, 1965).

Rodman, Hyman, "Mate Selection: Incest Taboos, Homogamy, and Mixed Marriages," Reading 4.

Hollingshead, August B., "In-group Marriage in the Upper Middle Class," Reading 5.

Sussman, Marvin B., *Sourcebook in Marriage and the Family*, third edition (Boston: Houghton Mifflin Co., 1968).

Hollingshead, August B., "Cultural Factors in the Selection of Marriage Mates," Reading 26.

Kirkpatrick Clifford, "A Statistical Study of the Psychoanalytical Theory of Mate Selection," Reading 28.

Winch, Robert F., and Goodman, Louis W., *Selected Studies in Marriage and the Family*, third edition (New York: Holt, Rinehart and Winston, Inc., 1968).

Hollingshead, August B., "Cultural Factors in the Selection of Marriage Mates," pp. 486–495.

Sugimoto, Etsu N., "Old Love and New," pp. 451–453.

Vogel, Ezra F., "Modern Japanese Marriage," pp. 453–454.

Katz, Alvin M., and Hill, Reubin, "Residential Propinquity and Marital Selection: A Review of Theory, Method, and Fact," pp. 496–503.

General References

Blood, Robert O., Jr., *Love Match and Arranged Marriage: A Tokyo-Detroit Comparison* (New York: The Free Press, 1967).

Brothers, Joyce, "What a Man Really Wants In a Woman," *Good Housekeeping*, February, 1967, pp. 58 ff.

Clarke, Alfred C., "Residential Propinquity as a Factor in Mate Selection," *American Sociological Review*, 17:17–22, February, 1952.

Hewitt, Lester E., "Student Perception of Traits Desired in Themselves as Dating and Marriage Partners," *Marriage and Family Living*, 20:344–349, November, 1958.

Korson, J. Henry, "Student Attitudes toward Mate Selection in Muslim Society: Pakistan," *Journal of Marriage and the Family*, 31:153–164, February, 1969.

Lind, A. W., "Interracial Marriage as Affecting Divorce in Hawaii," *Sociology and Social Research*, 39:17–26, October 19, 1964.

Mudstein, Bernard I., "Empirical Tests of Role, Complementary Needs, and Homogamy Theories of Marital Choice," *Journal of Marriage and the Family*, 39:689–696, November, 1967.

Snyder, Eloise C., "Attitudes: A Study of Homogamy and Marital Selectivity," *Marriage and Family Living*, 26:332–335, August, 1964.

Stephens, William N., *The Family in Cross-Cultural Perspective* (New York: Holt, Rinehart and Winston, 1963), Ch. 4.

Udry, J. Richard, "The Influence of the Ideal Mate Image on Mate Selection and Mate Perception," *Journal of Marriage and the Family*, 27:477–482, November, 1965.

Udry, J. Richard, "Personality Match and Interpersonal Perception as Predictors of Marriage," *Journal of Marriage and the Family*, 28:722–725, November, 1967.

Wallace, Karl, *Love Is More than Luck* (New York: Funk & Wagnalls Co., Inc., 1957).

Winch, Robert F., "The Theory of Complementary Needs in Mate Selection: An Analytical Descriptive Study," *American Sociological Review*, 19:241–249, June, 1954.

14

Religion in Mate Choice

The symbolism of the great religions of the western world is that of marriage and the family. The concept of bride, groom, father, son, brother, mother and child are central. The values and goals for human attainment are quite the same for both the family and the religious body. The fellowship in both the religious body and the family unit are described in similar terms. In fact, each of the three major faiths is comprehensible in terms of family interrelationships.

There is every reason to expect that those who are trained in the values supported by religion would succeed in marriage, that religious people would have the values, beliefs, and expectations internalized as guidelines for themselves that would help make marriage and family a success. There is the added fact that the religious body gives support to morality, stability, kindness, self-sacrifice, cooperation, goodness, in all aspects of human behavior. Church leadership is often able to provide wise counsel from the pulpit or in private, lending further social support in the direction of success in marriage and family life. The moral-religious system is the strongest restraint against sex outside marriage, both marital and premarital. Living by the sex code is favorable to marriage success.

If everyone could live up to the ideals of his religion, there could be no marriage and family problems, but these ideals are neither well taught nor acted out for the younger generation.

Religious bodies, stripped down to their bare ideal for humanity are quite alike. Unfortunately elaborate creeds are built up, and systems of taboos and procedural routines often become the main concern of the conscientious adherents.

The Sociological Problem

Religion has become one of the great cultural barriers in the western world, and the sabbath, the holy day of "segregation," with each major religious group going its separate way. This separate procession leads all the way to the cemetery. Among the dominant Protestant group, there are over 200 denominations and sects each with slightly different creed, many of them claiming to be the "only way." A framework of ritual, taboos, and beliefs, by which to justify their separateness, is maintained.

Each Protestant denomination has erected its own barriers by which it resists unity with the whole Christian body. Comparatively few of these barriers are ever torn down to allow merging to take place. Each perpetuates its teaching, bringing up a child in "the way he should go." Each depends largely upon the success of the upbringing of children in the faith for its growth and even its survival. Each strives to see that young people choose mates from the "in-group," if not the exact denomination, then one with similar tenets and sociomoral systems.

All church bodies are concerned with the mate choice of members and even more so with the way children of their members are trained in religion. The Jew and Catholic tends to require religious training. The Protestant groups are more permissive, even if no less concerned. They are more likely to depend on persuasion than on oaths or commandments, or cannonical pronouncements, but the goals are the same—to retain a body of believers through the generations.

Part of the reason for Protestant leniency is the more democratic approach to all matters of personal choice, the very essence of Protestantism itself. But Protestant bodies have less to fear, being the dominant group, proportionately, few marry outside their faith. They are less exposed to membership loss than either Jew or Catholic.

The sociologist's perspective considers the effect of religion on marriage and family outcome. The church is concerned for the survival of the religious institution as well. The sociological problem is the impact of religion on the total complex of family relationships; the church, life itself and human destiny.

Although the religious and sociological perspectives are different, they overlap. The very concern of church bodies about marriage, family life, and child training often interferes with the marriage relationship itself, particularly where there is a conflict of loyalties, as in the interfaith marriage. No matter how critical one may be about any given religious body's aggressiveness or arbitrariness about increasing the flock, many church leaders, perhaps most of them, have a deep human concern about the success of marriage and parenthood of their adherents. In their practical way, they are students of the marriage relationship and are more closely involved than sociologists possibly could be in marriage and family interactions and the problems involved in interfaith marriages.

The Ecumenical Trend

This decade has brought a strong ecumenical trend. The Catholic Church has accepted the reformation, not for itself, but for Protestants. Protestantism is becoming more merger-minded. The doctrine of segregation has been attacked in all fields of human relationships. Strong secular influences in American life have created a skepticism of church taboos and even ancient teachings, where these do not seem to tally with sociological knowledge and current concepts of human welfare. It has become much easier for young people, particularly young college people, to choose the rational at the cost of the traditional.

In this kind of world the question may well be raised as to whether religion is any longer a factor of concern to the student of marriage and family. Certainly most of the research in the field is outdated in the rapidly changing social climate of today. Even if it were fully current, it might well have less applicability to tomorrow than yesterday. However not all past research is invalid as a guide for the future.

Similar problems exist which have not been eliminated by changes in institutions or personal value systems. Marriages which cross barriers of faith still have certain unique problems to overcome that are not present in a marriage between persons of similar religious beliefs. Marriages between believers and nonbelievers have even more. Marriages of two people with no religious background will have greater difficulty still, as in the past. Sociological measures of degree of difficulty are faulty, but they point clearly toward special marriage problems in the interfaith marriage and those without a church tie.

Measurable Indices

There are various measurable indices of church-religious influence. Sociological studies have used them all in assessing the relationships between religion and success or failure of marriage. The assumption is that a positive relationship exists between church ties and marriage success.

Critical analysis may well challenge the casual relationship, thus robbing religion of its claim to making better people. Certainly the church either draws better people, or helps make them. Every church-religious index is associated with marriage success. The success index is not 100 percent by any means, but it is higher for those with religious connections than those without. Here are the usual indices used; frequency of church attendance, marriage by religious ceremony, Sunday-school attendance, being devout, being a member of a religious body.

Even interfaith marriages are favorable compared to marriages of persons outside all faiths. The evidence will be surveyed in due course.

The Interfaith Marriage

Interfaith marriages are likely to increase very rapidly in our nation of mixed religious backgrounds, growing religious tolerance, increasing secular orientation, and the bringing together of more young people in large groups in school and college where the issue of religious differences is minimal. The church academy and church college were once most effective in seeing that young people married in the faith, even in the particular denomination. They no longer handle much of the total youth population; the school atmosphere is generally secular, and campus life is not much given to religious exercise. Even the Greek houses are more tolerant and less exclusive in membership. Sororities have been the upper class mother's greatest assurance of her daughter marrying into the "right" race, religion and social class. It is true to a much lesser degree now.

While all of this means that the religious issue will in time become less significant in marriage, more people will be involved, even if their experience may be less serious than would have been true historically.

The Statistical Picture of Interfaith Marriages

In 1958 the Census Bureau published, for the first time, a nationwide picture of the extent of mixed marriages involving the three major religious groups in America—Protestant, Roman Catholic, and Jewish.[1] Data are for all persons 14 years old and over, and cover 36,576,000 couples. Here is the situation as reported:

Like Religion

Both Roman Catholic	8,361,000
Both Protestant	24,604,000
Both Jewish	1,258,000

[1] U.S. Department of Commerce, Bureau of the Census, "Religion Reported by the Civilian Population of the United States, March, 1957," *Current Population Reports: Population Characteristics*, Series P-20, No. 79, February 2, 1958.

Mixed Religion

Protestant-Roman Catholic	2,255,000
Protestant-Jewish	57,000
Roman Catholic-Jewish	41,000
	2,353,000

Proportionately, Catholics suffer most from interreligious marriages, over a fifth (21.2 percent) marry Protestants, and a few (0.4 percent) marry Jews. A detailed breakdown of the extent of interfaith marriages is presented in Figure 14–1. Of all marriages in the three major religious bodies, 6.4 percent were interfaith.

While these data suggest that the intermarriage problem is of significant dimensions, sample studies indicate that the actual number of persons crossing the major interfaith barriers in marriage is about twice as high as shown by the Census data. Many abandon their church before or after the ceremony. Although they are of different faiths in background, the difference has vanished as a statistical fact. The authorities of the U.S. Census Bureau have expressed the view that Census enumerators may have in some cases overlooked the fact that the husband and wife might be of different religions. Convincing studies have shown that the Jewish-Gentile marriages in the nation constitute about 13 percent.[2] Sample studies of Catholic marriages, although less extensive in scope, suggest that those of Catholic background cross the line in 35 to 50 percent of cases. Jesuit sociologist John L. Thomas of St. Louis University places the figures at almost half of all marriages, if the invalid (those not sanctioned by the church) are added to the valid interfaith Catholic marriages.[3]

These data may accurately represent the approximate ratio of outgroup marriages among the different major faiths, but in all cases, the number of these is approximately twice as high as shown.

Locke and his colleagues have proposed the thesis that, other things being equal, interfaith marriages will increase as the minority group decreases in ratio to the total population.[4] But in this area other things are never equal. The Jewish group is the smaller ratio group but maintains an in-group loyalty unmatched by the Catholic group.

The smaller the minority group, the greater its exposure to the outgroups is likely to be, but the factor of more importance than this is the strength of the religious tradition. Another important variable, too, is the degree of difference in the religious faiths pairs have to bridge.

[2] Erich Rosenthal, *Studies of Jewish Intermarriage in the United States,* Vol. 64, *American Jewish Year Book,* 1963. (Also in a reprint pamphlet.)

[3] John L. Thomas, *The American Catholic Family* (Englewood Cliffs, N. J.: Prentice-Hall, Inc., 1956).

[4] Harvey J. Locke, George Sabagh, and Mary Margaret Thomes, "Interfaith Marriages," *Social Problems,* 4:329–333, April, 1957.

FIGURE 14-1   INGROUP AND OUTGROUP MARRIAGES IN THE CIVILIAN
POPULATION, UNITED STATES, 1957 (36,576,000 MARRIAGES). Source:
U.S. Department of Commerce, Bureau of the Census, "Religion Reported
by the Civilian Population of the United States, March, 1957," **Current Population Reports: Population Characteristics,** Series P-20, No. 79, February
2, 1958.

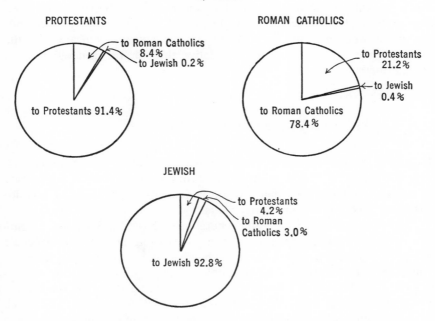

A high proportion of Catholics in our predominantly Protestant country
marry outside their faith. Actual rate of people marrying out of their faith
may run twice as high as shown here.

There are no legal barriers to marriage across religious lines, yet
most church groups advise against it. The Catholic group places important
restrictions on interfaith marriages, and the Orthodox Jewish group prohibits it altogether. Still, studies show that approximately half of college
students would cross these major religious barriers in marriage if other
aspects of the relationship were satisfactory.[5] Gordon[6] studied attitudes

[5] The initial study by Ray E. Baber asked, "All other things being satisfactory,
would you marry a person with a different religious faith (Catholic, Jewish, Protestant) than your own?" He received replies from 642 students in New York University. Ray E. Baber, *Marriage and the Family,* second edition (New York: McGraw-Hill Book Co., 1953), p. 119. Judson T. Landis repeated the question to 2,000
Michigan State students in 1947 and to 1,600 students in 11 colleges in 1952 and
repeated the study in 1967. See Judson T. Landis and Mary Landis, *Building a Successful Marriage,* fifth edition (Englewood Cliffs, N. J.: Prentice-Hall, Inc., 1968),
Ch. 18.

[6] Albert L. Gordon, *Intermarriage,* (Boston: Beacon Press, 1964), Ch. 2.

of 5,407 college students in some 40 colleges and universities of the nation. He found 37 percent of non-Jews would marry Jews; 56 percent of non-Catholics would marry Catholics. In the total sample, half did not favor marriage to a person of another religion.

Almost half of husbands in interfaith marriage studied by Prince[7] would be willing for their children to enter such a marriage, and well over a third of wives would be willing. Less than a fourth of husbands and wives were negative on this subject. This would indicate that the effect of interfaith marriage is cumulative through the generations that do intermarry.

Religion and Marriage Adjustment

Judson T. Landis[8] found a very positive association between religiousness and success of marriage. Those reporting no faith showed a high rate of marriage failure. These findings are consistent with findings of sociologists over a period of some thirty years.[9]

Rockwell Smith,[10] an astute churchman, has observed that religion is a very great socializing factor. During the dating period, young people are so completely wrapped up in each other and so completely satisfied emotionally that they tend to overlook the place of religion and church activities in their lives. However, when they settle down to the adjustments of marriage and community life, they wish to revive ties which have been most meaningful to them. Each then naturally turns to his own church and the church group he has found congenial.

If the couple are of the same religious faith, this building of the marriage into the larger fellowship of the church group is made easy and natural. If, however, they have different religious backgrounds, a great handicap faces them as they try to build church relationships. Instead of being able to participate naturally in the same kind of religious exercise in the community, there is a tendency to compete for church loyalty. The couple constantly finds a block in the way of their joint participation in any kind of religious activity.

[7] Alfred J. Prince, "A Study of 194 Cross-Religion Marriages, *The Family Life Coordinator,* 9:3–7, January, 1962.

[8] Judson T. Landis, "Religiousness, Family Relationships and Family Values in Protestant, Catholic and Jewish Families," *Marriage and Family Living,* 22:241–247, November, 1960.

[9] Carle C. Zimmerman and Lucius F. Cervantes, *Successful American Families,* (New York: Pageant Press, Inc., 1960).

[10] Rockwell Smith in Howard Becker and Reuben Hill, *Family, Marriage and Parenthood,* revised edition (Boston: D. C. Heath & Co., 1954), Ch. 20.

It is often only after marriage that the couple begins to realize, too, how deeply embedded are the philosophies of life and standards of behavior that form a part of any religious faith. A person who has had his life and goals oriented around the goals and aspirations that are the essence of his faith finds religion more significant in his life than he has realized. Often the person who has been quite casual in his religious attitudes has more deep-seated religious values than he is aware of until these values come into direct opposition to the values of a person whose core of religious philosophy is quite different.

These facts are probably the basis of the findings of sociological research which indicate that, where couples are not matched in religious background, their church participation usually decreases after the marriage. Many couples probably find this the only way to peace. Even though it may not bring satisfaction, it may at least help to reduce tensions. For example, Zimmerman and Cervantes found that about half the Catholic men they studied who were involved in interfaith marriages abandoned their faith.[11]

The issue comes to a head when children enter the family and the question arises as to whether or not to train them religiously, and if so, in what religion. It is then, most frequently, that the problem of religious differences becomes something besides a theoretical question between two individuals. How a child's faith will be directed and his life values established are certain to be of deep concern to parents. With this background, let us consider the findings of research.

Persons with and without Religious Connections

It was indicated that religious persons show evidence of greater success in marriage. There are various measures of church and religious affiliation as they relate to marriage. In 1967, Judson T. Landis related marriage survival to being married in church. This study of 581 couples married an average of 7 years showed that 84 percent had been married in a church. Of a control group taking counseling because of marriage difficulties only 41 percent were married in a church, and of a divorced group also compared, only 55 percent had been married in a church. Even interfaith marriages have a better record than those between persons without religious affiliation.

[11] Zimmerman and Cervantes, *op. cit.*

In Michigan, it was found that 18 percent of marriages in which neither parent had religious affiliations had ended in divorce as compared to 14 percent of mixed Protestant-Catholic marriages.[12] Of those in which the wife was a church member and the husband not, 16 percent ended in divorce.

A study[13] of interfaith marriages among parents of over 6,500 school children in Spokane, Washington, where the tradition of easy divorce prevails, found that 24 percent of the marriages studied ended in divorce when the couple was without religion as compared to 17.4 percent failure in mixed-religion marriages. A study of parents of 13,528 Maryland youths found a divorce rate of 17 percent in homes without religion compared to 15 percent for mixed marriages.[14]

Zimmerman and Cervantes[15] report that in marriages where one has religious affiliation and the other does not, the divorce, desertion, and delinquency rate of children are generally twice as high as in marriages in which both are affiliated with a religious group. Where both of the pair are without religion, the chances of divorce, desertion, and of child delinquency are four times as high as where there is religious affiliation.

Other studies have indicated that religious training makes a significant contribution to marriage success and happiness. Both men and women with strict religious training have been found to have higher happiness scores in marriage than those whose training was rated "considerable to none."[16] Those with many years of Sunday-school training also have been found to make a better adjustment to marriage than those with little or no training.[17]

Whether or not a couple remains actively associated with some church organization is also statistically important. Even as early as the engagement period, church attendance has been found to be a factor in the success or failure of the relationship. One study[18] found that more than half of the engagements in which the girl attended church more regularly than the boy were finally broken. This was also true of engagements in which neither had religious affiliations. Fewer engagements were broken among those couples who attended church once a month or more.

This association with a church, which contributes to success in en-

[12] Judson T. Landis and Mary G. Landis, op. cit., Fig. 18–2, p. 352.

[13] H. Ashley Weeks, "Differential Divorce Rates by Occupation," Social Forces, 21:336 ff., March, 1943.

[14] Howard M. Bell, Youth Tell Their Story (Washington, D.C.: American Youth Commission, Americal Council on Education, 1938).

[15] Zimmerman and Cervantes, op. cit.

[16] Lewis M. Terman and others, Psychological Factors in Marital Happiness (New York: McGraw-Hill Book Co., 1938).

[17] Ernest W. Burgess and Leonard S. Cottrell, Predicting Success or Failure in Marriage (Englewood Cliffs, N. J.: Prentice-Hall, Inc., 1939), pp. 392 ff.

[18] Ernest W. Burgess and Paul Wallin, Engagement and Marriage (Philadelphia: J. B. Lippincott Co., 1953), pp. 290–291.

gagement, is equally significant in marriage. Higher marital happiness scores were registered by couples who, after marriage, continued attending church regularly.[19] It has been found, too, that striking differences in marriage adjustment are associated with the circumstances under which a couple marries. Those who are married in a church or parsonage generally enjoyed a more successful marriage than those who took their vows outside a church before a civil officer.[20] This, of course, does not mean that the ceremony and the minister in themselves exert a lasting influence upon the fate of the marriage. It is, rather, further evidence that those with serious religious connections are more marriageable than others, since those who take their religion seriously more often choose to be married with religious sanction.

At least in some measure, religion meets its promise to make family life better. Carol L. Stone[21] studied 3,810 high school students and 1,469 college students comparing those active and inactive in church affairs. She found that (1) those active in church had a more harmonious home life, (2) the church group was more active in school social life, (3) the church group had a larger circle of friends, (4) the church group was more satisfied with and had few criticisms of their home community, (5) the church group was more optimistic and less worried in outlook, and (6) the church group was more service-motivated, more interested in helping others. It is clear that association with religious institutions produces a better functioning family.

Religions vary greatly, however, in their contribution to marital happiness. The degree of authoritarianism in religion seems to have some relationship. Chesser's[22] study in Great Britain of over 6,000 marriages indicates that the highest proportion of happy childhoods and happy parental marriages were found among the nonconformists, that is, the Protestants, rather than in the Church of England group. The lowest degree of happiness was among those with no religion. Jews were very close to second in producing the lowest proportion of happy marriages. Roman Catholics had the highest proportion of unhappy marriages and unhappy childhoods and highest rate of premarital intercourse.

The high rate of unhappiness among English Catholics is, in part, a reflection of their lower-class status. As in the United States, they are generally in a lower socioeconomic group due to their relatively more recent migration from southern and eastern Europe. But the prohibition against divorce itself consigns many couples and their children to a lifelong struggle.

[19] Burgess and Cottrell, *op. cit.*, p. 393.

[20] *Ibid.*, pp. 394, 417.

[21] "Church Participation and Social Adjustment of High School and College Youth," *Washington Agricultural Stations Bulletin*, No. 550, Pullman, May, 1954.

[22] Eustace Chesser and others, *The Sexual Marital, and Family Relationship of the English Woman* (New York: Roy Publishers, Inc., 1957).

Church Attendance

For the religion-no religion pair, attendance at church may be a major issue. The husband's work-week is time structured, often to the extent of commanding some of his leisure time. This and community activities may schedule most of his weekdays. Sunday is his free day, and he feels he should have a right to do as he pleases. He may even feel that the free use of this day for relaxation and esthetic enjoyment is the essence of religion itself. To the wife, on the other hand, the Sunday routine of Sunday school and church represents the one certain time in the week when she can dress up, have social contacts outside the home with the family as a unit, and can be seen in the company of her husband. She is likely to find the church service relaxing and stimulating entirely aside from the religious context, since it is a marked variation from her regular weekday routine, and a part of the religious training of the children.

The church today is more vital to women in another nonreligious sense. Much of the social activity of the church is in women's groups, as is much of its service-directed activity, both local and worldwide. The church offers women many leadership roles—for many housewives their only such opportunity. Participation in church-going may be essential to obtaining and retaining leadership roles in many of these less formal activities of the church, and to many wives this is of great importance. They could go to church alone, but their position is strengthened if their husbands are beside them.

Protestant-Catholic Marriages

Protestant and Catholic make up most of the interfaith-marriage combinations as shown by the Census data. Many develop out of dating which was never meant to get serious. The couple become attached to each other before the religious issue took on significance.[23]

The Catholic group, in most communities, is in the minority and consequently under some pressure to cross religious lines in order to find suitable mates. In fact, more than a fourth of all Catholic youths in the United States have ecclesiastical marriages to non-Catholics.[24] This takes no account of those Catholics who forsake the church in marriage outside

[23] Clifford Kirkpatrick and Theodore Caplow, "Courtship in a Group of Minnesota Students," *American Journal of Sociology*, 51:114–125, September, 1945.

[24] John L. Thomas, "The Factor of Religion in Selection of Marriage Mates," *American Sociological Review*, 16:487–491, August, 1951.

their religion. The highest rate of interfaith marriages is among those with higher education and with high socioeconomic status.[25]

The couple may well be close to the wedding day before the Protestant member is fully aware of what he must agree to in order to wed the Catholic party. The Catholic church, being still the true church from the Catholic point of view, makes the rules for the marriage with regard to birth control, wedding ceremony (sacred versus civil), permissibility of divorce, and most important, to the long-run adjustments of marriage, the training of children likely to be born to the union.

The Marriage Rite

Although all states require a license to wed, and most recognize the civil ceremony as being adequate, religious bodies require a religious ceremony. With Protestant denominations it is a ceremony with the church's benediction. In the Catholic church, the wedding is a sacrament.

To have a sacramentally valid marriage, the non-Catholic must participate in this rite and be married by a priest. He must make vows regarding noninterference with the faith of the spouse and rearing of children. Most likely the couple has already agreed on their own solution to the birth control question, and one or both may have doubts about having children "baptized and educated solely in the Catholic religion."

Although the marriage must be Catholic to be valid, the Second Ecumenical Council did grant the Protestant member the right of repeating the ceremony in his own church, a right formerly denied. Although a written oath on these matters, signed before a priest, is no longer required by the Catholic church, many dioceses do require an oral promise. It is in the nature of a solemn promise. It is doubtful that many mates of the out-group can give it the same seriousness that the Catholic member must.

The non-Catholic member is requested to be familiar with doctrines of the Catholic faith. There is no reciprocal requirement for the Catholic. The non-Catholic must agree not to interfere with the Catholic's exercise of his religion. This is also not a reciprocal agreement. In fact, if Protestant bodies had such requirements there could be no valid Catholic-Protestant marriages at all.

Finally, in granting the disposition for the interfaith marriage, the priest becomes a third party in the marriage and thereby has a right to

[25] Lee G. Burchinal and Loren E. Chancellor, "Survival Rates Among Religiously Homogamous and Interreligious Marriages," *Agricultural and Home Economics Experiment Station Research Bulletin 512,* December, 1962. See also Harold T. Christensen and Kenneth E. Barber, "Interfaith Marriage in Indiana," *Journal of Marriage and Family Living,* 29:461–469, August, 1967.

intervene if pledges are not kept. He does, in fact, acquire the right to involve himself in a way that no Protestant minister would consider doing.

The Indissolubility of Marriage

Since marriage in the Catholic Church is a holy sacrament, it may not be terminated except by death. While non-Catholics are undoubtedly very serious about the desire to make the union permanent, it is doubtful that many look upon it as indissoluble.

Margaret Mead has suggested[26] that an increasing number of Catholic mothers are advising their daughters not to marry in the church so they can get a divorce if they need one. For Catholics who do marry outside, this issue is resolved before marriage. For the faithful, it is a lifelong bond. Of course, if a mother does give a daughter such advice, it may well help ease the daughter's conscience in case she must leave the church for divorce.

It may well be that vows, seriously taken, help people tolerate difficult marriage adjustments that would otherwise be very difficult. Yet marriage is such an intimate relationship, it is doubtful that vows as such smooth the way.

Birth Control

The birth control issue has been of serious consequence in Catholic marriages and in interfaith marriages. Practice ignores teaching with increasing frequency, and there are many dissenting voices among the church leaders and laity. In fact, no single issue has so much challenged the authority of the Pope in recent times.

The following is the July 29, 1968 statement of George N. Lindsay, Chairman of Planned Parenthood-World Population, in response to the pronouncement of Pope Paul VI about birth control:

Pope Paul's pronouncement on birth control today marks a tragic turn in the history of the Catholic Church, and surely will be greeted with sorrow throughout the world. It is almost beyond belief that a man of Pope Paul's sensitivity, who has walked through the streets of Bombay and seen how overpopulation reduces human beings to misery and despair, can now feel compelled to limit the application of family planning. It must have been with great anguish that the Pope reached the decisions embodied in his statement, since

[26] "Margaret Mead's Sound Insights into the Furor over Shifting American Morals" *Life*, 65:30–34, August 25, 1968.

he must know full well the burdens thus placed on Catholic families and on the world.

His pronouncement may prove to be almost as futile as it is tragic for his Church. The number of Catholics who do indeed practice family planning, using effective medical methods, has steadily grown in recent years. The definitive Westoff-Ryder Study showed that in 1965, more than three-fourths of American Catholic wives practiced birth control, and more than two-thirds of these used forms of contraception other than the Church-approved rhythm.

Surveys also show that most U.S. Catholics believe that birth control assistance should become more widely available at home and abroad, and that 89 percent of Catholic wives under 35 years of ago believe that the present Catholic doctrine should be liberalized. . . .

There are predictions that the Pope must change his position. Yet the fact remains that it was taken after a large committee of Catholic scientists and church leaders, which he had appointed made their report, overwhelmingly recommending that the rules be changed. It will not be an easy position for him to change. It remains a matter of conscience for many devout Catholics.

The oath required of the Catholic-Protestant marriage no longer contains a pledge not to practice birth control, but it does require that the non-Catholic member "not interfere in any way with the Catholic party's exercise of the Catholic religion."

Should the Church change its position on birth control a source of potential conflict, health risk, economic hardship, and sexual stress would be removed. Unwanted children have been one of the serious burdens of the Catholic marriage, whether intra- or interfaith.

Official discouragement of interfaith marriages has been described as a "battle for babies," since recruitment of members is largely through births of children to members. Vincent[27] raised the question of whether churches would really be concerned with interfaith marriages if it could be proved that they added members to that particular religious body. He does not answer the question, but it has been answered by sample studies. Any particular church does lose members by interfaith marriages. Evidence will be cited later.

There is a certain cynicism in these comments which may be unjustified. Most religious leaders are very humane persons. They have wide experience with the most vital aspects of interpersonal relationships. Even priests, handicapped as they are by living outside wedlock and in a cloistered masculine world, hear the intimate confessions of members and know the anguish of people in trouble. Most church leaders may object to interfaith marriages quite as much, if not more, because of the troubles people experience in them as from the business angle of adding members.

[27] Clark E. Vincent, "Interfaith Marriages: Problem or Symptom?" In Marvin B. Sussman, (ed.), *Sourcebook in Marriage and the Family*, pp. 349–359 (Boston: Houghton Mifflin Co., 1963).

There is little question that child-training issue is a major concern of the interfaith marriage. Baber[28] was the first to point out that conflicts in Protestant-Catholic marriages centered around religious training of the child. He found that conflicts over the religious issue were about as numerous among those couples who were both rather indifferent in religion as among the devout.

Since the training of the children is the greatest troublemaker in the cross-religion marriage, Landis' research tried to find a statistical answer to child training and related questions by following "out-group" marriages into the second generation.[29]

It was found that among 4,000 parents of the college young people studied, over a third of one religion or the other had forsaken their faith to follow the faith of the other spouse. This change of faith usually took place before marriage, although in some cases it came later. Among those who did not change their faith, it was found that half of the children had been reared in the Protestant faith, 45 percent in the Catholic faith, and 5 percent in no faith at all. Obviously the pledge taken by all Catholics to raise their children in the faith is not easily followed. Thomas reports a loss to the Catholic group of 40 percent.[30] The Church seems justified in being wary of the cross-religion marriage.

Landis showed further that in these homes young people are subjected to various religious training programs. In more than a third of the cases, the mother took all the responsibility. In most of the other cases, the child was exposed to both faiths, sometimes by one parent, sometimes by both. In a few cases, he actually was taken to both churches in turn. These college students, looking at the mixed marriages of their parents, were inclined to feel that in general it had been a serious handicap in their home lives.

Prince, studying a small sample, found that the tendency was for the couple to raise the child in the faith of the mother, but with the likelihood that in the case of the two minority religious groups, training was likely to be in her faith.[31] Nationwide data for the Jewish group suggest that Judaism is losing about 70 percent of the children born to the mixed-faith couple. They may not be reared in the Protestant or the Catholic faith in many of these cases, but they are not reared in the Jewish faith.[32]

Zimmerman and Cervantes indicate that in 9,000 mixed marriages

[28] Ray E. Baber, "A Study of 325 Mixed Marriages," *American Sociological Review*, 2:705–716, October, 1937.

[29] Landis and Landis, *op. cit.*, Ch. 13 and Baber, *op. cit.*, also studied this problem with a small sample.

[30] John L. Thomas, *The American Catholic Family* (Englewood Cliffs, N. J.: Prentice-Hall, Inc., 1956).

[31] Alfred J. Prince, *op. cit.*

[32] Erich Rosenthal, *op. cit.*

they studied, 6 out of 10 children in the Catholic-Protestant mixed marriage end up rejecting all religion.[33]

There are also scattered data which suggest that the birth rate of the mixed marriage may tend to run lower than that in the marriage of like faith.[34] This seems particularly true in the case of the Jew. Whether it is the mixed marriage that is responsible of whether both the mixed marriage and the low birth rate are indicative of emancipation from tradition might well be asked.

A more recent study by Christensen and Barber[35] based on Indiana data found that interfaith marriages were of more secular pairs and that the pair tended to be older than average at the time of marriage. These factors would tend toward a lower birth rate.

It is apparent from widely scattered studies that the strong marriage pledge regarding rearing children in the Catholic faith is about as likely to be broken as kept. Pledges do not govern marriage behavior automatically. The amount of conflict that enters into violating the pledge is not known. It is likely that in many instances failure to keep it has involved stress between the couple themselves, with grandparents, in-laws, and perhaps church leaders.

Jewish-Gentile Marriages

In recent years, great alarm is expressed in the Jewish community, over the possibility of their disappearance as a people in the United States.[36] Jews have a low birth rate, but the principal basis of the concern is intermarriage and the loss to the Jewish faith of children born to the mixed marriages. The loss has been placed at 70 percent. The Jews place a premium on learning, and since greater tolerance pervades the college campus, there is free mingling in dating regardless of religious heritage.

The religious issue is the preeminent one in the above consideration, but the sociological one is important because of the likelihood of clash of values, rituals, and conceptions of life.

An early study showed that comparatively few young people of Jewish origin dated outside their religious group—slightly more than a fourth of Jewish male and only 15 percent of Jewish female college students at the University of Minnesota.[37] Jewish-Gentile marriages are not

[33] Zimmerman and Cervantes, op. cit.

[34] Ibid.; also Thomas B. Morgan, op. cit.

[35] Op. cit.

[36] Thomas B. Morgan, "The Vanishing American Jew," Look. May 5, 1964, pp. 42–46.

[37] Kirkpatrick and Caplow, op. cit.

as frequent as Catholic-Protestant ones. This results in part from religious observances, but it probably also reflects an attitude of anti-Semitism, which in most communities is a live prejudice.

About 13 percent of Jewish marriages are interfaith.[38] Studies of Jewish-Gentile intermarriage show that in most cases the marriage is between a Jewish man and a Gentile woman; comparatively few are between Jewish women and Gentile men. When such marriages do take place, they are between reformed or liberal Jews. Orthodox Judaism does not permit Jewish-Gentile marriages except in cases where the Gentile has been converted to the Jewish religion. The more liberal and reformed Jewish group, which is now in the majority in the United States, has no absolute prohibition against intermarriage, but does discourage it.[39]

There is a very close family supervision of the dating of Jewish young people, particularly of the Jewish girl. Any dating between Jews and Gentiles is frowned upon by the Jewish group.[40]

The real difficulty with the Jewish-Gentile marriage of the religiously emancipated Jew is that more differences than those of religion are involved. Judaism is a culture in and of itself, as is Christianity, not merely a religion. The Jewish world is a world of customs dating back through the centuries. Jews differ from Christians in observing a different day of rest, different religious holidays, different foods, and in numerous other ways. Not many young people reared in the Jewish culture can entirely forsake it, and few Gentiles reared outside this world can completely accept it.

One of the major handicaps in the Jewish-Gentile marriage has been that in approximately half the cases, one or the other or both families reject the new son or daughter[41] (see Figure 14–2). A second handicap is the prejudice against Jews exhibited in many circles. The Gentile in this marriage must face anti-Semitic prejudice against himself and his children.

It is often easy, when young people live far away from their own relatives, to forget how important religious differences can be when one joins two family lines in marriage. In these days of urban dating it is easy to forget that one marries, not only a person, but also a family. The Jewish family is a very closely knit group, and even though the Jewish

[38] This is the figure reported by Rosenthal, *op. cit.;* see also Ruby Jo Reeves Kennedy, "Single or Triple Melting Pot?: Intermarriage Trends in New Haven, 1870–1950," *American Journal of Sociology,* 57:56 ff., January, 1952.

[39] J. S. Slotkin, "Jewish-Gentile Intermarriages in Chicago," *American Sociological Review,* 7:34–39, February, 1942, classifies various Jewish types entering into Gentile marriages: the emancipated (most numerous), the rebellious, marginal, adventurous, promiscuous, and disorganized were the types found in his study of 183 cases of intermarriage in Chicago.

[40] Milton L. Barron, "The Incidence of Jewish Intermarriage in Europe and America," *American Sociological Review,* 11:12 ff., February, 1946.

[41] J. S. Slotkin, "Adjustment in Jewish-Gentile Intermarriages," *Social Forces,* 21:226–230, December, 1942.

FIGURE 14–2 FAMILY ACCEPTANCE OR REJECTION OF JEW-GENTILE
MARRIAGES. Source: J. S. Slotkin, "Adjustment in Jew-Gentile Marriages,"
Social Forces, Vol. 21, December, 1942.

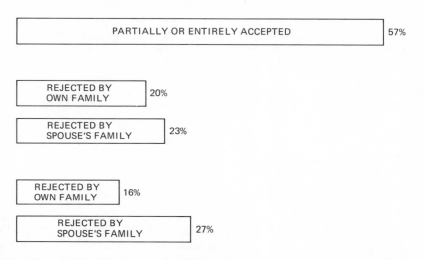

It is difficult for families to accept the Jewish interfaith marriage. The
growth of tolerance may have changed the situation somewhat since this
study was made, but many still face problems in relationships with parents
and grandparents.

young person may emancipate himself from his religion, he rarely emanci-
pates himself completely from his family and its influences.

Risks in Interfaith Marriage

Sociologists may have exaggerated the divorce problem of the interfaith
marriage. Yet studies over a period of years do consistently show higher
divorce rates than those of like faith, even engagements of those of different
faith are more fragile than those of like faith, according to studies of
Burgess and Wallin.[42]

A report[43] issued by the Department of Public Health in California
dealing with couples who had divorced or separated shows that the break
had come for interfaith pairs after a median duration of three to four
years for the various religious combinations; after a median of six to eight
years for those of like faith. Apparently serious trouble develops more
quickly between the mixed faith pairs who have serious difficulty or they
act more quickly in seeking separation as a solution.

[42] Burgess and Wallin, *op. cit.*, Figure 36, p. 290.
[43] Landis and Landis, *op. cit.*, Figure 12–3, p. 192.

Below are divorce rates in interfaith marriages at various times and in different locations:

Marriage Combination	Study I* Bell, Maryland 13,528 Couples	Study II† Weeks, Spokane, Washington 6,548 Couples	Study III‡ Landis, Michigan 4,108 Couples
Both Catholic	6.4	3.8	4.4
Both Protestant	6.8	10.0	6.0
Mixed, Protestant- Catholic	15.2	17.4	14.1
Catholic father- Protestant mother	—	—	20.6

* Bell, *op. cit.*, † Weeks, *op. cit.*, p. 336, ‡ Landis and Landis, *op. cit.*, p. 154.

Judson T. Landis[44] has suggested that the high divorce rate of the Catholic husband-Protestant wife combination may be due to the initiative that Protestant wives generally take in the matter of divorce, an initiative which the Catholic wife cannot exercise in the other combination. It may, however, be more than a technical issue. There is reason to believe that such a combination could lead to a maximum number of marital problems. Child training, for example, is generally a wife's function, but when the father is the devout Catholic in a mixed marriage, the job of religious training falls largely upon his shoulders. When, as must often be the case, he has neither the time nor the ability to assume this function, serious family problems seem likely to result, particularly if he blames the wife for her failure to qualify as his substitute.

Zimmerman and Cervantes, studying 40,000 urban families with children, found divorce rates three times as high in mixed Protestant-Catholic marriages as in those of like faith.[45] They found the failure rate of the Jew-Gentile marriage highest of all interfaith combinations.

Vernon[46] has rightly criticized such comparisons in tending to exaggerate failure. Numbers being small, percentage differences are large. The same percentages applied to successes would be smaller. For example, if the divorce rate in intrafaith marriages were 5 percent and in interfaith marriages 10 percent, the rate would be double. Yet the success rate is 90 compared to 95 percent, a very small percentage difference.

This kind of argument, however, does have a point. By this device

[44] *Divorce in California,* Department of Public Health, Bureau of Vital Statistics, October, 1967. Fig. 4–5, p. 43.

[45] *Op. cit.*

[46] Glenn M. Vernon, "Bias in Professional Publications Concerning Interfaith Marriages," *Religious Education,* 55:261–264, July–August, 1964.

sociologists may have overstressed negative aspects of the interfaith marriage. They may not have in terms of hidden meaning. Those close to it, counselors, ministers, parents, couples themselves, may well feel that divorce statistics do not begin to touch the problem.

The State of Iowa collects data on religious affiliation of marrying couples. These data, analyzed extensively by Burchinal and Chancellor, are presented by survival rates rather than divorce rates. These studies show clearly that the mixed marriage has a shorter duration and also that the marriages of unaffiliated persons are much shorter in duration than those with church connections (see Table 14–1). Duration of marriages, they found, is also related to age and to social status, older age and higher social status leading to longer duration rates.

Table 14–1   Percent of Marriages Surviving in the State of Iowa by Religious Affiliation

Spousal Religious Affiliation Type	Marital Survival Rate
Homogamous Catholic	96.2
Presbyterian–non–Catholic	94.6
Homogamous Lutheran	94.1
Lutheran–non–Catholic	93.0
Methodist–non–Catholic	92.9
Homogamous Methodist	91.4
Homogamous Presbyterian	91.0
Catholic–Lutheran	90.5
Baptist–non–Catholic	90.0
Catholic–Presbyterian	89.8
Homogamous Baptist	89.8
Catholic–Methodist	83.8
Catholic–Baptist	81.6
Homogamous–unaffiliated Protestant	35.0
Catholic–unaffiliated Protestant	28.7

Source: Adapted from Burchinal and Chancellor, *op. cit.*, Table 5, p. 758.

This study shows that the survival rates of certain interdenominational marriages are high, about as high as intradenominational marriages. Catholic-Protestant marriages show a high survival rate where marriage is with the more formal, liturgical denominations (Lutherans and Presbyterians). With the less formal, more evangelical denominations (Baptists and Methodists) survival rates drop to about 80 percent.

Numerically Baptists and Methodists make up more than half of the Protestant population of the nation, with a combined membership of over 40 million (see Figure 14–3). This being so, one would expect that most interfaith marriages of Catholics would be with Baptists and Methodists, where greater social contact exists. Regional distribution, however, is a factor. The Baptists are concentrated in the southern region of the nation where there are few Catholics. It is likely too that the evangelical denominations may less often cross the religious line than the more formal church adherents because a wider gulf of religious tradition is to be bridged.

For Catholics, divorce statistics are more significant than numbers would indicate. If one considers the stand of the Catholic church against divorce, he can appreciate the greater inner turmoil and marital conflict to which any divorce testifies. A Catholic cannot get a divorce and remain Catholic. For every Catholic who resorts to divorce there are no doubt many more who will bear great difficulty rather than take the forbidden step.

Whether he suffers more in interfaith marriages than in Catholic marriages, where the rule of indissolubility is doubly binding is unknown. But the fact that more interfaith marriages terminate in divorce may mean that they do face greater religious problems. Most church leaders assume that they do, and consistently warn against such marriages. It is likely that the church's concern is in part an outgrowth of unfavorable experience with marriages of this type and not solely a concern for future church membership.

It is among the nominal (unaffiliated) Protestants that the survival rate of marriage is very low (Table 14–1). The rate of survival is lower in Catholic-Protestant unions where the Catholic member is the husband, as seen in the Landis study.

Burchinal and Chancellor[47] have shown that the religious factor is less likely to terminate a marriage where husband and wife are older than average. High social class, too, lends to greater stability of the mixed marriage.

Christensen and Barber[48] in their study of Indiana data, report that couples in interfaith marriages have certain characteristics that tend to differentiate them from like-faith marriages: older at the time of marriage, more of them are entering a second or subsequent marriage, more are pregnant at time of marriage, more are from high status occupations, more have a civil ceremony, more live in urban centers.

[47] Ibid.
[48] Harold T. Christensen and Kenneth E. Barber, "Interfaith versus Intrafaith marriage in Indiana," *Journal of Marriage and Family Living,* 29:461–469, August, 1967.

FIGURE 14-3 RELIGION REPORTED BY CIVILIAN POPULATION, 14 YEARS OLD AND OVER, MARCH, 1957. Source: U.S. Department of Commerce, Bureau of the Census, "Religion Reported by the Civilian Population of the United States, March, 1957," **Current Population Reports: Population Characteristics,** Series P-20, No. 79, February 2, 1958.

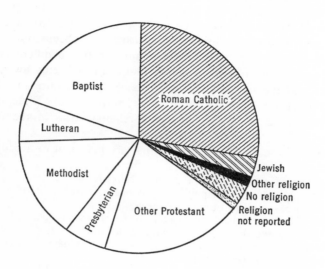

	Number	Percent
Total, 14 years and over	119,333,000	100.0
Protestant	78,952,000	66.2
Baptist	23,525,000	19.7
Lutheran	8,417,000	7.1
Methodist	16,676,000	14.0
Presbyterian	6,656,000	5.6
Other Protestant	23,678,000	19.8
Roman Catholic	30,669,000	25.7
Jewish	3,868,000	3.2
Other religion	1,545,000	1.3
No religion	3,195,000	2.7
Religion not reported	1,104,000	0.9

There are some 200 Protestant denominations. The membership of the larger bodies is shown here.

The cross-faith group seems to be, as one might expect, a more secularized, liberated group. This in itself would help explain the higher divorce rate although age and high social status should offset this factor. There is also a suggestion that there was a falling away from their religious affiliation prior to the marriage.

Weighing the Religious Issue in Advance

Professor James R. Hine has published a unique device for helping young people face religious differences before marriage. Sixty-five pairs of cards list items of religious belief. Each looks at his set and sorts the cards into "agree" and "disagree" piles. When all cards have been sorted, they compare cards and discuss each statement representing a difference in agreement. The discussion of these beliefs makes them keenly aware of differences in fundamental attitudes in areas such as nature of God, creed, prayer, the Trinity, man's purpose in life, salvation, the Bible, eternal life, miracles, sacraments, giving, missions, religious rites in the family, and so on.

Here are some of the questions that are pertinent to a couple's future plans:

1. Can one of us adopt the other's church?
2. If not, can we be happy going to one church or the other, or will we each go alone to our own church?
3. Will one or both of us break with the church altogether?
4. If we agree to keep our church attachments, what will we do about birth control, observance of special religious days, or eating customs?
5. What about benevolences?
6. How will our parents and friends accept the match?
7. How will our children be reared? In which faith, or in no faith at all?
8. If in the Catholic faith, can the Protestant member fully accept church supervision of the training of his child?
9. Can we stand the pressure of devout parents or grandparents, or representatives of our churches, who will bring pressure to have the children reared in their own faith?
10. In case of emancipation from religious connections, are we strong enough to stand alone when the crises of life overtake us in marriage, or will we, as so many do, revert to the security, certainty, and faith of our childhood religion? This question is particularly pertinent for the Catholic-reared member.
11. If it is a Catholic-Protestant marriage, the Protestant member should ask, Can I tolerate Catholic direction of my marriage and Catholic religious training of my children?

Interdenominational Marriages

Prince,[49] in his study of cross-religion marriages, included 52 marriages between different Protestant denominations. Although the sample is too

[49] Prince, *op. cit.*

small to justify wide generalization, two findings are strongly suggestive of outcome. (1) A very high percentage classed their marriage in the "entirely satisfied" or "very much satisfied" group compared to the interfaith marriages. (2) Only 19 percent retained their own separate denomination, compared to 55 percent of the interfaith group who retained their separate faith. In two-thirds of the cases the husband or wife adopted the other's faith. In 11.5 percent of the cases the couple adopted another denomination differing from the former loyalties of either.

If this research should receive further confirmation one would be justified in the conclusion that interdenominational marriages usually do not terminate the couple's adherence to some Protestant body, and generally the religious difference is not a major barrier to the marriage.

Burchinal and Chancellor calculated survival rates of interdenominational marriages and found them generally quite high (refer again to Table 14–1 p. 279).[50] They were, however, dealing with the more standard denominations, rather than fringe revivalistic groups. It is probable that these groups do not too often marry into the more conservative denominations with large memberships. The highest rate of failure was among the nominal (unaffiliated) Protestants.

Such marriages may be very hard on church membership in particular denominations. Bossard and Letts[51] have studied the problem of intermarriage by Lutherans, a rather conservative liturgically oriented group, through contacts with pastors. It was found that twice as many Lutheran women as men married outside their church. Although Lutherans are generally very loyal to their church, where they entered mixed marriages there was a loss of somewhere between 17 to 25 percent to the group.

One suspects that young people who are loyal to very orthodox or revivalistic religious groups would find themselves quite out of harmony with those who are members of the more formal or ritualistic churches. The formal and ritualistic group, too, is far different from the extremely modern fringe. Between such denominations, there is a vast difference in the level of religious appeal, esthetic appreciation, and emotional outlet.

While such differences may not be as great as Protestant-Catholic differences, for example, they are great enough to be grounds for caution. The dating period should be made to bring the couple, deliberately, into close relationships with the religious philosophy, the church, and the family of both young people. The liberal-minded person can generally feel little tolerance for the person who is extremely dogmatic or narrow in religious philosophy; it is often equally difficult for the one reared in a strict religious environment to liberalize his religion.

[50] Burchinal and Chancellor, op. cit., p. 758.

[51] James H. S. Bossard and Harold C. Letts, "Mixed Marriages Involving Lutherans—A Research Report," Marriage and Family Living, 18:308–310, November, 1956.

The sum of evidence to date would seem to be that interdenominational marriage probably leads to a considerable shifting of denominational allegiance, but does not seem to be a major handicap to marriage success or survival. Certainly the evidence is strong that church membership in and of itself is important to marriage success; that merely claiming to be Proestant or Catholic without practicing the faith is related to a high degree of marriage failure.

It is important that a young person who is a loyal member of a church think twice before marrying someone who has no interest in church and church affairs. The person with religious attitudes and church loyalties has had this slant toward life built into his or her personality for some twenty years before marriage. His particular values, attitudes, and aspirations are too deeply ingrained to be easily discarded or ignored. The Landis study[52] previously cited makes it clear that marriages between those who are loyal to a religious system and those who are not, are relatively hazardous from the standpoint of success and permanence.

In conclusion   It may be said that while religious differences account for many marital problems, religion itself is a powerful asset in making marriage succeed. Individuals with similar religious backgrounds, values, and opinions have a good chance to succeed in marriage. Even those who embark upon the uncertain path of an interfaith marriage have a better chance than the couple without religious convictions.

One may well wonder why this is so. Religious values are, in essence, the values that make for a well-adjusted personality, mature living, and emotional equanimity. The highest virtues of most religions are: meekness, kindness and consideration for others, helpfulness, self-sacrifice, putting off the immediate sensuous satisfaction for the sake of more distant goals, sacrifice of the temporal for the spiritual, the placing of ideals above ambitions, the placing of goodness above material gain, and many other such core human values. Persons who are able to hold and to live by these positive values in large measure cannot but be well-adjusted, forward-looking, peace-loving individuals.

Those who are truly religious possess the traits out of which good human adjustment and good family living spring. They have the values which make parenthood not merely an obligation, but a high achievement, not merely a duty, but a virtue, not merely a biological exercise, but a spiritual achievement.

It must, therefore, be expected that those who have captured the essence of religious virtues and who have learned how to apply them in social relationships, will be good prospects for marriage. This does not mean, of course, that people without church affiliations never possess any

[52] Landis and Landis, *op. cit.*

of these virtues—they may. On the other hand, there is greater likelihood of a person's having them if he belongs to church groups in which these values and aspirations are taught and practiced.

The problems which interfaith marriages encounter are not, as one might suspect, primarily the result of constant clashes in religious discussions. They are more frequently the outcome of differences over child training and over general values in life. Religion has an influence over far more than the spiritual life of its adherents. Major religious groups teach widely differing attitudes and value systems as well as beliefs. Young people are more often able to change their beliefs than the accompanying attitudes and values.

Problems

1. *Sociodrama:* A young man, religiously indifferent rather than agnostic or atheistic, has just proposed to a girl of serious religious faith. She refuses his proposal. The play begins with her refusal. Bring out her explanations, present his arguments, and include in the play their final decision.
2. Name several attitudes characteristic of a religious person which would be assets to him in marriage adjustment.
3. Would you say that a Protestant minister who advises young people against marrying either Catholics or Jews is probably prejudiced and intolerant?
4. Think of the ways in which children born to a marriage magnify the problems of an interfaith marriage. How would you handle the religious training of a child of an interfaith marriage?
   a. Let the father decide?
   b. Let the mother decide?
   c. Have some respected outsider decide?
   d. Try to combine the dogma of both faiths?
   e. Expose him to both faiths and let him decide for himself when he is old enough?
   f. Expose him to neither faith and let him decide in later years?
   g. Choose some other alternative?
5. In your opinion, what accounts for the greater degree of marriage failure among people without religious affiliation?
6. Catholic, Jewish, and Protestant faiths all share the same fundamental ethical codes. What, then, accounts for the many problems that confront marriages of mixed religion?
7. In most American homes is it the husband or the wife who assumes the religious leadership of the family? How would you explain this fact?
8. When individuals of different religious faiths decide to marry but maintain their separate beliefs, is there any justification for an intensive study by each of the faith of the other?
9. It has been said that the problems that arise out of interdenominational marriages often reflect differences in socioeconomic background rather than in religious belief. Does this statement make sense?

10. Is there anything that the churches could do to help make interfaith and interdenominational marriages more common and more successful? Do you believe that the churches should or should not make such an attempt? Why or why not?

11. Ask a marriage counselor or a family relations counselor, or a minister, priest, or rabbi to describe one or more actual instances of interfaith or interdenominational marriages. Ask the speaker to note specifically the kinds of problems reported by the couple or couples, the solutions sought, and whether or not their problems were solved.

Selected References

Articles in Books of Readings

Cavan, Ruth Shonle, *Marriage and the Family in the Modern World: A Book of Readings*, third edition (New York: Thomas Y. Crowell Co., 1969).
  Prince, Alfred J., "Attitudes of College Students Toward Inter-Faith Marriage," Reading 19.
Landis, Judson T., and Landis, Mary G., *Readings in Marriage and the Family* (Englewood Cliffs, N. J.: Prentice-Hall, Inc., 1952).
  Landis, Judson T., "Marriages of Mixed and Non-Mixed Religious Faith," pp. 203–210.
Rodman, Hyman, *Marriage, Family and Society* (New York: Random House, 1965).
Sussman, Marvin B., *Sourcebook in Marriage and the Family*, third edition (Boston: Houghton Mifflin Co., 1968).
  Vernon, Glenn M., "Bias in Professional Publications Concerning Interfaith Marriages," Reading 6.
  Thomas, John L., "The Factor of Religion in the Selection of Marriage Mates," Reading 27.

General References

Barron, Milton L., "The Incidence of Jewish Intermarriage in Europe and America," *American Sociological Review*, 11:12 ff., February, 1946.
Berman, Louis A., *Jews and Intermarriage: A Study of Personality and Culture* (Cranbury: New Jersey: Thomas Yoseloff, 1968).
Bossard, James H. S., and Letts, Harold C., "Mixed Marriages Involving Lutherans—A Research Report," *Marriage and Family Living*, 18:308–310, November, 1956.
Burchinal, Lee G., "Membership Groups and Attitudes toward Cross-Religious Dating," *Marriage and Family Living*, 22:248–253, August, 1960.
Burchinal, Lee G., and Chancellor, Loren E., "Survival Rates Among Religiously Homogamous and Interreligious Marriages," *Agricultural and Home Economics Experiment Station Research Bulletin 512*, December, 1962.
Burgess, Ernest W., and Wallin, Paul, *Engagement and Marriage* (Philadelphia: J. B. Lippincott Co., 1953), Ch. 6.

Christensen, Harold and Barber, Kenneth E., "Interfaith versus Intrafaith Marriages in Indiana" *Journal of Marriage and the Family*, 29:461–469, August, 1967.

Croog, S. H., and Teele, J. E., "Religious Identity and Church Attendance of Sons of Religious Intermarriages," *American Sociological Review*, 32:93–103, February, 1967.

Gordon, Albert L., *Intermarriage* (Boston: Beacon Press, 1964).

Heiss, Jerold S., "Interfaith Marriage and Marital Outcome," *Marriage and Family Living*, 23:228–233, August, 1961.

Hine, James R., *Religious Beliefs Inventory Kit* (Danville, Ill.: Interstate Printers, 1968).

Jacobson, Paul H., *American Marriage and Divorce* (New York: Holt, Rinehart and Winston, Inc., 1959).

Kennedy, Ruby Jo Reeves, "Single or Triple Melting Pot?: Intermarriage Trends in New Haven, 1870–1950," *American Journal of Sociology*, 57:56 ff., January, 1952.

Rosenthal, Erich, "Studies in Jewish Intermarriage in the United States," *American Jewish Year Book*, Vol. 64, 1963.

Samenfink, J. Anthony, "A Study of Some Aspects of Marital Behavior as Related to Religious Control," *Marriage and Family Living*, 20:163–169, May, 1958.

Slotkin, J. S., "Adjustment in Jewish-Gentile Intermarriages," *Social Forces*, 27:216–230, December, 1942.

Slotkin, J. S., "Jewish-Gentile Intermarriages in Chicago," *American Sociological Review*, 7:34–39, February, 1942.

Thomas, John L., "The Factor of Religion in the Selection of Marriage Mates," *American Sociological Review*, 16:487–491, August, 1951.

Zimmerman, Carle C., and Cervantes, Lucius F., *Successful American Families* (New York: Pageant Press, Inc., 1950).

15

Racial and Cultural 'Differences

Religion is a cultural barrier. Race is physical, but with significant cultural meaning. Religion is invisible. Couples may be mutually attracted and begin dating without knowledge of each others' religious inclinations and affiliations. Racial traits are always present. One usually does not become involved blindly.[1]

Arnold Toynbee[2] sees intermarriage as the ultimate solution of racial problems, but recognizes that English speaking peoples, along with some Western Europeans have retained deep prejudices against it. They have not intermarried as have people in Latin America, in the Arab world, and in many other parts of the globe. Myrdal,[3] Swedish population authority, studying the American Negro, has stated that the greatest intensity of discrimination is in the intermarriage area. Bogardus[4] reports the greatest social distance also exists for races in this area. The militant white racist fears most that sooner or later, if school integration is permitted, some Negro boy will be dating his daughter. Then will come "mongrelization" of the white race.

Gordon[5] in his study of student attitudes in 40 colleges and universities, obtained the reaction of 5,407 students to the question of intercultural

[1] It is estimated that 10,000 to 15,000 Negroes are legally classified as white. These are the lighter-skinned Negoes who are dominantly white in inheritance. See Paul H. Landis, *Introductory Sociology*, (New York: Ronald Press Co., 1958), pp. 354–358.

[2] "Arnold Toynbee Talks of Peace, Power, Race in America," with J. Robert Moskin, *Look*, 33:25–27, March 18, 1969.

[3] Gunnar Myrdal, *An American Dilemma: Negro Problem and American Democracy* (New York: Harper and Bros., 1944).

[4] Emory S. Bogardus, "Comparing Racial Distance in Ethiopia, South Africa and the United States," *Sociology and Social Research*, 52:1–10, January, 1968.

[5] Albert L. Gordon, *Intermarriage* (Boston: Beacon Press, 1964), Ch. 2.

and interracial marriage for themselves. Here is the way he classifies their answers:

Do not favor marriage to person of:	Percent
another color	91
another religion	50
another educational group	31
another nationality	16
a different economic class	13

Would find it easiest to marry a person with:	Percent
economic differences	64
nationality differences	58
educational differences	39
religious differences	27
color differences	6

The barriers are breaking down, integration is more nearly a reality than ever, and dating across color lines is taking place more frequently. Current research can scarcely foresee the outcome of marriages and child rearing in the cross-race situation.

The best guide we have is what is known of cross-race marriages to date. Some of the same situations will be faced, even if with less intensity. The prognosis is not good for the immediate future. The data are worth pursuing for their prognosis on outcomes.

Race mixture has been in process since the advent of slavery from the consequent sexual contacts that resulted. Racial intermixture has been so extensive that few pure Negroes remain. Since these sexual contacts were between white men and Negro women, it was the Negro race that experienced "mongrelization." A child from the union would remain with his mother and be considered a Negro. However, the racist fears contact between the Negro male and white female for then there will be a greater attempt to have the child accepted into white society. So far the child of an interracial couple has had a place only in black society.

The sociological fact is that wherever social distance between groups exists, whether it be the product of religion, nationality, economics, race, or other biological or cultural variables, once the process of integration and assimilation gets under way, amalgamation also begins. The ultimate step in integration is intermarriage.

As with all cases of conflicts involved in social distance, once affairs reach the point where intermarriage is considered, the hostilities which create problems are already vanishing.

Intercultural Factors

The cross-nation marriage, often confused with interracial marriage, bridges a cultural gap. Often both race and national heritage are involved. Sociologists have gained some insight into this problem also. Marriages crossing nationality lines in the United States are on the decrease as we are ceasing to be the melting pot of European nations. The new problem here is the marriage of thousands of service men to foreign brides while the former are stationed abroad. Cultural differences because of education of men and women are not so great as in a day when it was considered inappropriate for women to go to college. In many parts of the country there is nearly universal high school education. Cultural differences due to economics too tend to be obscured during the high school and college dating years and one suspects that an increasing proportion of marriages are between young people from families which have quite different levels of living. All in all intercultural factors are becoming less significant.

Interracial Marriages

Race crossings will be greatest among the educated who work together on the college campus and fight together in the crusade for equality. The Peace Corps, too, creates many interracial contacts. These social forces will bring a respectability to interracial marriages they have not had previously. The general climate of opinion will also be more tolerant toward the children of the mixed marriages, so that this will no longer be so great an anxiety-provoking factor in the experience of those who brave the color line in marriage.

Those who are shocked to anticipate the increase in interracial marriages will do well to remember that throughout the course of human history the races have mixed. One need not travel widely to be convinced of this fact. The racial crossing between all branches of the human race is fertile.

College campuses are becoming more cosmopolitan yearly. Any observer of campus life is aware that the taboos against white girls dating those of other races are breaking down, particularly where the dark-skinned male is from another country. Often marriages of this type mean marrying up into the aristocracy of the country from which the male student comes. This gives such marriages respectability. The next step is for dating and intermarriage to be less selective.

According to Knebel,[6] intermarriage today is causing an identity crisis among black women who are rebelling against black men who prefer white women in dating and marriage. Now through such means as The Miss Black America Contest black leaders are trying to elevate the status of black women and solve their identity problem.

Research guides   Adams'[7] early study of interracial marriage in Hawaii, where there is an indistinct caste-color line, and where two out of five marriages are racially mixed, showed that marriage problems were more a matter of cultural norms and sex roles than of social pressures affecting the marriage from the community standpoint. The native (Polynesian) Hawaiian woman marrying a Chinese or a white man of good character moved up in standard of living—and took pride in adopting the husband's way of life for herself and her children. In general these husbands were better providers than the native island males. The marriages in general did well.

In rare cases where the native male married a non-Polynesian female, marriages often turned out to be unsatisfactory. This male's standards of industry fell far below those of the Chinese or the white and the wife became intolerant of his easy-going ways and his lack of responsibility as a provider. These wives were, moreover, not willing to assume the customary tasks of the Polynesian wife.

Thus we have interracial-international marriages involving the same stresses turning out differently, depending on which combination of male and female are involved. The problem proves not to be racial, but rather one of subcultural differences, primarily in role expectations of male and female. This principle may well have wide applications in international and interracial cross-marriages everywhere.

One other principle discovered by Adams was that the degree of disorganization of the particular group or groups involved in marriages across race and nationality lines was a key factor in the divorce rate. Groups going through a period of rapid acculturation not only crossed the line in marriage more often, but also had very high divorce rates, both with in-race and cross-race marriages.[8] This behavior was particularly characteristic of such groups as Filipinos, Koreans, and Puerto Ricans. Japanese and Chinese tended to remain loyal to their culture and to marry outside very little. Those who did break with their race and culture groups had a high divorce rate.

[6] Fletcher Knebel, "Identity—the Black Woman's Burden," *Look*, September 23, 1969, pp. 77–79. See also Joan Aldous, "Wives' Employment Status and Lower-Class Men as Husband-Fathers: Support for the Moynihan Thesis," *Journal of Marriage and Family Living*, 31:469–476, August, 1969.

[7] Ronanzo Adams, *Interracial Marriage in Hawaii* (New York: The Macmillan Co., 1937), see particularly Ch. 5.

[8] *Ibid.*, see particularly Ch. 16.

Since World War II there has been opportunity to observe intermarriage, both of nationality groups involving the same racial strain and of interracial groups. For example, in the year 1946 alone there were 1,600 Air Force marriages to German girls, and thousands had married English girls. By the end of 1955, the American Embassy reported that there had been over 20,000 marriages of GI's to Japanese women. This was in spite of the fact that for a considerable part of the occupation period the Army forbade marriages with Japanese girls.

While comprehensive research is lacking, a few special studies throw some light on interracial marriage, particularly with the Japanese. Joseph Grant,[9] writer for the Associate Press, reports an interview study of 224 wives from Europe and the Far East by University of Hawaii sociologist, Yukiko Kimura. All of these women had married Hawaiian men and lived in Hawaii five years or more. Two out of ten considered themselves unhappy, wishing they had not come to Hawaii. Another three out of ten said they probably would not have married their husbands if they had it to do over again, thus making half who would not repeat their marriage. The largest percentage of unhappy women were Japanese who married "Nisei" husbands, that is, American men of Japanese ancestry.

The happiest marriages in this study were Japanese girls married to Caucasian husbands. The second group were Europeans married to "Nisei." Three-fourths of these European girls would marry their husbands again.

Apparently the main difficulty with the Japanese girl marrying the "Nisei" is with in-laws. The husband's family demands that the wife conform to Japanese old-world patterns. They expect her to work hard and be obedient. The modern Japanese girls do not wish to follow these patterns because most of them are from Japanese cities which have already been very much westernized.

It appears that the Japanese-American marriage in the United States since World War II has, for the most part, not fared too badly. The Schnepps and Masoko study of 40 couples indicates that the marriages have on the whole done very well.[10] Strauss' study in Chicago, based on interviews with 30 men and 15 women in American-Japanese marriages, indicates that in many respects marriage adjustment is eased by the combination of Japanese and American sex roles and marriage values.[11]

In a very comprehensive analysis of the cultural and social interactional factors involved in the Japanese-American marriages, Strauss concludes that one cannot arrive at the easy conclusion that interracial

[9] *Honolulu Star Bulletin,* June 27, 1957.
[10] Gerald Schnepps, Yui Schnepps, and Agnes Masoko, "Cultural and Marital Adjustment of Japanese War Brides," *American Journal of Sociology,* 61:48–50, July, 1955.
[11] Anselm L. Strauss, "Strain and Harmony in American-Japanese War Bride Marriages," *Marriage and Family Living,* 16:99–106, May, 1954.

marriages are necessarily doomed to destruction or even that they present unusually great problems of adjustment.

Such cultural values as the lack of vocational aspirations of the wife, the absence of strong institutional loyalties, even the lack of strong loyalty to the religious institutions of her nation, an attitude of acceptance of the American standard of living (which is far superior on every level to anything she has known), and the acceptance of the husband as he is, rather than pushing him to improve himself, all favor the Japanese wife. The Japanese philosophy of the girl shifting her allegiance to the husband's family when she leaves her home in marriage also helps her in making the adjustment to a new way of life.

Scoring happiness at 100 for very happy marriages, Baber's early study of 48 interracial marriages between whites and members of the black and yellow races rated their happiness at only 62, a score much lower than those of interfaith and mixed-nationality marriages. One-third of the couples had no children, although none of them had been married for less than three years, and the median period of marriage was ten years. Undoubtedly some of this group had refrained from having children because they did not want children born into an environment of discrimination and trouble. There was no way to know how large a proportion of such interracial marriages had already failed.[12]

Pavela[13] made a study of 95 Negro-white marriages in Indiana, where such intermarriages have been illegal since 1852 and where it has been illegal to perform rites for such couples. Of these, 69 were Negro men with white brides, 26 white men with Negro brides. He found couples more often entered marriage with a previous divorce and were older than average at the time of marriage. There was no evidence of the Negro male marrying down in occupational and social status, as is often assumed. Most were middle class. Few were married in a religious ceremony.

Pavela concludes, "It would appear that . . . interracial marriage occurs between persons who are, by and large, economically, educationally, and culturally equal and who have a strong emotional attachment, be it rationalization or real. The external pressures faced by the interracial couples are often great but certainly do not appear to be overwhelming."

He goes on to explain that with most couples, the children were still young and the real crises of adjustment may have lain ahead.

Jessie Bernard[14] finds that racially mixed black-white marriages, are about as homogamous as white-white marriages as to education. Wives of Negro men, regardless of color, tend to have more schooling than their

---

[12] Ray E. Baber, "A Study of 325 Mixed Marriages," *American Sociological Review*, 2:705–716, October, 1937.

[13] Todd H. Pavela, "An Exploratory Study of Negro-White Intermarriage in Indiana," Chicago Urban League, 1958–1959.

[14] Jessie Bernard, "Notes on Educational Homogamy in Negro-White and White-Negro Marriages," *Journal of Marriage and Family Living*, 28:274 ff., August, 1960.

husbands, because of the generally low level of schooling of Negro males.

Heer[15] believes that Negro-white intermarriage will help reduce the status gap between the races. He finds that most Negro-white marriages since 1950 have been between Negro husbands and white wives, the high-status male trading class advantage for the caste advantage of a white wife. He finds that Negro-white marriages are on the increase but sees no likelihood of sufficient increase during the next hundred years to bring, in and of itself, full equality.

The Child of Mixed Parentage

In the past, racially mixed pairs have accepted the fact that the child is classed as a member of the lower-status race. There is a long tradition for this in American society. It has been so with Negro-white offspring; and of the American Indian, down to the sixteenth part. (Influencing this was a Census definition, which was motivated by a desire to protect the child's share in tribal inheritance rights.)

Gordon,[16] after his comprehensive study of interrmarriage, concludes that the chance of failure of an interracial marriage is greater than of an interfaith marriage. Interracial marriages lack the social support which interfaith marriages have. Mass public opinion is opposed to the former. He goes on to comment about the fruit of such unions in these terms:

> The children born of Negro-white marriages in the United States are, I believe, among the most socially unfortunate persons in all the world if they seek or expect acceptance by the white community in America. . . . They must find their roots in the Negro community or remain unaccepted and unaccept-able to the white community.[17]

He finds unanimity of agreement among Negro-white parents that the teen-age years for their youngsters is the most trying period of their lives because of the taboos on interdating. He then raises the question of whether a couple in love have any moral right to create such problems for their children.

The long term view, of course, is that such problems would vanish if complete tolerance prevailed; but Gordon is no doubt right in his appraisal of the current situation and that it will not soon vanish from our society.

[15] David M. Heer, "Negro-White Marriage in the United States," *Journal of Marriage and Family Living*, 28:262–273, August, 1966.
[16] *Op. cit.*, pp. 348–349.
[17] *Ibid.*, p. 333–334.

Both the law and the weight of public opinion in American society stand in the way of intermarriage for certain groups. Yet crossing of ethnic and racial lines goes on. For some people there seems to be a fascination in unlike skin color which cultural taboos are insufficient to control. Stories are always afloat about the exotic flavor of interracial sexual ventures, and these encourage race crossing outside wedlock wherever peoples of different skin color inhabit the same territory.

There is no reason, from the hereditary standpoint, why race lines should not be crossed in marriage. There is even some indication that a kind of hybrid vigor results where pure strains are crossed, as is found in hybrid strains of plants and animals. In countries where race crossing is approved by custom there is no objection to intermarriage. Interracial marriages have taken on special significance in the United States only because of race prejudice, which expresses itself in segregation and discrimination. Prejudice is particularly severe against individuals crossing racial lines to marry and the child of mixed blood is in many situations accepted by neither racial group. Color prejudice is a social reality and no amount of idealism or faith on the part of young people in love can make it possible for them to evade this fact. It may still be generations away from disappearing.

It must be expected, however, that as America plays a leading part in world leadership, more and more of her young men are going to have the opportunity to marry girls of different racial and nationality strains while stationed abroad. Such marriages are often entered into from loneliness and during periods of great sex hunger. It is not likely that choices made at such times will be based on clear judgment and objectivity. There is often an inclination on the part of the youth to forget that his foreign wife will be expected to fit into a world entirely new and strange to her when he returns home. The transition is so great that few foreign women can be expected to make it without great difficulty and without considerable tolerance on the part of the husband and his family. The cultural differences here add to the racial difference.

The Education Factor in Marriage Adjustment

Education is the most potent cure for American ills as well as those of the underdeveloped nations. We expect much of it in every area of human improvement. Marriage is no exception. By this we mean not courses in marriage specifically, although they are increasing, but amount of education in terms of years spent in school.

Numerous studies going back as far as the basic researches of Burgess and Cottrell,[18] and those of Lewis I. Terman,[19] have found a relationship between years of schooling and happiness and duration of marriage. The 1960 Census shows a typical picture on a nationwide basis (see Table 15–1). More recently Luckey found[20] marital satisfaction positively related to years of schooling.

There can be no doubt about the association between schooling and somewhat more favorable chances for success in marriage. The reason for the association is not well understood. Several factors no doubt contribute. Those with higher levels of schooling marry later, have more maturity of judgment perhaps in mate choice by virtue of more extensive dating and

Table 15–1 Proportion of Ever-Married White and Nonwhite Men Age 45 to 54 in Stable Marriages, 1960, By Years of Schooling

| | Proportion in Stable Marriages | |
Years of Schooling	Nonwhite	White
0–4	53.5	73.0
5–7	57.3	76.4
8	57.5	78.4
9–11	55.9	77.3
12	59.2	79.6
13–15	54.8	78.2
16	65.2	83.5
17+	71.3	85.7

Source: *United States Census of Population, 1960, Marital Status,* Table 4, pp. 77, 81. From Jessie Bernard, "Marital Stability and Patterns of Status Variables," *Journal of Marriage and Family Living,* 28:421–439, November, 1966.

It will be observed that stable marriages within both white and nonwhite groups increase with level of education. (Stability is defined as a husband in his first marriage, living with a wife. In 89.9 percent of cases it was the wife's first marriage also.)

exposure to wider range of choice. Schooling in itself is a maturing experience. Greater tolerance for others and greater ease in making adjustments may be acquired. Perhaps those with more education develop superior problem-solving techniques. Certainly the way a couple approaches problems in their marriage is of prime importance to its success. Whatever the reason, the relationship exists. Marriages of college-educated couples turn

[18] Ernest W. Burgess and Leonard S. Cottrell, *Predicting Success or Failure in Marriage* (Englewood Cliffs, N. J.: Prentice Hall, Inc., 1939).

[19] Lewis I. Terman, *Psychological Factors in Marital Happiness* (New York: McGraw Hill Book Co., Inc., 1938).

[20] Eleanore Braun Luckey, "Number of Years Married as Related to Personality Perception of Marital Satisfaction," *Journal of Marriage and Family Living,* 28:44–46, February, 1966.

out far better than does the average marriage. (For convincing data turn to Figure 21–1, showing marriage happiness by occupation.)

Schooling is the gateway to stable income-producing occupations and professions. These give the kind of economic foundation associated with stable marriages. The college group moves into professional positions and the marriage is protected by more social pressures such as reputation, respectability, and social expectation.

The problem of degree of difference in education which can be tolerated between mates is of concern to many in the late high school and college years. Should the young man in college forget the girl who did not wish to continue or was not able to do so? Should a wife "put hubby through" at the cost of her own schooling? Should she go to school while he is in the military? These are recurrent questions in the peer group.

It is a well-established fact that most marriages are between those of similar education and intelligence.[21] This is to be expected in a country where everyone spends most of his dating years in school and associates for the most part with those of similar educational experience and achievement. High schools and colleges are sometimes humorously referred to as match factories.

Studies of college students indicate that girls prefer to marry men above themselves in education, while men generally prefer women their equals in education and intelligence. Two studies in particular[22] have sought to discover what educational requirements or preferences young people hold regarding prospective mates. Men, it was found, are generally willing to marry someone having less education or intelligence than they possess. Women are less willing to enter such a match although in the latter of the two studies, more than twice as many women (42 percent as opposed to only 18 percent in this first study) indicated that they would be willing to marry someone with less intelligence or education than themselves, other things being equal. This would indicate that women are much less demanding on the matter of education than they once were. This, in turn, probably reflects the great increase in opportunities for married women to earn and maintain the standard of living they choose. The majority,

[21] The problem of assortative mating by education and for ability is dealt with in the following: Paul Popenoe, "Mate Selection," *American Sociological Review,* 2:735–743, October, 1937; Lewis M. Terman and others, *Psychological Factors in Marital Happiness* (New York: McGraw-Hill Book Co., 1938), pp. 189 ff.; William S. Bernard, "Student Attitudes on Marriage and the Family," *American Sociological Review,* 3:354–361, June, 1938; Ray E. Baber, *Marriage and the Family,* revised edition (New York: McGraw-Hill Book Co., 1953), pp. 126–127; D. U. Mather, "The Courtship Ideals of High School Students," *Sociology and Social Research,* 19:169, 1934–35; Paul H. Landis and Katherine H. Day, "Education as a Factor in Mate Selection," *American Sociological Review,* 10:558–560, August, 1954.

[22] Ray E. Baber, *Marriage and the Family,* revised edition (New York: McGraw-Hill Book Co., 1953), p. 119; Judson T. Landis and Mary G. Landis, *Building a Successful Marriage,* second edition (Englewood Cliffs, N. J.: Prentice-Hall, Inc., 1953), p. 84.

however, still want a husband at least their equal in education and ability. This results in part, no doubt, from practical considerations, but much of it merely reflects traditional American conceptions of the perfect mate.

On education, findings indicate that only 1 percent of the girls studied preferred husbands with less education, 18 percent wanted equal education, and 81 percent preferred husbands with superior educational attainment.[23] Of the men, 9 percent wanted their wives to have more education, 9 percent less, 82 percent the same.

When it comes to actually selecting a mate, women come nearer to realizing their education ideal than do men. This is explained in part by the fact that more men than women reach the higher levels in education. It may also indicate that men attach much less significance to this qualification in their wives than do women in their husbands. In many instances, one suspects a young man actually in the marriage market discovers he does not want a wife who is his educational and intellectual equal.

Figure 15–1 shows the proportion of young college people marrying those who were educationally higher, equal to, and lower than themselves. Most college men married below themselves in educational status, but half the women succeeded in marrying educational equals. The further a young person went in college, the more likely he was to marry a person with some college training. Of those who graduated from college, 80 percent married persons with some college training.

The desire of women to marry up and the practice of men to marry down probably reflects basic differences in motivation in mate selection. The male, who is by custom the breadwinner, is usually judged by a woman, at least in part, by his ability to offer security by constancy of income. Since education has a direct bearing on economic success,[24] a good education has become an important selective factor by women's standards. The male has most to do with establishing and maintaining the general social status of the family, which is determined in our society by such factors as income, occupation, and standard of living. The young woman who can associate herself by marriage with a person of higher education and training is bargaining for a better standard of living than she could expect as a result of her own training and skills.

The man, on the other hand, in facing the problem of mate selection, is likely to consider criteria other than education of prime importance. Men are not particularly attracted to woman with college diplomas or other evidence of intellectual prowess. Attractiveness and feminine charm rate higher in our culture, and their importance is constantly reaffirmed

[23] Landis and Landis, *op. cit.*, p. 84.

[24] Paul H. Landis, "The Dollar Value of an Education," *Journal of the National Education Association*, 38:366–368, May, 1949; also Ernest Havermann and Patricia Salter West, *They Went to College* (New York: Harcourt, Brace & Co., 1952). Figure 21–1, shows the relationship between occupation and marital happiness.

FIGURE 15–1   EDUCATIONAL LEVEL OF MATES SELECTED BY COLLEGE
YOUTHS. Source: Paul H. Landis and Katherine H. Day, "Education as a
Factor in Mate Selection," **American Sociological Review,** 10:558–560,
August, 1954.

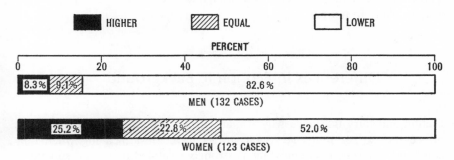

Most college men married below their level of education; very few married
higher. Almost half of all college women married equal to or above their
educational level—over a fourth above.

by pin-up girls, Miss America contests, and other symbols of the cult of
beauty.[25]

The belief in the intellectual superiority of the male has so long been
a part of American thinking that few men, and for that matter few women,
are comfortable in a relationship where the female is obviously the more
outstanding. A marriage having this relationship frequently brings feelings
of resentment, inadequacy, and frustration to the husband. Few men wish
to have their position of authority in the family threatened by the superior
educational qualifications of their wives. Popenoe believes the educated
man wants a wife who will flatter his ego.[26] Women reared in the popular
tradition wish to feel that their husbands actually are superior persons to
whom they may look up. Although one might think college women different
in these attitudes, numerous class discussions with upper division classes
have convinced the writer that college women hold this view also.

That this pattern of assortative mating is deeply rooted is suggested
by findings that women who marry above themselves in education are
more likely to be happy in marriage than those who marry below themselves.[27] In other words, the pattern is so well established that acting
contrary to it increases the danger of maladjustment in marriage.

In summary, the evidence favors the view that a similar amount of
schooling is desirable for marriage partners, and that if there is a differ-

[25] Various check lists show clearly that young men rate good looks more highly
than do young women in mate selection.
[26] Paul Popenoe, "Where Are the Marriageable Men?" *Social Forces*, 14:257–
262, December, 1935.
[27] Terman and others, *op. cit.*, p. 191.

ence in the amount of education, it is better for the husband to be the one with more education than the wife.[28] Even so, these differences are much less significant to marriage adjustment than religious and racial differences. Those with the kind of extreme educational differences that could be critical are not likely to marry.

Differences in Economic Background

Fiction and fairy tale have woven many a plot around the Cinderella-type prince-and-pauper marriage. Such stories have most meaning when they come out of a social system which is strongly stratified by class distinctions. The open-class system of the United States teaches that every man can be a king and attempts to ignore economic lines. This philosophy is encouraged by territorial mobility, which helps one shed his past, and by the prevailing belief in social climbing, which tends to obliterate class lines.

The lower-class girl, class theorists find, is the victim of the sexual exploitation by the upper-class boy when she is his date. If this is true, one might well ask whether the lower-class girl is in reality exploiting the boy's financial and status resources. Kinsey[29] finds that lower-class girls are no more accessible sexually than upper- or middle-class girls. Each seems to participate in premarital intercourse in about the same proportion of cases. Kinsey does not, however, go into the matter of whether the joint participants in the sex acts are of the same social strata.

Although many studies have shown a tendency to date and marry within similar socioeconomic classes, lines are by no means rigidly drawn. Where differences in economic backgrounds are great, certain difficulties may logically be anticipated. Men and women alike who consider marriage into different social backgrounds or into families with very different ways of life must expect to overcome certain handicaps and make difficult adjustments in order to find happiness in marriage.

It is easier for a man to marry down the economic ladder than for a woman to do so. The man is not criticized too severely for picking a girl who comes from a lower social, economic, or educational level. If a woman is beautiful, he is excused, often envied, even though she falls short in many other qualities. At the same time, many social groups are critical of the woman who marries a socially, economically, or educationally inferior man. This is not particularly because she is giving up a higher standard of

---

[28] *Ibid.*
[29] Alfred C. Kinsey and others, *Sexual Behavior in the Human Female* (Philadelphia: W. B. Saunders Co., 1953).

living. Actually, the criticism such a woman draws upon herself results from a complex of social attitudes and traditions. First, she is bucking custom—tradition says each woman should find someone to care for her and protect her, someone to give her all of the things she "deserves." It is popularly believed, too, that one's choice of a mate is a reflection upon one's self. The first question which is likely to enter the minds of her friends is, "Couldn't she do any better than that?" Finally, marrying "down" is generally taken as an admission of personal or social inadequacy.

The average girl can adjust more easily to a higher than to a lower standard of living. There is always some risk in marriage when the young wife is accustomed to a much higher level of living than her new mate can provide, although few girls should expect to start on the level their parents have attained by middle age. Only an unusual girl can face low-income living, even in her own home. The man who marries under these circumstances owes it to his own future happiness, as well as to that of his fiancée, to make clear that he cannot hope to maintain the level of living to which she is accustomed.

If the wife, in order to maintain her past standard of living, begins to depend on her family as a source of income or to obtain accustomed luxuries and recreation, this becomes a source of embarrassment to her husband, whom society expects to provide for her. Sometimes the wife's family wants to save their daughter from hardships or presumed hardships. They cannot bear to have her going without things they themselves have, things she has been used to in her childhood home. In fact, they are even unwilling to have her go through the struggles that they themselves went through.

In summary, the lesson that stands out most clearly in the area of racial and cultural variables discussed in this chapter is that for the most part those most nearly alike in racial and national heritage, in schooling, in socioeconomic background, and adding the findings of Chapter 14, in religion, have fewer handicaps to overcome and more often find satisfaction in marriage.

There are always those who beat the odds in any gamble, and in most of the areas discussed the gamble is not a great one. The odds are likely to be increased by ignoring differences in too many areas. Interracial marriages are more likely to work where there is similar education, religion, and economic background. The status of the children will be higher if both are educated and if there is adequate income. If the pair have a strong bond of like religion they do not have to solve this problem for their children, along with the race relations problem.

Awareness of these facts in the early stages of dating can often guide young people away from unnecessary problems and appreciably simplify the task of mate selection.

Problems

1. *Sociodrama:* The honeymoon is over, figuratively as well as literally, and a wealthy, well-educated, young woman and her husband of humble background and little education are trying to plan their leisure hours together.
2. Charles and Katherine are graduate college students in a northern university. They have known each other since early high school days and are familiar with one another's values, ideals, and ambitions. They are both from wealthy families, both plan to be chemists, and both tend to be introverts with little interest in or need of outside friendships.

   After five years of dating during which their attachment has steadily grown, Charles finally broached the subject of marriage, though none too courageously, for Charles is a Negro and Katherine is Irish by descent. In your opinion should Katherine:
   a. Refuse outright?
   b. Talk the matter over with her parents and minister?
   c. Consent?
   d. Consent but plan to move to another country?
   e. Consent but insist that they have no children?
   f. Delay her consent until she has discovered whether or not Charles would be accepted by her friends, parents, and community?
   g. Consent and plan to identify herself with his family and friends if they will accept her?
3. What might account for the attraction many girls feel for men ten to thirty years their senior? What might be the advantages in such a marriage? What are the disadvantages?
4. If there is a foreign war bride in your community ask her to describe some of the adjustments demanded by an international or interracial marriage.
5. "Marriage," they say, "is a private affair." Why, then, should an individual hesitate to marry someone of another race whom he sincerely loves?
6. In what way do children complicate the adjustments of interracial marriages?
7. Do you believe that encouraging interracial marriages among those who are unprejudiced would tend to reduce interracial hatred and intolerance in general?
8. Marie is from a patriotic French family. Otto was a German pilot in World War II. They both live in the United States now. They have lost their accents and few people could tell from looking at them that they are not of the same nationality. In what way, then, might nationality stand in the way of their achieving marital happiness?
9. What arguments can you think of in favor of marriages in which the wife is a few years older than her husband? What might the disadvantages be?
10. What age relationship between husband and wife do you consider ideal? Why?
11. A wealthy young man has proposed to a friend of yours from a lower-class home. Would your advice be:
    a. "Jump at the chance. This is every girl's dream."
    b. "His background of wealth doesn't make any difference in America, so don't let that influence you."

    c. "Don't marry him; you could never be happy together."
    d. Some other advice.
12. In our society, tradition favors a woman's marrying above rather than below her economic station in life. In your opinion, has the time come to do away with this practice as outmoded? Justify your answer.
13. What do you believe accounts for the fact that men generally prefer wives of equal or slightly less education than themselves?
14. Do you believe that the responsibilities of caring for a home, financial management, and child rearing make a college-educated woman a better wife?
15. What educational relationship do you believe ideal for husband and wife? Why?
16. The Duke of Windsor's story (in his book, *A King's Story*) is one of the great romances of history involving those of very different background. Discuss and appraise the former king's choice.

Selected References

Articles in Books of Readings

Landis, Judson T., and Landis, Mary G., *Readings in Marriage and the Family* (Englewood Cliffs, N. J.: Prentice-Hall, Inc., 1952).
    Baber, Ray E., "A Study of 48 Inter-racial Marriages," pp. 210–214.
Rodman, Hyman, *Marriage, Family and Society* (New York: Random House, 1965).
    Rodman, Hyman, "Mate Selection: Incest Taboos, Homogamy, and Mixed Marriages," Reading 4.
Sussman, Marvin B., *Sourcebook in Marriage and Family*, third edition (Boston: Houghton Mifflin Co., 1968).
    Heer, David M., "Negro-White Marriage in the United States," Reading 15.
Winch, Robert F., and Goodman, Louis Wolf, *Selected Studies in Marriage and the Family*, third edition (New York: Holt, Rinehart and Winston, Inc., 1968).
    Heer, David M., "Negro-White Marriage in the United States," pp. 481–485.
    Udry, J. Richard, "Marital Instability by Race, Sex, Education, Occupation, and Income Using 1960 Census Data," pp. 572–578.

General References

Adams, Ronanzo, *Interracial Marriage in Hawaii* (New York: The MacMillan Co., 1937).
Aldous, Joan, "Wives' Employment Status and Lower-Class Men as Husband-Fathers: Support for the Moynihan Thesis," *Journal of Marriage and Family Living*, 31:469–476, August, 1969.
Bernard, Jessie, "Note of Educational Homogamy in Negro-White and White-Negro Marriages," *Journal of Marriage and the Family*, 28:274–276, August, 1966.

Bescancency, P. H., "On Reporting Rates of Intermarriage," *American Journal of Sociology*, 70:717–721, May, 1964.

"Black and White Dating," *Time*, July, 1968, pp. 48–49.

Bogardus, Emory S., "Comparing Racial Distance in Ethiopia, South Africa, and the United States," *Sociology and Social Research*, 52:149–156, January, 1968.

Burma, J. H., "Interethnic Marriage in Los Angeles, 1948–1959," *Social Forces*, 42:156–165, December, 1963.

Golden, Joseph, "Patterns of Negro-White-Intermarriage," *American Sociological review*, 19; 144–147, April, 1954.

Gordon, Albert L., *Inter-Marriage* (Boston: Beacon Press, 1964).

Heer, David M., "Negro-White Marriage in the United States," *Journal of Marriage and the Family*, 28:262–273, August, 1966.

Knebel, Fletcher, "Identity—the Black Woman's Burden," *Look*, September 23, 1969, pp. 77–79.

Lind, A. W., "Interracial Marriage as Affecting Divorce in Hawaii," *Sociology and Social Research*, 49:17–26, October 19, 1964.

Myrdal, Gunnar, *An American Dilemma: Negro Problem and Modern Democracy* (New York: Harper & Brothers, 1944).

Pavela, Tood H., "An Exploratory Study of Negro-White Intermarriage in Indiana," *Journal of Marriage and the Family*, 26:209–211, May, 1964.

Schmitt, Robert C., "Age and Race Differences in Divorce in Hawaii," *Journal of Marriage and the Family*, 31:48–50, February, 1969.

Schnepps, Gerald, Schnepps, Yui, and Masoko, Agnes, "Cultural and Marital Adjustment of Japanese War Brides," *American Journal of Sociology*, 61:48–50, July, 1955.

Strauss, Anselm L., "Strain and Harmony in American-Japanese War Bride Marriages," *Marriage and Family Living*, 16:99–106, May, 1954.

16

Age for Marriage

"To everything there is a season, and a time for every purpose under heaven." This quote is taken from Ecclesiastes and a current popular song takes up the theme. Young people think in more personal terms: "Shall we marry before he finishes his military service?" "Shall we wait until he (she) graduates?" "Do we want to put it off until he is through med school?"

Readiness for marriage admittedly cannot be determined by chronological age alone. Yet it is difficult to acquire a mature perspective on life without attaining the experience which comes with the years. Success in marriage is, in part, a matter of readiness in the broad sense of having reached the age at which one can fit it into life plans, accept and carry the obligations marriage involves. Levy and Munroe[1] believe that emotional readiness for marriage is much more important than any particular personality trait. They believe that persons who have the proper mental attitude toward marriage can work out a way of life together and make a good adjustment, just as such people do in a field of work which may not be the most ideal from the standpoint of their interests and needs.

This view considers that "when to marry" is the real question and that this is answered in terms of one's own development. It holds that acceptance of the marriage relationship is of major importance—to be able honestly to practice the words, "to love, honor, and cherish, for better or for worse, until death do us part." It holds that a husband and wife can have a lot of conflicts and face many problems, but if they have this attitude of certainty toward their marriage, they can work problems out to a solution. They feel that an experimental approach to marriage is a sure signpost to Reno.

There is a finality about marriage, and only those persons should marry who have reached the time when marriage is more important to them than

[1] John Levy and Ruth Munroe, *The Happy Family* (New York: Alfred A. Knopf, Inc., 1938), p. 43.

anything else. One's age at marriage, his preparation, the particular time in world affairs, the stage of one's career development, one's achieved state of social, emotional, and economic maturity—all have a bearing.

Age for Marriage

It is a commonly held belief that early marriages are likely to work out well, because of the adjustability of youth. The person who is older is pictured as habit-ridden and fixed in his ways. This notion may have had substance in the fixed relations of agrarian societies. In a rapidly changing society it is likely that the person who has lived a few more years and has gained a greater breadth of experience is more adjustable than the teen-ager with his limited horizon and circumscribed existence. The experiences of leaving home, changing communities, meeting and working with strangers, and planning one's life seldom come before the late teens or early twenties. These experiences might be expected to contribute appreciably to one's ability to adjust.

Teen-age Marriages

For many years there has been great concern over teen-age marriage and the problems it presents to parents, school systems, community welfare systems, and agencies working with young people. It is often disastrous when the young take on adult responsibilities and fail at them.

The number of marriages in the younger group has declined. There are fewer girls marrying under 18 years than 15 to 20 years ago (see Figure 16–1). Of women marrying 15 years ago, 23 percent were under 18, now only 15 percent. Not many young men ever did marry under 18, but the proportion doing so is less than 15 years ago, and the proportion marrying under 20 has also dropped substantially.

Still far too many marry too soon, but a reversal of this trend has taken place. There are several possible reasons for this: more young people plan to have a college education, the military service creates a shortage of marriageable males at home, an awareness among young people that early marriages generally are headed for trouble (some have opportunity to observe this fact among their classmates who may be married and divorced), and perhaps the use of the pill[2] and other sophisticated birth control methods, warding off pregnancy and thus avoiding the forced marriage.

[2] It is believed that parents in some cases have the family doctor prescribe the pill on pretense of curing menstrual irregularities in order to protect the daughter from pregnancy.

FIGURE 16–1   PERCENTAGE OF PERSONS WHO MARRIED BEFORE SPECI-
FIED AGE, 1966—BY AGE AND SEX. Source: Robert E. Parke, Jr., and Paul
C. Glick, "Prospective Changes in Marriage and the Family," **Journal of
Marriage and the Family,** 29:249–256, May, 1967.

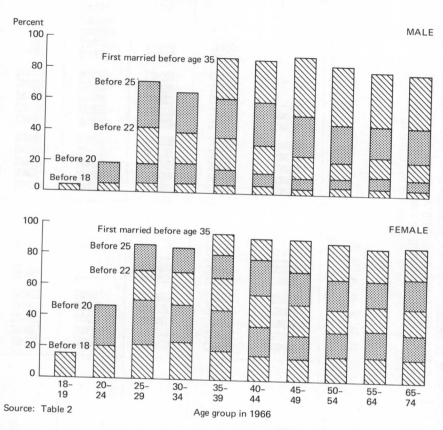

Source: Table 2

Age group in 1966

Marriages of young teen-agers are on the decline, having reached a peak
some 15 to 18 years ago.

The Success Record of Teen-Age Marriage

For thirty years students of the family have been examining the relationship
between age at marriage and success or failure. One of the first such studies[3]
compared adjustments of individuals in various age groups of more than 500
upper-middle-class couples. It was found that the likelihood of good ad-

[3] Ernest W. Burgess and Leonard S. Cottrell, *Predicting Success or Failure in
Marriage* (Englewood Cliffs, N. J.: Prentice-Hall, Inc., 1939), pp. 115–117.

FIGURE 16-2 RELATIONSHIP BETWEEN MARITAL ADJUSTMENT AND AGE OF HUSBANDS AND WIVES AT TIME OF MARRIAGE. Source: Based on data from Ernest W. Burgess and Leonard S. Cottrell, **Predicting Success or Failure in Marriage** (Copyright 1939, by Prentice-Hall, Inc, New York). Reproduced by permission of the publisher.

W I F E

AGE AT MARRIAGE	POOR ADJUSTMENT	FAIR ADJUSTMENT	GOOD ADJUSTMENT
16-18	46.9%	34.4%	18.7%
19-21	28.5%	29.2%	42.3%
22-24	20.9%	29.1%	50%
25-27	22.5%	27.5%	50%
28 AND OVER	17.7%	24.2%	58.1%

PICTOGRAPH CORPORATION

Almost one-half of the wives who married under 19 made poor adjustments in marriage; few made good adjustments. Husbands who married under 21 had considerable chances of poor adjustment. Data are for middle-class, urban couples. We do not know whether the same relationship holds for rural couples.

justment for women between the ages of 16 and 30 years increased steadily with later marriage (see Figure 16–2). Among the cases studied, more than twice as many women nearing 30 were found to have made a good marital adjustment as had women marrying under 18.

Men who married before the age of twenty-two stood considerable chance of poor adjustment. Those who married between twenty-eight and thirty took the least risk. However, men who married after thirty were found to make good adjustments less frequently. This probably indicates, not that men become less marriageable as they pass thirty, but merely that by this age those with the best potentialities have already been selected.

Divorce rates are much higher among marriages that occur at an early age.[4] Burchinal and Chancellor,[5] studying marriages that ended in divorce, found that when both were nineteen or under, the marriages lasted only half as long as when they were twenty or older. Where the husband was of low occupational status, duration of the marriage prior to divorce was also briefer than when he was of high occupational status. Age of marriage and occupational status are inevitably related since training is a prerequisite to high occupational status.

Glick, studying Census data, found divorce of those married before age eighteen almost as three times as high as of those marrying between twenty-two and twenty-four.[6]

Christine H. Hillman analyzed inquiries to an advice column in a newspaper. She found that 66 percent of these inquiries came from married individuals and that 72 percent of the inquiries of the people who were or had been married were from those who had married before their 18th birthday. The median age of first marriages of these people was 16.8 years.[7]

There are many reasons for the unhappiness and frequent failure of the teen-age marriages. They are often induced by pregnancy. No accurate statistics are available, but various studies and estimates place the figure at 50 to 75 percent for high school marriages.

[4] Harvey J. Locke found that a relatively high proportion of divorced women in a group studied in Indiana had married before age eighteen; and of divorced men, before age twenty-one; see his *Predicting Adjustment in Marriage: A Comparison of a Divorced and Happily Married Group* (New York: Henry Holt & Co., Inc., 1951), pp. 101-102. Judson T. Landis, studying 1,051 marriages, found a divorce rate of 14.3 percent where both married under 20. The rate dropped consistently to 2.3 percent where both were over 30. Judson T. Landis and Mary G. Landis, *Building a Successful Marriage*, fourth edition (Englewood Cliffs, N. J.: Prentice-Hall, Inc., 1963), pp. 127-131.

[5] Lee G. Burchinal and Loren E. Chancellor, "Survival Rates Among Religiously Homogamous and Interreligious Marriages," *Agricultural Experiment Station Research Bulletin 512*, December, 1962.

[6] Paul C. Glick, *American Families* (New York: John Wiley & Sons, Inc., 1957), Table 72, p. 112; see also Paul H. Jacobson, *American Marriage and Divorce* (New York: Holt, Rinehart and Winston, Inc., 1959).

[7] Christine H. Hillman, "An Advice Column's Challenge for Family-Life Education," *Marriage and Family Living*, 16:51-54, February, 1954.

The forced marriage is unfortunate at any age[8] and has even more counts against it with teen-agers. Many do not have the physical development to perform the normal functions of adult life, including work responsibilities and the biological functions of reproduction and child care. The human female is not fully ready for the reproductive function until long after puberty. Adolescent sterility has long been noted by anthropologists observing primitives who have no taboos on sexual intercourse among adolescents. Full fertility and biological capability of producing sound offspring are not reached, on the average, until the early twenties. Ashley-Montagu's studies show a high rate of infant and maternal mortality among adolescent mothers, and a high rate of premature births, miscarriages, and stillbirths.[9] Guttmacher, however, places the ideal age from an obstetrical viewpoint at between ages seventeen and twenty-one.[10]

Young people may lack a good educational and vocational foundation to meet the economic demands that a family brings. Too often they are unready to give up teen-group activities and settle down; this is likely to be especially true of the male. Young couples are not old enough to win a respected place in the adult community; often not mature enough to stand the daily pressures and tensions that married living and children bring. These pressures are likely to be multiplied when the children are not wanted.

The comment of a young mother of three children, divorced at twenty-one, may be typical of many. When asked if she had been too young at marriage, and if that was why it failed she replied, "I wasn't too young, but he was." She went on to explain that she made the adjustment, but that her husband found being tied down to the support of wife and children too much for him.

In some cases he may have been tied down involuntarily because of the girl's pregnancy, and he escapes his problem by terminating the marriage. This adds to her problems and to the social burden of the community supporting his children. Thus the male economic role is transferred to the tax roll.

In some small communities a major problem of landlords is fending off applications for rent by the young divorced woman with small children. In self-defense they often reject her as an unsuitable tenant. Her funds are at best limited, and alimony is undependable. She is likely to be entertaining males in the home in her quest for a new husband and father, and she may marry and leave without notice.

[8] Harold T. Christensen, and Hannah H. Meissner, "Studies in Child-Spacing: III—Premarital Pregnancy as a Factor in Divorce, *American Sociological Review*, 18:641–644, December, 1953.

[9] M. F. Ashley-Montagu, *The Reproductive Development of the Female* (New York: Julian Press, Inc., 1958).

[10] Dr. Allan F. Guttmacher, Obstetrician and Gynocologist in *Reader's Digest*, p. 34, June, 1969.

Parental Relations in Early Marriage

Margaret Mead concludes[11] that today romance is less a factor in early marriage than twenty years ago. Now girls get married "to get away from their mothers." The small nuclear family has no place for two women in the household. Under the large family system this urgency did not exist.

But in marrying young many do not get away. A 1967 study by the U.S. Bureau of the Census shows[12] that 19.2 percent of marriages in which the husband is under 20 were living with relatives, only 5.7 of those 20–24. Less than 2 percent of any other age group prior to retirement, lives with relatives.

These data suggest that there is a high degree of dependence on parents and other relatives and a risk of interference from relatives in the new marriage. Privacy is limited and the chance for the couple to adjust to each other and maintain their own counsel is likely to be limited.

The young bride and groom are much more vulnerable to parental interference from both sides,[13] and invite a real in-law problem. It is likely that parents on both sides feel freer to criticize a young couple and are inclined to feel it is their right if the couple is drawing support from them. The young are more likely to seek emotional support from the parents, and with it may come advice which one or the other of the pair resents.

The "Glick Effect"

Paul Glick[14] first called attention to the fact that both high school and college women who drop out to marry have the highest rate of divorce in their respective age groups. Jessie Bernard[15] finds a similar relationship in her analysis of 1960 census data and refers to the lower marital stability of the dropout group as the "Glick effect."

There has been considerable discussion as to whether factors in the background of the girl explain both her dropping out of school and her

[11] "Margaret Mead's Sound Insights into the Furor over Shifting American Morals," *Life,* 65:30–34, August 25, 1968.

[12] "Marital Status and Family Status: March 1967", Population Characteristics, Series P–20, no. 170, February 23, 1968, United States Census, Table B, p. 2.

[13] Judson T. Landis and Mary G. Landis, *Building a Successful Marriage*, fifth edition (Englewood Cliffs, N. J.: Prentice-Hall, Inc., 1968), Figure 17–3, p. 338; see also Robert O. Blood, Jr. and Donald M. Wolfe, *Husbands and Wives,* (New York: Free Press of Glencoe, Inc., 1960), p. 247.

[14] Paul C. Glick, *American Families* (New York: Wiley and Sons, 1957), p. 154.

[15] Jessie Bernard, "Marital Stability and Patterns of Status Variables," *Journal of Marriage and Family Living*, 28:421–439, November, 1966.

failure in marriage. A whole complex of disadvantages are involved in the failure of the marriage, some of them residual in the childhood environment, some induced by leaving school and some by premature entry into marriage.

The very circumstances of entering marriage may also be a factor. Hungerford[16] has pointed out that girls often enter into sex relations in the hope that this will lead to marriage. This brings the forced marriage. Since the boy was only interested in sex, he resents the responsibilities he is forced to assume.

Marriage while in College

There are two types of college marriage. The first is the student, already past the average marriage age, who marries and may begin his family while in college, or before coming to college. The other is the average-age student who marries before the rest of his peers consider marriage desirable. The problems of the two groups are considerably different.

The number of older married students increased sharply after World War II, when veterans flooded the campuses and married, requiring colleges and universities to face the problems of college housing and other aspects of the care of families and children.

Considerable sociological study of the veteran's group has been made, and findings are likely indicative of problems faced by today's veterans and older married students. Research has centered on relative success in school performance of married and unmarried couples, on their success in marriage itself, and on special problems the college marriage faces.

A Wisconsin study, for example, showed that even couples with children made better than average grades.[17] The divorce rate during the first few years of college marriages is lower than among educated people generally. Judson T. Landis' study[18] of 544 couples at Michigan State College in 1947 indicated that not only do these married students have a better grade average than the unmarried group, but that they have a greater sense of security and feel more settled. The men queried felt that a wife was a help rather than a hindrance in their college life. Of these couples, 95 percent gave themselves a rating of happy or very happy in appraising their marriage.

Some husbands were critical of the wife's interest in having more

[16] Mary Jane Hungerford, "Preventing High School Marriages," *Family Life,* 28:1-4, September, 1968.

[17] Svend Reimer, "Married Students Are Good Students," *Marriage and Family Living,* 9:11-12, February, 1947.

[18] Judson T. Landis and Mary G. Landis, *Building a Successful Marriage,* fourth edition (Englewood Cliffs, N. J.: Prentice-Hall, Inc., 1963), pp. 114-116.

social life than the husband could take time for, but on the whole, college marriages were considered successful.

Lawrence L. Falk studied 40 married and 40 single students, comparing their grades and finding no difference. Those who married while in school kept the same grade level or improved.[19]

Christensen and Philbrick's study at Purdue University in 1950 asked student couples whether or not, knowing what they knew now, they would marry again while in school.[20] Three-fourths said they would marry while in college if they had it to do over again. A fourth of the group felt that the difficulties of making a living, of finding housing, and of doing satisfactory college work offered too great handicaps. The researchers, however, suggest the probability that some of these gave external factors as rationalizations, that in many of these instances the marriage itself was one which had little hope of surviving because of deep psychological problems. (Lower happiness ratings were in evidence in the group that would have deferred marriage because of college.)

It must be remembered that most of the marriages were government subsidized, so that economic worries were greatly reduced. While many sociologists, the author among them, believe that it would be wise social policy to subsidize the marriage of able and socially mature college students, such a program does not exist. This means that nonveterans are on their own when they marry, unless they can work out and willingly accept some sort of subsidy or loan from parents.

One of the possible eugenic benefits to the nation of college postwar marriages was that the birth rate of the college group increased. This, however, often created personal problems that college couples did not anticipate. The Michigan State study showed that two-thirds of the pregnancies among this group had not been planned; one-third admitted carelessness; the other third had done everything possible to avoid pregnancy. Clearly, a college couple must take into account the possibility, or even the probability, of having children.[21] Christensen and Philbrick found similar results in a study of student-couple pregnancies at Purdue involving 346 couples.[22] Of course, birth control is more certain now than when these studies were made, but this will not take care of the carelessness factor. This study further reports that children proved to be a serious handicap to college performance, taking time, making study difficult, requiring loss of sleep, and eventually wanting to play when the parents got

[19] Lawrence L. Falk, "A Comparative Study of Problems of Married and Single Students," *Marriage and Family Living*, 26:207-208, May, 1964.

[20] Harold T. Christensen and Robert E. Philbrick, "Family Size as a Factor of Marital Adjustment of College Students," *American Sociological Review*, 17:306-312, June, 1952.

[21] Judson T. Landis and Mary G. Landis, *op. cit.*, pp. 150-151.

[22] Christensen and Philbrick, *op. cit.*

home from school or work. Johannis[23] reports that two-thirds of the parent couples he studied in Oregon felt that children brought difficult problems for the student marriage—crowding, high rent costs, problems of getting baby sitters and paying for them, and lack of play space for children. Medical care costs are also found burdensome.

The Younger College Marriage

There has been much criticism of the underclassman marriage, and considerable research into its special problems. Any teacher who has discussed the topic with college classes becomes aware of the disadvantages students see in marriages of the usual-age college student, particularly if he marries during the first years of college.

He cuts himself off from much of the teen-age social life which is such a vital part of the college experience. His chances for leadership are undoubtedly greatly reduced, as well as his chance for developing special talents such as are demanded in the numerous extracurricular activities of the campus.

He has a compensating social life among married young people which may replace some of these disadvantages. Yet class discussions in marriage problems courses lead one to think that the average young college person feels it would be a decided loss to have been married during the early years of college, entirely aside from the economic hardship that is likely to be faced. There is also, of course, the practical problem of the great risk of pregnancy before the educational career is terminated.

Margaret Mead, in lectures on college campuses, has expressed concern over the trend toward early marriages which threatens intellectual development and makes earning a living take precedence over scholarly achievement.[24] Unlike European society, where men of great ambition were encouraged to put off family responsibility, youth in our society are pushed into it. This, she believes, tends to deny them the chance to explore, challenge. She fears men can no longer be expected to strive for great achievement when they must give priority to earning a living and caring for babies. Babies have "engrossed women for a thousand years, and it now looks as if they were going to engross men, too." She goes on to ask the question whether anyone will have time for "statesmanship, art, science, exploration of outer space?"

[23] Theodore B. Johannis, "The Marital Adjustment of a Sample of Married College Students," *The Coordinator*, 4:4, June, 1956.

[24] These ideas have been published by Margaret Mead in *U.S. News and World Report*, June 6, 1960.

No society can have both men and women devoting their time to infants. This makes for a "settled, security-loving, unadventurous people." This she views as serious in an age when countries like the Soviet Union and China have women as well as men striving for great achievement, feeling that the future belongs to them and is worth sacrificing for.

"If we retire into a kind of fur-lined domesticity, in which everyone is concerned with his own little family and his own little house, I think it is going to curtail seriously the contribution that we can make as a nation to the development of civilization on this planet," Mead believes.

Kingsley Davis,[25] in a satirical vein, has commented on the early-marriage trend in the United States, with reference to the college group particularly. He points out that it tends to destroy the ambition of women, since they are becoming increasingly content to enter marriage and bear children without other significant contribution to society. Thus they sacrifice professional and creative aspirations and fail to make a contribution to the labor force as, for example, they do in Russia where there are many women engineers and doctors. He feels that we are seeing a strong return to primitivism in the behavior of women. Too many women have abandoned ambition and sacrificed careers to their college-attending husbands.

The American girl seems too eager to enter into marriage as soon as she reaches approximate physical maturity. Many women sacrifice their future status as effective wives by cutting off their training while helping their husbands through school. Davis feels that often they cheat themselves out of the reward of high status in marriage and also risk their marriage, as the husband outgrows them in training and sophistication.

He suggests that the early-marriage rate tends to make young people, particularly girls, dawdle through school. They have little motivation to pursue academic interests seriously. He sees the young married generation becoming a generation of spongers, depending on parents to put up the money for school, for down-payment on a house, for doctor and hospital bills when the baby comes, for loans to buy the automobile or other luxuries.

Marshall and King[26] have focused on the inadequacies of most of the research into college marriages and point out reasons for inconsistent results of the various studies. Such variables as age, social class, amount of government subsidy, economic background, and other socioeconomic factors affect marriage adjustments, as well as hardships the pair encounter, amount of leisure time, the difficulties of parenthood, whether the wife has to work, and whether the wife must drop out of school. All of these should be considered by researchers.

---

[25] Kingsley Davis, "The Early Marriage Trend," *What's New*, summarized in *WSC News*, 7:3, October, 1958.

[26] William H. Marshall and Marcia P. King, "Undergraduate Student Marriage: A Compilation of Research Findings," *Journal of Marriage and the Family*, 28:350–359, August, 1966.

A study by Eshleman and Hunt[27] suggests the social class variable may be a deciding factor in the couple's adjustment to both marriage and children. They find a higher ratio of marriages among those from lower class backgrounds, and greater approval of the idea of marriage while in college. Husbands were less disturbed in their studies by having children in the home, perhaps from having grown up under more crowded conditions.

The authors feel that marriage may be made possible at an earlier age for the lower socioeconomic classes by college low-cost housing rentals, and opportunities for the wife to earn. Adjustments may be easier too, because the wife has lower educational aspirations than women in the higher socioeconomic classes. And the male may be less disturbed by the fact that grades do not usually improve over high school, since his educational background is often weak and he may have a lower level of scholastic aspirations.

Recurrent Problems of Campus Marriages

Although studies differ in many details of their findings, there are certain recurrent problems in college marriages. Many of them might exist outside the campus environment had these same people married at the same age, but our central question here is whether it is better to marry during one's schooling period or to wait.

Economic hardship is a feature of campus marriages. In the Eshleman and Hunt study this was found to be true regardless of social class.[28] According to all studies, three-fourths of the males and 60 percent of the wives were employed forty or more hours a week. Veteran's subsidies, of course, help relieve this situation.

The education of the couple is threatened and may be terminated. There is a strong tendency for marriage to terminate the wife's schooling even if marriage and children permit the husband to struggle through.

Social life will be limited, as will extracurricular activities. The time and cost factors are significant here, as is living apart from group houses and dormitories. The wife's social life particularly will be limited, and even the simple home relaxations of radio and television will be restricted by the husband's need for quiet. Faced with such difficulties the older couple will tolerate them with greater equanimity than the younger couple.

However, the college marriage receives some social support not given marriages in the world off campus. Low-grade housing is less humiliating

[27] J. Ross Eshleman and Chester L. Hunt, "Social Class Influences on Family Adjustment Patterns of Married College Students," *Journal of Marriage and Family Living*, 29:485–491, August, 1967.

[28] *Op. cit.*

because most students are equal in this respect. There are many campus organizations catering to the married couple and to student wives, and there is an interest on the campus in children and their development. Nursery schools and child-care centers are likely to be more available than in the average community.

The college campus probably offers more protection from sideline romances than do work situations in the world outside. Yet a wife may gain a distinct impression that her husband considers the girls he associates with in the classroom and in the college student union building, very attractive. It is not unusual for him to roam during her pregnancy and the campus offers ready opportunity. On the college campus there is likely to be more criticism of disloyalty than in the average industrial or other work situation, but extramarital ventures are not uncommon.

Whether advantageous or not, college couples have a basis for rationalizing their marital and family difficulties. They can justify their economic hardship, their bickering, their sacrifice of living standards, their denial of recreation, and their hardship for the children as a sacrifice of present pleasure for future gain. Even those in serious difficulty with marriage problems likely defer a decision regarding divorce, hoping that all will be well when they get out of college. But if they choose to seek it, they can more often find counseling help on the campus than they could outside.

The Danger of Differential Rates of Growth

There is danger of the husband outgrowing the wife if she drops out of school to support him, or to become a homemaker, and thus isolates herself from many of the social experiences which would, for a single woman, bring a great deal of growth during these late teen years.[29] The husband may outgrow the wife in training and sophistication and he may reach the time in college or later when he feels the need for a more worldly (in the broadest sense) woman to share his role as a professional or business man and to influence his career as the wife he has now outgrown never could.

Margaret Mead[30] sees an underlying psychological basis for the breakup of marriages after graduation from college or professional school. In putting her husband through, the wife takes over the role much like that of a parent. The husband feels little guilt in dropping her once he has reached his goal of schooling and has acquired his independence. She also may have pushed him to study and to finish school, much as a parent

[29] Lester A. Kirkendall finds this a real risk in his "Married Undergraduates on the Campus: An Appraisal," *The Coordinator*, 5:2, December, 1956.

[30] "Margaret Mead's Sound Insights into the Furor over Shifting American Morals," *Life*, 65:30-35, August 25, 1968.

would, and may have even encouraged having children so that he could not leave her. As he would with a parent, the husband drifts away from his wife.

The problem of differential rates of growth, while exaggerated on the campus, is certainly not confined to campus marriages. Differential rates of growth and personality change explain many postwar divorces, when men return from world-wide travels with broadened experience and find the interests of wives or fiancees too limited. That women should have the same opportunities, and travel at public expense, is perhaps the strongest argument for drafting women, since most jobs in the military are clerical, administrative, and technological.

Differential growth rates is a life-long problem for married couples in our day of rapid change, often taking the male into broader circles than the female. Whyte, studying wives of management for *Fortune* magazine, learned that in the managerial hierarchy industry does not object to a man getting a divorce, for it is felt he will choose a woman more compatible to the aims of the corporation when he chooses again.[31] Industry recognizes that perhaps one of the main reasons why men on the climb get a divorce is because their wives did not climb with them.

The Optimum Time

Marriage in the early twenties seems to offer the maximum advantages in contemporary American culture, although the late twenties would be better from the standpoints of adjustment and finances. But fears of not finding a mate, of being abnormal sexually or otherwise, a desire to fit the norm, pressures of parents and peers, and many other influences bear on personal decision. In addition, in times of military buildup there is a certain fatalism which makes some hasten to finalize relationships and build security.

College women who are not engaged or married by the last semester of the senior year seem anxious to marry and sometimes make a hasty choice. It appears that some men at this time reach a similar stage or at least a point of greater receptivity to marriage. However, a very strong career drive, requiring considerable training beyond college tends to delay marriage for both men and women, particularly for women.

The optimum time is in part the time when opportunity comes. Women are more aware of this than are men, and they should be. Their chances of finding a mate decline rapidly with age.

By the time a woman reaches thirty, for example, her chances of

[31] William H. Whyte, Jr., "The Wives of Management," *Fortune,* 44:86 ff., October 1951; also his "Corporation and the Wife," *Fortune,* 44:109 ff., November, 1951.

marriage are little more than fifty-fifty. After forty-five the chances fall
to one in ten (see Figure 16–3).

The discipline and competitiveness that may characterize such a
woman after a long period of schooling and business activity are in complete contradiction to those qualities most men regard as attractive in a
mate. But there are several other handicaps, too. The young men she knew
as a girl are already married. The professions into which women most
often go—school teaching, social work, library work, and nursing—are,
for the most part, female occupations offering few opportunities to meet
marriageable men.

These women are further handicapped because men their own age are
usually more attracted to younger women. By the time a man is thirty-five
he usually marries, not a woman of thirty-two, but rather a woman in her
late twenties. Likewise, a man in his late twenties is more likely to marry
a girl in her middle or early twenties than one near his own age. This
means that the professional woman in her late twenties must seek a partner
among men approximately thirty-five years of age. Most men who are
interested in or suited to family life are already married before they reach
that age. A woman in her late twenties or early thirties is likely to find her
best chance to marry among widowers and divorced men. There are some
very desirable marriage partners among this group, but divorced men are
a 50-percent greater risk, as far as marriage success is concerned, than
men entering their first marriage.[32]

One can argue that these figures simply reflect the fact that women
who delay marriage until the later ages are a select group of the unmarriageable who choose careers as their only alternative. But if this argument
is not the right one, then age must become a practical consideration in a
woman's thoughts of marriage.

These facts are important not only to those young women who wish
to delay marriage to pursue a business or professional career, but to those
who for other personal reasons delay marriage until well into the twenties.
Among this group are those who want to enjoy a relatively long period
of freedom prior to settling down to the responsibilities of a home. Some
want to earn enough to travel, thinking that after marriage they may never
have an opportunity to satisfy this desire. Marriage seems so final to many
girls; in fact, it means the end of many liberties that their education and
experience have caused them to consider highly desirable. For a time at
least the girl may place more value on these liberties than on marriage. In
some cases in which the girl does not feel this way, her parents may.

Girls sometimes delay marriage primarily because they are cautious
rather than because of a desire to achieve another goal in life. They want
to be sure they have reached an age when they know what kind of husband

[32] Paul H. Landis, "Sequential Marriage," *Journal of Home Economics,* 42:625–
628, October, 1950. Data are presented in Ch. 34, pp. 717–721.

they want. They may want the security of a career to fall back on if their marriage should fail or if untimely death should take their husband.

FIGURE 16–3   CHANCES OF MARRIAGE FOR SINGLE WOMEN. Source: U.S. Department of Commerce, Bureau of the Census.

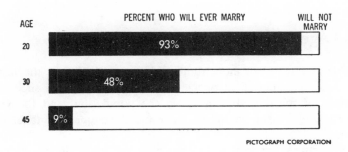

To remain single until 30 reduces chances for marriage by half; until 45, to about 1 in 10.

All of these are worthy motives and each must decide for herself whether the goals she seeks to realize before marriage are important enough to justify the risk of finding herself at an age and in a work situation where establishing close friendships with the opposite sex is difficult.

With all the advancement in work opportunities, the desire to marry has remained uppermost in the plans of most women. Whether the "new feminism" will prompt an increasing number of capable women to undertake careers that require years of preparation and involve the likelihood of giving up marriage and motherhood remains to be seen.

The growth of singles' clubs and the increase in housing and recreational facilities for the single person are factors in the movement toward single life. Today spinsterhood does not necessarily mean sex denial, although sex outside marriage does not offer the security and continuity desired by most people. The sentiment in the scientific community that in a world rapidly becoming overcrowded the single state should be encouraged for increasing numbers of women may also lessen the value placed on marriage by most women.

The college man at the close of his education has to face certain problems with respect to the time he wishes to marry. Although he is already well past the age when he might reasonably marry, he is likely to endure economic hardship if he marries immediately. If he is entering a profession, he will have a relatively low income for a period of several years. He may, in the face of these economic handicaps, choose to delay marriage. If he delays marriage itself but becomes engaged, there is the difficult problem of living as an engaged person for a long period of time. He may, on the other hand, decide to remain a bachelor, delaying any serious interest in engagement and marriage until he becomes established in his profession and has sufficient income to support the home and family that he desires. There is some danger in this case that he may lose all interest in romantic attachments and fail to marry.

Age Difference of Marriage Mates

Few problems have been more thoroughly researched over the last thirty years than the possible effect of age difference on marriage success. With the shortage of marriageable males in the population, and the necessity for many young women to marry older men, the question takes on new significance.

Most couples are similar in age, with the male slightly older. This is true in part because girls mature somewhat earlier and wish to marry sooner than men do, and also because the male is still the principal bread winner and must think in terms of earning capacity.

As women have come to earn, the age differential of males has declined. The age difference was 6 years in 1890, when census data were first assembled, now it is 2.6 years. In Europe there has been a wide gap in age of husbands and wives historically for economic reasons. The age difference is still greater there than in the United States, but it is declining as prosperity spreads.

Age difference of the pair is one of the least significant variables studied. As far as getting along together, whether the couple is equal in age or far apart seem not to be measurably important. We have already pointed out that if both are young, there is little chance of a successful marriage. Perhaps if one partner had married an older mate, he might have succeeded.

When marriage age differs by eight to ten years or more, the relationship frequently takes on the character of a father-daughter relationship when the man is older, and a mother-son relationship when the woman is the older. Some such marriages do achieve great happiness, but it is possible that such marriages are entered into only when the persons involved prefer the parent-child relationship to a relationship of equality. That is, such marriages may be selective according to particular personality types.

Certain obvious difficulties are inherent in these marriages. If the wife is considerably older, the couple's ability to have children may be greatly decreased; if the husband is decidedly older, the wife is almost certain of a long period of widowhood. If the husband is older by a period of many years, this widowhood may well come while she still has dependent children (see Figure 16–4).

Sex powers of the older person may wane, particularly the male, opening the way for jealousy and suspicion of the younger wife's behavior. The problem is likely more his than hers; many women are quite content with less sexual attention of a man whom they greatly respect and who can provide well for their needs and those of the children. The marriage of the young girl to the older man usually involves marrying up economically and guaranteed financial security.

Time devoted its essay of February 21, 1969, to the theme "In Praise of the May-December Marriages" and made a strong case for them when the male is the older.

FIGURE 16–4 CHANCES OF MATE SURVIVAL BY AGE DIFFERENCES. Source: Metropolitan Life Insurance Company, **Statistical Bulletin,** September, 1953.

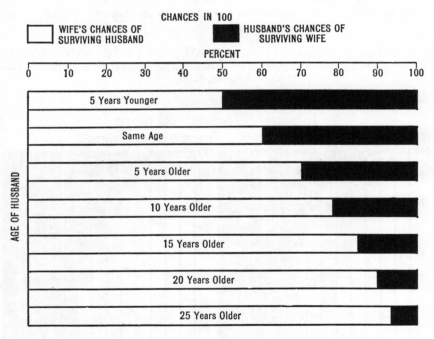

The longer life span of women, and the fact that they are usually the younger member of the pair means from few to many years of widowhood for the wife in the average marriage. The June-December marriage, where the male is older, greatly increases the likelihood of a long period of widowhood.

The article pointed out how much more common such marriages were in our society in an earlier day, when so many wives died in childbearing, and also how much more usual they have been in Europe than here. *Time* predicts that with the increased length of life, and the number of divorces in the later years of marriage, now that marriages last so long, May-December marriages are sure to increase. They quote the old saying that "it is better to be an old man's darling than become a young man's slave," and add that "it may sometimes be better to be a young woman's darling than an old woman's curmudgeon."

Marrying the Widowed or Divorced Person

The widowed may have had a successful marriage which can be a good credential for a future spouse. This is not so true of the divorced, who make up most of the eligibles in the older group. Second marriages are

FIGURE 16–5   PREVIOUS MARITAL STATUS OF BRIDES AND GROOMS IN 14 STATES, 1950. Source: Metropolitan Life Insurance Company, **Statistical Bulletin,** June, 1953.

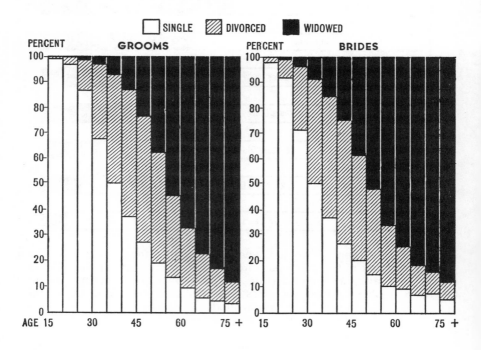

Most of those who marry late in life marry someone who has previously been married.

more risky than first marriages, and remarriage of the divorced woman is somewhat more risky than that of the divorced man, as far as likelihood of another divorce[33] is concerned.

Judson T. Landis[34] finds that persons entering their second or subsequent marriage do so with fewer formalities such as formal weddings and engagement rings, and there is less often parental approval. They have more often had sexual intercourse with others than a spouse, and in 75 percent of cases have had premarital coitus before consummating the second or subsequent marriage.

The older girl in the city is particularly likely to face this question of marrying a divorced man, for of the men approaching thirty—the group to which she is most attracted—there are few single ones who are marriageable.[35] Many in this group have faced repeated rejection and so a widower or divorced man may seem to be a much better marriage prospect. Even college students are not as strongly opposed to marrying divorced persons as some might expect. Judson T. Landis[36] has asked large numbers of college students in twelve universities, and at two different periods of time, the question, "All other factors being satisfactory, would you marry a person who has been divorced?" In both studies, it was found that 48 percent of the college women would do so; 54 and 56 percent, respectively, of the college men.

Census data show that the rate of failure in second and subsequent marriages is much higher than in the first marriage. The divorced man is a 50 percent higher risk than the single man and the divorced woman is a somewhat higher risk still.[37] Divorce rates increase with increase in the number of remarriages.[38]

Thomas P. Monahan,[39] studying divorce statistics for Iowa during the years 1953 to 1955, found the rate to be 16.6 per hundred marriages for those in their first marriage. Where one had been divorced the rate jumped to 36.6 per hundred marriages.

Most marriages in the older age group are of persons previously married; in fact, 23 percent of all marriages are second or subsequent mar-

[33] Paul H. Landis, op. cit.
[34] Judson T. Landis and Mary G. Landis, op. cit., Table 2, p. 151.
[35] This problem of "marriageability" is discussed at length in Ch. 30.
[36] Judson T. Landis and Mary G. Landis, op. cit., p. 84.
[37] U.S. Department of Commerce, Bureau of the Census, Marital Status, Number of Times Married, and Duration of Present Marital Status: April, 1948, Series P–20, No. 23, March 4, 1949. See p. 654 of this text for a summary of statistical data or Paul H. Landis, "Sequential Marriage," Journal of Home Economics, 42:625–628, November, 1951, for an analysis of the Census data; see also Paul H. Jacobson, American Marriage and Divorce (New York: Holt, Rinehart & Winston, Inc., 1959), Chs. 5 and 6.
[38] Thomas P. Monahan, "How Stable Are Remarriages," American Sociological Review, 58:280–298, November, 1952.
[39] Thomas P. Monahan, "The Changing Nature and Instability of Remarriage," Eugenics Quarterly, 5:73–85, June, 1958.

riages. Figure 16–6[40] shows the proportion of each age group marrying which is single, divorced, or widowed. During the years thirty-five to forty-five, the divorced make up the highest proportion of those marrying. After forty-five, the overwhelming proportion is the widowed, and this increases with age. Above sixty-five, more than four in five marriages are of widowed persons.

In conclusion, because people seek to realize various goals in life, and because some of them can be realized only by delaying or sacrificing others, a choice must be made. Marriage promises to fulfill several basic wishes, but others may have to be sacrificed if one marries too soon. Work is for many girls a satisfying and creative experience which they want before marriage. Some young people want freedom to earn and spend as they please, to travel, to date widely and make new friends, to strive for economic security. For them these desires must be satisfied before assuming the obligations of the family life.

In the final analysis, one's own answer to the question of when he should marry is determined by the wants he expects to satisfy. Early marriage will assure the immediate realization of some goals, but it may well make the realization of others virtually impossible. Good questions to ask oneself are:

1. How many of the other goals which I wish to achieve in life must be forgotten or delayed by my marrying now?
2. How important are these goals to me?
3. Will I be content if my marriage should make the attaining of any or all of these goals impossible?

Problems

1. In the light of evidence studied so far in this course, do you feel it is better for a girl to marry a little too young rather than take the risk of not having a chance to marry when she is older?
2. What are your views on the desirability or undesirability of college marriages? Consider your answer from the following standpoints: economics (for example, would you feel it right for the wife to carry the economic burden until the husband is through school?) parenthood, the change in recreational life and freedom involved, studies, risk to completing education, and other problems you foresee. Would you be willing to marry while in college?

[40] Metropolitan Life Insurance Company, "Current Patterns of Marriage and Remarriage," *Statistical Bulletin*, 34:6–8, June, 1953.

3 Beth and Keith are juniors in college. They have dated since their freshman year and have been engaged for over a year and a half. They are quite certain of their compatibility but have serious doubts about advisability of marriage. Beth has one more year to complete her education and Keith must continue for at least another six years before he is prepared for his vocation. He cannot hope to support a wife and home until his education is completed, and since his family is already contributing financially to his education he can expect little more financial aid from them. Beth feels that it would be a mistake to delay marriage for six years, at which time both would be twenty-six years old. What would be your advice?

a. Wait the full six years?
b. Marry now and get as much financial help from both families as possible?
c. Marry now but delay parenthood for the six years?
d. Postpone marriage until Beth's graduation and plan to have her support the family?
e. Other advice?

4. *Sociodrama:* A high school senior girl is wondering about the desirability of marrying her twenty-year-old fiancé before he is drafted. She discusses the problem with an older girl whose husband is overseas.

5. Which area or areas of maturity do you consider most essential as prerequisites to marriage?

a. Physical maturity—a fully developed body.
b. Intellectual maturity—a fully developed mind.
c. Emotional maturity—understanding and perspective with reference to your own feelings.
d. Vocational maturity—definite vocational goals.
e. Philosophical maturity—a fully developed and satisfying philosophy of life.

Discuss the importance of these kinds of maturity and thing most essential.

6. Here are three individuals, *A, B,* and *C,* from whom you are to select a marriage partner. None of them is ideal. Choose the one with that combination of traits you consider most important.

A is—
physically immature
intellectually very mature
emotionally immature

B is—
physically very mature
intellectually immature
vocationally mature
emotionally mature

C is—
physically mature
intellectually immature
vocationally immature
emotionally very mature

7. Discuss the experiences you have had since high school graduation which have affected your values and tastes in mate selection. Answer such questions as:

   a. Is your "ideal" mate today different from the ideal you held during high
     school days?

   b. Has your attitude toward having children changed?

   c. What specific experiences have contributed most to any change or ma-
     turation you observe?

8. *Research exercise:* Poll the class on the ideal age at which a man and a
woman should marry. Tabulate results and make a four-way comparison:
men's view of ideal age for man and for woman, women's view of ideal age
for woman and for man. If differences are found try to explain them in
terms of (*a*) economic factors, (*b*) customs, (*c*) sex interests, (*d*) maturity,
and any other factors that may seem important.

9. *Sociodrama:* A mother tries to discourage her nineteen-year-old daughter
from marrying a man twenty years her senior.

Selected References

Articles in Books of Readings

Cavan, Ruth S., *Marriage and the Family in the Modern World: A Book of
Readings*, third edition (New York: Thomas Y. Crowell Co., 1969).
   Ellis, Albert, and David, Lester, "Should Men Marry Older Women?" Read-
   ing 38.
   Christensen, Harold T., "Why All These Young Marriages?" Reading 39.
Landis, Judson T., and Landis, Mary G., *Readings in Marriage and the Family,*
(Englewood Cliffs, N. J.: Prentice-Hall, Inc., 1952).
   Popenoe, Paul, "A Study of 738 Elopements," pp. 127–132.
Sussman, Marvin B., *Sourcebook in Marriage and the Family,* third edition
(Boston: Houghton Mifflin Co., 1968).
   Moss, J. Joel, "Teenage Marriage: Crossnational Trends and Sociological
   Factors in the Decision When to Marry," Reading 16.

General References

Anderson, Wayne J., and Latts, Sander M., "High School Marriages and School
   Policies in Minnesota," *Journal of Marriage and the Family,* 27:266–270,
   May, 1968.
Atkyns, Glenn C., "School Administrative Policy Related to Motherhood,
   Pregnancy, and Marriage," *The Family Coordinator,* 17:69–73, April,
   1968.
Burchinal, Lee G., "Trends and Prospects for Young Marriages in the United
   States," *Journal of Marriage and the Family,* 27:243–254, May, 1965.
Farber, Seymour M., and Wilson, Roger H. L., eds., *Teenage Marriage and
   Divorce* (Berkely, Diablo Press, 1967).

Lowrie, Samuel H., "Early Marriage: Premarital Pregnancy and Associated Factors," *Journal of Marriage and the Family*, 27:48–56, November, 1965.

Samenfink, J. Anthony, and Milliken, Robert I., "Marital Status and Academic Success: A Reconsideration," *Marriage and Family Living*, 23:226–227, August, 1961.

Wallace, Gerald R., "High Schools and Married Students—Are They Compatible?" *Marriage and Family Living*, 24:295–296, August, 1962.

17

Engagement

The marriage commitment is legal, and meant to be final. There are many steps in emotional and semi-contractual commitment between the beginning of serious intentions and the marriage license. None of them need be taken. The expression of commitment depends on the social class of the couple, local customs, whether they are in school and other such factors. In the high school and college community exchanging tokens—class rings or pins, sorority or fraternity insignia, athletic sweaters, charm bracelets, love beads, medallions or other symbols precedes the more serious pledge of engagement, usually accompanied by the engagement ring.

Research suggests that these various stages leading up to engagement are taken more seriously by girls than boys, as perhaps they should be.[1] Girls tend to be more marriage oriented than boys, and winning in a competition in which they have to play the more passive role is more of an achievement.

Desirability of Engagement

Students of marriage find engagement a desirable intermediary step. Elopements, most of which involve no engagement, or a short one at best, are one test of marriage without engagement. Popenoe's study[2] of 738 elopements shows that in nearly half of them, there was parental objection to

[1] Judson T. Landis studied this problem extensively among college students on the Michigan State University campus and the University of California campus. See Judson T. Landis and Mary G. Landis, *Building a Successful Marriage*, fourth edition (Englewood Cliffs, N. J.: Prentice-Hall, Inc., 1963), pp. 227–228.

[2] Paul Popenoe, "A Study of 738 Elopements," *American Sociological Review*, 3:297 ff., February, 1938.

the marriage, and that less than half led to happy marriages. When the motive was economic, or the wish to avoid publicity, over half were happy, but when the reason for elopement was pregnancy, only a third were happy.

Judson T. Landis'[3] follow-up study of 581 couples married an average of seven years, comparing them with 155 couples in the California Court of Conciliation and with 164 divorced persons, shows that 88 percent of the first group had been formally engaged, while only 37 percent of the group seeking counseling and only 57 percent of the divorced persons had been formally engaged.

Length of Engagement

Early studies[4] show a positive relationship between long engagements and success in marriage, those of two or more years having a high ratio of success, whereas those under six months show a high rate of marriage failure, with few leading to good marriage adjustment. Whether these findings still have validity is open to some question. As far as the college generation is concerned, they do not consider long engagements necessary or wise. The writer's classes, almost without exception, unanimously favor engagements of not more than four to six months.

Their reasoning is based on the fact that there are so many preliminary steps preceding formal engagement that many of the issues once deferred to the engagement period are now resolved prior to the engagement. Also, many of the intimacies, confidences, and plans once deferred to engagement are shared prior to the engagement. They seem to feel also that during this preannouncement stage many relationships that would not have weathered the formal engagement period end, and with less public exposure. To the extent that this is true, the length of the engagement ceases to be a primary criterion of the degree of understanding and adjustment.

Today, when young people associate so closely and when considerable physical contact is customary, many authorities are inclined to look upon an engagement of more than a year as producing too much sex tension to be justified, although points of view differ on this subject.[5]

[5] Ernest W. Burgess and Paul Wallin find that sexual intercourse is more frequent among couples engaged sixteen months or over than among those of engagements of shorter duration; see *Engagement and Marriage* (Philadelphia: J. B. Lippincott Co., 1953).

[4] Lewis M. Terman and others, *Psychological Factors in Marital Happiness* (New York: McGraw-Hill Book Co., 1938), p. 199; Ernest W. Burgess and Leonard S. Cottrell, *Predicting Success or Failure in Marriage* (Englewood Cliffs, N.J.: Prentice-Hall, Inc., 1939), p. 168; Landis and Landis, *op. cit.*, fourth edition, p. 240.

[3] Landis and Landis, *op. cit.*, fifth edition, *Building a Successful Marriage*, Table 2, p. 79.

Burgess and Cottrell's[6] study of over 500 married couples showed that only a fourth of those married after an engagement of less than three months made good adjustments in marriage; half of them made poor adjustments, the rest only fair. Those who had no engagement also showed a high proportion of maladjustments. With an engagement period of up to two years or over, the proportion of happy marriages greatly increased. In fact, of those who were engaged two years or more, only 10 percent were characterized by poor marital adjustment. Other studies have shown similar results.[7]

It is open to argument whether length of engagement, as such, is the primary factor, or whether people of more steady temperament tend to prolong their engagement; but one thing is certain: a fairly long engagement eliminates many romances that could not have succeeded in marriage.

It is likely that a long acquaintance before engagement is more significant than the long engagement itself. Burgess and Cottrell's early research[8] showed that long acquaintance was associated with good marriage adjustment. Judson T. Landis'[9] follow-up study of 581 couples who had been married an average of seven years, comparing them with 155 couples in the California Court of Conciliation and with 164 divorced persons, shows that over 40 percent of each of the two latter groups had known each other less than a year before marrying, whereas only 16 percent of the couples still outside divorce or counseling groups had been so hasty in entering marriage.

If a couple has known each other for a long time and has had a long period of going steady, a lengthy engagement may be less important than if each has known little about the other's background and if they have gone together only a few months before engagement. The really important thing is not how long the engagement is but what is accomplished during the period. Getting really well acquainted is the most valuable outcome of any engagement, and in nearly all cases getting acquainted takes time.

It is important, too, that a couple be engaged long enough to see whether they can work out patterns of adjustment which will assure the continuing development of an ongoing companionable relationship. A long engagement, however, can do nothing for the couple who are not going in the right direction in their adjustment to each other. They should learn that they never can develop a satisfactory relationship. But a long engagement can give those who are moving in the right direction the opportunity to learn what kinds of adjustment techniques work for them. Both results are equally important—the one in blocking unwise marriages;

[6] Burgess and Cottrell, *op. cit.*

[7] A summary of several of these studies appears in Landis and Landis, *op. cit.*, pp. 232–235.

[8] *Op. cit.*

[9] Landis and Landis, *op. cit.*, fifth edition, Table 2, p. 79.

the other in building assurance that the pair relationship has qualities that will endure in marriage.

Some young people today are inclined to feel that marriage can be speeded up. Such a philosophy is particularly prevalent in wartime, and probably explains the high rate of failure of postwar marriages. Getting acquainted was deferred until after marriage and then the couple found that each had married a strange and incompatible person.

Today, the period of serious association is probably no shorter than in an earlier day. Koller followed the length of going together through three generations, and in all three the serious period of going together covered a median period of a year and a half.[10] The real difference was that in the earlier generations it was not unusual for the couple to have known each other for a lifetime. Today a couple must spend a great deal of time merely getting acquainted with each other's background, personality, and aspirations. This makes time all the more important in preparing the way for a successful marriage.

In his 1967 study of thousands of college students in a number of universities, Judson T. Landis[11] found that the time between first date and engagement is about the same as his study of twenty years earlier showed. The route from first date to marriage takes about three years for the college group. The buildup to a close relationship is slow; the typical pattern is casual dating five months, steady dating eight months, during which time they have an "understanding," and six months of formal engagement.

This cautious pattern may well explain why college marriages turn out well in a larger proportion of cases. There are the factors of added age and the maturing effect of the educational experience.

Disagreements During Engagement

There is considerable evidence that engagements are seldom calm periods of perfect happiness. With growing intimacy and understanding, and with more frequent and less formal contacts, disagreements are common, and actual quarreling may begin.

Burgess and Wallin's study[12] of 1,000 engaged couples was focused upon discovering exactly what does happen during the modern engagement. Figure 17–1 shows the result of a series of questions to test extent of agreement. It will be seen that, among the couples studied, agreement on most

[10] Marvin R. Koller, "Some Changes in Courtship Behavior in Three Generations of Ohio Women," *American Sociological Review*, 16:366–370, 1951.

[11] *Op. cit.* Table I, p. 217.

[12] *Op. cit.*, p. 246.

issues was the rule. On every topic the study covered, some couple disagreed, though the proportion of disagreement varied greatly on different items. As many as one couple in four experienced disagreement on some issues.

The one area in which there was most agreement dealt with dating. Since engagement is primarily a matter of association during dates, this perhaps would be expected. The next highest area of agreement dealt with demonstration of affection. The third was "arrangement for marriage." The areas of most frequent disagreement were questions of conventionality, philosophy of life, and ways of dealing with each other's families. This latter indicates that in-law problems actually begin before marriage for at least a fourth of the couples.

Table manners and conventionality, were points of disagreement with the fiancé.

A more detailed analysis of replies showed that only 17 couples out of the 1,000 always agreed in all areas of their relationship. Only 185 always or almost always agreed in all areas of their relationship.

Concluding their analysis of the experience of engaged couples, Burgess and Wallin indicated that about two-thirds of the couples experience some strain. They described the engagement period as one in which the couple attempts to adjust "conflicting differences in the interest of the survival of their relationship."[13]

These researchers also asked whether the couples experienced jealousy often, occasionally, or never. Men are the more jealous sex. Their answers were: often, 16.4 percent; occasionally, 55.1 percent; never, 28.5 percent. Forty percent of the women were never jealous; 49.5 percent, occasionally; only 10.5 percent, often.

This analysis shows that some insecurity is present during most engagements because of previous dating of the partner, or because of lack of mutual trust, the one doubting the affection of the other. Men seem to suffer from a greater sense of doubt regarding loyalty in the engagement relationship than do women. The authors conclude that young people should not expect the engagement period to be "one of continuous bliss and ecstasy."

The disagreements which arise during the engagement period may conclude in a variety of ways. Frequently they are resolved and the relationship is strengthened for having weathered conflicts. In other cases, the disagreements as they increase in number begin to create serious doubt in the minds of one or both about the desirability of marriage. It was found, in fact, that about half of the men and women studied felt hesitant about the marriage at some time during the engagement period. A fourth of the women and a fifth of the men wished they had never become engaged, and

[13] *Ibid.*, p. 271.

FIGURE 17-1 AGREEMENT OF 1,000 ENGAGED MEN AND WOMEN IN SELECTED AREAS. Source: Ernest W. Burgess and Paul Wallin, **Engagement and Marriage** (Philadelphia: J. B. Lippincott Co., 1953). Reproduced by permission of the publisher.

EXTENT OF AGREEMENT OR DISAGREEMENT (Percent)

AREA	REPORTED BY	Always agree	Almost always agree	Disagree*	Other reply**
Dates with one another	Men	70.0%	21.9%		2.4% / 5.7%
	Women	70.6%	22.4%		2.4% / 4.6%
Demonstration of affection	Men	53.6%	33.9%	9.7%	2.8%
	Women	53.3%	32.2%	11.7%	2.8%
Arrangements for your marriage	Men	50.9%	31.1%	11.9%	6.1%
	Women	53.2%	29.0%	11.7%	6.1%
Religious matters	Men	49.8%	22.0%	16.0%	12.2%
	Women	50.0%	21.4%	16.4%	12.2%
Table manners	Men	48.4%	26.2%	13.2%	12.2%
	Women	51.0%	22.3%	14.5%	12.2%
Matters of conventionality	Men	38.9%	33.1%	21.8%	6.2%
	Women	39.8%	32.3%	21.7%	6.2%
Matters of recreation	Men	38.2%	46.0%	14.3%	1.5%
	Women	44.9%	41.2%	12.4%	1.5%
Philosophy of life	Men	35.9%	34.8%	20.5%	8.8%
	Women	38.9%	35.5%	16.8%	8.8%
Money matters	Men	33.8%	41.7%	17.1%	7.4%
	Women	33.3%	43.4%	15.9%	7.4%
Ways of dealing with your families	Men	32.8%	33.5%	24.6%	9.1%
	Women	36.0%	30.2%	24.7%	9.1%
Friends	Men	29.6%	46.2%	22.0%	2.2%
	Women	32.0%	45.9%	19.9%	2.2%

* Occasionally or more frequently.
** Never discussed and a few cases where a given item was not checked.

It is rarely possible for two people to agree in all areas of their relationship. This research shows that engaged men and women are no exception. Relatives, money matters, friends, and philosophy are areas in which a fourth or more of the couples disagree. (Data are for 1,000 engaged men and women.)

about as many at some time seriously contemplated breaking the engagement.

At such times it is very common for young college people to discuss the advisability of marriage with those in whom they have confidence. Approximately two-thirds of the men and women discussed the advisability of marriage with their respective mothers; over a third, with their respective fathers; a fourth, with friends; and a smaller percentage, with other relatives, with doctors, etc.[14] Almost half of both men and women at some time during the engagement felt hesitant about marrying the person to whom they were engaged.[15]

About one in four engaged couples, at some time during the relationship, broke off temporarily. Moreover, 16 percent of the men and 23 percent of the women had had previous engagements, and 15 percent of the couples studied, later broke their engagements.[16]

These data indicate quite clearly that among college engagements, at least, there are frequently serious doubts and uncertainties about the desirability of following through to marriage. Burgess and Wallin conclude that the love relationship desired in the American marriage could scarcely be realized without considerable association between men and women before marriage; that there is reason to believe "that various combinations of men and women differ considerably in their probabilities of developing into more or less durable love relationships." Trial and error, they feel, is necessary in order to insure the maximum number of desirable combinations. Often the relationship proves to be inadequate.

Burgess and Wallin also conclude that one of the serious weaknesses of the engagement period is that it is too often carried on exclusively in an atmosphere of recreation and play, giving an unrealistic picture of what marriage will be like.

Engagement Confessions

Mark Twain is reputed to have said, "Confession is good for the soul, but bad for the reputation." The very real feeling of interrelatedness of those deeply in love often induces a mood of confession and repentance. During the engagement period, or even before, young people frequently feel a strong urge to confess all their past sins to each other, the girl to test his love, the boy to shed his guilt.

This seems to be a normal phase in the development of love, particularly for the male. Sometimes this way of relieving guilt feelings for past misconduct is an asset, not only to the individual, but to the couple. It may be an indication that the couple has become intimate enough to want to share with each other secrets known to no other. It may also indicate a strong sense of mutual need and trust.

[14] *Ibid.,* p. 178.
[15] *Ibid.,* p. 180.
[16] *Ibid.,* p. 136.

The question of the desirability of confession at such a time is not so simple, however, as it initially appears. One might well ask himself, "Will the other person have the background to absorb these confessions with understanding, or will it only raise doubts and uncertainty about the advisability of marriage?"

Of course, it all depends upon the kind of thing being confessed and whether or not it has a bearing on the marriage. Certainly if there are factors in one's background that might have a direct or serious bearing on the marriage, the person one intends to marry should know about them.

Judson T. Landis[17] in his early research found that all engaged students he studied of both sexes confessed nervous breakdowns, suspected bad hereditary traits, previous marriage, and having a child out of wedlock, although, of course, few had such serious issues in their background. Almost three-fourths of boys who had had sex experience with another girl confessed it; two-thirds of girls with previous sex experience confessed it. Petting experiences were confessed in approximately 60 percent of cases, a higher proportion of boys with experience than of girls with experience confessing.

His restudy in 1967[18] found that almost all students do confess their past necking and petting experiences, and most of those having had premarital sexual intercourse confessed (91 percent of men and 86 percent of women). Those who had serious family problems also revealed them.

If one is in doubt as to whether it is the kind of confession that might help or hinder the marriage and whether it actually needs to be made, it is often better to talk to a physician, counselor, minister, or other confidant first. It is useful to get the advice of a third party before taking the risk of revealing matters which may have no significance whatever to the marriage and may actually create mistrust. It is not wise to confess matters which are of no consequence to the marriage and which may be held against one later.

The Premarital Examination

A premarital physical examination is required in many states. Often it is only to check for venereal disease. Sometimes it includes other possible problem areas, but, in general, it should be more extensive than it is. The examination is usually sought immediately before the marriage. A much better practice, for the girl, is for her to visit a doctor, marriage clinic, or specialist in women's problems three months before marriage so that

[17] Landis and Landis, *op. cit.*, fourth edition, *Building a Successful Marriage*, p. 250.
[18] *Ibid.*, fifth edition, Table 7, p. 243.

she may benefit by a long period of counsel. In cases where the hymen has to be stretched, or special treatment given, this can be carried on for a period of time before marriage. There is also the advantage of gaining confidence and understanding by discussing the sexual aspect of marriage with someone who is objective and understanding. This has great value for those women who have strong taboos regarding sex teachings and sex behavior. During this period, there is time for the woman to acquire knowledge of contraception from her doctor, to be fitted with a contraceptive device, and to learn how to use it, or to build pregnancy immunity with "the pill."

By starting early the couple will also have time to investigate with a specialist their hereditary backgrounds, possible defects of organic development, and other factors that might have a bearing on successful adjustment in marriage and the rearing of children. Couples should be able to discuss sex matters and attitudes together and with the doctor. They should not hesitate to discuss with a doctor or marriage counselor the psychological as well as the physical aspects of sexual adjustment. They should read books which will give them information as to techniques and attitudes appropriate to the sexual relationship in marriage.

FIGURE 17–2   COMPARISON OF TWO GENERATIONS ON DISCUSSION OF CHILDREN WITH PROSPECTIVE HUSBANDS. Source: Paul H. Landis, "Marriage Preparation in Two Generations," **Marriage and Family Living,** 8:155–156, November, 1951.

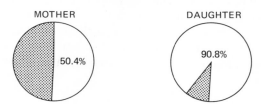

There has been a marked increase in discussion of children among engaged couples. Only half of the mother's generation discussed the question prior to marriage; almost 91 percent of the daughter's generation did.

The latter part of the engagement period should, of course, be a period in which the young people enter into a serious discussion of aspirations with regard to children and family. This is the time to understand fully each other's attitudes and interests in children. Some states grant an annulment if one party can prove that the other had decided prior to the marriage not to have children. Although most young people plan to have children, not all do so. The prospective mate has a right to know this beforehand.

·A study of two generations shows that the present generation of married college women and wives of college students, much more often than their mothers, discussed children with their prospective husband before marriage[19] (see Figure 17–2) and also sought premarital advice (see Figure 17–3). This is desirable and should become universal.

FIGURE 17-3   COMPARISON OF TWO GENERATIONS ON SEEKING PRE-MARITAL ADVICE. Source: Paul H. Landis, "Marriage Preparation in Two Generations," **Marriage and Family Living,** 8:155–156, November, 1951.

MOTHER   DAUGHTER

25.2%   55%

Premarital Counseling

Intelligent young people with access to marriage clinics should not hesitate to seek advice there and to put their love under critical examination by counselors experienced in the complexities of human relationships (see Figure 17–4). The counselor is the best person to consult about the biological and psychological aspects of marriage, and he can advise on conflicts and differences that may have led to doubt in the relationship, and on any other problems that may seem important. A counselor does not moralize or condemn. His business is to see the client's problems from the client's viewpoint, to help the client view them objectively, and to assist, when necessary, in working out mutually satisfying solutions. The counselor can also give advice on practical matters dealing with marriage itself: legal steps in obtaining a license, how much to pay the preacher, etc. In the well-developed marriage clinic, too, there is a medical specialist who gives full time to pelvic examinations, problems of birth control and sterility, and various other psycho-sexual aspects of the marriage relationship.

The oldest marriage clinic in America, the American Institute of Family Relations at Los Angeles, has for many years given premarital emotional maturity tests to couples coming for advice previous to marriage. These tests, combined with a thorough physical examination, make up a

[19] Paul H. Landis, "Sex Education: The Facts about Two Generations," *The Clearing House,* 24:451–455, April, 1950; also his "Marriage Preparation in Two Generations," *Marriage and Family Living,* 8:155–156, November, 1951.

major part of the premarital counseling. Couples who go through the clinic and who are reassured of their suitability for one another show a high rate of success in marriage.

FIGURE 17–4 COMPARISON OF TWO GENERATIONS ON SOURCE OF PREMARITAL ADVICE. Source: Paul H. Landis, "Marriage Preparation in Two Generations," **Marriage and Family Living, 8:155–156,** November 1951.

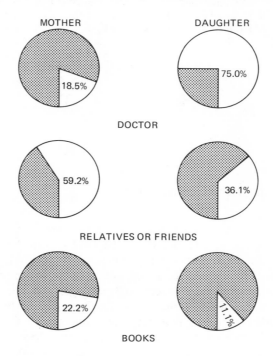

Of the mother's generation only a fourth sought premarital advice; of the married daughters, 55 percent. Among mothers, few sought advice from anyone but relatives and friends. Three-fourths of the daughters who sought advice consulted a doctor. None in the parent's generation sought the advice of a minister or teacher. One in ten daughters consulted a minister; one in thirty-five, a teacher.

Dr. Paul Popenoe, the founder, says that not one divorce occurred among couples who came to the Institute for premarital assistance during the first eight years of its existence. This record is outstanding, for the clinic is in the city of Los Angeles where the divorce rate is high.

Marriage fitness tests have been used extensively in the marriage clinic at Pennsylvania State University. Writing a few years after it was established, Clifford Adams, psychologist and director of the marriage clinic stated:

. . . hundreds of couples who were tested before marriage at the Marriage Counseling Service are checked periodically after marriage to find how they are making out. Of all the marriages which the service predicted would be successful, not one has yet ended in divorce or separation. Most of the people who went ahead despite the clinic's cautions are already in serious trouble or have been divorced.[20]

While this testimony is convincing, it does not necessarily mean that all divorces would be done away with if all young people would go to a premarital clinic for counsel and heed its advice. Since the marriage clinic is a new institution, it is to be expected that most of those who have used it have been the intelligent and serious persons who are willing to face facts and to follow wise counsel. This may mean that most young people who have used the clinic would have been successful in marriage anyway. There can be no doubt that specialists in counseling can be most helpful to any prospective marriage.

Time to Get Acquainted— An Indispensable Precaution

Of all the simple precautions to assure marriage happiness, the most obvious and readily accessible one is time—time enough to know that the match is a suitable one. Most marriage failures are courtship failures.[21] This point cannot be overstressed.

The key to success seems to be through acquaintance—being together enough before marriage to know whether or not there is a basis for compatibility. Marriage, in order to last, must be based on lasting qualities, which cannot be tested in whirlwind romances ending in premature marriages. Of course, almost everyone knows of a marriage like this that has succeeded, but research evidence suggests that such marriages are among those lucky accidents in life. Most marriages hastily contracted do not survive.

Figure 17–5[22] dealing with 526 married couples, gives a characteristic picture of research on this subject. It indicates that less than a fourth of the "under six months" couples made a good adjustment. (Remember that the couples who divorced quickly have been eliminated, since this is a study of married couples.) Half of these survivors in marriage considered

[20] Clifford Adams and Vance Packard, *How to Pick a Mate* (New York: E. P. Dutton & Co., Inc., 1946), Preface.

[21] Dr. Henry Bowman feels that this is so, judging by views expressed in lectures. Burgess and Wallin (*op. cit.,* p. 302) go so far as to suggest that the breakup of engagements probably saves many divorces and that if more engagements were broken there would be fewer divorces.

[22] Burgess and Cottrell, *op. cit.,* p. 164.

their marriage adjustment poor. The proportion of good adjustments increased with increased length of acquaintance.

Whether people with short get-acquainted periods represent a type of temperament that fails in marriage, or whether these same people, had they prolonged their dating and engagement, would have broken up their relationship, we can only guess. It seems reasonable to suppose that the length of the period is not in itself the only reason for unsuccessful marriages, although it could be an important factor. The early stages of dating are often very romantic; marriage at this time might lead a person to expect more than any marriage can realize. A lengthened, steady-dating period usually brings about a more reasonable understanding of the person, and diffuses the halo effect of early romance.

FIGURE 17–5 RELATIONSHIP OF MARITAL HAPPINESS TO LENGTH OF ACQUAINTANCE. Source: Based on data from Ernest W. Burgess and Leonard S. Cottrell, **Predicting Success or Failure in Marriage** (Copyright 1939, by Prentice-Hall, Inc., New York). Reproduced by permission of the publisher.

Short acquaintance before marriage means great risk.

Danger Signals

Length of acquaintance alone will not guarantee a successful marriage. Many people marry who know each other so well already that they have serious misgivings about their compatibility, and yet move ahead toward marriage and later regret. So this rule must be added: "Heed the danger signals!"

A case comes to mind of a minister's wife who, after fifteen years of marriage, had to end her marriage. There were two children, a boy and a girl. When she left her husband to prepare for teaching, she took the boy with her and left the daughter with the husband. In leaving the church, she faced great opposition. There was a serious threat to her husband's position in the church as well as great pressure from the bishop to get her to continue, merely to put on a proper front if for no personal reason. She finally told him that even if it wrecked the whole church she could tolerate the marriage no longer; it was a question of breaking up the marriage or going to a mental institution. She admitted she had no one to blame but herself for the fifteen years of misery she had endured. During the eight years they were going together his intolerance, tendency to dominate her, his refusal to genuinely accept her as an equal, his coldness, all troubled her greatly. But, he was a good man, he was a Christian, he was a minister. She felt that there must be something wrong with her. The prestige of his work and her desire to share in it, and the service it represented, made a great appeal to her. She said that she hoped that, by some magic, marriage would change the situation with regard to their interpersonal relations; she went ahead into a marriage which almost destroyed her.

A Canadian girl wrote and asked whether or not she should marry a person she had been going with for some years. She described him and her many reactions to him. Among her comments was, "He has a way of talking which I find rather obnoxious."

Why should a young lady need advice as to whether or not to marry under these circumstances? If she finds certain traits very obnoxious on an occasional date, how is she going to tolerate this man across the table three times a day?

Judson T. Landis' follow-up study[23] of 581 married couples who had been married an average of seven years, comparing them with 155 couples in the California Court of Conciliation and with 164 divorced persons shows that only 29 percent of the first group had considered breaking their engagament, 44 percent of the group in counseling, 50 percent of the divorced persons. The successful group had only 9 percent who had temporarily broken their engagement, the others 26 and 22 percent respectively. Of the successful group 90 percent had felt confident the marriage would be happy, 83 percent in the counseling group and only 71 percent of the divorced persons. This would seem to indicate that seriousness of adjustment problems is somewhat predictive of marriage difficulties and outcome, and that their own expectations for the marriage had some predictive value.

It appears there was considerable unwarranted optimism.

In this same Landis study,[24] parent's approval or disapproval was a

[23] See Landis and Landis, *op. cit.*, Table 2, p. 79.
[24] *Ibid.*, Table 2, p. 79.

more predictive factor as to wisdom of the marriage than the couple's own faith as to outcome. Of the successful couples, 84 percent had approval of the marriage from both sets of parents, while only 58 percent of the groups in serious difficulty had approval.

Engagement Failure

Various studies place the rate of failure of engagements at from one-third to one-half. Even so, some students of marriage feel that more should be broken, basing their opinion on the number of marriages which fail after a short time.

Reasons for failure in serious affairs was investigated extensively among college students at the University of Minnesota some years ago.[25] Here are the most common causes of conflict in serious affairs involving college students:

Cause of conflict	Male affairs (Number 314) percent	Female affairs (Number 582) percent
Jealousy	28.0	23.2
Possessiveness	22.0	23.7
Criticism	21.0	17.9
Irritability arising from emotional tension	19.4	15.3
Dislike of friends	19.1	13.4
Accusations of loss of interest	15.3	14.1
Disagreement about the future	13.1	17.3
Dominance	9.6	8.9
Dependence	3.2	4.3
Exploitation	1.4	3.5

While the issues mentioned cause a lot of grief in serious affairs, these specific reasons were not given as the ones responsible for the breaking up of love affairs. The 71 men in this study who reported broken love affairs had broken 230 affairs in all; the 121 women interviewed accounted for a total of 414 unsuccessful affairs. Here are the reasons given.[26]

[25] Clifford Kirkpatrick and Theodore Caplow, "Courtship in a Group of Minnesota Students," *American Journal of Sociology,* 51:114–125, September, 1945.

[26] *Ibid.,* p. 123.

Cause of breaking affair	Male affairs (Number 220) percent	Female affairs (Number 414) percent
Parents	5.2	8.6
Friends	3.1	5.8
Subject's interest in another person	15.1	32.2
Partner's interest in another person	29.7	15.3
Mutual loss of interest	46.9	39.1

Much of the dissimilarity between these two lists can probably be accounted for on the basis of specificity. Loss of interest, and interest in another by one or the other or both, which accounts for the termination of about 90 percent of the affairs in the second list are, without doubt, the result of such factors as jealousy, possessiveness, criticism, etc., that rank high in the first list.

Affairs where both lose interest are the easiest to terminate. There is little explaining or rationalizing to do and presumably no one is seriously hurt. Where one causes the breakup because he or she has found another, it is a different matter. Here there is the possibility of the deserted partner suffering jealousy, defeat, humiliation, and other feelings which the love relationship is capable of producing.

Parental influence is often a factor in the girl's reasons, perhaps indicating that parents watch the mate-selection process of the girl more than that of the boy. Would these same types of conflict issues be equally operative in the breakup of noncollege couples or in the breaking of engagements? There has been little attempt to study the noncollege population. Undoubtedly parental influence is often a factor in the termination of affairs among younger teenagers and is likely to be exerted before engagements take place.

What proportion of serious college affairs break up? The study[27] above shows that 71 percent of the serious love affairs of the girls had been broken; 73 percent of those of the men. The median age of the group at the time of the study was twenty-two years.

About what proportion of couples make a go of their affairs up to engagement? Burgess and Wallin's study of 1,000 engagements showed that only 20 to 30 percent of young people have never gone steadily with anyone except their future spouse.[28] Most college students have gone with two or more persons before becoming engaged.

The average engagement is not without its periods of doubts and conflicts. These alone cannot be reason enough for breaking an engage-

[27] *Ibid.*
[28] Ernest W. Burgess and Paul Wallin, *Engagement and Marriage* (Philadelphia: J. B. Lippincott Co., 1953), p. 148.

ment. Are there any clues to indicate when a couple should cease their attempts at adjustment and turn instead to new relationships? In any serious affair, whether it involves a ring, a pin, or a promise, the following situations should be considered definite indications that the relationship holds little promise of future success:

(1) *When many reforms in the partner are planned for after marriage:* Changing one's ways—habits, ideas, and values—is a difficult job, one that takes time and effort. It always seems easier to try to change the other person to fit one's own way of life than to make fundamental changes in oneself.

This reluctance to change one's own ways, coupled with the desire to erase the annoying or distasteful habits, attitudes, and manners in the prospective mate, is the cause of many major difficulties in marriage. When one marries, he or she is taking a "person" with a fully developed personality, not a piece of clay that can be molded into any desired form. The man or girl who marries with the expectation of remaking the new spouse into a more desirable person is in for a rude awakening.

Everyone carries into marriage the same ways of meeting problems that were used before marriage. The girl who escapes into illness rather than meet the unpleasant issues of life will likely resort to this same escape in marriage, where there are even more issues to be faced. The man who thinks this technique of adjustment will be changed by marriage is fooling himself.

The boy who has used drinking as an escape from problems before marriage will find even more worries to escape after marriage. In times of crisis he is likely to resort again to drinking rather than face and attempt to solve his problems. A girl who thinks she will change this is usually kidding herself.

Irritability, intolerance, moodiness, lack of respect and consideration, placing blame on others rather than shouldering it oneself—these and many other such traits are likely to be magnified rather than cured by marriage.

The writer once conferred with a college couple who failed in part because the husband tried to correct the way his wife walked. His nagging became intolerable. Another couple failed in marriage when the husband kept trying to get his wife to correct a slight lisp in her speech which dated back to her childhood and which she probably could not correct. Why should these men have married these girls if they found such traits obnoxious? Why didn't they choose girls they wouldn't have to remake? Many other men would have had no objection to these traits.

One suspects it was not until after marriage that they realized these traits might reflect unfavorably on them in professional circles. Maybe they did object to the traits before marriage and sincerely thought they could change them. It may be that these traits became the object of attack, when more basic matters were involved.

Mutual respect is an essential of the marriage relationships. If one finds himself losing it during engagement because of traits that seem obnoxious, that prove embarrassing in social relationships, or that threaten to reflect unfavorably on one's work, conventions, or reputation, it is time to be wary.

There are young marriageable people whom one will not need to reform, if one is realistic. If one's standards are so impossibly high that everyone of the opposite sex seems to have many annoying traits, then successful marriage is out of the question anyway. If one must do a lot of reforming, it is better to attempt to do it before marriage. Then, the chances are that the marriage will not take place and both will be saved a lot of trouble.

(2) *When the couple recognizes failure in adjusting toward a compatible relationship:* The patterns of adjustment that are established during the serious stage of dating will be the ones carried over into marriage. If roles of dominance and submission are evident then, they will characterize the marriage. If equality is the pattern established, this will likely continue into marriage. If quarreling is the method of adjustment, rather than discussion and working out of solutions to problems, this will probably carry over into marriage. If one or the other of the pair puts parents, brothers, or sisters first in his emotional attachments, marriage will not cure this. An objective appraisal of the relationship by oneself, or better still by fair-minded friends and relatives who observe the match, will tell a great deal about what the marriage is to be. So, also, will an objective analysis by a marriage counselor or other professional person of wide experience. Such case-history observations are valid measures of the potential marriage, allowing for the margin of error that enters into all such human judgments.[29]

The most extensive study of serious love relationships to date, that by Burgess and Wallin, has related engagement success to later marriage success. The authors work on the assumption that the type of interpersonal relationships begun during the period of going steady and being engaged, will not be radically altered in marriage, and that, therefore, the adjustment made during the engagement is predictive of the kind of adjustment that will be made in the marriage.[30]

Among the engagement factors which were found to offer a basis for forecasting the success of the marriage are: (a) the nature and degree of love of the couple, (b) their temperamental compatibility, (c) their emo-

---

[29] Burgess and Wallin (*ibid.*) find that such judgments have considerable merit in forecasting the outcome of a marriage.

[30] *Ibid.*

tional interdependence, dependence, and independence, (d) their common interests, including their attitude toward children, (e) their method of making decisions and the locus of their authority, (f) their adaptability, (g) their vulnerability to adverse factors such as interference by relatives and friends, economic difficulties, etc.[31] This research suggests that the adjustment level reached during engagement sets a couple's pattern for the marriage and offers a basis for forecasting its success.

On a statistical basis, this study reports a correlation of .50 between engagement history and other engagement factors, and marriage success. The researchers explain the lack of a higher correlation by such factors as the inadequacy of tests of success of engagement, inadequate measures of sucess in marriage, and by dynamic factors which enter into the relationship in marriage that were not foreseen.

(3) *When one or both lose interest:* Loss of interest is one of the most frequently given reasons for the termination of an engagement or serious affair. This is actually only a simple way of indicating any one of a number of things. Dissimilarity of backgrounds, interests, and values generally lead to gradual loss of attraction, as may the more or less serious personality deficiencies or unpleasant personal traits in one or the other —traits which were not discernible or were easily forgiven early in the affair. Loss of interest may merely indicate that the relationship was never intended to lead to marriage—that it was, in fact, only a "grown-up" version of going steady. Many such casual affairs do become serious without the couple's giving up their intention to refrain from marriage. This is often true of young people in school or professional training. When the motivation of marriage is lacking, attraction generally eventually dies of its own accord. When the attraction gets out of control and problems of deeper involvement, particularly of a sexual nature, begin to threaten, such couples usually change their plans in favor of marriage or they break up.

The common expression for the undesirable deep emotional involvement is "getting too serious," by which women mean that the male has begun to demand a sexual relationship, and by which men mean "she wants to get married."

Breaking Up

Occasionally, a couple feel trapped in their relationship with each other. When they say this, they may mean several things—emotional involvement that they find difficult to break, physical attachment where a com-

[31] *Ibid.,* p. 590–591, 620.

plete sexual relationship has been established, social responsibility in the cases of pregnancy, or involvement of family and friends and possessions. Men more often feel trapped in the serious relationship than do women, although Kirkpatrick and Caplow's study shows only 7 percent often felt that way and 23 percent occasionally felt too involved.[32] Where sexual intercourse is involved, this study suggests that the man more often feels trapped than does the woman, since he may believe it unfair to terminate the relationship. If an affair has been of long duration the man may feel, too, that it is unjust to drop the woman after having kept her restricted for so long.

The emotional damage of the breakup is, of course, the important thing from the standpoint of facing the future. Unless the relationship terminates by mutual agreement and on the basis of loss of interest, there are likely to be severe readjustment problems for at least one of the mates. Most student reactions indicate that there is considerable emotional turmoil in the breakup of a serious affair.[33] In fact, one suspects that the breakup of love affairs is responsible for the most serious emotional crises facing young people today.

In the background of the breakup are such factors as repeated misunderstandings, conflicts, and a growing awareness of differences in background, aspirations, values, and life plans. There may be opposition of parents or of other relatives and friends, coldness due to separations or to a growing recognition of undesirable personality traits, and an awareness of cultural, economic, religious, or other differences that foreshadow trouble.

Assuming this kind of background in the couple's love development, there are five steps through which the breakup goes, according to the most extensive study made to date:[34] (1) difficulties involving misunderstandings and quarrels, (2) the actual breaking of the engagement which may be an abrupt act or a tapering-off process, (3) the emotional crisis, the severity of which depends somewhat upon the extent to which it has been expected by both parties, (4) the rebound experience which often leads to a new emotional involvement with someone else, (5) a reappraisal of the engagement experience in terms of future behavior. This study finds that the person is often more cautious in making a new commitment, sometimes even cynical concerning the fidelity of the opposite sex.

The period of time required "to get over it" varies little between broken engagements and other serious affairs. In both cases the range is from one or two weeks to over two years.[35]

[32] Kirkpatrick and Caplow, *op. cit.,* p. 121.
[33] *Ibid.*
[34] Burgess and Wallin, *op. cit.,* pp. 297–301.
[35] Landis and Landis *op. cit.,* Table 5, pp. 222–227.

College students studied at the University of Minnesota were asked by Kirkpatrick and Caplow[36] about various "adaptive reactions" in an attempt to get some insight into the emotions and problems that followed the breakup of serious affairs.[37] Findings appear here:

Adaptive behavior	Male affairs (Number 230) percent	Female affairs (Number 414) percent
Frequenting places with common associations	11.3	10.0
Avoiding places with common associations	2.9	3.4
Avoiding meetings	4.7	5.1
Attempting meetings	5.9	4.3
Remembering only unpleasant things	2.3	3.9
Remembering only pleasant things	15.6	15.8
Dreaming about partner	15.5	11.2
Daydreaming	14.3	11.4
Imagining recognition	6.4	7.9
Liking or disliking people because of resemblance	5.5	5.4
Imitating mannerisms	1.8	2.1
Preserving keepsakes	7.0	10.8
Reading over old letters	6.8	8.7

There is considerable evidence here of daydreaming and of thinking about pleasant bygone dating days.

About half of the group, this research shows, got over the affair immediately, but a third of the men and a fifth of the women said it took them several weeks. Another fifth of the women and 7.7 percent of the men said it took them several months. Five percent of the men and 5.3 percent of the women said it took a year. The real sufferers, 5.3 percent of women and 2.3 percent of the men said it took several years. One may well suppose that some of this group will never get over the broken affair to the point of being able to love and marry.

Getting over an engagement is similar. The time required may range all the way from a week or two to over two years. Judson T. Landis indicates that over two-thirds of young college people get over the emotional effects of a broken engagement in less than six months, and only 12 percent suffer ill effects after a period of two years.[38]

[36] Kirkpatrick and Caplow, op. cit.
[37] Ibid., p. 125.
[38] Landis and Landis, op. cit.

His study of 1,059 students in eleven colleges showed that the typical reaction of the young college person to the breakup of love affairs is to remember the association as a pleasant one. About two-thirds have this reaction.[39] Almost as many soon begin dating somebody else as an aftereffect of the breakup of the engagement. More than a fourth continue to daydream about the lost lover.

Almost a third of the girls preserve keepsakes from the previous love affair; few boys do this. Half of the young people report trying to avoid meeting him or her afterward. About an equal number attempt to meet him or her. Girls are more likely to reread old letters, to remember pleasant associations, frequent places where the couple have been together, daydream, and so forth. It is only rarely that one or the other thinks of suicide.

No doubt the kind of emotional reaction that follows a broken love affair depends somewhat on the way the break is made. There are mean ways to break up, just as there are mean ways to carry out any other social relationship. If the couple discusses the situation reasonably and tries to face a solution together, as adults, the aftereffects should not be too serious. The most tragic affairs, no doubt, are those in which one person is still very deeply attached and wishes to continue the relationship to marriage and the other, seeing no possible future in the situation, breaks it abruptly without discussing the matter with the partner. This is particularly serious for the individual who is left with the feeling that something is seriously wrong with him or her, personally.

The broken affair or engagement becomes a serious threat to future marriage prospects if the lost partner was idealized to the point that all future affairs pale. The "phantom lover" experience is less common today, when most young people have dated enough to know they have another chance. The seriousness with which most breakups are taken may be more an indication of lack of previous experience than it is a measure of love. One who has dated widely before becoming serious can probably face the future with optimism; those with little or no previous dating would be more likely to take the experience seriously and suffer bereavement on its involutary termination.

In summary, affairs of the heart in our romance-minded culture often come to an untimely and unexpected end, and this is undoubtedly as it should be. The opportunity to correct a mistake, once recognized, is an important one. The chief difficulty arises when the people involved do not agree that the time has come to part. Even though not all engagements and serious affairs are of the stuff that promises permanency and happiness, "breaking off" is often a difficult, even heartbreaking business.

This chapter suggests that the game of love has its brutal and pain-

[39] *Ibid.*

ful aspects. Reverting to age-old custom and letting someone else do the mating would be an easy cure, but the price of individual choice is risk of failure. Individual mate-seeking is an emotionally wasteful and, in rare cases, a tragic process, but as Kirkpatrick and Caplow[40] conclude from their study of college students, "Pending the advent of a social engineer who can guide young people directly to their ideal mates, a more or less painful process of selection and rejection—of making and breaking court-ships—must take place."

Problems

1. After an engagement of sixteen months which of the following discoveries would probably lead you to break your engagement?
   a. He or she has an uncle in a mental institution.
   b. He or she confesses to having had sexual relations with another person at the age of thirteen.
   c. He or she refuses to join your church.
   d. He or she suggests not inviting a certain old friend to the wedding be-cause "he wears such odd clothes people would laugh."
   e. He or she refuses to establish a home in another community because of parental wishes.
   f. He or she still enjoys flirting with casual acquaintances.
   g. He or she shows slight tendencies toward characteristics of the other sex.
   h. He or she looks down upon the social and economic status of your family.
   i. He or she keeps asking questions about your past instead of reassuring you of unqualified devotion.
   j. He or she suddenly suggests that you extend your engagement for an-other six months and that three of these months be spent in separation to test the love.
2. Your close friend is brokenhearted because his girl has just returned their engagement ring. What would your advice to him be?
   a. Forget her and start dating Jean who thinks you're attractive.
   b. Ask her to give you one more chance.
   c. Try to make her jealous by dating other girls.
   d. Talk it over with her parents.
   e. Spend most of your free time on something else for a little while—reading, outdoor life, traveling.
   f. Make sure that some of the other girls know that breaking up was her decision.
   g. Decide once and for all that it's better to date than to ever get serious.
3. Do you believe that if a young man begins to tire of his fiancée he should:
   a. Tell her outright and break the engagement.
   b. Gradually show his loss of interest.

[40] Op. cit., p. 121.

    c. Ask a friend to tell her.

    d. Be seen with someone else.

    e. Wait for her to break the engagement no matter how long it takes.

    f. Initiate the subject deviously even if it takes several weeks to make the point.

Do the views of the boys and girls in the class tend to differ in their choice of alternatives and the arguments by which they support them?

4. List the advantages of a broken engagement over a broken marriage.

5. Bob and Marcy are physically very much attracted to one another. They enjoy the same books and sports, they agree on family size and politics, but Marcy suggests breaking the engagement when she discovers how different are their codes of ethics. Think of a number of situations in which ethics might seriously endanger a marriage.

6. *Sociodrama:* Jim and Kay thought they were "made for each other," but now Kay is suggesting they break their engagement. Let their friendly but serious discussion touch upon some of the situations or discoveries that have brought them to the point of breakup.

7. *Sociodrama:* The wedding is a week away. Most of the gifts have arrived; the wedding gown is finished, the wedding invitations have been sent out, and reservations have been made for a honeymoon. The young bride-to-be has just admitted to herself what she has subconsciously known for a long time, that she has been in love with love, not with her fiancé. In a burst of fear and uncertainty she rushes to her parents for advice and comfort.

    The drama pictures the attitudes of a levelheaded father, the excited mother, and the very upset daughter.

8. Should a couple refrain from breaking their engagement because of the embarrassment it would cause and the talk it would create?

9. *Sociodrama:* A young woman visits a marriage counselor and, among other things, brags that she and her fiancé "never disagree on anything." The counselor is dismayed. Continue the discussion emphasizing the questions the counselor might ask.

10. Study the following list of items about which an engaged couple might find themselves in disagreement. Be ready to discuss areas where disagreement would cause you to question the desirability of marriage.

    a. Whether or not to have a large formal wedding ceremony.

    b. Number of children desired.

    c. Whether or not to have children.

    d. Politics.

    e. Religion.

    f. Whether or not "the man runs the family."

    g. What is "good" in music and art.

    h. How children should be disciplined.

    i. Whether to buy a home or spend the money on a long trip.

    j. Leisure time interests.

11. An engaged couple who are deeply in love ran across a "marriage success" test in a popular magazine. The test, composed by an outstanding man in the field, indicated that their chances for marriage success were very slim. What would your advice to this couple be?

12. Clifford and Madelaine were engaged. While Clifford was stationed overseas he had a brief affair with an English girl. Should he:

    a. Describe the whole affair to his prospective wife?

b. Let her know there was such an affair?

c. Say nothing about it?

13. Are there psychological as well as physical reasons for the premarital physical examination?

14. What are your reactions to the idea that couples who are in love can take tests which will tell them whether or not they can succeed in marriage with one another?

15. Under what circumstances would it be unwise for an individual to confide all his past history to his prospective mate, or do you feel each should tell everything about his past?

Selected References

Articles in Books of Readings

Cavan, Ruth Shonle, *Marriage and the Family in the Modern World: A Book of Readings,* third edition (New York: Thomas Y. Crowell Co., 1969).
   Ktsanes, Thomas and Virginia, "Factors in Broken Engagaments," Reading 22.
Vincent, Clark E., *Readings in Marriage Counseling* (New York: Thomas Y. Crowell Co., 1957). Readings 11–17.
   A Symposium, "Premarital Sex Relations: The Facts and Counselor's Role in Relation to the Facts," pp. 104–117.

General References

Bolton, Charles D., "Mate Selection as the Development of a Relationship," *Marriage and Family Living,* 23:234–240, 1961.
Bossard, James S. H., "The Engagement Ring—A Changing Symbol," *New York Times Magazine,* p. 32 ff., September 14, 1958.
Burgess, Ernest W., and Wallin, Paul, *Engagement and Marriage* (Philadelphia: J. B. Lippincott Co., 1953), Chs. 5, 8, 9, 10.
Israel, S. Leon and Nemser, Sondra, "Family-Counseling Role of the Physician," *Journal of Marriage and Family,* 30:311–316, May, 1968.
Kirkpatrick, Clifford, and Caplow, Theodore, "Courtship in a Group of Minnesota Students," *American Journal of Sociology,* 51:114–125, September, 1945.
Koller, Marvin R., "Some Changes in Courtship Behavior in Three Generations of Ohio Women," *American Sociological Review,* 16:366–370, 1951.
Landis, Paul H., "Marriage Preparation in Two Generations," *Marriage and Family Living,* 8:155–156, November, 1951.
Mudd, Emily Hartshorne, *The Practice of Marriage Counseling* (New York: Association Press, 1951).
Popenoe, Paul, "A Study of 738 Elopements," *American Sociological Review,* 3:297 ff., February, 1938.

18

The Research Score on Premarital Sex Experience

Much is written in the popular press regarding the "sexual revolution," particularly on the college campus. Some deny its existence, others greatly exaggerate its manifestations—few are neutral. Behavioral scientists have tried to learn by in-depth studies on campus, what is happening and the circumstances, particularly as to degree of emotional commitment, under which coitus takes place.

Promiscuity is not a universally accepted pattern on campus for any significant number of either sex. There has been much less altering of behavior than of conversation and of attitudes. For most young people, guilt feelings are still a part of violating the moral code in the sexual area. The proportion of girls who engage in premarital coitus has increased, particularly among women in the junior and senior years of college. Even so, violators of the moral code suffer a great deal of anxiety. It is believed that the proportion of males having premarital sex relationships has been relatively constant.[1]

Even those who restrict themselves are reluctant to condemn another for sex relationships with an engaged partner. A common statement runs something like this: "I could not have sexual relationships until I marry, but I do not blame those who can and do."[2]

In 1967, Judson T. Landis conducted a study[3] of 1,005 men and 2,184 women in 18 colleges and universities, and compared attitudes toward premarital sex relations with a similar study he made in 1952 and

[1] These observations are based on the reading of student autobiographies in the writer's classes. The autobiographies are written anonymously each semester. See also research reports listed at the end of the chapter.

[2] This trend toward greater tolerance is very marked in anonymous student autobiographies submitted over the years.

[3] See Judson T. Landis and Mary G. Landis, *Building a Successful Marriage* fifth edition (Englewood Cliffs, N. J.: Prentice-Hall, Inc., 1968), Table 2, p. 168.

a Cornell study in 1940. More permissive attitudes are reflected. In 1967, more than three times as many males as in 1940 believed sexual relationships were proper for both. (15 percent compared to 47 precent). The proportion of women holding this view had risen from 6 percent to 21 percent. Only 24 percent of men and 39 percent of women felt both should be chaste.

In a 1969 survey for *Time,* the Louis Harris Poll studied changing American morals.[4] Marked changes in sexual morality were evidenced among professionals, college graduates, prosperous citizens of suburbia, and those under thirty. Those over fifty, the less educated, and less prosperous still clung to traditional sexual morality.

In the area of adultery, 36 percent reported knowledge of particular cases as compared to 24 percent in 1964; the percent "virtually admitting to adultery in their own family," rose from 10 to 15. As to abortion, 64 percent believed it should not be a matter of law but of personal choice; 60 percent of Catholics held this view.

There is a growing tendency to evaluate sex, not in terms of right and wrong, but of whether or not it is a genuine expression of affection. The test becomes a psychological rather than a moral one. The question has changed from "Is it right?" to "Is it right under the circumstances which exist between us?"

While there can be little doubt that the vast majority of college girls live by traditional codes, an increasing number are willing to grant others the right to live according to their own conscience. Perhaps the greatest risk in this kind of atmosphere is that many girls, who have a built-in conscience clearly defining right for themselves, try to embrace the other code and find themselves inflicted with deep psychological wounds. Their rationalizations, their reading of supporting literature from "experts," their discussion with peers do not quiet their conscience.

This is by no means a female problem only. The male is more immune from restrictions of morality because few families instill in the male so strict a code, yet there are college men who suffer deeply from having reached beyond the bounds of their internalized moral values. There are also more college men who live by a strict moral code than the popular magazines would lead one to believe.

A Broad View of Premarital Sex Experience

An anthropological study by Murdock of 250 societies throughout the world shows that 70 percent permit sexual experimentation before mar-

---

[4] "Changing Morality: The Two Americas," *Time,* pp. 26–27, June 6, 1969.

riage.[5] Even among the 30 percent which place a taboo upon premarital sex relations, the taboo most often applies only to girls. In many of these societies, marriage comes soon after puberty. The prohibition against premarital intercourse is actually a prohibition against prepubertal intercourse. In most societies also the taboo is upper class only.

This study concludes that there is nothing in human societies generally to indicate that a taboo on premarital sex relations has any value to survival of the group. In most societies it is assumed that premarital intercourse has no relationship to postmarital fidelity (all societies seek postmarital fidelity); in other words, it does not seem to interfere with the function of the family institution, once marriage has been entered into.[6]

Where premarital sexual relations are sanctioned, intercourse usually is not extensive or promiscuous. The society recognizes it as a means of preparing for marriage, rather than as a means of indulging in sexual excitement as such.

So much for human experience in the broader perspective. Are there reasons why our society should differ in this matter from the general norm? Does it actually differ?

Reasons for and against Premarital Coitus

The question of premarital coitus is one of the most important issues facing couples today from the beginning of their casual contacts through the engagement period. Numerous reasons for and against premarital coitus are advanced. Kinsey has summarized these arguments as found in the marriage manuals.[7]

Reasons for Premarital Intercourse

1. It may satisfy a physiological need for a sexual outlet.
2. It may become a source of immediate physical and psychological satisfaction.
3. If there is no guilt, it may increase one's ability to function more effectively in other, nonsexual fields.
4. It is more valuable than solitary sexual activity for developing one's capacity to make emotional adjustments with other persons.
5. It may develop one's capacity to make the particular sorts of emotional adjustments which are needed in marital relationships.

[5] George P. Murdock, "Sexual Behavior: What Is Acceptable?" *Journal of Social Hygiene,* 36:1–31, 1950.

[6] Evidence that it may do so in American society is presented later in this chapter.

[7] Alfred C. Kinsey and others, *Sexual Behavior in the Human Female* (Philadelphia: W. B. Saunders Co., 1953), pp. 307–309. By permission of Dr. Kinsey.

6. It may provide training in the sorts of physical techniques that may be involved in marital coitus.
7. It may test the capacities of two persons to make satisfactory sexual adjustments after marriage.
8. It is easier to learn to make emotional and physical adjustments at an earlier age; they are learned with greater difficulty after marriage.
9. Failure in a premarital relationship is socially less disastrous than failure after marriage.
10. Heterosexual experience may prevent the development of a homosexual pattern of behavior.
11. Premarital coitus may lead to marriage.
12. In at least some social groups, an individual may acquire status by fitting into the group pattern for behavior.

Reasons against Premarital Intercourse

1. The danger for the female of pregnancy.
2. The danger if abortion is used to terminate a pregnancy.
3. The possibility of contracting a venereal disease.
4. The undesirability of a marriage which is forced by a premarital pregnancy.
5. The traumatic effects of coitus which is had under the inadequate circumstances which are supposed to attend most premarital relations.
6. The damage done by the participant's guilt over the infringement of the moral law.
7. The guilt at the loss of virginity, and its subsequent effect on marriage.
8. The fear that males lose respect for and will not marry a female with whom they have had coitus.
9. The damage done when guilt feelings are reawakened after marriage.
10. The guilt resulting from fear of public disapproval.
11. The risk and fear of social difficulties that may follow discovery of the relationship.
12. The risk and fear of legal difficulties that may follow any discovery of the relationship.
13. The possibility that premarital coitus which is satisfactory may delay or prevent altogether the individual from marrying.
14. The possibility that the coitus may make one feel obligated to marry the sexual partner.
15. The possibility that guilt over the coitus may break up an otherwise desirable friendship with the sexual partner.
16. The overemphasis which premarital experience may place on the physical aspects of friendship and marriage.
17. The likelihood that premarital irregularities will lead to later extramarital infidelities, with consequent damage to the marriage.
18. The possibility that the female will be less capable of responding satisfactorily in her marital coitus because of the traumatic effects of premarital experience.
19. The fact that premarital coitus is morally wrong.
20. The principle that abstinence from such activities may develop one's will power.

Statistical Trends

Kinsey found that all forms of sex experience showed a marked increase between the generation born in 1890 and that born in the 1900–1910 period.[8] The increase in sex activity among those born since the 1900–1910 decade was not striking, although the most recent decade of births dealt with was 1920 to 1929. Other research confirms these findings.[9] The 1952 study[10] of 1,600 students in 11 universities shows that only about 10 percent of the girls reported having had premarital intercourse. A study[11] of a Florida university group reported similar findings. It is possible, of course, that college girls may not always report this fact accurately. Half of the unmarried women in Kinsey's sample had had sexual intercourse. Of the unmarried men in his sample, 85 percent had had coitus. The educated group in the Kinsey study of the male had had coitus less often than had the uneducated.[12] Of his sample of college girls less than 20 percent had had sexual relations.

Data dealing with engaged couples in the higher educational levels show a far higher rate of sexual intercourse previous to marriage than these general statistics present. Burgess and Wallin's[13] study of a thousand engagements reported that about 45 percent of their couples had had premarital coitus. Kanin and Howard,[14] studying 177 wives of college students at a midwest university, show about the same ratio (43.5 percent). This study also reports what other studies have shown regarding the influence of social class and religion as factors: the lower the social class of the wife, the more likely she is to have permitted sexual intercourse before marriage, particularly if she is engaged to an upper-class male. Seriousness about religion is a great deterrent to premarital sexual intercourse. Concerning social class, Kanin and Howard suggest that more than differences in class mores are in operation; the upper-class male

[8] *Ibid.* Comparisons throughout the book are made by decade of birth.

[9] Lewis M. Terman and others, *Psychological Factors in Marital Happiness* (New York: McGraw-Hill Book Co., 1938). Terman finds an increase with younger age of couples in his sample.

[10] Landis and Landis, *op. cit.*

[11] Winston W. Ehrmann, "Student Co-operation in a Study of Dating Behavior," *Marriage and Family Living*, 14:4 ff., November, 1952; also his *Premarital Dating Behavior* (New York: Henry Holt and Co., 1959).

[12] Alfred C. Kinsey and others, *Sexual Behavior in the Human Male* (Philadelphia: W. B. Saunders Co., 1948).

[13] Ernest W. Burgess and Paul Wallin, *Engagement and Marriage* (Philalphia: J. B. Lippincott Co., 1953).

[14] Eugene J. Kanin and David H. Howard, "Postmarital Consequences of Premarital Sex Adjustments," *American Sociological Review*, 23:557–562, October, 1958.

is probably exploitive of the lower-class female in a way he is not with one of his own status or above; the lower-class female, lacking other devices of attraction, uses sex to the maximum advantage in winning her man.

The Landis study[15] of students in 18 colleges and universities found 12 percent of women and 29 percent of men had sex relations during casual dating. During steady dating it rose to 48 percent of men and 45 percent of women during formal engagement. Packard[16] reports that 43 percent of college educated women had had coitus before they married, compared to a 27 percent for the Kinsey sample of the earlier period. The trend is in the direction of permissiveness with affection, and even greater permissiveness with engagement commitment.

Trends in Coeducational Housing

The trend toward less restricted visiting in dormitories and in off-campus apartments has been in progress for several years and will increase. This will give students even more freedom of choice in the sexual area than the automobile did.

The number of coeducational dormitories, long existing in Scandinavian countries, will undoubtedly increase. Even living together off campus may well cease to be grounds for expulsion from colleges and universities. Sexual morality is certain to become more a matter of personal choice rather than of adherence to rules imposed by institutional authorities.

The effects are as yet unpredictable. Whether opportunity will greatly increase premarital sexual activity, or whether traditional personal codes will prevail remains to be seen. Closer association may even alter relationships and attitudes of men and women toward each other.

Joseph Katz[17] has studied coed housing in Stanford and finds not only that 95 percent of the students favor it but also that it has lead to "at least a partial moratorium on sex." Shared dining and classes avoids over-idealization, reduces "mutual teasing and destructive behavior characteristic of campus dating, leads students to regard each other more like brothers and sisters." He concludes it may modify sex relationships and strengthen marriage.

[15] *Op. cit.,* Table I, p. 167.

[16] Vance Packard, *The Sexual Wilderness* (New York: David McKay Co., Inc., 1968).

[17] News item in *Family Life,* 28:4, May, 1968.

Sex and Sin

Earlier studies by sociologists and the Kinsey Sex Institute left little doubt that the sin conception of sex out of wedlock was a very strong element in social control. The deepest form of guilt from days prior to Hawthorne's *Scarlet Letter,* was sex guilt.

The sin concept of sex has weakened and with it, social control. Young people who are serious about finding a positive answer to their doubts and queries even find a church atmosphere in which positive assurances are less often given. Where there was certainty in the church leadership as to what the moral code in the sexual area should be, there is now debate by the clergy and less moralizing about sexual matters. Where there was prohibition, there is now a tendency to be permissive or silent. Those who wish an answer may seek in vain for an authoritative guide.

As Packard[18] points out, some ministers and religious journals have been arguing seriously about the *Playboy* philosophy, rather than rejecting it outright. While some parents when faced with religious leaders who fail to take stands may feel less guilt and anxiety about their children it is Packard's opinion that others seek a church where their children will have the guidance of a minister who "preaches what is right."

Even with the weakening of religious controls, they are still among the strongest in our culture. Judson T. Landis'[19] 1967 study of 3,189 students in 18 colleges and universities sought to learn reasons for refraining from premarital sexual intercourse of 44 percent of men and 75 percent of women who wanted to wait until marriage. Family training and religion were strong motivating factors, although about a third of both sexes feared pregnancy.

The Conflict of Professional Opinion

A few counselors take a strong position in favor of premarital sex experience. Walter Stokes,[20] for example, holds that the best sexual development is possible through premarital sex experience under emotionally favorable conditions. He believes that in women there is a relationship between the sex response and the development of vaginal musculature. He takes no

---

[18] Vance Packard, *op. cit.,* p. 40.

[19] *Op. cit.,* Table 3, p. 169.

[20] See discussion on the Stokes article, *Marriage and Family Living,* 15:39–49, August, 1953.

stock in the idea that we should teach that sex is beautiful and proper, but that there should be no experience with it until after marriage.

He bases his argument largely on clinical evidence, finding that the young male who comes for counsel previous to marriage boasting that he has never masturbated, or had any sex experience, offers almost hopeless prospects for success in marriage. He goes so far as to say that all of the chaste young men turn out to be impotent to the degree of requiring extensive psychiatric treatment. Dr. Stokes finds, also, that girls who have had no sex experience are more likely to faint during vaginal examination and to otherwise exhibit the tenseness and fear that grow out of lack of sex training and experience.

The unanswered question is, of course, would these same types have been any different had they had premarital sex experience? Or would the conditioning which led to these negative attitudes toward sex also lead to the same consequences which he observes had they attempted more intimate forms of sex experience.

He does present limited positive evidence[21] for his position. He indicates that he has worked experimentally with a group of patients who came to him some years ago at the time of their marriage. He has helped these patients train their children without the usual sex inhibitions, and reports that when these youngsters are ready for marriage, he finds an amazing zest for sex enjoyment, greater maturity, and greater sense of responsibility than is usual in young people of their age.

Dr. Albert Ellis,[22] clinical psychologist and counselor in New York City, likewise takes the position that virginity and chastity represent cultural lags in our thinking about marriage preparation. He believes that extreme sexual difficulties in his clients are directly attributable to taboos against premarital sex relations and masturbation.

Sociologically, this view has a certain weakness. Social systems have always operated on the assumption that maximum physical satisfaction is rarely or never possible in human relationships—that only through restraint on biological appetite, by restricting it to customary channels of expression, can human society as such exist. The sex impulse is, therefore, always regulated in relation to the goals and objectives of the family itself. Societies are concerned not with maximum satifaction of the individual from the sexual act, but with establishing controls which act as a bulwark to the family system.

Most counselors are firmly convinced that conventions must be given a place in appraising premarital sex behavior, and they feel just as certain that, conventions being what they are, premarital chastity is desirable. Among counselors and authors who are strong in their support of the

---

[21] *Ibid.,* p. 267.

[22] Albert Ellis, *Marriage and Family Living,* 15:242–244, August, 1953. Discussion.

mores are David Mace, Harold T. Christensen, Abraham Stone, and Emily Mudd.[23]

The Unprotected Mother and Child Problem

Fear of pregnancy is often said to be less of a force in controlling pre-marital coitus, since risks have largely been eliminated. However, the increasing illegitimate birth rate indicates: a) either contraception as used by the unmarried is most risky, b) it is not used; c) one party or both seeks pregnancy; d) girls are more inclined to see pregnancy through rather than seek an abortion. Illegitimate birth rates in the United States rose from 7.1 per 1,000 unmarried women in 1940 to 24.4 per 1,000 in 1968 for all races combined. For whites the figure rose from 3.6 to 11.6 births per 1,000 unmarried women, for the nonwhites from 35.6 to 97.6 (see Table 18–1). The National Center for Health Statistics placed births out of wedlock at 339,200 in 1968.[24]

Katherine Brownwell Ottinger of the Childrens' Bureau estimates[25] that 44 precent of babies born out of wedlock are born to mothers 13 to 19 years of age, and that in 1969 there will be 74,000 babies born to school-age girls 17 or younger.

The table shows the distribution of births by age groups. We can see that the ratios are highest, not among the young and ignorant, but among the older group who should know most about contraception. The illegitimate births exceed 24 per 1,000 among unmarried white women 25–29 years of age. Obviously contraception is not the full answer. We are dealing here with very complex motives.

The difference in the figures for whites and nonwhites is due to two or more factors. Nonwhites are less likely to seek an abortion, and are also less likely to marry soon after discovering pregnancy, often waiting until a child or two is born before marrying. The child born out-of-wedlock is more accepted in the nonwhite family and nonwhite community, and there too, the lower-class Negro male feels less responsibility for the economic liabilities of parenthood. Negro women are more often the support of the family than are white women.

As more is understood about the poor, it is increasingly evident that those in this subculture have very different family and marriage values

[23] See discussion on the Stokes article, *Marriage and Family Living,* 15:39–49. August, 1953.

[24] Of white children, 16 percent are born within 8 months of the marriage, of nonwhite, 41 percent. Table A, "Trends in Illegitimacy, United States—1940–1965," National Center for Health Statistics, Series 21, Number 15, Washington, D.C., February 1968.

[25] News item in *Family Life,* 29:5, February, 1969.

from the middle class. Among the poor, consensual unions without ceremony are the rule and are preferred by women as well as men. Men show little promise of being able to offer the family steady support or inheritance. They do not want the legal entanglements which marriage and divorce imply. Women prefer not to be tied down to men who feel superior to women and are "immature, punishing, and generally unreliable." Without marriage, women have some of the freedom always claimed by men and retain full right to the children if they choose to leave the man or are abandoned by him. The house and any other property belong to the woman if she forces the man to leave. The family is matriarchal in character.

In the United States, the consensual union is most common among nonwhites where poverty is concentrated. This subculture has a definite bearing on the illegitimacy statistics of nonwhites.

Table 18–1. Estimated Number of Illegitimate Births Per 1,000 Unmarried Women 15–44, by Age and Color of Mother in the United States, 1940 to 1965

White	1965	1960	1950	1940
15–44 years	11.6	9.2	6.1	3.6
15–19	7.9	6.6	5.1	3.3
20–24	22.1	18.2	10.0	5.7
25–29	24.3	18.2	8.7	4.0
30–34	16.6	10.8	5.9	2.5
35–39	4.9	3.9	3.2	1.7
40–44			0.9	0.7
Nonwhite				
15–44 years	97.6	98.3	71.2	35.6
15–19	75.8	76.5	68.5	42.5
20–24	152.6	166.5	105.4	46.1
25–29	164.7	171.8	94.2	32.5
30–34	137.8	104.0	63.5	23.4
35–39	39.0	35.6	31.3	13.2
40–44			8.7	5.0

Source: Table B, "Trends in Illegitimacy: United States 1940–1965," National Center for Health Statistics, Series 21, No. 15, Washington, D.C., February, 1968.

One can speculate at length about the reasons for the increase in illegitimacy rates in the "Pill Age," but he cannot deny the seriousness of the consequences to society. In addition to the unfair burden on the mother and the unprotected child, society must take over the task that belongs to the responsible adult male, the support and training of his offspring.

Aside from the question of morality, society has great economic stakes involved. More than a fifth of all these children are cared for on welfare rolls. Where there is no father to assume the economic burden, parents, other relatives, persons who adopt, or welfare agencies must bear it. One need only compare the number of illegitimate children in this country with that in the Latin American cultures to realize how serious the problem can become should morality become obsolete. In this respect northwestern European culture and that of Scandinavian countries are in striking contrast. In Scandinavia, the state is custodian of the child, through welfare guardians.[26] It is the responsibility of the state to locate the father and give the child his name. The law provides that the child will have equal rights to inheritance with the child of any marriage the father may have. There is no compulsion to marry, but the father assumes the same financial responsibility of parenthood that he would assume if he were married. The child has all the rights he would have if the couple married. The mother has the regular protections of social security available to all mothers in addition to certain extra benefits. This situation permits the equal freedom of men and women to participate in the sex act, both before marriage and in extramarital sexual relationships—a basic necessity in sex equality.

In the cultures of northwestern Europe and Scandinavia, relationships between the sexes tends to be courtship-centered rather than dating-centered. By limiting association to one male at a time, the girl is assured of being able to legally fix responsibility for paternity. Second, the intent of the couple from the beginning of their serious relationship is marriage; pregnancy may mark the actual beginning of marriage plans.[27] In a culture

[26] In 1950 there were 84,393 children in Sweden born out of wedlock, and under the supervision of child-welfare guardians. Paternity had been established for 76,798 or 85.2 percent of these by acknowledgement of the father, and 14.8 by court decision. There were only 7,595 cases in which paternity had not been established; see *Social Sweden* (Stockholm: Social Welfare Board, 1962), pp. 214–218. See also Linner, Birgitta, *Sex and Society in Sweden* (New York: Pantheon, 1967).

[27] In Sweden, about 10 percent of children have been born out of wedlock during recent years; in Denmark, about 10 percent. The proportion was as high as 15 percent in Sweden during the 1920s and 1930s. It is estimated that 50 to 55 percent of first births in these countries and about 27 percent of births in Holland take place prior to 9 months of marriage. These figures were given the author by population and birth control authorities in the various countries in 1953. For Swedish data on children born out of wedlock, see *Social Sweden, loc. cit.* In Copenhagen rates are 90 percent for women married under age 20. See Sidney Goldstein, "Premarital Pregnancy and Out-of-Wedlock Births in Denmark, 1950–1965," *Demography*, 4:925–926, 1967.

A comparison of Norwegian and American college students shows that among Norwegian students 80 percent consider full sex relations proper during engagement. Only about 28 percent of American college students agree. See William Simenson

FIGURE 18-1   TWO SYSTEMS OF PAIR RELATIONSHIPS.

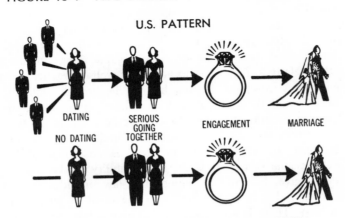

U.S. PATTERN

DATING

NO DATING

SERIOUS
GOING
TOGETHER

ENGAGEMENT

MARRIAGE

CONTINENTAL AND SCANDINAVIAN PATTERN

PICTOGRAPH CORPORATION

Under the first system of pair relationships premarital coitus carries a much
greater risk than under the second. The first kind characterizes the United
States; the second, Western Europe and Scandinavia.

like our own where dating is simply a game between a girl and boy,
marriage comes later, if ever, in the plans of most couples. It is not until
they have settled down to dating one person for a considerable length of
time that ideas of a permanent pair relationship even enter into their
plans (see Figure 18-1).

Sex activity in the premarital period, therefore, if it comes before the
time of serious intentions, is hazardous from the standpoint of the girl.
In our mobile society with its casual dating, it is difficult to fix responsibility for paternity. If premarital sex activity were condoned the girl
would possibly find herself without protection for a child, and age-long
expectation of society that the male will provide for the female and helpless young would be defeated. Under such circumstances, a society can
hardly permit sex relationships during the dating period, and can scarcely
sanction them during the engagement period, for dating is so extensive
in our culture that even engagement is a tentative relationship—not less
than one in three engagements is broken.

and Gilbert Geis, "Courtship Patterns of Norwegian and American University Stu-
dents," *Marriage and Family Living,* 18:334–338, November, 1965; see also Harold
T. Christensen, "Cultural Relativism and Premarital Sex Norms," *American Socio-
logical Review,* 25:31–39, February, 1960; also Harold T. Christensen and George
R. Carpenter, "Value-Behavior Discrepancies Regarding Premarital Coitus in Three
Western Cultures," *American Sociological Review,* 27:66–74, February, 1962; also
their "Timing Patterns in the Development of Sexual Intimacy," *Marriage and Family
Living,* 24:32–35, February, 1962.

Of course, our customs are not so well reasoned out as this argument suggests. The mores rather than any well thought out social policy are the major factor in the control of sex behavior. American morality, based on our Puritanic culture, is sex-centered. Morality has become almost synonymous with being discreet in sex matters. If one inquires or comments about another's morals, he is usually thinking entirely of his sex attitudes and conduct, not of his general honesty, his truthfulness, his loyalty to persons or causes.

This commonly accepted conception of decency, powerful in itself as a means of controlling sex activity, receives further support from the threat and fear engendered by public opinion. Unlike the Scandinavian peoples, we still make much of the term "illegitimacy"; and the woman who bears a child out of wedlock has more than her own conscience to reckon with. Regardless of the circumstances, she is generally met by a hostile and unsympathetic community.

Scandinavian society accepts premarital pregnancy and believes that the child and the mother should have the same protection as in wedlock. Zetterberg's study[28] shows that 93 percent of Swedish people interviewed approve sexual intercourse for the engaged or those going steady, 99 percent feel that children of unwed parents should have the same rights as children born in wedlock, and 98 percent feel that unwed mothers should have all the rights of the married. The terms *illegitimate* and *bastard* have long been replaced by the term *children of unmarried mothers.*

The social problem of premarital coitus is that of providing protection to mother and child, not of sanctifying sexual relationships. Every child has a right to be wanted. In a highly mobile society, which assumes that each pair will build their own and their children's security, and which considers a father's name a mark of respect and status for the child, premarital chastity must remain the social standard. Otherwise we must develop many institutions in support of the unprotected mother and child and must radically modify concepts of legitimacy and respectability.

Factors in the High Pregnancy Rate

Some males regard having sexual relations with a girl as a proof of masculinity, and have no concern for the consequences to the girl or a possible child. For many women, pregnancy proves their femininity, and some actually want to have a child of their own regardless of other consequences. Some girls get pregnant to spite parents, or to trap a mate,

[28] Hans L. Zetterberg, *On Sexual Life in Sweden,* Report on the Royal Commission on Sex Education, summary in J. Robert Moskin, "The New Contraceptive Society," *Look,* February 4, 1969, p. 50 ff.

while others feel that any preparation spoils the spontaneity of the sex act. Many who are troubled in conscience could not consider preparation including the pill which takes much foresight. Most girls will not take the pill in advance because of guilt they feel about what they might do. Perhaps psychologically it represents a form of aggressive behavior which they cannot accept for themselves.

McCandless[29] gives a motive for pregnancy among the lower working-class which it will be difficult for the average college student to understand. For them the only "genuine creation" may be the "production of something perfect"—the bringing into the world of a baby.

Vincent[30] says middle class girls are more ego involved than lower class girls. They must be sure that sex becomes a means for self-enhancement, they want intense emotional involvement as a proof that they, not just sex favors, are meaningful to the male. Lower class girls are interested in winning the boy through sex and use it as a way of gaining affection.

In addition, there is much ignorance about sex and carelessness. Some consider the forms of contraception they know unsanitary; some trust unreliable methods. Other couples fail to comunicate with each other and assume the other has taken the necessary precautions.

Universal and honest contraceptive information given to all prior to puberty would help alleviate the problem, but as a society, we are far from accepting this goal. Long term immunity to pregnancy would be another approach, but it would require parental consent, or else radical modification of law regarding treatment of those under age by the physician. Neither of these goals are readily attainable now. The morning after pill now in the experimental stage could help if used.

Judson T. Landis reports in his 1967[31] study of college students that 50 percent of those who had broken an engagement reported having had sexual intercourse with the partner without having taken reliable contraceptive precautions. College students would be expected to practice more than average restraint, and to have fair knowledge of contraception and access to contraceptive devices. Apparently accessibility to contraception is not enough to avoid pregnancy.

The Scandinanvian experience indicates that the goal of security for children within marriage in a society which sanctions premarital sexual intercourse is not attainable. With extensive contraceptive knowledge and widespread trial marriage, which implies no compulsion to marry even when the girl is pregnant, about half of brides in Sweden are preg-

[29] Boyd McCandless, "The Devil's Advocate Examines Parent Education," *Family Life Coordinator,* 17:149–154, July, 1968.

[30] Clark Vincent, *Unmarried Mothers* (New York: Free Press of Glencoe, Inc., 1961), pp. 92 ff.

[31] Landis and Landis, *op. cit.,* p. 241.

nant at their wedding and approximately 10 percent of children are born out of wedlock.[32]

Those societies have had to develop, as we have seen, a system of social institutions and of mores to supplement the family in order to meet the needs of unmarried mothers and their children. We have no such institutions.

Effect of Premarital Sex Experience on Engagement

The sharing of sexual experiences, providing they are mutually sought and satisfying, does much to strengthen the close relationship of husband and wife. When intercourse takes place during the engagement period it can be assumed that it does so by mutual agreement. It may be mutual only in the sense that the female yielded to a great deal of pressure from the male. The decision to refrain may be by mutual agreement or by female denial. Do mutually sought sexual relations at this time have the same beneficial effects upon the engagement as they have upon a marriage relationship?

In studying couples during the period of their engagement, the most authoritative study[33] to date asked 81 engaged men and 74 engaged women the effect of premarital intercourse on their relationship. Over 90 percent of each group said they thought it strengthened the relationship. Slightly over 5 percent of of the women thought it had a weakening effect, but only 1 percent of the men thought so. The others thought that it had no effect at all on their relationship.

These reactions, of course, must be weighed in light of the long-term effects on engagement and marriage; the temporary effect may be to strengthen the relationship, but the long-term effects may be quite different. It is possible too that couples at the time of the interview might have been rationalizing considerably. In any case, it was found that engagement adjustment scores were somewhat higher for the group that was not having intercourse. On the question of whether engaged men and women had had sexual relations with persons other than the affianced, adjustment scores were slightly higher for those who had had no such relations, but there was no significant difference between those who had had sexual relations with the affianced only and with the affianced and others. Nor did frequency of intercourse with the affianced or with others

[32] Zetterberg, *op. cit.*
[33] Burgess and Wallin, *op. cit.,* p. 372.

seem to have any relationship to the problem of adjustment. Whether or not they had intercourse at all seems to have been the significant factor.

This study shows further that more couples who had had intercourse than those who had not had intercourse broke their engagements. Although the sample dealing with broken engagements is small (31 cases), it lends support to the view of some doctors and counselors that the male's desire for marriage is lessened when his sex needs are being regularly satisfied outside marriage. This is an important point since sex is generally one of the most powerful incentives of the male to marry.

Among the reactions most often reported by couples engaging in intercourse were relief of physical tension and confidence that they were going to be married. Among unfavorable feelings most frequently reported were fear of social disapproval, which was mentioned by more than a fifth of both men and women, and fear of pregnancy, which was mentioned by a fourth of men and 26 percent of women. Sixteen percent of women also reported feelings of guilt.

The researchers consider it significant that none of the group, in reporting feelings or justifications that accompanied premarital sex relations, mentioned sexual experience as a test of sexual compatibility. They conclude that premarital sex relationships, therefore, are not entered into as a guide to physical compatibility; rather they occur, not with any long-time definite purpose in mind, but as a relief for "frequent and intensive erotic stimulation."

Kirkendall's study has accumulated the case histories of 250 premarital relationships of college students, focusing interest on the quality of the interpersonal relationship which is associated with premarital intercourse.[34] The author of the study concludes that "practically all the premarital coitus in the preengagement period takes place under conditions which, in both the short and the long run, result in more suspicion, distrust, and less ability to set up a good relationship later." Some engaged couples are drawn closer together by coitus during the engagement period, but this study reports other cases where the couple was also drawn closer together by a decision not to have intercourse, indicating that an intimate level of communication may be the main factor in drawing them closer together. Kirkendall concludes that sexual intercourse usually weakens the relationship, and often terminates it.

He finds that motives of men and women differ, and this often leads to misunderstanding. The man usually enters into a sexual relationship merely for the physical thrill, to make himself feel a man, or to accomplish what some of his friends boast about accomplishing. A woman is

[34] Lester A. Kirkendall, "Premarital Sex Relations: The Problems and Its Implications," *Pastoral Psychology,* April, 1956; see also his *Premarital Intercourse and Interpersonal Relations* (New York: Julian Press, Inc., 1961).

more likely to enter the relationship to hold the man, or to push him into marriage. After the sexual relationship she may become possessive, show great anxiety to make the relationship permanent, and talk a great deal about marriage. The boastful man begins to feel more sober and senses that he is being trapped. Men in this situation are generally much less interested in marriage than are women.

Women generally sense more guilt than do men when they break the moral codes. This also leads them to encourage the marriage idea. With the loss of virginity, marriageability has been somewhat weakened as far as other prospective mates are concerned. If her violation of the code is discovered she is much more exposed to shame and social censure than is the man, so she feels much less safe. Often the greatest threat to her reputation comes from the man, who may be very indiscreet in boasting about his conquest to friends. This not only threatens the woman's reputation but makes it more likely that other men will expect sex favors if the pair breaks up.

Men are not undamaged by casual sexual experience. Many find it hard to settle down when the time comes to marry. Some are forced into marriage before they are ready by a sense of guilt, because a girl with whom they have had intercourse becomes pregnant, or fears she is pregnant, or merely claims to be to force marriage. (Pregnancy can be determined in a few minutes by any reliable physician.)

LeMasters feels that coitus tends to gloss over serious differences between couples so that these do not appear until after marriage. He believes many couples "neck their way out" of problems before marriage, rather than facing them. Sex thus becomes a confusing force during mate choice.[35]

In talking with engaged couples one frequently hears a young woman say, "My fiancé is always tense and cross before a weekend is over, but I'm sure the problem is sex tensions." This may well be. It may be desirable, however, to take a second look at the relationships, and make sure that even the restrained sex play entered into is not an effort to keep from facing the real issues, or a device for forcing complete sex relations.

Refraining from sexual intercourse during the engagement period is, of course, often extremely difficult, especially today when close physical contacts are customary.[36] Sexual intercourse, Burgess and Wallin found, is more often entered into by those who have prolonged their engagement 16 months or more.[37] Kinsey finds too that the incidence of premarital coitus increases with delayed marriage. The likelihood of women having

[35] E. E. LeMasters, *Modern Courtship and Marriage* (New York: The Macmillan Co., 1957), pp. 195–196.

[36] Ernest W. Burgess and Paul Wallin, *Engagement and Marriage* (Philadelphia: J. B. Lippincott Co., 1953), pp. 386–390.

[37] *Ibid.*, Ch. 11.

an orgasm in premarital intercourse also increases with age. In other words, delay of marriage increases both the incidence of premarital coitus and of orgasmic experience. He finds too that those females who begin coitus early, marry early. Those who attain higher levels of education are more likely to have had premarital coitus by the time of their marriage because of later age of marriage.

Some feel that petting to the point of orgasm may be a part of the natural psychosexual development of this period, a satisfactory substitute for coitus, and a desirable preparation for marriage. It does permit the cultivation of sublimated forms of sex expression in the male and thus prepares him for the more complex and sympathetic part he is often expected to play in the sexual life of the modern married couple. It has the advantage of deferring pregnancy till marriage in cases where couples find it necessary to reduce sexual tension. Use of this outlet depends upon the extent to which intimate petting can be engaged in without guilt, perhaps more than on actual physical factors.

It must be recognized too that most young people have difficulty in petting to the point of orgasm without running considerable risk of actual intercourse. For many couples intercourse occurs, not after mutual agreement, but after mutual stimulation has erased their combined self-control. There are other possible disadvantages to this solution. It frequently brings satisfaction to only the male, and, in addition, it is likely to leave some individuals with as great a feeling of guilt as would sexual intercourse.

Effect of Premarital Sex Experience on Sexual Adjustment in Marriage

A rationalization frequently used by young people to justify premarital sexual relations is the wish to prove their adequacy for the sexual aspects of marriage, and also to prove that they are "physically mated." It is likely that some adolescent girls yield to this argument of the male because although they have no real sex interest they feel they should have. They may be told that they are frigid and cold because they do not feel a sex drive comparable to that of their male partner.

There is abundant evidence that the average woman, especially in her teens or even in her early twenties, has less capacity to respond sexually than she will have later.[38] It is not too likely that the average girl, during a short period of premarital sex experimentation, will develop the capacity to experience orgasm unless she is much more precocious sex-

[38] Evidence is presented in Ch. 22.

ually than the average. Her failure to respond may create anxiety concerning her ability to respond when there is no real reason for such anxiety.

To learn whether or not premarital sexual intercourse affects sexual adequacy in marriage, Burgess and Wallin interviewed couples during engagement and again after several years of marriage.[39] This study shows that orgasmic adequacy in marriage is favorably related to premarital sex experience—the more sexual experience the wife has had, the more likely she was to experience a full orgasm in her marital relations. This generalization held true both for women who had had sexual relations only with their future spouse and those who had had sexual experience with other men as well. These findings correspond to those reported by Terman[40] and Kinsey.[41]

Confirming support for this view is found by Kanin and Howard in studying the degree of sex satisfaction on the wedding night and during the honeymoon of 177 wives of married students on a college campus in a midwest university.[42] The more complete their sex activity before marriage, the greater the likelihood of satisfaction. Far more of the wives with premarital sexual experience, however, had sex difficulties during the early days of marriage, and of the 14 women who reported long-time difficulties beginning during the first two weeks of their marriage, all had had premarital sexual intercourse. Five of these women reported that they felt like "sex servants." This suggests that the woman who engages in sexual relations before marriage may have no argument in restraining her husband after marriage.

In further study of this group, Kanin[43] reports that the upper-class girls reported least frequency of premarital coitus; the middle class, next; and the lower class, greatest frequency. He found that premarital coitus was associated with avoidance of a honeymoon, abbreviated dating histories (couples tended to move quickly into marriage), decrease in the use of premarital counseling, and a decrease in the usual psychological disturbances of the wedding day.

The American Institute of Family Relations collected some 2,000 questionnaires, predominately from among college graduates in the United States. The initial orgasmic response of those women who were virgins at marriage was 28 percent, compared to 39 percent of those who had had experiences of premarital intercourse. The differences vanish quickly with

[39] Ernest W. Burgess and Paul Wallin, *Engagement and Marriage* (Philadelphia: J. B. Lippincott Co., 1953), Ch. 12.

[40] Terman and others, *op. cit.*

[41] Alfred C. Kinsey and others, *Sexual Behavior in the Human Female* (Philadelphia: W. B. Saunders Co., 1953), p. 383.

[42] Kanin and Howard, *op. cit.*

[43] Eugene J. Kanin, "Premarital Sex Adjustment, Social Class and Associated Behavior," *Marriage and Family Living*, 22:258–262, August, 1960.

sexual experience in marriage. At the end of the first year, the following results were reported:

| | Percent having orgasm | |
	Virgins	Nonvirgins
Younger wives	67	63
Wives over 30	63	59

These data suggest that even with marriage greatly delayed (into the thirties) orgasmic response is not dependent on the cultivation of early response through premarital sex activity. Popenoe believes that there is evidence here, and in clinical observation as well, that a large part of "premarital sexual experience of young women is neurotic rather than normal."[44]

Confirming this view are Reevy's findings[45] concerning premarital petting and other forms of sexual activity, including sexual intercourse and marriage predictability scores. He summarizes his conclusions thus, "The group with unfavorable marital predictions can be characterized as being more active sexually than the group with favorable marital predictions."

Shope and Broderick[46] compared the marriage adjustment of 80 virgins with 40 women who had experienced orgasm during sexual intercourse prior to marriage and 40 who had had sexual intercourse without orgasm. The virgins made better overall sexual adjustment, although differences were not greatly in their favor. The girls who had had orgasm did not differ in marital happiness or sexual adjustment from those who had not.

Kinsey makes a strong case for the biological desirability of premarital sex experience, holding that long abstinence, restraint, and avoidance of physical contacts and emotional responses before marriage may well lead to the building of inhibitions which damage the capacity of the organism to respond sexually in marriage.[47] Petting to orgasm, intercourse to orgasm, or even masturbation to orgasm, he believes, help prepare the organism to react physiologically.

Those who masturbate extensively prior to marriage are more likely than others to have orgasm in marriage,[48] and there is a close relation-

---

[44] Paul Popenoe, "Premarital Experience No Help in Sexual Adjustment after Marriage," *Family Life,* 21:1–2, August, 1961.

[45] William R. Reevy, "Premarital Petting Behavior and Marital Happiness Prediction," *Marriage and Family Living,* 21:349–355, November 1959.

[46] David F. Shope and Carlfred B. Broderick, "Level of Sexual Experience and Predicted Adjustment in Marriage," *Journal of Marriage and Family Living,* 29:424–427, August, 1967.

[47] *Sexual Behavior in the Human Female,* p. 383.

[48] *Ibid.,* p. 391.

ship between the experience of intercourse to the point of orgasm prior to marriage and ability to reach it during the first year of marriage.[49] These findings, of course, may only mean that highly sexed female is the one who engages in various kinds of sex stimulation prior to marriage.

One of the great faults of the Kinsey work was that he interpreted findings from the standpoint of biology. Sociologists have to recognize that moral reality is quite as binding on human beings as are biological impulses. In fact, moral suasion has precedence over biological impulse in societies everywhere. Man cannot satisfy his sexual desires in defiance of moral codes and go unblemished either in self-conception or reputation.

Sociologists have pursued their study beyond the point of simple physiological response. In a study of the total sexual adjustment scores of 600 men and women in marriage, no relationship, favorable or unfavorable, was found between sexual adjustments scores of husbands and wives and premarital intercourse.[50] It was found, however, that there was a slight favorable relationship to good adjustment where each had had sexual experience with both the future spouse and others. (The sexual adjustment score was based on answers to questions relating to various aspects of the sexual relationship with the marriage partner.) Clearly, ability to achieve an orgasm is not a complete test of the adequacy of the sexual relationship.

On the other hand, even this sociological study concludes that there is no statistical foundation for the belief that premarital intercourse is unfavorable to sexual adjustment in marriage. It recognizes, however, that people who are most likely to suffer from fear, or guilt, and anxiety because of premarital intercourse do not engage in it.

This research carried the investigation one step further in an attempt to relate premarital sex experience to total adjustment in marriage as measured by (1) marital happiness, (2) general marital satisfaction, (3) love, and (4) marriage permanence.

The findings in general agree with those of Terman,[51] Davis,[52] Popenoe,[53] and Locke,[54] that virginity prior to marriage is most favorable to total marriage success.

This suggests that the total pattern of marriage adjustment is something quite different from sexual adjustment alone. It may well be that

[49] *Ibid.*, p. 329.

[50] Burgess and Wallin, *op. cit.*

[51] Terman and others, *op. cit., pp.* 324–330.

[52] Katherine B. Davis, *The Factors in the Sex Life of 2,200 Women* (New York: Harper & Bros., 1939), p. 59.

[53] Popenoe, *op. cit.*

[54] Harvey J. Locke, *Predicting Adjustment in Marriage: A Comparison of a Divorced and a Happily Married Group* (New York: Henry Holt & Co., Inc., 1951), pp. 133–137. Locke found that a higher proportion of the divorced than the successfully married had had premarital sex relations.

secondary reactions to the premarital sexual experience are the decisive ones rather than sexual adjustment as such. Guilt and anxiety, a lack of mutual confidence, a suspicion that a pattern of disloyalty has been established which may lead to extramarital coitus—such feelings may be lurking in the background.

Kinsey finds striking proof that those having had premarital coitus are more likely than others to have premarital coitus again, and also that those having had premarital coitus are much more likely than others to have extramarital relations.[55] (See Figure 18–2.)

FIGURE 18–2   INTENT TO HAVE PREMARITAL COITUS. Sources: Alfred C. Kinsey and others, **Sexual Behavior in the Human Female** (Philadelphia: W. B. Saunders Co., 1953). Reproduced by permission of Dr. Kinsey.

Females without premarital coital experience generally are positive that they will not engage in it. Almost half of those who have had premarital coitus intend to repeat it. The Kinsey research shows that experience in premarital coitus also increases the likelihood of extramarital coitus.

Data relating premarital to extramarital coitus of women show, for example, that those who have had premarital coitus are twice as likely as others to have extramarital coitus. Moreover, a greater proportion of those who had had extramarital coitus than those who had not, thought they would do the same again.[56] This would seem to give some justification to the fear of disloyalty although change of custom and morality may well lead to greater stability in time. Zetterberg[57] finds no evidence of increased marital disloyalty among the Swedes with their greater permissiveness and experience with sex prior to marriage.

On the moral issue, however, there is not too much evidence of a carryover of guilt in Kinsey's data. Only about 31 percent of the unmarried females who had had premarital coitus regretted it afterward. Only 23 percent of the married females regretted it. The incidence of regret

[55] *Sexual Behavior in the Human Female,* Ch. 10, pp. 427–431.

[56] *Ibid.,* Charts pp. 318–319.

[57] Zetterberg, *op. cit.*

was not even particularly high among females who had experienced premarital pregnancy. As would be expected, knowing the nature of the human conscience, those who had experienced the greatest amount of coitus over the greatest period of time were least likely to have regrets. Those without religion were less subject to regret than those who were devout (see Figure 18–3).

Again, of course, one is dealing with the group who do have sexual relations, and with their after-adjustments. This is the morally liberated group. Average reactions of all persons to premarital sex experience would undoubtedly be quite different.

FIGURE 18–3 RELATIONSHIP BETWEEN REGRET AFTER PREMARITAL COITUS AND RELIGIOUS BACKGROUND. Source: Alfred C. Kinsey and others, **Sexual Behavior in the Human Female** (Philadelphia: W. B. Saunders Co., 1953). Reproduced by permission of the publisher.

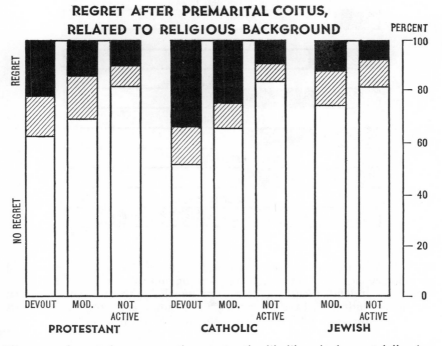

REGRET AFTER PREMARITAL COITUS, RELATED TO RELIGIOUS BACKGROUND

The more devout the woman, the greater the likelihood of regret following premarital coitus. Intermediate shading indicates some lesser degree of regret. Devout Catholics most ofter suffer regret.

These findings may be challenged too on the ground that an expression of "no regret" may not tell the whole story. In fact, Lester Kirkendall, teacher and marriage counselor, in his study of 250 college couples having sexual intercourse shows that many who claim no regret, at the same time tell of experiences of hurt feelings, recriminations, bitterness, distrust, etc.[58] Some boys who report no regret also tell of girls trying to "trap" them into marriage. Even in cases where there is no sense of guilt, there is often a sense of distrust, suspicion, and disrespect, which indicates that the human relationship involved has degenerated because of the sex experience.

FIGURE 18–4 FACTORS RESTRICTING PREMARITAL COITUS GIVEN BY WOMEN. Source: Alfred C. Kinsey and others, **Sexual Behavior in the Human Female** (Philadelphia: W. B. Saunders Co., 1953). Reproduced by permission of Dr. Kinsey.

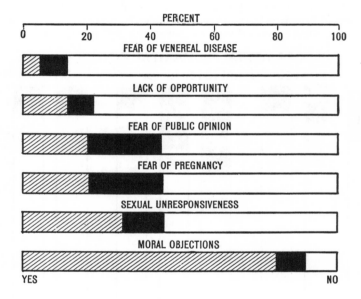

Moral factors are the major control against premarital coitus, and sexual unresponsiveness the second. Black shading indicates replies falling between yes and no, including data from females with and without coital experience. Judson T. Landis currently finds family and religious restraints the more effective ones (**Op. cit.,** Table III, p. 169).

Studies by Hillman of inquiries to an advice column of a metropolitan paper indicate that premarital sexual intercourse had brought more problems to the column than any other single factor; 3,371 letters dealt with problems arising from this source. The second most frequent problem arose out of unfaithfulness on the part of the other party. This type of

[58] Kirkendall, *op. cit.*

inquiry brought 1,887 letters. Alcoholism was third, with almost as many inquiries.[59]

In the final analysis, the question of premarital sexual relations must be weighed in terms of morality and notions of propriety rather than of biology alone.

Religious and moral convictions are the strong controls on sexual behavior. One may well suspect that when persons who hold these convictions violate sexual mores, they suffer most. Kinsey finds religion the most powerful influence among both men and women in deferring sexual relationships until after marriage[60] (see Figure 18-4). Judson T. Landis found that more than a third of the men in the 11 colleges studied in 1952 gave this as a reason for refraining, and 31 percent of the women concurred. In the Cornell 1940 study, 21 percent of the total group refrained for religious reasons.[61] (Both of these groups placed family training far above religious beliefs as a reason for refraining, and more also gave as a reason simply wanting to refrain until after marriage.)

Dedman found religion a strong deterrent to premarital sexual relations,[62] as did also Kanin and Howard.[63] Of engaged couples who were both regular in church attendance, in the latter study only 28 percent had premarital sexual intercourse; of the couples with one regular attender and one nonregular, 48 percent; of the nonregular attenders, 61 percent.

Although American data show very clearly that religion is a great restraint on premarital and extramarital sexual activity, there is no doubt a great difference related to the particular church attended. Chesser's study of over 6,000 marriages in England shows that almost half of the Roman Catholic women had had sexual intercourse before marriage, by far the highest proportion of any religious group studied. Only one-fourth of the Protestant group had had sexual intercourse before marriage, and only one-fifth of the Jewish women.[64]

It is apparently on the grounds of religion, morals, parental attitudes, and their own conception of their future that most young people refrain from premarital sexual intercourse rather than on the basis of biological considerations. As one girl expressed it in her term paper "I want to have a honeymoon that means something new to me. I don't want it compared with another place, another man. And I never want a husband who could throw it back to me that I was pregnant, that he had to marry me."

[59] Christine H. Hillman, "An Advice Column's Challenge for Family-life Education," *Marriage and Family Living*, 16:51–54, February, 1954.

[60] *Sexual Behavior in the Human Female*,

[61] Landis and Landis, *op. cit.*, fourth edition, p. 175.

[62] Jean Dedman, "The Relationship Between Religious Attitude and Attitude Toward Premarital Sex Relations," *Marriage and Family Living*, 21:171–176, March, 1959.

[63] Kanin and Howard, *op. cit.*

[64] Eustace Chesser and others, *The Sexual, Marital, and Family Relationships of the English Woman* (New York: Roy Publishers, Inc., 1957).

Mental Health and Premarital Sexual Relations

Mead suggests that young people are moving away from the position of feeling guilty about sleeping with somebody, to feeling guilty if they are not sleeping with someone.[65] This shocking statement may be good journalism, but there is no support for it in the researches known to the writer. Undoubtedly there is more pressure to sleep with someone although not just anyone, simply because it is less taboo; but the pressure is not the result of feeling guilty because one does not sleep with someone. There may be cliques which regard such behavior as a mark of belonging, and it may be a male status symbol in certain circles, but researches show clearly that it is the sleeping with someone to whom one is not married, not refraining from it, that brings a sense of guilt to many males and to most females.

Indications are that in time the guilt feelings subside, as they do with any repeated violation of conscience, but whether they are suppressed and later surface to cause guilt and become a factor in neurosis can scarcely be revealed by studies.

Evidence is far too meager to indicate what lasting influence premarital sexual relations have on the personality and mental health of the individuals involved. We do know this—most young people in the United States develop, as they mature, a rather exacting code of right and wrong on sexual matters. These codes are generally centered about religious teachings, but whether they are or not, religious ethics act as nearly inflexible yardsticks by which persons judge their own behavior and that of others. When one allows himself to act contrary to these codes, society seldom has to punish him; conscience does the job.

In this area there is little or no statistical evidence available. Clinical data is available, however, indicating the results of self-betrayal. An illustrative case from a counselor's experience is described below.

Virginia, daughter of a small-town minister, migrated from her home in Tennessee to a large northern city shortly after her graduation from high school. She lived in a furnished room with a girl friend, became active in church affairs, and obtained steady employment in a clothing store.

George, one of her co-workers, was attracted to Virginia and they dated one another irregularly for a year and a half. There followed a period of six months when they dated one another exclusively, spoke often of marriage, and after considerable urging on George's part had sexual intercourse more or less regularly.

Even though they used a contraceptive device, Virginia became pregnant.

[65] "Margaret Mead's Sound Insights into the Furor Over Shifting American Morals," *Life* 65:30–34, August 25, 1968.

After two unsuccessful attempts at abortion by pills, she confided in George who willingly agreed upon an early date for their marriage.

The marriage itself proved to be a generally happy and successful one. When Virgina occasionally became depressed concerning the circumstances of their marriage, George reassured her. None of their friends or acquaintances learned of the untimely conception.

After the birth of the first child, however, Virginia's periods of depression became more numerous and lasting. The climax came when she attempted to enter the date of her marriage and of the birth of her child in her Bible. She found herself incapable of writing the birth, or of inscribing false dates. She began to dwell constantly upon the matter, feeling a deep sense of guilt and unworthiness. She could no longer go to church, associate with her friends, or even feel at ease with her husband.

In the end, a period of intensive professional counseling was necessary merely to enable her to continue even somewhat effectively in her roles as wife and mother. At this time, three years after the birth of her first child, she still experiences periods of dangerous depression in which suicide plans figure vaguely, but persistently.

Not all such cases reach the attention of professional counselors. It is safe to say that, though the percentage of persons so haunted may not be great, the pain and guilt they suffer make their cases highly significant. For every young person who takes lightly the risks involved in premarital sexual intercourse—and the temptation to do so will increase as contraception becomes more dependable—there remains one basic question, "what will the experience mean relative to my own self-respect and mental health?"

Until the moral teachings of most American families undergo very fundamental changes, there will be many young people who suffer as much or more from psychological repercussions as from the potential social consequences of intercourse prior to marriage.

The basic moral development of the child begins very early in the family. It becomes relatively fixed at an early age, and does not change with rationalizations that "other people do, why can't I?" This is the conclusion of Robert F. Peck and his colleagues after a sixteen-year study[66] of a group of children. They reported:

"It appears, in summary, that the basic qualities of personality structure and interpersonal attitude are predominantly created by the child's experiences with his parents."

Pregnancy Risks of Exposure

In a Kinsey sample of 2,094 single white females, ranging in age from adolescence to forty years, who had had premarital coitus, 476 or 18

[66] Robert F. Peck and others, *The Psychology of Character Development* (New York: Wiley and Sons, 1960).

percent had become pregnant—almost one in five. Many of this group were not yet married, so the likelihood of even a greater proportion becoming pregnant prior to marriage is, of course, to be taken for granted.

Fifteen percent of those who had become pregnant had been pregnant more than once. While this seems like a high proportion of pregnancies, Kinsey finds that for any given act of intercourse among this group the average is only one pregnancy for each thousand single acts of intercourse. Such statistics are, of course, deceptive. The individual who is highly susceptible to pregnancy is vulnerable, whereas a sterile couple, or near-sterile one, is not at all.

There is no doubt that the Kinsey sample was of women who were abnormally sexually active and exposed to pregnancy.[67] Yet the risk is always there. No matter how effective birth control becomes, it will not eliminate premarital pregnancy.

The "contraceptive society," as Zetterberg has labeled[68] modern society, particularly referring to Sweden, has succeeded to a remarkable degree in separating sexual intercourse from procreation. His study of Swedish couples shows that there are 1,100 acts of sexual intercourse for each birth. Contraceptive knowledge is more available to the unmarried there, contraceptive devices more accessible, and moral codes less condemnatory than here.

Handling Premarital Pregnancy

One must assume that in American society premarital pregnancy is rarely if ever desired. When it occurs there are three alternatives—marriage, abortion, or unmarried motherhood. The third has been discussed; the other two merit consideration.

Marriage is the ideal solution if the couple are ready for marriage and have favorable attitudes toward life together and toward parenthood, which is unlikely when there has been no period of close association prior to pregnancy. Even where there has been, the very fact of being forced to marry sooner than the couple had expected may be a handicap, and if problems arise about the marriage, one partner may be quick to accuse the other of responsibility for the pregnancy. Both have been hurt by the obligation to terminate other plans in order to settle down to the responsibilities of homemaking and parenthood; both have suffered some sense of shame and humiliation in being "caught." They may have a feeling of guilt, too. And they may, in fact, because of all of these unfavorable

---

[67] For convincing argument and evidence see Judson T. Landis, "The Women Kinsey Studied," *Social Problems,* 1:139–142, April, 1951.

[68] Zetterberg, *op. cit.*

factors, actually have lost their love and respect for each other before they entered into the marriage.

Christensen and Rubenstein have studied the problem of premarital sexual intercourse primarily from the standpoint of the effect of pregnancy on later success in marriage.[69] These studies leave no doubt that premarital pregnancy is a hazard to successful marriage. Premarital pregnancy is associated with an abnormally high divorce rate (see Figure 18–5). They suggest that it may be associated with other unfavorable factors like venereal disease, incurring anxiety and guilt, and inciting social condemnation. Locke's study, which compared backgrounds of divorced and happily married couples, showed a fairly high number of pregnancies previous to marriage among the divorced.[70]

FIGURE 18–5   RELATIONSHIP BETWEEN PREMARITAL PREGNANCY AND DIVORCE. Source: Harold T. Christensen and Hanna H. Meissner, "Studies in Child Spacing: III—Premarital Pregnancy as a Factor in Divorce," **American Sociological Review,** 18:641–644, December, 1953.

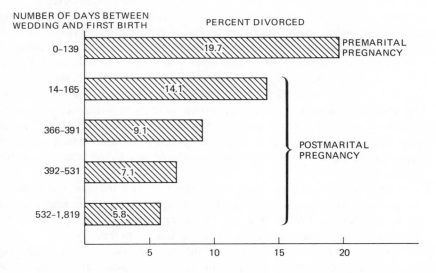

Judson T. Landis'[71] study of 581 couples, married an average of seven years, comparing them with 155 couples in the California Court of Conciliation and with 164 divorced persons, shows a much higher

[69] Harold T. Christensen and Betty B. Rubenstein, "Premarital Pregnancy and Divorce: A Follow-up Study by the Interview Method," *Marriage and Family Living,* 8:114–123, May, 1956; see also Harold T. Christensen and Hanna H. Meissner, "Studies in Child Spacing III—Premarital Pregnancy as a Factor in Divorce," *American Sociological Review,* 18:641–644, December, 1953.

[70] Locke, *op. cit.,* p. 92.

[71] Landis and Landis, *op. cit.,* Table 2, p. 79.

incidence of premarital sexual relationships with the spouse and of premarital pregnancy for the two problem groups.

Swedish social workers reported to the 1953 European Study Tour on Marriage and Family, of which the author was leader, that many divorces are caused there by marriage having been entered into because of premarital pregnancies. Yet in Sweden there is no pressure whatever from social workers or public agencies to encourage marriage if the couple involved in the pregnancy do not wish it.[72] This suggests that even where all conditions in the society favor premarital pregnancy, it seems to work to the disadvantage of marriage.

In our culture, even with the strong taboos against premarital pregnancy, marriage counselors do not recommend marriage if the young couple involved are no longer interested in each other.

Abortion offends the moral sense of all but the most callous, yet many girls resort to it to avoid shame for themselves and their child. The death rate for women from illegal abortion is more than twice that for the death rate for women from childbirth. The risk of causing sterility is great, as is the risk of permanent damage or disease to the female organs.

Great quantities of drugs are sold annually in the United States for inducing abortion. Such drugs are either dangerous or worthless, except that they may keep a woman who thinks she is pregnant from going to an abortionist. However, in many cases the woman is not, according to Dr. Nadina Kavinoky, Gynecologist and Past President of the National Council of Family Relations, who has estimated that as many as half of the abortions carried out by illegitimate practitioners among unmarried girls involved no pregnancy at all. In Sweden, of 1,200 girls dying of illegal abortions, 100 were not pregnant and of every hundred tested for pregnancy in the clinic of the National League for Sex Education, 40 are not pregnant.[73]

The shock of first intercourse, or the fear and tension that come to one having sexual intercourse outside marriage, often retards menstruation for a considerable period of time. The abortionist exploits the girl's fear and carries out the abortion even when there is no pregnancy.

Compared to preventing conception, induced abortion is a costly way of disposing of unwanted pregnancy in terms of physical, emotional, moral, and economic considerations. Yet even in the "contraceptive society," it is much in demand.

[72] In Holland, pressure is more often exerted to bring about marriage in case of premarital pregnancy.

[73] Data given by Elsie Ottesen-Jensen, founder and director of the League, in a lecture to a Marriage and Family Life Student Tour in the Summer of 1953. Unlike the United States, Sweden has legalized abortion for many reasons. For example, abortion is legal if the mother contracts German measles during the early period of pregnancy.

Zetterberg finds that in Sweden, perhaps as permissive in the area of premarital sex as any Euro-American people, abortion is approved by most women and they feel it should be provided free by the National Health-Care System of medical insurance.[74]

There is much agitation today for a radical revision of abortion laws in the United States, and a few states have already developed new and more liberalized codes. Public demand is still ahead of the legislative process in most, if not all states. Since abortion is primarily a solution for the married, rather than the unmarried, a more complete discussion of the problem appears later (Chapter 26).

The girl who chooses unmarried motherhood may seek the counsel of a social worker or a legitimate physician. In most instances she will be directed to an institution offering proper care to her and the child and facilitating its adoption if this is her wish.[75]

In conclusion, much evidence has been presented on the topic of sexual behavior during the years previous to marriage. This topic has been the subject of much research. The biological evidence is not against premarital intercourse. It would seem to slightly favor the position that, considering the physical side only, the exercise of genital musculature is conducive to biological responsiveness.

But the adjustment of two human beings in a close and lasting interpersonal relationship is dependent on so much more than biology that the mere ability to respond to each other sexually is a very small, even though very important, part of the relationship.

There is little evidence that premarital sexual relationships improve the adjustment of a couple prior to engagement. In some instances it appears to do so after engagement, yet even here there are many exceptions. Disrespect may lessen the male's desire to marry in certain instances. Awkward situations may arise, and data seem to indicate that the likelihood of the engagement breaking will be increased. At least, broken engagements are more often found among those who do than those who do not have coitus.

Evidence available to date suggests that marriages of the chaste are most successful under the culture pattern of the United States. This may merely mean that the conventional are the best marriage risks. Under a different moral order, personal and marital problems resulting from pre-

---

[74] Zetterberg, *op. cit.*, p. 50 ff.

[75] *The Directory of Maternity Homes and Residential Facilities for Unmarried Mothers,* published in 1966 by the National Council on Illegitimacy, lists 194 maternity homes and private agencies providing residential care for unmarried mothers in the United States. For each agency the following points of information are covered: auspices, admission requirements, method of application, services available, and capacity. The 206-page book is paperback and may be obtained from the National Council on Illegitimacy, 44 East 23rd Street, New York 10010.

marital sexual relationships would no doubt be greatly reduced, but the moral system exists and is a reality with which all must reckon. Perhaps the greatest risk in premarital sex relationships is the frequently resulting feeling of self-betrayal and the inner conflicts which this brings.

Society must operate on the principle of safety first. Here the personal impulse and group responsibility clash. The burden on society of caring for the unprotected mother and child increases yearly as mores weaken.

Problems

1. *Research exercise:* Poll the class or some other student group on the questions, "Do you believe in premarital sexual relations? Why?" According to tabulations:
   a. Does most of your class favor or oppose premarital sexual relations?
   b. Does favorableness to premarital relations tend to be associated with one or the other sex in your group?
   c. What reason is most often given in favor of premarital relations?
   d. What argument is most often given against it?
2. Discuss the institutional changes that would be required if premarital sexual relations were condoned in the United States?
3. In the long run would premarital sexual relations tend to increase or decrease the freedom of young people?
4. As a group do you feel that sexual relations are less objectionable during an engagement that before an engagement?
5. Your friend's fiancée has become pregnant but both agree that had it not happened they would have broken their engagement. What would your advice to him be?
   a. Get out of town.
   b. Take her to an abortionist.
   c. Marry her and try to make it work.
   d. Marry her with the understanding that you will get a divorce when the child is one year old.
   e. Take her to an institution for unwed mothers and put the child up for adoption.
6. A very religious girl, in a moment of excitement, consents to sexual relations with her fiancé and discovers two months later that she is pregnant. List the possible social and psychological consequences if:
   a. They marry after her third month of pregnancy.
   b. They decide not to marry at all.
7. In your opinion how might parents and institutions, such as church and school, best help young people to avoid the dangers of premarital sexual relations?
8. Discuss the statement, "The chief danger of premarital sexual relations is to one's mental health rather than physical well-being."

Selected References

Articles in Books of Readings

Cavan, Ruth S., *Marriage and the Family in the Modern World: A Book of Readings*, third edition (New York: Thomas Y. Crowell Co., 1969).

Symonds, Percival M., "Expressions of Love and Sex," Reading 25.

Herzog, Elizabeth, "Unmarried Mothers: Questions to be Answered and Some Answers to be Questioned," Reading 31.

Vincent, Clark E., "Unmarried Fathers," Reading 32.

Christensen, Harold T., *Handbook of Marriage and the Family* (Chicago: Rand McNally & Co., 1964).

Ehrmann, Winston, "Marital and Nonmarital Sexual Behavior," Ch. 15.

Goode, William J., *Readings on the Family and Society* (Englewood Cliffs, N. J.: Prentice-Hall, Inc., 1964).

Hamblin, Robert L. and Blood, Robert O., "Premarital Experience and the Wife's Sexual Adjustment," Ch. 13.

Rodman, Hayman, *Marriage, Family and Society* (New York: Random House, 1965).

Ehrmann, Winston W., "Being in Love, Going Steady, and Sexual Intimacy," Reading 1.

Sussman, Marvin, B., *Sourcebook in Marriage and the Family*, third edition (Boston: Houghton Mifflin Co., 1968).

Ehrmann, Winston W., "Premarital Dating Behavior," Reading 24.

Reiss, Ira L., "Social Class and Premarital Sexual Permissiveness: A Reexamination," Reading 25.

Vincent, Clark E., *Readings in Marriage Counseling* (New York: Thomas Y. Crowell Co., 1957).

Kirkendall, Lester A., "A Viewpoint on the Premarital Sex Problem," pp. 117–126.

Winch, Robert F., and Goodman, Louis Wolf, *Selected Studies in Marriage and the Family*, third edition (New York: Holt, Rinehart & Winston, 1968).

Martz, Helen E., "Extent of Illegitimacy in the United States," pp. 198–199.

Goode, William J., "Legitimacy, Illegitimacy, and the Family," pp. 200–205.

General References

Bernard, Jessie, *The Sex Game* (Englewood Cliffs, N. J.: Prentice-Hall, Inc., 1968).

Birdwhistell, Miriam, "Adolescents and the Pill Culture," *The Family Coordinator*, 17:27–32, January, 1968.

Broderick, Carlfred and Bernard, Jessie (eds.), *The Individual Sex and Society* (Baltimore, Md.: Johns Hopkins Press, 1969).

Brecher, Ruth, *An Analysis of Human Sexual Response*, New American Library, Signet Book.

Christensen, Harold T., "Child Spacing Analysis via Record Linkage: New Data Plus a Summing Up," *Marriage and Family Living*, 25:272–280, August, 1963.

Christensen, Harold T., "Studies in Child Spacing: I—Premarital Pregnancy as Measured by the Spacing of the First Birth from Marriage," *American Sociological Review*, 18:53–59, February, 1953.

Christensen, Harold T., and Meissner, Hannah H., "Studies in Child Spacing: III—Premarital Pregnancy as a Factor in Divorce," *American Sociological Review*, 18:641–644, December, 1953.

Clark, LeMon, M.D., and Rubin, Isadore, *150 Sex Questions and Answers* (New York: Health Publications, 1960).

Clothier, Florence, "The Unmarried Mother of School Age as Seen by a Psychiatrist," *Mental Hygiene*, 39:631–646, October, 1955.

Dalrymple, Willard, *Sex Is for Real: Human Sexuality and Sexual Responsibility* (New York: McGraw Hill, 1969).

Dedman, Jean, "The Relationship Between Religious Attitude and Attitude Toward Premarital Sex Relations," *Marriage and Family Living*, 21:171–176, March, 1959.

Duvall, Evelyn M., *Why Wait Till Marriage* (New York: Association Press, 1968).

Ehrmann, Winston W., *Premarital Dating Behavior* (New York: Holt, Rinehart and Winston, Inc., 1959).

Ellis, Albert, "Symposium on Premarital Sex Views," *Marriage and Family Living*, 15, August, 1953.

Falk, Ursula and Gerald J., "The Unmarried Mother: A Sociological Profile, *The Family Life Coordinator*, 14:17–19, January, 1965.

Finck, F. H., "Groups Counseling the Unmarried Mother," *Journal of Marriage and the Family*, 27:224–229, May, 1965.

Furstenberg, Frank, Jr., Gordis, Leon, and Markowitz, Milton, "Birth Control, Knowledge and Attitudes Among Unmarried Adolescents: A Preliminary Report," *Journal of Marriage and Family*, 31:34–42, February, 1969.

Hardin, Garrett, "Abortion or Compulsory Pregnancy?" *Journal of Marriage and the Family*, 30:246–251, May, 1968.

Kanin, Eugene J., "Premarital Sex Adjustment, Social Class, and Associated Behavior," *Marriage and Family Living*, 22:258–262, August, 1960.

Kanin, Eugene J., and Howard, David H., "Postmarital Consequences of Premarital Sex Adjustments," *American Sociological Review*, 23:556–562, October, 1948.

Kinsey, Alfred C., and others, *Sexual Behavior in the Human Female* (Philadelphia: W. B. Saunders Co., 1953).

Kinsey, Alfred C., *Sexual Behavior in the Human Male* (Philadelphia: W. B. Saunders Co., 1948).

Kogan, William and Pox, Earling, "Personality Changes in Unwed Mothers Following Parturition," *Journal of Clinical Psychology*, 1–13, January, 1968.

Levy, Dorothy, "A Follow-up Study of Unmarried Mothers," *Social Casework*. 36:27–33, January, 1955.

Linner, Birgitta, *Sex and Society in Sweden* (New York: Pantheon, 1967).

Masters, William H. and Johnson, Virginia E., *Human Sexual Response*, (New York: Little, Brown and Co., 1966).

Murdock, George, "Sexual Behavior, What Is Acceptable?" *Journal of Social Hygiene*, 36:1–31, 1950.

Packard, Vance, *The Sexual Wilderness* (New York: David McKay Company, Inc., 1968).

Parker, Seymour and Kleimer, Robert J., "Characteristics of Negro Mothers in Single-Headed Households," *Journal of Marriage and the Family*, 28:507–513, November, 1966.

Poffenberger, Thomas, and others, "Premarital Sexual Behavior: A Symposium," *Marriage and Family Living*, 24:254–278, August, 1962.

Pope, Hallowell, "Unwed Mothers and Their Sex Partners," *Journal of Marriage and the Family*, 29:555–567, August, 1967.

Reevy, William R., "Premarital Petting Behavior and Marriage Happiness Prediction," *Marriage and Family Living*, 21:345–355, November, 1959.

Reiss, Ira L., *Premarital Sex Standards in America* (New York: Free Press of Glencoe, Ill., 1969).

Reiss, Ira L., *Social Context of Premarital Sexual Permissiveness* (New York: Holt, Rinehart and Winston, 1967).

Shipman, Gordon, "The Psychodynamics of Sex Education," *The Family Coordinator*, 17:3–12, January, 1968.

Shope, David F. and Broderick, Carlfred B., "Level of Sexual Experience and Predicted Adjustment in Marriage," *Journal of Marriage and the Family*, 29:424–427, August, 1967.

"Startling Story of Illegitimate Children in U.S.," *U.S. News and World Report*, 63:84–85, October 2, 1967.

Terkelsen, Helen E., *I'm Going to Have a Baby and I'm Not Married* (Philadelphia: Fortress Press, 1968).

Vincent, Clark E., *Unmarried Mothers* (New York: Free Press, 1969).

Walker, Brooks R., *The New Immorality* (New York: Doubleday & Co., 1968).

Young, Leontine R., "Personality Patterns of Unmarried Mothers," in Roberts, Robert W., editor, *The Unwed Mother* (New York: Harper and Row, 1966), pp. 81–94.

5
MARRIAGE ADJUSTMENT

19

Marriage Adjustment

"How do they get along together? Do they love each other? Are they compatible?"—these are the key questions concerning a married pair in our culture.

They are meaningless in terms of the values of the institutional system of an earlier day in our culture, or in the traditional joint-family system operating today in India or Pakistan, for example. In East Africa an Indian wife, learning that the writer worked in the field of marriage problems, asked quite seriously and sincerely, "But what could there be to write about?" In a family system rooted in tradition which still outlines a rigid framework of roles, authorities, and values for the man-and-wife relationship as in India, there is little to write about. What happens is taken for granted; defined institutional relationships are not viewed as individual problems or subjects for analysis.

Social status, economic survival, and caring for offspring are sufficient to justify the marriage relationship quite apart from personal considerations. If an intimate personal relationship is lacking, there is adequate social and emotional support in the primary group: the large kin group, the tribal group, or the close-knit rural neighborhood. Few lack close ties somewhere in this circle. A dependable confidant is there, a loving friend, a source of constant social support. One is not alone, even if the mate proves distant, hostile, or impersonal.

This is not so in societies created by the urban-industrial complex. Children rarely form close ties with relatives. Neighborhoods disintegrate with mobility; and rapid change may destroy the neighborhood locality altogether.

Our society is one of special interest groups, rather than all-inclusive primary groups. Special interest groups draw only a segment of the personality into their orbit, and even that with reservations. Life is never complete in such relationships. There must still be an all-embracing

393

relationship which in childhood the family represented for the individual. This is sought in marriage. This is why a marriage can be successful by all the old values—satisfactory social status, property, children, and still fail.

We who study the pair relationship are increasingly aware that in the marriage system of our culture, failure in the interpersonal relationship of man and wife is responsible for an undetermined amount of ill health and emotional crisis. Sanity itself is at stake in the poorly adjusted relationship of man and wife, and their woes are passed on to their children. Unhappy parents, at odds with each other, can destroy the security of their children in the nuclear family.

Adjustment is not a fictitious norm in the marriage-family system which has emerged in our society—it is the key to married life, almost to adult life itself.

The Honeymoon

The early days and months of marriage involve a subtle series of interactions by which each partner is trying to reshape the other in his or her own image of what a mate should be. True, this is not always subtle, and it does not necessarily begin after marriage. If the marriage lasts, it will continue and take a decidedly different turn when children are born. The honeymoon is a special adjustment period. Popularly looked upon as a time of supreme bliss, it may actually be one of the most strenuous of adjustment periods. There is some truth in novelist Philip Wylie's contention that "Honeymoons Are Hell."[1] Others have spoken of post-marriage depression.

The honeymoon at its best, however, can be an enjoyable and not too strenuous event. Understanding the significance of the honeymoon can save a couple months of more difficult adjustment. When the honeymoon is unrealistically planned, however, it can actually become a liability rather than an asset to the new marriage.

The least successful honeymoons, from the standpoint of marital happiness, are those that seek to cram into a week or two all of the activity, adventure, and travel which the couple should not expect to afford for another five or ten years. Parents are often guilty of encouraging couples to undertake too much. Since the length of the honeymoon trip, and the people and places one visits, are frequently reported in the hometown paper, the honeymoon is often used as a testimony to one's social and economic status rather than one's good sense.

The most desirable honeymoons from the standpoint of all-around happiness are those which are planned for rest, for being alone, and for spending time with others and group activity.

[1] *Redbook,* November, 1952.

Time for rest   The commercialization of the wedding has been called a "National Scandal," almost equaling the funeral scandal.[2] The wedding industry is a seven billion dollar enterprise, with caterers, florists, dressmakers, photographers, printers, musicians, jewelers all making a profit. The public wedding takes on many elements of conspicuous consumption, rather than of a solemn religious occasion.

The bride particularly enters the honeymoon in a state of extreme fatigue. In this condition of nervous and emotional exhaustion, the couple begin their life together. Regardless of how well acquainted they have become during their engagement period, marriage is bound to raise new situations requiring thought, sensitivity, and tact. Nervous and physical exhaustion make it doubly difficult for the young couple to meet these inevitable circumstances with wisdom and patience. The awkwardness which frequently accompanies this period of initial intimacy is easily exaggerated by fatigue, until the loved one—so familiar only yesterday —may begin to seem strange and more than a little frightening. Research suggests that not more than half of couples can expect early sexual adjustment.[3]

The couple's first venture into sexual relations is likely to be discouraging. Strain, fatigue, and awkwardness often make intercourse difficult or unpleasant for the new wife. The long-awaited experience often turns out to be a frightening and completely disillusioning experience. As one young women commented about her honeymoon, "If I ever see that doctor again, I'm going to give him a piece of my mind for the buildup on sex he gave me." She indicated how awkward and embarrassed she was about sexual intercourse even though she was informed and knew what was expected of her. She concluded with, "It was not till weeks later that the wonder of it came to me."

Time for being alone   Dating and engagement activities normally lead a couple along a path of steadily growing intimacy. By the time they begin to seriously consider marriage, sexual attraction and desire have already begun to loom as significant factors in their relationship. By the day of the ceremony, this desire for complete fulfillment has generally reached its peak. Yet, sexual fulfillment for the new wife usually is not a simple matter of sexual intercourse. Her greatest satisfaction and happiness may come primarily from the hours of intimate companionship, wooing, and the gradually increasing sexual play that precede intercourse.

When a couple spend their honeymoon in an atmosphere of hectic social activity their opportunities for these periods of gradual sexual preparation are lost. Not only does the sex act itself fall short of expecta-

[2] Kitty Hanson, *For Richer or For Poorer,* (New York: Abelard-Schuman, 1968).
[3] Data are presented in Ch. 22.

tions, but also the full meaning of emotional oneness is seldom realized.

Sexual adjustment is not the only justification for planning time to be alone. During engagement couples oversell themselves to be sure of winning the mate. Now, during the early days of marriage, this idealized mate becomes more and more a real person, both actually and in the eyes of the spouse. The honeymoon should be a time of getting reacquainted. The new person who emerges from a period of continuous intimacy is likely to be very different in many respects from what was expected. Problems and uncertainties may even be aroused in the process of this awakening and they can seldom be met and solved in a crowd or among relatives and friends.

Time to be with others and for doing things in a group   Before marriage many couples find it difficult to be apart a single moment. They feel that they want to spend every moment of the rest of their lives alone together. Yet, experience shows that honeymoons spent in complete isolation from other people and from all group activities are more than most young people can take.

Many hotels, lodges, and resorts cater especially to honeymoon couples. They provide lengthy meal periods and a variety of activities from which couples may choose and thus live at whatever pace they desire. Such institutions assure the couple the companionship of their age group but of a nonintimate nature.

Whether a couple select such an institution or prefer to make their own arrangements it is important that they consider a number of factors in making the decision: (1) amount of money to be spent; (2) length of honeymoon; (3) activities both would enjoy; (4) amount of travel involved; (5) opportunities for rest as well as recreation.

All Make Adjustments

The first days of marriage, if all goes well, involve erotic pleasure and a degree of ecstacy. This level of emotion cannot be sustained, since it is emotionally impossible and in any case would hinder the adjustment to demands of new relationships and practical problems which arise.

The role of homemaker is thrust rather abruptly on the young bride today. She has little preparation for its demands and even less advance opportunity for making this role significant to herself, and fitting it into her scheme of values.[4]

The degree of adjustment that takes place in marriage is determined in

---

[4] Helena Znaniecki Lopata, "The Life Cycle of the Social Role of the Housewife," *Sociology and Social Research,* 51:5–22, October, 1966.

considerable part by what takes place previous to marriage. Some couples work out techniques of adjustment during the days preceding marriage and carry the same patterns over. Some couples, it may be supposed, never had major adjustment problems in their relationship before marriage and do not have them once they are married. There are others who have many problems of adjustment because they should never have married in the first place.

Burgess and Wallin's[5] study of married couples whose engagement periods had been studied when they were in college showed that more than half of husbands and wives were aware of no major adjustment in marriage. Significantly these were for the most part couples who made their adjustments during the engagement.

Adjustment problems in marital relationships may arise over such factors as sex, social life, religion, economic problems, in-laws, friends, or recreation.[6] They may also develop about problems of temperament, adaptability, and children.[7] All such issues are possible of solution if the couple approach them cooperatively and with a will to succeed. As someone has said, "The only failure in life is failure of purpose."

Burgess and Wallin's research, one of the most comprehensive sociological studies to date, finds that a person's adaptability has the most to do with successfully fitting into the marriage relationship. Adaptability is defined as "the person's capacity to change his roles, his attitudes, and his behavior in order to adjust to those of the other person or to a new or modified situation."[8]

Adaptability, it is believed, is determined by the person's "empathy, flexibility, command of appropriate attitudes and roles, and motivation to adjust." By empathy is meant understanding of the other person to the point of recognizing and appreciating his motives. This trait in the marriage relationship, the research shows, is dependent to a great extent upon the husband's and wife's ability to communicate with each other, for understanding to the point of empathy is possible only as they confide, talk, and discuss issues fully.

Flexibility, the study shows, is partly psychogenic, that is, determined by the early years of conditioning. It consists essentially in being able to vary one's responses within a situation. On the matter of motivation to adapt, findings indicate that the couples most in love are most willing to adapt to each other. New situations, crises, and a will to succeed all have a bearing on the person's motive to adapt. It is also reported that asso-

[5] Ernest W. Burgess and Paul Wallin, *Engagement and Marriage* (Philadelphia: J. B. Lippincott Co., 1953), Ch. 18.

[6] Judson T. Landis, "Length of Time Required to Achieve Adjustment in Marriage," *American Sociological Review*, 11:668 ff., December, 1946.

[7] Burgess and Wallin, *op. cit.*

[8] *Ibid.*, p. 623.

ciating with an intimate group with similar motives is a strong factor in motivating the individual toward particular kinds of adjustment. For example, the young wife who does not want children may readily and almost unconsciously change her motivation by association with a young married group with babies and an interest in them.

There are at least three types[9] of decision-making in the marriage relationship: (1) the authoritarian type, in which the decision is handed down by the spouse who assumes the superior role; (2) verbal coercion, whereby one mate forces his opinion upon the other after strong argument; and (3) the democratic type, in which there is mutual discussion with husband and wife each entering into the decision.

Various researches extending over a period of more than thirty-five years show that the democratic partnerships are the happiest.[10] This, of course, does not mean that other kinds of relationships cannot and do not succeed. Rather, the democratic partnership, probably the hardest of all to practice, brings great rewards to those who succeed with it. It is without doubt among those who try it and fail that the highest middle-class divorce rate is found too.[11] Highly individualistic men and women often can settle for nothing short of the ideal.

Wives Adjust More Than Husbands

The ideal of democratic cooperation on the basis of mutuality is seldom fully realized, although it is probable that each generation is nearer to it. There is no precise way of knowing how close the average marriage comes to approximating genuine equality.[12]

In the late 1930's a study of over 500 marriages showed that in the American marriage at that time the wife was doing the major part of the adjusting. Burgess and Wallin's later study[13] of college-educated

[9] Bernard Farber, cited in Burgess and Wallin, *op. cit.,* 643 ff.

[10] Burgess and Wallin, *op. cit.;* see especially pp. 336–337; see also Judson T. Landis, "A Re-examination of the Role of the Father as an Index of Family Integration," *Marriage and Family Living,* 24:127 ff., May, 1962.

[11] Alver Hilding Jacobson finds it so in "Conflict of Attitudes Toward Roles of the Husband and Wife in Marriage," *American Sociological Review,* 17:146–150, April, 1952. Our studies show that divorce rates are highest in families where the democratic philosophy of child training is practiced; see Carol L. Stone and Paul H. Landis, "An Approach to Authority Pattern in Parent-Teenage Relationships," *Rural Sociology,* 18:233–242, September, 1953; also, Paul H. Landis, *The Broken Home in Teen-age Adjustments* (Pullman, Wash.: Washington Agricultural Experiment Station, April, 1953), Bulletin No. 542.

[12] Ernest W. Burgess and Leonard S. Cottrell, *Predicting Success or Failure in Marriage* (Englewood Cliffs, N. J.: Prentice-Hall, Inc., 1939), pp. 341–349.

[13] Burgess and Wallin, *op. cit.,* Ch. 8.

couples reported that either husband or wife may make most of the adjustments in marriage, or they may adjust equally, but more often both husband and wife agree that the wife has made the greater adjustment. Wives generally fit into marriage more easily than husbands because home, husband, and children are still the central interests in the plans of most women, whereas profession or business are the core interest of the middle-class male.

It may be inevitable that women will adjust somewhat more than men because of the demands of marriage itself. A man rarely changes his vocation or place of residence for the sake of his marriage. A woman must often drop out of the work world entirely and move to the location in which the husband is employed. This puts the major burden of vocational adjustment on her. The woman who has been gainfully employed must shift the entire routine of her life in taking over the management of her home, even though she may continue to work. Where she formerly had independence and directed her life to suit her own convenience, she is now required to make this secondary to the interests and work activities of the husband.

Some years ago Hughie Call, writing for *Reader's Digest,* entitled her article "Sheep Come First." A city girl, she had married a sheep rancher in Wyoming. She learned from the rigorous life at a sheep ranch that at lambing time and at many other times, sheep are much more important than women.

When children come into the family the wife faces the most difficult adjustments of all. The man's role is little affected. In our nuclear family, being a mother is the most demanding, exacting, and time-consuming task the modern woman faces during her lifetime. To be constantly tied down by the helplessness of the small child is a nerve-testing, exacting routine for women, particularly those who face it with an attitude of frustration, rather than one of pleasure and pride.

Throughout the entire period of child rearing, the demands on the mother are much more rigorous than those on the father, and come from various sources—children, husband, and from groups in which the children participate. In a real sense, there is a long period in the life of the mother when there is little opportunity to think in terms other than family needs. Too few come to motherhood prepared for the transition.

This fact makes for more difficult adjustments in the later years, too, when the children leave home and she must develop new interests for herself. The husband continues in his chosen work throughout a lifetime and faces no adjustment crises in his routine until retirement. The whole lifetime of the married woman is almost inevitably one of continuous adjustment.

Time vs. Technique

Judson T. Landis[14] studied the time it took couples to reach a satisfactory state in six general areas of adjustment—sex, money matters, social activities, in-law relations, religious activities, and mutual friends. Except for the first two areas, which will be discussed in separate chapters, adjustment was satisfactory for two-thirds to three-fourths of the couples from the very beginning. The marriages analyzed had lasted for an average of well over twenty years at the time of the study. A third to a half of those who had not made an early satisfactory adjustment in these four areas never did, and were still maladjusted.

In about 10 percent of the cases, the adjustment was satisfactory for one spouse, but not for the other at the beginning of their marriage. This, no doubt, reflects differences in values and expectations of men and women as to what the marriage should be.

Does time bring the necessary adjustment? Landis implies that it does for a certain proportion of couples. Burgess and Wallin are positive that time has nothing to do with adjustment. They say:

> The point needs to be made that the passage of time in itself does nothing. Of course, a spouse having endured an unsatisfactory condition may at last come to accept it. But any emphasis on time as a curative factor may result in a laissez-faire attitude toward dealing with an adjustment. . . .
>
> Our review of the interviews of adjustment made in the first three to five years of marriage suggests that adjustments do not happen with the passage of time. They are either made or they are not made.[15]

The decisive factor is whether husband, or wife, or both are adaptable. According to this view, then, technique is all-important. Either during the engagement or in early marriage a couple adopts techniques which lead to a satisfactory working relationship or else they are likely to remain at odds.

The truth probably lies somewhere between these positions. There is no doubt that some couples mature in marriage and become more considerate and understanding in their relationship to the mate. An in-law problem may be cured by time, through death or migration, for example. Time is an important factor in the pair relationship both before and after marriage. Many, no doubt, follow an arbitrary and unyielding pattern after marriage which was already apparent during the engagement. Accommodation or failure are the only alternatives for these people. Time alone will only fix the already established relationship.

[14] Judson T. Landis, "Length of Time Required to Achieve Adjustment in Marriage," *American Sociological Review,* 11:668 ff., December, 1946.
[15] Burgess and Wallin, *op. cit.,* pp. 617–618.

The Importance of Early Adjustment

Whether adjustments are made prior to or early in marriage, the earlier the better the chances for the couple. First, during engagement and early marriage most couples are more eager to make their relationship succeed; there is greater motivation to success. Second, they are at a period in life when adjustments come more naturally than they will later. Third, and perhaps most important, is the fact that marriage habits have not yet developed. A new relationship is flexible. As the marriage pattern becomes increasingly crystallized around certain ways of acting and reacting, the problems involved in changing become increasingly complex.

The important thing is not just reaching a verbal agreement, but mutually practicing insofar as possible the agreed-upon behavior. A young man, for example, may be talked into agreeing that his wife rather than his mother should decide questions about his new home, but unless he is willing to act accordingly from the very beginning, there is little hope that he has really been convinced.

In the matter of general marital adjustment, the following rules are practical ones to follow:

1. Work out mutually satisfactory solutions to major differences before marriage.
2. Problems (such as those that might grow out of sexual relations) which cannot be met before marriage should be solved as early in the relationship as possible.
3. Throughout married life, problems and differences should be met and solved as they arise. The longer an unsatisfactory marriage situation is allowed to persist, the greater the problems involved in changing it.

The scriptural admonition, "Let not the sun go down upon your wrath," is an excellent guide in marriage.

In-Laws

Throughout history mothers-in-law have been considered troublesome. Most societies have inflicted severe penalties on a man if he and his mother-in-law meet.[16] In Northern Australia, a man who speaks with her must be put to death, and in the South Pacific, both parties would commit suicide if they should meet. In Yucatan, a man who meets his mother-

[16] John M. Shlien, "Mother-in-Law: A Problem in Kinship Terminology," Article 16 in Hyman Rodman, *Marriage, Family and Society: A Reader* (New York: Random House, 1965).

in-law face to face will be made sterile for life, he believes. Since Navaho men believe they will go blind if they see their mother-in-law, she may not attend the wedding.

Apparently fear of seduction of the young husband by the mother-in-law, or some such incest taboo, is present in many of these restrictions. Little is feared from the intrusion of the husband's mother into the marriage.

In parts of India, where the joint-family system of the Asiatic world is meeting the individualistic nuclear family of the Western World, social workers report that suicides are greatly on the increase among young wives. The bride who has learned Western ways is not happy to become a servant in her husband's parents' household, and be ordered, persecuted, and outrivaled for her husband's affection by the husband's mother and sisters. An ex-governor of Bombay felt the situation was so serious that he proposed a law providing punishment for such in-law persecution.[17] All over India the mother-in-law is proverbially considered a devil. With the joint-family system, and patrilocal residence of the young couple, such a concept of the husband's mother is not surprising.

In the United States, the in-law crisis, if it does not come before marriage, reaches its worst proportions soon after. Each family is appraising the new addition. Parents have a hard time letting go and continue to hope to direct the lives of their children in a proper and helpful way. As actress Spring Byington said in her TV show, *December Bride,* "When my daughter got married, I made a vow that I'd let her live her own life, even if I had to show her how to do it."[18]

The in-law conflict in the United States is unpredictable since it is a matter of interpersonal relationships and not an institutional arrangement. This is very unlike most cultures where the relationship of in-laws is rather explicitly institutionalized, the culture defining the claim that parent family and the adopted family will have on the new members. Usually in the joint-family system, particularly if it is patrilocal, the son's mother has rather comprehensive claims on the new daughter. Until she has borne a son, the young wife is expected to have a rating quite like that of the servants in the household, and to be subject to the mother-in-law's command.

As American marriages get established, parents are somewhat less likely to interfere. They learn that advice is not wanted and will be ignored, or they come to see that the new pair are capable of handling their own affairs. Also, the longer a marriage has existed, the greater likelihood that parents will have died and, therefore, have been removed from the possibility of interference. This, of course, is not by any means

---

[17] N. P. N. Pillai, *Journal of Family Welfare*, Bombay, March, 1956, p. 90.
[18] *Look,* March 3, 1959.

always the case. Sometimes when one parent dies the other moves in with the young couple, adding to the problems of adjustment.

In a very real sense every family has its own distinctive way of life. Marriage adjustments are often intensified because each member of the pair tries to reestablish the way of life of his own childhood family. For this reason, in-laws may get blamed for problems they are only indirectly responsible for causing.

On the other hand, both parental families are judging the new in-law addition by their own standards. It is particularly true that the husband's family is likely to be looking the new daughter-in-law over very carefully, trying to form a judgment as to whether or not she is going to be able to fit their family pattern. The son's relatives are often guilty of trying to make his wife over to fit their pattern. Their ideas of her duties as a wife may be quite different from her own, and, in fact, quite different from what her responsibilities as a wife should be. If they start out to reform her, she may soon find her husband and all his family in agreement as to what she should become to be the good wife.

Actually, the new marriage may require quite a different marriage relationship than that which has been made by either set of parents. Yet it is not unusual for the new wife to find herself hemmed in by their expectations, being gradually forced to conform to their family customs. Undoubtedly, the extent to which the wife is subjected to scrutiny depends on the degree to which premarital acquaintance has been thorough and carried on in close contact with the husband's parents. In such cases much of this adjustment has been made in advance.

Yet there are those who marry knowing there is going to be trouble. Judson T. Landis[19] in 1967 studied 581 marriages. Of those who reported an in-law problem, 41 percent indicated they had been aware of it before they married.

Husband's mother more often intrudes   Folklore holds that there are times when any young wife may find it comforting to run home to her mother, instead of establishing from the outset the habit of talking over her problems with her husband. The fact is, however, that the husband's mother is most often the problem in-law in the modern marriage. The attachment between mother and daughter is a very strong one, but mothers cling even more tenaciously to a son and become a greater nuisance in a son's than in a daughter's marriage.

One might, of course, expect young women to feel that their husbands' mothers were the greater problem since they would naturally be more tolerant of their own mothers than of the husbands'. But these young

[19] Judson T. Landis and Mary G. Landis, *Building a Successful Marriage*, fifth edition (Englewood Cliffs, N. J.: Prentice-Hall, Inc., 1968), Figure 15–5, p. 285.

women had discovered what research also shows regarding the in-law problem in contemporary marriages. The husband's mother has much more difficulty in letting go than does the wife's mother.

This, perhaps, is not the only factor. The husband's mother identifies the wife's role in marriage with her own and, therefore, is likely to be extremely critical. The wife's mother is less likely to be critical of her own daughter, since she follows housekeeping and marriage patterns which the mother has instilled. The wife's mother is not likely, either, to interfere so much with the young husband's role, since she has no close identification with the male role.

Judson T. Landis,[20] studying in-law-relationships of 544 student couples, found the mother-in-law was the cause if a problem did exist. For the wife, the mother-in-law was causing friction in half the cases, for the husbands in 42 percent of the incidents. The next most troublesome person was the sister-in-law, who caused friction for 16 percent of husbands and 13 percent of wives.

Blood and Wolfe[21] find, as did Landis, that the younger the couple, the more difficulty with in-laws. It is apparent that parents feel more free to interfere with the youthful couple. Parents undoubtedly see more mistakes, more often mistrust judgment of the young bride or groom, and the young more often solicit advice and financial help. The young have more often married against parental advice, for reasons of pregnancy, and consequently lay themselves open to criticism.

A 1967 study[22] by the United States Bureau of the Census shows that 19.2 percent of marriages in which the husband is under 20 were living with relatives, only 5.7 of those aged 20–24. Less than 2 percent of any other age group prior to retirement lives with relatives.

Duvall analyzed case-history documents of over 1,800 in-law relationships. She found the husband's mother (the wife's mother-in-law) the most trouble-causing personality. Next was the wife's mother, with the husband's sister a close third.[23]

The in-law adjustment is twofold. Newlyweds must reckon with the impact of relatives on the family, and also with their own ties to parents and relatives as they affect the new marriage. Although parental ties are supposed to be fairly well-broken by attachment to the new mate prior to marriage, and fully severed in an intimate sense when the marriage is consummated, the break is not always so complete.

[20] *Ibid.*, Table 1, p. 331.

[21] Robert O. Blood, Jr., and Donald M. Wolfe, *Husbands and Wives* (New York: Free Press of Glencoe, Inc., 1960), p. 247.

[22] "Marital Status and Family Status: March 1967," United States Census, Population Characteristics, Series P–20, No. 170, February 23, 1968, Table B, p. 2.

[23] Evelyn Duvall, *In-Laws: Pro and Con* (New York: Association Press, 1954).

Winch[24] found, in a study of the carry-over of attachments, that the mother is the preferred parent of both husband and wife; that the son is the preferred child; and that the mother-son relationship is the strongest family relationship. He believes that the strong attachment of the son to the mother impedes his mate choice and also his adjustment in marriage. Burgess and Wallin, in their study of engaged and married couples,[25] find that both son and daughter carry over strongest attachments to their mothers.

These and other authorities[26] seem to agree that though both son and daughter carry over close attachments to the mother, the son having been away from home more has emancipated himself more completely from attachments to his mother prior to his marriage. Even though his mother may cling to him more than the wife's mother to her, his prior independence from her and the cultural expectation that he be independent may make his emancipation from his mother as easy, if not easier, than that of the daughter from her mother.

Time and distance factors   About one in ten couples, according to Landis's study, had not worked out a satisfactory adjustment with relatives after more than twenty years of marriage; another 7 percent had taken one to twenty years to do so.[27] If this group is typical, the in-laws problem is a difficulty of considerable importance over a long period in one of every five or six marriages. The study does not indicate whether parents are responsible, the clinging of the husband or wife to a parent, or whether both situations are responsible. It is probable that in many cases the strong attachment to a parent on the part of one of the mates is a two-way attachment and that the difficulty in the marriage is ultimately resolved only by the death of the parent.

Actually, the in-law problem may not now be as serious as it once was. In our mobile society young people usually live in a separate residence, and often in a separate community from their parents. Moreover, social security has helped remove the necessity of children caring for the widowed parent in their own home.

Positive contribution of in-laws   The in-law relationship has been discussed as a problem. It is not always so. Many married couples do not have in-law problems at all. Duvall's case histories show that in many

---

[24] Robert F. Winch, *The Modern Family* (New York: Holt, Rinehart and Winston, Inc., 1952), p. 299.

[25] Burgess and Wallin, *op. cit.*, pp. 598–599.

[26] See Mirra Komarovsky's conclusion in Burgess and Wallin, *op. cit.*, p. 599.

[27] Judson T. Landis, "Length of Time Required to Achieve Adjustment in Marriage," *American Sociological Review*, 11:688 ff., December, 1964.

cases the young wife appreciates the husband's mother as a second mother, loves her and finds her helpful.[28] And the husband sometimes finds the wife's mother a substitute for his real mother who has died, or a second mother if his mother still lives. Many times the in-laws help with the children, take the wife in while the husband is away in military service, and care for her and her children in case of his death or their divorce.

Duvall's study also shows that the in-laws sometimes suffer from the neglect, or inconsiderateness of children. They do not know quite what role to play with their married children, and later, with the grandchildren. This is a new situation and unique to our type of marriage-family system. Such role-relationships are never left in doubt in the ancient cultures of the world. In the in-law area, as in so many relationships of the married pair in urban industrial society, roles must be worked out through the adjustment process because they are no longer defined by custom.

Schlesinger's[29] in-depth study of 84 successful remarriages of Canadian couples—middle class, somewhat superior in intelligence and schooling, and still fairly young, who had made a success of their marriage—suggests that in-law relationships was a major area of adjustment for them.

It is undoubtedly true that during the divorced period spouses have "returned to mother" in a certain degree, reviving the parent tie. Parents may have a difficult time releasing the child a second time. Often in the case of divorce, there are children, usually left with the mother. Here too the daughter is often required to reestablish parental ties. This may make it doubly hard for grandparents to release her and their grandchildren to a new husband who is not the father of their grandchildren.

Disillusionment with Marriage

One of the more significant of all early adjustments is the discovery that marriage is after all primarily a routine way of living. During the early days of marriage there is a preoccupation with the personal feelings and responses of the mate. This is gradually lessened as a living routine is established. Men suffer more from disillusionment than women. Loss of freedom, new household obligations, and economic responsibilities are a part of the normal cost of marriage. Romance decreases in reality.

Hobart finds some evidence of postmarital disillusionment in both men and women. The disillusionment shows up most in the areas of personal freedom, marital roles, having children, in-law relationships, values of neatness, values on control of money, and attitudes toward divorce. He

[28] Duvall, *op. cit.*
[29] Benjamin Schlesinger, "Successful Remarriage after Divorce," *Family Life,* 29:1–4, January, 1969.

believes his data show some evidence of a relationship between degree of romanticism prior to marriage and disillusionment.[30]

In marriage the sexual tension of the chaste engagement eases in the satisfying release of sexual relations. The "put on" self of the engagement period becomes the more routine self, with ups and downs of moods and tempers. "Woe unto him or her who cannot understand and accept this 'disillusionment' of marriage," say Levy and Munroe.[31] "The person who must have glamour, who cannot take the disillusionment of settling down, is not ready for marriage."[32] This kind of person, even though he resorts to divorce, will find that a new marriage will not help. He has not yet come to accept himself or to know what his own needs are. He will not find them in marriage. "Glamour in marriage cannot be continuous, but it needn't be absent."[33] All human beings must learn sooner or later that man is not capable of living at a high pitch of glamorous excitement.

If dating has carried the couple well beyond the first excited stage of love, considerable realism should have entered the relationship before marriage. In such cases disillusionment should not be great. Marriages entered into hastily, and in the overly excited first stages of the pair relationship, may be in for a most painful period of disillusionment.

Some couples sense this risk. During World War II, a young woman who had married the day before her new husband, a young man she had known only briefly, had left for a foreign post with the military, expressed her anxiety over the fact that her husband was writing her an average of 35 letters a week. They were long letters in which he was pouring out his heart in an over-romanticized love.

She was still working in her home county as a home economist with the Agricultural Extension Service, was of a more practical nature, and still felt herself a part of real life. She feared the reality he would have to face when they were able to live togther as husband and wife. "I'm no angel," she said. "In his dreams now I seem to be. I'm not sure whether he can accept the discovery or not."

For some, the disillusionment of marriage comes quickly, and the relationship is on its way to early termination from the outset. This is not surprising, for many marry who are not suited to marriage. Some never will be, others will be only after disillusionment which shocks them into a greater sense of reality about the marriage relationship.

Others marry for the wrong reasons, or for no conscious reason at all. It may well be that most people marry for wrong reasons, but are

[30] Charles W. Hobart, "Disillusionment in Marriage and Romanticism," *Marriage and Family Living,* 20:156–162, May, 1958; see also E. E. LeMasters, "Parenthood as a Crisis," *Marriage and Family Living,* 19:352–355, November, 1957.

[31] John Levy and Ruth Munroe, *The Happy Family* (New York: Alfred A. Knopf, Inc., 1938), p. 67.

[32] *Ibid.,* p. 74.

[33] *Ibid.,* p. 77.

adjustable enough to reappraise the situation and work out a marriage of reality. Men particularly are at a loss to give a reason for marriage. Ask the question of them unexpectedly and they are likely to falter. A woman is more likely to answer in terms of the fine qualities of the man she married.

The underlying motives for marriage are, of course, often very complex. The insecure seek an anchor, the sex hungry seek a partner, and the pregnant seek respectability and relief from guilt. Those from troubled families seek to escape them, some marry to spite another, and others marry on the rebound. Some marry because they fear time is running out for them. The supply of eligibles they depended on is dwindling. Some seek social status in their marriage. Some wish to escape the pressure to marry exerted by family and friends.

Little wonder that some become disillusioned.

In conclusion, realism is important to adjustment during the first months of marriage. Levy and Munroe begin a chapter in a very significant book on marriage with this statement, "Nine-tenths of human misery in the world is sheer nonsense."[34] The authors go on to elaborate man's amazing ability to imagine all kinds of troubles for himself. In this, they consider he has more ingenuity than any other creature on the face of the earth. The book concludes that the "mental cruelty" of the imaginative modern wife is of greater consequence than was the physical cruelty of the Neanderthal caveman to his wife. It also points out that the suffering of a wife today for a mink coat is probably more serious than was the suffering of the Neanderthal women who lacked clothing altogether.

The moral of the story is that the modern marriage suffers not so much from lack of fulfillment of physical needs, as from the lack of fulfillment of the thousands of complicated expectations and desires that have been built into young people's personalities through an elaborate process of social conditioning.

These authors, in the tradition of psychiatry, believe that people marry for motives beyond their understanding, mostly nonrational motives, and that whether or not their marriage succeeds is dependent in large part on unconscious factors since human beings are not primarily rational.

There is much to be said for this emphasis in understanding marriage and its adjustments. Many motivations are hidden and people rationalize them in other terms. Each person is conditioned to respond favorably or unfavorably to certain situations and certain traits. Presumably, one marries the kind of person to whom he can respond favorably in most situations. This is the whole idea of dating and engagement, and of getting thoroughly acquainted before marriage. Those who have failed in these respects will soon learn the price. Theirs must be a super effort and de-

[34] *Ibid.* Ch. 2.

termination to make their life together a success in spite of surprising discoveries after marriage.

Problems

1. Ralph and Evelyn are trying to decide how and where to spend their honeymoon. They are young, out-going, and companionable, but neither has a serious hobby. Their list of possible choices has been narrowed down to six. Which of the six would you oppose and why?
    a. Visit Evelyn's aging but lovable grandparents on their little Iowa farm.
    b. Visit Ralph's uncle who owns a dude ranch in New Mexico.
    c. Rent a secluded little island hide-a-way off the Florida coast.
    d. Spend a week in New York City seeing the current plays, buying clothes, seeing all the sights, and if possible, landing a job for Ralph.
    e. Join two other honeymoon couples who are going from Florida to South America on a small yacht.
    f. Spend a more-or-less unscheduled week in Miami.
2. Couples who are happy and report that no adjustments have been necessary are probably:
    a. Well-mated.
    b. Lying.
    c. Delaying the adjustments until a more appropriate time.
    d. So used to adjusting that they are unconscious of doing it.
    e. Unusually successful in their sexual adjustment.
3. In the marriage of your parents or acquaintances, is there any evidence that adjustments are still taking place? Without giving names, describe a situation in which you have observed an adjustment in a marriage that has lasted over five years.
4. List the circumstances under which you would agree to have either your father-in-law or mother-in-law share your home.
5. Married students in the class describe your early relationships with your in-laws. In what areas did problems most often arise?
6. *Research exercise:* Poll the class or some other student group on the question, "In what areas do you anticipate the most numerous adjustments in the early weeks of marriage?"
    a. Diversity of ethical codes.
    b. Recreational interests.
    c. Sexual relations.
    d. Little things such as habits of daily living.
    e. Religious beliefs.
    f. Home management.
    g. Life philosophies.
    h. In-law relationships.
    Tabulate results. Does the class tend to agree on areas of greatest likelihood of difficulty? Do the areas of anticipated adjustment differ according to sex?
7. Do you believe that women usually have to do more adjusting in marriage than do men? That marriage changes their way of life more completely than that of men?

8. *Sociodrama:*
   a. A doting mother whose only son has recently married visits the young couple regularly and explains, "I only want to help out; I know how much a young bride has to do and how many things she has to learn." Tension mounts with each visit and the play opens with the young bride finally telling her mother-in-law how she feels about the situation.
   b. A young bride, after a month of marriage, discusses with an older married sister, her disillusionment with marriage.

Selected References

Articles in Books of Readings

Cavan, Ruth S., *Marriage and the Family in the Modern World: A Book of Readings,* third edition (New York: Thomas Y. Crowell Co., 1969).
   Blood, Robert O., Jr., and Wolfe, Donald M., "Reciprocal Interdependence," Reading 35.
   Duvall, Evelyn Millis, "Marriage Makes In-Laws," Reading 41.
Christensen, Harold T., *Handbook of Marriage and the Family* (Chicago: Rand McNally & Co., 1964).
   Bernard, Jessie, "The Adjustment of Married Mates," Ch. 17.
Haimowitz, Morris L. and Haimowitz, Natalie Reader, (eds.), *Human Development: Selected Readings* (New York: Thomas Y. Crowell Co., 1966).
   Corman, Rena, "Close-up of the 'Normal' Wife," Reading 10.
   Berne, Eric, "Games People Play," Reading 35.
Landis, Judson T., and Landis, Mary G., *Readings in Marriage and the Family* (Englewood Cliffs, N. J.: Prentice-Hall, Inc., 1952).
   Landis, Judson T., "Time Required to Achieve Marriage Adjustment," pp. 169–180.
Rodman, Hyman, *Marriage, Family and Society* (New York: Random House, 1965).
   Shlien, John M., "Mother-in-Law: A Problem in Kinship Terminology," Reading 16.

General References

Dean, Dwight G., "Emotional Maturity and Marital Adjustment," *Journal of Marriage and the Family,* 28:454–457, November, 1966.
Duvall, Evelyn M., *In-Laws: Pro and Con* (New York: Association Press, 1953).
Hobart, Charles W., "Disillusionment in Marriage and Romanticism," *Marriage and Family Living,* 20:156–162, May, 1958.
Kirkpatrick, Clifford, *The Family as Process and Institution,* second edition (New York: The Ronald Press Co., 1963), Ch. 18.
Landis, Judson T., "Length of Time Required to Achieve Adjustment in Marriage," *American Sociological Review,* 11:666–667, December, 1945.
Phillips, Clinton E., "Some Considerations for the Newlyweds," *Family Life,* 28:4–6, December, 1968.

20

Patterns of Adjustment

In any kind of close living or working arrangement between human beings, some way of getting along together must be worked out if the association is to last. Business partners must divide privileges, responsibilities, and work, as well as profits. Roommates in a dormitory must each modify some of their ways if they are to spend a year together. Bachelor girls sharing an apartment must agree on many things, or agree to disagree—on hours for doing certain things, on food, and furniture. This necessity is even greater with married couples, for the possible areas of conflict are more numerous than in any of the other pair relationships mentioned.

In all human relationships, whether of individuals or groups, certain interaction processes and adjustment devices are characteristic. The simplest of these is *dominance* and *submission*. This pattern is seen everywhere—in the chicken yard, where psychologists have spotted the dominant hen by her ability to outpeck all the others and make them bow to her demands; among the forest animals, where the most powerful male wins the female after defeating all comers; among children in their play; among adults in many work and social situations. Once the relationship of dominance and submission has been established, quarreling and conflict cease. The superior need no longer fight to hold his own, for the inferior has already been cowed.

Conflict is another common interaction pattern between persons. At its worst, it aims at annihilating the enemy. In its more gentle forms, it is expressed in quarreling, which is an attempt to annihilate the opponent on the ego level. Where conflict exists, adjustment has not been reached. In fact, conflict is one of the common ways of striving for an adjustment. The difficulty with this device is that someone always has to lose before there can be peace, unless there can be compromise and both can be content to call it a draw.

411

Accommodation is a sociological term which means about what is meant by the common phrase "agree to disagree." It is settling issues by permanent compromise of differences. Conflict is tiring, even in the form of quarreling. There comes a time to call a halt and stake out neutral territory if there is to be any getting along at all.

Competition is a common pattern of American life and to some extent of life almost everywhere. It aims at outdoing the other person by superior performance. Modern business is geared to perpetual competition. Success in modern education for the most part is measured by one's ability to outdo his classmates—by landing a little higher toward the "A" side of the normal curve. Men live in a competitive world throughout a lifetime. Women live competitively in school and college.

Cooperation is the goal of adjustment. Instead of a couple's outdoing each other, their mutual aid and mutual sharing are the pattern of cooperation. It gives to each the other's strength. The cooperative couple is the adjusted couple.

Each of the above processes appears in some form in every marriage. The device employed most often and the kind of adjustment arrived at determines the happiness of the marriage.

Dominance and Submission

The story is told of a strapping big lieutenant who married a girl of small stature inclined toward bossiness. After carrying her across the threshold, he took off his pants, handed them to her, and commanded her to put them on. She put them on, then protested, "Why, Bill, they're three times too big for me."

His reply was, "Don't forget that."

In the relationships of husbands and wives, dominance and submission has been the most characteristic pattern of man-wife relationships, with the male historically more often assuming the dominant role. This solution to the problems of the marriage can be simple, clear-cut, and remarkably effective if each member of the pair can accept it. There is little quibbling over issues and little time spent in family councils.

Many of the peaceful marriages in which there were never any real quarrels are explained by this clear distinction in the authority of man and wife. If Grandpa was the patriarch that most men in his time were, he blew off steam and his wife humbly took it, slipping off in the bedroom to cry rather than fighting back. Other women had their way by subterfuge. They had to recognize the superior physical strength of the husband but resorted to their wits to outmaneuver him. *Life with Father* depicts the strong male figure well but also the wife who knew how to get her way in a situation where open conflict would have been futile.

Rainwater's study[1] of authority patterns by social class suggests that equality in decision making is most likely to be found among middle-class couples. At the working-class level, particularly among Negroes, but also to a certain extent among whites, the wife is most likely to dominate in decision making.

Judson T. Landis studied the marital happiness of 3,000 marriages of parents of his students. He found the democratic marriages far more often happy than those in which either husband or wife were definitely dominant. Strong wife dominance was least often related to happiness. A tendency toward male dominance was quite favorable to happiness but not equal to the 50–50 pattern.[2]

Among couples in trouble to the point of seeking counseling help, Landis found the husband dominant in half of them, the wife dominant in 31 percent, and in only 29 percent 50–50 dominance.[3]

A survey covering 2,596 well-educated families attempted to learn not only who was boss but also whether or not the couple was happy with the arrangement. Students in three colleges—the University of California, Oklahoma Agriculture and Mechanical College, and Columbia University—were asked by Paul Popenoe of the American Institute of Family Relations to rate couples with whom they were well acquainted and who had been married at least five years as to (1) who was boss in the family and (2) happiness of the marriage. It was found that men were dominant in 35 percent of the cases and women in 28 percent; in 37 percent of the cases there was a democratic partnership. Of the democratic partnerships, almost nine out of ten were found to be happy; of the male-dominated couples almost two-thirds were happy; of the wife-dominated marriages, less than half.

David Mace emphasizes the point that there are many patterns of marriage which can succeed. He believes that the marriage in which dominance and submission are the characteristic pattern often has a place, concluding that "there are people who want to be dominated—and not all of them are women."[4]

The democratic ideal, while it is a norm for the urban-industrial marriage, certainly need not be attained by all persons in order for them to be happy. Many couples can and do live together very successfully in

[1] Lee Rainwater, *Family Design: Marital Sexuality, Family Size, and Contraception* (Chicago: Aldine Publishing Co., 1965), pp. 28–60.

[2] See Judson T. Landis and Mary G. Landis, *Building a Successful Marriage,* fifth edition (Englewood Cliffs, N.J.: Prentice-Hall, Inc., 1968), Figure 5–8, p. 298.

[3] *Ibid.,* Figure 15–9, p. 299.

[4] David R. Mace, "Personality Expression and Subordination in Marriage," *Marriage and Family Living,* 15:205–207, August, 1953.

a relationship of dominance and submission. It is when one insists on this kind of relationship and the other finds it incompatible that trouble begins.

Quarreling

It is an unusual couple who have not had some very serious quarrels during their engagement period. Those who do not are probably not well enough acquainted or have failed to be together in enough different situations to learn some of their real differences.

For those who have no misunderstandings before marriage, the first real clash after marriage is likely to be unusually disturbing. The chances are that the young couple will wonder how two people so much in love could possibly quarrel so.

Quarreling near universal   The American Institute of Public Opinion in one of its national surveys asked couples whether or not they had marital disputes. Four out of five couples admitted that they did. The researchers in interpreting these data suggested that they suspected the other fifth either had had some pretty serious marital disputes, or else were still honeymooners, or were people who had passed their golden anniversary and forgotten a great deal.

Absence of quarrels is too often regarded as a criterion of successful marriage. Usually it means little more than indifference—a superficial placidity attained by shallow people or those whose real interests lie outside the home, or those who, with or without a day of reckoning, habitually bury their antagonism under the thick cotton pad of polite behavior.[5]

Quarreling in marriage is one indication that husband and wife both recognize their equal status in the marriage. The way a young couple handle a quarrel is the thing that tells whether they will build a cooperative union. The issues about which a couple quarrel indicate areas where adjustments have to be made.

Judson T. Landis' 1967 study[6] of 581 married couples, one of whom had been in his college marriage classes at a prior time, showed that discussion and compromise is the effective way to get along. Arguing and quarreling led to negative reactions, yet more than two-thirds engaged in this kind of behavior. Over half at times refused to talk to each other. Avoidance in the area of difference was reported as behavior practiced by

---

[5] John Levy and Ruth Munroe, *The Happy Family* (New York: Alfred A. Knopf, Inc., 1938), p. 76.

[6] Landis and Landis, *op. cit.,* Table 1, pp. 292–293.

about two-thirds, 62 percent of husbands reported that wives cried at times, and 48 percent that she denied him sex relations.

The most extreme reaction reported was becoming physically ill from encountering differences. This reaction was reported by 16 percent of husbands as a reaction of their wives and by 7 percent of wives as a reaction of their husbands.

David Mace[7] states that although a couple are drawn together by such affinities as a need for sexual fulfillment, the need for comradeship—that is, to share a common destiny and to avoid loneliness—and the need for a sense of belonging, it is just as certain that at some point in their relationship, hostilities must appear to protect the ego of the individual against too great an encroachment by the other party. This is the only way, he believes, that the personality can avoid destruction. Couples must learn where the point of equilibrium is.

Harold F. Searles[8] has concluded that people become schizophrenic partly by reason of "a long continued . . . unconscious effort on the part of some person or persons . . . to drive him crazy." This can be a family conspiracy, even though unconscious. Better to tell another member of the family "you're crazy" now and then than to let matters fester to the point where there develops the "unconscious need to drive somebody else crazy so that an unhealthy state of mutual dependence can continue despite anxieties and frustrations."

Mace believes that because of this inevitable hostility, quarreling has a proper and useful place in marriage in that it lets off emotional steam, whereas intellectual interchange on the discussion basis fails to do so. He feels that the couple needs at some time to feel the heat of each other's points of view and needs. To quarrel without either partner giving ground, until emotion is dissipated and they are drawn together by some affinity, most likely sexual need, is likely to be disastrous. No equilibrium is reached, and the marriage simply fluctuates back and forth between hostility and attraction. Also, for one partner to give in for the sake of peace is not good. In this case, one member becomes the tyrant and the other submits.

Discussion of issues is a rational substitute for quarreling and argument. Quarreling is a direct attack on an opponent. It is an attempt to in some measure destroy him. Discussion, by contrast, is an attack on issues to be settled. The one is personal; the other is impersonal. The one leads to chronic nagging; the other brings out issues on which the couple differ, airs them, and tries to work out an intelligent solution. But discussion does not vent hostilities and is not an adequate substitute if there are deep hostilities.

[7] Mace, *op. cit.*
[8] *Time,* April, 1959, p. 73.

Quarreling vs. Other Reactions
to Marriage Frustration

Psychologists and counselors recognize the likelihood of the average marriages needing to vent hostilities, to the extent that various counseling techniques have been developed which encourage domestic battle, often in group situations. A recent book, *The Intimate Enemy*,[9] stresses the virtues of quarreling and sets forth fair rules for it. Television presentation has outlined two steps. They stress the motto "Couples who fight together, stay together," "A fight a day keeps the doctor away." They stress that the fight must be a fair fight.

Bach claims that couples he has taught his "fight-training" are living more satisfying lives than before.[10] He has trained many in his marathon group sessions.

Whether results are from his unique genius in working with people or could generally be used by others it is too soon to know. And whether all couples could benefit from intensive, often violent, fighting therapy, is seriously to be doubted. There may well be many types who would be destroyed by it.

Quarreling like many adjustment devices, though never a constructive means is often a better alternative than many others that are likely to be needed if provoking circumstances exist. One is reminded of the old Quaker with his gentle philosophy of living. The cow had switched him all during the milking and finally dragged her tail through the milk and slapped it around his neck. He jumped to his feet, grabbed her tail and said, "I will not smite thee, I'll not curse thee, but I will twist thy dern tail!"

Situations can reach the point where some kind of action has to be taken or the inner disturbance costs more than venting the emotion externally. The intimate husband-and-wife relationship requires so much encroachment on the private domain of the other's ego that an explosion may be needed to release tension and establish balance. The explosion clears the air for discussion by venting the emotional pressure. It may open the way for the couple to work out a more clear and understanding relationship, and thus strengthen their relationship with each other.

In the violent quarrel, the real issues are more likely to come out than they are under other circumstances. The making-up process often leads to a deeper level of intimacy than existed before, for the sequel is often a confession or admission of mutual guilt and mutual responsi-

[9] George R. Bach and Peter Wyden (New York: William Morrow, 1969).
[10] See "Marriage: Fight Together, Stay Together," *Time*, February 21, 1969, pp. 64–65.

bility. People who can quarrel are much less likely to get involved in serious psychological problems than are those whose recourse is sulking, or avoidance. Quarreling is a better adjustment device than brooding, walking out, or running home to mother or to a neighbor. It is better than the neuroses which may develop from constantly ignoring or repressing hostility issues. It is better than escaping in drink, in desertion, or in a romance outside the marriage. It is even better, although some authorities disagree, than quietly and passively resigning oneself in religion as an antidote for adjustment.

This is not to say that a couple who can live without a quarrel is not a happier or more perfect pair. There is no doubt that they are. But most couples cannot, at least in the early stages of their marriage, expect to live at this level of perfection. The problems to be worked out are usually too numerous. Quarrels begin with trivialities, but they uncover much more. The triviality is the trigger. The built-up hostilities, frustrations, and aggravations are the background for the explosion. As the emotionally charged quarrel breaks loose and the destructive impulses of one mate are vented on the other, the real issues of the quarrel are likely to be exposed. As the heat of wrath grows, that standard phrase comes forth, "And another thing," and with it an exposure of the vital issues. The issues are no longer trivial; they are the very issues that determine marriage survival or failure.

Compromise not enough   Whether the quarrel leads toward adjustment or carries the marriage toward disaster will depend on the outcome. Of these there are several possibilities. Compromise is a more logical outcome perhaps than one would expect in a really heated quarrel. Genuine contrition allows the couple to each recognize his faults and ask forgiveness for them. This may bring the partners to a deeper level in understanding of each other's needs and thus may result in a more perfect love. People who have never had issues to overcome perhaps cannot understand how this can be. This kind of outcome leads to the building of closer marriage relationships and decreased hostilities. It leads to mutual acceptance and increased mutual respect. This is perhaps the finest outcome possible in any kind of human conflict, for it is not merely the peace of compromise that points the way to accommodation (discussed in the next section) but it is also a genuine approach to mutual identification and to becoming one in spirit and in aims as well as in flesh. Genuine compromise is, of course, a step forward. And in some marriages, compromise of a purely rational character is necessary. Compromise is not enough, however, where it proves only to be a truce in a cold war. The same hostilities are there if the issues over which the quarrel took place are still there.

If each continues to feel that the other is wrong, that the other is to blame, that the other person is the one who must change, the truce cannot last. It will revive again and continue, and perhaps with each battle the road back to genuine mutual understanding will be made more difficult.

If the result is a draw and each recognizes and respects the other person, then the ground is laid for an accommodative relationship in the particular areas of tension.

The quarrel may end in one party or the other being completely cowed. Such a marriage can last. It may be that the wife can recognize and respect her husband and be willing to be subservient to his demands and needs. She may be able psychologically to accept this without neurosis. She (or he) can, however, in being cowed, be put on the way toward the development of psychosomatic illness which are the ego's way of expressing frustration.

In an earlier day, many women, when they had lost all hope of being treated fairly in their marriage, found solace in religion, sufficient solace to retain their sanity. Many today, with less faith but with equal provocation, end up in a mental institution. *The Deseret News Telegram* in a "Confidentially Yours" column by Mary Marker published the account of a woman who found solace in prayer and faith in a marriage where many years of crying had brought no solution. The account goes:

> I never express my needs to my companion but rather to my Heavenly Father. He is our friend and will fill our needs if we trust Him. I have had many things I have wanted badly. Because I knew my husband would be cross and angry if I mentioned them to him, I asked only my Heavenly Father. Many of them came slowly but surely.
>
> Early in my marriage I learned that for peace there had to be a 100 percent husband marriage. So for peace, here I have had to take the mental attitude that I am the hired girl working in his home with no more rights than a hired girl. I talk of only things he is interested in, and when I am with him, I do the things he likes to do.
>
> With this attitude, I can be grateful for all the crumbs he shares with me. To me, the house, furniture, money, children—all things are his and I am fortunate to be able to be in his home that I might care for and be with his children.[11]

One suspects that few psychiatrists would agree with this woman's solution. In fact, it is doubtful that many moderns could accept it for themselves without being victimized by their frustrations to the point of emotional collapse.

In quarreling there is always such a thing as victory without a solution. Certainly the situation that tends to neurotic symptoms proves to be of this character. There may be victories where neither is left cowed but

---

[11] Mary Marker, "Confidentially Yours," *The Deseret News Telegram,* Salt Lake City, June 14, 1956.

where one is left rebellious, even though silent—more hostile, more deeply determined that in the end he or she must win, must destroy the other or the marriage. If this is the solution, the divorce will take place in the atmosphere of vengeance.

Human nature is complicated, and it is most difficult to spell out all types of situations, the hurts, and the solutions that couples arrive at through venting antagonisms. The list of outcomes mentioned must be considered only as suggestions.

Vicarious relief   Critics may well say that mature persons do not use quarreling in the marriage relationship to vent frustrations. But where is one to find a world of such human beings? True, the more mature person learns vicarious ways of venting hostilities undamaging to others. All can practice in this direction.

The old-fashioned butter churn offered many a mother and grandmother a wonderful relief from the aggravations and frustrations of a dominant and contrary husband. They gritted their teeth and slammed the plunger down. The vigor depended on the extent of their hostility and the depth of their feelings of aggression, which they dared not vent directly on the husband. The result was good—the butter came more quickly, and their feelings were relieved without being taken out on their children.

Some vent hostilities in driving an automobile. A psychiatrist living in the outskirts of the Los Angeles area indicated that he enjoyed the long drive to work through the Los Angeles traffic very much. "It vents my hostilities," he said. Drivers are dangerous when venting their hostilities while driving through traffic; many seem to get the thrill of combat in dodging traffic, or in speeding, or in outwitting the traffic patrol. This is not a recommended way of relieving one's emotions.

The batting of a ball, the playing of handball, any vigorous physical activity, is for many a wonderful way of easing the spirit of tension and aggression. Perhaps one of the great psychological benefits of hunting and fishing, mountain climbing, and the conquest of nature lies here. The revival of interest in these activities in our day, when so many live under heavy social pressure, lies in part in the fact that conquest of nature restores the ego.

Every person needs to learn how to vent hostilities in vicarious, harmless ways, whether this be by pounding the piano keys or by throwing darts. Thus it is possible to restore one's own ego without destroying another person.

When children enter the marriage, quarreling or even arguing vigorously often gives the children a disquieting sense that there is deep trouble in the family. Couples who must continue to do a certain amount of quarreling and arguing should be particularly careful that it is done in such a way, or at such a time, as not to give the children a sense of insecurity.

Accommodation—The Imperfect Path

Barbara Steel reports asking a friend the secret of her long and happy marriage.[12] The reply was that the friend and her husband discovered early in their marriage "that there was no subject on which we could reach an agreement. And so . . . we've never tried." Hanna Lees, writing for the *Saturday Evening Post,* titled an article "How to Be Happy though Incompatible" and made a very strong case for her thesis.[13] She declares that men give no thought to the problem of compatibility. Wives may as well face the fact, and a lot of emotional probing won't improve matters at all. She feels that few men give wives the attentions they feel they need because husbands are preoccupied with other things and take marriage for granted. Almost every marriage, she concludes, has many areas of incompatibility. It is to be expected.

There is much sense in this. Of course, the crux of the matter is: How many areas of incompatibility can be tolerated? And, how serious is the incompatibility to those aspects of the relationship which are most vital?

If the husband is inclined to direct or correct all the wife's moves when she goes bowling or when they sit at the bridge table, they may find it essential to seek their recreation separately.

The wife may not like the fact that the husband wants an occasional weekend to hunt with the boys, but she comes to recognize that escape into the male subculture provides a type of recreation he needs and likes; and so she accepts it, even though it means that she has to be alone sometimes. At first she may have quarreled about this; then she probably realized that there was no use quarreling about it the rest of her married life. Such weekends were important to him, and she recognized this fact, even though she would have liked to have it otherwise.

The husband may not like the fact that his wife—say she is a former teacher—takes occasional work as a substitute teacher. Her working inconveniences him. He storms about it at first because his meals are not ready on the days she teaches. She explains that she needs to get out of the home and keep in touch with people and activities that she likes. He grumbles for a while but learns to step aside and let his wife work out this part of her life to suit herself rather than him.

The petty irritations of living are often the worst irritations of all.

[12] Reported in *Reader's Digest.*
[13] *Saturday Evening Post,* February 16, 1957.

Dr. Lester Kirkendall, family specialist emeritus at the University of Oregon, tells of a young wife in one of his classes who was irritated almost beyond endurance by the fact that her husband left his socks on the floor. Dr. Kirkendall asked the class of young women what they would do.

"Nail them to the floor," one said. "Put them on his desk," another suggested. And so the answers came—a dozen or more—all of them solutions which would have increased the tension between husband and wife.

Finally one girl, registering a tone of disgust at her classmates' answers, said "They're not very heavy. Pick them up!"

"But," the wife protested, "he's got *no right* to expect me to pick things up!"

A marriage is in for difficulties when either husband or wife insists on living by rights. There are many instances in any human relationship where someone must go the second mile, and there are many second miles to be walked in a successful marriage. It will sometimes be the husband who walks them and sometimes the wife. When both are willing to do this, there is a kind of sharing that raises the marriage relationship to the highest level of happiness.

How much one can give and take very often depends on what the issue symbolizes for him or for her, as the example of the socks so well illustrates. Many women can pick up the socks day after day, and, though they dislike it, they take it as part of their work routine and come to accept it. But the wife who protests "He's got no right to expect," "It's not democratic," etc., has much more at stake than household routine. Ego and status values of great depth are apparently at stake in her case. She no doubt feels herself in servile status picking up socks. If this is so, the giving will probably have to be on the husband's part.

Without doubt, the greater the number of areas of accommodation, the less likelihood there will be of a completely happy marriage. Yet in most marriages there must be some acceptance of the mate in spite of certain incompatibilities. Topics on which the couple can never agree are not discussed. A "Keep off" sign is posted over these topics. It is far better simply to let them lie. There are certain fields of activity which the couple must avoid altogether.

Avoidance may not meet the ideal of the romantic marriage, yet if couples, by avoiding certain subjects, certain issues, certain places, or even each other completely for periodic separate vacations or other breaks, can thus keep the peace, they may find this the most satisfactory way of marriage for them. Many cannot submerge their personalities fully in marriage. There are vital zones of overlapping, but this is all there ever can be. Those who learn this about themselves and their mate may well find their marriage quite satisfactory, in fact, as satisfactory as any marriage could be for them.

Competition vs. Adjustment

The ego and the love motives in human personality are forever at odds, yet the ego must be preserved from extinction even in marriage. In a society where the game of competition has become the most engrossing activity of life, love is always threatened. In love, one cannot count marks and scores, dollars and cents, honors and distinctions, prizes and awards. These are part of the ego-expressing game. Love cannot be measured in the balance of fair exchange. It gives without asking in return.

The educational and occupational worlds are worlds of competition for survival. Success and status are dependent upon the development of this trait in the personality. In most relationships of adult life in American society, equality assumes competition. Competition involves rivalry— the spirit of excelling and outdoing. This spirit has come to characterize the lives, not only of men but also of women. It is the predominating pattern of school activities from earliest childhood through the college years.

Work relationships in industry and in offices and the vying for social position and standard of living also show this pattern. Admittedly, competition is an invigorating characteristic of a society which has always preached the doctrine of social climbing—a faith of a people who believe that there is room at the top.

Marriage, by contrast, is an institution of close complementary cooperation. Its success or failure depends upon the couple's ability to work together as a team and to get along. Among young people today, each of whom has gone to college and competed both educationally and in the work world, the competitive habit often brings great difficulty to marriage because it is hard not to carry over the competitive spirit into the marriage relationship.

If both continue to work, they may feel they are competing with each other in the amount of income they earn, in the type of expenditures they are able to afford, and in many other aspects of their personal relationship. This is one of the great difficulties faced by the emancipated couple in this age. Instead of being able to bolster each other and strengthen each other's roles in the community and work world, each finds himself trying to detract and run down the mate as a way of maintaining or building up his own status. The wife may envy the husband in his work if she is confined to the home; if both work, they may feel competitive in seeking status, just as couples who are friendly in school sometimes feel competitive over athletic or social success or grades. This competition destroys the couple's feeling of security in each other. The wife feels humiliated by the husband's success, or the husband feels outdone by the wife's achievements, whether they are in social life or the work world.

Rather than being able to share the joy of the partner's achievement, the mate then is likely to suffer from inferiority feelings. Rather than push the mate forward to further success, each tries to draw the other down to his own level. Rather than bolstering the husband's or wife's feeling of self-importance, the mate tries to "cut him down to size." Rather than the marriage being a cooperative sharing, it is subjected to the same strain as business and social life outside the family, where rivalry for position and influence replaces a genial spirit of working together. This is one of the important reasons that every marriage for the well-informed modern couple is a marriage of constant adjustment.

This problem is often presented as one peculiar to the modern wife. It is so only because men have by custom so long been granted authority that the wife gets blamed for her attempt to realize equality in the marriage. Something has to give in such marriages, for affection evaporates and the marriage becomes comparable to a business relationship, with the same ruthless driving for success, the same quest for recognition. As love dies, the craving for status and recognition become more desperate. Human nature is so constituted that if one has a full and understanding love, his ego requires little satisfaction in the marriage relationship; without love the ego makes great demands. If the love relationship is lost in marriage, the ego becomes immense, demanding satisfactions and recognitions that are entirely beyond reasonable expectations.

Popenoe says that the American male wants a woman who will bolster his ego—give him sympathy, warmth, and security—not outdo him. In writing to college-trained women, he has warned that even in our sophisticated age, men are not interested primarily in women with college degrees. They want a woman in marriage to satisfy emotional needs that cannot be met in the competitive activities of work life. This is no doubt the great appeal of the foreign girl to the American male.[14]

Women, too, in marriage are, in the final analysis, looking for the emotional security that comes from being wanted, loved, and cared for. They crave a sense of belonging. They want this without paying the price of sacrificing their right to be individuals.[15]

The American marriage today sets before men and women the highest ideal of which man has ever dreamed—that of sharing on the basis of complete equality, or recognizing each other as full, complete, and self-sufficient individuals, with rights, privileges, and aspirations to be satisfied both within and outside the marriage. This type of marriage

[14] For research bearing on this, see Ch. 15.

[15] For a discussion of many facets of this problem see Seymour M. Farber and Roger H. L. Wilson (eds.), *The Potential of Woman* (New York: McGraw-Hill Book Co., 1963).

is a much finer relationship than one based on dominance and submission, and yet it is one which is increasingly difficult to attain. This is not because men and women do not realize its merits but because they are built for a competitive relationship and cannot meet the demands of such a marriage. Consequently, most marriages are a compromise.

The secret of a happy marriage, like a happy romance, is cooperative, self-sacrificing sharing. It is the part of each spouse to bolster, support, and build up the ego of the other. Both men and women seek to satisfy their wish for emotional security in marriage. Both must also find success and recognition to be happy.

Realism in Expectations

Marriage, in its interpersonal relationships, is not a highly standardized institution. It is, rather, highly individuated, and a pattern satisfactory for one couple would not be for another. For the most part, research to date has been drawn from the middle and upper-middle classes. There is no doubt that family patterns of her lower classes differ considerably in many respects and that the kinds of adjustment described in many situations in the preceding pages would not be satisfactory for certain couples.

The ideal marriage relationship—the goals for which young people should strive—has been outlined. One should not be discouraged if he does not fully realize the ideal of cooperation. One meets couples who seem to be happiest together after a good spat. They have let off steam and seem closer for it. And there are some wives who seem sure of their husband's love only after he has given them a good beating.

Most such marriages are among couples from national cultures where the expression of violent emotions is sanctioned by customs and where male dominance is still accepted in the culture pattern. The book and film previously cited, *The Quiet Man,* depicted a marriage relationship in which the American male failed to conform to the expectations of Irish culture and lost the respect of both his wife and the community. Only when he became his wife's master did he regain a place of respect.

If a couple has found a satisfactory life together along these embattled lines, who is to say that their roles should be revised for the sake of an ideal? Such couples might find a peaceful life a monotony. Often the wife who requires such treatment of a husband in order to love him has been punished or severely dominated by her father during her upbringing.

But in the genuinely democratic marriage of sharing and cooperation —the ideal of the American family system today—adjustment rather than conflict is the accepted goal. This is for most couples the road to understanding. In general, it is assumed that such a philosophy of adjustment offers a far superior type of human relationship to that which is sometimes attained by means of a struggle for mutual acceptance.

In a definite sense, every family pattern in the United States is different. In fact, some authors talk about family culture, referring to the unique characteristics of each individual household. Any young couple should get valuable hints and guides from the foregoing discussion and the research upon which it is based. On the other hand, one should not be anxious about his future if his pattern of life does not exactly fit the norm which this or any other book presents. The important thing is that the pattern of life established create a mutually satisfying family environment and provide a home in which children feel secure. This is a point which has been stressed repeatedly throughout the book and which cannot be overstressed. Human life is not patterned so specifically that any two people can fit into an identical mold, nor would they be happy in doing so if they could.

Husbands and wives cannot, in all situations, see eye to eye, and most marriages would be monotonous affairs if they did. Adjustment, after all, is a relative thing. It assumes a working relationship which is satisfactory in most respects for the persons involved in it. It need not satisfy neighbors, friends, even relatives, and it need not satisfy every criteria of research or of marriage books.

Successful marriage adjustment is not for the perfectionistic, nor yet is it for the callous and inconsiderate. The democratic marriage of today offers a sharing between human beings of their strengths and weaknesses and their troubles and anxieties. The way any particular couple work out their life together is their own problem. The institution of marriage no longer standardizes the roles of husbands and wives. In fact, at many points, their roles interchange. The important thing is that the couple work out a way of life that is satisfactory to them. It need not conform to the kind of life their parents found satisfactory or to the norms by which other people live. The important test is that the marriage satisfy a sufficient number of their needs so that their lives run more or less smoothly. There is much evidence from the study of even the better marriages that marriage cannot satisfy every need and that even at best it is not a perfect institution. The demands of close daily association are rarely met without occasional frictions and the numerous forces which impinge upon the marriage from outside make constantly recurring adjustments almost inevitable.

Young couples need to avoid constantly taking their marital temperature and worrying about the state of their relationship together. They need to be realistic and practical about the marriage and recognize what it can and cannot do. Within the family, as in other institutions, there is always the tendency of the individual to want to have life ordered to suit him.

However, the institution itself survives only as life is ordered to suit the group. The struggle between these two forces has always gone on in every marriage. It is particularly active today with the recognized equal status of family members. With equality of status becoming socially approved and men and women becoming more specialized and individualistic, the struggle between individual interests and group interests becomes more evident.

If the central purpose of the couple is to maintain a working relationship together and to face life's issues together, most of the minor differences will be submerged in the longer and more distant goal. Much divorce today takes place over petty issues because the couple have not decided in their own minds that their marriage is going to be a success, that it has a future, and that its central purpose will be fulfilled regardless of the many fringe adjustments which must be made in the relationship together.

In conclusion, marriage is a highly individuated institution, and patterns of adjustment will vary. Some marriages will have considerable conflict and yet be generally satisfactory; others will reach a high degree of harmony and cooperation. Some spouses can accept, even enjoy, a relationship of submission. Some marriages can perhaps survive considerable competition. In an individualistic age, most marriages require a certain amount of accommodation. The degree to which a given pattern will be employed will vary with family and ethnic background of the pair as well as with their temperament and disposition.

Problems

1. If one or the other spouse tends toward dominance in marriage, do you think it should be the husband or the wife, or does it matter? Upon what grounds would you justify your position:
   a. Tradition.
   b. Pattern of your parental home.
   c. Family well-being.
   d. Natural law.
   e. Economic factors.
   f. Intellectual differences.
   g. Other factors.
   Do the men and women of the class agree? What is the most common justification offered?
2. List several areas of a marriage in which accommodation rather than adjustment is likely to occur.
3. Mary and Jarvis are both college graduates with responsible and well-paying jobs in a large, highly competitive advertising agency. Their jobs rest on their ability to think up schemes for outdoing other firms and outselling other products. They even compete with one another at their jobs,

since their salary and prestige depend upon the number and quality of ideas that each submits. How might they guard their private lives from the competitiveness they must feel while on the job?

4. List several situations or personal qualities to which you would refuse to adjust, or even to accommodate, in marriage. Does there tend to be consensus among class members on any of these adjustment limitations? Do men's and women's views differ?

5. Describe a situation in which a quarrel might serve as a desirable adjustment device.

6. *Research exercise:* Poll the class or some other student group on the question, "In your own home what pattern of adjustment seemed to prevail?" Tabulate results by sex. What patterns of adjustment are most often found? Do men and women have a different conception of adjustment patterns in their homes?

7. Do you believe that some men, as well as some women, are happier in marriage when they have a mate to dominate them and make decisions for them? If so, how do you explain such personalities?

8. Do you believe that an occasional quarrel is as necessary to a marriage as a pressure valve is to a pressure cooker, that both provide means for letting off steam and keeping the lid from blowing off?

9. Do you believe that competitiveness is on the increase or gradually being reduced in the relationship of the sexes before marriage? After marriage?

10. *Sociodrama:* Stage a quarrel between husband and wife over some common problem such as money, recreation, friends, or religion. At the end, let the group discuss the quarrel as an adjustment device. Would another pattern have produced better results?

11. What is your opinion of "fight-training" for marriage partners?

Selected References

Articles in Books of Readings

Cavan, Ruth S., *Marriage and the Family in the Modern World: A Book of Readings*, third edition (New York: Thomas Y. Crowell Co., 1969).
    Blood, Robert O., Jr., "Resolving Family Conflicts," Reading 47.
Landis, Judson T., and Landis, Mary G., *Readings in Marriage and the Family* (Englewood Cliffs, N.J.: Prentice-Hall, Inc., 1952).
    Roth, Julius, and Peck, Robert F., "Social Class and Marital Adjustments," pp. 197–199.

General References

Clark, Alexander L., and Wallin, Paul, "Women's Sexual Responsiveness and the Duration and Quality of Their Marriages," *American Journal of Sociology*, 71:189–196, September, 1965.
Hallenbeck, Phyllis N., "An Analysis of Power Dynamics in Marriage," *Journal of Marriage and the Family*, 28:200–203, May, 1966.

Mace, David R., "Personality Expression and Subordination in Marriage," *Marriage and Family Living*, 15:205–207, August, 1953.

Nye, F. Ivan, and Hoffman, Lois Wladis, (eds.), *The Employed Mother in America* (Chicago: Rand McNally & Co., 1963), Part 3.

Peterson, James A., *Education For Marriage*, second edition (New York: Charles Scribner's Sons, 1964), Ch. 13.

Stephens, William N., *The Family in Cross-Cultural Perspective* (New York: Holt, Rinehart and Winston, 1963), Ch. 6.

21

Marriage Happiness

Happiness is an elusive quality, perhaps more often found by those who do not seek it directly than by those who do. In marriage it is in part a by-product of assuming responsibility. It is also affected by temperament. Some are more gloomy and pessimistic than others. General health and energy affect it, and certainly basic to it is conditioning by the childhood home. Unhappy homes produce unhappy children, who become unhappy adults.

Happiness is in part a matter of perspective. We have spoken of the disillusionment of early marriage. The perspective here is that of young people who have not quite forgotten the romantic dreams of the courtship period. But old people, looking back over the years, choose as happiest, not the so-called carefree years of youth but the busy years of family rearing.[1] Concepts change with time and experience.

Proportion of Marriages Attaining Happiness

Intangible and elusive as the quality "happiness" may be, most husbands and wives recognize it once it has been attained. It has been found that husbands and wives usually agree in their estimates of their marital happiness and also that outsiders who know the couple well generally agree with them in estimating the degree of their happiness.[2] Research has also shown that the happiness ratings of a couple do not change much over short periods of time.

[1] Judson T. Landis, "What Is the Happiest Period in Life?" *School and Society*, 55:643–645, June 6, 1942.

[2] Ernest W. Burgess and Leonard S. Cottrell, *Predicting Success or Failure in Marriage* (Englewood Cliffs, N.J. Prentice-Hall, Inc., 1939), Ch. 3.

More than thirty years ago Burgess and Cottrell had 526 couples rate their marriages as to happiness. These are their replies:[3]

Happiness rating	Number	Percent
Very happy	224	42.6
Happy	108	20.5
Average	76	14.4
Unhappy	71	13.5
Very unhappy	42	8.0
No reply	5	1.0
Total	526	100.0

It will be seen that over 63 percent classified their marriages as either happy or very happy and that only 21.5 percent classified them as unhappy or very unhappy.

Judson T. Landis,[4] studying 3,189 marriages in 1967, found that about the same proportions of marriages were happy or very happy, average, unhappy, or very unhappy.

A study at Stanford University of 792 couples living in the urban and semiurban areas of California showed similar results.[5] The group was in the middle and upper-middle classes. Each person was asked to fill out a questionnaire independently of husband or wife. Husbands and wives rated themselves as follows:

Happiness ratings	Husbands (percent)	Wives (percent)
Extraordinarily happy	29.5	34.6
Decidedly more happy than average	36.8	35.9
Somewhat more happy than average	16.3	14.7
About average	12.9	9.2
Somewhat less happy than average	2.9	3.0
Decidedly less happy than average	1.6	1.8
Extremely unhappy	0.1	0.8
Total	100.0	100.0

[3] Ibid., p. 32.
[4] Judson T. Landis and Mary G. Landis, Building a Successful Marriage, fifth editon (Englewood Cliffs, N.J.: Prentice-Hall, Inc., 1968), Table 3, p. 11.
[5] Lewis M. Terman and others, Psychological Factors in Marital Happiness (New York: McGraw-Hill Book Co., 1938), Ch. 7.

This group had even more happy couples and fewer unhappy couples than did the other studies. Women clearly run more toward the extremes in their expression of happiness or unhappiness than do men. It is likely that a wife's happiness is more exclusively dependent on the marriage than is that of the husband.

These studies probably give a little brighter picture of marriage than actually exists if all marriages are taken into account. Presumably the most unhappy marriages end in divorce. These studies excluded divorced individuals. The Stanford University study did, however, include some couples who had visited family clinics and who were, therefore, known to be having trouble with their marriage. In all studies a high proportion of the couples were well educated, and as has been previously shown, success and happiness are realized more often in marriage by those who have gone on to the higher levels of education.

A study of marital happiness of 17,533 couples as reported by their close friends showed the following:[6]

Rating	Number	Percent
Very happy or happy	10,798	61.6
Average	3,322	18.9
Unhappy, very unhappy, or divorced	3,413	19.5
Total	17,533	100.0

At the University of Southern California, a study of 2,080 married men showed that 58 percent were happy; 15 percent doubtful; 27 percent unhappy; and that of 2,176 married women, 58 percent were happy, 15 percent doubtful, and 27 percent unhappy.[7] The ratings were by graduate students and were made for educated couples of their acquaintance.

Chesser's study in Great Britain, dealing with over 6,000 women, shows that happy marriages are closely related to happy childhood there, as they are in the United States. Childhood happiness is, of course, dependent largely upon the happiness of the parent's marriage. Happily married women, he found, are as much in love with their husbands after marriage as before. They do not regret their marriages and would marry again. The unhappy women's love has diminished since engagement and the first year of marriage. Three-fifths of them would marry different men if they married again, and a third, if they had their choice, would not marry

---

[6] Richard Lang, Ph.D. thesis at the University of Chicago, summarized by Burgess and Cottrell, *op. cit.,* p. 139.

[7] Paul Popenoe and Donna Wicks, "Marital Happiness in Two Generations," *Marital Hygiene,* 21:218–233, 1937.

at all. Three-fourths of these women found after marriage that their husbands were not the sort of people they thought they were before marriage. Most of those who were happy found their husbands as they thought they were prior to marriage.[8]

These studies are fairly consistent in showing that approximately 60 percent of marriages are considered very happy or happy by the couples themselves or by friends, and that 15 to 20 percent are considered unhappy or very unhappy. Apparently, then, a fairly high proportion of marriages that last do lead to happiness. It is possible also that some of the couples who at the time of questioning were unhappy may have been happy earlier in their marriage.

Of course, these statistics, except for the Lang study, omit those marriages that have already terminated in divorce.

Qualities of Happy Mates

Terman tried to determine the principal traits that characterize the happy and the unhappy husband and wife. Here are the traits he found most indicative:[9]

Happy wives	*Unhappy wives*
have kindly attitude toward others	often have feelings of inferiority
like to help underdogs	tend to be defensive or aggressive
tend to be conventional	are easily annoyed, irritated
are cooperative	often join clubs only to get an office or
have strong urge to save money	recognition in them
are optimistic about life	are extreme in their views
do not take offense easily	are more likely to be neurotic
are less interested in social activities	lose tempers easily
such as dances	are impressed by thrilling situations
like to teach children	seek spectacular activities
put less importance on clothes	want to be on the move, are romance
are systematic homemakers	seekers
do less daydreaming	show little interest in others

[8] Eustace Chesser and others, *The Sexual, Marital, and Family Relationships of the English Woman* (New York: Roy Publishers, Inc., 1957).
[9] Terman and others, *loc. cit.*

Happy husbands	*Unhappy husbands*
have greater stability	often have feelings of inferiority
are cooperative	compensate by browbeating wife and
get along well with business associates	subordinates
are somewhat extroverted	dislike details
are conservative in attitudes	are more radical about sex morality
are willing to take initiative	are inclined to be moody
take responsibility easily	are argumentative
do not get rattled easily	like recreations that take them away from home
	are likely to be careless about money

Clearly, many of the attitudes and behavior traits mentioned in these lists are rooted in early training. Some of these factors may, of course, relate to the character of the marriage itself. For example, whether or not a husband likes recreation outside the home may depend a great deal on the kind of home his wife provides. The unhappy wife's restlessness, too, may depend on the kind of security and ego satisfaction the husband provides.

In one of its series of polls, the American Institute of Public Opinion asked respondents what they considered the most important qualities of husbands and wives. The question was worded thus: "What would you say is the most important quality in a good husband (wife)?" Here are the five most frequently given answers:

Qualities men want in a wife	*Married men (percent)*	*Single men (percent)*
good homemaker, good housekeeper, etc.	47	28
agreeable, good company, pleasant disposition	18	21
faithfulness, loyalty	15	16
cooperative, a partner	13	8
patience, understanding	11	9

Qualities women want in a husband	*Married women (percent)*	*Single women (percent)*
good provider	42	28
faithfulness, steadiness	22	24
kindness, consideration	20	13
agreeable, good company	14	16
cooperative, a partner	55	1

In this day of restaurants, delicatessens and laundries, it is a little surprising to find that almost half the married men mentioned the old-fashioned quality of being a good homemaker and housekeeper. This, along with good cooking, is about the same standard that their great-grandparents probably would have set. In fact, it is the trait Solomon emphasized centuries ago in his description of the good wife:

> She seeketh wool, and flax, and worketh willing with her hands. She is like the merchants' ships; she bringeth her food from afar. She riseth also while it is yet night, and giveth meat to her household. . . . She perceiveth that her merchandise is good: the candle goeth not out. She layeth her hands to the spindle, and her hands hold the distaff. She is not afraid of the snow for her household; for all her household are clothed. . . . She looketh well to the ways of her household, and eateth not the bread of idleness.[10]

Even in this day of great stress on companionability and compatibility, only a small portion of men mention these traits. Married women are quite old-fashioned, too, in one respect. Almost half of them want the husband to be a good provider, but with them the cooperative partner is even more important. This latter attitude suggests that women hold the new concept of marriage in much higher regard than men.

When one compares the standards of single and married men and women, he sees why some adjustment in marriage is necessary. Little more than a fourth of the single men thought of housekeeping and home-making as of great importance, but almost half of the men with experience in marriage considered it of great importance. Similarly, single women were much less often concerned about marrying a good provider than were married women.

Some 19 percent of both single men and women didn't know what qualities they wanted in a mate. This group perhaps will have few adjustment problems. More likely, they will know what they want if they fail to find it in the person whom they marry.

The Happiest Period

Adjustment to marriage and family life is a progressive thing. Better or worse rather than stationary relationships are likely to characterize most human associations. Into every family, factors intrude from the outside. There are relatives, social activities, clubs of one member or the other, friends, children and their problems, obligations to city, church, and school. There are always various influences that infringe upon the family to affect its relationships—economic hazards for which the couple is in no sense re-

---

[10] Proverbs 31:13.

sponsible, health difficulties of relatives or of the members of the family, tragedy due to the death of near relatives or death within the family, tragedy due to sideline romances. All these factors—in fact, everything which enters into the experience of one or both members of the pair—affect the marriage relationship in one way or another.

Some of these factors make for greater solidarity. Many couples, as they share an increasing number of experiences together, grow closer to each other in understanding, sympathy, and mutual dependence. In other cases, experiences divide the family and force members further apart, so that in every marriage there tends to be greater or lesser satisfaction with the marriage partner as time goes on.

Even marriage conflict and divorce are seldom events that happen suddenly. There is usually a long period of increasing friction and conflict prior to the divorce,[11] and even in the best-adjusted families there is often a long history of adjustments, some of which were not wholly pleasant. Marriage, like other relationships, is not always ideal; in fact, it is doubtful whether it is ever ideal. The storybook concept of a couple marrying and living "happily ever after" is a beautiful illusion. Marriage, like every other human relationship, is a developing, growing, changing affair. The degree of its satisfaction depends upon many factors, not the least of which is the ability of people to find in personal relationships the kinds of responses which satisfy them.

In our day of intimate interpersonal relationships, most marriages face the supreme test at some time during their duration. Even happy marriages may approach the point of divorce when certain forces impinge upon the relationship: disloyalty of one mate, financial crisis, in-law crisis.

Burgess and Cottrell's study of happiness in marriage according to years of marriage shows that happiness scores are higher during the first year of marriage. They drop about 10 points during the first six or eight years. After many years of marriage they seem to be somewhat higher again but not so high on the average as at the beginning.[12]

Lang's study of the happiness of 7,393 couples, as reported by friends rather than by the couples themselves, finds more couples happy and fewer unhappy during the first two years of marriage than during the later years of marriage.[13] The number of discontented couples, according to the study, slowly increases with the number of years married.

Hamilton's study of 200 married men and 200 married women reports that the first four years of marriage are the happiest.[14]

Cuber and Harroff[15] studied the marriages of persons of the upper

---

[11] Discussed with data in Ch. 30.

[12] Burgess and Cottrell, *op. cit.,* pp. 246–248.

[13] Lang in Burgess and Cottrell, *op. cit.,* p. 139.

[14] G. V. Hamilton, *A Research in Marriage* (New York: A. & C. Boni, Inc., 1929).

[15] John F. Cuber and Peggy B. Harroff, "The More Total View: Relationships

middle class in the age group thirty-five to fifty-five, all stable (married for at least a decade), and rated them in terms of relationship that seemed to prevail. Categories were "conflict-habituated," "devitalized," "passive-congenial," "vital," and "total."

The authors conclude that there are very few good marriage relationships, i.e., "deeply satisfying," as appraised by themselves. Couples reported that more vital relationships were often found outside the marriage but that the marriage continued out of "habit, tradition, and austere social sanctions." The researchers conclude that at this stage in life "the good man-woman relationship in marriage is the exception rather than the rule."

DeBurger's analysis[16] of letters addressed to the American Association of Marriage Counselors for help shows that problems connected with "affectional relations tend to increase as length of marriage increases." Not so with the sexual relationship of the husband. His problems decrease with length of marriage. The wife's sexual problems, though less often present, persist.

Luckey found[17] that couples married for approximately eight years saw less favorable personality qualities in their mates, the longer they were married. This was true of both those who were satisfied with their marriage and those who were not.

Counselors are aware of a late "middle-age slump" in many marriages. Clinton E. Phillips, director of the Department of Counseling of the American Institute of Family Relations, lists it in his outline of marriage phases as: "Disenchantment (threats of divorce) process,"[18] children are leaving home, the couple may already be grandparents at age forty-five or soon after, they are beginning to look forward to thirty to fifty years together in the empty nest, they need new meaning in their lives.

The wife may be absorbed in the emotional adjustments of menopause or consumed with lonesomeness over the children's departure from home and community. She neglects the husband or is callous to his feelings of loss and loneliness, which may be as strong as her own. The husband at this time is particularly susceptible to the romantic lure of a younger woman, who may seem to promise him his lost youth and a new lease on life. He may even plunge into an adolescent love affair with all the violence and emotional turmoil of an sixteen-year-old in his first throes of puppy love in compensation for his first awareness that youth is past,

among Men and Women of the Upper Middle Class," article 8 in Hyman Rodman, *Marriage, Family and Society: A Reader* (New York: Random House, 1965).

[16] James E. DuBurger, "'Marital Problems, Help-Seeking, and Emotional Orientation as Revealed in Help-Request Letters" *Journal of Marriage and Family Living,* 29:712–721, November, 1967.

[17] Eleanore Braun Luckey, "Number of Years as Related to Personality Perception of Marital Satisfaction," *Journal of Marriage and Family Living,* 28:44–46, February, 1966.

[18] "Some Considerations for the Newlyweds", *Family Life,* 28:4–5, December, 1968.

much opportunity gone, and ambition unfulfilled. If fulfilled, he may wonder now about the purpose of it, with the children gone and security already built for the future.

This experience of middle age provokes the saying "There's no fool like an old fool." Unless the wife shows unusual wisdom or unless social restraints of the community are strong, this affair of the late forties or early fifties may actually break the marriage, for in some cases the husband learns too late that he is not so young as he thought he was. For the ventures of a new sex experience, of which he may tire quickly, he has sacrificed a companion who could share the wisdom and understanding of his years. With that sacrifice he has lost the lifetime continuity of experience which they share in each other and in their families.

This is the time for the couple to find outside interests, hobbies, companionship, and all the other things they have dreamed of during the busy days of hard work and family rearing.[19] Now comes the time to enjoy their postponed travel and leisure.

Gradually, the grandchildren will become the focus of attention and a new emotional outlet. They will give the aging couple a grasp on the future and revive a close family bond.

Occupation and Happiness

One of the most important and continuous outside forces that impinge on marriage is occupation. Lang's extensive study[20] dealt with this problem, classifying the happiness of over 17,500 couples according to the husband's occupation, ratings being made by friends of the couple. Marked variations are observed. Whether these statistics mean that occupation is in part responsible for marital happiness or whether marital happiness is primarily a value of the upper and middle classes is uncertain. Whatever the meaning one assigns to the differences, they are striking (see Figure 21–1).

A third to almost a half of the marriages in the occupational groups at the top were rated "unhappy" by friends who knew them well, and only 10 to 15 percent of those at the bottom were rated "unhappy." Lang advanced the theory in explanation that (1) occupational groups that are mobile are less happy and (2) groups over which the community exercises less control are less happy.[21] The latter point reminds one of the comment of an early Greek philosopher, who observed that a man's troubles begin when he is free to do as he pleases. It will be seen that most of the group shown at the top of the chart move about from place to place a

---

[19] Leland J. Axelson, "Personal Adjustment in the Postparental Period," *Marriage and Family Living,* 22:66–68, February, 1960.
[20] Lang in Burgess and Cottrell, *op. cit.*
[21] Burgess and Cottrell, *op. cit.,* pp. 139–143.

FIGURE 21-1 HUSBAND'S OCCUPATION AS A FACTOR IN MARITAL HAPPINESS. Source: Richard O. Lang in Ernest W. Burgess and Leonard S. Cottrell, **Predicting Success or Failure in Marriage** (Copyright 1939, Prentice-Hall, Inc., New York). Reproduced by permission of the publisher.

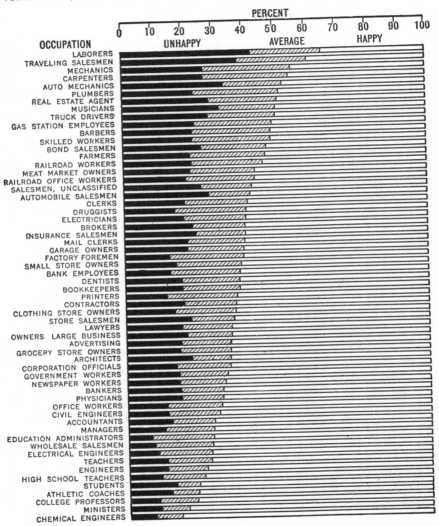

The results of ratings made by friends of 17,533 marriages, in which the husbands were engaged in the occupations listed in this chart, seem to show that professional men have the happiest marriages. Those in the occupations requiring mobility have more unhappy marriages.

great deal in their occupations, and the communities in which they live exercise little control over them. The traveling salesman is the folklore stereotype of the worker who escapes community control.

At the bottom of the chart are occupational groups which require little migration and over which the community exercises strict control— ministers, college and high school teachers, and students and administrators.

Popenoe's study of 3,528 marriages, in broad occupational groups, showed that farm marriages were the happiest of all occupational groups, over two-thirds of them being happy. At the other extreme were the marriages of unskilled laborers, less than half of which (only 42 percent) were happy.[22] Professional groups ranked next to farmers in happy marriages, semiskilled groups ranked next to the bottom, and business groups fell in the middle. The happiness ratings in the study were made by students at the University of California and at Colorado State College of Education. They rated only marriages that they knew well and had lasted five years or more.

Burchinal and Chancellor,[23] studying the duration of marriages in Iowa, found that among those who divorced, the couples having high

Table 21–1   Proportion of Ever-Married White and Nonwhite Men Age 45 to 54 in Stable Marriages, 1960, by Occupation*

Occupation	Proportion in Stable Marriages	
	Nonwhite	White
Professional and technical workers	69.1	84.2
Managers, officials, proprietors	63.2	82.0
Clerical workers	64.6	81.1
Sales workers	64.9	79.8
Craftsmen, foremen	61.2	79.5
Operatives	60.5	78.8
Service workers	54.2	73.6
Laborers	58.6	77.2

* *United States Census of Population, 1960, Marital Status,* Table 7, pp. 96, 99. Note that marriages are more stable for white than nonwhite, and within each racial group, for those in occupations which provide regular income and offer higher status. Source: Jessie Bernard, *loc. cit.*

[22] Paul Popenoe, "Farm Marriages Are the Happiest," *Family Life,* 8:1–2, May, 1947.

[23] Lee G. Burchinal and Loren E. Chancellor, "Survival Rates among Religiously Homogamous and Interreligious Marriage," *Agricultural Experiment Station Research Bulletin 512,* December, 1962.

economic status stayed together longer than did those having low economic status. In general, those of low economic status marry earlier, too. Their study further showed an early dissolution of marriages in which both partners were nineteen or under.

Jessie Bernard,[24] using 1960 census data, measured marriage stability, (defined as men from forty-five to fifty-five in their first marriage living with a wife, not necessarily a first wife—90 percent were the wife's first marriage). Table 21–1 shows that stability of marriage as so defined is lowest for those at the lower end of the scale of occupations and highest for the more stable and better-paid occupations.

The evidence of such studies as the above suggests that finding happiness consists in part of finding an occupation in which people either place a value on happiness and find it as a consequence or in which happiness is more nearly an inherent part of the total life pattern. At least it is quite evident that happiness in family life is related to occupation.

Income and Marriage Stability

Happiness of marriage and its duration are probably related. There is considerable evidence that certainty and regularity of income are favorably related to success in marriage and have been for many years. Burgess and

Table 21–2   Proportion of Ever-Married White and Nonwhite Men Age 45 to 54 in Stable Marriages, 1960, by Income*

| | Proportion in Stable Marriages† | |
Income 1959	Nonwhite	White
No income	38.5	57.9
$1 to $999 or less	49.9	64.8
$1,000 to $2,999	55.6	73.7
$3,000 to $4,999	58.2	78.0
$5,000 to $6,999	62.8	80.5
$7,000 to $9,999	68.0	82.0
$10,000 and over	69.0	84.7
Median income	$3,079	$5,613

* United States Census of Population, 1960, Marital Status, Table 6, pp. 113, 116. Marriage stability increases for both white and nonwhite with increase in income.
Source: Jessie Bernard, loc. cit.
† Stable marriages refer to marriages in which men have been married only once and wife is present. In 90 percent of the cases it was also the wife's first marriage.

[24] "Marital Stability and Patterns of Status Variables," Journal of Marriage and the Family, 28:421–439, November, 1966.

Cottrell, in their classic study of the 1930's, first reported the relationship.[25] Parke and Glick during the 1960's cite[26] the elimination of poverty as one of the two factors which will probably reduce the divorce rate of the future, for they found stability of marriage related to stability and amount of income.

Bernard's 1960 study[27] related income to marriage stability (stability defined as explained above). It will be observed in Table 21-2 that nonwhites and whites alike show greater stability with greater income.

Problem Areas on Which Happiness May Hinge

Certain cultural conceptions have much to do with determining differences, the resolving of which husbands and wives consider essential to their happiness and success in marriage. In order to get some idea of what these basic issues are considered to be, the writer asked over 1,100 women —college girls, wives of college students, and the mothers of these two groups, what the five most important things were in making happy and unhappy marriages.[28] This gave a picture of the views of women through two generations and of both single and married women in the present generation. The answers of these groups were not far different, indicating that the same problems persist and are recognized now, as in the mother generation, and by single as well as by married women. In Table 21-3 are shown the percentages of women who named the items listed as one of the five most important in marriage.[29]

The most striking fact is that economic and financial problems take first place in the opinions of women, both in their list of factors causing happy and unhappy marriages. Separate chapters are devoted to adjustment to money problems of marriage.

The next most important field has to do with fidelity,[30] general sexual compatibility, affection, and love. If one combines these items in the

---

[25] *Op cit.*

[26] Robert Parke, Jr., and Paul C. Glick, "Prospective Changes in Marriage and the Family," *Journal of Marriage and the Family,* 29:249–256, May, 1967.

[27] Jessie Bernard, *loc. cit.*

[28] This was not a checklist. Women wrote in a blank space the items they considered important.

[29] Paul H. Landis, *Two Generations of Rural and Urban Women Appraise Marital Happiness* (Pullman, Wash.: Washington Agricultural Experiment Station, March, 1951), Bulletin No. 506.

[30] In studies by the Institute for Sex Research, one woman in four, or 26 percent, admitted to having relations with another man or other men during their marriages. Usually it was only once, or occasionally, and often was not premeditated. Only 1.2 percent thought they had become pregnant by another man, and of these only 5 in

Table 21–3   Conceptions of Two Generations of Women as to Factors
Producing Marital Happiness and Unhappiness

Factors Producing Unhappiness in Marriage	Percent of 1,138 Women of Two Generations Listing Factor	Factors Producing Happiness in Marriage	Percent of 1,071 Women of Two Generations Listing Factor Marriage
Financial and economic		Lack of financial problems	48.5
problems	51.9	Similar social interests	41.7
Infidelity, unfaithfulness	35.3	Understanding and	
Personality clashes	34.5	consideration	40.5
Vices (drinking gambling)	32.6	Children	40.1
Religious differences		Affection, love, devotion	30.9
(no religion)	28.4	Agreement on religion	24.7
Sexual incompatibility	21.3	Sexual compatibility	18.2
Lack of understanding		Lack of personality clashes	16.5
and consideration	19.3	Confidence and faith	
Different social interests	18.9	(trust)	14.4
Selfishness, wanting		Unselfishness	13.6
own way	16.7	Similar education	
Lack of confidence		and ability	12.7
(jealousy)	16.1	Lack of vices	4.0
Childishness	15.2	Lack of interference	
In-law trouble (relatives		of relatives	3.1
interfering)	14.6	Others	68.6
Differences in education			
and ability	10.6		
Lack of affection	7.2		
Others	59.4		

list, this area of adjustment is mentioned by more women than any other.
Asked to mention the one thing most disastrous to marriage, more women
listed the problem of infidelity than any other. A separate chapter will
be devoted to the area of psychosexual adjustment.

Trouble Areas

A second approach to this question of happiness or misery in marriage is
to study areas of trouble among those actually seeking help. DuBurger

---

32 cases allowed the pregnancy to develop. In most cases, abortions were performed.
See Alfred C. Kinsey and others, *Sexual Behavior in the Human Female* (Philadelphia: W. B. Saunders Co., 1953).

has made a tabulation[31] of "help-request" letters received by the American Association of Marriage Counselors. It will be seen that the affectional aspect of marriage problems is uppermost in the wives' lists, the sexual in the husbands'. (See Table 21–4.) It may well be that they are talking about the same problem viewed from the perspective of female and male subcultures. At least the two areas have some relation. Personality relations are another area of considerable trouble. Money problems do not show up in this study, probably because most couples do not seek financial help from this source.

Alcoholism   The prominence of alcoholism in contemporary society and its disastrous effect on marriage and family life make some understanding of it of more than incidental importance (see Figure 21–2). There are more than five million alcoholics in the United States. In fact, we have one of the highest rates of alcoholism in the world; and alcoholism, and the excessive use of alcohol short of the disease, may well be one of the major problems of marriage adjustment today. For alcoholism is not only a problem in and of itself but also brings with it many concomitant problems: nonsupport, infidelity, abuse, lack of companionship, and loss status.[32]

Alcoholism is basically due to an inadequate psychological constitution, to feelings of inadequacy. Studies of marriage combinations where alcoholism is involved indicate that the wife is not always blameless. In the case of the alcoholic wife, the husband is not always blameless. Research suggests that the wife of the alcoholic husband is often a very difficult person, that there is considerable sense in the expression "she drove him to drink."[33]

There is also evidence that the wife of the alcoholic often gets some kind of deep satisfaction out of his plight. It may be a way of expressing her superiority, or it may be that she gets pleasure in punishing him. Clinicians find that sometimes, even though the alcoholic is cured, the wife is not happy till she creates pressures that make him an alcoholic again. She seems to like his dependence.

One of the tragic effects of alcoholism is on the children. It is particularly likely to build hostilities between the father and the adolescent son.[34]

Joan K. Jackson, psychiatrist, has outlined seven stages in the cumulative pattern of alcoholism. First, there is the stage in which the victim

---

[31] *Op. cit.*

[32] John L. Thomas has stressed such factors in relationship to the problem of alcoholism in the Catholic family. He finds it is not unhappiness that drives the mate to drink. The drinking habit is in itself dangerous for many. See his *The American Catholic Family* (Englewood Cliffs, N.J.: Prentice-Hall, Inc., 1956); see also Albert L. Gordon, *Intermarriage* (Boston: Beacon Press, 1964), Ch. 4.

[33] Marian M. Kalashian, "Working with the Wives of Alcoholics in an Out-Patient Setting," *Marriage and Family Living*, 20:130–133, May, 1959.

[34] *Ibid.*

Table 21–4 Major Problems Revealed by Husbands and Wives in 1,412 Help-Request Letters*

Category	Husband (percent)	Wife (percent)	Total (percent)
Affectional Relations	11.5	31.0	27.6
Spouse cold, unaffectionate			
Spouse is in love with another			
Have no love feelings for spouse			
Spouse is not in love with me			
Spouse attracted to others, flirts			
Excessive, "insane" jealousy			
Sexual Relations	42.1	20.6	24.4
Sexual relations "unsatisfactory"			
Orgasm inability; frigidity, impotence			
Sex deprivation; insufficient coitus			
Spouse wants "unnatural" sex relations			
Role Tasks-Responsibilities	0.0	6.0	4.9
Disagreement over 'who should do what'			
Spouse's failure to meet material needs			
Parental-Role Relations	0.0	1.7	1.4
Conflict on child discipline			
Parent-child conflict			
Intercultural Relations	11.5	11.4	11.4
In-law relations troublesome			
Religion and religious behavior			
Situational Conditions	4.0	3.4	3.5
Financial difficulties, income lack			
Physical illness, spouse or self			
Deviant Behavior	7.5	8.7	8.5
Heavy drinking, alcoholism of mate			
Own heavy drinking or alcoholism			
Spouse's "loose" sex behavior			
Own illicit sex behavior			
Compulsive gambling			
Personality Relations	23.4	17.2	18.3
Spouse domineering, selfish			
Own "poor" personality, instability			
Clash of personalities; incompatible			

Table 21–4 (continued)
  Spouse's violent temper tantrums
  Spouse withdrawn, moody, "neurotic"
  Spouse quarrelsome, bickering, nagging
  Spouse irresponsible, undependable

Total	100.0	100.0	100.0
		$n = 252$	
		$n = 1160$	
		$N = 1412$	

*Chi-square $= 91.80$; $P < .001$ (8 categories $\times$ husband-wife status).

An analysis of letters addressed to the American Association of Marriage Counselors. Source: James E. DuBurger, "Marital Problems, Help-Seeking, and Emotional Orientation as Revealed in Help-Request Letters," *Journal of Marriage and Family Living*, 29:712–721, November, 1967.

denies the disease.[35] After each drinking bout, there is an attempt to define it as normal. The main anxiety at this time is the social risk of drinking behavior. Both husband and wife feel that if it becomes widely known, the status of the family will be threatened. This proves to be of greater anxiety to the wife than to the husband. Normal behavior is rationalized by attempting to compare the husband's behavior with that of friends.

The second stage involves an attempt to eliminate the problem. This is done by becoming more isolated socially as the family becomes consciously more drink-centered. Drinking tends to become the symbol for all the conflicts between the spouses as well as between parents and children. The children are shielded from the father's behavior, and attempts are made to hide it from the employer by lying. Alienation between spouses increases. The more the wife expresses her hostility, the more the husband drinks. Discussions as to what the cause of the problem is and how it can be solved seem to be increasingly unproductive. The wife feels inadequate as a wife, as a mother, and as a woman. She begins to feel that she is inadequate to meet her husband's needs. She tends to devaluate herself. In spite of all the attempts to reorient values, the drinking continues.

The third stage is disorganization. The attempts of the husband to control his drinking are more sporadic or are given up entirely. The wife adopts a fatalistic attitude. The family shows increasing demoralization. It is no longer possible to conceal from the children the father's behavior. The father has pretty much lost his status in the family. The sexual relationship between the spouses has usually been severely disturbed. They resort now to public agencies for support, a procedure which damages

[35] Joan K. Jackson, "The Adjustment of the Family to Alcoholism," *Marriage and Family Living*, 18:361–369, November, 1956.

FIGURE 21–2   THE TYPICAL ALCOHOLIC AS FOUND AMONG PATIENTS OF THE CHICAGO ALCOHOLIC TREATMENT CENTER. Source: **Chicago's Alcoholic Treatment Center News,** 1:2, September, 1964. By permission of Chicago's Alcoholic Treatment Center.

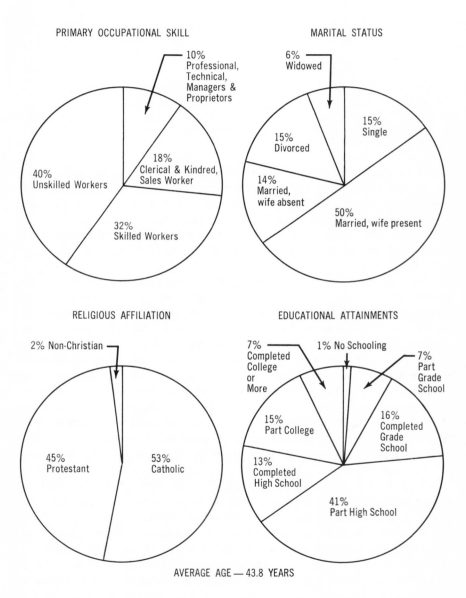

PRIMARY OCCUPATIONAL SKILL

10% Professional, Technical, Managers & Proprietors

18% Clerical & Kindred, Sales Worker

40% Unskilled Workers

32% Skilled Workers

MARITAL STATUS

6% Widowed

15% Single

15% Divorced

14% Married, wife absent

50% Married, wife present

RELIGIOUS AFFILIATION

2% Non-Christian

45% Protestant

53% Catholic

EDUCATIONAL ATTAINMENTS

7% Completed College or More

1% No Schooling

7% Part Grade School

15% Part College

16% Completed Grade School

13% Completed High School

41% Part High School

AVERAGE AGE — 43.8 YEARS

Alcoholism disrupts the lives of all family members and makes for widespread unhappiness.

self-respect. The wife may begin to worry about her sanity and find herself engaging in behavior which is often random and senseless as she becomes more anxious and hostile. She finds that she has deviated widely from her former self and feels that she is no longer "the real me."

Stage four is usually produced by some subsidiary crisis like an accident or arrest. It requires that some decisive action be take if the family is to survive. The wife takes over the husband's role; the husband comes to be ignored and is assigned the status of a delinquent child. The wife begins to recognize her obligations to her children as parallel to her obligations to her husband. As feelings of pity and protectiveness arise, the hostility tends to decrease. The husband's attempts to reenter the family ranks are rebuffed more and more. The wife begins to rationalize the situation so that she no longer has to relate his drinking to herself or to other family members. She assumes control of the family, regains a sense of worth, worries less about her sanity, and begins to plan long-time goals for the family. She may be helped in this by numerous agencies. Her shame decreases. If she happens to contact Alcoholics Anonymous, she gets a new perspective on the drinking problem and therefore loses her sense of shame and comes to see the problem as an illness. She begins to renew extrafamily social contacts among people who are not disturbed by her husband's drinking problem.

Now comes a period of unemployment, imprisonment, or hospitalization. Other women have usually come into the life of the husband. He may not even hesitate to bring them to his own home. Finally the husband recognizes that he needs help with his problem. The family begins to mobilize itself, to try to reinstate him, and to help him get into contact with agencies which may offer a cure. Roles are reshuffled as an attempt at attitude changes is made. Then there follows bitter disappointment if treatment fails.

In stage five comes an effort to escape the problem by separation. This means usually legal separation or divorce for the wife. The husband may accept it passively or resist. In this stage, the family may be threatened by physical violence or actually experience it. The husband may give up drinking for a short time. This action often leaves the wife confused as to what course to pursue. It is hard for her seemingly to desert him in an hour of crisis. She may resort to help from public agencies to ease her conscience or to make it possible for her to live alone.

Stage six brings the reorganization of family life into separate households. The wife must reshuffle her roles, adjust her emotional reactions, work out her feeling of bereavement, and go through the other crises of any divorce action. There is the added problem, however, that the alcoholic may feel that he has to get even with the family for deserting him.

Stage seven is defined as the stage of reorganization of the whole family as a unit if the husband achieves sobriety, with or without separation. Even if there is a complete cure and the restored marriage lasts, there are many role adjustments. The mother has long been accustomed to managing for the family, to assuming the father and manager role, that numerous role adjustments have to be made. There are also the numerous debts and other obligations that have to be met along with current needs. Children may be unable to accept the father in his restored role. They may carry over deep hostilities or distrust. They may refuse to accept his judgment. The wife therefore hesitates to relinquish control in her role as the decision maker. It is very hard for any member of the family to forget the past. The father himself may be more demanding than is justified. He may feel superior because he has overcome his difficulties.

Gradually the memories of the drinking problem fade into the past; its influence remains, however. Whether the wife will be allowed to drink at parties or whether the children will be allowed to drink are problems of unusual significance, for here is a husband who knows that to drink again is to again become a victim. If the husband has been restored through Alcoholics Anonymous, he often throws himself so fully into these activities that he neglects the wife and family. Even though the wife is free from alcoholism within her own family, she is not free from alcoholics, since the husband may keep the house full of men he is helping.

Haberman finds[36] that children of alcoholic parents have many more symptoms of maladjustments than those of a control group of non-alchoholics and a control group of parents with stomach trouble. Of the eight problem symptoms compared, all were more common in children of alcoholic parents; the most difference was found in the area of temper tantrums, fighting with peers, and trouble in school. Children of alcoholic families were also more often known to correctional and school authorities as troublesome.

Gambling   Compulsive gambling is destructive to family life. Like alcoholism, it is considered a disease, and a most difficult one to cure. It, too, has its roots in a disturbed childhood environment and feelings of rejection. The gambler uses money to buy love and borrows money to support his gambling.

Compulsive gambling leads to the neglect of wives and children and, at times, to their support by relatives. It often leads to bankruptcy, yet the compulsive gambler returns to his betting again and again.

It is believed that compulsive gamblers may be as numerous as compulsive drinkers. A "Gambler's Anonymous," patterned after Alco-

[36] Paul W. Haberman, "Childhood Symptoms in Children of Alcoholics and Comparison Group Parents," *Journal of Marriage and Family Living*, 28:152–154, May, 1968.

holics Anonymous, founded some ten years ago, has a following numbering in the thousands.

Drugs   Until recently, our nation has been relatively free of drug addiction. The more frequent use of drugs—for "kicks," for emotional release, and because it is the thing to do in many circles—undoubtedly means that many families of the future will have to reckon with this problem. There are always those who will come to depend on drugs and for whom one drug leads to a more potent one. In time these insecure persons' lives become absorbed in a quest to satisfy the drug hunger to the neglect of their wives and families.

In conclusion, when one considers the differences in values of men and women to be reconciled in marriage, the complexities of the world in which the average couple lives, the intimate and demanding nature of the marriage partnership, and the high ideal of adjustment for which the couple strives today, the record of successful adjustment is surprisingly high. Few business partnerships survive for more than a year or two, and many of them end in great bitterness. Seventy percent of all businesses fail in less than five years. The marriage contract is perhaps still the most successful of all human ventures in terms both of its durability and its realizations. When one adds to all the personal complications the forces that impinge on the marriage from without in the modern world, the survival of so many marriages is almost a miracle.

Problems

1. After interviewing the community's oldest couple on their golden wedding anniversary, the newspaper reported cheerfully asked, "Does all this publicity thrill you? Tell me, are you as happy together today as when you were courting?"

   The old lady snapped back, "Listen young fellow. We're a dozen times happier today than we were when we were young, but it isn't the publicity that makes us so. You'd have to be married fifty years before you could understand just how happy we really are and why!"

   What are some of the things that might account for increasing marital happiness with the passage of time?
2. Betty is neither pretty nor witty. She wanted to marry young but she was almost thirty before someone finally proposed. Now she is determined to make her marriage a success by making it happy.

   Her plan is that Bob's income should take care of their everyday needs. Her own income—for she expects to continue working—she calls the "fun fund." It will provide them with two vacations a year, a new car every second year, a show or theater three evenings a week, and funds for enter-taining every weekend.

Betty feels sure that in their old age they will look back upon an unusually happy marriage. What is the logic of Betty's reasoning? What important factors has she failed to consider?

3. Aside from the actual size of their incomes, compare the way of life of a judge with that of a man who goes from one selling job to another. What circumstances suggest that the judge's family has a greater chance of realizing a happy life? (Consider status in community, self-appraisal, security, leisure time, companions, social controls surrounding each, etc.)

4. American wives are frequently criticized for their "refusal to grow up and grow old gracefully." Is this criticism justified in your opinion? What indications are there of its validity or inaccuracy? If true, does it have a bearing on realizing lasting marriage happiness?

5. Which of the following factors would you consider least important to marriage happiness:
   a. Size of income.
   b. Stability of income.
   c. Vocational adventure.
   d. Health.
   e. Community satisfaction.
   f. Job security.

6. Do the older childless couples of your acquaintance seem:
   a. Less happy?
   b. More happy?
   c. Just as happy as those with families?

7. Most writers in the field of marriage relations argue that conscious effort and planning are more conducive to marriage success than the attitude "If we love one another, we're bound to succeed." Does this mean that couples are more likely to be happy if they make happiness an end in itself and keep this goal constantly in mind?

8. Discuss the statement, "Happiness is the by-product of a productive way of life."

9. Much is written about divorce, separation, and marital discord in our times. Has America finally reached the point where most marriages fail to achieve happiness?

10. A young student in a preparation for marriage course voiced the following opinion, "Couples should probably postpone parenthood for at least five years, for it is only in early marriage that couples may be said to be happy. After they have the responsibility of children, they have to forget about themselves and dedicate their lives to child rearing."

    Do you agree that happiness is bound to fade with the passing years? What does the evidence suggest?

11. How do you explain the fact that stability in occupations is associated with marital happiness?

12. What factors probably account for the apparently high rate of failure and unhappiness among Hollywood marriages?
    a. Instability of income.
    b. Temperament of actors.
    c. Neurosis.
    d. Cultural standards unlike those of United States in general.

    e. Competition to get to the top.

    f. Marriages for publicity only.

    g. Marriage failures are not numerous, just overly publicized.

13. *Sociodrama:* Two young wives discuss the marriage of a mutual acquaintance in such a way as to reveal the grounds upon which a marriage is rated as either happy or unhappy.

14. *Sociodrama:* A mother criticizes her married daughter's decision to postpone parenthood in order to maintain a "happy marriage."

Selected References

Articles in Books of Readings

Cavan, Ruth S., *Marriage and Family in the Modern World: A Book of Readings,* third edition (New York: Thomas Y. Crowell Co., 1969).

    Jackson, Joan K., "Alcoholism and the Family," Reading 44.

    Eliot, Thomas D., "Adjusting to the Death of a Loved One," Reading 46.

Landis, Judson T., and Landis, Mary G., *Readings in Marriage and the Family* (Englewood Cliffs, N. J.: Prentice-Hall, Inc., 1952).

    Straus, Robert, "Excessive Drinking and Its Relationship to Marriage," pp. 313–332.

    Bossard, James H. S., "War and the Family," pp. 323–332.

Sussman, Marvin B., *Sourcebook in Marriage and the Family,* third edition (Boston: Houghton Mifflin Co., 1968).

    Cuber, John F., "Five Kinds of Relationships," Reading 35.

    Vincent, Clark E., "Mental Health and the Family," Reading 53.

Rodman, Hyman, *Marriage, Family and Society* (New York: Random House, 1965).

    Hill, Reuben, and Waller, Willard, "Habit Systems in Married Life," Reading 7.

    Cuber, John F., and Harroff, Peggy B., "The More Total View: Relationships among Men and Women of the Upper Middle Class," Reading 8.

General References

Berardo, Felix M., "Widowhood Status in the United States: Perspective on a Neglected Aspect of the Family Life-Cycle," *The Family Coordinator,* 17:191–203, July, 1968.

Brayshaw, A. Joseph, "Middle-Aged Marriages: Idealism, Realism and the Search for Meaning," *Marriage and Family Living,* 24:358–364, November, 1962.

Day, Barbara Ruth, "Alcoholism and the Family," *Marriage and Family Living,* 23:253–257, August, 1961.

Hatch, David L., and Hatch, Mary G., "An Unhappy Family," *Marriage and Family Living,* 24:213–223, August, 1962.

Jackson, Joan K., "The Adjustment of the Family to Alcoholism," *Marriage and Family Living*, 18:361–369, November, 1956.

Jellinek, E. M., *The Disease Concept of Alcohol* (New Haven: Hillhouse Press, 1960).

Kalashian, Marian M., "Working with the Wives of Alcoholics in an Outpatient Setting," *Marriage and Family Living*, 20:130–133, May, 1959.

Landis, Judson T., "Some Correlates of Divorce and Nondivorce among the Unhappy Married," *Marriage and Family Living*, 25:178–180, May, 1963.

Landis, Judson T., "What Is the Happiest Period of Life?" *School and Society*, 55:643–654, June 6, 1942.

Landis, Paul H., *Two Generations of Rural and Urban Women Appraise Marital Happiness* (Pullman, Wash.: Washington Agricultural Experiment Station, March, 1953), Bulletin No. 506.

Peterson, James A., ed., *Marriage and Family Counseling: Perspective and Prospect* (New York: Association Press, 1968).

Pineo, Peter C., "Disenchantment in the Later Years of Marriage," *Marriage and Family Living*, 23:3–11, February, 1961.

Rosenbaum, Bernice, "Married Women Alcoholics," *Quarterly Journal of Studies on Alcohol*, 19:79–89, March, 1958.

Roth, J., and Peck, R. F., "Class and Mobility Factors Related to Marital Adjustment," *American Sociological Review*, 16:478–487, August, 1951.

Scanzoni, John, "Occupation and Family Differentiation," *The Sociological Quarterly*, 8:187–198, Spring, 1967.

Stephens, William N., *The Family in Cross-Cultural Perspective* (New York: Holt, Rinehart and Winston, 1963).

Whitney, Elizabeth D., *Living with Alcoholism* (Boston: Beacon Press, 1968).

22

Sexual Adjustment

The physical ability to separate coitus from procreation is an attainable goal. For most elements of the population, the moral right to do so has been won. These victories in and of themselves have few parallels in man's forward march in controlling his economic and social destiny. But helpful as they may be, they do not settle for the individual couple their own interpersonal relationships in the biological or emotional areas of sex.

Letters to the American Association of Marriage Counselors seeking help were heavily concentrated in the area of sexual problems, as we have seen (Chapter 21).[1]

Continuity of the Sexual Bond

In nature, sexual adjustment is not a problem. Generally, there is no continuity of relationship between mates, although there are exceptions. Some birds and a few animals pair for life. In general, animals do not. Even those birds which mate for life, like geese, confine their sex life to the rhythm of the biological season. Their interest in the opposite sex is momentary, when nature calls for sexual expression. Beyond that, the male's responsibility usually ceases, and the female's maternal instincts take over the problem of nurturing the young.

It is not so with human beings. Society demands a continuity in the relationship between male and female that is institutionalized everywhere in the world in some form of marriage-family relationship, as are social

[1] James E. DuBurger, "Marital Problems, Help-Seeking, and Emotional Orientation as Revealed in Help-Request Letters," *Journal of Marriage and Family Living,* 29:717, November, 1967.

pressures for providing this continuity and numerous rules for terminating the pair relationship. Not all pairings of mates can last, but the assumption of all societies is that in adulthood there will be a continuity in the male-female relationship. This is usually a paired relationship, although it may involve multiple mates. Whatever the sanctioned relationship, it is certainly far more than a sexual relationship. In fact, the sexual relationship is made subservient to economic and status relationships. It is also made subservient to the marriage rules of the culture and its sex taboos. The institutional aspects of the man-woman relationships are so elaborate in all cultures that the sexual aspects become a relatively incidental matter. For man, sex is not merely a biological fact; it is one of the most significant sociological, psychological, and emotional facts of existence. Culture makes sex more than a biological act. For man, there is no such thing as mating without emotional connotations.

One of the unique facts about the human biological mechanism is that both male and female seem to be without a conspicuous seasonal period such as one finds throughout animal life, where the coming into heat of the female, or of rut in the male, causes each to aggressively seek to copulate. There is no specific period of rut in the human male, and there is serious doubt whether there is a period of heat in the human female. (Evidence pro and con is presented in a later paragraph.) The sex act is primarily a factor of social, psychological, and emotional rather than biological motivation. This is the basis for a continuing sexual relationship between male and female, a relationship which need not and does not in most of its functioning have any relationship to procreation at all. After a woman comes to share bed and board, the provider expects to have sexual access, subject to whatever codes and taboos exist in the culture. By virtue of customary regulations of the marriage system, it is assumed that the husband has this right as part of his bargain to support a family. The wife must therefore give his needs priority over her own feelings.

The male is capable of copulating with an unaroused and even un-interested female. In some marriages the sex act is performed without the female's interest. Its timing is determined primarily by the male's readiness, as is its consummation by the male's period of response. This pattern is not found elsewhere in nature but is established in the adjustment of the human male and female in the institution of marriage, where romantic love, economic motives, mutal aid, and many other such values become blended with sexual drives into a highly complex system of motivations.

The human female's accessibility in marriage is to quite an extent a matter of logic rather than desire. In marriage, coitus is expected and customarily sanctioned. The husband, though his desires are not periodic, does have regular sexual needs because of the build-up of semen in the glands. Only as he is taught to go through the courting period, to be considerate of the female's feelings, to recognize that her arousal is a part of his obligation, does he sense any need to regard her feelings in the matter at all.

In our culture, where the wife is not only mother but mistress, she is given few of the customary protections by which she may be relieved temporarily from the sexual advances of her husband. Many cultures, both historic and present, taboo intercourse during pregnancy, during menstruation, and when she is nursing her young—with primitives this may be two or more years—and some taboo it during periods of activities demanding the concentrated expenditure of male energy—in periods of battle, when the hunt is on, when fish are to be caught, when artistic products are to be made, when praying needs to be done.

If the female is taught by the culture to be sexually passive, her rewards are not considered important. It is enough that she have children. If she is taught to be assertive, then the male's courting gestures, his ability to arouse and inspire and finally to satisfy, put him to a sexual test. It is under this type of marriage philosophy that the concept of sexual adjustment has become a serious consideration. Such it is in the United States today.

No Estrus Phase in the Human Female

The period of heat is marked in apes[2] and in baboons[3] by swelling of the vaginal area and by changes in behavior. In the wild baboon troop, the female in estrus seeks out males of her choice to satisfy her desire, beginning usually with one of lower status and working up in status until her needs have been fully met.

Research among both single and married women fails to show any of the psychological characteristics of an estrus period. That there is a rise in body temperature of a fraction of a point near the time of ovulation (most often falling between the eleventh and fourteenth day from the beginning of menstruation, see Chapter 26) is a well-established biological fact. Benedek finds endocrine and dream reactions at ovulation that give some evidence of an estrus period.[4] But if this is a physiological estrus, overt behavior does not betray it.

Most research shows a slight shift in intensity of sex desire at certain

---

[2] R. M. Yerkes and J. H. Elder, "Estrus Receptivity and Mating in the Chimpanzee," *Comparative Psychology Monographs*, 1–39; also J. H. Elder and R. M. Yerkes, "The Sexual Cycle of the Chimpanzee," *Anatomical Record*, 67:119–143, 1936.

[3] Sherwood Washburn, Professor of Anthropology at the University of California, in address at Washington State University, Spring, 1959.

[4] Therese Benedek, "Psychosexual Functions in Women," in her *Studies in Psychosomatic Medicine* (New York: The Ronald Press Co., 1952).

times of the month, but in any particular study the rise in the curve is slight, and the research of different workers with different groups leaves the whole matter open to question. It is likely that slight statistical differences at different periods in the month are social rather than biological. Research suggests that the time of greatest desire is just before or immediately after menstruation, the least likely times for pregnancy to occur.

Landis,[5] studying a sample of 181 college girls, found that more report increased sexual desire directly before menstruation than at any other time. The second peak is after menstruation. Terman[6] has found that half of the married women who reported on periods of greater desire placed them either just before or just after menstruation, with about twice as many after as before. Hamilton[7] reported that 81 percent of women he studied recognized greater sexual desire just after menstruation. Davis' study[8] of 868 single women found their period of greatest sexual interest preceding menstruation.

None of the data show an increase in sexual desire at the time of ovulation, as might logically be expected if nature provides an estrus in the human female. As we have seen, Margaret Mead, from her knowledge of numerous cultures, many of them permitting premarital sexual experience, concludes that prior to marriage the female controls the timing of the sex act, after marriage, the male.[9] This change would not take place if it were regulated by nature, as in the case of animals, where the female is approachable only in times of heat,[10] or as in the case of those animals among which the male is potent only seasonally. Nonbiological factors are operative.

It appears that sexual desire among modern women is largely a function of the psychological climate produced by contact with the male, both before and after marriage. In marriage, frequency of the male's demands may well determine whether the wife has any desire at all, other than as aroused by her sexual partner. If she has, in most instances it will likely be after menstruation, since with most young couples this is the longest period of abstinence. This being the period of estrogen pickup, many have renewed energy, which may also be a factor. Others who suffer

[5] Judson T. Landis, "Physical and Mental-Emotional Changes Accompanying the Menstrual Cycle," *Research Studies of the State College of Washington*, 25:155–167, June, 1957, p. 160.

[6] Lewis M. Terman, *Psychological Factors in Marital Happiness* (New York: McGraw-Hill Book Co., 1938), p. 351.

[7] G. V. Hamilton, *A Research in Marriage* (New York: A. & C. Boni, Inc., 1929).

[8] Katherine B. Davis, *Factors in the Sex Life of Twenty-two Hundred Women* (New York: Harper & Bros., 1929).

[9] Margaret Mead, *Male and Female* (New York: Mentor Books, 1955), pp. 156–160.

[10] Yerkes and Elder, *op. cit.*

considerable discomfort and depression prior to menstruation may well seek the comfort and loving which sex involves, not from physical desire as such but for the secondary reasons which are most important at this time.[11] There is, however, a pickup in energy due to an increased metabolic rate just before menstruation, which is undoubtedly a factor. Finally, pre-menstrual desire may be in part a rational and planned matter. The wife, knowing that a period of continence lies ahead, if she enjoys the sexual re-lationship, is interested in intercourse as a means of abbreviating the time until the menstrual flow is over and the rhythm of sex can begin again. Her awareness of her husband's needs may also be a factor in her en-couraging his advances and courting; or he may, if he is aware of the coming period of continence, be more aggressive than usual, stimulating both her interest and his own. Thus part of the peak of sexual interest prior to menstruation may be like "banking" sex until the period of de-privation is past.[12]

This kind of speculation illustrates how complicated by conscious, psychological, and biological factors the human sex urge is and how far it can be removed from a rhythm of nature, if such exists.

The highly socialized character of the sexual experience, its romantic connotations in our culture, and its diversity of meaning in the interactions of individuated men and women have apparently largely romoved it, for the female, from the level of physical desire and made it secondary to the whole area of sociality and of generalized feeling. The lack of an estrus period in the female and a period of rut in the human male and his frequent readiness are undoubtedly important factors in this trend of the psychosexual orientation of the female.

Sexual Adjustment as a Goal

Every society faces the problem of resolving the strain involved in the different biological natures and sexual proclivities of male and female. Many societies have solved the problem by denying female sexuality and leaving not only initiative but satisfaction to the male alone. Polygynous societies, in their favored classes, try to balance male sexual needs with

[11] Judson T. Landis, *op. cit.,* suggests this as a likely reason for premenstrual sex desire.

[12] Many years ago, Carl G. Hartman commented on many phases of the sex desire cycle in his book, *The Time Ovulation Cycle in Women* (Baltimore: The Williams & Wilkin Co., 1936).

those of the female by providing sufficient wives so that when one is incapacitated by sickness, pregnancy, or childbirth, another will be accessible. The mistress system, where sanctioned by custom, permits a similar male outlet, as does concubinage. The monogamous systems of the world have historically sanctioned prostitution as a device for balancing out the male's greater needs for sexual expression.

In polygynous societies, males complain of too many demands from their wives, as each tries to tempt the husband to her bed.[13] In monogamous societies, generally it is the male who is perpetually unsatisfied because of deprivation or because of the monotony of one wife.

The romantic marriage in America has perhaps put a greater strain on both men and women in sexual adjustment than has any other system. The wife plays the role of both mistress and wife, attempting to meet the husband's sexual needs fully. The pledge of romantic loyalty compels the husband to confine his advances to the marriage bed. This means that he must make adjustments to incapacities of the wife and deny himself sexual expression at times for the sake of the romantic bond.

The Meaning of Sexual Adjustment

Sexual adjustment is not synonymous with equality of their sexual desire or frequency of the orgasmic response. Neither does the concept of sexual adjustment involve the regular subordination of one mate's interests to those of the other. Adjustment is a matter of the satisfaction of both. One couple may be spoken of as sexually better adjusted than another. The difference between them is not a matter of frequency or intensity of the sex act but of the differing degrees to which each couple obtains satisfaction and happiness from whatever relationship they have. Complete satisfaction comes from the unrestrained sharing of these moments of greatest marital intimacy.

This does not mean, however, that both partners must experience similar responses to the sex act. For the male, intercourse brings orgasm and accompanying tension release; for the wife it may bring no physical climax at all but only a feeling of being loved and needed. As long as each partner is satisfied with what he or she obtains from the act, their adjustment may be said to be a good one.

When there are marked differences in the desire of the two mates,

[13] Mead, *op. cit.*, p. 161.

adjustment is difficult. Whether they want intercourse only once a month or several times a day is not the point. The significant consideration is whether the frequency of desire in one mate is compatible with the desire of the other or whether a mutually acceptable compromise can be worked out.

The desire of the husband—particularly in the early years of marriage—tends to exceed that of the average wife. Good adjustment generally requires that each make some concessions to the needs of the other. The husband withholds his advances when the wife seems genuinely uninterested. The wife must occasionally participate when she does not really desire satisfaction herself.

Equality of orgasmic response seems to have even less bearing on sexual adjustment, providing both mates accept the difference as a relatively unimportant one. Males experience an orgasm as an inherent part of semen discharge. Wives vary greatly, but it has been found that in the average marriage considerably less than half of the women can expect always to have an orgasm, and during the early months of marriage as many as half of wives experience few if any orgasmic responses at all.

Today the wife should, and usually does, expect satisfaction in the sexual relationship. Unless she has been hemmed in by taboos and irrational fears in her sex education, she is in most instances capable of as deep a physical and emotional satisfaction in coitus as is her husband, although frequently these reactions are of a different kind. All modern scientific study shows that the sexual relationship is normal and beneficial alike to both male and female.[14]

Healthy Sex Attitudes

Inability to perform or respond sexually is in most cases psychological rather than physical. Much literature and clinical experience favor this point of view. This concept brings up the important problems of acquired attitudes as fundamental factors in conditioning.

Current conceptions of sex are varied, even within the confines of an average American community. To a few sex is sin; to others it is an activity to be indulged in for procreation only. To some its primary purpose is pleasure. For still others it represents the highest form of human

---

[14] Marie Stopes, *Married Love,* published in Britain in 1918, first declared woman's right to sensuous enjoyment in the sex act of marriage. The book was long banned in the United States, but has to date sold more than a million copies.

sharing. Even in marriage, sex can mean different things at different times, depending on the total relationship of the pair. Instead of being an experience in sharing and affectional expression, it may turn out to be an experience in male conquest, domination, or exploitation.

There has been a great deal of speculation on the degree to which a child's early conditioning affects his later capacity to give affection and to respond to sexual stimuli. Freudian-oriented literature assumes that the child's relationship with the parent of the opposite sex has decided influence on psychosexual development. More likely it is the total family pattern which conditions one's attitude toward members of his own sex, toward the opposite sex, and to marriage, rather than one's particular relationship with a member of the opposite sex within the family. This total influence is so complex that simple generalizations regarding a unilateral factor in determining psychosexual development are likely to lead to more error than insight. Of this much we can be sure—fundamental attitudes as well as actual behavior patterns basic to a development of the capacity for affection are learned in the family and have much to do with a person's psychosexual development. This point was stressed in Chapter 9 and need not be dwelt on at length here.

Tenderness, ability to show affection, and responsiveness are developed in the child by his relationship with the parent. In loving a responsive parent, the child develops a capacity to love others. With expanding contacts, the child develops ability to show affection to others as others show affection to him. In normal development, the mother and other love objects recede into the background as heterosexual love emerges.

The child born in a home without affection is likely to develop without any real capacity for it or any means for expressing it. If he has constantly been rebuffed by his mother and rarely shown affection, he keeps what feelings he has to himself and rarely can relax in the presence of affection. By such a simple process of conditioning, the capacity to love is limited. The child's relationship with the parents is therefore the critical experience in the development of capacity to give and respond to affection in later years.

The attitudes expressed in a child's home are also important in determining his later adjustment in marriage. Even in families where affection and warmth are openly exhibited, sex itself often remains an unmentionable subject, surrounded with mysteries that are suggestive of sin and immorality. It is not enough to shield a child from undersirable or frigthening sexual experiences. To assure him of healthy attitudes some positive sex education is necessary. Complete silence is not really neutral. To a child's inquiring mind, this is influence in a negative direction.

Thus, it is not uncommon for a young person (usually the girl) from an otherwise conscientious home to enter marriage with fears and misgivings about the sexual side of the relationship. Such fears are not easily overcome. While such fears are probably not so common today as in our earlier folk culture, it is true that marriage ceremonies do not have the magic power to redraw mental pictures and attitudes concerning sex which have been built up during childhood and adolescence. The marriage ceremony removes only the legal and moral restrictions.

Below is a listing of some of the most common attitudes that are conducive or detrimental to sound and early sexual adjustment in marriage.

Attitudes Conducive to Sexual Adjustment
Early in Marriage

1. Coitus is a normal, right, and re-creative experience as well as a creative experience.
2. Both husband and wife are capable of sexual gratification.
3. Both husband and wife should be considerate, sympathetic, and patient in sexual relations.
4. Sexual expression is usually a more direct urge in the male, and while he can cultivate some sublimative arts, the male is not to be criticized for his greater preoccupation with coitus as a purely physical act.
5. Consistent with physical well-being and mutual interest, there are no restrictions that need be placed upon the sexual expressions of a couple, either upon the method, frequency, intensity, or duration of expression throughout the couple's lifetime.
6. Coitus can serve different functions at different times. It can be for pleasure, for comfort, to express love, for relief from tension, for the serious intent of having children, or for rejuvenating a tired body or spirit. It is the closest form of human sharing.

Attitudes Detrimental to Sexual Adjustment
Early in Marriage

1. When a husband really loves his wife, pleasant conversation and intimacy become much more satisfying to him than coitus.
2. Men are like animals in that coitus can never acquire any spiritual meaning for them.
3. Women can never get the pleasure from coitus that men do; they should accept it, therefore, simply as one of their duties as wives.
4. Nice girls, because of their higher values and ideals, do not lose themselves in sexual play; they remain patient and reserved and do not show a great interest in the matter.

5. Only a very vulgar or degenerate man is pleased by experimentation in sex play outside the common pattern.
6. Sexual intercourse is inevitable in marriage, but talking about it before or after is bound to be embarrassing and detracts from its spiritual quality.
7. In a marriage between modern, enlightened people, the wife who cannot equal her husband in desire or response should consider psychiatric or medical attention, for she must be either physically or emotionally defective.
8. It is a husband's duty to woo his wife from reluctance to eager anticipation before each sex act. The husband who does not or cannot accomplish this, who sometimes becomes impatient, is inadequate and failing in his function, for no wife can become interested otherwise.
9. Coitus is a private affair. To seek outside help, to get books from the library on the subject, or to talk about what's wrong with one's mate is an admission of failure.
10. Once a man has saddled his wife with a house and children he has no right to complain if she loses her interest in coitus.

Variety in the Monogamous Marriage

The sexual relationship of the happily married couple can represent one of the most creative and distinctively individualistic and rejuvenating aspects of their life together. In most instances, the husband is the aggressor. Yet many couples find mutual satisfaction in the wife's occasionally reversing the roles. This is but one of the many variations they develop to add to the freshness and adventure of their sex life.

Frequency of coitus, positions during sexual intercourse, the amount and nature of the foreplay, and the degree to which the couple speak of the relationship varies from time to time. Levy and Munroe, psychiatrists, suggest the variety of uninhibited married sex life:

Study of the sex activity of relatively uninhibited happily married couples demonstrates very beautifully both the unorthodox nature of their impulses and the ease with which they are integrated into a "normal" heterosexual pattern. Sometimes the pair will be close and affectionate. Tenderness will pass into a rather solemn passion, a confirmation of their abiding love for each other. At other times their mood will be wholly frivolous. Intercourse then will be just a rattling good time without deeper implications. Or the husband will seek protection and cuddling at his wife's breast. Or he will lie like a girl while she takes possession of his body. At times he will vulgarize the act with smutty words or take a fine pleasure in hurting his wife and forcing her to his will. Or the couple may play at an illicit relationship, acting out a little seduction farce for their own benefit. They will try out odd positions and experiment with unusual parts of the body. Often, too, intercourse will be a routine satisfaction of a bodily need about as romantic as orange juice, toast, and coffee for breakfast. Our uninhibited happily married couples will take all of these variations and find them good.[15]

The limits within which variations should be practiced are few and simple. They should bring neither physical nor emotional harm to either mate. They should be indulged in only by mutual inclination, for atypical behavior can bring disastrous consequences if not understood or appreciated as normal and legitimate by the mate.

This does not mean that the couple must share similar views of this matter from the outset. Very few do. It is important, however, that the individual who initiates a typical behavior does so only gradually and with utmost care in observing responses. In this, as in all sexual development, the male usually is the teacher.

Frigidity

Too little understood but much talked about are frigidity in the female and impotence in the male. A woman is not frigid simply because she may not experience an orgasm in sexual relationships or does so only on rare occasions. If she is capable of affection and of sharing the sexual relationship without a feeling that it is obnoxious and repulsive, she is not frigid. Frigidity rightly refers only to those few cases in which the psychological and emotional block is such that she cannot accept the sexual relationship and its affectional expressions. Such feelings of repulsion are due to deep-seated psychological problems, sometimes to tragedy, shock, or faulty upbringing, and are problems for mental therapy. Many happily married women rarely or never have an orgasm.

Impotence in the male likewise is a condition of emotional blocks which make it impossible for him to participate in the sex act. In cases where it exists, it is rooted in the emotions and can be cured only by psychological therapy. Seldom is it biological in origin. Freud[16] described it as the ailment the practicing psychiatrist was most often called upon to treat. He spoke of psychological impotence as "the most prevalent form of degradation of erotic life." He says further,

[15] John Levy and Ruth Munroe, The Happy Family (New York: Alfred A. Knopf, Inc., 1941), p. 129.
[16] Sigmund Freud, "The Most Prevalent Form of Degradation in Erotic Life," No. 10 in The Anatomy of Love, A. M. Krich (ed.) (New York: Dell Publishing Co., 1960).

This strange disorder affects men of a strongly libidinous nature, and is manifest by a refusal on the part of the sexual organs to execute the sexual act, although both before and after the attempt they can show themselves intact and competent to do so, and although a strong mental inclination to carry out the act is present.

It often applies to only certain sexual objects or to certain women.

Fear is sometimes a predisposing condition, needless fear. For example, many males worry about the size of the penis or if it is not straight when in erection, about its difference from other males' in these respects. These are matters in which there is great individual variation, and they have no bearing on the ability of the male to satisfy a mate, any more than does the size of the vagina have a bearing on satisfaction of the male.

Female aggression is an increasing factor in male impotency, as viewed by practicing psychiatrists and counselors.

Homosexuality

Homosexual tendencies represent a common type of sexual abnormality and in some instances affect marriage relationships. It is fairly well established that such tendencies are not inborn but are due to conditioning. Just as man is born to hunger but without any definite notion as to what is fit to eat, so he is born with sex drives. His social experience tells him how they can be satisfied.

Some cultures have elevated homosexual experience to a position far above the heterosexual. The Greeks in the period of their historic glory did so, considering marriage a practical child-rearing arrangement but homosexual love the true romantic love. Women in the Isle of Lesbos, which lies between Greece and Turkey, elevated love between women to the supreme level. This is the origin of our word *lesbian* for female homosexuals. Our culture abhors homosexual behavior and condemns it both by law and custom. The most effective approach to the cure of homosexual tendencies is through some form of psychological therapy.

Confirmed homosexuals usually do not marry, some even fearing to test their sexual adequacy with members of the opposite sex. But many married males do seek homosexual outlets during periods of separation from their wives for long periods of time, as in the military and in prison. They also seek outlets for variety and for other personal reasons. A serious problem here, in addition to the break that homosexual activity may cause if the wife should learn of it, is that it can lead to public disgrace of the family, to the man's loss of position, or to his being blackmailed.

The homosexual wife's problem is not likely to lead to public exposure or blackmail, for it is of less social concern. It will more likely express itself in denying coitus to the husband and in forming close ties with another woman or women to the neglect of the marriage affectional bond.

Sexual Fidelity

Few cultures have confined sexual relations strictly to marriage: prostitution, the mistress system, secret liaisons, and special occasions like festivals and initiation rites allow the satisfaction of erotic interests without attachment of family liability.[17] Concubinage is also a supplement to the marriage, but it adds part of the responsibilities of marriage, in that the male supports the wife and children on a permanent basis.

Infidelity is seldom found to accompany happiness or adequate sexual adjustment in our romantic marriage. The crucial question is, however, which of the two comes first and tends more frequently to cause the other? It is easy to understand how one who discovers infidelity in his or her mate is likely to feel bitter and unloved and thus to lose whatever pleasure he or she might have found in coitus. Thus infidelity might logically be said to cause sexual maladjustment. On the other hand, the husband or wife who charges that the mate's infidelity has ruined his marriage may be ignoring an important fact—the mate may have been unhappy with the marriage before an illicit affair could appeal.

Since the law forbids but usually ignores adultery, and does not attempt to control extramarital relations except where it makes them grounds for divorce, in this as in most other areas of marital adjustment, the crucial consideration is not an arbitrary rule but an analysis of how the mates involved view the infidelity. In some marriages, a husband's obligations are considered to center around providing and caring for his wife and family. Companionship, love, and faithfulness, while desirable, are not considered the crucial demands of marriage. At the other extreme, unfaithfulness may be taken lightly because marriage itself is taken lightly. There are even a

[17] Bernard Farber, *Family: Organization and Interaction* (San Francisco: Chandler Publishing Co., 1964), pp. 91–96.

few happily married couples who consider extramarital relations of no importance to the marriage itself.

The marriage vows, which most take seriously, reflect the traditional American view that when two individuals marry it is for better or for worse and for a lifetime. Sexual fidelity is considered not only desirable but obligatory. One does not run out on a mate because of financial problems, sickness, or disability; neither does one break his vow because of disappointment over their sexual life together. The relationship is assumed to be a binding one and the interests of the family are considered to far outweigh those of the individual.[18]

Many of these traditional views are justified on religious grounds as well as personal ones, and the general welfare of society lends additional argument to their continuance. Where the individual family rather than any other institutional agency is held responsible for the care and upbringing of children, there is considerable logic in the widespread rejection of extramarital relations. A more stable family and consequently a more stable society are thought to result from the expectations and demands for fidelity placed upon both husbands and wives. Husbands like to feel that the children they support are their own. This may be the basic reason that adultery is so widely forbidden in human society.

The Kinsey research group found that of people studied, approximately 26 percent of women and half the men had had extramarital sexual relations. Forty-one percent of the sexually unfaithful wives had had sexual experience with only one partner.[19] For almost a third of those who were unfaithful, the act of unfaithfulness had occurred only a few times, often only once. This experience was for many unpremeditated.

The attitude of the younger generation toward extramarital intercourse under special circumstances seems to be more or less one of toleration. A study of the attitudes of 223 engaged men and 215 engaged women toward extramarital relationships showed that approximately half of both men and women would justify extramarital relationships for both men and women under certain circumstances.[20] Women were less tolerant toward infidelity for women than were men.

Over half the men would justify it in case of frigidity in the wife. A fourth of women would justify it in case of their unsatisfactory response

---

[18] A worldwide survey of 250 societies found that in only five (2 percent) are adulterous relationships sanctioned; see George P. Murdock, "Sexual Behavior: What Is Acceptable?" *Journal of Social Hygiene*, 36:1–31, 1950.

[19] Alfred C. Kinsey and others, *Sexual Behavior in the Human Female* (Philadelphia: W. B. Saunders Co., 1953). Because of the nature of the Kinsey sample, incidence of infidelity reported is probably higher than average.

[20] Ernest W. Burgess and Paul Wallin, *Engagement and Marriage* (Philadelphia: J. B. Lippincott Co., 1953), pp. 400–402.

from the husband. Twenty percent of men and 16 percent of women would justify it in cases of general dissatisfaction with the spouse. Twenty-three percent of women and 18 percent of men would justify it in case of strong attraction for another person. Almost half thought it would be justified in case of repeated unfaithfulness of the spouse.

The romantic marriage is based on sexual loyalty. It is interesting to observe that most of the reasons recognized as adequate for unfaithfulness are those which indicate that mutual sexual responsiveness is not present in the marriage.

A *Time*–Louis Harris poll reports[21] a striking increase in marital infidelity during the years 1964 to 1969, with the changing moral standard being most pronounced among the upper-socioeconomic, upper-educated, suburban population and among young people under thirty. Conventional standards are still strong among the lower-income, less well-educated population, particularly those who live in small towns. He thus finds two American attitudes in regard to moral standards.

In cases of marital infidelity where there has been public exposure, one of the difficulties in restoring confidence between mates is that the offended party feels disgraced in the eyes of the community. He is made to feel that he is doing less than his duty (more often her duty) if the spouse's offense is tolerated. If tolerated, it may also require tolerating the lying and deception that is used to cover it up. In many circles, it is more or less expected that the innocent spouse divorce the disloyal one, thus exacting the ultimate penalty.

From the standpoint of reconciliation of the pair, it may be important to analyze reasons for the adultery. Was it momentary sex hunger during a period of absence? Was it a means of defying the mate? Was it an escape from some frustration or defeat? Was it venturing in quest of variety? Does the offending person still love the mate and wish to continue the marriage?

Often the husband and wife themselves do not know the answer to these questions. By visiting a marriage counselor or psychiatrist or by discussing the problem with a person who approaches the situation not as one of guilt, but as one in human relationships, they may be able to maintain a marriage relationship which is vital to both and to their children.

Problems

1. Helen and Tom are the pride of their community—happy and very much in love after six years of marriage. Tom is called the perfect husband—

[21] Changing Morality: The Two Americas," *Time*, June 6, 1969, pp. 26–27.

thoughtful, considerate, and proud of his wife. And who could want a better wife than Helen? She is pretty, efficient, and devoted. Only her closest friends know that sexual relations have never given her pleasure, and they admire her for never having hurt Tom by mentioning this fact. What would you say about Helen?

 a. She has shown more realism in her sexual expectations than most women.

 b. She is reasonable and has therefore made a satisfactory sexual adjustment.

 c. She has cheated herself and her husband by not telling him of her problem.

 d. Her sexual life could probably be improved.

2. What relationship do you believe exists between a happy marriage and sexual adjustment? Would you say that happiness in marriage:

 a. Is the result of satisfactory sexual adjustment?

 b. Produces satisfactory sexual adjustment?

 c. Is not closely related to satisfactory sexual adjustment?

 d. Is neither cause nor effect but is generally associated with satisfactory sexual adjustment?

 e. Is primarily a matter of attitude rather than of physical satisfaction as such?

3. In a popular book which promises to teach its readers *How to Achieve Sex Happiness in Marriage*, approximately three-fourths of the writing is devoted to discussions of techniques in sex. About one-fourth of it is devoted to helping the reader form healthy general attitudes toward sex in marriage. In your opinion, which of the two areas, technique or attitudes, is responsible for most of the problems that trouble sexually unadjusted couples?

4. In almost every American city one may see motion picture theaters crowded with men who enjoy the sexually suggestive skits and jokes and the seminude female performers. Are these audience made up mostly of:

 a. Sexually abnormal men?

 b. Sexually immature men?

 c. Sex-starved men?

 d. Men who are probably normal?

Upon what grounds do you base your opinion?

5. A happily married woman who feels that the sexual adjustment she and her husband have made is a good one suddenly notices her husband reading books on sex techniques. Later he begins to initiate certain new and somewhat unconventional sexual practices into their relationship. In your opinion should she:

 a. Talk about it with a psychiatrist?

 b. Let her husband know she is worried about him?

 c. Read the books with her husband?

 d. Reexamine his background for a hint of some sexual abnormality?

 e. Accept his behavior as natural?

6. For what specific reasons is sexual fidelity generally considered basic to sexual adjustment?

7. Are there any circumstances under which you consider sexual infidelity justifiable in a happy marriage?

8. *Sociodrama:* Two mothers discuss the attitudes toward sex their fifteen-year-old daughters are learning from their high school course in preparation for marriage. One mother favors the course; the other is shocked by it.
9. What do you know about the nature and extent of homosexuality? As a class, or through a committee, study this problem in America today. Discuss it along the following lines:
    a. What are believed to be its causes?
    b. Is there a cure?
    c. What is our legal and social treatment for the homosexual?
    d. Is a slight homosexual tendency dangerous?
    e. What better program and/or attitude might be adopted with reference to homosexuals?
10. In your opinion, if a couple begins to talk together and joke about their sexual relations, are they apt to detract from its spiritual quality and reduce it to a mere physical act?

Selected References

Articles in Books of Readings

Coser, Rose Laub, *The Family: Its Structure and Functions* (New York: St Martin's Press, Inc., 1964).
    Foote, Nelson N., "Sex as Play," pp. 184–191.
Vincent, Clark E., *Readings in Marriage Counseling* (New York: Thomas Y. Crowell Co., 1957).
    Stokes, Walter R., "A Marriage Counseling Case: The Married Virgin," pp. 256–270.
    Ellis, Albert, "Marriage Counseling with Couples Indicating Sexual Incompatibility," pp. 270–279.
    Stone, Abraham, and Levine, Lena, "Group Therapy in Sexual Maladjustment," pp. 342–355.

General References

Deutsch, Ronald M., *The Key to Feminine Response in Marriage* (New York: Random House, Inc., 1968).
Kinsey, Alfred C., and others, *Sexual Behavior of the Human Female* (Philadelphia: W. B. Saunders Co., 1953).
Landis, Judson T., Poffenberger, Thomas, and Poffenberger, Shirley, "The Effect of First Pregnancy Upon the Sexual Adjustment of 212 Couples," *American Sociological Review*, 15:767 ff., December, 1950.
Money, John, *Sex Research—New Developments* (New York: Holt, Rinehart and Winston, 1965).
Levine, Lena, and Gilman, Mildred, *The Doctor Tells the Bride and Groom*, revised edition (New York: Planned Parenthood Federation of America, 1953).

Levine, Lena, and Gilman, Mildred, *Frigidity* (New York: Planned Parenthood Federation of America, 1952).

Mead, Margaret, *Male and Female* (New York: William Morrow & Co., Inc., 1949), Ch. 14.

Murdock, George P., "Sexual Behavior: What Is Acceptable?", *Journal of Social Hygiene*, 36:1–31, 1950.

Novak, Emil, *The Woman Asks the Doctor* (Baltimore: The Williams & Wilkins Co., 1944).

Stone, Abraham, M.D., and Levine, Lena, "Group Therapy in Sexual Maladjustment," Reprint of the Marriage Counseling Service of the Margaret Sanger Research Bureau, New York.

Stone, Abraham, M.D., Levine, Lena, and Stone, Hanna H., M.D., *A Marriage Manual*, revised (New York: Simon & Schuster, Inc., 1968).

23

Sex Expectations

Knowing what to expect of sex in marriage can do much to help young people over the first difficult hurdles in their life together. For some, expectations need to be toned down—movies, fiction, and campus "bull sessions" have led them to expect more than the average marriage is capable of giving. For others, expectations need to be raised—they expect so little or fear so much that they are bound to relegate sex to a negative position or one of insignificance. There are even those who hope for a sexless marriage. For a large number of young people, however, what is needed most is simply some facts—facts that will help them develop a realistic pattern of sexual relations, facts that will encourage them, reassure them, and guide them and inform them of what they can expect in the all-important partnership they hope to enter.

Although our culture is one in which sex is more talked about, and used more extensively in entertainment and advertising than in almost any other part of the world, sex ignorance is appalling. The masses do not have a scientific sex vocabulary. Otherwise informed leaders are often grossly ignorant of the facts of human biology and psychology where sex is concerned. For example, McHugh and Moskin studied the attitudes and information of ministers in the area of sex.[1] They found most of them grossly ignorant, uninformed, and incompetent as counselors. Less than 15 percent were actually competent to counsel, and 50 percent preached that sex is evil. Their study of 451 young ministers concerning their information about reproduction showed that 35 percent did not know the period of greatest likelihood of pregnancy and almost half thought menstruation cleared the womb of the unfertilized ovum. Almost three-fourths

[1] G. McHugh and J. Robert Moskin, "What Ministers Are Learning about Sex," *Look,* November 25, 1958, pp. 79–86.

considered a woman slightly ill when menstruating. Forty percent thought a woman's sex interest ceased at menopause.

It is very likely that many doctors would not score much higher on some of the psychological and emotional aspects of sex as it affects the marriage relationship.

Sexual Intercourse

Preparation   The male is responsive to a wide range of psychic and physical stimuli. The female may require considerable love play, called "foreplay" in counseling literature. In this the male is normally the aggressor; the female pursued. Love play in marriage is likely to be bypassed by the husband. If it is, he need not be surprised that his wife often cannot share the sexual act to the fullest. Mutual sexual enjoyment usually requires that the act of courting be maintained in marriage. The courting consists of stimulating the more sensitive zones of the female's body. This brings about the flow of lubricating fluids in the vaginal tract, preparing her for the sex act. It also stimulates lubricating fluids in the male. This, with the psychological readiness, is complete readiness for the sex act.

The sex act   The sex act involves stimulating with increasing ecstasy until one or both reach an orgasm, which is a series of spasmodic contractions. In the male, climax is accompanied by the discharge of a tablespoon or two of seminal fluids carrying the sperm. In the female, there is no such discharge with the spasmodic contractions, but there may be a sucking motion in the uterus which can help draw the sperm up through the opening of the cervix, thus increasing the likelihood that the sperm will reach the Fallopian tubes and meet the egg cell. To reach an orgasm usually requires that both participate in spontaneous rhythmic motions. For the male the glans penis is the principal area of stimulation; for the female the clitoris is the focus of stimulation.

Any form of foreplay or stimulation which proves exciting and any physical position for the sexual act that they wish to assume are proper. The usual face-to-face position, with the male surmounting the female is not the universal position as human cultures go.

Mutual enjoyment should be the determining factor in the position or positions assumed, although what is customary in the local culture will seem more natural.

Afterplay   The male is usually relaxed and ready for sleep on concluding the sex act. The wife usually desires further courting play, in an atmosphere of "delicious langour" in which she senses great tenderness for the male. This is a time for strengthening the love bond and often for close confessions of differences and for patching up difficulties that have entered their life. This is called the period of afterplay.

The Importance of Spontaneity

Margaret Mead has stated as a principle that the more a creature thinks, "the less he may copulate, unless copulation and thought are skillfully integrated at each level."[2] She goes on to elaborate this view, indicating that in cultures where goods are considered to be limited, the expenditure of energy in sexual activity is likely to be conceived as a loss from productivity.

She believes that the sexual functioning of the male is most effective when it is most automatic, a response to simple signals such as the exposure of the female and her gestures, and that conceptions of romance, moral qualms, and other abstractions complicate the sexual functioning of the particular group or social class involved.

She finds that in the upper-class groups these inhibitions are likely to be most common and that in such groups numerous indirect culturally conditioned practices for stimulating the male are invented. Among the lower classes such stimulations are not found and are not needed. The male's approach to sex is direct, uninhibited, and automatic.

Length of Time Required
for Sexual Adjustment

Among those whose expectations need to be deflated are the "enlightened youth" who feel sure that they have a head start toward sexual adjustment because they recognize that such an adjustment will be necessary. As one young man explained to his friend, "Marian and I have taken all the courses and read all the books. We know just what kind of things have to be worked out, so it's not likely to take us more than a week or two to overcome any of the problems we're likely to experience."

This young man may have been correct. For a few the adjustment does come easily, and certainly being well informed is an asset. But sexual adjustment is much more than knowing the right answers. It involves one's most deeply rooted attitudes, habits, and values; and when everything else is normal, it may require time, practice, and patience. Judson T. Landis

[2] Margaret Mead, *Male and Female* (New York: William Morrow & Co., Inc., 1949), pp. 158–164.

found that sex is the one area in which couples least often experience mutual satisfaction from the beginning. (Other areas studied were spending, social activity, in-law relations, mutual friends, and religion.) His study dealt with 409 couples who were the parents of college students at Michigan State, and compares the periods of time they required to make adjustments in their sexual relationship.[3] It will be seen from Figure 23–1 that few more than half agreed that sex relations had been satisfactory from the beginning; in another 12 percent of cases, one member had thought the relationship unsatisfactory. At the far extreme are 12.5 percent who never made an adjustment in sex relations, and yet they were still married at the time of the study.

His 1967 study[4] of length of time it took 215 wives to achieve orgasm, shows that there is still a time lag after marriage. Only 58 percent experienced orgasm during the first four weeks of marriage, 22 percent took a month to a year, 7 percent more than a year, and 13 percent had never experienced an orgasm.

FIGURE 23–1 TIME AS A FACTOR IN SEXUAL ADJUSTMENT OF 409 COUPLES. Source: Judson T. Landis, "Length of Time Required to Achieve Adjustment in Marriage," **American Sociological Review,** 11:668 ff., December, 1946.

PICTOGRAPH CORPORATION

Note that only half of the couples made a satisfactory adjustment at the beginning of their marriage.

Kinsey reported that adjustment problems appeared at some time during the marriage in two-thirds of the relationships he studied.[5] Our study of marital happiness of two generations indicates that more young married women than their mothers considered sex adjustment an important factor

[3] See Judson T. Landis and Mary G. Landis, *Building a Successful Marriage,* fifth edition (Englewood Cliffs, N. J.: Prentice Hall, Inc., 1968), Figure 15–4 and pp. 283–284.

[4] *Ibid.,* Table 1, p. 316.

[5] Alfred C. Kinsey and others, *Sexual Behavior in the Human Female* (Philadelphia: W. B. Saunders Co., 1953).

in happiness (see Table 23–1).[6] While we have no way of knowing the extent to which this view reflects difficulties in the younger generation's own experience, we assume that it probably does.

Table 23–1   Percentage of Two Generations Listing Sexual Compatibility or Incompatibility as One of Five Factors Which Most Affects Marriage Happiness or Unhappiness

| | Sexual Compatibility | | Sexual Incompatibility in Unhappy Marriage | |
	Number	Percent	Number	Percent
Mothers	83	16.1	90	16.7
Single Daughters	74	16.6	113	23.2
Married Daughters	38	35.2	39	35.1

Sex education, at the college level particularly, has led the new generation of women to expect completeness in their sexual life. Literature given to newlyweds also stresses the possibility of women's full participation in sex experience. This literature often gives rather elaborate information of physical positions to be taken in sex relations and other intimate details of sex functions. It is possible that the new generation, in their conscious effort to achieve completeness in sex relations in marriage, may hinder rather than help sexual adjustment.

The overemphasis on sex in modern marriage may be another factor. Because of women's great hopes for complete sexual relations, many are dissatisfied with the adjustment they are able to make. It is possible that many seek divorce on grounds of sexual incompatibility who in another generation would have been content because their expectations were more modest.

It is possible also that some daughters were still so recently married as to be in the early stages of sexual adjustment. It may be, too, that some were facing difficulties imposed by different sexual patterns introduced into their marriage that their husbands learned in their military experience abroad.

Whatever the cause, the problem of sexual adjustment seems to be one that unduly preoccupied the thinking of the newly married group here compared with the other two groups studied.

Those who do not achieve sexual adjustment after a few months of

[6] Paul H. Landis, *Two Generations of Rural and Urban Women Appraise Marital Happiness* (Pullman, Wash.: Washington Agricultural Experiment Station, March, 1951), Bulletin No. 524.

marriage should seek the advice of a family clinic or of an understanding physician. To enjoy the sexual relationship in marriage is a desirable goal for both men and women. Those who are lacking in health, who have been shocked by punishment when a child for exploring sex organs, or who for other reasons have thwarting attitudes, who are emotionally too deeply attached to parents, or who are lacking the basic knowledge of how to participate in the physical act—these may fail to achieve it. There is a cure for many of these cases.

Unrealistic expectations concerning the length of time adjustment may require are very serious but probably not so common as other types of misconceptions that may affect the adjustment process. Many young people enter marriage with no ideas, or only false ideas, about what the physical and psychological responses of each mate are likely to be. What is a realistic expectation?

Orgasmic Reaction

In only half of the marriages of young couples can it be expected that the wife will experience an orgasm during the honeymoon and the first four weeks of marriage. In a fourth of the cases, it will take from a month to a year.[7] Whether biology alone is responsible for the fairly high proportion of married women in our culture who are slow to experience an orgasm is, of course, an unsettled question. It is known that the female has a much less localized sex interest than the male (see Figure 23–2). Most virgins have little or no localized sex desire, and most women who achieve it do so only after experience in marriage. Sex feeling is much more diffused throughout the body of the female and more closely related to affection and general emotional satisfaction.

With the male, sex can often be isolated from love feelings. No doubt the same thing is possible for many females, but as the female is trained in the middle and upper classes of our society, affectional factors are highly important to sexual responsiveness.

Some authors today believe that practically all women could develop orgasmic adequacy if training from childhood were adequate and there were no shocks or other developmental factors to interfere with normal maturation. These authorities are inclined to blame sexual maladjustment almost exclusively upon psychic factors, which have deep roots in childhood development or which grow out of the ignorant blundering of the male during the early period of marriage. Some counselors believe that skillful

---

[7] Kinsey's data suggest this in *Sexual Behavior in the Human Female;* see also Eugene J. Kanin and David H. Howard, "Postmarital Consequences of Premarital Sex Adjustments," *American Sociological Review,* 23:556–562, October, 1958.

FIGURE 23-2   TOTAL SEXUAL OUTLET IN MALES AND FEMALES. Source: Alfred C. Kinsey and others, **Sexual Behavior in the Human Female** (Philadelphia: W. B. Saunders Co., 1953). Reproduced by permission of Dr. Kinsey.

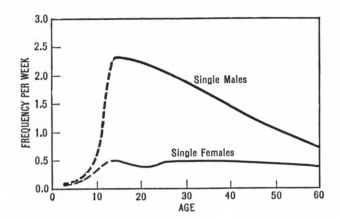

Striking differences in sex activity are indicated at all ages. (Lines show median frequency of orgasm in total sexual outlet. Dotted lines represent estimates for the prepubertal period.)

counseling and direction can cure most of these cases.[8] In this age of counseling and optimism concerning female sexual adequacy, it is probable that these views overstate the case.

Kinsey and his co-workers found that about 50 percent of wives experience an orgasm at least once during the first month of marriage and that about 75 percent do so by the end of the first year. This rises to above 80 percent by the fifth year and to a peak of almost 90 percent by fifteen years of marriage.[9] These data refer not to regular orgasm but to having had the experience at least once.

There is of course great variation. Some wives have multiple orgasms during a single act of intercourse; others have an orgasm only once or a few times in a lifetime. Approximately 10 percent of married females in Kinsey's sample had never reached an orgasm at any time in their marital coitus. About 75 percent had responded at least once in the first five years of their marriage. Generally speaking, the older a woman (up to age forty), the greater the likelihood of her having an orgasm. The peak period in women's experience seems to be age thirty-one to forty. Lack of orgasm is very common in the younger marriage group. For example, between the ages of thirty-one and forty, 90 percent of the females had reached an

[8] See, for example, Oliver M. Butterfield, *Love Problems of Adolescents* (New York: Emerson Books, Inc., 1941), p. 45.

[9] Kinsey, *op. cit.*, p. 349.

orgasm at least once, whereas, among the married females sixteen to twenty years of age, only 71 percent had done so. After forty, the incidence declined somewhat.

The Kinsey researchers found that 70 to 77 percent of coital experiences in marriage produce an orgasm for the wife. The incidence is much less in the early years of marriage than in the later years, ranging from an average of only 63 percent in the first year of marriage to 85 percent in the twentieth year of marriage. The exact findings are as follows:[10]

Year of marriage	Percent of coital experience producing orgasms in the wife
first	63
fifth	71
tenth	77
fifteenth	81
twentieth	85

The figures need some interpretation. During the early years of marriage, coitus is more frequent and is engaged in for the sake of the husband, whether or not it brings satisfaction to the wife. These are his most active years, sexually speaking, while at the same time the wife is most heavily burdened by pregnancy and the care of small children. In the later years of marriage, the husband's sexual needs have diminished and more nearly equal those of the wife. The wife loses her fear of unwanted pregnancy and may participate in sexual activity without this inhibiting fear. Also, she is in a period of life when family burdens are light.

In the average marriage, somewhat less than 40 percent of women can expect always to have an orgasm. The proportion will be considerably lower than this for those with lower education levels and considerably higher for those with higher education levels. The proportion will be somewhat less during the early years of marriage and somewhat higher in the later years, according to the Kinsey findings.[11]

The Significance of Orgasmic Response

It cannot be emphasized too often that orgasms cannot be taken as the sole criterion for determining the degree of satisfaction which a female may de-

---

[10] *Ibid.*, p. 375.

[11] Judson T. Landis finds that the Kinsey sample of women was probably a very highly sexed group and that therefore norms for women in general would be much lower; see his "The Women Kinsey Studied," *Social Problems*, 1:139–142, April, 1954.

rive from sexual activity. Considerable pleasure may be found in sexual arousal which does not proceed to the point of orgasm, and in the social aspects of a sexual relationship. Whether or not she herself reaches orgasm, many a female finds satisfaction in knowing that her husband or other sexual partner has enjoyed the contact, and in realizing that she has contributed to the male's pleasure. We have histories of persons who have been married for a great many years, in the course of which the wife never responded to the point of orgasm, but the marriage had been maintained because of the high quality of the other adjustments in the home.

So Kinsey and colleagues conclude from their studies. Whether one is concerned with general marital adjustment or with sexual adjustment alone, the facts seem to indicate that the purely physical aspect of sex is being greatly overemphasized today.

No two women will respond exactly alike. For some the orgasm is a muscular spasm of almost epileptic proportions; for others it is nothing more than a relaxing sigh. For still others it does not exist at all, and yet they enjoy the close contact of the sexual embrace and feel content in helping the husband satisfy his needs.

The ability to respond is more often a matter of psychology than physiology. In women, sexual response is likely to be identified with a whole complex of attitudes centering about genital functions. The woman who dreads menstruation and who dreads pregnancy may also find sexual response difficult. The woman who has welcomed menstruation as a normal function and who is eager for childbearing and motherhood is more likely to make a good sexual adjustment.

The male usually experiences an ejaculation and the accompanying orgasm in sexual intercourse. There is no evidence to indicate that all women can reach an explosive climax. The female has no organ of sexual sensation fully comparable in importance to the male organ. In many women, there is no developed clitoris and even in those who have a developed clitoris, the organ in no way corresponds in size or area of sensitivity to that of the male. Generally speaking, the woman's sensation awaits development by the male sex organ.

In many societies all that is expected of women is that they be passively receptive. Whole societies can ignore the climax as a part of female response, Mead[12] finds. She also finds that in some societies, as in Samoa, where males have an elaborate repertoire for stimulating the female, some women cannot respond to sexual stimulation. Mead states the probability that an undeveloped clitoris, lack of tone in vaginal muscles, poor general health, or other weaknesses may be factors. Even though the female probably has more sensitive erogenous zones capable of sexual stimulation and orgasm than the male, as a matter of fact, sexual response is less universal than among males. Responsive sexuality in the female is a learned reaction.

[12] *Op. cit.,* pp. 164–170.

The American Institute of Family Relations has found, among wives coming to the clinic for help, that a lack of tonus in the pubococcygeus muscle is a key factor in lack of female response. By teaching them to strengthen this muscle through exercise, which consists essentially in flexing the muscle as in shutting off urination, they are able to improve response in many instances.[13] Maxine Davis, in her book, *Sexual Responsibility in Marriage*, claims that "orgasm adequacy" is less rare than once thought, if women can be taught to use the "magic muscle." Even she, however, recognizes that too much emphasis has been placed on the orgasm leaving "everybody expecting too much." She recognizes that for some women the orgasm is very mild; for some, almost as intense as labor pains.

In the current popular conception of sex, the test of marriage seems to be the ability of husband and wife to realize a mutually satisfying physical climax in their sexual relationship. The suggestion that such coordination is not always necessary and often even impossible is difficult for most young couples to believe at a time when so many doctors, psychiatrists, counselors, and writers have emphasized the physical aspects of sex.

Orgasm Not the Only Test of Sexual Adjustment

Coitus, as an expression of love and mutual regard in marriage, as a thing which encompasses the personalities of husband and wife, is a symbol of their oneness. As a mechanical process to be judged by the intensity and coordination of physical release alone, it is no more significant than such release among creatures of the barnyard. By making the perfection of this mechanical process the goal of sexual life in marriage, many marriages are found wanting. Yet it is known that there are and always have been happy and otherwise successful marriages that have failed to reach this physical goal, just as there have been many marriages that were sexually satisfying that have ended in the divorce court.

Because of the current narrow and unrealistic concept of sex, some men and women fear to marry. Others go through married life with unnecessary feelings of personal guilt, frustration, and failure. Dr. Nadina Kavinoky, a gynecologist and past president of the National Council on Family Relations, believes that the fear of inability to measure up to this standard has given us frigidity, impotence, and many other marriage prob-

[13] A significant book on this subject is that of Ronald M. Deutsch, *The Key to Feminine Response in Marriage* (New York: Random House Inc., 1968). See also, for a brief summary, Ronald M. Deutsch, "A Key to Feminine Response in Marriage," *Reader's Digest*, October, 1968.

lems.[14] Dr. Edward A. Strecker, a psychiatrist, agrees.[15] He believes that the physical rewards of the perfect sexual relationship have been too greatly emphasized by his own profession as well as in fiction and so-called scientific literature.

Much of this current misconception of what sex in marriage should be is centered on the kind of sexual satisfaction a woman should receive. It is popularly believed that she or her husband is inadequate, if she fails regularly to achieve an explosive physical climax. This belief persists in spite of the contradictory nature of the facts concerning orgasmic response which were presented above.

Realistic expectations are important to marital adjustment for a marriage cannot long survive in an atmosphere of failure and frustration. Too many marriages crumble under the weight of sexual disappointment that would have been unnecessary had the couple but known the facts.

A young divorcée still thinks with tenderness about a marriage that broke up because of this striving to reach an impossible goal. She confided to the author:

We would have been the happiest couple in the world if, somehow, we could have forgotten all the "stuff" we ever heard or read on the subject of sex. My happiest moments were when we were together. I loved to feel his nearness and wanted nothing more than to satisfy his every wish. But he was sure that I should get the same excitement out of sex that he did. We never relaxed and enjoyed the intimate life that could have been ours; instead we searched for a kind of mutual ecstacy that was forever out of reach. Our sex life became a time of tension and awkward experimentation that left us more and more upset and dissatisfied. After a while, I lost the simple but deep happiness I had known in our intimate life, and from there on our marriage seemed of little value or meaning to either of us.

While very different from the explosive climax promised in most books, this couple might have been content with their sex life had they not expected so much from the physical side alone. The pleasure the wife received from mere intimacy with her husband was amply rewarding in itself. Many happily married wives share this woman's feeling of joy in sharing themselves with their husbands, a joy which often fully compensates for their own lack of physical excitement. Many wives do not need peaks of sexual excitement. They are quite content with simple intimacies —the nearness of a husband, the protectiveness and security of his body, the touch of his hand, a kiss.

The woman who has not expected too much and who is not guilt-

[14] Nadina Kavinoky, "Premarital Examination," *Western Journal of Surgery, Obstetrics, and Gynecology,* 51:315, October, 1943.
[15] Edward A. Strecker, "A Doctor Looks at Marital Infidelity," *This Week Magazine,* June 8, 1952, p. 22.

ridden and frustrated by her inability to match her husband's sexual desire can nevertheless establish a completely happy marriage which leaves none of her husband's needs unsatisfied.

Dr. Kavinoky believes that the pendulum in sex teaching has swung to the extreme of a "narrow physical concept of the act.[16] She believes that it is time we consider sex "in its relationship to the entire life of the two people concerned." She is less concerned about a specific organic reaction to the sexual relationship than that the couple find in it adventure, excitement, release from tension, contentment, unity and spiritual oneness, and, in times of sorrow or trouble, even comfort and consolation.

If this concept of sex can be accepted, young people will be less concerned over their failure to consciously attain certain specific organic reactions. In removing anxiety, it will be possible to relax and find genuine physical satisfaction. This will also permit those who fail to do so to live happily without guilt.

Technique Is Not Enough

This does not mean that physical techniques are never important. They are, and couples should try to adjust to each other's needs by discussing them frankly and, when necessary, even seeking help from a doctor or counselor. But the first criterion of success should always be whether the two people themselves are happy in their sexual life. If the wife finds that a physical climax in some sort of complete and explosive form is necessary to her satisfaction and her husband is, through faulty timing or techniques, unable to achieve this condition, she may be frustrated and unhappy. A good marriage counselor or doctor can sometimes offer help to the couple in attuning their responses. The importance of such an adjustment cannot be dismissed lightly. Often it is only a matter of faulty sex education that is to blame. The husband may not realize that courting prior to the sex act is often essential to her response. Or the wife may not understand her own sensitivities and her powers of bringing the greatest degree of pleasure to both her husband and herself.

Techniques are not of first importance. More often what may be required for harmony is not refinement of technique, but rather, "a mutual generosity of body and soul.[17] Many will obtain the explosive reaction by

[16] Kavinoky, op. cit.
[17] Simone de Beauvoir, The Second Sex, edited and translated by H. M. Parshley (New York: Alfred A. Knopf, Inc., 1953), p. 402.

preliminary love play and improved timing; others, with the best love play, will never reach it but with proper attitudes can find pleasure in the intimacy and sharing that can come to all happily married people.

Love and trust constantly expressed are great satisfactions in themselves. Despite Hemingway's classic description, the earth need not always move in the ecstasy of sexual love.

Two final facts should be mentioned in connection with sexual adjustment and the orgasmic response of the female. First, such an ability has no necessary connection with her capacity for becoming pregnant.[18] Second, neither is the capacity to respond with orgasm affected by menopause and cessation of capacity to reproduce, as many generally well-informed people suppose it to be. Many women experience an upsurge when the fear of pregnancy is gone.

Dr. Chesser's study of sexual adjustment among English women and their happiness in marriage showed that one-half of the happiest women had a great deal of satisfaction in sexual intercourse; only one-tenth of the unhappy women did. On the other hand, it must be pointed out that half of the happily married women did not get a great deal of satisfaction out of the sexual relationship as such.[19]

Burgess and Wallin report guilt feelings among men whose wives did not respond to orgasm.[20] This they suspected was a middle-class norm which had not yet affected the lower classes. Bettelheim[21] states that "today the boy wants his girl to prove him a man by her 'orgastic experience.'" In trying to have one for him, she becomes anxious and often ends up pretending.

Ruth Cavan[22] has stressed the fact that "anxiety and intense effort to achieve only add to difficulty" and goes on to state that the "great concern with . . . lack of orgasm . . . is not limited to the wife's feelings of deprivation, but may become a contentious subject leading to lack of satisfaction . . . for both husband and wife."

Bettelheim blames the "alarming rise in homosexuality" to such factors in the relationships of husbands and wives."[23]

---

[18] Oliven does express the view that orgasm may set up a sucking motion in the uterus and aid in pregnancy, but this action is not necessary to pregnancy; see John F. Oliven, *Sexual Hygiene and Pathology* (Philadelphia: J. B. Lippincott Co., 1955).

[19] Eustace Chesser and others, *The Sexual, Marital and Family Relationships of The English Woman* (New York: Roy Publishers, Inc., 1957).

[20] Ernest W. Burgess and Paul Wallin, *Engagement and Marriage* (Philadelphia: J. B. Lippincott Co., 1953).

[21] Bruno Bettelheim, "Growing Up Female," *Harper's*, 225:120–128, October, 1962.

[22] Ruth Cavan, *The American Family*, third edition (New York: Thomas Y. Crowell Co., 1963), p. 397.

[23] Bettelheim, *op. cit.*

Religion and Sex Activity in Marriage

Wallin has studied the degree of religiosity as it relates to sexual gratification.[24] He finds that religion apparently is a sublimating factor in women's sex-marriage relationships, for low sexual gratification scores of religious women depreciate their overall marital satisfaction scores less than do low sexual gratification scores of the nonreligious. This relationship is not clear in the case of men.

Frequency of Coitus

Two major variables affect frequency of sexual intercourse: (1) the sexual conceptions of the culture pattern, (2) sexual energy of the pair. The first area sets out for every man and woman the pattern of expectations for both self and mate. The second accounts for the wide range of variations from couple to couple.

There are cultures which hold norms that by our standards would represent great excess. Sexual intercourse several times a night is expected. Other cultures aim at the goal of eliminating sex from the marriage. We have cited the Manus tribe (Ch. 3). In Hindu culture, around age forty a man enters the age of contemplation and is expected gradually to merge sexual energies in philosophical contemplation.

Our culture falls between such extremes. Norms differ with length of marriage, age of the couple, and perhaps much more between social classes than we know from research. But we do have sort of a general norm from sample studies. And we have norms for husbands and wives. These do not reflect the range of individual variation. Some males rarely want sexual intercourse, and quite a percentage of women rarely or never experience orgasm, yet there are couples who have sexual intercourse nightly or even more frequently. Kinsey notes a case of a woman who reported seventy orgasms weekly.

Terman, studying psychological factors in marital happiness of 792 couples, found that husbands on the average wanted coitus somewhat more frequently than wives (see Figure 23–3). To summarize briefly Terman's findings according to the way his married couples matched up sexually,

[24] Paul Wallin, "Religiosity, Sexual Gratification, and Marital Satisfaction," *American Sociological Review*, 22:300–305, June, 1957.

the following table is given, showing what proportion of wives and husbands were satisfied with the frequency of their sexual relations:

	Wives (percent)	Husbands (percent)
Too frequent intercourse	24	3
Just the right amount	53	54
Too little intercourse	22	44

Frequency is largely determined by the biological rhythms of the couple, particularly of the male. The buildup of seminal fluids, along with psychological stimulation operate here. Sexual appetite is, of course, variable with amount of activity and with degree of restraint and self-control. Frequency is not a matter of morals in the view of most married people today. It is a recreative activity without being an intentional act of procreation, except on rare occasions. The norm of younger people is two to three times weekly, but variations up and down from this norm are to be expected.

The degree of resulting stimulation—the extent to which the couple feel tired and irritated or rejuvenated and more energetic—is the practical measure of desired frequency. Usually the husband is more eager and must temper his demands to the wife's tolerance; otherwise she becomes fatigued, irritable, and may in time dread his approaches. If the wife is the more eager, too great demands may lead the husband to the point of impotence, since the male usually must take the initiative in order to feel psychologically safe.

It is very likely that the degree of sexual satisfaction in coitus will depend on the degree of mutuality. In this there appears to have been some improvement in recent generations, possibly due in part to the male's increased recognition of the need for restraint in order to meet the wife's norm. Of wives in the Kinsey research born before 1900, marital coitus had a frequency of 3.2 per week; of those born after 1900, the frequency was 2.6.[25] This research also finds a greater variety of techniques and more foreplay among couples at the later period;[26] also that more wives responded to orgasm—37 percent of those born prior to 1900 and 42 percent of those born later.[27]

All these findings would seem to point toward greater mutuality in

[25] Alfred C. Kinsey and others, *Sexual Behavior in the Human Female* (Philadelphia: W. B. Saunders Co., 1953), Table 97, p. 397.

[26] *Ibid.*, pp. 360–366.

[27] *Ibid.*, pp. 380–381.

the sexual aspect of marriage and to greater satisfaction of sexual needs.

Happy is the person who is married to a mate with similar desire frequency. The average for couples in the United States seems to range between ten and fifteen times a month. In other words, the cycle of the usual marriage is one to three times a week. Figure 23–3 shows the average difference in desire for intercourse of couples of different ages. It will be seen that the men at all ages feel the need for coitus more often than the wives. These data are, of course, averages. In some couples the wife is more strongly sexed. Kinsey's data show the range of extremes more variable in women than in men.

At the beginning of marriage, intercourse daily is not unusual, with a gradual tapering off as the novelty of it passes, until the couple adjusts to their normal cycle of needs. After this point there is a slow decline in frequency until the late fifties. From then on coitus may continue until old age with declining frequency, depending on the physical energy and psychological outlook of the pair.

Studies of the great biologist Raymond Pearl and some later studies suggest that sexual intercourse is most frequent among farmers, second among people in the business classes, and least frequent among those in the professions. Such differences might well be explained in terms of diversity of interest, habits of living, physical energy, variety of other recreational outlets, and psychic stimulation outside the marriage, rather than by differences in biological drives.

FIGURE 23–3   PREFERRED FREQUENCY OF INTERCOURSE. Source: By permission from Lewis M. Terman and others, **Psychological Factors in Marital Happiness** (Copyright 1938, McGraw-Hill Book Co.).

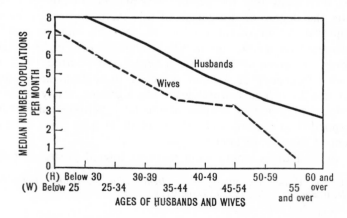

At all ages the wife's preferred frequency averaged less than the husband's. Such averages, of course, do not depict the wide range of individual differences in both men and women. (Data are for 792 married couples.)

Sexual Denial In Marriage Bargaining

The most extensive commercialization of sex is found in prostitution. But it is used extensively in bargaining in dating, particularly where the male pays the bill for dates. We have cited Margaret Mead's statement that prior to marriage it is customary everywhere for women to determine when and whether the sex act takes place. In marriage the male makes these decisions.

No doubt this broad statement has quite general application, but there are times in the marriage relationship when wives use sex for bargaining. Perhaps they always have. Herodotus describes the affiliation of Greek wives, intent on stopping war. They were to put on fine garments, allure their husbands, and excite them sexually, then deny them sexual relations unless they agreed to stop warfare.

Wives have no doubt always used their sexual bargaining powers even if with less altruistic motives. Males are much less likely to do so. Wives may also use denial more often than husbands as a penalty for disagreement and tensions in the marriage.

In 1967, Judson T. Landis surveyed 581 couples, of whom one member of each had been in his marriage classes at Berkeley at a previous time (average for all, seven years previously.) His data show that 48 percent of the husbands reported that their wives at times denied them sex relations, as a reaction to marital differences, 40 percent of wives admitted denial.[28] Only 24 percent of wives reported husbands refusing to have sex relations.

The Duration of Sexual Activity

Many young people are inclined to think that sexual attraction and sexual drives are characteristic phenomena of youth but have no significance in the later years of married life. This notion is very persistent, and it is also completely inaccurate. Although youth is the more highly romantic age, and although, for the young male particularly, sexual drives may seem overwhelming, the facts are that sexual attraction and interest in sexual intercourse persist throughout most of the years of married life.

Kinsey's data deal with large samples of both males and females in the later years of life. The young male reaches his maximum capacity during the teens, having on the average an orgasm approximating two

[28] See Judson T. Landis and Mary G. Landis, *Building a Successful Marriage,* fifth edition (Englewood Cliffs, N. J.: Prentice Hall, Inc., 1968), Table I, p. 293.

and a half times per week during this age period. His sex activities decline consistently thereafter. But at sixty, only 5 percent of males, he finds, are inactive; at 70, only 30 percent. Some are still active at 80 or older.[29]

The average female during the early teens has little capacity for sexual responsiveness. Even at twenty, her medium orgasm is about one every three weeks. She reaches her peak of orgasmic response—about one every two weeks—at around thirty years of age, and remains near this level till past fifty. At age sixty her capacity to respond by orgasm remains almost as high as it was at age 20.

FIGURE 23-4   DIAGRAMMATIC VIEW OF FEMALE REPRODUCTIVE SYSTEM. Source: C. L. Anderson, **Physical and Emotional Aspects of Marriage** (St. Louis: C. V. Mosby Co., 1953). Reproduced by permission of the publisher and Dr. Anderson.

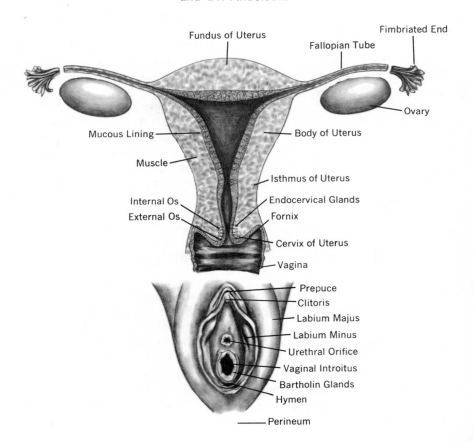

[29] *Sexual Behavior in the Human Female* (Philadelphia: W. B. Saunders Co., 1953), pp. 231–235.

Genital Structure

This is not the place for an extensive discussion of human physiology. Presumably most young people will have made some study of human physiology before they study a book of this kind. On the other hand, there are always those who have had no training even in the fundamentals of reproduction. To enter marriage in such a state of ignorance can bring serious consequences in the fields of sexual and general adjustment.

Figure 23–4 gives a detailed frontal view of the female reproductive system, with a cross-section view in the lower part of the diagram. The point of deposit of semen by the male is in the vaginal tract near the cervix. The sperm must be sucked in or swim through the cervical opening and travel up through the uterus to the Fallopian tube to reach the

FIGURE 23–5   DIAGRAMMATIC VIEW OF MALE REPRODUCTIVE SYSTEM. Source: C. L. Anderson, **Physical and Emotional Aspects of Marriage** (St. Louis: C. V. Mosby Co., 1953). Reproduced by Permission of the publisher and Dr. Anderson.

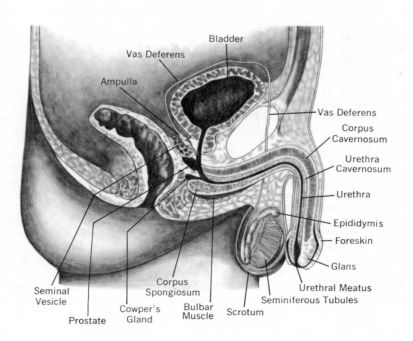

ovum. The ovum, or egg, and sperm can meet only during a short period of the month, usually seven or eight hours.[30]

The second diagram (Figure 23–5) shows the male reproductive organs. Millions of sperm are manufactured daily in the testicles, which lie outside the body in the scrotum,[31] are stored in the seminiferous tubules and are discharged through the penis at the time of the male orgasm in sexual intercourse. In normal sexual intercourse millions are deposited, along with fluids from Cowper's gland and the prostate gland, in the upper end of the vaginal vestibule of the female.

Problems

1. It has been stated that, with reference to their sexual expectations, "American women have gone from one extreme to another. They used to expect nothing; now they expect everything. Of the two extremes, today's is probably the more dangerous." Discuss.
2. What are your reactions to the proposal that it would be desirable for each young couple to set a time limit of, say, one year in which to achieve sexual adjustment? During the year they would read about sex, patiently experiment, and seek help if necessary. At the end of the period they might reasonably say that they had done everything possible, and, if they still feel dissatisfied, they should seek a divorce.
3. What would your advice be to a women who has experienced no orgasm by her third year of marriage?
   a. Visit her doctor.
   b. Visit a psychiatrist.
   c. Keep trying.
   d. Discuss the matter with her husband.
   e. Accept the fact gracefully and recognize that she need not match her husband in orgasmic response.
   f. Some other alternative.
   Defend your choice.
4. Most couples with children believe that their marriage is a happier one than it would have been had they remained childless. Why then is some form of birth control often considered important to marital happiness?
5. What stand does the Catholic Church take on birth control?
6. Sexual relations, even in happy marriages, are thought by most young people to cease by middle age. It is difficult for many to realize that older people could find one another sexually interesting and attractive. In general, what are the facts concerning duration and frequency of sexual activity among older couples?
7. While no class is a typical cross section of young people, your class nevertheless represents various levels of opinion and knowledge. Poll the class

[30] Charles H. Best and Norman B. Taylor, *The Living Body: A Text in Human Physiology*, fourth edition (New York: Holt, Rinehart and Winston, Inc., 1958), p. 657; also Edmund J. Farris, *Human Ovulation and Fertility* (Philadelphia: J. B. Lippincott Co., 1956).

[31] Sperm require storage in a temperature lower than normal body temperature.

on their sex knowledge as it was prior to reading this chapter with the following statements.

Before reading this chapter I believed that:

a. Sexual adjustment was generally a matter of (1) hours, (2) days, (3) weeks, (4) several months, (5) a year or so, (6) a lifetime.

b. Most women experience an orgasm (1) generally, as do men, (2) almost always, (3) about half the time, (4) occasionally, (5) very seldom.

c. In order for both mates to be happy, the wife (1) must experience an orgasm, (2) should experience an orgasm occasionally, (3) need never experience an orgasm.

d. The average young couple engages in sexual relations (1) nightly, (2) almost every night, (3) about once a week, (4) infrequently.

e. That sexual relations between couples tends to cease (1) after the first five years of marriage, (2) after about twelve years, (3) in middle age, (4) after menopause, (5) when the couple become very old.

In analyzing the results of this poll, consider the degree to which the answers (a) agree with the facts in the chapter, (b) differ by sex.

Selected References

Articles in Books of Readings

Krich, A. M. (ed.), *Women: The Variety and Meaning of Their Sexual Experience* (New York: Dell Publishing Co., 1954).
Mead, Margaret, "Potency and Receptivity," pp. 11–135.
Krich, A.M. (editor), *Men: The Variety and Meaning of Their Sexual Experience* (New York: Dell Publishing Co., 1954).
Menninger, Karl A., "Impotence and Frigidity," Ch. 4.
Walker, Kenneth, "The Art of Love," Ch. 13.

General References

Benedek, Therese, "Psychosexual Functions in Women," in *Studies in Psychosomatic Medicine* (New York: The Ronald Press Co., 1952).
Brecher, Edward and Ruth, *An Analysis of "Human Sexual Response"* (Boston: Little, Brown & Co., 1965; New York: New American Library, Signet Book). A summary and professional opinion of the Masters and Johnson work.
Chesser, Eustace, and others, *The Sexual Marital and Family Relationship of The English Woman* (New York: Roy Publishers, Inc., 1957).
Clark, LeMon, *One Hundred and One Intimate Problems Answered* (New York: New American Library, Signet Book, 1967).
McCarey, James Leslie, *Human Sexuality* (Princeton, N. J.: D. Van Nostrand Co., Inc., 1967).
Masters, William H., and Johnson, Virginia E., *Human Sexual Response* (Boston: Little, Brown & Co., 1966).
Wallin, Paul, "Religiosity, Sexual Gratification, and Marital Satisfaction," *American Sociological Review*, 22:300–305, June, 1957.

24

Economic Values
in Marriage Interaction

There is a tendency among the young to take affluence for granted. A large proportion of those of the middle class and above have known no severe economic hardship. For many, their parents have provided a level of spending they will have difficulty attaining after marriage. There is even a large idealistic group who deprecate the value of economic security altogether. And at the far extreme are those who condemn economic security as something evil, a reflection of a corrupt establishment.

Some prefer adventure to a vocation of security and some choose a voluntary poverty in order to spend themselves in various welfare causes: neighborhood projects, the Youth Corps, Head Start, the Peace Corps, VISTA, and many such ventures.

Much of this is worthy, but when it comes time to marry, success will be based in part on a realistic appraisal of the economic costs and on the use of income wisely. Money problems are the big problems of marriage today, equaling if not, in fact, surpassing sex problems as a trouble area.[1]

Symbolic Meanings

Thorstein Veblen, the brilliant iconoclastic economist, saw material goods as a means to status. This theory he enlarges upon in one of the most cutting satires in social science literature, his *Theory of the Leisure Class.* Leisure itself is the key to social status: it testifies that here is a man who lives with little work; he has plenty. His wealth is spent in costly publicity-

[1] See data in the latter part of Ch. 21; also see Judson T. Landis, "Length of Time Required to Achieve Adjustment in Marriage," *American Sociological Review,* 11:688 ff., December, 1946.

gaining activities—at the races, golfing, hunting, gambling, and in lavish entertainment of the "right" people. Conspicuous consumption (lavish spending in ways that are obvious to others) is another device of status-seeking, as is conspicuous philanthropy.

Veblen saw this pattern as affecting not only the wealthy but all who imitate them, or nearly everyone in our culture. He saw deeply into the mainsprings of human nature in the area of economic motivation. However, the motivations he saw operating in our economic life seem to be more typical of nonindustrial civilizations, where there is no middle class, than of modern American society. The American, in spite of his supposed greed and moneymindednes, is less driven to conspicuous consumption than are many peoples of the world. Yet the use of goods for status does operate here and it is a factor in the relationships of men and women. The Veblen views point up the fact that the adjustment struggle centering about money in marriage is of much deeper significance than monetary values as such. Money is at the roots of status seeking in the value systems of men and women, and what money means to a particular individual must be understood in this broader framework.

Economic Adjustments after Marriage Rather than Before

The property problem in the institutional marriage systems of the world is negotiated in advance of marriage by the families concerned. Economic values, as we have seen, are critical in mate choice where elders are in control of matchmaking. Property and family status are the criteria of appropriate mate choice, not personal characteristics of bride or groom. In our propertyless concept of mate choice, however, love and companionability are what count. Property matters are considered later.

Money, or, more broadly, economic values, have become the symbol of innumerable needs and satisfactions; and because they have, money values become the supreme issues in many aspects of husband-wife adjustment in the marriage. The real problem of the modern marriage is not merely how money shall be earned or how it shall be spent but rather the kind of values in life which the couple seek to obtain through its use. Differences in ideas concerning the use of money in the marriage are symbolic of basic differences in personal values and aspirations, for money actually has a place in the personal values of everyone, and the ends the individual pursues with money are symbolic of his total value system.

The person with a background of thrift and practicality may, for example, experience real satisfaction and boast at length about the bargain-counter purchase of a dress at a fourth of its regular price. In this person's scheme of values, such a purchase represents a shrewd and wise way of overcoming economic limitations and of actually achieving success and status. Those reared in a luxurious environment and those who aspire to a higher social status are likely, by contrast, to achieve satisfaction through buying a garment that is conspicuously expensive or that bears the label of the most exclusive shop.

Value Differences of Men and Women

A *Fortune* poll some years ago asked men and women to indicate which sex they thought was the more extravagant. A majority of both men and women felt that women are the more extravagant. Undoubtedly, this feeling is the basis of much of the conflict between men and women over economic values.

Probably the reason women have gained the reputation of being more extravagant is that they do such a high proportion of the spending. It usually falls to the wife to do most of the day-to-day shopping.

Far too often the male role becomes that of supercritic of all the purchases. Frequently, he does not mean to be a critic; he wants to know what is going on. When he notices new curtains at the living room windows, he asks, "Where did these come from?" The wife, if she is sensitive, may anticipate the next question, "What did they cost?" When beefsteak appears on his table, the husband asks, "Where did you get this steak?" perhaps meaning, "It's a fine piece of meat. Go there more often." Or he may mean, "We're buying more steak than we can afford," or "Steak like this costs more than we can afford." In either case, the wife has the feeling he is questioning her judgment. If the steak happens to be a tough one, he is likely to growl, "Where'd you get that piece of leather?" Immediately he implies that her judgment in purchasing meat is not to be trusted.

So the interactions centering about the wife's role as purchasing agent in the marriage go on. In this role she is inclined to receive little praise and a great deal of blame unless the husband, too, has absorbed a large measure of the commonly held attitude that you've got to "put on" to "get on" in this world.

When it comes to the large purchases, like the family car, a house, life insurance, or investments, the husband acts. Women's judgment is not appreciated in such circumstances. They don't know the business world. When the husband makes an investment error, which he is as likely to do as not, he prefers to live above censure, but if called upon to justify his move, he rationalizes that one must, in investment ventures, expect to make some mistakes, that the man who does not venture never has anything.

At the nonthrifty extreme are those husbands who are always out for a quick deal which promises to bring the family immediately to the luxury plane. It may be the horses that fascinate them, the stock market, the long shot in a business venture, or any one of the thousands of deals that bait the speculation-minded with a gambler's hope of quick success. Certainly some wives are guilty of this, too, but generally speaking the husband is the culprit, while the patient, or impatient, wife protests, guided by the sound evidence of past example.

It is difficult even yet for men to recognize that one of the most influential newspaper financial columnists and authors on income tax matters today is a woman (Sylvia Porter)—a married woman. For years she used only her initials in order not to betray the fact that she is a woman. It was feared that she would have no readers if her sex were known.

Women, the bargain hunters   Women, much more than men, are bargain hunters when it comes to buying. Considering their time of little value, they are inclined to do a great deal of footwork and sometimes drive the family automobile a considerable distance to save a few cents. They work on the philosophy that anyone can get an article at the full price but that it takes a shrewd woman indeed to find a bargain. At some social levels, there is prestige as well as personal satisfaction in such achievement, particularly if it is learned that some unwitting friend or neighbor paid two cents more for the same article. In certain instances, bargain hunting becomes such a fascinating game that sale items are bought in excess and the total outlay far exceeds the savings. If purchases are confined to the actual need, however, there is a saving.

Men, the discount seekers   There are many exceptions, but generally women do not believe in arguing the seller down in price. They feel guilty in trying to do so. Perhaps they feel it is giving the impression they can't afford the article. Verbal bargaining's where the male shines. He wants to do his shopping in a hurry and without unnecessary footwork. He is aware that nothing is saved by driving the car about hunting for the cheapest article in town, but he likes the game of beating the seller down. He will argue that the markup is for time customers, to cover worthless trade-ins, that such items are not moving any more—anything to bring the seller to his terms. And he is always ready for a chance to gloat about his bargain and to strut his success before his less brazen neighbor who was sucker enough to pay the full price. Buying wholesale, too, has become a great American game.

Merging roles   With the entry into the work world by women, the traditional clashes between husbands and wives over economic values have been modified. Where both work, both often shop together in the supermarket. While the wife is filling her shopping cart with canned goods, the husband is over at the meat counter selecting the steak or roast that strikes his fancy or his purse. And where both earn, they are more likely to talk over investments and plan them together.

The wife who has had experience in earning also may realize as clearly as does the man how much labor goes into earning the money for a particular expenditure. Such wives' standards of value may in time become similar to those of the husband in spite of different values dominating the childhood training of boy and girl.

The old division of labor within the household tends to break down, too, as sex roles become modified to fit modern economic roles. Where both husband and wife work for wages, the hard-and-fast line no longer exists in their division of labor in the home.

While it is assumed that the disappearance of rigid lines of division of labor have for many couples eased the friction and increased the co-operative spirit of the household, all is not peace. The very fact that roles are no longer strictly defined, and the division of labor is no longer clear, is the basis for many a family argument.

Where division of labor is fixed, each accepts his place and carries out his appointed task. Where there is no real division of labor, the couple must define each new work situation for itself. This calls for the maximum of tolerance, good humor, and cooperation. It also calls for a great deal of good sense.

So the problem is ramified into hundreds of struggles between husbands and wives in their attempts to define a satisfactory division of labor and a compatible scheme of economic values. Maximum adjustability is required if marriage is to be a truly cooperative economic venture.

Property Owernship vs. Comforts

In the rural economy of an earlier day—and some of those values still survive—the accumulation of possessions was symbolic of a person's accomplishments. The contrasting urban value is to "live well" whether one actually owns anything in the way of tangible assets or not. There is a world of difference in the two approaches to life, and where the two meet in marriage, as they often do, a major compromise is required.

The roots of the first series of values, so deeply imbedded in history, persist and merit a brief examination. In an agricultural economy a man's character and accomplishments were measured by the time he went into the field in the morning, the acres and fertile land he acquired, the success of his crops, and the size of his flocks and herds. Woman was a helpmate in these achievements and shared a sense of accomplishment and respect in them. She also acquired success and respect in a domain of her own. The successful agrarian housewife was respected for the good bread she baked, her pies, cakes, doughnuts, or noodles, or for some other specific art in which she excelled her neighbors. For her homemaking and general ability to carry her share of the farm load, she received unspoken but deeply felt gratitude from her husband and respect from her neighbors.

The new world of wages and salaries and the new setting of urban industrial civilization have shifted emphasis from the desire to accumulate possessions or to achieve in domestic spheres where accomplishment was once significant. The values of the ordinary person now center about earning in order to spend for a higher level of living. This means greater comfort, greater leisure, even greater luxury. The quest for security in land, house, and other real property has receded. Women's domestic arts now have to compete with the processed products of the great factory, with its packaged cake mix, pie crust, and frozen foods.

The economic world is no longer family-centered, nor are economic values so clear-cut in the personalities of either man or wife. The comfort-minded and the possessions-minded are merely two points of view among many contrasting types of value systems around which personalities are oriented today.

Investments in Male and Female Subcultures

Gain made by investment of money for long-term goals of family security has been largely in the area of the male subculture. Many wives think that when they spend money for something they want, they are making an investment; some even consider this saving. These ideas shock the investment-minded husband.

Such subculture value differences may bring arguments and misunderstanding in early married life and can be serious indeed in later life if the wife is left with property which must be managed if she is to remain independent and live in the comfort which her husband's management of money may have provided.

Because women live longer, they inherit much of the wealth in houses, farms, livestock, lands, stocks, bonds, life insurance, and cash. It has usually been the husband's money management which has led to whatever estate has been accumulated. Suddenly, usually without prior training on the part of the wife for the responsibility, it is hers to use, to manage, and, if she has the capacity, to multiply until such time as it is passed on to the children and grandchildren or to whatever charity she may choose as an alternative to passing on the inheritance to her descendants.

Albert E. Schwabacher, Jr.,[2] has commented with the wisdom of wide experience of an investment banker on the weakness of widows. He expresses the view that women probably own half the property but control only about 20 percent, since most husbands and estate planners leave it in such a form that control is provided for through pensions and other plans. But when they are left free to control their money, they usually turn to professional managers, most of whom are men.

As a manager of money, Schwabacher has found that women with understanding of money and property management are rare. Only a few are informed, intelligent, and competent in this area of operation. He finds that with many, discussing business is a waste of time. Often he finds that women appraise investment situations strictly in personal terms and by impulse. "Buy Aunt Sally Candy Company stock!" Ask her why, and her answer is "I like candy." The fact that the stock earns no money makes no difference. "Don't buy any Safeway stock." Ask her why: "A Safeway clerk was rude to me."

He finds that many want to sell a good stock—one that should be kept —on impulse, while others want to keep a stock that has no future "because my departed husband bought it."

As a manager of money, he feels that the female subculture is weak. Women are not taught the principle of risk involved in investment—to invest in a capitalistic economy means risk, the possibility of losing. A capitalistic society is always short of risk capital, and women tend to hoard wealth or have it managed too conservatively, so that much of it is of little use in expanding the economy.

Satisfactions of Productivity

One of the principal roads to personal satisfaction and high social standing in our culture is still through productivity. The wealthy in America have failed to fit Thorstein Veblen's picture of the leisure class. They have not, in fact, been a leisure class; they have been among the most productive individuals in the economic system, for here a man's measure is still, in part, his ability to contribute something worthwhile to monetary wealth.

Being productive brings a feeling of importance and the admiration of others. The desire to feel important and to be admired explains in

[2] Albert E. Schwabacher, Jr., "The Repository of Wealth," in Seymour M. Farber and Rober H. L. Wilson (eds.), *The Potential of Woman* (New York: McGraw-Hill Book Co., 1963), pp. 241–254.

large part the acquisition of wealth and property throughout history. The flocks and herds, the apartment houses and factories, the finery and gadgets, and particularly the material comforts and luxuries, are means. Possession shows the world that this man or woman, or this man and woman together, has been able to get ahead in the highly competitive struggle for financial success.

The urban worker employed by others, particularly the salaried worker, has found it difficult to find as much satisfaction in productivity as the self-employed man usually does today. In fact, the tendency of the labor union movement and of labor union philosophy has been to play down production and play up income received for production. Slowdown and other devices have tended to make the worker feel that to produce more than the man working at his elbow is disloyal to labor and tends, in the long run, to reduce the number of jobs available for workers, This value, of course, is in direct contrast to the old rural value under which a man's productive effort was a measure of his character, almost of his religion.

This need to feel productive is still to some extent characteristic of the great majority of Americans, but there is evidence that it varies greatly among individuals and can be cultivated or largely destroyed by early training. The average male exhibits it more consistently than does the average female. In most communities, however, as has been stressed, a man is still judged and judges himself primarily in terms of his productivity, not by his success as a father, a husband, or a human being. He may be happy and well adjusted, but until he makes his business a prosperous one, he is likely to remain a failure in the eyes of his neighbors. He may have ulcers or suffer from high blood pressure and constant worry, but among his acquaintances he is known as a "go-getter," because he has put himself—his time, money, energy, and perhaps his health—into achieving vocational success.

This difference in values, or in the emphasis upon values, is no serious problem on a national or even community-wide basis. Such differences, in fact, tend to complement one another, and both extremes can find satisfaction in our culture as well as in our economy. A real problem does arise, however, when such differences clash head-on in marriage. Clashes of this kind are not uncommon, since the value of personal productivity is much more strongly emphasized in the rearing of boys than of girls.

Women judge themselves and one another more consistently in terms of consumption. The location of one's residence, the conversation pieces, and the number of one's labor-saving devices rather than what one can produce determine one's success and status in the community.

In many marriages, then, the husband is largely production-oriented, the wife consumption-oriented. When an adjustment is not reached or when funds do not allow for the satisfaction of both, a clash almost inevitably results.

Overemphasis on productivity   The well-known practice of the farmer building a good barn before considering a new house for the family is often ridiculed, but the farmer is production-minded. He makes his living from the barn. Without it he feels he cannot afford the new house, the running water, or the bathtub. It takes a rurally reared woman of the old school to have sympathy with such standards, and if one is to read meaning into the extensive migration of girls from farming areas immediately after high school, one must surmise that a decreasing proportion of farm girls are willing to sacrifice their comfort to a production philosophy of farm living.

It is characteristic of the older generation of farm families to become so production-minded that even when they can afford the higher level of consumption that would spell comfort for parents and children, they continue to draw all their satisfaction from producing, living on in the same old, inconvenient way. This is often a point of conflict between parents and teen-agers in the farm family. The teen-ager becomes ashamed of his home and living conditions and tries to make his voice heard in getting the house improved so that he will not feel embarrassed when bringing his friends there.

The vice of undue production-mindedness is not entirely one of the rural male. The struggling small-town or urban businessman, particularly in the eyes of a consumption-minded wife, may also be guilty of wanting to plow everything back into the business. He justifies this in terms of greater comfort and wealth in the future. The wife often wants her cake now.

Then there is the aspiring professional man who feels disposed to plow all family surplus into his further training rather than permit the wife to raise the level of family living. Legitimate as such a goal is, wives and husbands may not see eye to eye, and of course there are no doubt many husbands who are too willing to sacrifice interests of the marriage to their own ambitions. At least there are often legitimate points of difference between husbands and wives centering on the philosophy of the utilization of money as an investment in future productivity rather than as an investment to improve the family level of living.

In thinking of production-mindedness and consumption-mindedness, one finds striking examples of types in the movie colony. John Barrymore made millions but lived it up in "wine, women, and song" and ended up in debt, with even his household goods confiscated by creditors. That is consumption to the limit. Walt Disney's daughter, in writing about her distinguished father, told how at home there was never much ready cash.

Beyond the necessary living, everything was going into her father's latest project: a new cartoon series, Disneyland, etc. Production-mindedness is in evidence here. Rockefeller taught his sons the same lesson, as did Henry Ford.

Woman's Need for Productive Outlets

Much is written today of the failure of competent women to live up to their promise, of their great readiness to settle down into an early marriage, childbearing, and domesticity.[3] Much is written also of the fact that many find later in life that they settled for too little. They find life boring, domesticity less satisfying than they had hoped, and themselves unprepared for the kind of work roles they might have found satisfying had they pursued education to its conclusion. They awake too late to the fact that the last thirty to forty years are important ones, those years after children are no longer dependent.

Betty Friedan declares, "If women do not put forth, finally, that effort to become all that they have in them to become, they will forfeit their own humanity."[4] She discovered after writing the *Feminine Mystique* that a surprising number of women have found a new "fourth dimension" of productivity that makes their lives complete.[5]

The woman's need for productive outlets is one which many husbands, busy in their own work or creative hobbies, fail to appreciate when their wives insist on working outside the family. For many women housework alone does not provide sufficient recognition and creative satisfaction to justify their existence to themselves. In order to live the full and complete lives which they desire, and in order to avoid the neurotic developments which come from a feeling of uselessness, they must seek activity in outside employment. This explains why women today, by and large, are more willing to engage in gainful employment than men are to have them do so. Polls of young people show that many more girls than

[3] Farber and Wilson, *The Potential of Woman, op. cit.*, deals with many aspects of this subject. Betty Friedan, in her best-selling *The Feminine Mystique* (New York: W. W. Norton & Co., Inc., 1963), made much of it. Margaret Mead in lectures on college campuses has been critical of this pattern of female performance; see her views in *U.S. News & World Report*, June 6, 1960. Rosemary Park, president of Barnard, warns girls of the need to be able to use the last forty years of their lives; see Terry Ferrer, "Rosemary Park: New President of Barnard," *Saturday Review*, April 20, 1963, pp. 66–68.

[4] Friedan, *op. cit.*, p. 324.

[5] "Woman, the Fourth Dimension," a special issue of the *Ladies' Home Journal*, June, 1964.

boys think girls should work before marriage and also after marriage.[6] This difference in viewpoint can become an issue in marriage and is an area where an adjustment must definitely be worked out.

For some women the home alone is not enough and cannot be. The job means a great deal as an escape from the monotony of home and as a way of expressing the need to achieve and create. Previous to the time that children are born, particularly, the average young wife can escape loneliness and monotony only by being given an opportunity to work and to secure the recognition that comes with earning. The husband who blocks his wife in her work endeavor is inviting trouble for himself, for her, and for the whole family. Research confirms this view.[7]

Those women who are able to find a sense of productivity in household activities alone and in the rearing of their families are happy indeed. The ability of a woman to do so depends, no doubt, on a number of factors. The conception of what a wife should be, what she may do, and how she may act is usually learned in early life as she observes her mother and absorbs her mother's attitudes concerning a wife's role. These early impressions are very strong and frequently account entirely for the later attitudes and behavior of the grown girl. They are not incapable of modification, however. Other women whom the child admires, a school curriculum emphasizing career training rather than preparation for a domestic life, or a husband who gives little credit and recognition for housework— any or all of these help account for the overwhelming personal need of many wives and mothers to find work outside the home.

In the end a large proportion of women must find a place outside the home to feel content. Family life is a transient experience, largely over by age forty. Then, if not sooner, most women need new outlets. For the woman who completed school early and is inadequately trained, this offers serious problems. Most women may need to return to school to brush up or to improve work skills. These necessary adjustments also require the sympathy and understanding of the husband. Such adjustments cannot be appraised primarily in terms of increased earning power but rather in terms of increased self-esteem for the wife who may no longer feel useful.

Husband's appreciation needed   At all stages of their married life, appreciation by the husband is needed. The appreciation he gives the wife in her domestic roles is frequently the deciding factor, as well as his

---

[6] Howard M. Bell, *Youth Tell Their Story* (Washington, D.C.: American Council on Education, 1938); *Youth and the World of Work* (Lansing: Social Research Service, Michigan State College, 1949); also *Purdue Opinion Poll for Young People*, 15:4a, February, 1956.

[7] Ernest W. Burgess and Leonard S. Cottrell, *Predicting Failure or Success in Marriage* (Englewood Cliffs, N.J.: Prentice-Hall, Inc., 1939), pp. 266 ff., finds that if a woman wishes to work, it is an asset to good adjustment in marriage that she work.

recognition of the savings occurring to the household from the labor contribution she makes. Often, in fact, the husband is far too little aware of her very great economic contribution and is quick to criticize and slow to praise her for her part in making the family an economic success.[8]

In the early years of marriage, husbands and wives alike generally exert considerable influence over the role attitudes of their mates. The man who marries a working girl and takes her out of her earning role, for example, can do much to make her transition to housewife and mother an easy and unregretted one if he greets each of her domestic efforts with praise and real appreciation. The young wife, wanting very much the recognition of her husband, generally enjoys the cultivation of qualities and abilities which he admires. If, on the other hand, he challenges every expenditure, asks her to justify every bill, and rarely if ever expresses any appreciation for her thrift and saving or her long hours of regular work in providing for a comfortable home, she can take little pleasure or pride in her new wife-homemaker role.

The need for recognition of the homemaker role is particularly acute in urban homes, in cases where the wife does not continue in gainful employment. Farm women still take great pride in their productive activity within the household, recounting at every opportunity the number of quarts of this and that they have canned, the glasses of jelly made, the pickles and preserves, and the jars of sauerkraut and pickles in their basements. One reason they can do so is that their husbands and their communities rate this productive role favorably.

The Strain of Overconsumption

The average urban housewife takes comparatively little pride in the kind of productive activity that goes on in the home. Her satisfactions, therefore, have to be derived largely from the kind of consumption in which the family can engage. The well-furnished home and well-dressed children are a means to a feeling of recognition and importance for her. To the extent that this is true, her personal satisfactions among her neighbors and relatives is dependent on the amount of money she can spend for the improvement of the level of living in the family. It is her source of pride and personal satisfaction. What the husband considers extravagant may be necessity for her, basic to satisfying her need for feeling important.

This all goes to say that the expenditure of money is not always the

[8] Some estimates place her economic contribution through domestic activities at $7,000 to $8,000 per year.

same to the man as to the woman, and one has difficulty in understanding the other unless he tries to appreciate what the motivation may be. The motivation may not be too evident. In fact, one must assume that the economic acivities of both men and women are deeply fraught with significance in terms of the recognition they bring to their personalities of the individuals involved.

One hears less today about the underworked and overshopping housewife, but no doubt she is still present in many circles, making marriage adjustment quite difficult, particularly for those husbands whose training has built into them a wide streak of thrift. Such husbands must recognize that the cure for such a wife is some other outlet for personal recognition.

Actually today the pressure on all sides is to encourage the new couple to overstrain their economic resources in an effort to match the pace of friends, fellow workers, or neighbors. The luxury goal of living is evidenced in the whole trend of American invention. Once a particular invention has reached a stage of relative mechanical perfection, the manufacturers compete in terms of beauty and ornamentation. In fact, this becomes the final level of appeal in modern advertising, for here there is no satiation point. There is a limit, for example, to the amount of horsepower that is desirable in an automobile engine. That limit may have been reached or even exceeded in the present state of highway development. But when the automobile market becomes highly competitive, the major emphasis shifts to styling and design. In this there is no limit to the creative imagination of man. One new model can follow another year after year by a change in style. This keeps up the hunger to buy and puts competition of new-car ownership strictly on the basis of prestige rather than utility. If only automobiles were involved, the matter might be quite simple, but the luxury-ornamentation motive is no less characteristic there than in dress, eyeglasses, bathtubs, telephones, and almost every other item of daily use.

The American standard of living has risen so precipitously that young couples in many instances are able to begin married life on or near the level of comfort which their parents achieved only after years of struggle and thrift. Aspirations for a high level of living, in fact for an increasingly higher level of living, are a part of the American heritage. The common laborer shares it along with the middle and upper classes. An open-class system sets no limits to human aspirations. There is no standard by which one knows when he has reached a satisfactory level and can rest content in his achievements.

Modern business is sales-minded and uses every possible means of contact and communication to whet desire and raise aspirations—the display window, the talking mannequin, the demonstration, pseudo and real scientific opinion, high pressure salesmen, advertising by press, radio, and television. There is no end to what a couple can want, for new models and styles, and even new products, are flashed before them in a continuous flow of advertising.

To make it all easy, and nearly painless, there is the generous time contract by which the couple may mortgage their income for two to three years ahead even with readily consumable goods to say nothing of twenty- to twenty-five year mortgage contracts or life-long insurance contracts. One can mortgage any share of his future income he chooses years before it is earned.

"Keeping ahead of the Joneses" is a favorite American game and no doubt explains some of our remarkable progress as a nation toward new and better things. This spirit keeps the family on its toes, too, but it can readily become a vice, particularly for those young housewives whose aspirations far exceed their husband's earning power. In many marriages, basic conflicts in values of husband and wife center on consumption standards and values. Such conflicts are almost inevitable in many marriages today.

The Two-Income Family

We have spoken at length about the need for a feeling of productivity as a motive for the outside employment of housewives. What about the simple consideration of "making ends meet"?

According to one woman who has successfully combined a career with motherhood, women's rights and individual development are no longer the crucial considerations. Among young married women today it has become simply a "matter of bookkeeping."[9] "Under present circumstances, a single pay envelope will not meet the needs of a white-collar family. It is as simple as that."

It should be added, however, that the justification for working to supplement income, while sometimes easier to understand, is no greater than working to satisfy personality needs. The woman who "works out" in order to keep up payments on the new car but who worries over neglecting her children, is probably doing herself and her family greater harm than if the car were allowed to revert to the creditors. At the same time, the wife who, because of unjustifiable guilt feelings or because of uncertainty about her role, forces herself to stay at home full time and pass up opportunities for an interesting job is inviting frustration and bitterness that can easily undo many of the advantages of being a full-time wife and mother.

[9] Nancy Barr Mavity, "The Two-Income Family," *Harper's Magazine,* 203:57–63, December, 1951.

Mutual Role Acceptance

Whether the young bride becomes a full-time housewife, combines her new role with a part-time job, or devotes her daytime interests and energies to a full-fledged career is not the point. The important consideration to marital adjustment is whether husband and wife agree on the course of action taken and are mutually satisfied with the kind of family life it entails.

The wife who does not work outside the home, for example, has no right to expect the same amount of sharing of her domestic duties as has the wife who works the same length of day as her husband in gainful employment, yet she may do so. The husband whose wife works may expect the same leisure and attention at home as though his wife were not working and be negative toward any suggestion that he share the housework or care of the children. There are no set rules to follow. The husband in this instance is trying to live by the division of labor that may have existed in his parental home, not realizing that he hasn't established the same sort of family.

The choice of several possible roles is not the exclusive right of wives. Husbands, too, must decide whether or not they will divorce themselves completely from housework, household interests, and child-rearing activities. A good marital adjustment is seldom achieved unless husband and wife can genuinely accept whatever role the other decides to assume.

Whether or not she decides to work outside the home full or part time, the average wife soon discovers that, in our culture, the husband's work activities usually take precedence over her own. There are numerous exceptions, but they are exceptions nevertheless. A "good wife" is still expected to look up to her husband in the matter of making a living and to show an interest in his productive activities. If she fails to do so before marriage, she is likely to lose her man in spite of her personal attractiveness. A wife who fails to develop an interest in her husband's work, investments, and other productive efforts and to grow in knowledge and understanding of such activity is bargaining for a lonesome future.

He may or may not leave her, but he will find much of his conversation, companionship, and true friendship in quarters where there are men or women who appreciate the things that are vital to him. The most vital interests of most successful males are centered on productivity. If their work is uninteresting, it may be hobbies or avocations that give life zest for them.

This does not mean that a wife should lose her own interests and hobbies and become a drudge of the home. Far from it. To be the wife most men want she must keep alert, informed, have her own vital and stimulating interests, and also understand his world of activity and meaning.

This takes the young wife through one step after another of adjusting to the husband's world. In spite of romantic considerations, most wives must learn early in marriage to share a great deal of the husband's time with his job. Many professional men and others ambitious to get ahead in their work are inclined to spend longer hours with their profession or business than they should, sometimes to the unnecessary neglect of the wife. Some employers also are inconsiderate of their employees, requiring a great deal of overtime work. With men, work tends to come first, although every man should realize that marriage takes time and that the wife's interests must be given consideration.

The demanding, possessive woman had better marry a man who has no deep male recreational or occupational interests. Otherwise, either he or she or both are likely to be unhappy in marriage. For example, she should never marry a doctor. She will either succeed in ruining him as a doctor and as a man, or she will have to suffer from seeing him devote a great deal of his interests and time to his profession. Similarly, if she wants a great deal of attention, she should not marry an ambitious college professor or, in fact, any individual who expects seriously to pursue a highly competitive vocation. She may actually succeed in shaping him to her will, but if she does, his career will be ruined. Few men can forgive a woman for being so demanding.

The same is true for a man who marries a woman with her heart set on a vocation and insists on confining her to the home after marriage. He will have on his hands a person disillusioned with marriage as soon as she realizes that it has robbed her of satisfactions which mean more to her than housekeeping or even marital romance.

Most wives recognize that a great deal of a man's time and energy will be consumed in work; most of them are willing to have the attention of their husband in the family for only a limited portion of the time, recognizing that the husband's devotion to his occupation is essential to the family's economic well-being. But there are some wives who are too demanding to make such adjustments.

In the case of a few highly intellectual individuals, it seems to be possible to have a marriage that permits each member to continue very much the independent life he has lived before marriage, each continuing with his own work and associations, knowing, well before they marry, that married life will make demands on only a relatively small part of their time and attention. Such couples usually do not plan to have children, and each plans to retain a high degree of individual self-interest within marriage. The average marriage, however, cannot be of this character.

For most couples, give and take to a degree never required of them before is necessary in the early weeks and months of marriage. The blending of two distinct personalities into one way of living is for most people something more of a task than they expected. But it can be done by those who are determined to succeed.

The adjustments of the early years of marriage, even in the companionship family, are generally more demanding of the wife than of the husband. This is why, as we have seen in an earlier chapter, a girl looking forward to marriage must have a great deal in the way of character and courage to succeed. It is the wife's way of life that is usually reshaped to fit the husband's. This will probably be true as long as men earn the living in most families.

While most couples follow in the traditional pattern, the significant issue is not that they do so but that they do so willingly and with a mutual respect for whatever role the other takes in the home as well as in the world of work.

Problems

1. Describe specific American traditions or customs, and specific instances from American education and advertisements that seem to produce differences in values held by men and women.
2. Modern society has greatly increased the number of areas in which women may play productive roles. Why then is the modern wife likely to feel less productive than the wife of two generations past?
3. Is it possible to educate women away from the need they feel to be productive? Describe a way of life in which feminine productiveness is frowned upon. Why would such a role be unacceptable to most American women today?
4. *Sociodrama:* A young doctor and his wife have come to live in a new community. The wife realizes how important it is to make the right impression in order to gain standing in the community. In order to make this impression, she is willing to spend all their savings and mortgage most of their future earnings in possessions. The husband is beginning to be concerned about the fact that they have no children, no real savings, no money for relaxation and adventure. Dramatize a discussion or argument between them in which their values are pictured, in which the dangers of overconsumption are suggested, and in which the arguments for the wife's point of view are presented.
5. If a young couple agree that the wife shall work for a limited time, are there any rules they should agree upon as to how her income shall and shall not be spent?
6. Marilyn was a graduate student in interior decoration with a brilliant career awaiting her, when she fell in love with Mike. Mike is not a tyrant, but he firmly believes that a home can be happy only when the wife devotes herself full time to her roles as wife and mother. He believes that she should channel her professional talents into her own home and forget about the career that might have been. Still, she feels that life would never be complete without a little success in the competitive world outside marriage. Would you advise her to:

   a. Forget about marriage; Mike is unreasonable?
   b. Postpone marriage a few years in order to further her interests?
   c. Marry and try to forget the career?
   d. Try some other alternative?
   In weighing and discussing each alternative, consider its possible risks as well as its advantages.

7. Describe several common customs or practices that illustrate the consumption-mindedness of modern Americans.
8. Poll the class on the problem: If, upon marrying, you were able to live in a comfortably but simply furnished apartment and save $100 a month, would you prefer to:
   a. Save the $100 without specific purpose?
   b. Use the $100 for recreation?
   c. Buy a car?
   d. Invest the money?
   e. Begin having children?
   f. Buy furniture?
   g. Buy a home or property?
   h. Travel and have some adventure?
   i. Use the $100 for attractive wardrobes, eating out, and entertaining?
   j. Divide it in half and let each mate spend $50 as he chooses?
9. After tabulating the anonymously submitted data, do you find that:
   a. Most students tend to agree on economic values?
   b. Students differ according to sex.?
10. If no agreement can be reached on how to spend the family's income, how should the dilemma be solved and why?
   a. Husband's values prevail?
   b. Wife's values prevail?
   c. Some other arrangement?
Discuss.

General References

Farber, Seymour M., and Wilson, Roger H. L. (eds.), *The Potential of Woman* (New York: McGraw-Hill Book Co., 1963), Parts 3, 4, 5.

Goode, William J., "Economic Factors and Marital Stability," *American Sociological Review*, 16:802–812, December, 1951.

Ladies' Home Journal, June, 1964. This is a special issue devoted to "Woman, the Fourth Dimension."

Landis, Judson T., "Length of Time Required to Achieve Adjustment in Marriage," *American Sociological Review*, 11:688 ff., December, 1946.

Mavity, Nancy Barr, "The Two-Income Family," *Harper's Magazine*, 203:57–63, December, 1951.

Neisser, Edith G., "Emotional and Social Values Attached to Money," *Marriage and Family Living*, 22:132–138, May, 1960.

Springer, John L., *Make the Most of Your Income* (Englewood Cliffs, N. J.: Prentice-Hall, Inc., 1961).

U.S. Department of Labor, Women's Bureau, *American Women*, Report of the President's Commission on the Status of Women, Washington, D.C., 1963.

25

Finance Management

Most young couples in the early years of their marriage, when they are struggling to get ahead, look forward to a day when they can have just about anything they want. That day probably will never come, for wants will most likely multiply more rapidly than resources. One of the most certain things about the money aspect of marriage is that there will never be enough money. Wise management will be necessary if even a substantial portion of wants of all family members are to be met. The word wants is used advisedly; most families in the United States have their needs met quite adequately. Wants are as flexible as human aspirations, and tend to grow Veblenian fashion, as members of the family use money to keep pace with the demands of their social circle, the husband with other men in the male subculture—business, club life, recreation—the wife with other women, primarily in the female subculture—clothes, beauty care, household furniture and equipment, club life—and as children grow, each with his age group in toys, appropriate clothes, and gadgets from the cowboy outfit to the first dress suit of the budding adolescent.

A few years ago *Life* carried an editorial based on a study by William H. Whyte, Jr., for *The Wall Street Journal*. It was titled "Is Thrift Un-American?" and described the spending habits of 83 young couples with incomes of $5,000 to $7,500. He found typically that their incomes were "hocked" far in advance, so that they never had cash. For example, he found of a $500 gross monthly income, only about $45 remains after all commitments for the month are met: time contracts, food and lunch money, but no savings. The system is to have oneself committed to regular monthly payments for all major items. In buying, cost is disregarded. The question asked is "What is the monthly payment?" There is more concern in the fact that it is $12.73 a month than in the total price. And there seems to be a complete disregard of the fact that 12 to 18 percent interest piles up. In big expenditures like automobiles, Whyte finds that buyers take dealer "packs" without even calculating the total amount, and often end up suckers.[1] Not only has Yankee thrift vanished but so has Yankee shrewdness, he suggests.

His sampling of the $13,000 to $17,000 junior-executive group shows a similar pattern of being committed far in advance, carrying a large amount of debt in as many as fifteen different loans. Saving, he concludes, is no longer identified with morality.

In the average family, the difference between success or failure in money matters is largely a matter of money sense, no matter what the income level. One can always be in debt regardless of salary, and with the possible exception of the very lowest income group, savings are usually possible. Barring major illness or other such misfortune, success is simply a matter of money management.

There is no significant or consistent relationship between the amount of income and marital happiness.[2] The economic security of the family, as measured by the proportion of the income being saved, has been found to bear an association with poor and good adjustment in marriage, as does regularity of employment and income.[3] This may mean that the desire or ability to save is an index to a certain type of character which adjusts well in marriage. It is more definitely established that occupation and steadiness of income are related to successful adjustment in marriage. Managerial and professional occupations, where income is regular, show greater happiness scores than the less-regular-income occupations.[4]

Money Management

Advice is always cheap, yet in the field of money management it is always in demand. By and large, the American family's success at money management falls far short of an ideal standard. Loan sharks by the dozens flourish in every city. Other finance agencies with greater respectability but equally excessive hidden interest rates abound in cities, states, and even on a nationwide scale. Installment financing is often offered at more than twice a normal bank rate of interest.

In the field of life insurance and investments, the average couple are

---

[1] This situation became so bad that the government entered the field, requiring that actual interest rates be shown and that the cost of the car be made known, to protect the gullible buyer.

[2] Ernest W. Burgess and Leonard S. Cottrell, *Predicting Success or Failure in Marriage* (Englewood Cliffs, N.J.: Prentice-Hall, Inc., 1939), p. 404.

[3] *Ibid.*

[4] *Ibid.* Refer again to Figure 23–1.

"babes in the woods" with little or no knowledge to help them in judging when they are or are not buying wisely. In the daily purchases of the household, many wives have too little knowledge to provide a sound basis for wise purchases of furniture, fabrics, and nutritious foods. A great deal of consumer education is needed.

Although one cannot assume that wise money management would ease all the family tensions that arise over money matters today, it undoubtedly would help. Not all prospective housewives can take a broad course in home economics, nor can all men be trained in money management, but some money sense is essential to successful home management.

FIGURE 25-1   MEDIAN   FAMILY   INCOME,   UNITED   STATES,   1966—BY RACE AND YEARS OF SCHOOL COMPLETED. Source: "Consumer Income," **Current   Population   Reports,**   Series   P-60,   No.   53,   December   28,   1967, Table 7, p. 27.

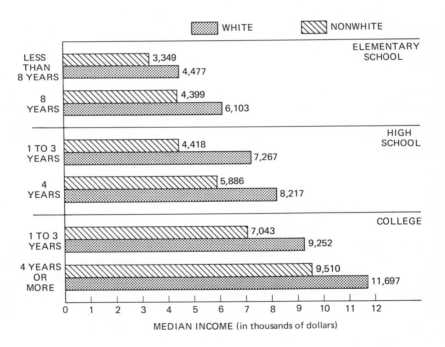

Education and race are factors affecting family income. Among both whites and nonwhites, the more schooling the higher the income. At current salary rates a college graduate will provide $410,000 to $500,000 income for his family during his working lifetime, depending on his race; a high school graduate $250,000 to $350,000, and a grade school graduate only $190,000 to $265,000. Schooling is also the most important gateway to occupational security.

The average young man who makes it through college will earn about $11,697 for his family. It will be less at the beginning, more as he climbs. To have more for luxuries, either his wife must earn or he must learn to save and invest wisely to increase income later on as family responsibilities increase. There are only two ways to obtain income: (1) earn it as a reward for services performed or (2) add value to investments.

A Picture of Family Income

A realistic conception of probable earning power is important to success in marriage. In the modern world, income is closely related to the schooling of the family head (Figure 25–1). This is inevitable, since a high

FIGURE 25–2   MEDIAN INCOME, U.S. FAMILIES AND PERSONS, 1966— BY OCCUPATION. Source: "Consumer Income," **Current Population Reports,** Series P–60, No. 53, December 28, 1967, Table 9, p. 29.

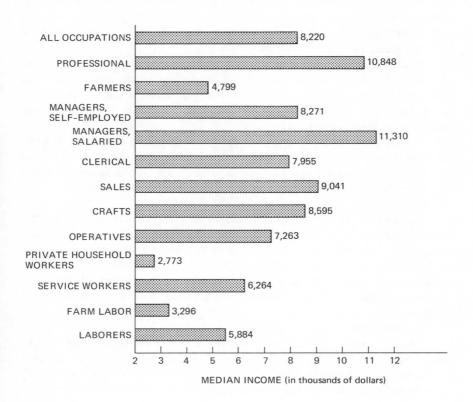

MEDIAN INCOME (in thousands of dollars)

level of training is prerequisite to both the better-paying and more stable occupations. Whites with less than grade school education have a median income level of $4,477; those with eighth-grade schooling, of $6,103; high school graduates, of $8,217; and college graduates, of $11,697. Non-white families receive substantially less income than white families at all levels of education, but among them, also, more training brings a higher median level of income.

The occupation decided on will also have a direct bearing on earnings. Most of the college-trained seek positions at the professional and managerial levels. These salaried fields are now the best paid, providing the highest median income, which in each field exceeds $9,000 (see Figure 25–2). More important still to the security of family life, they provide regularity of income.

The Cost of Money

Whether or not a young couple of average or above average income will be economically secure at age forty-five or still living beyond their income will depend in considerable part on their learning early in their married life, or before, the cost of money.

Money used for *investment debt* is cheap money. It is used in the purchase of tangible assets which have permanent value and which often increase in value with the passage of time. Investment capital is usually to be had at a simple rate of interest. Land, a house, a business are examples of investment debt.

Money borrowed on *consumer debt* is high-priced money. It is used for consumable items, which perish with the using and the value of which rapidly diminishes with the passage of time. Cars, refrigerators, washing machines, furniture, clothes and boats are examples of consumer debt. (See Table 25–1.)

Investment debt is financed by *simple interest*, that is, interest on the unpaid balance. In other words, the amount of interest declines with each payment on the principal. Consumer debt is financed by *discount interest,* or *hard interest,* that is, interest which is charged on the whole amount for the whole period of the loan. The interest is charged in advance and does not decline as monthly payments are made, so it is actually almost twice the simple-interest rate. Actual interest rates range usually from 10 to 35 percent on consumer debt.

Money is made by the use of borrowed money for investment debt in assets which will increase in value. The borrower pays, say, 6 percent simple interest, expecting with the passage of time that his investment will grow in value far beyond the purchase price and accumulated interest.

Agreement on Who Is to Handle Family Spending

A seemingly simple but frequently contentious aspect of money management is the handling and the spending of the family income. In every marriage an early decision must be made concerning who shall handle the money and how it shall be handled. With some couples, the question does

Table 25-1   Comparative Costs of Consumer Credit by Source
(Hard or Discount Interest)

Lender	Type of Credit	Dollar Rates	Annual Real Rate* (percent)
Banks	Personal Loans	$4.50 per $100	8
Credit Unions	Loans to Members	2/3 of 1%–1% per month	8–12
Small Loan Companies	Small Loans	1½%–3½% per month	18–42
Banks	Auto Loans	$4.50–$6 per $100	8–12
Finance Companies	Auto Finance (Installment)	$6–$7 per $100 for new car $9–$17 per $100 for used car	12–14 18–34
Department Store Charge Account	Revolving Credit (up to set limit)	1½% per month	18
Department Store Installment Contract 1–3 yrs.	Expensive Items (appliances, T.V.)	$9–$10 per $100	18–20 (and up)
Banks or Savings & Loan Associations	Home Modernization Loans	$5 per $100 up to $2,500; $4 per $100 from $2,500–$3,500	10

* The annual real rate is the simple interest rate on the money used at a given time.

Source: A Guide to Consumer Credit, Public Affairs Pamphlet No. 348, New York.

not come out in the open. Circumstances seem to decide the answer before it ever becomes an issue. With others there is a good deal of experimentation, and sometimes quite a contest develops before a mutually satisfactory arrangement can be reached. There are at least five possible methods of handling money: (1) the husband may control all the spending; (2) the wife may control all expenditures; (3) the husband may control the income but give his wife an allowance for meeting household expenses, her own personal needs, and the needs of the children; (4) the husband and wife may have separate incomes and bank accounts, each one controlling his own funds, and each agreeing to meet certain of the family's financial obligations; (5) the husband and wife may maintain a joint bank account, each drawing upon it at will.

This question appears on the surface to be one of simple expediency. It is that, but it is much more, too. The decision reached influences how the family shall live and also has an effect upon attitudes and relationships of family members. Problems of domination, submission, insecurity, inferiority feelings, and many others are frequently created or exaggerated by the circumstances surrounding the spending of the family income.

The following case, reported by a family relations counselor, illustrates a characteristic difficulty as well as the importance of reaching a mutually satisfactory decision:

Jim and Gertrude married during their senior year in college. Jim was receiving veterans' schooling benefits and Gertrude had a part-time typing job. Their combined income allowed for few luxuries and only by careful planning were they able to finish their schooling without outside assistance.

At first, they handled the money together, both planning and worrying about making ends meet. After a few months, however, a budget was worked out and Gertrude took over the routine jobs of bill paying, grocery buying, etc. Since there was no "extra money," no question or argument ever arose as to how any of their income *should* be spent.

After graduation, Jim obtained an excellent position with a local insurance office. His income rose steadily and, by mutual agreement, they invested in a new car and began the accumulation of household furnishings. Gertrude maintained her position as the family money manager and as Jim's pay increased she regularly revamped their budget to allow for larger expenditures on furniture and appliances.

When Jim occasionally complained about his own lack of spending money or about the absence of extra cash for unplanned-for expenditures—magazines, books, records, or a show—Gertrude would reassure him that after next month, "when the TV set is paid off, we'll have plenty for extras."

Months passed but the day when there would be plenty for extras was always a month or two away. Jim finally exploded over a situation in which he, a man earning $9,000 a year, should "have to borrow from somebody every time I want a pack of cigarettes or a cup of coffee!"

Gertrude, in turn, felt accused and unappreciated for her hours of budget planning. For several months the atmosphere remained bitter and the problem unsolved. Sometimes Jim handled all of the money himself, but bills went unpaid and insufficient funds were being put aside for groceries and living expenses. Then Gertrude took over and the old problems reappeared.

In their third year, they reached the point of considering divorce because of the constant bickering and frustration over money. A friend induced them to take their problems to a local family relations clinic. They did, and after several weeks of "talking things over" with a counselor they began to understand one another's values and wishes in money matters. After months of effort they finally reached a solution in which both could find satisfaction. Only by giving up a few of the furnishings that Gertrude had set her heart on was Jim able to carry sufficient money in his pocket to regain his sense of confidence and pride in himself as a successful money-earner. Gertrude continued to handle most of the routine spending, but whenever the question of a new purchase of any significance arose, they talked over its desirability and the effect it would have upon their regular way of life.

This is but one of an endless number of possible situations which can grow out of money handling. Because of the importance money plays in the satisfaction of our needs and wishes, it is desirable that every couple face personality needs, as well as economic considerations, in deciding who shall handle the money and how. There is no one best answer. The policy adopted by one couple is bound to differ from that of others even in the same income group.

It may be said, however, that in general a mutually acceptable routine plan for money spending is more conducive to happiness than the policy of meeting each month's financial demands as if they were a new experience. Money matters can become the foremost issue in every family discussion. To allow this is to invite poor management as well as hard feelings. To prevent it, however, demands mutual concern, give and take, and a real desire to make money a tool of happy family life rather than the family's master.

Since financial patterns are a matter which must vary among families, no one system can be given to suit all needs. There are, however, certain basic considerations in financial planning which should help most couples in working out a program suited to their own needs.

Financial Planning

Every family, regardless of the amount of its income, has to face the problem of dividing up that income according to the use that will be made of it. This may be done according to plan or simply by deciding what one wants and spending the money without any systematic plan, but in either case it will be divided up in some way in an attempt to meet the needs of the family.

To develop a family budget requires, first, an estimate of income; second, an estimate of the various kinds of expenses which the family wishes to accept for a given period of time; and third, a plan for dividing this income among these various expenditures. Usually involved is a cash record of the expenditures, so that it is possible to know whether or not the plan of the family budget has been carried out.

The amount of income determines not only the amount there is to be spent but also the ratio of income that can be spent for different things. Generally speaking, the smaller the income, the greater the proportion spent for food, clothing, and the necessities of life; the larger the income, the smaller the proportion spent for necessities and the greater the proportion spent for comforts, luxuries, and savings.

By developing a family budget, it is usually possible to make money go further to obtain the things that are most important to the family. It also has the advantage of making all members of the family plan together for the use of money to be spent. Thus, neither partner is so likely to blame the other if the money runs short.

No family should become a slave to the family budget, even though they may plan out in advance each year or each month the amount they are going to spend for a given class of items. Such exact accounting has certain advantages, but it may, like any other exact scheme, become a source of irritation and conflict. Some people can probably do better without any written budget at all, but families should give some thought to the way they will spend their income in order to get the most satisfaction from it.

Frequently the difficulties over a family budget come not in planning how to spend the money but rather in trying to keep an exact accounting of what each penny was spent for. At least keeping such an account will show where the seepages are. Many couples are amazed to discover how these small expenditures mount into many dollars.

The expenditures for every family are in most respects quite standard, at least for major items, which usually fall into the following categories: food, shelter (which may be broken down into rent or, if the person owns property, taxes, mortgage, and so on), clothing, transportation, operating expenses (under which come the costs of keeping up the home, heat, light, electricity, and telephone), charity, and recreation (under which may come expenditures for personal items, vacations, candy and tobacco), education (under which comes the purchase of books, papers and magazines), and savings (under which come life insurance, a fund for emergencies, and other investments).

The amount that can be allotted to these various items depends, first, upon the amount of income the family has to divide, and second, upon the interests of the members of the family.

The American Institute of Family Relations (Los Angeles) has worked out a practical guide sheet to help couples in setting up a spending plan and in anticipating major items of expense. Here is their outline:

Steps in Setting Up a Spending Plan

1. Decide for what you want to plan: the most important thing you want to accomplish; things of lesser importance but desirable.
2. Decide for how long you want to plan. (Six months, a year, etc.)
3. List the income from all sources that can be depended upon each month.
4. Next set down the various fixed expenses, placing the amount of each under the month when it must be paid.
5. Then calculate the amount which must be set aside each month to meet these fixed expenses which occur less often than monthly (insurance, taxes, etc.).
6. Set up some sort of reserve fund to take care of these expenses. This might be done by:
   a. Having a separate envelope for each of these items and placing the specified sum in each, each month.
   b. Adding together the monthly allowances for the various items to make up a reserve fund which must be set aside as a whole each month. This can go into a temporary savings fund or account, or into the checking account provided it is not used for purposes other than those decided upon.
7. Subtract the total of the fixed expenses for each month from the income for each month. This difference is what is available for the less predictable expenses or those that can be adjusted or varied.
8. Out of this, set aside first a small sum to take care of small unexpected demands or miscalculations. If it is not needed, it can be used for some special pleasure or item.
9. Make an estimate of the amount needed for each of the variable expenses. For this, one can go for information to:
   a. His own past experience.
   b. What he considers essential, or his own standards.
   c. The experiences of others.
   d. Studies of how others spend.
   e. Scientific information.
   f. Suggested divisions of the budget.
   g. "Standard" budgets.
10. Make adjustments until the total of all of these expenses for the month does not exceed the sum available for the variable expenses for that month. Where there are larger expenses which do not occur monthly (larger items of clothing, Christmas gifts, etc.), make some provisions for accumulating the necessary amount through additions to the reserve fund mentioned above, a separate fund, or the like.
11. Select some method for keeping a record of what is spent.
12. Decide who is to be responsible for keeping the record of expenditures, paying the bills, and being responsible for the business management of the household—or which person it to be responsible for which things.
13. Try out the plan for a month, keeping a record of expenditures. Make any adjustments that seem necessary, then try it out again. Continue this until a satisfactory plan is developed.
14. When the budget is running smoothly, simplify the work of account-keeping as much as possible.
15. Measure the success of the plan frequently in terms of what you hoped to accomplish with it.

16. Strive continually to maximize the satisfactions possible from the income available through:
    a. Independence and originality in choice making.
    b. Careful buying.
    c. Intelligent using.

Fixed Expenses

Taxes (state, federal, local): personal, income, automobile, real estate, assessments.
Insurance: life, accident, health, automobile, fire, and theft.
Licenses: car, business, pets.
Fixed payments for medical or hospital care.
Union or professional dues or fees.
Rent, after a decision is made.
Minimum charges for utilities; telephone.
Tuition: fees, special lessons, books, and equipment.
Newspapers and magazines if on a yearly subscription basis.
Installment payments and interest on debts.
Obligations for the support of others.
Pledges made to church or to civic organizations.
Savings: government bonds, savings accounts, investments.
Reserve fund: A fund set aside to take care of larger expenses occurring less often than monthly.

Variable Expenses

Food
    meals at home, lunches, other meals away from home, entertaining
Clothing

outer garments	materials	cleaning and pressing
underwear	dressmaker, tailor	laundry (if not under
footwear	clothing repair	*Household Operation*)
hats, accessories		

Personal Care
    barber and beauty parlor services, shaving supplies and equipment, cosmetics, toilet articles, dental supplies
Housing
    rent, if not already determined; improvements, repairs, and depreciation on owned home.
Furnishings and Equipment

furniture, rugs, carpets	kitchenware
draperies, curtains, shades	cleaning and laundry equipment
silver, china, glass	lamps, fixtures, vases
linen, bedding	clocks, etc.

Household Operation
    utilities, fuel, refrigeration, laundry, household service, household supplies, small equipment, stamps and stationery (if not taken from *Personal Allowance*)
Transportation
    car, train, bus fare; running expenses of automobile; car repairs and upkeep

Health
> doctor, dentist, hospital, medical supplies, devices or equipment

Education
> books, magazines, newspapers, lectures, technical journals, supplies, tuition and special lessons unless a fixed expense, miscellaneous school expenses

Recreation
> travel, vacation, sports, hobbies, musical instruments, music, records, toys, club and organization dues, concerts, opera, theater, movies, dances, meals out, entertaining, races

Gifts
> to members of the family
> to others: wedding, shower, baby, birthday, Christmas, etc.; flowers
> to community welfare: Community Chest, church, Red Cross, etc.

Personal Allowance or Spending Money
> An amount allocated each member of the family for pocket or spending money. In the case of children this might be gradually increased as an educative measure to provide for additional items—school supplies, lunches, clothing, etc.

Estimating the Cost of Children

Family planning has come with urban industrial civilization. Because children are a heavy drain on the family budget, their numbers are limited in most families and the couple tries to save up for the extra cost. In agricultural societies, by contrast, children are workers and are desired in part for the contribution they will make to the family income.

FIGURE 25-3 COST OF A CHILD IN TERMS OF FATHER'S YEARLY INCOME. Source: Based on estimates from Metropolitan Life Insurance Company, **Statistical Bulletin.**

The rearing of each child in the average family requires 3 years of the father's income.

Table 25–2   The Cost of Rearing a Child

	Family of $2,500 Income	Family of $5,000 to $10,000 Income
Cost of birth	$ 300	$ 750
Food	2,272	3,628
Clothing	710	1,697
Shelter	2,648	5,774
Education	82	283
Medical care	297	846
Transportation and recreation	1,127	2,787
Sundries	327	572
Total	$7,763	$16,337

What does a child cost? The initial cost will depend a great deal on the level of living of the couple, their income, and their standard of medical care. The upbringing will vary with the same conditions. To provide couples with a standard for planning, the Metropolitan Life Insurance Company once estimated the cost of rearing a child from birth until he is eighteen years of age, for the family with an annual wage of $2,500, at $7,763. This was on the basis of price levels prevailing in 1935–36, the cost being divided as shown in Table 25–2. Data are also given for a higher-income family, where the cost totals $16,337. These depression-period costs are approximately doubled today.

An analysis of costs per child from birth to wedding estimates it at between $11,000 and $12,000 for farm families to as high as $30,000 for city and suburban families who send their children to private schools.[5] Birth costs now range from $500 to $1,000, care costs through the eighth grade average $14,000, high school costs are approximately $7,000, college costs approximately $8,000, and marriage costs the parents from $1,000 to $1,500. These costs vary with income level of the family and the sex of the child and are at best rough approximations. They do indicate, however, that before he is established in a home of his own the child will represent a substantial investment for the parent.

The cost of rearing a child to maturity, regardless of price levels, may be calculated roughly as requiring three years of the father's income. One child will take three years of the father's earnings; three, nine years, etc. (Figure 25–3).

[5] These cost figures were developed by T. J. Mayo in "The High Cost of Parenthood," *This Week,* September 27, 1965, pp. 26–27.

Three Major Economic Issues

Three major issues face the newlywed couple, each involving very important financial considerations and each fraught with serious consequences to the success of the marriage. They are (1) life insurance, (2) housing, and (3) installment buying. The way these matters are handled has a great deal to do with the couple's financial security and with the long-run success of their joint effort to become a successful economic unit. Let us consider each of these items briefly.

Life Insurance

The young are relatively propertyless, yet they have major responsibilities once children become dependent upon them. This means that in case of the untimely death of the breadwinner, they will have no estate, unless it is provided for by life insurance. By the mere passing of a physical examination and paying of a premium on a policy, an estate of considerable value can be had immediately, the amount of the estate depending on the amount of insurance purchased.

This is the only kind of estate that may be had for a small outlay of cash. It is, therefore, the only kind of estate that the young marriage can afford. Even so, unless wisdom is used, even this estate will be too small to provide for the emergency of death of the family earner. Where investment funds are limited, as they are in the average young marriage, the goal should be to buy the maximum protection for the least cash outlay.

Assuming that the couple will soon have three dependent children, that the husband is earning $6,000 per year, that the couple has the average number of debts and the average standard of living for the beginner in the professions, adequate protection would seem to call for an insurance policy that would replace three or four years of his income if he should die. In other words, he should think of providing an insurance estate with a minimum value of $20,000 to $25,000. This would help pay off pressing debts, in case of his death, and give the family security while the wife was getting back into the work world. If the husband is covered by Social Security and is paying in the maximum contribution the insurance load can be cut in half, since income from this source will carry about half the family burdens of the family with a $6,000-per-year-income.

To be able to afford this much insurance requires that the young man spend his insurance dollar where it will buy the most protection. A look at the chart will show quickly where the greatest protection lies for the least cost—term insurance.

FIGURE 25-4   VALUE OF INSURANCE POLICY BOUGHT FOR $100 YEARLY
PREMIUM.

Different types of insurance policies provide different kinds of protection.
Insurance can have two principal values—protection against risk and savings. Renewable term policies give maximum protection against risk for
those with little to spend from present income. The 20-year endowment
policy gives least protection but maximum savings. Which is the more
appropriate for the young married man with a child and low income? Why?

The shorter the term for which he buys insurance, the less it will cost,
since the risk of death goes up each year, and therefore the cost of coverage
increases slightly with each year of age.

Unfortunately, in certain instances, life insurance is sold for the
benefit of the insurance salesman or broker rather than for the customer.
This is certainly the case when young couples of low income are sold high-
priced endowment policies which net the agent the greatest commission.
Often these policies appeal to uninformed young people because an endowment policy pays something back while they are living. The salesman
calls when the announcement of the birth of their baby appears in the
local paper. At this time, couples uninformed about insurance will do
well to make sure that they are dealing with a reliable and well-informed
agent, of whom there are many today. Endowment policies should be
bought only by those who are in a position to save money. In an endow-

ment policy, a person is buying not only insurance but a savings plan which returns only 4 to 6 percent interest on money deposited beyond the cost of insurance—a return that is little if any more than he can get from government bonds.

There is no objection to the endowment or other type of savings policy for the prosperous, but the beginning family usually cannot afford the low interest return. If it is bought, it is usually at the expense of an adequate protective coverage for dependents. Some are talked into these

FIGURE 25-5   COMPARISON OF NET PREMIUMS FOR $1,000 INSURANCE. Source: Jerome B. Cohen, **Decade of Decision** (New York: Institute of Life Insurance, 1958), p. 11.

The cost of a **straight life** insurance policy is level throughout a person's lifetime. The amount he pays depends on the age at which the policy is taken. The younger the person, the less the death risk and the less he pays per year. Of course he pays a larger sum years before death. In this kind of policy he pays far more in the younger years than it costs to cover the risk of his death; he pays in excess of cost until he is into his fifties, as shown above.

Term policies increase each year in cost, but in the younger ages rates are very low because death risk is low. A five-year term policy, for example, taken at age 25 costs what it costs to cover the death risk between the years 25 to 30 only. This is why term insurance offers maximum coverage at very low costs for the young family, providing the wife and children an immediate estate in case of the death of the husband.

policies, being told that insurance will cost them a much higher rate later on in life. This is true enough, but they will also be earning more and will have a shorter term to go until they collect by death. The facts are that the average couple will have very little need for heavy insurance coverage after age forty to forty-five for their children will have passed the age of dependency. Besides, by then the shrewd couple will have built an inheritance of other business or property assets to protect each other.

FIGURE 25-6   TWENTY-YEAR ENDOWMENT POLICY. Source: Jerome B. Cohen, **Decade of Decision** (New York: Institute of Life Insurance, 1958), p. 16.

The **endowment policy** insurance offers a maximum amount of protection for the money and the maximum amount of savings. A 20-year endowment policy for $1,000 pays $1,000 at the end of 20 years because the buyer has paid in a small amount for insurance and a large amount for savings which draw interest at a low rate. If cashed at the end of 20 years, insurance ceases. This kind of policy is not recommended for the young family because premiums are so high that it is impossible to create an adequate estate for those dependent on the father's income.

Some are enticed into buying high-cost endowment policies by the thought that they will get all their money back in twenty years, or whatever the period of maturity may be. Only the survivor will get the insurance money back, and then only if the insured person dies before his time. At around age twenty-five it costs about $6.00 per year to insure a young man. This rate is based on actuarial tables which show the likelihood of death in a given million, or other large number of people in this age group. These premiums go to pay death claims. Some will die in their twenty-fifth year, in a large group some even the day after the policy is written, others the twenty-sixth year, but some will still be living at one hundred years of age. The company charged enough to pay off each person's inheritors at his death, regardless of his age, and retain a profit. On endowment

FIGURE 25-7 FAMILY INCOME POLICY PROTECTION VALUES. Source: Jerome B. Cohen, **Decade of Decision** (New York: Institute of Life Insurance, 1958), p. 20.

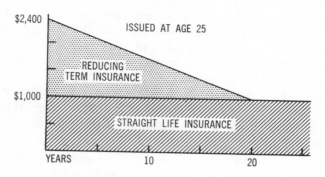

This policy combines **straight life** insurance—giving a small amount of permanent insurance—with a **reducing term** of almost two-and-a-half times the value of the straight life insurance. The reducing term is very cheap since it declines in value with increased age and cuts off entirely before death risk becomes great. This policy costs slightly more than term insurance. For those who have bought costly insurance policies before marriage, adding the declining term rider to the existing policy offers a good solution to the problem of providing a maximum estate while children are most dependent.

policies, one does not get his insurance back. He gets the extra money back which he invested, plus accumulated compounded interest.

Assuming that a young couple can afford, say, $150 per year for life insurance, the choice is clear. For this $150 they can buy around $25,000 renewable term insurance, or at the other extreme, they can buy a twenty-year endowment policy worth around $3,000. If they choose the latter, the widow may not have enough left to pay medical and funeral expenses, to say nothing of providing for herself and the children during the transition back to a normal life.

For a brief graphic comparison of the more common types of policies, see Figures 25-4 to 25-7. The ideal type of insurance for the young couple who can afford a little more than the average beginner is the type depicted in Figure 25-7. Here one is getting a small amount of permanent insurance. Onto this is attached a reducing-term rider, which greatly increases his protection at very low cost for the term in life when his load of dependents is greatest.

Much insurance today is carried through group plans rather than on a personal basis. The military, federal, state, and local governments, public institutions, business corporations, and many other employers have group plans under which employees are covered, usually at advantageous rates.

Often the employer assumes part or all the cost. In the teaching field, the Carnegie Foundation has established the Teachers Insurance and Annuity Association,[6] which is nonprofit. A legal-reserve life insurance company, incorporated in New York State and operating without agents, this company, in addition to funding the retirement plans of colleges and universities, also issues specially designed life insurance policies for college staff members. Here the teacher pays standard rates, but at the close of each year, when the profits are known, refunds are made. Most industries have group plans at very favorable rates.

The need of the young couple for life insurance is depicted statistically in Figure 25–8 which shows the chance of a child's being orphaned now compared with his chance at the beginning of the century.[7] The chances

FIGURE 25–8   CHANCES IN 1,000 THAT A NEWBORN CHILD WILL BE ORPHANED BEFORE AGE 18. Source: Metropolitan Life Insurance Company, "Family Responsibilities Increasing," **Statistical Bulletin,** 40:3–5, April, 1959.

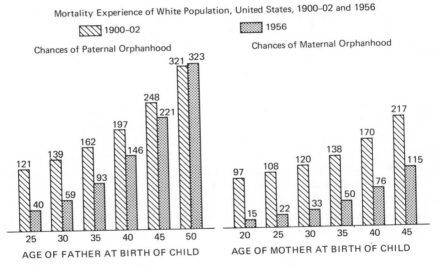

Although the chances of death of a parent have greatly decreased, there is still sufficient risk to justify purchase of insurance on a basis which will assure maximum protection for the young couple without property, rather than provide for savings in old age. Study figure 25–4 and see that $100 a year can buy $17,500 worth of protection or $3,000 worth of protection plus the investment feature.

[6] Address: 730 Third Avenue, New York, N.Y. 10017.

[7] Metropolitan Life Insurance Company, "Family Responsibilities Increasing," *Statistical Bulletin,* 40:3–5, April, 1959.

are much less now than then, but still there is sufficient likelihood of the father's dying before the child has reached eighteen to justify carrying a reasonable amount of protective coverage.

In case of divorce before the family is reared, there is still need for life insurance protection. In fact, disposition of insurance increasingly enters into divorce suits.

Home Ownership

In acquiring home-ownership debt, the couple is in the area of simple interest money and investment use of credit. Not only are houses looked upon as investment debt in credit circles, they are considered the safest of all debts. For this reason, home finance is the cheapest in the market-place of money. In fact, the bulk of insurance company loans, much labor union retirement fund money, and much bank capital is invested in real estate. And throughout the nation are numerous savings and loan associations which use most of their capital in home finance. Those with federal charters guarantee the money deposited by investors on the same basis as deposits are insured in banks with federal charters.

Home ownership should be an aspiration of most young couples, and separate living quarters, even though a rented house or apartment, are almost necessary today, when a rather complete economic break from the parental family is expected at marriage.

Whether one can buy a home depends very much on the kind of credit arrangements that can be made, the down payment, and the interest rates. Houses are almost always bought on credit, and ordinarily in the younger years should be. This kind of debt is creative, in that a house, with a little work by the couple in improving it, usually increases in value.

The general standard is that one can buy a house valued at twice his annual income and not be overreaching himself. In other words, the $7,000-a-year man can safely buy a $14,000 house. He may go higher if he gets low interest and a low down payment.

The importance of housing to the success of marriage and family life has never been adequately studied, but certainly living arrangements have much to do with the personal relations of husband and wife and of parents and children. Living with in-laws results in congested living arrangements and lack of privacy, as well as in a tendency of relatives to interfere with the couple's adjustment to each other.

In Great Britain during World War II, when family members were forced to live in one room because of the heating problem, many families found it necessary to impose the rule of silence on the family. Only by this means could they tolerate the close and congested living that was forced upon them.

One only has to investigate the matter casually in Europe to know the terrible strain and frustration of inadequate housing. In France, Holland, and Germany, for example, into the 1950's, people who had more than an average of one and a half rooms per family member were required to take in an additional family. Many young people could not marry because they were unable to find housing. Some married and had to live apart a good deal of the time. Even in Sweden and Denmark, where such rules of combining households were not in force, many of the same problems of housing shortage existed, hindering marriage and increasing unmarried motherhood and other problems.

Low-cost government-insured bank loans have been a major factor in the development of private family housing in the United States since World War II. It has made possible extensive home ownership even during a period of high building costs. Over half of American nonfarm families now own their own homes. Home ownership is certainly a factor in family stability, both from a psychological and a mobility standpoint.

Undoubtedly some young couples have overextended themselves economically in order to acquire a new home, or too high-priced a home, but there are others who would have been much further ahead had they bought rather than paid high rental rates. When can one afford to buy a house?

It is not necessary to be rich to buy a house, but usually a down payment of about one-tenth of the price of the house is required. (More liberal terms have been granted to veterans.) A rough standard by which one may judge what amount he should pay for his home in relation to his earnings is the following:

If income is	Family can afford a home costing
$ 5,000	$10,000 to $12,500
10,000	20,000 to 25,000
20,000	40,000 to 50,000

The Chicago Metropolitan Home Builders' Association has set up the following even more specific table to help persons determine how much of the family's monthly income may be invested safely in a home. It does not contradict the preceding—in fact, it agrees quite closely with that standard—but does spell it out in greater detail. Here are monthly payments on a home that families of different months incomes can handle ranging from the safe side to the risky side:

Monthly income after taxes	Safely	Probably	Risky
$200	$ 58	$ 66	$ 75
250	64	72	83
300	68	78	91
350	74	84	100
400	78	90	109
450	82	96	118
500	86	102	127
550	89	108	135
600	92	112	142
650	96	118	149
700	99	124	156
750	101	130	161
800	103	136	168

Home Financing

The amount a couple can pay for a home and the monthly payment load they can carry will vary with the number of children, the number of high-interest installment contracts they carry, their habits of thrift, their ability to handle maintenance and make improvements themselves, and many other factors in their living habits and spending practices. But one of the basic factors is the kind of financing they are able to get at the outset in buying a house.

Few pay cash for a house, rather houses are usually bought on contract with a small down payment and monthly payments. The monthly payments include principal and interest. If the buyer pays 10 percent down on a new development house, the balance will be paid in equal monthly payments over a period of twenty-five years. (Federal Housing Administration loans, available through banks and other lending agencies, government-insured, may run up to thirty years. Most insurance companies and savings and loan associations lend for a maximum of twenty-five years.) Let us say this house is bought for $15,500. The buyer, then, has paid down $1,550 (10 percent). He will owe $14,000 on the mortgage. It will require a monthly payment of $98.95 for 300 months (twenty-five years) to pay off the balance with interest on the declining balance at the rate of 7 percent. On a house of this value, insurance will run around $20 per year and taxes around $220. (Rates will vary from community to community. Small towns usually have lower taxes than this; larger cities have much higher taxes.) Most couples prefer to pay the taxes and insurance monthly. If they are paid in this way rather than in a lump sum annually, the $240 required for taxes and insurance will raise monthly payments by $20. This brings the total monthly payment to $118.95.

Upkeep   Home ownership involves upkeep. How much will be required depends on the condition of the house. Here we are dealing with a new house (an old one would require more upkeep). But even with a new house, plumbing can become clogged, and in time paint and other maintenance will be necessary. At the beginning, landscaping and fencing may be required, or widow screens, screen doors, or gutters may be needed. Also, one must allow some money for unexpected upkeep. Let us say the total allowance for upkeep will be $10 per month. The actual cost of ownership then becomes 128.95 per month. Couples who are handy with tools and paint brush can keep maintenance costs low; others can expect them to be much higher.

Interest costs   In considering home purchase, the interest rate on the contract is very important. Suppose the young couple in shopping for a house are offered the same house with an 8 percent interest rate instead of 7 percent. Then the contract payments for the 300 months would be $108.06 or $9.11 more per month before insurance, taxes, and upkeep. Over the life of the contract this interest rate makes the house cost $2,277.50 more.

House finance is the cheapest money the family can borrow, but even so, a one-half percent difference in interest rate can affect the family budget. At the start of the 70s, interest rates on home financing are so high as to make purchase prohibitive for the young buyer. Rates of 8.5 to 9.5 percent make monthly payments out of the range of most family budgets.

The down payment   If the buyer has an extra $1,000 beyond the required down payment, should he add it to the down payment? Old ideas of American thrift would lead one to advise "yes." In the present pattern of American life, the answer is "no." Keep the extra thousand for other investment or for other use.

The typical young couple, in three to six years, will be moving to a larger house in a new city or new neighborhood of the same city. They will want to get their equity back for the down payment on a higher priced home. Even with the small down payment and the equity gained from monthly payments, the new buyer must have quite a sizable down payment to repay the seller's investment. This will be particularly true if the sellers have improved the house and landscaping and raised the price a thousand dollars or so to gain a little profit from their investment and effort. The chances are that if the extra thousand-dollar down payment had been made, the buyer would be priced out of the market, if the sellers expected to get it back in cash. To sell, they would likely have to take a second mortgage and take years to get the extra thousand back in small monthly payments.

The buying situation   There are some localities and some towns and cities where real estate is depressed. If one is certain he is going to live there the rest of his life and in the same house, bargains are plentiful. But for a young couple on the way up, this is not a buying situation. There may be no market when they move on to the new job or the bigger house.

In buying, consultation with someone who knows conditions in the new locality—a banker, builder, or realtor—can reduce risk.

It is also important to consider community services and institutions. Distances to a shopping center, to schools, and to churches are important. On selling, convenience of location with reference to such institutions will be a factor in demand and sale price.

Profit possibilities   The young couple on the way up should buy only in a community where they can expect to make a profit when the advancement in position requires that they sell. With "do-it-yourself" skills, this is a realistic goal in the average growing community. A great deal will depend, however, on the energy the pair puts into improving the house and landscaping. Improvements usually add more value than they cost, particularly if the couple do the work, and the improvements will add to family comfort. As the family increases in size, the couple will likely want to add a room or two to meet space requirements.

Installment Credit

Here we enter the world of hard-interest money, or discount interest. Rates usually range upward from 10 percent, with the average in the 15 to 20 percent range. Can one get ahead paying a fifth of his income for the use of money? This is a question to which few young families today give serious thought.

The American family is time-contract-minded. The merits of this philosophy of economics is widely debated, and, of course, even from the standpoint of the individual family, there are two sides to the question. There is no doubt that a young couple can get off to a quicker start by buying on contract to the full extent of their credit. But they burden themselves with an interest load which reduces their capacity to buy for one or two years ahead, particularly if they load themselves with contracts with excessive interest rates. Yet in periods of inflation part of the excess interest is offset by price rises in goods over a two-year period.

Interest-charge abuses have been so great that consumer credit is now regulated by the "Truth in Lending Law," passed by Congress to protect the consumer from excessive hidden interest charges. All time contracts must show the true rate of interest in terms of simple interest. In financing cars, for example, the claim of 6 percent can no longer be made. Cars are sold at discount or at hard-interest rates. The 6 percent is closer to 12 percent on a simple-interest basis, and this must be shown in the contract. The actual simple-interest charge on credit-card accounts and store-credit balances must also be shown.

On consumer goods interest rates have to be high to cover the cost of collection, bookkeeping, loss on goods not paid for, repossession of goods, and their resale.

Many couples justify purchases with high carrying charges in terms of immediate comfort, convenience, or necessity. There are no doubt instances where such added costs are justified, but to make installment buying a habit in family living is to sell oneself short in making the most of income. In cases where quick credit is needed, those who, after a period of thrift and saving, have established sound credit, can usually borrow on a straight bank loan at 7 to 10 percent simple interest on the unpaid balance.

Factors In a Personal Credit Rating

Banks and other agencies which lend money rate those who apply for credit. Here is a standard form used by many banks that is quite like the I.Q. test used in school placement.

The bank wishes to know the following:
Income? _____
How long on present job? _____
Credit experience? _____
Equity in real estate? _____
Down payment you can make on purchase? _____
Total Score _____
From information below fill out your credit rating above.

Income per week:	*Points*
Under $75	0
$76 to $100	150
Over $100	200
Wife earning	50

Length of time on job:

Less than a year	0
One to four years	100
Four to ten years	150
Over ten years	250

Credit experience:

None	0
Favorable for six months (one source)	250
Favorable for six months (from another source)	100
Good record from previous loans from bank	100
Unfavorable credit references	−100

Equity in property:

Little or unknown but do own	100
Equity twice minimum, or five years' ownership	200
Property owned clear	300

Down payment you can make:

0 to 10 percent	0
10 percent to one-third	100
Over a third	200

(A score of 600 will usually be sufficient for small loans.)

Source: "A Guide to Consumer Credit, Public Affairs Pamphlet No. 348, New York.

There Will Never Be Enough Money

As was stated at the outset, one of the most certain facts that any young couple must face in planning for their economic future is that they will never have enough money to meet all their needs. A nationwide survey of attitudes on this point by the office of Public Opinion Research of Princeton showed that most Americans are not satisfied with the amount of money they make. The less than a third who felt that they were more or less satisfied with their incomes were not necessarily the most prosperous; in fact, they were more likely to be farmers and businessmen who were self-employed and felt that they controlled their own economic future.

The most dissatisfied group of all was the professional group, where income is generally fairly adequate but where aspirations for an improved level of living are apparently extremely high. Another finding of opinion polls is that people who define happiness in terms of making money actually are not as likely to achieve happiness as those who consider love, family, and wisdom the essentials in life.

Probably the greatest worry of the American family is in making ends meet. This struggle between the amount of money the family makes and the number of things they want suggests that perhaps the majority of American families never really learn to live within their incomes.

The family with a $5,000 income is sure its members would have everything they wanted with $10,000; but the family with the $10,000 income is just as certain, and perhaps even more so, that it could meet all its needs with $15,000. Yet Spectorsky's study of "exurbanites"[8]—the high-pressure New York advertisers and promoters who live in the lavish mansions with acreages out beyond the suburbs—shows that not only are they living high on the hog, but they are also so deeply in debt that the $40,000 man must look forward to moving up another $10,000 to $20,000 a year to ever get out, and the man already up there is as bad or worse off.

Credit counseling clinics are now common in many communities to keep the couples from falling into the hands of loan sharks and bankruptcy courts. Help in locating such clinics may be had by writing: National Foundation of Consumer Credit, 1819 H Street, Washington, D.C. 20006.

In summary, the secret of happy family life from the standpoint of its economic adjustment would seem to be largely a matter of limiting desires to one's ability to pay. The worry over unmet bills can become chronic in those families which are constantly living beyond their income. The habit of thrift, of cautious and wise spending, probably has no relationship whatever to amount of income earned. These habits either are or are not deeply ingrained in the training of the child and in the philosophy of the individual as he learns to use money. Those who are thrifty can save, even on a small income, and can limit their expenditures to their prospective income. Those who are of extravagant habit and who see no virtue in saving seldom realize a secure and prosperous living on any amount of income. This has been shown repeatedly in the lives of sons of American millionaires, who in many instances have been able to run through their parents' acquisition of millions in a matter of years and end up in poverty.

Money is the road to purchasing many of the satisfactions that make life worth while, but whether it actually does so is a matter of judgment, taste, values, and buying habits, much more than the amount of money the family handles.

Problems

1. Discuss this statement with reference to marriage happiness, "Dollars alone are not enough. You've got to have dollars and sense."
2. Lawrence earns a comfortable income, but he and Jane are only recently married, and there are a hundred ways in which each extra dollar could

---

[8] A. C. Spectorsky, *The Exurbanites* (Philadelphia: J. B. Lippincott Co., 1955).

be spent. When Lawrence handles the money, he and Jane have a lot of fun, but at the end of the month there are always bills he forgot to pay. When Jane handles the money, the bills get paid and they are able to buy some of the extra things they want—furniture, records, etc.—but Lawrence feels that they have no fun and resents the fact that he is given an allowance like a child. What alternative method of money management might you suggest that would satisfy the economic-psychological needs of both Lawrence and Jane?

3. Poll the class on the questions, "What income are you likely to receive in the occupation you plan to enter? Do you believe that it will be more or less than ample for your needs and wishes?" Tabulate and discuss the class expectations with regard to future income. Do the expectations of the group seem to be realistic?

4. A marriage counselor advised a childless couple after their fifth year of marriage, "If you wait until you can afford to have children, you'll never have them." How accurate do you consider his observation? What merit is there in estimating the cost of children?

5. *a.* Nat and Alice are twenty-eight and twenty-six, respectively. They have two children, age two months and two years, and plan to have one more after a few years. Nat has a relatively secure position, and Alice has a temporary half-time job. Their combined incomes total $6,700 a year before taxes. What type of insurance and what amount would you advise them to buy?

b. With a saving of only $1,000 would you advise Nat and Alice to consider buying a house? If so, what price range should they consider? Under their circumstances, what are the advantages, or disadvantages, of apartment living?

6. What is the appeal of installment buying? Under what circumstances is it justified? Some couples argue that it helps in budgeting if almost everything is bought on the installment plan. In what way is this true? What argument is there against it?

7. One occasionally hears of people with fabulous incomes who are sued for indebtedness. How can this situation be explained in the case of honest, well-meaning people?

8. *Sociodrama:* A young man and wife who have not yet begun their family disagree on how the income should be handled. The play opens as the husband suggests, "Let's pay all the bills at the beginning of each month; put the rest in a big purse and trust one another to draw from it wisely. We'll save whatever is left over each month."

Selected References

Articles in Books of Readings

Landis, Judson T., and Landis, Mary G., *Readings in Marriage and the Family* (Englewood Cliffs, N.J.: Prentice-Hall, Inc., 1952).
    Cyrus, Della, "Problems of the Modern Homemaker-Mother," pp. 392–402.

General References

Cohen, Jerome B., *Decade of Decision*, revised edition (New York: Institute of Life Insurance, Educational Division, 1967).

Hafstrom, Jeanne L., and Dunsing, Marilyn M., "A Comparison of Economic Choices of One-Earner and Two-Earner Families," *Journal of Marriage and the Family*, 27:403–409, August, 1965.

Matteson, William J., and Harwood, E. C., *Life Insurance from the Buyer's Point of View* (Great Barrington, Mass.: American Institute of Economic Research), annual revisions.

Metropolitan Life Insurance Company, "The Widows and Widowhood," *Statistical Bulletin*, 47:3–6, 1966.

Morgan, James N., "Family Use of Credit," *Journal of Home Economics*, January, 1968, pp. 21.

Ross, Irwin, "When You Borrow, When You Buy—Watch Those Interest Rates," *Reader's Digest*, November, 1963, pp. 157–165.

Schwabacher, Albert E., Jr., "The Repository of Wealth," in Seymour M. Farber and Roger H. L. Wilson (eds.), *The Potential of Women* (New York: McGraw-Hill Book Co., 1963), pp. 241–254.

The Women's Division of the Institute of Life Insurance, 448 Madison Avenue, New York, N.Y. 10022, publishes certain free materials of value to the average couple; for example, *The Money Manager* (a work-sheet for a family budget); *A Discussion of Family Money; How Budgets Work and What They Do* (Informal Study No. 3).

6

PARENTHOOD

26

Family Planning

The growing awareness of world hunger, and the imminent catastrophe of mankind as it approaches the time when, even with the best possible distribution of food resources, there will not be enough, have made having children a matter of thoughtful consideration for every couple. Awareness of the population explosion has undoubtedly been a factor in the falling birth rate (down from 25 per 1,000 population in 1957 to 17.9 now)[1] in the United States.

Even with this drop, the birth rate is still about twice what we need for population replacement. There are 9.5 deaths per thousand per year, compared to the above 17.9 births. The immigration-emigration ratio is the only other factor that can affect rate of growth, and immigration is now strictly regulated.

It is likely that our nation will develop population policies to greatly lower the birth rate in the immediate years ahead. In fact, these efforts are already under way on a modest scale as a means of alleviating the burden of children on families of the poor, and of breaking the poverty cycle in families living on welfare generation after generation.

During the life time of the present college population the time will likely come when having more than two children will be considered a matter of great social concern, or even of prohibition. Nations with less abundance of space and food, may even see moratoriums on births altogether for longer or shorter periods of time.[2]

More attention will be given to quality also. In highly competitive agriculture, plant and animal eugenics are the key to survival. We will likely

[1] The ratio for whites is 17.4, for nonwhites, 26.1, according to Natality Statistics of the National Center of Health Statistics.

[2] Paul R. Ehrlich, "World Population: Is the Battle Lost?" *Stanford Today,* Winter '68 Series 1, No. 22: see also in *Reader's Digest,* pp. 137–140, February, 1969.

see national registration of families with known defects that are transmissible, and control of marriage where the statistical chances of polluting the genetic stream are high.

With increasing knowledge of genetics, control will be more certain than at present. With rapid strides in the study of genetic material, less control in some areas will be necessary, because of ability to determine heredity and make corrections in the uterus.

As having children becomes more of a privilege and less an inherent right, children will be a greater source of joy, and many of the burdens of having children will be removed. Resources will be more adequate, children will be more healthy and parents will less often have to ask themselves, "Will my child be normal?"

How Life Begins

Each girl is born with a lifetime supply of many thousands of immature eggs in her ovaries. During her fertile lifetime only some 400 to 500 eggs will ripen, at the rate of one per twenty-eight days. About the twelfth day after the beginning of menstruation, an egg cell is released from an ovary and floats into the opening of the Fallopian tube. Its capacity to survive in the tube is limited, perhaps to a maximum of eight hours. To be fertilized, the thick wall of the cell must be penetrated by a sperm cell. If it is met in the tube by sperm, which have been discharged into the vagina and have swum up through the uterus and into the Fallopian tube, the fertilized egg then begins to divide and to move down into the uterus (or womb). Here it attaches itself to the wall, which is fully lined with bloodfilled tissues to cushion the egg and nourish it.

One ovulation occurs, normally every 28 days, from one ovary or the other. This will usually be between the tenth and sixteenth day. During most of the ovulations that take place in the woman's fertile life cycle, no sperm will be there to meet the egg, or even if they are there, they may not succeed in penetrating its wall. As a consequence, rather than the womb performing its function of nursing the egg, the microscopic-sized unfertilized egg floats on through and is discharged. Since the blood-filled uterine wall is unused, some fourteen to sixteen days later it breaks down and passes out in the menstrual flow.

After the cessation of the flow, the rebuilding of the womb lining begins again preparatory to another ovulation, which takes place, as is mentioned above, about the twelfth day after the beginning of menstruation.

There is a slight rise in temperature near the time of ovulation. The temperature change is due to hormone changes and often does not conform exactly to the period of ovulation. Some women feel the egg burst through

FIGURE 26–1 FETUS JUST PRIOR TO BIRTH. Source: C. L. Anderson, **Physical and Emotional Aspects of Marriage** (St. Louis: C. V. Mosby Co., 1953). Reproduced by permission of the publisher and Dr. Anderson.

The magnified section shows the sinuses in which the mother's blood circulates. Only the thick lining of the sinuses separates the maternal bloodstream from that of the fetus.

the wall of the ovary, with a sharp cutting pain (called *mittelschmerz*) but most are not aware of the time of ovulation.

In sexual intercourse, approximately a tablespoon of semen, containing some 500 millions of sperm, is deposited in the upper part of the vaginal tract, near the *cervix*, or neck of the *womb* or *uterus*. The cervix is a strong muscle with an opening that is normally very small, but it can stretch to permit the passage of the baby at birth. Vaginal fluids are hostile to sperm, but if pregnancy is to result, some sperm must swim rather quickly through this tiny opening (or be sucked through with the orgasmic contractions of the uterus) and travel the long distance up through the womb to meet the female ovum in the Fallopian tube. The five-inch journey of the sperm has been likened to a man's five-mile swim upstream. If the egg meets the sperm, and one finally breaks through its tough wall, the egg is fertilized. The fertilized egg becomes the *zygote*, and as cell division proceeds, the *embryo*, which after birth becomes the child.

The point at which the zygote becomes attached to the uterine wall develops into the umbilical cord and provides the nutritional contact between mother and child. Here the blood streams of mother and child flow side by side, permitting nutrition to pass through the thin wall by osmosis from the mother's blood stream to the embryo's, and permitting the embryo's wastes to pass into the mother's blood stream.

In the womb the embryo grows the normal nine months (known as the *gestation period*), when contractions in the uterus warn the mother that the birth of the child is imminent (see Figure 26–1). [For an excellent film showing all these processes, see *Human Reproduction.*]

Heredity in Family Planning

Many young people enter marriage with groundless fears about their heredity. Others who enter marriage with hereditary defects should be concerned about them, but are not. The field of heredity is a highly technical one and only a competent eugenist can give adequate advice on specific problems. Suffice it here to give some general information.

The marriage of close relatives has been condemned in most primitive and modern societies. Yet the question comes up frequently as to whether cousins can marry. In the Arab culture cousin marriage is still extensive. The difficulty of cousin marriages arises out of the simple fact that all human strains carry certain undesirable and usually hidden traits in the germ plasma. These pathological genes are recessive. When two recessive genes combine they can produce an individual with the undesirable trait. The likelihood of relatives combining the recessive genes is many times greater than of nonrelatives doing so. Cousins, therefore, have a greater chance of producing offspring with genetic abnormalities than do people with completely different blood lines.

A study of 106 first-cousin marriages showed that while there was little ill effect prior to birth, insofar as spontaneous abortions and still-births were concerned, damage began to appear after birth and increased with age.[3] The death rate was three times that of marriages outside the bloodline, and abnormalities were twice as numerous—major abnormalities, even more than twice as numerous.[4]

Fortunately for mankind, most defective traits are recessive, and affect offspring only when both husband and wife carry the defective gene; in such cases, the chances are one in four of the offsprings' inheriting it. Cystic fibrosis is a fatal genetic trait, which causes offspring to die after a few weeks, months, or years. It is a chronic disease of the pancreas beginning in infancy and manifesting itself in inability to digest food and difficulty in breathing. About one in every 20 adults carries the defective gene, and about one in 800 white children inherit it. It is rarely found among Negroids and mongoloids.

The predisposition to diabetes, epilepsy, certain forms of heart disease, high blood pressure, and some forms of mental illness may be inherited. By this is meant that they appear more readily under certain conditions of environmental stress in people with these diseases in their hereditary background than among others, even though the diseases themselves may not be transmissible in the genes.

On diabetes, Amram Scheinfeld[5] presents these facts: (1) one in four diabetics has a diabetic relative; (2) if one identical twin has diabetes, the other will also, in almost every case; (3) diabetes is inherited in some strains of mice.

In addition to the known million diabetics in the United States, the Health Information Foundation says there are a million unknown diabetics.

There are only one in twenty chances that a parent who is an epileptic will have an epileptic child, and in only about one case in seventy will seizures become chronic. The type of epilepsy which develops after age thirty has no hereditary basis at all.

Huntington's chorea (deteriorating brain disease with onset of middle age) is definitely hereditary and dominant. Hemophilia and color blindness are sex-linked hereditary defects (carried by the mother but appearing in the male line). There are numerous other less common diseases which are known to be of genetic origin.

[3] Herman M. Slatis, Raymond H. Reis, and Robert E. Hoene in the *American Journal of Human Genetics,* December, 1958, summarized in *Family Life,* 19:2–4, March, 1959.

[4] For study of a line degenerated by inbreeding see Carl Mydans, "Far-Off Exiles of Tristan," *Life,* July 12, 1963, pp. 72–78.

[5] Amram Scheinfeld, *The Basic Facts of Human Heredity* (Philadelphia: J. B. Lippincott, 1961), p. 80.

Genetic Counseling

The unanswered question of all expectant parents is, "Will our child be normal?" One of the heaviest burdens parents have to bear is having a defective child. There is about one chance in 33 that a child will be born with some defect.

The time to seriously consider this question is before marriage. Certainly not all defects can be anticipated. Even those of sound heredity may have a defective child—for reasons that will become evident later in this chapter. But most young people do not even think of counseling in this area until they have had one or more defective children. Then they are inclined to react with a sense of guilt: "What have I done to deserve this?"[6]

Unlike Denmark, where all defective families are registered, in the United States it is up to prospective parents themselves individually and together to analyze their backgrounds for similar recessive defective traits. Because of the very common use of drugs for medicinal reasons and as a means of escape, x-ray effects of radiation, and many other factors, genetic counseling is advisable for many couples. Some have anxieties based on common myths, or about consequences of racial mixture and want to allay their fears in this area.

Genetic counseling for those who have had a defective child helps them decide whether the risk of a repetition of the defect in other children they may wish to have is too great. Doctor J. A. Fraser Roberts, of London's Guy Hospital, has worked out the ratio in which hereditary defects will reappear. If the risk is as high as one in ten, it is a high risk. Muscular dystrophy, hemophilia, and some forms of mental retardation are in the high-risk group, as is cystic fibrosis, with a risk of one in four. In the low-risk group, Dr. Roberts places those diseases with a less than one in twenty-five chance of reoccuring.

Where the risk is statistically too great, the couple may choose sterilization. If they wish to have a family, they can adopt.

Some couples will need to choose sterilization before marriage if they intend to meet their social obligation. Knowing that they each carry recessive traits that may come out in their offspring, or that one carries a dominant defect, they have to choose between further pollution of the genetic pool, refraining from marriage, or seeking sterilization. Most states have sterilization laws, which were designed to eliminate certain defective strains, but they have not been widely used. Probable reasons are: (1) the

---

[6] William M. Rose and Walter J. Burdette, "Some Sociological Aspects Inherent in Genetic Counseling," *Journal of Marriage and Family Living,* 28:204–205, May, 1966.

uncertainty about what is hereditary and what is not, particularly in the area of mental deficiency and mental disease; (2) uncertainty about hereditary factors involved in many physical diseases and defects which tend to run in families; (3) uncertainty about hereditary factors in such areas as criminality and moral deficiency; (4) resistance of certain religious groups to interfering with man's capability of reproduction; (5) some political resistance to the state's deciding who may and who may not reproduce.[7]

New techniques now make possible the correction of certain hereditary defects very early in the intrauterine period. As more is being learned about the chemistry of the cell, eugenicists look forward to the time when they can control human heredity by selecting gene combinations. Some predict that this will be the most significant development of the next century.

The following are the institutions with the major human heredity clinics in the United States and Canada:

United States
  Bowman Gray School of Medicine, Winston-Salem, N.C.
  Children's Memorial Hospital, Chicago, Ill.
  Dight Institute, University of Minnesota, Minneapolis, Minn.
  Johns Hopkins University Medical School, Baltimore, Md.
  Medical College of Virginia, Richmond, Va.
  Minnesota Dept. of Health, University of Minnesota Campus,
      Minneapolis, Minn.
  New York State Psychiatric Institute, New York, N.Y. 10032.
  Tulane University Medical School, New Orleans, La.
  University of Chicago, Dept. of Zoology, Chicago, Ill.
  University of Michigan, Ann Arbor, Mich.
  University of North Carolina, Chapel Hill, N.C.
  University of Oklahoma, Norman, Okla.
  University of Texas, Austin, Tex.
  University of Utah, Salt Lake City, Utah
  University of Washington Medical School, Seattle, Wash.
  Western Reserve University, Dept. of Biology, Cleveland, Ohio

Canada
  Children's Hospital, Winnipeg, Manitoba
  Children's Memorial Hospital, Montreal, Quebec

[7] The National Association for Voluntary Sterilization, formerly called Human Betterment Association for Voluntary Sterilization, once published statistics annually on eugenics sterilizations performed in the various states (their report of December 31, 1963, showed that 63,678 such operations had been performed, mostly for the mentally ill and mentally deficient). Now their emphasis is on voluntary sterilization as a means of controlling population.

Hospital for Sick Children, Toronto, Ontario
McGill University, Toronto, Ontario
University of Alberta, Edmonton, Alberta
University of British Columbia, Vancouver, British Columbia

Sterility

Some 10 to 15 percent of marriages throughout the world are sterile; at least, this proportion never bears children throughout their married life. This is the conclusion of The First World Congress on Human Infertility, held in New York City in May, 1953, with 1,300 physicians from fifty-three nations in attendance.[8] United States Census data show that childlessness ranges from 9 percent of rural marriages in the United States to over 17 percent in urban marriages. It is assumed that most of the sterility is involuntary. Although a few marriages, of course, are voluntarily childless.

Of the Kinsey Institute for Sex Research sample of women, 20 percent of marriages proved infertile.[9] Women who married youngest proved to be the most fertile, in that they became pregnant most often and in a higher percentage of cases. Of those who married before the age of 21, pregnancy occurred among 90 percent and they averaged 3.5 pregnancies. Pregnancy occurred among 86 percent of those who married between 21 and 25, and they averaged 2.8 pregnancies. Of those who delayed the marriage until after age 30, the Institute reports that not more than half became pregnant, although the sample of this age group was rather small. They cite confirming evidence that after age 30 very few women in any of the samples become pregnant, even those who had previously demonstrated their fertility. From age 46 on there is only one chance in 500 of a woman's becoming pregnant.

Throughout history sterility has been considered a tragedy, and has universally been looked upon as a defect in the wife. This is no longer so. Absolute sterility is thought to characterize only a small percentage of the childless marriages and where it exists it is now recognized that the husband is as responsible as the wife. In fact, Dr. Edward Tyler estimates that more sterility is caused by lack of male sperm count than any other single factor. He blames this for 40 percent of all cases of infertile marriages.[10]

[8] For a brief summary of this conference see Abraham Stone M.D., "World Conference on Human Fertility," *Marriage and Family Living*, 15:231–233, August, 1953.

[9] Paul H. Gebhard and others, *Pregnancy, Birth and Abortion* (New York: Harper & Bros. and Paul B. Hoeber, Inc., 1958).

[10] Reported in a television address. Dr. Tyler is with Planned Parenthood in the Greater Los Angeles area. He practices in the Venice, California Clinic.

In general, the treatment of infertile husbands is less successful than the treatment of sterile wives. Hormone and drug treatments have for the most part proved disappointing. A recent development is the use of pituitary hormone to bring about ovulation in women who do not ovulate.[11] The hormone, at first taken from the glands of the dead, is now extracted from the urine of postmenopausal women. The drug (Pergonal, for gonad) often causes ova to break out of both egg sacs at once so that nearly half who become pregnant have twins. A few have quadruplets.

Various medical and surgical techniques have been developed to treat sterility. Knowledge of them may be obtained from doctors, specialists, and clinics. It is, however, important to know that the likelihood of barrenness increases somewhat with delay of pregnancy; each year pregnancy becomes more difficult. This leads some practicing gynecologists to advise the young woman with an underdeveloped uterus or other symptoms which might indicate difficulty in becoming pregnant to have her first pregnancy early in the marriage.

That emotions can affect fertility is becoming well established.[12] The Margaret Sanger Research Bureau in New York City studied 500 cases of sterile couples. Of these, 122 couples were found to be sterile because of psychological tensions.[13] Once the tensions were removed by counseling and reassurance, they became pregnant. Only five of the 122 needed psychotherapy. It may well be that this is nature's way of keeping the nervous mother from conceiving offspring who would be damaged during development by her extreme stress. As is shown in a later paragraph, extreme nervous tension of the mother can produce a child who is neurotic at birth.

Alternatives to Natural Conception

In many cultures of the world, perhaps in most of them historically, a fertility ceremonial has been institutionalized. This may consist of a sanctioned period of license, in which mating with others than the spouse is more or less taken for granted. There is a survival of these practices in many advanced cultures. In the West German Catholic areas, for example, especially in the Rhineland, Swabia, and Bavaria, there is an annual ceremony called the *Karneval.* (In rural areas it is called *die Fastnacht.*) It is a Mardi Gras type of celebration, with riotous parties and a carnival atmosphere that takes over the community. Drinking and carousing are the

[11] Isabella Taves, "New Adventures in Female Fertility," *Look,* May 19, 1964, p. 91 ff.

[12] "Emotions Affect Fertility," *Science News Letter,* 61: p. 308, June 14, 1952.

[13] *Family Life,* 16:5, February 6, 1956.

order of the day. It is said that the spouse who would attempt to sue the mate on grounds of infidelity which occurred during Bavaria's carnival time would be laughed out of court.[14]

Such practices are a boon to the spouse of an infertile mate, but they are hardly an acceptable solution to this problem in our society. Artificial insemination now offers scientific help to the apparently sterile couple. In cases where both husband and wife are fertile but conception fails to take place, instrumental insemination using the husband's semen is sometimes successful.

Thousands of artificial inseminations have been successfully carried out. It is, however, according to some authorities, still hazardous to the marriage. Husbands rarely suggest artificial insemination. Even when his consent is willingly given, and in spite of the fact that he is present when the act of insemination is performed, the husband may become jealous and suspicious, feeling that the wife has been disloyal. It should not be undertaken, using a donor's semen, without being discussed fully.

The emotional impact of artificial insemination is found by Farris to be less serious than these warnings suggest. He reports, for example, that there may be the same emotional complications in the case of adoption, when there is resentment against the adoption agent. Artificial insemination does meet the desire of the couple to experience pregnancy, and promises 50 percent heredity, which gives promise of a closer tie than does adoption. It also protects the husband's pride, in that no one but he and his wife know the child is not his. He also finds that couples he studied who had a child by artificial insemination would unanimously agree to have another.[15]

Student attitudes generally favor artificial insemination by the husband but not by a donor. Vernon and Broadway, studying attitudes toward artificial insemination, both by donors and by husbands at Central Michigan College, reported a great preference for adoption over artificial insemination by any means.[16] Only 73.5 percent would approve artificial insemination using the husband's semen, compared to 90 percent studied by Greenberg at Colorado, and only 17 percent would approve it by a donor compared to 52 percent at Colorado studied by Greenberg. Religious reasons were among those given for condemning artificial insemination. The more conservative attitudes, as would be expected, were among

[14] *Time*, February 27, 1956, p. 35.

[15] Edmund J. Farris, *Human Ovulation and Fertility* (Philadelphia: J. B. Lippincott Co., 1956).

[16] Glenn M. Vernon and Jack A. Broadway, "Attitudes Toward Artificial Insemination and the Variables Associated Therewith," *Marriage and Family Living,* 21:43–47, February, 1959; also Joseph H. Greenberg, "Social Variables in Acceptance or Rejection of Artificial Insemination," *American Sociological Review,* 16:86–91, February, 1951.

the Catholics. Whether a difference in the classroom atmosphere in which artificial insemination was discussed is the real variable here, or regional differences, or whether students are actually becoming more conservative in this matter is debatable (Greenberg's study was made earlier). It seems unlikely that the statistical differences found represent real differences in attitudes. It may well be that attitudes have changed since the latter study was made.

The legitimacy status, and inheritance rights of the child sired by the donor's semen are in question. So far most courts have ruled such children illegitimate unless the husband adopts the child. Some courts have ruled that the act of siring a child by such means is adultery.[17]

Family Life[18] called a 1968 decision of the California Supreme Court without precedent when it ruled that a husband was criminally negligent for the nonsupport of a child born to his wife by artificial insemination, even though they had already been divorced.

Legal problems will no doubt be solved with the increased use of artificial insemination. Scientists are already advocating sperm banks for eugenics reasons, particularly as a protection of human stock from possible radiation damage. The storage of deepfrozen semen[19] was recommended by Nobel Prize winner, Hermann J. Muller to the American Institute of Biological Sciences. So far the preservation of human sperm has not been achieved with the same degree of success as has been the case with cattle-sperm storage. It is, however, at least in the area of practical possibility.

Fetology

Fetology is a new science that has developed techniques for studying the interior of the womb from the time of conception to delivery. By puncturing the mother's abdomen with a hollow needle, fluid is drawn from the sac in which the fetus floats. Its color, chemical composition, and volume indicate the sex of the fetus, health or illness, and can reveal certain genetic abnormalities. It is even possible to remove the placenta from the mother's body in order to perform surgery on the fetus and return it to her body. When genetic abnormalities are discovered by analysis of chromosomes in the fetal fluid early in the pregnancy, an abortion can be performed.

It is possible also to detect the extent of Rh damage, and the effect

---

[17] For a sample case, see "Test-tube Test Case," *Time,* December 27, 1954, p. 52.
[18] Vol. 28, July, 1968.
[19] "Frozen Fatherhood," *Time,* September 8, 1961, p. 68.

of maternal diabetes on the fetus, and to determine when to take remedial action, such as early delivery or transfusion. Transfusions can be performed routinely by inserting the hollow needle into the blood stream of the fetus.

Prenatal Influence—Myths vs. Science

The "old wives' tales" about the baby's harelip being caused by the mother's being frightened by a rabbit is not so far from the truth as was once supposed. Experiments with animals show that damage to lip and palate can be caused by drug injection or severe emotional stress, which has the effect of releasing chemicals into the blood stream. Two variables determine the degree of damage to the embryo: (1) time of influence— it must be when the jaws and lips are being formed, (2) extent of in- fluence—it must reach a degree of intensity for damage to result.

Study of harelip and cleft palates among human beings shows that most persons with these defects were born to mothers who experienced the damaging influence between the sixth and eighth weeks, the time when jaw structures form in the human embryo.

Such research has led to a reevaluation of the arbitrary opinions re- garding the possibility of the mother's health, nervous stability, and emotional experiences affecting the child. Instead of writing all prenatal influences off as old wives' tales, research is now trying to assess the specific effect of the prenatal environment on the unborn child. Briefly, for this is too highly complex a subject to present in any detail, evidence to date suggests the following:

Prenatal marking   The idea that if a mother is scared by a snake the child will have the print of a snake on its back; or by a rabbit, and the harelip will result; and many other such folk tales are strictly myth. Extreme fright at a time when given embryo structures are forming can, however, create developmental damage.[20]

Prenatal chemical damage   Certain chemicals injected into the body can affect the development of the embryo, as experiments with animals have clearly demonstrated. X-rays and radiation can damage an embryo. Women should avoid x-ray and fluoroscopic examination during the first half of the month while the egg is forming.[21] Cigarette smoking by the mother, while it will not produce a yellow baby as folk myth holds, may

---

[20] "Link Cleft Palate with Stress in Early Pregnancy," *Science News Letter,* 20:217 ff., October 6, 1956; see also Sylvia Brody, *Patterns of Mothering,* (New York: International Universities Press, Inc., 1956).

[21] *Children Limited,* 7:18, May, 1958.

cause premature births.[22] It constricts blood vessels in the abdomen and cuts off oxygen supply.

LSD seems to be particularly damaging to the fetus, according to preliminary studies, and some of the more potent drugs may even affect genetic material. To date the latter point is unproven.

Prenatal nutritional damage   Lack of vitamins may damage the embryo. During the stress of war, when carbohydrates were burned up by mothers in excessive amounts, babies were born light in weight but of normal length, since mineral elements that form bone structure were not consumed in excess.[23]

Prenatal disease damage   Virus diseases of the mother, particularly German measles, have been responsible for as much as 30 percent of cerebral palsy; but even chickenpox and diabetes may also damage the embryo, causing deformity or mental retardation.[24] This is so well recognized as a hazard during the first three months of pregnancy that having German measles is legal grounds for abortion as a eugenics measure in Sweden,[25] and in some American states under new legislation.

Recent research shows that even children who show no symptoms of having been damaged prenatally by German measles, may pass the disease on to others, thus spreading the disease among women who may be pregnant, and who may come in contact with pregnant women. Fortunately a new vaccine shows great promise of eliminating German measles (rubella), the worst intrauterine crippler and killer.

An untreated syphilitic mother can transmit syphilis to the child during the embryonic stage. Although the blood stream of the mother and the fetus are separate, syphilis can pass through the placenta wall by osmosis, in the same way as food and waste materials.

Prenatal emotional damage   Extreme emotion causes release of chemicals into the blood stream, which can very decidedly affect the embryo, just as can externally injected chemicals.[26]

Dr. Sontag's studies show such effects in mothers undergoing ex-

---

[22] Winea J. Simpson of Loma Linda, California, studied 7,500 women in three San Bernadino hospitals. Premature births increased with number of cigarettes smoked daily. *American Journal of Obstetrics and Gynecology,* vol. 17, April, 1957. The U.S. Public Health Service report on Smoking and Health, p. 343, finds that babies of women who smoked during pregnancy are lighter in weight. They also find that smokers have a significantly greater number of premature deliveries.

[23] For a summary of this significant research see Lester W. Sontag, "War and the Fetal-Maternal Relationship," *Marriage and Family Living,* 6:3–4, 1944.

[24] "Dangers before Birth," *Time,* June 10, 1959, p. 76.

[25] *Social Sweden* (Stockholm: Social Welfare Board, 1952).

[26] Gladys D. Schultz, "The Uninsulated Child," *Ladies Home Journal,* June, 1956, p. 61–62; see also Sontag, *loc. cit.*

treme emotional stress. Fetal activity is greatly increased, too, and the fetal movements last longer than stress of the mother, causing it to burn up excessive carbohydrates. Infants born to mothers undergoing extreme emotional stress are hyperactive after birth, want to be fed frequently, and have frequent bowel movements. They are in a real sense born neurotic. Ashley-Montagu's research confirms the fact of the neurotic child being born to the extremely nervous mother. He also summarizes other research confirming this view.[27]

In the animal field, breeders have long recognized the necessity of a calm gestation period, particularly for captive wild animals like foxes and mink. Perhaps with continued research we will have equal insight into the effect of maternal temperament on prenatal environment.

Prenatal damage from Rh disease   Intrauterine damage to the fetus due to the clash of the mother's and the child's blood is rare now, but once resulted in jaundice, anemia, heart defects, and mental retardation to some 20,000 children per year, 10,000 still births, and accounted for 10 percent of cerebral palsy cases.

Rh incompatibility (named for its discovery in rhesus monkeys) occurs when the mother is Rh negative and the fetus is Rh positive like the father.[28] The mother is normal and healthy but the pregnancy sets up antibodies, as if the fetus were a virulent disease or transplant. There is little of this reaction until the placenta breaks at the birth of the child causing some of the child's blood to get into her blood stream. The first child is not affected, but following children, if they are Rh positive, will be damaged.

Blood transfusions immediately after birth, and more recently blood transfusions in the uterus itself have helped offset damaging effects. Recently a means for building immunity in the mother, so that her system will not attack the fetus, has been developed and promises elimination of Rh disease where proper medical treatment precedes pregnancy.

Protein deficiency   As hunger, throughout the world and within our nation, has become a matter of increasing social concern, it has been discovered that malnutrition may retard mental and physical development in the womb and after birth. Particularly critical is protein starvation, a factor in prematurity and in retarding brain growth.

Eating clay, a practice of many of the poor in the South, particularly

[27] M. F. Ashley-Montagu and Gertrude Schweitzer, "There Is Prenatal Influence," *Ladies Home Journal,* 71:43 ff., February, 1954; for animal experiments see William S. Kroeger, "Influence of Prenatal Maternal Anxiety on Emotionality of Young Rats," *Science,* 125:698, April 12, 1957; see also, William S. Kroeger, "Baby May Be Neurotic if Mother Is Disturbed," *Science News Letter,* 63:376, June 20, 1953.

[28] The Rh negative factor is found in 15 percent of white people, 7 percent of Negroes, and 1 percent of Chinese and Japanese.

of Negro women, replaced in the northern city by eating starch, is disastrous from the standpoint of nutrition.[29] It leads to such obstetrical problems as premature birth, low weight of fetus, placenta complications, low resistance to infection, and mental retardation of the newborn child.

The Risks of Youthful Pregnancy

Ashley-Montagu[30] has found that full female maturity for purposes of reproduction is reached only very slowly, and not until years after puberty. Pregnancy before full biological maturity is risk-laden. The principal risks which he finds are: (1) a high death rate among children born to young mothers; (2) a high death rate among young mothers themselves during or following childbirth; (3) many spontaneous abortions among young mothers; (4) high stillbirth rate among young mothers; (5) more frequent toxemia among the younger mothers.

Surveying the evidence, he concludes that we should not only discourage young marriages, but that where young people in their teens do marry, they should delay the first pregnancy for several years.

Hazards of Birth and Birth Timing

Birth damage to children is extensive. Dr. Meyer A. Perlstein's research in the area of cerebral palsy, which affects one child in every 215 born in the United States, suggests that about 3 percent is caused by forceps delivery, but that 60 percent is due to brain hemorrhage and contusions during a difficult natural delivery,[31] and to oxygen starvation.[32] Illness of the mother during pregnancy, notably German measles, anemia, and diabetes may account for 30 percent, and the Rh factor about 3 percent. Childhood injuries account for the rest.

Premature births are another problem of great significance. About half of the infant deaths are among this group. Extremely careful handling is necessary not only to save life but to protect the premature

[29] Richard T. Cooper, "The Clay Eaters: A Tragic Price Paid in Health," *Los Angeles Times,* Part 1, p. 1. February 12, 1969.

[30] M. F. Ashley-Montagu, *The Reproductive Development of the Female with Special Reference to the Period of Adolescent Sterility* (New York: Julian Press, Inc., 1958).

[31] This makes all the more risky the practice of delaying births until the doctor comes, etc. See "Cruelty in the Maternity Hospital," *Ladies Home Journal,* November, 1957; May, 1958.

[32] For a part of Perlstein's work, see "Against Cerebral Palsy," *Time,* December 16, 1957, p. 39.

from brain damage due to bile pigments which the liver cannot handle, and from blindness due to an excess of oxygen in the incubator. The excess of bile pigment usually requires blood transfusion.

About 12 percent of births are delayed about two weeks beyond due date, and 4 percent are delayed three weeks. Research by Dr. Mitchell J. Nechtow has found the death rate of the latter group three times that of normal term babies.[32] His explanation is that the placenta may shrink, causing the baby to live off its own tissues, thus losing weight. Difficulty of delivery also increases with more frequent breach births and use of forceps and Caesarean sections, all of which bring risk of injury.

Multiple Births

Throughout much of human history and, among peoples of most cultures, twins have been considered omens of either good or bad luck. In much of black Africa they are put to death to protect the group from evil. Certain Canadian Indian tribes which accept them as good omens, have elevated them to enviable places in the group. In our sophisticated culture, superstitions concerning twins have disappeared, but twins do attract attention, require special care in rearing, and have become the subject of studies for testing the relative influence of heredity and environment.

Identical twins begin with a single ovum which has been fertilized by a single sperm and which later divides to form two embryos, each having the same pattern of genes and therefore the same common inherited characteristics. They are, of course, of the same sex. If the egg divides late after fertilization, the twins may be *mirror images* of each other rather than identical images; that is, their hair will part on opposite sides, one will be left-handed and the other right-handed, etc.

The handwriting and fingerprints of identical twins are very similar. Their skin is so identical that skin grafts can be made on each other's bodies interchangeably and without difficulty.

Numerous studies of identical twins show that they have the same general characteristics of temperament, interest, and even hereditary weaknesses. Researchers[34] find few twins in the list of distinguished persons. There seems to be frequent intellectual retardation among them, possibly linked to premature birth. Some think a factor of retardation is speech-caused. The twins are able to communicate with each other and do not have to learn normal vocabulary.

[33] See "Premature and Past Due," *Time,* April 20, 1959, p. 77.
[34] Frank Sandon so concludes after studying thousands of records of English twins, *Eugenics Review,* July, 1958.

The statistical chance of twins is about one in 85 births, of triplets, one in 7,000, of quadruplets, one in 50 million, of quintuplets, one in 57 million (only 60 sets have been reported in the world during the last 500 years). Twins do tend to run in families, both male and female can carry the twinning characteristic. Older mothers more often have twins than young mothers. The death rate of multiple births is high—of twins even three times as high as in single births.

Fraternal twins (nonidentical) make up 75 percent of all twins. They are born of two different eggs which have been fertilized by two different sperms. The fertilization may even take place in different acts of intercourse, even by different males, as has been proved in tests of paternity. Such twins may be of either sex and are no more alike in heredity than siblings born separately.

A rural myth of long standing holds that mixed-sex twins are sterile. It apparently originates from the "free martin" situation in cattle. In the case of mixed-sex twins, the female is almost always sterile. The reason seems to be that the placenta surrounding the calves is very thin, permitting the male sex hormone to dominate the female's sexual development and making it sterile.

The Control of Pregnancy

The ability to control conception is at the very heart of the companionship marriage. For the welfare of the children, too, child spacing is considered an essential in providing the maximum social and economic advantages. Effective timing and spacing of children requires medical technology and constant vigilance. Most couples will have consulted a physician or visited a clinic prior to marriage, ideally three months before. Methods of conception control will have been provided so that the marriage insofar as possible is protected from unwanted pregnancy. There are many approaches to conception control. Various devices are used to keep sperm from entering the cervix. The most effective of the mechanical means are the condom, used by the male, and the diaphragm, used by the female. The chemical means include creams, suppositories or foams introduced into the vagina prior to sexual intercourse. They may be used along with the diaphragm for extra safety. Douches are used after intercourse as means of conception control. They are among the least effective means, for the sperm may already have moved through the cervix into the uterus.

Withdrawal prior to ejaculation (*coitus interruptus*) is an ancient method of conception control among peoples who know the relationship between sexual intercourse and conception. It is unreliable, as some semen may be leaked prior to withdrawal; in addition, withdrawal takes more strength of will than many males are able to command.

Intrauterine inserts have come into wide usage. They consist of a ring, coil, or loop—the shape does not seem to matter—which uncoils after insertion. It is the foreign object in the uterus which protects from pregnancy. Plastic or stainless steel, it is noncorrosive and when inserted by the doctor may be left for years without side effects. It is inexpensive, requires no daily planning, or preintercourse ritual. It has been widely used in India as the best approach to date to an economical mass-method of population control.

However, some women expel the device, some for various reasons remove it. In this country Planned Parenthood finds more than 30 percent discontinue its use. Generally the device is not recommended until after the first pregnancy.

Rhythm

The rhythm method is based on the assumption that a couple may determine quite exactly the time of ovulation and by avoiding sexual intercourse then, avoid conception. The rhythm method, although usually identified with spacing births or limiting births, is of equal importance in achieving pregnancy. It depends for its effectiveness upon accuracy in determining the time of ovulation.

Edmund J. Farris has reported research which casts considerable doubt on existing theories about the specific period of ovulation. He finds that in 90 percent of the cases, ovulation takes place between the 10th and 16th days from the beginning of the menstrual flow, and that in the majority it takes place between the 11th and 14th days, the 12th day being the most common. He is very doubtful that the ovum can be fertilized later than 8 hours after its rupture from the egg sac or that sperm cells are potent for more than 24 hours after ejaculation.

He recommends that women who wish to establish the time of ovulation either for purposes of birth control or conception determine the midpoint of the cycle and subtract two days from this number. This is the time of most likely ovulation. The earliest possible day of fertility then would be two days before this date and the latest five days afterward. He believes that the temperature method of determining ovulation is not reliable in more than half the cases.[35]

Farris has indicated that to assure conception it is desirable to re-

[35] Edmund J. Farris, *Human Ovulation and Fertility* (Philadelphia: J. B. Lippincott Co., 1956).

frain from sexual intercourse until just five days prior to ovulation to assure maximum development of the husband's sperm.[36] Then at the period when ovulation is expected, the couple should have sexual intercourse daily for three days before the midcycle day.

As a means of birth control, the "safe period" is the only means approved by the Catholic Church, and even this method is approved with reservations by some of the Church leaders. For limiting offspring it is highly ineffective.

A careful mathematical analysis of the reliability of the "safe period" has been made by André J. DeBethune. He finds that even if the fertile period is no longer than 12 hours, a couple who wish to space children two years apart are limited statistically to two acts of coitus per menstrual cycle. Those who expect to space children by four years are limited to one act of coitus per cycle. He concluded his analysis with the observation, "It is not surprising that the rhythm method has become a source of mental torture to many couples."[37]

In addition to being ineffective as a means of birth control, rhythm may, when it fails, produce a totally malformed child. The difficulty is stale sperm, or a stale egg. The supposition is based on the substantially higher rate of serious malformations found among Catholic than Protestant or Jewish offspring.

Dr. Raymond G. Cross[38] of Dublin found anencephaly (absence of brain, and failure of spinal column to close), to run 2.8 per thousand among Catholics, 2 among Protestants, and 0.7 among Jews. Professor Carlo Sirtori of Milan agrees with this finding and adds mongolism to the list of defects from stale reproductive cells. Dr. Alan Guttmacher, president of the Planned Parenthood Federation in the United States, indicates that the stale-egg theory has been confirmed in animal experiments.

"The Pill"

The most revolutionary and the surest approach to pregnancy control has been the oral hormone inhibitor. The most frequently used pill employs estrogen, which inhibits ovulation during a woman's pregnancy. When taken in the right dosage twenty times per month on successive days beginning five days after the onset of menstruation, it inhibits ovulation just as pregnancy does. Ovulation begins when the pill is no longer used.

[36] Ibid.

[37] André J. DeBethune "Child Spacing: the Mathematical Probabilities," Science, 142:1629–1634, December 27, 1963.

[38] "Contraception: Hazardous Rhythm," Time, August 30, 1968.

A Rating of Birth Control Methods

Time,[39] reporting particularly on the latest intrauterine devices for contraception, places them on a par with the pill in effectiveness. (The risk is that they may slip out of the uterus. A tail is now attached to some of the devices so the woman can check. The risk with the pill is that they may not be taken regularly.) *Time* concludes that:

If 100 wives use:	*Number of pregnancies per year*
nothing	90
rhythm	40
diaphragm and condom	2 to 20
intrauterine devices	1
pill	1

It is likely that a survey made now would give the intrauterine devices (coil, loop, ring, etc.) a lower rating than that shown here. Subsequent studies rate it much lower than the pill in effectiveness.

Chevalier, writing for *McCall's* (March, 1969) "What's New in Medicine" column, reports 3 to 4 percent of women who depend on the pill will get pregnant, and that about 9 percent find they cannot use it.

The Side Effect Risks

The extent to which a given device or chemical controls pregnancy is but one significant measure of the desirability of its use. The basic question, particularly with chemical methods, is that of side effects. Using this as a standard, of the two most effective methods, the intrauterine device rates higher in safety. The pill involves the user's entire hormone balance affecting as it does the pituitary gland and the ovaries. The effect of the IUD is localized, for it lies harmlessly in the uterus.

The pill as used today by some 5,000,000 women is to date the most effective of methods. The side effect of most concern from the pill has been that its long-continued use may cause blood clots in certain women, as well as other less serious side effects. In September 1969,

[39] *Time,* July 31, 1964, pp. 48–49.

the Food and Drug Administration released its in-depth study on oral contraceptives. Although they report that the death risk is 4.4 times greater for pill users than non pill users, the drug is well within the limits of safety.

H. W. Stinson, M.D., president of the Association for Voluntary Sterilization, commenting[40] on the findings, says, "It is well to keep in mind that child-birth deaths are 1,700 percent greater than pill death." Use of the pill over long periods of time does require medical supervision, and doctors do not recommend its use for those with a history of cancer or vascular diseases.

Side effects of the pill have been about as few as with most drugs in general use and no doubt will decrease in the future. The dosage of the long-used twenty pills a month has been cut to one-tenth the original dosage, but the pills do require medical approval and supervision. Other pills are being and will be developed also which will mark further improvement insofar as human tolerance is concerned. And pills for "morning after," once a month, once a quarter, and longer periods are in the experimental stage, as are pills providing male sterility for a period of time.

Population pressure is so critical in many parts of the world, and food shortages so recurrent, that it is probable that temporary immunity to pregnancy may be introduced to large populations through chemicals placed in water or food supply. Social concern is so great that new means for the control of pregnancy are receiving much research attention.

Certainly much can be expected in the way of improvement of chemical immunization in the immediate years ahead, by use of pills, injections, implantation of capsules under the skin to release inhibitors continuously, and temporary sterilization agents for the male. The Poverty Program is experimenting with injections which give three month's immunity.

Sterilization for Family Limitation

Vasectomy involves the tying off and cutting of the *vas deferens*, an operation of approximately seven minutes duration, requiring an incision into the scrotum. Usually the male can return to work within a day or so after the operation. Ligation or salpingotomy involves opening the abdominal cavity of the female to tie and cut the Fallopian tubes. Since this involves surgery of considerable seriousness, it is usually not used in this country except when the abdominal cavity is opened for other

[40] News release of the Association for Voluntary Sterilization, Inc., September 5, 1969.

reasons or when serious medical reasons exist. In Catholic countries like Puerto Rico, it has been used extensively by women who usually give as their reason, "one confession is sufficient," whereas with birth control repeated confessions are necessary.

Vasectomy is being promoted by the government of India as one of the principal means of population control. Some states give a payment to the male submitting to the operation, and some also a reward payment to the recruiter, and in some states impose a fine on those having more than three children. Vasectomy for family limitation is on the increase in the United States. Neither vasectomy or ligation is illegal in the United States, and the male operation is so economical in terms of discomfort and cost (as low as $50) that it offers a final solution to the problem of unwanted pregnancies for couples choosing to use it. The Association for Voluntary Sterilization is promoting voluntary sterilization throughout the world.

The great concern of males considering the operation is with the physical, psychosocial, and marital implications of the operation. Landis and Poffenberger[41] studied 2,007 vasectomy records of physicians and obtained follow-up questionnaires from 330 couples. Most couples appraised the results as beneficial to their sexual life and to their marriage; almost none regretted it. Greater frequency of sexual intercourse was reported by most couples. The principal motive for the couple's joint decision to have the operation was their desire to fix the size of their families, even though most of the couples had small families.

The one serious objection to sterilization has been its finality. Some couples change their mind about the number of children they want, and some remarry after widowhood or divorce. In the past, comparatively few operations have been reversible to the point of restoring fertility. For some time Dr. P. S. Jhaver, an Indian surgeon, has been working with plastic devices for blocking the sperm tubes (vas deferens). One is a plastic tube inserted in the *vas* with a plug that can be opened. The other is the Jhaver clip, which pinches the *vas* shut and can readily be removed by the physician. Some such device soon will remove the objection to sterilization[42] as regards finality.

For couples who have achieved the family size they wish, sterilization offers an easy solution to their problem. As a device for national policy in population control among impoverished urban groups and in

[41] Judson T. Landis and Thomas Poffenberger, "The Marital Adjustment of 330 Couples Who Chose Vasectomy as a Form of Birth Control," *Journal of Marriage and Family Living*, 27:57–58, February, 1965. See also Judson T. Landis "Attitudes of Individual California Physicians and Policies of State Medical Societies on Vasectomy for Birth Control," *ibid.*, 28:277–283, August, 1966.

[42] See *Progress Report* of the Association for Voluntary Sterilization, Inc., 14 West 40th Street, New York, N. Y. 10018, September 30, 1968.

isolated pockets of rural poverty, this method offers great hope if it should receive adequate backing and promotion.

Abortion

Throughout countries where birth control is extensively practiced, particularly where groups promoting it are legally permitted to operate, as in the Scandinavian countries, Holland (in Holland the Society for Anticonception was initiated more than seventy-five years ago), and in many parts of the United States, effective contraception is considered a deterrent to abortion.[43]

From a social and health standpoint, contraception is much less costly than induced abortion. Nevertheless, abortion is a major problem in the United States and is much more common among the married than among the unmarried.

Of all the pregnancies among married women studied by the Kinsey group, only 66 percent resulted in birth of the child; 17 percent ended in miscarriage; 17 percent, in induced abortions.[44] Their data show that the most frequent patron of the abortionist is not the unmarried girl, nor the widow or divorcée, but the wife. The younger the wife, the higher the proportion of miscarriages and of abortions. Women who start having abortions under twenty also tend to have abortions later. A married

Pregnancies in marriage terminated by induced abortion

Year†	Percentage
1925	23.6
1930	24.3
1935	18.3
1940	13.5
1945	12.3
1950	10.4

† Year given is mid-point of decade.

Source: Paul H. Gebhard and others, *Pregnancy, Birth and Abortion* (New York: Harper & Bros. and Paul B. Hoeber, Inc., 1958), p. 205.

[43] *Social Sweden* (Stockholm: Social Welfare Board, 1953), pp. 320 ff., also *The National League for Sex Education* (Stockholm, 1949).

[44] Paul H. Gebhard and others, *Pregnancy, Birth and Abortion* (New York: Harper & Bros. and Paul B. Hoeber, Inc., 1958).

woman under 20 who has an induced abortion will have an average of 2.4 abortions in her married lifetime, according to these research data. The lower wives are on the socioeconomic ladder, the greater the abortion rate.

Devoutness in religion is inversely related to the abortion rate. The devout have few abortions; those who lack devoutness have relatively more.

There is something hopeful in these data, if generations are compared. Young wives are having fewer induced abortions than did their mothers. In fact, since the depression years of the 1930s, abortions have been on the decline. The researchers conclude that wives of later generations are more eager for motherhood than wives of earlier generations studied.

Another factor must, however, be taken into account. Contraception has become more widely known and more effective over the years studied.

Table 26–1   Unfavorable Consequences of Illegal Operative Abortion Reported by White Nonprison Females and Males by Marital Status at Event

Unfavorable Consequences	Female Report (Percent)				Male Report (Percent)
	Pre-marital	Marital	Post-marital	Total	Total
None	67.7	81.8	78.4	74.2	86.6
Mild physical	4.1	2.0	2.7	3.2	3.2
Moderate physical	7.7	5.4	6.8	6.8	2.5
Severe physical	6.4	6.8	6.8	6.6	2.8
Psychological	13.6	4.1	5.4	9.0	4.2
Social	3.6	0	0	1.8	1.1
Legal	0	0	0	0	0
Total	103.1	100.1	100.1	101.6	100.0
Number abortions, consequences known	220	148	74	442	283
Number abortions, consequences unknown	92	363	36	491	406

Source: Paul H. Gebhard and others, *Pregnancy, Birth and Abortion* (New York: Harper & Bros. and Paul B. Hoeber, Inc., 1958), p. 205.

Reliable contraception is without doubt the most effective preventative for abortion. Sweden considers it so.[45] In Japan, where abortion rates have been unusually high and effective in holding down population growth, promotion of contraception is now considered the method of reducing abortion.

Statistics in the area of abortion for the population at large are of necessity estimates. It is believed that the abortion rate is much higher than for the generations shown in the Kinsey samples. Estimates place the abortion ratio, considering single and married together, as high as one for four pregnancies. Certainly if this even approximates the actual situation, pregnancy wastage by voluntary abortion among single and married together approaches a million a year. All authorities agree that the majority of abortions are among those married, and usually by those who already have all the children they want and can care for.

Abortion Law Reform

The demand for new and more liberalized abortion laws reverberated in the legislative halls of many states in 1967 and 1968. The situation existing in almost every state was that a woman could obtain an abortion legally only if the doctor, or hospital panel of doctors, was willing to swear that "it was to save her life." However, the influential could persuade hospital staffs to sanction an abortion, for example, if they felt it would seriously disturb the woman's emotional life. Making extensive use of this clause, reputable physicians operated without legal challenge.

The masses of the needy had to resort to the undercover operator, with the risks to health and life this has entailed (see Table 26–1). It is believed that this operation has caused 25 percent of all maternal deaths. First Colorado, then North Carolina, Georgia, Maryland,[46] and California remodeled their nineteenth-century laws.

The essential provisions of the new laws, as passed in these states, and discussed in many others where bills were considered, permit abortions for reasons of threat to the physical or mental health of the mother, pregnancy from rape or incest, and likelihood of the child's being born defective, as in cases where the mother has had German measles during the first three months of pregnancy.

[45] Hans L. Zetterberg, *On Sexual Life in Sweden,* Report of The Royal Commission on Sex Education, summarized in J. Robert Moskin, "The New Contraceptive Society," *Look,* February 4, 1969 p. 50 ff. See also Birgitta Linner, *Sex and Society in Sweden* (New York: Pantheon, 1967).

[46] For a brief summary of new laws and their effect on medical practice in the area see "Progress on Liberalized Abortion," *Time,* pp. 61–62, November 19, 1968. For a study of change in moral attitudes toward abortion, see "Changing Morality: The Two Americas, A *Time*–Louis Harris Poll," *Time,* pp. 26–27, June 6, 1969.

No doubt most states will remodel laws as public pressure mounts. After a year under these liberalized laws, no state or city has become an abortion mecca, although legal abortions have increased.[47] It is apparent in these states too that most abortions are still performed illegally. Legal abortions take time for clearance and are very expensive because of medical consultations and other factors, but they are safe.

In September, 1969, the California Supreme Court, in ruling on an abortion case, raised the question whether restriction on the right of abortion was an "improper encroachment on womens' fundamental right to choose whether or not to bear children." *Time* (September 19, 1969, p. 66) pointed out that the action may cast "constitutional doubt on rigid abortion laws in no fewer than 41 other states." The proceedings also questioned the right of a particular church to impose its religious views on the state.

With the new feminism now beginning to crusade on such issues, radical changes in abortion restriction may be in the making.

Effective contraception is certainly the better alternative but even in Sweden, which is very free with contraceptive information, there is still need for abortion. Most women approve it, and feel it should be given as part of the free medical service under the socialized medical program of the nation.[48]

We have already suggested that a high percentage of abortions among the unmarried are performed on women who are not pregnant. Frequently women who have been divorced or separated from their husbands also cease menstruation due to nervous tension and anxiety and immediately fear they are pregnant. These women are also easy victims for the abortionist, as are married women who fear pregnancy and fail to go to a realiable physician for a pregnancy test before visiting an abortionist.

A very simple test is now used to determine pregnancy which gives a conclusive answer in minutes.

Child Spacing

The problem of spacing children is one which must depend largely upon the couple's own desires. An early study of maternal and child development by Dr. R. W. Woodbury, in 1915, recommended that children be spaced at least two years apart for the sake of the health of the mother. More recent research and medical opinion suggests that the nearer the children can be spaced, the better for the health of the mother.

Close spacing of births does increase the percentage of premature

[47] *Ibid.*
[48] Zetterberg, *op. cit.*

births, according to records of the University of Pennsylvania School of Medicine. Researchers find the following:[49]

Months since previous pregnancy	Percentage of premature births
More than 23	7.8
12–23	10.3
Less than 12	18.0

From the standpoint of social development of children there is something to be said in favor of having children as close together as possible. It provides a play group of similar ages in the home even if a highly competitive one. Of course, it takes a sturdy mother to effectively care for two or three very small children at the same time, particularly if the family does not have the financial resources to hire help with housework and child care.

Coitus During Pregnancy

There is much folklore about sexual intercourse during pregnancy. Actually, pregnancy usually does not reduce interest in sexual intercourse until the later stages. In fact, the wife's desire may actually increase during the early stages of pregnancy. During the final stages, particularly the last two weeks to a month, when the neck of the uterus is likely to be somewhat open and the nearly full-grown embryo may be expanding the uterus down into the vaginal canal, intercourse is not wise, at least intercourse by deep penetration of the vagina.

The belief that having sexual intercourse during pregnancy will make the child oversexed is strictly myth, as is also the notion that intercourse will make the delivery easier.

After childbirth, intercourse may begin as soon as the wife feels ready for it. Unless there has been surgical damage, she is usually ready in three to six weeks. The need for contraception by those who wish to space children will be greater after delivery than before. Because of the dilation of the cervix a new pregnancy is often very easy following childbirth. The notion that a nursing mother cannot become pregnant has no basis in fact.

[49] S. Leon Israel and Sondra Nemser, "Family-Counseling Role of the Physician," *Journal of Marriage and Family Living*, 30:311–316, May, 1968.

Psychological Adjustments to Pregnancy

Folklore and old wives' tales have given the young wife a picture of what pregnancy may be expected to be. The symptoms are so familiar that the woman who does not have her morning nausea, often accompanied by vomiting and symptoms of dizziness, considers herself almost abnormal. Motion pictures have contributed to this image by having the young husband act solicitous when the young wife announces that they are going to have a baby.

The particular symptoms of pregnancy are, in part, a matter of custom and culture. This is well demonstrated in Margaret Mead's analysis of the extent of nausea that exists among women in various cultures.[50] In cultures where the nausea feeling is considered the universal experience of pregnant women, practically all women have it; in societies which ignore the phenomenon, nausea is rare, although it may be felt by some women. She explains this by the fact that nausea and even vomiting are biological capacities of the organism, but that a culture may elaborate these to the point where they become important and customary. Or the culture may neglect, ignore, or even frown on such reactions so that they are not so frequently in the consciousness of the pregnant woman.

She also finds that cultural expectations very much affect the reaction of the woman to the menstrual period. In some cultures where pain is glorified, women may almost all feel severe symptoms during the menstrual period. In cultures where menstrual pain is ignored, the woman may simply rub her body with stinging nettles to obscure a real feeling of menstrual pain and go about her day, attempting to ignore it completely.

Some women do have nausea and vomiting and a great deal of discomfort during pregnancy. A few are even confined to bed for considerable periods of time in order to avoid miscarriage. For many healthy young women, however, none of these symptoms appear at all. In fact, a woman is more likely than not to feel better during pregnancy than at any other time. This may be due to the release of certain hormones which prepare the uterus, particularly, and the entire physiological system to some extent, for handling the fetus.

A current theory is that nausea is possibly due to the mother's system trying to reject the fetus as a foreign object, just as it would a transplant. This view came from the observation that pregnant women reject transplants less violently than nonpregnant women, leading to the presumption that certain restraints against rejection are present in her system during

[50] Margaret Mead, in A. M. Krich (ed.), *Women: The Variety and Meaning of Their Sexual Experience* (New York: Dell Publishing Co., Inc., 1954).

pregnancy. Even so, some women miscarry, thus expelling the foreign object.

Sex Life During Pregnancy

Judson T. Landis and co-workers at the University of California, asked a group of 212 wives who had completed their first pregnancy the question, "What effect, if any, did pregnancy have upon your sexual adjustment?"[51] Husbands and wives generally agreed as to the answer. Their answers were:

Effect	Husbands (percent)	Wives (percent)
No effect	58	58
Unfavorable	28	25
Favorable	19	17

Of those who indicated that the effect had been favorable, most had had poor sexual adjustment previous to conception. Of those who reported an unfavorable effect, a considerable proportion had had a good adjustment before pregnancy. In general, husbands and wives reported a decrease in sexual desire with the duration of the pregnancy. Toward the end of the pregnancy, many women were found to lose interest in sexual contact, or found it painful. Others quit because of doctors' advice for fear of hurting the baby.

A significant effect of pregnancy is the decreasing of the husband's desire. About 10 percent felt "it didn't seem right" or that they didn't enjoy intercourse. Almost all the wives felt that their husbands were more considerate of them and exhibited more sensitivity concerning their feelings during the pregnancy than before.

Childbirth

Childbirth is another field in which much has been done to banish superstition and needless fear. One of the most influential factors has been the publication by the late Grantly Dick Read of his world-famous book,

[51] Judson T. Landis, Thomas Poffenberger, and Shirley Poffenberger, "The Effects of First Pregnancy Upon the Sexual Adjustment of 212 Couples," *American Sociological Review,* 15:766–772, December, 1950.

Childbirth Without Fear. This book's spontaneous acceptance by modern women, who had been reared on traditions of childbirth as painful travail, was one of the marvels of changing family life in the postwar generation. Young mothers, particularly, approached doctors and hospitals with requests for childbirth following this procedure. Classes teaching women the way to cooperate with nature became popular, and the entire birth process came to be looked upon as a challenge rather than something to be dreaded.

Dr. Read, in 1953, to see how his theories worked out in a state of nature, carried his research on childbirth into Africa. In *No Time for Fear,* he reported that among Bushmen, Basutos, Hottentots, and Masai, from 95 to 98 percent go through childbirth with no pain. Confirming evidence that fear is an inhibiting factor in the birth process and induces pain was discovered among adulterous women, some of whom struggled in painful labor two or three days. Dr. Read reports that when persuaded to confess their adultery, they would suddenly relax and release the child.

The essence of the Read philosophy is that the mother approach childbirth in pleasant anticipation and without fear. She is expected to understand natural muscle reactions that take place during childbirth and to take certain exercises which make it possible for her to cooperate with nature. Read believed from his experience with women in childbirth that too many modern women, fearing the process and considering it an ordeal, tensed themselves and fought the natural muscle spasms, thus making childbirth much more difficult than nature intended.

The Read approach stresses the great emotional reward of natural childbirth and promises that release from tension will reduce the pain of childbirth. American doctors, although they have been profoundly influenced by the Read movement, use a combination of conscious childbirth, and often the training for it beforehand, with local anesthetics like the saddle block, which in no way affect consciousness. In cases of complications, they use modern anesthetics which do not make the infant groggy at birth, as those of forty years ago did.

Like many innovations, natural childbirth exaggerated the advantages of the method. Even with maximum cooperation with nature, with full and proper use of muscles as nature intended, and with the complete absence of fear, childbirth can be excruciatingly painful in some instances. In case of complications the use of anesthetics and surgery are essential.

Many doctors believe that the great spiritual value of conscious childbirth has been exaggerated. And some women who attempt natural childbirth feel guilty because they have to ask for anesthetics during the painful part of delivery.

Hospital experience, where preparation for childbirth is standard procedure gives convincing evidence that such training reduces the tension of labor, shortens labor, and in general makes for a more favorable total childbirth situation.[52]

The "Birthsuit"

Professor O. S. Heyns at the University of Witwatersrand, South Africa, has been using the suit for some years to reduce the pain of labor and to minimize risks of complication for mother and child.[53] Various American doctors are experimenting with pressure "bubbles."

The mother sits in the suit with her arms free. She can regulate the pressure in the suit. Regulation of pressure keeps the uterus in a normal position, avoiding the painful muscle spasm in the uterus. Painful labor, shock, and mental distress are eliminated. South African reports say that 90 percent of women who used it got relief from labor pains or eliminated them completely. Labor time has been cut by half in most instances. Chances of brain damage, cerebral palsy, mental deficiency, and stillbirth of the child are greatly reduced. It is estimated that fetal distress is cut 80 percent.

The most amazing aspect of the method is that babies are superior in tone and behavior from the beginning. Researchers feel that the level of mental ability is substantially increased in that there is no longer damaging oxygen deprivation during birth. Use of the pressure suit keeps up the free flow of blood to the fetus, thus keeping up the oxygen supply. It is even recommended that the suit be used for half-hour daily periods during the latter stages of pregnancy to increase the oxygen saturation of fetal blood.

These beginnings would seem to promise something revolutionary in the fields of technological improvement over nature in childbirth.

The Hospital Situation

Along with the Read plan for childbirth another movement of significance has developed, that of rooming-in, also called the *Cornelian Corner*.

[52] For an excellent discussion of the significance of the Read movement and also for contrasting case histories of women who approach childbirth with fear and women who approach it after adequate education, see Frederick W. Goodrich, Jr., "Natural Childbirth," in A. M. Krich (ed.), *op. cit.*, pp. 149–170. See also Herbert Thoms and Robert H. Wyatt, "One Thousand Consecutive Deliveries Under a Training for Childbirth Program," *American Journal of Obstetrics and Gynecology*, 61:205–209, January, 1951; also Herbert Thoms, *Training for Childbirth* (New York: McGraw-Hill Book Co., 1950).

[53] Ora Mendels, "A Revolution in Childbirth?" *Ladies Home Journal*, Winter, 1963, p. 40.

With the development of the modern hospital, the practice of partially isolating the infant from the mother during the period of her stay in the hospital had become more or less customary. Now, rooming-in provides that the child be placed with the mother a great deal during her period in the hospital; that she nestle and cuddle it, give it affection, and nurse it. It is believed that the basis is laid here for a more secure personality, in addition to the satisfaction and comfort given to both mother and child.

A new group of nurse-midwives has been trained, assuring the mother more prompt and continuous attendance during the uncomplicated childbirth than the busy doctor can give.

Problems

1. Few couples consider it necessary to have more than the conventional physical examination prior to marriage. Under what circumstances would an analysis of one's physical heredity seem warranted?
2. A happily married couple who want children have failed to have any by the end of their third year of marriage. Which of the following courses of action would you advise, and why?
   a. Consult a marriage counselor.
   b. Consult a psychiatrist.
   c. Consult a doctor.
   d. Consider adoption.
   e. Concentrate on keeping their marriage a happy one in spite of their failure.
3. *Sociodrama:* A young woman whose husband is sterile seeks the counsel of her doctor (this doctor may be either male or female) on whether and how she and her husband may have a family. Through a question-and-answer type discussion the two of them consider the advantages and disadvantages (physical, psychological, etc.) of such alternatives as: (a) adoption, (b) artificial insemination, (c) remaining childless.
4. What do we know about the effect of prenatal conditions on a child? For example:
   a. Can a child be physically "marked" as a result of traumatic experiences happening to its mother during pregnancy?
   b. Can a child be physically affected by certain physical conditions of its mother during pregnancy?
   c. Can a child be psychologically affected as a result of traumatic experiences happening to its mother during pregnancy?
5. Is there any way in which an individual can increase the chances of bearing twins?
6. What are the various common techniques for controlling pregnancy? Which method seems to be the most effective? Are any of them 100 percent effective? What are the psychological advantages and disadvantages of birth control devices?
7. Giving birth out of wedlock to an unwanted child can bring tragedy to many people: to the couple whose life plans must be changed, to the

infant who is unwanted, and to the families of the girl and boy involved. Why then is abortion unlawful? Are there any circumstances under which abortion is legal? Do you think the grounds for legal abortion should be broadened?

8. *Sociodrama:* A young mother whose children are one and three years old respectively is sorry that she followed the advice of her pediatrician in spacing her children. Her older sister whose two children are now six and eight defends the pediatrician's advice. Show how both have good arguments for their positions.

9. In what way is our culture, rather than nature, responsible for many of the pains and problems of pregnancy and childbirth?

10. Describe the physical and psychological arguments in favor of the "rooming-in" maternity wards that are now increasing in American hospitals.

Selected References

Articles in Books of Readings

Haimowitz, Morris L. and Haimowitz, Natalie Reader,(eds.), *Human Development: Selected Readings* (New York: Thomas Y. Crowell Co., 1966).
Ashley-Montagu, M. F., "Constitutional and Prenatal Factors in Infant and Child Health," Reading 19.
Krich, A. M. (ed.), *Men: The Variety and Meaning of Their Sexual Experience* (New York: Dell Publishing Co., Inc., 1954).
Goodrich, Frederick W., Jr. "Natural Childbirth," pp. 149–170.
Krich, A. M. (ed.).*Women: The Variety and Meaning of Their Sexual Experience* (New York: Dell Publishing Co., Inc., 1954).
Marshall, F. H. A., "Physiology of Reproduction," Ch. 6.
Landis, Judson T. and Landis, Mary G., *Readings in Marriage and the Family* (Englewood Cliffs, N.J.: Prentice Hall, Inc., 1952).
Stern, Curt, "The Rh Blood Factors," pp. 221–227.
Landis, Judson T., Poffenberger, Thomas, and Poffenberger, Shirley, "Effects of First Pregnancy on Sex Adjustments," pp. 228–234.
Greenberg, Joseph H., "Artificial Insemination," pp. 234–237.
Bartemeier, Leo H., "The Practical Application of Basic Mental Hygiene Principles by the Cornelian Corner," pp. 257–260.
Levy, David M., "Maternal Over-Protection and Rejection," pp. 269–274.
Winch, Robert F. and others, *Selected Studies in Marriage and the Family,* third edition (New York: Holt, Rinehart and Winston, Inc., 1968).
Ferreira, Antonio J., "The Pregnant Woman's Emotional Attitude and Its Reflections on the Newborn," pp. 259–265.

General References

Anderson, Ray C., "The Influence of Heredity on Family Health," *Marriage and Family Living,* 19:136–141, May, 1957.
Ashley-Montagu, M. F., and Schweitzer, Gertrude, "There Is Prenatal Influence," *Ladies' Home Journal,* 71:43 ff., February, 1954.

Campbell, Arthur A., "The Role of Family Planning in the Reduction of Poverty," *Journal of Marriage and the Family*, 30:236–245, May, 1968.

Comstock, George W., M.D., and Landen, Frank E., Jr., M.D., "Parental Smoking and Prenatal Mortality," *American Journal of Obstetrics and Gynecology*, 98:708–718.

Crawley, Lawrence Q. and others, *Reproduction, Sex and Preparation for Marriage* (Englewood Cliffs, N.J.: Prentice-Hall, Inc., 1964), Ch. 2.

Davids, A., De Vault, S., and Talmadge, N., "Anxiety, Pregnancy and Childbirth Abnormalities," *Journal of Consultive Psychiatry*, 25:74–77, 1961.

Diehl, Harold S., *Tobacco and Health: The Smoking Controversy* (New York: McGraw-Hill Paperback Series in Health Education, 1969).

Emery, Alan E. H., *Hereditary Disease, and Man* (Berkeley: University of California Press, 1968).

"Family Planning in Modern Societies," symposium, *Marriage and Family Living*, Vol. 25, February, 1963. This issue covers family-planning practices in various countries of the world.

Farris, Edmund J., *Human Ovulation and Fertility* (Philadelphia: J. B. Lippincott Co., 1956).

Freedman, Ronald, and others, *Family Planning, Sterility and Population Growth* (New York: McGraw-Hill Book Co., 1959).

Gebhard, Paul H., and others, *Pregnancy, Birth and Abortion* (New York: Harper & Bros. and Paul B. Hoeber, Inc., 1958).

Gilbert, Margaret Shea, *Biography of the Unborn* (Baltimore: The Williams & Wilkins Co., 1938).

Guttmacher, Alan F., *Birth Control* (New York: Ballantine Books, Inc., 1969), paperback.

Guttmacher, Alan F., *New Facts about Birth Control* (New York: Public Affairs Pamphlets) No. 136B.

Hellegers, Dr. Andre E., "Abortion, The Law and the Common Good," *Medical Opinion and Review*, pp. 76–93, May, 1967.

Heredity and Marriage Counseling (Los Angeles: American Institute of Family Relations), Pamphlet.

Herndon, C. Nash, "Medical Genetics and Marriage Counseling," *Marriage and Family Living*, 16:207–210, August, 1954.

Hill, Reuben, and others, *The Family and Population Control* (Chapel Hill: University of North Carolina Press, 1959).

Kroeger, William S., "Influence of Prenatal Maternal Anxiety on Emotionality of Young Rats," *Science*, 125:698, April 12, 1957.

Landis, Judson T., "Attitudes of Individual California Physicians and Policies of State Medical Societies on Vasectomy for Birth Control," *Journal of Marriage and the Family*, 28:277–283, August, 1966.

Landis, Judson T., Poffenberger, Thomas, and Poffenberger, Shirley, "The Effects of First Pregnancy Upon the Sexual Adjustment of 212 Couples," *American Sociological Review*, 15:767–772, December, 1950.

Landis, Judson T., and Poffenberger, Thomas, "The Sexual and Marital Adjustment of 330 Couples who Chose Vasectomy as a Form of Birth Control," *Journal of Marriage and the Family*, 27:57–58, February, 1965.

Mead, Margaret, *Male and Female* (New York: William Morrow & Co., Inc., 1949), Ch. 11.

Poffenberger, Shirley, Poffenberger, Thomas, and Landis, Judson T., "Intent Toward Conception and Pregnancy Experience," *American Sociological Review*, 17:616–620, October, 1952.

Poffenberger, Shirley, and Poffenberger, Thomas, "Vasectomy as a Preferred Method of Birth Control," *Marriage and Family Living*, 25:326–330, August, 1963.

Read, Grantley Dick, *Childbirth Without Fear* (New York: Harper & Bros., 1944).

Rodgers, David A., Ziegler, Frederick J., Rohr, Patricia, and Prentiss, Robert J., "Sociophysiological Characteristics of Patients Obtaining Vasectomies from Urologists," *Marriage and Family Living*, 25:331–335, August, 1963.

Rodgers, David A., Ziegler, Frederick J., Altrocchi, John and Levy, Nissim, "A Longitudinal Study of the Psycho-Social Effects of Vasectomy," *Journal of Marriage and the Family*, 27:59–64, February, 1965.

Scheinfeld, Amram, *The Basic Facts of Human Heredity* (New York: Washington Square Press, Inc., 1961), paperback.

Schellen, A. M. C. M., *Artificial Insemination in the Human* (Princeton: Elsevier Press, Inc., 1957).

Schultz, Gladys D., "The Uninsulated Child," *Ladies Home Journal*, June, 1956, pp. 61–62.

Schur, Edwin M., "Abortion," *The Annals*, 376:136–147, March, 1968.

Smith, Virginia, "The Public Health Nurse's Role in Family Planning," *The Family Coordinator*, 17:15–17, January, 1968.

"Sterilizations in India," *Family Life*, 29:6, March, 1969.

Stone, Abraham, "World Conference on Human Infertility," *Marriage and Family Living*, 15:231–233, August, 1953.

"Test Tube Babies: The Controversy Over Artificial Insemination," *Good Housekeeping*, pp. 163 ff, February, 1968.

Underwood, Paul, "The Relationship of Smoking to the Outcome of Pregnancy," *American Journal of Obstetrics and Gynecology*, 91:270–276, January, 1965.

Vellay, Pierre, *Childbirth without Pain*, Translated from the French by Denise Lloyd (New York: E. P. Dutton & Co., Inc., 1960).

27

Parents and Children

The young human is interwoven with an entire family situation. With the birth of a baby a total family structure is modified. Figuratively speaking, a grandparent is produced, or a brother. Status relationships are drastically altered. An empire may be snatched away, a war started, or a multimillion-dollar fortune redirected. Metaphorically, scripts are issued for new roles to be played by family members in adjustment to the new role of the infant actor.[1]

No single relationship in life has greater and more lasting significance than that between parent and child. The connection is more than one of blood; there are deep ties of emotion and lasting marks of influence that affect both throughout their lives. No experience can cause so much growth in the personality as that of parenthood, and certainly no single circumstance in the life of the child is so fateful as his relationship with his parents. Ashley-Montagu[2] sees the development of every human being as a loving person who is capable of realizing his full potential in cooperative relationships with others as the great challenge to our society and especially to mothers who are so intimately connected with the development of the individual.

The following chapters do not pretend to substitute for a course in child development, nor can they summarize all of the significant information young couples should consider. They are designed, rather, to point up a few of the basic issues and to give some insight into problems of parenthood.

[1] Clifford Kirkpatrick, *The Family* (New York: The Ronald Press Co., 1963), second edition, p. 206.
[2] M. F. Ashley-Montagu, *Education and Human Relations* (New York: Grove Press, Inc., 1958).

Timing Parenthood

We have reached an era when it is theoretically possible for children to be born only when a couple wishes. The child need not be the victim of accident and fate. Many are, of course, particularly those conceived premaritally. Barring this circumstance, the newlyweds may, if they choose, decide the time in their marriage when they will have their children.

In European cultures, delaying marriage and delaying children in marriage has been a necessity for economic reasons until quite recently. Studies of American college students made twenty-five years ago indicated a desire to delay children until the marriage was well established in terms of companionability and finance.[3] Later there developed a trend toward bearing children earlier in the marriage.

This trend may have passed its peak. The birth rate is dropping, and there seems to be increasing resolution on the part of college students to postpone having children until they have discovered their own identity.

Morton M. Hunt, writing for *Redbook,*[4] developed the case for delaying parenthood into the thirties, until the pair have realized fullness in their lives together, and developed their personal potential. The idea may have merit, but is not the usual pattern for the new marriage.

Hunt's article drew many letters of protest, among them one by Alan F. Guttmacher, Director of Obstetrics and Gynecology at Mount Sinai Hospital in New York. Dr. Guttmacher says the years 17 to 21 are the best years for childbearing.

Typical comments of young people who wish to have children soon after marriage are: "We wish to have them while we are young enough to enjoy them," or "We want to get this part of marriage over while we are young."[5]

The question of the best time to start a family is one which is likely to trouble every young couple as they plan their life together. It is safer from the standpoint of the wife's health and life to have the first child while she is still in the twenties. With the low maternal death rates of today, however, having a child somewhat later is not a serious risk. Life-conserving techniques improve from year to year. Financial considera-

[3] William S. Bernard, "Student Attitudes on Marriage and the Family," *American Sociological Review,* 3:354–361, 1938.

[4] "Parenthood Should Wait," October, 1968; also in *Reader's Digest,* February, 1969, pp. 49–54.

[5] Reprinted in *Reader's Digest,* p. 34, June, 1969.

tions and the status of the couple's marital adjustment are more often the issues which need to be faced, rather than the health risk. Sterility, however, does increase with age. This is a concern only to those who marry when the wife is well past the average age of marriage.

Children should be planned for only after the couple are confident that their own relationship is established on a secure basis.

Well-meaning people sometimes advise couples who are in difficulty in their marriage to have a baby, assuring them that this will likely make their marriage a success. There is no scientific opinion to support this view, and the risks of bringing a child into a situation of tension are great indeed. Research and clinical observations indicate that a home in which there is severe tension between parents is the worst possible situation in which a child can be placed. Prenatal damage may result. (See pp. 553–554.) The additional work and worry accompanying the birth of a child is more likely to add problems to the already difficult situation.

Much research, too, has shown that there is a close relationship between the happiness of the parental home and the happiness of the child.[6] Unhappily wed people usually have a negative attitude toward children, which may account in part for the failure of children in such homes to obtain happiness. Unhappiness as a parental attitude frequently leads to a lack of harmony in the parent-child relationship also.[7]

Differences in the divorce rate of couples with and without children are not so great as has been supposed. Although divorce is more frequent among the childless in the early years of marriage, there is no difference in the rate after thirteen years of marriage. Even the differences in rates which exist in the early years of marriage are probably not explained by the presence or absence of children.[8] Young couples who are not happy will seldom become so by having children. If they cannot work out techniques of adjustment during the childless period of family life, there is little likelihood that they will be able to face the complicated adjustments that are involved as the family grows.

The circumstance under which the birth of a child might be expected to save a failing marriage is that in which childlessness itself is at the root of the marital discord. When an otherwise compatible couple begin to find life meaningless and empty but feel, for example, that they cannot yet afford the children they both want, they must reexamine their

[6] Ernest W. Burgess and Leonard S. Cottrell; *Predicting Success or Failure in Marriage* (Englewood Cliffs, N.J.: Prentice-Hall, Inc., 1939); also Lewis M. Terman and others, *Psychological Factors in Marital Happiness* (New York: McGraw-Hill Book Co., 1938).

[7] Paul Wallin and Howard M. Vollmer, "Marital Happiness of Parents and Their Children's Attitude Toward Them," *American Sociological Review,* 18:424–431, August, 1953.

[8] Paul H. Jacobson, "Differentials in Divorce by Duration of Marriage and Size of Family," *American Sociological Review,* 15:235–244, April, 1950.

values and ambitions in order to save their marriage. As one counselor advised a group of newlyweds, "Young couples who are determined to get somewhere in this world will probably never feel that they have reached the place where they can afford children. At some point they must merely decide to compromise ambition for the sake of their own happiness."

All the evidence points up the conclusion that only those couples who genuinely want children should have them and that only those couples who are well adjusted in marriage should plan to have children.

Marriage Happiness and Children

There is some evidence that having a child during the first year of marriage interferes somewhat with the happiness of the couple.[9] This would seem to agree with the popular opinion that the couple should be alone during the first year or so of their marriage and not have the interference of a third member. It is assumed that a period of adjustment to marriage and to the community is desirable before confinement. Marriage books and clinicians usually advise a delay of a year or two to permit time for adjustments in the marriage and in social and community relationship.

Some couples fear that the pregnancy and the child will in some measure interfere with their love life. Studies of marriage happiness show that the happiest years are those early in marriage before children come.[10] Old people looking back on their lives, however, indicate the years when the children were growing up in the family as their happiest in terms of total life satisfactions.[11]

Some of the early births are a result of marriage forced by pregnancy, which no doubt is a factor in reducing happiness. Evidence shows that the highest rate of failure in marriage is among those who become pregnant premaritally.[12] Happiness ratings for those who become pregnant early in the marriage are lower than for those who become pregnant after a year or more of marriage.

There are, however, arguments in favor of having a baby fairly early

[9] Harold T. Christensen and Robert E. Philbrick, "Family Size as a Factor of Marital Adjustment of College Students," *American Sociological Review,* 17:306–312, June, 1952.

[10] Burgess and Cottrell, *op. cit.,* pp. 246–248.

[11] Judson T. Landis, "Social-Psychological Factors of Aging," *Social Forces,* 20:468–470, May, 1942.

[12] Christensen has made extensive studies in this area. For representative results see Harold T. Christensen and Betty B. Rubenstein, "Premarital Pregnancy and Divorce: A Follow-up Study by the Interview Method," *Marriage and Family Living,* 8:114–123, May, 1956; see also Harold T. Christensen, "Child Spacing Analysis via Record Linkage," *Marriage and Family Living,* 25:272–280, August, 1963.

FIGURE 27–1 RELATIONSHIP BETWEEN DESIRE FOR CHILDREN AND
MARITAL ADJUSTMENT. Source: Based on the data from Ernest W. Burgess and Leonard S. Cottrell, **Predicting Success or Failure in Marriage**
(Copyright 1939, by Prentice-Hall, Inc., New York). Reproduced by permission of the publisher.

*Not desired by husband, or wife, or both.

Results are for 526 middle-class couples.

in the marriage, provided the wife is physiologically mature.[13] The longer
the couple is together in a pair relationship, the greater the difficulty in
breaking the established routine and habits in order to make room for a
third party. The companionship marriage, which emphasizes the partnership role of husband and wife, is in fact the one most likely to suffer
severe problems of readjustment of husband-wife relations. The more
traditional family system had no place for marriages in which the role of
wife was distinct from the roles of housekeeper and mother. Where a
high level of companionship has been established by the couple in their
marriage, the effect of a small child, with his rigorous demands on the
mother and the requirement that the entire routine of the couple be changed,
is often serious.

An English statesman, in commenting on the problems of the contemporary family, observed that the main trouble with the companionship
marriage is that couples get to be so companionable that they have no
place for children in their lives. This foreboding has certainly not been
justified in the United States. Margaret Mead, writing for *U.S. News and
World Report* (June 6, 1960), criticized the young wife for wanting to
be a mother to the neglect of her obligations as a wife. She fears the trend

[13] See David R. Mace's statement on this problem as presented in "Should You
Have a Baby the First Year?" *Woman's Home Companion*, 76:38 ff., December, 1949.

toward overdomesticity which draws the young male into the safe shelter of the home, thus curbing his creative, adventurous outlook.

The question of whether there can be a happy marriage without children will be of increasing concern in the days ahead, as the pressure of world population reaches an ever more critical point. The question has not been given the attention it deserves. Burgess and Cottrell's[14] classic study of 526 married couples is suggestive that a desire for children is the key, not actually having children. This trend might even change, as population pressure mounts to the point of radically changing reproductive values. Their findings are the best guide we have at present. (See Figure 27–1).

It will be seen that poor adjustments were few among couples who had no children but who wanted children. Good adjustments were high among this group. The group which had one or more children and desired them also showed a high percentage of good adjustments. But those who had children that were not desired showed the greatest proportion of poor adjustments, and very few of these couples showed good adjustment.

The Baby and Family Routine

The coming of the first child into the family calls for numerous readjustments in the habits of the parents. Much of the routine of family life must be centered around the child. Times of rising and retiring, sleep habits, recreational habits, the time spent outside the home—all these things have to be viewed from a new perspective when young people face the responsibilities of parenthood.

The first baby is one of the most significant educational experiences in the life of any person. This is especially true now because an increasing number of young people have had no experience with babies, even in their parental home. Their first experience comes with their own first baby.

The young parent learns that a baby is quite a different physiological mechanism. The heart beats around 135 times a minute, rather than 72 times, as in the adult. The infant breathes 35 times a minute instead of 16. Although much more susceptible to dietary upsets than an adult, he recovers from fevers and many diseases, and from injuries, much more quickly than will the adult. His temperature-adjusting mechanism is much more flexible, permitting quick adjustments to hot and cold. This is true to a considerable extent throughout childhood. And the abounding energy of the young child and older child is unmatched in the adult. Growth and development are very rapid; so also is the repair of damage to tissue.

[14] Burgess and Cottrell, *op. cit.*

Emotional Adjustments to a Third Family Member

The coming of the first baby quite frequently creates emotional problems centering around the relationships between husband and wife. This may occur immediately after the child's birth or come when he is a few weeks old, and the couple begins to sense the change parenthood has brought into their lives. The wife goes through a honeymoon period with the baby, a time in which the insecure husband is likely to feel sadly neglected. In some cases the mother from that point on makes the child, rather than the husband, the emotional center of her life. The wife who relegates the husband to the position of merely earning the money, giving all her attention and emotional life to the child, cannot expect to continue to have a satisfactory home life.

There are other cases where the wife resents the coming of the child because his birth means sudden and unwanted termination of her career, her independence, or some other special status she enjoys. The wife may also fear that the coming of the child will interfere with the relationship between husband and wife.

No matter how much the baby is wanted or how happy the couple may be on its arrival, the home life or the husband-wife relationship will never be the same. Babies are in their own innocent way tyrants in the home. As Levy and Munroe[15] have so well expressed it,

> No matter how going a concern a marriage may be, the advent of children causes severe strain between parents. Newborn babies cannot be taken in their stride; they have none. Their very physical disorganization sets the pace for their influence on marriage ties. Children are as disturbing to marriage as their own physical eccentricities. Any orderly, smooth, satisfactory relationship carefully worked out between husband and wife is broken up the very first night the child is home from the hospital. The inability of a child to do anything for itself means that demands are made on parents which create a new relationship between husband and wife. Their time and energy are no longer their own for companionship or intimacy. The little tyrant need only raise its voice a tiny bit to break up the parents' closest embrace. The warmth of the adult relationship is forever being disturbed by the child's demands for physical attention. At any hour of the night the newborn youngster can separate husband and wife without repaying them for their loss with even a friendly smile. The child's physical requirements have the right-of-way over their feelings toward each other and toward the child. No matter how much one or both of them may resent this intrusion, their only choice is to obey the child's call and sacrifice their own need for each other. Babies are tyrants.

[15] John Levy and Ruth Munroe, *The Happy Family* (New York: Alfred A. Knopf, Inc., 1938), p. 243.

On the other hand, children always bring to the home a new focus of interest which is usually of decided advantage. They also bring new responsibilities which may intensify the loyalty of parents to each other and intensify their loyalty to the family itself.

LeMasters has made a case-history study of the adjustments of 46 couples to the coming of the first child.[16] Of this group, 38 couples, or 83 percent, reported "extensive" or "severe" crisis in adjusting to the first child. This was a joint rating of the parents. LeMasters concludes that adding a child to the urban middle-class married couple constitutes a crisis.

Most of these couples actually wanted and planned for the child, so this was not a case of unwanted children; and most of them considered their marriages good marriages, so it was not a matter of husband-wife conflicts. Much of the difficulty was due to a romanticized rather than a realistic conception of what parenthood and babies are like. Mothers had not anticipated the loss of sleep, the chronic tiredness and exhaustion, the confinement to the home, the curtailment of social contacts, the drain on income, the isolation, the washing and ironing, the seven-day-and-night week, the worry over the child and their ability to meet its demands adequately, that are a part of parenthood. Women with professional work experience suffered a crisis in every case.

Fathers added to these adjustments the decline in sex interest of the wife, the loss of her earnings, putting a greater burden upon him, and worry about future pregnancies and income. LeMasters reports that the husbands quickly became disenchanted with the parental role.

He concludes that there is a great deficiency in preparing young people for the parent role in our culture. They anticipate with great hope the mate role but not the parent role. The first child destroys the pair role relationship and creates the triangle relationship. The husband no longer has priority in the wife's interests and attentions. The first child painfully forces the couple to take the last step into the adult world.

Most of the group LeMasters studied eventually made the transition into successful parenthood. Even though the transition was painful, most felt it was worth what it cost.

Robert O. Blood, Jr., and Donald M. Wolfe of the University of Michigan found, in a study in the Detroit area over a five-year period, that "the arrival of children constitutes the gravest crisis that the average marriage encounters."[17]

---

[16] E. E. LeMasters, "Parenthood as a Crisis," *Marriage and Family Living,* 19:352–355, November, 1957. This research was confirmed by findings of Everett D. Dyer, "Parenthood as Crisis: A Re-study," *Marriage and Family Living,* 25:196–201, May, 1963.

[17] *Husbands and Wives: The Dynamics of Married Living* (New York: Free Press of Glencoe, 1960).

This they found to be true even though children are more popular than ever and practically all couples want them. The mothers stressed such factors as loss of companionship between husband and wife, economic hardship, loss of sleep and other disruption of their lives, and being tied down to the home.

Alice Rossi agrees that motherhood exacts a big price on mothers in a society without the kinship group. It is a question of deprivations versus rewards. She feels that women do not have a realistic appreciation of the cost of motherhood. "What has not been seen is the more general point that for the first time in the history of known society, motherhood has become a full-time occupation for adult women."[18]

But she thinks it wrong to call it a crisis. Most women do adjust. It is, therefore, to be viewed as a role transition, a developmental stage.

Women used to expect pregnancy soon after marriage. Marriage was, for them, the transition. Now that pregnancy can be delayed, the transition is that to parenthood. The real shock of parenthood is that the role is abruptly assumed and with it a twenty-four-hour task from which there is no reprieve.

In many cities, infant-care classes are offered for prospective mothers and fathers. These are valuable not only in that they help young people gain confidence in handling and caring for a baby but also they place the couple with others who are enthusiastic about parenthood.

Parent Maturation

One of the rather surprising things the young couple has to learn when the first baby comes is that the role of the mother in the family is quite different from that of the wife and that the role of the father is quite different from that of the husband. The coming of the child, in fact, calls for a recasting of attitudes of the parents toward each other.

Dorothy Canfield Fisher, the novelist, once discussed the topic "How Children Educate Their Parents" in *Progressive Education*. She says:

Most mothers and fathers at the beginning of their career as mothers and fathers are immature, egotistical, raw, spoiled children, whom society has not been able to "educate" in any real sense of the word; at whom life has not been able to get, through the thick barrier of protection set up around the young; in whom the most careful training has been able only to plant the barest germs of what we know as "character." Their ideal of life, expressed or subconscious, is the childish, shallow unrewarding one of doing as they like, and leaving somebody else to take the consequences. They have been (I speak

[18] Alice M. Rossi, "Transition to Parenthood," *Journal of Marriage and Family Living,* 30:26–39, February, 1968.

of course only of the majority of cases) cherished more or less wisely, protected more or less wisely, protected more or less completely, looked out for by their families. In the back of their minds has always been the feeling that if things got too bad, or difficulties too steep, or the water too deep, one could always fall back on the older generation.

She then shows how being a mother or father puts many young people on their own resources for the first time and concludes, "The great majority of ordinary human beings would be unbearable if they had no children to bring them up."

The proper emotional attitude of the parent is all-essential in providing the child with a proper atmosphere for development. The infant at birth has a capacity to learn but no knowledge, emotions but no orientation of them around persons or things. Experience, the social traditions, moral beliefs of parents and other social groups must be acquired. The mind is plastic, highly impressionable, capable from the outset of receiving an almost unlimited number of impressions. This plasticity of mind and receptivity of the nervous system makes possible the cultivation of his emotional life and the passing on to the child of the experiences of the race.

The family atmosphere surrounding the child in early infancy and childhood is the most important single factor in personality development for he absorbs the atmosphere of the life about him. Impressions and attitudes resulting from these early experiences carry over through the individual's lifetime, affecting many other relationships. The relationships between the parent and the child are important factors in the happiness of the child as he grows to adulthood and to his later success in marriage.

Nursing vs. Bottle Feeding

Recent research reports that only about half as many mothers in the United States breast-feed as ten years ago. The breast-feeding mothers are predominantly college-educated, affluent, and "warmly relaxed about sex." The bottle-feeding mothers are reported to have more psychosexual disturbances and to dislike nudity and sexuality.[19]

Contemporary research on breast feeding, suggests that the isolation of the infant from the mother, as in many modern hospitals, may be wrong. Research by Ashley-Montagu confirms the fact that the child should be allowed to nurse from the beginning.[20] Research by Paul G.

[19] Michael Newton and Niles Newton, *New England Journal of Medicine,* reported in "Research Notes" of *Family Life,* 28:3, June, 1968.
[20] M. F. Ashley-Montagu, *Anthropology and Human Nature* (Boston: Porter Sargent, Publisher, 1957), p. 20.

Gyorgy, professor of pediatrics at the University of Pennsylvania, shows that the colostrum which is in the mother's breast prior to the flow of milk is necessary to the growth of microorganisms important to the infant, giving it resistance to disease.[21] Cow's milk has only 1/13 to 1/15 the amount of fortification against disease as has human milk.

Ashley-Montagu's research shows that, for the mother, the sucking of the infant immediately after birth sets up contractions in the uterus which help to constrict blood vessels, guard against post-partum hemorrhages, and cause the immediate detachment of the afterbirth and its ejection. This immediate nursing of the infant is nature's way of getting the uterus to return to normal size. The contractions in the uterus produced by nursing last as much as 20 minutes after the infant ceases sucking. Where nursing is delayed as much as 20 hours or more, blood oozes into the uterine cavity, causing irregular spasmodic contractions. The mother whose baby has nursed immediately will not suffer afterbirth pains and will return more quickly to her prepregnant condition.

What is known as the "let-down reflex" in the mother may start the milk flowing even before the infant begins sucking. There is a definite erotic feeling in connection with this reflex that is a factor in the emotional bond between mother and child.[22]

The contractions of the uterus which accompany nursing and continue even beyond the completion of the breast feeding seem to be of the same character as those experienced during orgasm in the sexual act. The nursing reaction, therefore, not only brings close contact with the child but also brings emotional and physical satisfaction to the mother. In many primitive cultures, nursing extends beyond a two-year period, in some as long as four or five years, perhaps accounting in part for the built-in security of the child.[23]

On the other hand, the long-nursed primitive child may suffer great trauma when weaning time comes. When a new babe goes to the breast, he may feel greatly rejected. Today, the nursing period is confined to a few months, and the baby gradually shifts to soft foods. There is little trauma at weaning because it is so gradual and takes place well before a rival sibling enters the scene.[24]

[21] *Ibid.*

[22] Niles, Newton, "The Influence of the Let-Down Reflex in Breast Feeding in the Mother-Child Relationship," *Marriage and Family Living*, 20:18–20, February, 1958. For further study of the "milk-ejection reflex" and the relationship of nursing to psychosexual factors, see Edward M. Brecher, "We Are All Our Mothers' Daughters: What Sex Research Reveals about Unhappy Wives," *Redbook*, 138:71 ff., November, 1969.

[23] For a brief current summary on this topic, see "Maternity," *Time*, July 19, 1968, p. 53.

[24] Refer back to Ch. 9 for a further discussion of this topic.

The Second Baby

The following is the experience of a young couple, the father with a Ph.D. in sociology, the mother with an M.A. in psychology:

> Well, we seem to have weathered the worst of it; not without scars, however. Five weeks have passed and things are beginning to seem almost normal again. Our problem came from the least expected source—not the baby, but our two-year-old, Sue. After two days of angelic behavior she hit the baby with a toy truck, grabbed her bottle and finished it off and the battle was on. Since then she has kept us under a more or less constant trial by fire—up late at night, at any and all hours of the night and at 5:30 or 6:00 every morning; temper tantrums, whining ill-humor, and all of the other horrible things that a child of mine "just wouldn't do." At the first signs of what was happening we hastily read all the books we should have read six months ago on the peculiarities of the two-year-old and sibling jealousy. Bill ended up playing mama to the baby, while I became a 24-hour-a-day mama to a very babylike Sue.
>
> Within the last couple of days she has begun to get sick of me, which is the sign I've been waiting for, and to return to much of her former independent activity. If this is really about the end of it, I guess we've gotten off fairly easy, although the weeks since it began seem much more nearly like four months.

At the time the second pregnancy is known, preparation of the first child for the sibling's coming is highly important. This will be a momentous event in the life of the firstborn. He has had a world in which the affection of parents has been his exclusively. He cannot share his rights, privileges, and attention without a great deal of adjustment.

Parents need to begin early by telling the child he is to have a brother or sister playmate and helping him to look forward to the coming of the baby with happy anticipation. This also will be a time for a new step in the sex education of the child. If he is old enough, he is certain to ask where babies come from, how they grow, who brings them, or some similar question which opens the way to explain that the baby grows inside the mother. When he asks how it gets out, the question must be answered by a simple statement such as, "through the birth canal," or "it comes out through a very special place that opens at that time." It is important that questions be answered honestly, up to the level of the child's understanding.[25]

When the mother returns from the hospital, full attention should be given to the child who has been left at home and not to showing off the

[25] An interesting development is the location of the maternity ward on the ground floor, with low windows, so the older child may visit his mother while she is in the hospital, and building the nursery on the outside wall, too, and with low windows, so the child can see his new brother or sister while the baby is in the hospital.

new baby. As much attention must be given to him in the days following as is possible, to avoid jealousy and the development of aggression of the child toward the new baby. Even then a perfect relationship should not be taken for granted.

Factors Influencing Number of Children

This aspect of family life was very much in the lap of the gods historically. There was little control over reproduction, so the number of children was in ratio to the couple's fecundity and years married. Today, size of family reflects in part, differences in values and goals and to some extent differences in self-control and ability to consistently pursue whatever ideal has been set for the size of the family.

There is some evidence that family size is a matter in part of family tradition, for there seems to be a definite family-size relationship running through the generations. Those children who come from large families tend to have large families. This is more true if the mother comes from a large family than if the father does, although it holds true somewhat for both. It seems also to hold for all social classes.[26]

Census data on size of family by education show that those with least education have the largest families; those with the most education, the smallest families. High school and college graduates tend to have small families (see Figure 27–2).

One must recognize, of course, that this association between education and size of family is a two-way relationship. Parents with a large number of children are able to give them less education, and therefore the large-family pattern persists.[27] Families with a small number of children can educate their children, so the small-family pattern persists.

Another important variable in determining the number of children has been, and is still to some extent, religion. The Catholic birth rate has been considerably higher than the Protestant, owing to restrictions placed on birth control by the Church.[28]

Economic factors too have been operative. In Western society it is

[26] For a summary of findings on this point and analysis of original data dealing with 1,482 families see J. Berent, "Family Size of Two Successive Generations," *Milbank Memorial Fund Quarterly*, 31:39–50, January, 1953.

[27] Paul H. Landis, *Teenage Adjustment in Large and Small Families* (Pullman, Wash.: Washington Agricultural Experiment Station, April, 1954), Bulletin No. 549.

[28] The subject of differential birth rate has been of concern to demographers and sociologists for generations. For a summary of studies see Paul H. Landis, *Social Problems in Nation and World* (Philadelphia: J. B. Lippincott Co., 1959), Ch. 33.

FIGURE 27-2 RELATIONSHIP BETWEEN EDUCATION AND NUMBER OF CHILDREN BORN, 1964—PER 1,000 WOMEN EVER MARRIED AGES 15-44. Source: "Fertility of the Population: June 1964 and March 1962," **Current Population Reports,** Series P-20, No. 147, January 5, 1966, Table 4, p. 16.

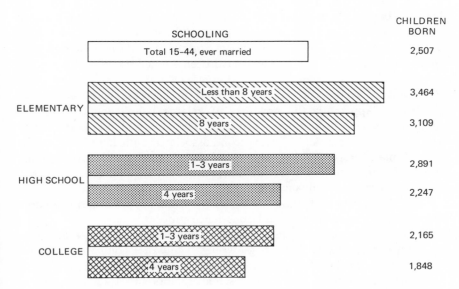

	SCHOOLING	CHILDREN BORN
	Total 15–44, ever married	2,507
ELEMENTARY	Less than 8 years	3,464
	8 years	3,109
HIGH SCHOOL	1–3 years	2,891
	4 years	2,247
COLLEGE	1–3 years	2,165
	4 years	1,848

The educated tend to have smaller families. This is partly because they marry at a later age, but important factors no doubt are also different motivational and aspirational goals from those with less education.

generally those least able to support children who have the largest families.[29] This is in part both cause and effect. The large family makes heavy economic demands, but on lower socioeconomic levels birth control techniques are less effective and motives less strong or less implemented.

With any couple, motives governing size of family are certain to be complex, being affected by family tradition, by their scheme of values, by the way children are viewed in fulfilling or hindering their life purpose. And even with the best resolves and best technology, couples do have children they did not plan for.[30]

[29] *Ibid.* This issue is of current political concern. The issue now is whether the poor and the nonwhites among them, should be helped with birth conrtol and sterilization by the use of public funds in order to help solve the recurrent problem of poverty through the generations.

[30] Lynn Landman claims the nation has 5,300,000 women age 18–44 in need of subsidized family planning. A program for this will cost $100 million a year, he says. "United States Underdeveloped Land in Family Planning," *Journal of Marriage and Family Living,* 30:191–201, May, 1968.

Number of Children and Quality
of Family Life

The number of children in a home has the effect of remaking it as an environment. It is a much different place with one child than, say, with six. It becomes a different environment for the parents and for the children. Both aspects of the problem have been studied.[31]

Happiness of parents   Happiness tends to decrease with the size of the family. Apparently the pressures of a large family detract from the ability of the couple to enjoy marriage.[32] The ability of a couple to control the size of their family seems to be associated with happiness. In the case of many large families, they have failed in this objective and are burdened with children they are not adequately equipped to care for, either emotionally or financially.

In this group are undoubtedly many Catholics who have children they felt they could not in good conscience prevent.

Although couples in small families seem to be happier, they resort to divorce more readily if things go wrong. The writer compared[33] divorce rates in large families (six or more children) and small families, using as a sample the parents of 4,300 high school seniors and 1,424 college students. In this sample only 6 percent of homes in families of six or more children were broken by divorce and 16 percent by death. In the broken only-child families, 11.5 percent had been broken by divorce, 10 percent by death. There was a 50–50 chance of divorce and death in the broken two- and three-child families.

Parent-child relationships   An intensive study of 100 large families by Bossard and his coworkers led them to a comparison of large families with the general small-family systems and to the development of some hypotheses concerning the characteristics of each.[34] In the small family, planning is one of the basic characteristics, along with the spacing of chil-

[31] For a concise summary of studies on this problem and original data, see Christensen and Philbrick, *op. cit.*

[32] *Ibid.;* also Robert B. Reed, "Social and Psychological Factors Affecting Fertility. VIII: The Interrelationship of Marital Adjustment, Fertility Control and the Size of Family," *The Milbank Memorial Fund Quarterly*, 25:383–425, October, 1947. See also Ivan Nye, "Adolescent-Parent Adjustments: Age, Sex, Sibling Numbers, Broken Homes, and Employed Mothers as Variables," *Marriage and Family Living*, 14:327–332, 1952.

[33] Landis, *op. cit.*

[34] James H. S. Bossard and Winnogene Pratt Sanger, "The Large Family System," *American Sociological Review*, 17:3–9, February, 1952; also, James H. S. Bossard and Eleanor Stoker Boll, *The Large Family System* (Philadelphia: University of Pennsylvania Press, 1956).

dren and a strong emphasis on child rearing. Educational aspirations are high; the quest for status is conscious and deliberate, pointing toward a career for the child. Parenthood is intensive, with a great deal of professional care being given the child. In many cases, both parents are working; often the mother has a career-oriented personality. Family life is generally democratic, with the child having a voice in the family discussions. The full development of the child is the objective of the family atmosphere, so that the pattern is essentially one of cooperation, with the parent being conscious of numerous emotional problems of the child. The parent is always comparing his child with other children in the social group. There is great pressure on the child to measure up and great anxiety on the part of parents if the child fails to measure up. There is little discipline from siblings and little direct interaction between the child and other children. The child's resentments, because of his limited contacts, are directed against a few persons—often the parents. The same is true of his affections. In most conflict situations, it is two against one rather than there being a large group in the conflict unit. In the small-family pattern, it may be one parent and child against the other parent—a struggle, in effect, between the parents for the favor of the child.

Summarizing the characteristics of the small family, Bossard and Sanger say:

> The small family rests upon the ideas of planning, individualization, democratic co-operation, social isolation and intensive pressures. The small family system is the quality system, chiefly at the middle-class level. Its driving force is one of ambition, in an open class system; its social justification, if one may thus speak of it, is that it represents an adjustment to a rapidly changing society, with its train of attendant insecurities.[35]

These writers find that the large family is different in almost every respect and that it produces quite different personality types. Involved in the birth rate itself is a different philosophy of life. When the large family is intentional, it is usually a desire of either husband or wife, rather than of both. In nonplanned large families, children are accepted as a product of fate.

The large family provides an environment in which there are constant readjustments to the vicissitudes of life. Things are always happening in the large family, and there must be a constant shifting of roles, statuses, and responsibilities of various members to meet events. The family group is the unit of first concern in the large family, whereas in the small family the individual is the unit of concern. In the large family, each person's wishes are always subservient to those of the group. Sleeping arrangements, dress, dates, every aspect of living are limited by the economic resources, crowded conditions, and constant pressure of

[35] *Op. cit.*

family members upon each other. The large family is more rigidly organized within and therefore tends to be more authoritarian, with one or more persons being dominant. A greater degree of executive direction and arbitrary control is necessary. This control is usually by the father or mother but sometimes by an older sibling. Authoritarianism is almost an inevitable part of the large-family system. This, the writers suggest, is probably why the early American family was authoritarian in character.

This research also finds that in the large family there is a great deal more specialization of roles among family members. One girl may be a household drudge, a son may be a father substitute. One child may be a gadabout, one a whiner, another a tattletale, and so forth. Obviously such specialized roles cannot be played in the small family. The young child in the large family has fewer choices of roles, as many roles are already taken by the time he appears on the scene.

In the large family, parents and children are likely to be less demanding in attitude and less tolerant of neurotic tendencies of members than in the small family. It is impossible for the child in the large family

FIGURE 27–3   FAMILY PATTERNS OF HIGH SCHOOL SENIORS. Source: Paul H. Landis, **Parent Teen-age Relationships in Large and Small Families** (Pullman, Wash.: Washington Agricultural Experiment Station, April 1954), Bulletin No. 549.

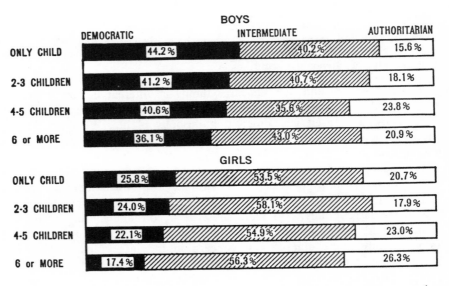

The larger the family the more authoritarian it tends to be. Data are for 4,377 high school seniors in the state of Washington and show the percentages of these young people living under family administrative patterns by size of family.

to receive the much-emphasized individual attention so characteristic of family philosophy in small families. The crowded space of the home, it is believed, tends to lead young people to want to leave home early and to marry early.

The writer has been able to test some of these hypotheses further with a group of more than 4,300 high school seniors and 1,424 college students.[36] This study gives statistical confirmation to many of the differences suggested by the Bossard and Sanger case studies.

In the writer's study, also, it was found that the large family (large families, those with six or more children) does tend to be authoritarian, the small family democratic (Figure 27–3). The small family was found to be much more education-oriented than the large family. Even those representatives of large families who finished high school and went to college were less academically oriented, had lower educational aspirations, and were less successful in their school performance. Those from large families were more certain they knew the vocation they wanted to go into, which probably indicated a limited range of choice rather than actual preparation for a wide range of choice.

Much evidence of economic pressure and home crowding was found in the large family. This is inevitable in a society where wages and salaries are based on individual performance alone, with no subsidy being made by industry or government for children. The boy from a large family adjusts well; girls from large families do not. In fact, girls from large families have more problems of adjustment in senior high school and college years than others. They are more often friendless or have few friends and seldom exercise leadership. Girls from the small family, particularly from the only-child family, are far superior in their adjustments as measured by number of friendships, number of activities, and leadership roles at this period in life to those from large families and, in fact, have a more prominent place in leadership than any other group.

Historically, this may not have been true. Formerly the girl's life was submerged in the family. The modern girl who finishes high school, and particularly the girl who goes to college, is venturing far out into the individualistic world of contemporary life. She is sampling competitive values that were once the privilege of the male only. Her training in the individualistic family, under the small-family pattern, has led to the maximum of independence and self-sufficiency, and she has, therefore, formed her personality more appropriately for living in an individualistic society. The girl in the large family, by contrast, has had her personality so submerged in the family that she is not particularly well fitted for the adjustments of our highly individualistic teen-age world.

It may well be that the personality deficiencies of the teen-age girl in

[36] *Op. cit.*

the large family are due largely to the fact that she has been tied down with being an assistant mother or housekeeper to younger children. This is often the case with the older girl in the large family. She is thus hindered from making the plunge into her peer group at the puberty period. This may be for the girl what the psychologists call a "critical period";[37] it must either be done then or she can never feel at home with her peers. In any case, we know that she tends to develop a feeling of friendlessness.

There is much evidence from our study of teen-agers that boys are never so submerged in the family as are girls and are seldom so completely subject to authoritarian patterns, regardless of family size.[38] This is probably a factor in the adjustability of the boy by type of family background. The boy in the only-child family probably suffers from overmothering, making his adjustment outside the family difficult. He is also an only rival of his father for his mother's affection.

The problems faced by teen-agers in large families tend to be largely external in nature—schooling, living space, money, and vocational problems. The only child suffers more from problems that are introspective in character. He more often has problems in his relationships with family members, with his age mates, and in boy-girl relations. He also tends to have more problems in the area of morals and religion.

Elder and Bowerman[39] studied the effect of family size and composition on child-rearing patterns with a sample of 1,261 Protestant seventh-grade pupils. They found that with the increase in family size, the lower-class girl was more likely to perceive her father as being authoritarian and both parents as being less communicative, more controlling and given more to physical punishment and less to praise than was the case in the smaller family.

Among the boys, it was in the middle-class family that authoritarian traits more clearly emerged as the family pattern with increase in size: more physical punishment, more parental dominance, less communication.

Hawkes and his colleagues found that the small-family environment did not have a detrimental effect on the personalities of children they studied—a fifth-grade group. They found no evidence favoring the bene-

---

[37] For a discussion of this concept see J. P. Scott, "Critical Periods in Behavioral Development," *Science*, 138:949–956, November 30, 1962.

[38] Paul H. Landis and Carol L. Stone, *The Relationship of Parental Authority Patterns to Teenage Adjustment* (Pullman, Wash.: Washington Agricultural Experiment Station, September, 1952), Bulletin No. 538; also Carol Larson Stone and Paul H. Landis, "An Approach to Authority Patterns in Parent-Teenage Relations," *Rural Sociology*, 18:233–242, September, 1953.

[39] Glen H. Elder, Jr., and Charles E. Bowerman, "Family Structure and Child-rearing Patterns: The Effect of Family Size and Sex Composition," *American Sociological Review*, 28:891–905, December, 1963.

ficial effects of the large family. Generally speaking, they concluded, children from the small family probably fare better psychologically than those from larger families.[40]

These studies suggest that the pattern of life of the family and the personality formation of children will be very much affected by the size of the family a young couple has. The evidence is sufficient to suggest that there is no one pattern that may be considered ideal. One cannot accept the folklore notion that a large family is ideal for the adjustment of the child because brothers and sisters knock the rough spots off personality. The large family seems to hold no disadvantage for the boy in his later adjustments, but it is a decided handicap for the girl. We must also modify current conceptions about the only child, particularly in cases involving the girl, if results of the above study are found to be generally characteristic. She adjusts better in many of her social relationships than do girls from families with more than one child.

Finally, families of all sizes have their characteristic problems in marriage relationships as well as in parent-child relationships.

Sibling Relationships

There probably never was a family with more than one child in which a certain amount of jealousy, rivalry, and bickering, or hidden suffering, did not take place in the relationship between siblings. An early account of family relationships is the bitter jealousy between Cain and Abel, which led to murder. Joseph's relationship with his half brothers is an account of the interplay of family relationships in a large patriarchal family—their envy of his coat of many colors given him by a doting father, their sale of him into bondage, his later forgiveness, when as a member of Pharaoh's household he was able to save them from famine. The Cinderella story and numerous other tales of fiction and fact, as well as historical biography, tell of struggles, rivalries, jealousies, and resentments, as well as magnanimity of sibling relationships.

These relationships require insight on the part of parents. The nature of the sibling relationship is of life-long importance. Jessie Bernard, who has studied the literature on sibling relationships thoroughly, concludes her review with this statement:

If, standing on a crowded street corner, we could see all the adults about us in terms of their sib relationships, we would see not the seemingly independent,

[40] Glenn R. Hawkes, Lee Burchinal, and Bruce Gardener, "Size of Family and Discipline of Children," *Marriage and Family Living,* 20:65–68, February, 1958.

self-resourceful individuals who pass before us, but rebellious little sisters fighting against parental discrimination, resentful little brothers hating older sisters whose superiority in age and maturity frustrated their male egos, jealous older sisters resenting the attention bestowed on little sisters, sisters of all ages envying the privileges of brothers of all ages. Most of us, on becoming closely acquainted with men and women of apparent maturity, have found that in certain aspects of their personalities they are still much under the influence of brother or sister, still smarting under childhood patterns. It does not matter that they are now successful in their own right; they must still convince brother or sister of their success. One man's whole life is spent in achieving goals which his sister unconsciously set for him years ago; he must prove to her that he can do it. One woman's life is shattered because of her ambivalent attitude of hatred and love for a brother who dominated her childhood.[41]

Parents cannot hope that children will be alike in temperament, disposition, or lovability or that each will be able to accept the other fully. Some children will live under the shadow of a brother or sister for a lifetime, even though they are far separated by marriage. Others carry in their personalities the experience of dominance or submission which was established early in life by a relationship with a brother or a sister. This may affect their choice of a mate. Still others will carry a long resentment against a sibling, always fighting against anyone who interferes with their development because they are still subconsciously fighting a dominating brother or sister.

The autobiographies of college students describe sib influences as a determining force in the development of their personalities. Take, for example, the young person who has suffered from an overshadowing relationship with a domineering or brilliant brother or sister and who has literally shaped his life in the sibling's image. Some describe how painful and discouraging such a relationship is as they continue to live under this shadow, even when they go to school, being faced by their teachers all the way from grade school to college with the record of an older brother or sister who happened to achieve high standards. Such a person may never get over the feeling of inferiority and hostility this constant unfavorable comparison has brought.

Parents can do much to keep down the bitterness and rivalries between children in the family, but wisdom and understanding and a great deal of patience are required. The best book which has come to the writer's attention for giving insight and removing anxiety of parents in the little rivalries and difficulties that normally develop in the family is that by Edith G. Neisser, *Brothers and Sisters.*[42]

[41] Jessie Bernard, *American Family Behavior* (New York: Harper & Bros., 1942), p. 312.
[42] New York: Harper & Bros., 1951.

Adoption

Because of the low death rate of parents today, there are comparatively few orphan children available for adoption. Most children for adoption are born out of wedlock. Of these, there are more than 300,000 born yearly.

To secure a child for adoption through an agency, hopeful foster parents must submit to the most careful social-work investigation which will appraise not only, or even primarily, their economic resources but also their emotional resources and the success of their marriage. Reliable adoption agencies today are legitimately concerned with whether or not the home is going to be adequate in meeting the social, psychological, and emotional needs of the child. In fact, children placed in homes of adopted parents probably have a better opportunity for an ideal home environment than the child who comes by birth. But all has not gone well.

Some religious groups have orphanages, as do fraternal organizations. They have vested interest in maintaining them; they solicit funds for their maintenance. They do not seek to have the child released for adoption. Many religious groups have restrictions on who can adopt, often requiring that the foster parents be of their own religion. Adoption across religious lines is prohibited by law in several states and is quite generally looked down upon by placement agencies everywhere, making it very difficult for the mixed Protestant-Catholic couple, for example, to adopt a child.

While it must be recognized that orphans are rather few in our culture compared with those in underdeveloped areas of the world, there are, nevertheless, large numbers of children for adoption who have little chance of escaping the custodial care of the institution in which they have been placed. The public reaction to the difficulty of adoption has been to bypass the recognized agencies of placement. Actually, the cost of getting a child through the gray market (through the lawyer or the doctor who represents the girl having her baby out of wedlock) is much less than getting it through the standard agencies. Most of the agencies charge costs of placement.[43] Many doctors or lawyers require only the cost of their services—in the case of the doctor the cost of the pregnancy and delivery, and perhaps of the hospital, if a hospital is used. The lawyer's fee is the cost of legal counsel and adoption papers.

Vincent has studied adoption in relation to the type of doctor to

[43] Elizabeth I. Lynch and Alice E. Mertz, "Adoptive Placement of Infants Directly from the Hospital," *Social Casework*, 36:450–457, December, 1955.

whom the girl goes if she has the baby delivered rather than seeking an abortion. Of unorthodox adoptions, many are arranged by doctors and lawyers.[44] An increasing number of agencies, like the Salvation Army, are adopting directly. Many hospitals now are adopting directly rather than going through the complicated channels of agencies and risking that the child will never be adopted at all.

Lynch and Mertz in a study of direct placement conclude very positively that the best adjustment and physical development of babies comes when they are adopted directly from the hospital at the age of 3 to 10 days.[45] These authors feel that this is due to the fact that only in this way can the child from the beginning get the affection and love which all children need. They advise the following precautions. If these are met, they feel direct adoption is safe:

1. Adoptive parents are eager for the child.
2. The prenatal records of the mother are complete and show no difficulties.
3. The delivery was normal.
4. The child at birth is in good health.

Ernest and Francis Cady, in their excellent book *How to Adopt a Child*,[46] report that half the adoptions today are independent, that is, arranged directly by the physician, an attorney, or other persons who bypass the child-placement agencies. In some states as many as three-fourths are placed through the gray market, which is no more costly than the voluntary contributions, fees, and so on of the usual adoption agency (ranging from $500 to $1,000). The black market is quite a different matter. Almost any price may be charged. The difference between the black market and the gray market lies in the motivation, the black-market operator being in the business for profit rather than trying to recover fees for helping a girl who became pregnant out of wedlock.[47]

The Cadys point out that many people bypass the agencies because of the rather forbidding atmosphere of the placement agency and its personnel, their lack of warmth, and their apparent lack of genuine interest in the prospective foster-parent. They find also that agencies do not look too favorably on applications of people who quibble about fees or gifts expected by the orphanage.

With the great increase in number of "preferred" children (whites

[44] Clark E. Vincent, "The Adoption Market and the Unwed Mother's Baby," *Marriage and Family Living*, 18:124–127, May, 1956.

[45] Lynch and Mertz, *op. cit.*

[46] Ernest Cady and Francis Cady, *How to Adopt a Child* (New York: William Morrow & Co., Inc., 1956).

[47] Although children for adoption are more plentiful now than at any time since World War II, owing to the increasing out-of-wedlock birthrate, black markets still flourish. In mid-1964 the U.S. Congress started a nationwide investigation into this racket. They reported fees for babies running as high as $7,500. A million-dollar racket in baby placement was reported (Associated Press release, June 18, 1964).

with good health and heredity) born out of wedlock, adoption regulations are becoming less severe. The age range during which couples are eligible is being liberalized, there is less restriction as to number of children a couple may adopt; children need not be in perfect health; and waiting period is greatly reduced.

For those willing to take a child of a minority race—Indian, Negro, Mexican-American, and of mixed parentage—there are large numbers of children waiting for adoption.[48]

The way to respectable motherhood without marriage is being opened through adoption by single persons. Few states have encouraged the program, but for women who will take other than the "preferred" children particularly, the challenge is great. Their lives can be enriched by adopting a child or children and giving him the love and care he needs. This is socially important. As Charles Mangel has stated, "It is the loveless man and woman who threatens our national life and culture."[49] Children raised without love cannot fit into society in a normal way.

Single men may also find a challenge in adopting the older child.

It is generally believed that the sound procedure in handling an adopted child is to make his adoption clear to him from the time he is able to first understand it. By frank handling of the situation, without overdoing it, the child will develop normally and naturally without any anxiety about the situation—probably, in fact, with less anxiety than many children who feel insecure with their natural parents. Many of the latter at times daydream that they are adopted.

Problems

1. Childlessness in marriage may result from physical or emotional factors, sterility, voluntary control of pregnancy, continued delaying of parenthood, or the conviction of one mate that children are undesirable. Under which of these circumstances do you think a childless marriage will most likely remain happy? Under which circumstances is the marriage most likely to be doomed?
2. Cases X and Y below are taken from a marriage counselor's file. In the first of the two cases the counselor advised the couple to seriously consider having a child; in the second, he discouraged parenthood. After studying the cases discuss:
   a. Why the counselor advised as he did.
   b. Whether or not his advice seems justified.
   c. What the future of the two marriages will probably be if the couples follow the counselor's advice.

[48] Charles Mangel, "An Unmarried Mother for Mike," *Look,* February 4, 1969, pp. 56 ff.

[49] *Ibid.*

    d. What the future of the two marriages will be if the couples do not follow the counselor's advice relative to having a child.

    Case X: Wife and husband, aged 26 and 30, respectively. Married six years. Report that, while still compatible and in love, marriage seems to be losing its joy. Both feel despondent and sad. Wife reported, "We just don't have anything to stay married for or even to stay alive for, for that matter." Couple childless because their financial circumstances would not, as husband puts it, "allow us to raise the children with the advantages we would want them to have."

    Case Y: Wife and husband aged 25 and 27, respectively. Married three years, during which they have separated briefly twice but have not considered divorce because of religious convictions of wife. Report that, while they occasionally enjoy things together, marriage has lost much of its meaning. Wife wants to continue working but husband disapproves of a wife's earning money. Husband thinks wife would "settle down" if she had a child. Wife is unsure but tends to think that the way to save their marriage is for both of them to work and make money "so we can start having some fun again."

3. *Sociodrama:* A wealthy but conservative young wheat grower sells his farm, moves to New York, and later becomes engaged to a young office worker. Dramatize a scene in which they disagree about how long they should wait before having their first child. Let their backgrounds, role conceptions, and values determine the arguments they present.

4. A man and his wife in looking back at their early months with their two children admit: "Actually they were both very much alike—neither cried excessively, neither was sick or unusually demanding, both followed much the same sleeping and eating schedules. Why then," they wonder, "did the first seem like such a terrible problem? How could it have so disrupted our lives and spoiled our relationship when the second seemed so angelic and undemanding?" How would you explain the difference in the way they felt about the two infants who acted so much alike?

5. Do you consider the role of the mother or that of the father more important in child rearing? Do you believe it is unnecessary, rather silly, or very important for men to be formally prepared for their roles as fathers? Why?

6. In terms of social and psychological (rather than economic) advantages, what size family do you consider ideal? What, if any, are the advantages of growing up in a very large family? What, if any, are the advantages of being an only child or one of two children?

7. When couples are unable to have children, adoption is considered by many to be a desirable alternative. Why should couples be urged to think long and hard about the disadvantages of adoption when childlessness is their only alternative?

Selected References

Articles in Books of Readings

Cavan, Ruth S., *Marriage and the Family in the Modern World: A Book of Readings,* third edition (New York: Thomas Y. Crowell Co., 1969).
    Cobliner, W. Godfred, "Some Maternal Attitudes towards Conception," Reading 52.

Rossi, Alice S., "Transition to Parenthood," Reading 53.

Bain, Katherine, "Adoption: United States Philosophy and Team Approach," Reading 54.

Chappelear, Edith, and Fried, Joyce, "Helping Adopting Couples Come to Grips with Their New Parental Roles," Reading 55.

Haimowitz, Morris L. and Natalie (eds.), *Human Development: Selected Readings* (New York: Thomas Y. Crowell Co., 1966).

Breckenridge, Marian E., and Vincent, E. Lee, "What are Some of the Laws Which Govern Growth?" Reading 20.

Thomas, Alexander, and others, "Behavior Individuality in Early Childhood," Reading 24.

Levy, David M., "Maternal Overprotection," Reading 47.

Krich, A. M. (ed.), *Men: The Variety and Meaning of Their Sexual Experience* (New York: Dell Publishing Co., 1954).

Benedek, Therese, "The Meaning of Fatherhood," Ch. 7.

Sussman, Marvin B., *Sourcebook in Marriage and the Family*, third edition (Boston: Houghton Mifflin Co., 1968).

LeMasters, E. E., "Parenthood as a Crisis," Reading 52.

Winch, Robert F., and Goodman, Louis Wolf, *Selected Studies in Marriage and the Family*, third edition (New York: Holt, Rinehart and Winston, 1968).

Maccoby, Eleanor F., "The Choice of Variables in the Study of Socialization," pp. 242–253.

Maccoby, Eleanor F., "The Communication of Child-Rearing Advice to Parents," pp. 254–258.

General References

Aarons, L. I., "Adoption Laws," *New Republic*, 156:10. January 28, 1967.

Ashley-Montagu, M. F., *Anthropology and Human Nature* (Boston: Porter Sargent, Publisher, 1957), p. 20.

Blanton, Smiley, *Love or Perish* (New York: Simon and Schuster, Inc., 1955).

Bossard, James H. S., *The Sociology of Child Development*, third edition (New York: Harper & Row, Publishers, 1960).

Bossard, James H. S., and Boll, Eleanor S., *The Large Family System* (Philadelphia: University of Pennsylvania Press, 1956).

Bowerman, Charles, and Irish, Donald P., "Some Relationships of Stepchildren to Their Parents," *Marriage and Family Living*, 24:113–121, May, 1962.

Burch, Thomas K., "The Size and Structure of Families: Analysis of Census Data," *American Sociological Review*, 32:347–363, June, 1967.

Campbell, Arthur A., "The Role of Family Planning in the Reductions of Poverty," *Journal of Marriage and the Family*, 30:236–245, May, 1968.

Carner, Charles, "What's New in Adoption?" *Today's Health*, 45:44 ff, August, 1967.

Chappelear, Edith M., and Fried, Joyce E., "Helping Adopting Couples Come to Grips with Their New Parental Roles," *Children*, 14:223–226, November–December, 1967.

Christensen, Harold T., and Philbrick, Robert E., "Family Size as a Factor in the Marital Adjustments of College Couples," *American Sociological Review*, 17:306–312, June, 1952.

Devereux, Edward C., Bronfenbrenner, Urie, and Rodgers, Robert R., "Child

Rearing in England and the United States: A Cross-National Comparison," *Journal of Marriage and the Family,* 31:257-270, May, 1969.

Erickson, M. T., and others, "Intelligent-Parental Environmental Influence," *Science,* 157:1210 ff, September, 1967.

Hawkes, Glenn R., Burchinal, Lee, and Gardner, Bruce, "Size of Family and Discipline of Children," *Marriage and Family Living,* 20:65-68, February, 1958.

Hobbs, Daniel F., Jr., "Transition to Parenthood: A Replication and an Extension," *Journal of Marriage and the Family,* 30:413-417, August, 1968.

Kammeyer, Kenneth, "The Feminine Role: An Analysis in Attitude Consistency," *Journal of Marriage and the Family,* 26:295-305, August, 1965.

Kammeyer, Kenneth, "Sibling Position and Feminine Roles," *Journal of Marriage and the Family,* 29:494-504, August, 1967.

Landis, Judson T., "A Re-examination of the Role of the Father as an Index of Family Integration," *Marriage and Family Living,* 24:124-128, May, 1962.

Landis, Paul H., *Teenage Adjustment in Large and Small Families* (Pullman, Wash.: Washington Agricultural Experiment Station, April, 1954), Bulletin No. 549.

LeMasters, E. E., "Parenthood as a Crisis," *Marriage and Family Living,* 19:352-355, November, 1957.

Loomer, Alice, "The Myth of the Only Child," *Parents' Magazine,* March, 1967, pp. 55 ff.

McCandless, Boyd, "The Devil's Advocate Examines Parent Education," *The Family Coordinator,* 17:149-154, July, 1968.

Mead, Margaret, *A Creative Life for Your Children* (Washington, D.C.: U.S. Department of Health, Education and Welfare, 1962).

Messer, Alfred A., "The Only-Child Syndrome," *New York Times Magazine,* February 25, 1968, p. 84.

Myerhoff, B. G., and Larson, W. R., "Primary and Formal Family Organization and an Adolescent Socialization," *Sociology and Social Research,* 50:63-71, October, 1965.

Niles, Newton, "The Influence of the Let-down Reflex in Breast Feeding in the Mother-Child Relationship," *Marriage and Family Living,* 20:18-20, February, 1958.

"On Being an American Parent," *Time,* December 15, 1967, pp. 30-31.

Rossi, Alice S., "Transition to Parenthood," *Journal of Marriage and the Family,* 30:26-39, February, 1968.

Scott, J. P., "Critical Periods in Behavioral Development," *Science,* 138:945-958, November 30, 1962.

Skard, Aase Gruda, "Maternal Deprivation: The Research and Its Implications," *Journal of Marriage and Family Living,* 27:333-343, August, 1965.

Spock, Benjamin, *Baby and Child Care,* revised edition (New York: Pocket Books, Inc., 1968).

Taylor, Katharine Whiteside, *Parents and Children Learn Together* (New York: Teachers College Press, 1968).

Tomasson, Richard G., "Social Mobility and Family Size in Two High Status Populations," *Eugenics Quarterly,* 13:113-121, June, 1966.

Tulema, Jacob, and Regan, Richard A., "Size of Family and Behavioral Problems in Children," *Journal of Genetic Psychology,* 3:151-159, December, 1967.

Wintour, Eleanor, "Bringing Up Children: The American vs. the British Way," *Harper's Magazine,* 229:58-63, August, 1964.

28

Bringing Up Children

The way children are trained is a part of folk wisdom in all cultures, and, therefore, methods are transmitted through the generations without much reasoning about consequences of methods used to arrive at the end product. For some time our society has struggled to replace folk wisdom in child training with scientific wisdom. This is not an easy thing to do, and has not been done effectively.[1]

Learned theories have not been constant. New research has brought changes with great rapidity. Different social classes accept the new with differing degrees of readiness, and there are always critics who challenge the validity of the new as a means of justifying their clinging to the old. The teacher in the college classroom still finds two attitudes prevailing: (1) I want to treat my children as my parents treated me; or (2) I am not going to bring up my children like my parents brought me up. In making these statements, students are commenting on methods of discipline, their parents' ways of informing them about sex, and other such specific matters.

The fact that students still tend to think in terms of folk wisdom does not necessarily mean that they are uninterested in what has been learned in child psychology and child development. They are interested but try to fit the new knowledge in with what folklore has given them. Which will predominate in the training of their children is problematic. Perhaps most will make a combination of both, as they must do when man and wife bring two family cultures to bear on the rearing of their children.

It is doubtful that many young people are fully aware how much the way they handle, teach, and discipline their children will have to do with the kind of people they become in capacity to love, to learn, and to

[1] Comment based on the writer's experience in reading thousands of anonymous student autobiographies, and class discussions.

603

function well in the society of which they become a part. Few societies have placed so much responsibility on the pair, and particularly the mother, for doing the job alone during the most critical early years as ours has. The joint family provides many teachers and disciplinarians. Western cultures once had more kinfolk in the home, and servants and "nannies" to share child training.

Few cultures have provided such a rich environment outside the home, so that by the teen years most of the training is by agencies which supplement the family.

Even so, the young mother has many professional guides. They do not always quiet her anxiety as to whether she is doing the right thing. Sometimes they give her a guilty conscience because she does not live up to the best she reads or hears about, but she is not likely to run to her mother for assurance and comfort in solving her problems. The college woman particularly is likely to trust the guides who speak with the voice of scientific authority.

There Is No One Best Way

If one surveys the leading cultures of the world, he finds a great variety of child-training methods.[2] The end product in adulthood is quite different, of course. Englishmen, Germans, Japanese, Frenchmen, and Tahitians are made by the way infants and children are handled. The product may be a stern, unaffectionate administrator, an overly disciplined military type, or it may be an affectionate, home-loving, domestically oriented type who loves and is loved by the opposite sex.

The differences in training begin at birth. Tight wrapping in swaddling clothes may be customary; there the child lies bound hand and foot for two to three days. Being tucked in beside the mother's warm body and given the breast immediately may be the custom, or the child may be separated by a glass cage in the hospital, comforted by the sounds of a tape-recorded heart beating out the pulselike rhythm to which he was accustomed in the womb.

No people has a panel of experts in child psychology and child development sit down and try to picture the kind of man and woman they want or need in the next generation and then outline steps to achieve the product desired. In sort of a vague way cultures do this, and so does every pair of parents.

Parents want bright children, able to meet intellectual challenges.

[2] William N. Stephens, *The Family in Cross-Cultural Perspective* (New York: Holt, Rinehart and Winston, 1963).

They want their children well enough mannered to function in social relations and in work situations. They want children who know the moral rules and practice the sexual and other impulsive restraints sufficiently to become dependable community members and eventually marriage partners and parents.

The American philosophy of child training, for instances is in direct contrast at many points to that of certain European and English societies. In France and England the visitor gets the impression that children are reared by tea-time etiquette and are made young adults from the very beginning. The French child meets his schoolmate on the street and shakes hands with him as an adult would do. An English boy will ask his boyfriend in for tea in midafternoon. Adult standards of etiquette and behavior seem to prevail. British training methods are still stern,[3] perhaps a carry-over from the day when the British upper-class male was trained to rule the empire.

In the United States, children are seldom thought of or treated as miniature adults. They are credited with different standards, values, and interests. They are treated as children and adults are very much surprised if they do not act as such. Scandinavian cultures conceive of childhood in much the same way. The world of a child is believed to be a world of play and independent activity. He is not expected to live entirely, or even primarily, by the manners, codes, and restraints of adults, or to share in their responsibilities and problems. He is to have a warm and affectionate relationship with parents, but otherwise live in a child's world.

His attachment to parents is emotional and affectional, whereas the child in European society tends to be reared in an attitude of respect, honor, and obedience to parents, much as in the patriarchal family of America some generations ago.

The British want their children quiet, clean, polite and respectful of adults. They are left outdoors for long periods unattended in perambulators as infants. Their crying is ignored. The child is often left to the care of a "nanny." Even guests of the family do not see the children. They are kept out of the way. By our standards they are "repressed, unresponsive, and unchildlike."[4] It is still the practice of many families to send the child "off to school," which means off to live in a boarding school at an early

---

[3] *Time* reports a great deal of cruelty to children still. Caning is heavily used in home and school. A recent Gallup poll, they report, showed that 70 percent of British men and 76 percent of British women urge the flogging of young criminals. A British doctor is reported to have said, "Instead of feeling a sense of horror on hearing of some father brutally belting his son, many people instinctively think that the little bastard probably deserved it." They report that the National Society for Prevention of Cruelty to Animals was founded in 1824; 58 years later some protection for children came into law. The penalty for mistreating a child is $70.00; an animal, $140. See also Eleanor Wintour, "Bringing Up Children: The American vs. the British Way," *Saturday Review*, 229:58–63, August, 1964.

[4] Eleanor Wintour, *ibid.*

age. By the age of eight, the boy's training is usually taken over by men schoolmasters.

A study of the home life of 158 children in Milwaukee suggests that there are a great variety of practices and ways of doing things in families within the United States and that good adjustment is associated with no particular technique.[5] Some of the factors that are generally associated with good adjustment, however, are "love and affection, being wanted, being appreciated, being trusted, being accepted as a person, being looked upon with respect as individuals."

It must always be kept in mind, too, that personality formation is a continuous and never-ending process, that it goes on throughout childhood and the teen years into adulthood, and that forces outside the family have their part in it.

The Love Anchor

The development of love in the personality is so basic that it was discussed at some length in an earlier chapter (Chapter 9). This brief statement is by way of review and to reinforce the necessity of understanding that it is of first importance in the building of normal personality.

Love is the basis for one's feeling of security. Without it the world is an unfriendly place. Psychologists believe that one's sense of belonging is established by relationships with those closest to him, the mother or mother substitute during the first two or three years of life. If a mother by affection makes her child feel that he is wanted and important to her, he acquires a sense of security which carries over to other relationships. If, on the other hand, she is irritable or hostile and makes him feel that he is unwanted, he develops a sense of insecurity which is difficult to eradicate in later years.

Socialization begins early with the body warmth and loving care of the mother or mother figure. By five or six months of age, a child differentiates between the mother and others to the extent that her absence brings separation anxiety. Up to about three years of age, he has such an undeveloped sense of time that her short absences give him great anxiety. After the child is three, she can begin to increase the length of her absences. By two and a half, he has already become very much aware of his sex identity.

Dr. Spock observes that it is at about five months that the baby begins to discriminate between familiar and strange people.[6] From this time on, through three years of age, he needs a familiar figure for love, comfort, approval, play, gentle kidding, and curbing. Dr. Spock feels that this is the critical time of socialization, when the child gets his self image, which builds in him a sense of being a good or bad person, of a world that is hostile or loving. After three, he believes, the child can be left by the mother in the care of a reliable substitute without anxiety being provoked.

Dr. Spitz[7] finds that if emotional deprivation starts late, in the third quarter of the first year, a condition develops which resembles depression in the adult. If the deprivation lasts no longer than three months, reestablishment of sociality is possible. If it lasts longer than five months, no improvement is shown after restoration of social contacts.

The Developmental Goal

The current emphasis in child training is developmental, not regimental. It is assumed that natural growth should be encouraged and directed, but not suppressed. Initiative is to be encouraged rather than curbed. Human nature is good, not evil.

In our culture it has been easy for parents to accept a negative view of human nature and to curb their natural impulse to love the child. Our culture is rooted in a theological conception which held that human nature is evil, that the child is born in sin, and that before he can be good his nature must be changed. A maxim of parental training of an earlier day held that the child is by nature willful, sinful, and carnal, that before goodness could even begin, his will had to be broken. "Spare the rod and spoil the child" was one expression of this philosophy.

Scientific study of human nature leaves no basis for such a view of childhood. Gesell, who has spent a lifetime in child-study research, declares, "The intrinsic charm and goodness of childhood still constitute the best guarantee of the perfectability of mankind."[8] He further observes, "The most ameliorative force . . . is an intensified conservation of the development of infants and children."[9]

Here we see an expression of the scientific view: that human nature is to be accepted, cultivated, developed, and brought to its full potentialities. Good and bad are in the training system, not in the nature of the child.

[7] René A. Spitz, "The Role of Ecological Factors in Emotional Development in Infancy," *Child Development*, Society for Research in Child Development, Inc., Purdue University, 20:145–155, 1949.

[8] Arnold Gesell and Frances L. Ilg, *The Child from Five to Ten* (New York: Harper & Row, Publishers, 1946), p. 453.

[9] *Ibid.*, p. 454.

Maslow has criticized child training which employs fear, punishment, witholding love and threat of abandonment. He finds that children and adults who feel safe, loved, and respected were trained by positive rather than negative methods. They were taught to please, to make others happy; they were taught truth, logic, justice, consistency, right, and duty. Their personalities were not built in an atmosphere of anxiety, fear, insecurity, guilt, or shame but in one where reality, fair play, fitness, beauty, and rightness were stressed.

Maslow sees need for nourishing goodness in human nature, not negative and suppressive tactics, as the route to desirable character. Rather than seeing child-parent relationships as a chance primarily to make mistakes, as a set of problems, he sees them as "a pleasure and a delight, a great opportunity to enjoy."[10]

The Self Image

Self image is formed very early, mainly during the first three years of life, as was shown in Chapter 9. It is largely the product of relationships with the mother during the period from five months to three years of age. It is she who makes the child feel he is good or bad, accepted or rejected, that the world is hostile or friendly. Self image is added to and modified later by others in the primary group, and as the child ventures outside the family, by secondary groups, but the foundation is laid very early.[11]

Freud and his followers no doubt made too much of toilet training as a factor in determining the trend of personality development. The significant fact may well be that the control of elimination is taught during the critical period of socialization. It is then that the attitudes of the mother toward the child have so much to do with the building of his self image. Whether the child will be a confident and assured person or a fearful and guilt-ridden one depends very much on the mother's early treatment of him.

It is important that the child have self-esteem if he is to feel secure and meet life with courage and vigor. Lacking this he is cringing in his attitude, fearful of new experiences and new challenges.

If the self image given by parents is that the child is bad, there is a tendency to live up to expectations. Studies in the field of delinquency show that self image is an important factor in the route a boy takes. Those

[10] A. H. Maslow, *Motivation and Personality* (New York: Harper & Row, Publishers, 1954), pp. 376–378.

[11] Charles H. Cooley was one of the first sociologists to be keenly aware of the importance of self image. He discussed at length the "looking-glass self" and its importance to behavior. See his *The Individual and the Social Order* (New York: Charles Scribner's Sons, 1909).

with a good self image from the family can be insulated against delinquency even in areas where a delinquent subculture makes violating the law seem natural for most.[12]

A Climate for Growth

Few young people realize how much the intellectual growth of their child, the manners and morals, the character formation, the response to responsibility will be dependent upon their attitude toward the child from the date of his birth, in fact, from the time of his conception.

Every prospective parent needs a course in child development. But a brief review of some of the developments in the area of child training here will at least give a start toward incorporating current concepts.

Every young mother needs to have some of the vision of the one who said, "I've lived all my life to be ready for this time: *to teach my children the things I have learned that will help them be what they can be.*"

Aspiration Level

Parents do most to set the aspiration level for their children, as they do the patterns of creativity and adventure. Whether a child expects great things of himself or the mediocre is determined in large part by parental expectations and their ways of expressing them.

The way the child's imagination and curiosity are treated in the home will have much to do with his mental and emotional growth.[13] Far too often parents dismiss the child's imaginative activities, stories, and dreams in such a way that he becomes discouraged and falls back into the routine which most human beings follow. His "silly ideas" may well have been the ones that indicated a spirit of creativity and originality.

The National Merit Scholarships tests for high school students seek evidence of creativeness in the persons considered. No longer are grades the sole measure for college entrance in even the most exclusive universities.

[12] Walter Reckless and others, "Self Concept as an Insulator Against Delinquency," *American Sociological Review,* 21:745, 1956. See also Morris L. Haimowitz, "Criminals Are Made, Not Born," Article 44 in *Human Development,* second edition, Morris L. Haimowitz and Natalie R. Haimowitz (eds.), (New York: Thomas Y. Crowell, 1966).

[13] For some thinking on this subject, see Margaret Mead, *A Creative Life for Your Children* (Washington, D.C.: U.S. Department of Health, Education and Welfare, 1962); also T. F. James, "New Route to Excellence," *This Week* Magazine, April 26, 1964, pp. 4–5. Also Robert E. L. Faris, "Ability Dimensions in Human Society," *American Sociological Review,* 26:835–842, December, 1961.

If one wants to develop a genius, he will do it by encouraging the maximum learning and by encouraging the child's ventures rather than scorning them.

Genius is, in part, the product of a home which frustrates least and which provides maximum stimuli toward growth. Children tend to become what parents expect them to become and what parents trust them to become.

Intellectual Growth

One of the most important lessons learned in the study of poverty during the last half of the 1960s was that poverty brings intellectual blight. "Head Start" was a courageous effort to introduce corrective measures. That decade brought to focus study on the learning of the very young child. Discoveries have been revolutionary.

Response to stimuli begins in the womb. It is now believed that 20 percent of the child's basic abilities are developed before his first birthday. The most rapid period of learning of his lifetime is the preschool years. By the age of four, he will have gained half of his basic abilities and intellectual growth.

From the very beginning, the infant needs an environment rich in sights, sounds, colors, textures, heat and cold, light and darkness; and, as soon as there are toys, articles which offer a great variety of manipulative possibilities. He needs to lie on his stomach and squirm and reach, twist neck and body. He needs as much freedom from clothing and playpens as can be permitted in order to explore his world and try out his senses.

Much is learned by touch, and he should therefore be given a wide variety of textures, coarse and smooth, wet and dry, hot and cold, so that his senses may experience the full range. Objects are tested by his lips, where sensation is most acute.

During long periods in bed when he is awake, he should be in a lighted room so that he can learn to focus his eyes and study objects about him, their color and form. There can be no visual learning in darkness. Colors in wid range should be presented to him. Exposure to a wide variety of sounds is important to the cultivation of the auditory sense. He should be read to and talked to, long before he can speak. Learning is going on, even though he can give no vocal response. He learns words long before he can speak. His mind is like a computer, processing information. A wide range of foods and odors are important to cultivating the sense of taste and smell. Different food textures and temperatures are important in the learning process. The infant exhausts the learning potential of most toys in a minute or so, according to critics of toys. As soon as he has seen their color, felt them, tried them in his mouth, their learning value is gone. They offer little chance for manipulation.

Opportunities for wide use of the senses give the child a head start in learning and are important to his development.

The parents need not push the child into learning. It is enough to provide rich opportunity. He already has the motive if it is encouraged, and capacity for learning is unlimited. It was once thought that early learning might damage the child and that those who started later would surpass him. Not so. A head start means a permanent advantage. The whole idea of the national project "Head Start" is based on the knowledge that those who have limited exposure to experience and vocabulary during the preschool years are already seriously handicapped in school competition.

Exceptional Ability

Terman's *Genetic Studies of Genius,* which took a large group of high-ability children and followed them through into productive life, making periodic studies of their life adjustments and achievements, banished the old myths that genius is a form of insanity, "Early ripe, early rot," "Usually one-sided in talent."

The group was high in scholarly achievement, and also in life activities generally. Their high creativity shows up early, and the myth that geniuses are often dull later in school and early in life is found to be just that—a myth.

Terman concluded that although children of high ability should not be pushed through school, they should be allowed to progress more rapidly than others so they can move into productive after-school life while at the peak of youthful creativity.[14]

The most recent follow-up of Terman's gifted group of children, first studied in 1921–22, found that family environment, and not genius mentality, was a major factor in differential lifetime achievement of the 100 most successful and 100 least successful.[15] The parental home, in providing emotional stability, in giving motivation and encouragement, seems to be most important in the actual achievement of children of genius capacity.

[14] For a summary of Terman's life-long studies of superior children, see "The Discovery and Encouragement of Exceptional Talent," article 72. (This article carries a bibliography of Terman's studies); see also W. Drayton Lewis, "Some Characteristics of Very Superior Children," article 73. Both articles are in Haimowitz and Haimowitz, *op. cit.*

[15] Melita H. Oden, *Genetic Psychology Monographs,* 77:3–93, 1968.

A composite picture of the home in which genius grows to its maximum potential, as judged by these findings, is one where parents:

1. Place a high value on education.
2. Encourage independence and initiative.
3. Expect a high level of accomplishment.
4. Provide an atmosphere of security and emotional stability.
5. Encourage perseverance, self-confidence, motivate toward leadership, friendships, academic success, excellence in work, and recognition for accomplishment.

Here are a few hints that may help the child in the direction of creative development:[16]

1. Treat the child's questions with respect.
2. Encourage his imagination.
3. Show him that his ideas have value.
4. Let him do things experimentally within the limits of safety.
5. Let him create things for himself.
6. Remember that undirected play is highly creative. As Suttée has said, "Necessity is not the mother of invention, play is."[17]

Good Sense in Child Training

Being informed about the latest theories is important, as is knowing general stages in child growth and development. Yet every child is very much an individual and has his own distinct problems of growing up and of making adjustments to the family, to brothers and sisters, to his own age group, and to adults outside the family. These adjustments may not follow in the order the parents think they should, and they may not all be made without pain on the part of the child and considerable anxiety on the part of the parent. Life is not abnormal when this is so. A lot of trial and error goes into the formation of a personality. As one psychiatrist put it, "All children have difficulties."[18]

Parents need to have confidence that growth itself will work wonders

[16] For literature in the area of creativity, the following are useful: J. W. Getzels and P. W. Jackson, *Creativity and Intelligence,* New York: John Wiley & Sons, 1962; D. W. MacKinnon, "The Nature and Nurture of Creative Talent," *American Psychologist,* 7:484–495, 1962; E. P. Torrance, *Guiding Creative Talent* (Englewood-Cliffs, N.J.: Prentice-Hall, 1962); P. S. Weisburg and K. L. Springer, "Environmental Factors in Creative Function: A Study of Gifted Children," *Archives of General Psychiatry,* 5:554–561, 1961.

[17] Ian Suttée, *The Origins of Love and Hate* (New York: Julian Press, 1952), p. 18.

[18] John Levy and Ruth S. Munroe, *The Happy Family* (New York: Alfred A. Knopf, Inc., 1938), p. 28.

in the experience of the child. The adjustment that he finds so difficult to make at a particular time in his development may be made almost automatically and as a matter of course as he acquires a little more age and experience. Time itself will cure many of his problems.

Neither do parents need to have great anxiety that some serious period of maladjustment in the child's early life is going to maim him permanently as a human being. Personality is a constantly growing and developing affair. Many of the mistakes of the past can be corrected and many of the wounds that have been suffered through rather severe periods of maladjustment can be healed by time. The child's confidence and assurance can be rebuilt as his path into the future is plotted with greater certainty.

Growth and development are most amazing phenomena and very interesting to watch. The parent, if he is not overly anxious, will see in his child's growth and maturation the fascinating and miracle-working power of nature as it transforms the personality with age and experience. A few parental blunders are not going to ruin a child. These are merely some of the bumps he experiences in growing up. It is the long-persistent, seemingly incurable situations in the environment that work the damage, not the little day-to-day ups and downs that are characteristic of the normal experience of childhood.

In summary, the parent who would provide a family with a climate in which development is healthy and growth toward full potential is possible can do so by applying such principles as follows to the child:

1. Give him no reason to doubt your love. Do not use threat of love withdrawal as a disciplinary measure.
2. Stress what he does well instead of condemning what he does poorly. Praise rather than condemn and criticize.
3. Remember that what he accomplished by himself is all-important. Let him gain satisfaction from his own achievement.
4. Give him freedom of choice within the limits of his physical and moral safety. Let him make his own decisions.
5. Keep lines of communication open. Anticipate his questions, and treat them with consideration and respect. Talk with him about many things.
6. Remember that undirected play is highly creative. As Suttée has said, he will know his limits.
7. Build positively. Stress goals and virtues rather than building guilt by prohibitions.
8. Respect him. Trust him. Help him build a self image of which he can be proud.
9. Let him know by your confidence and trust that you expect much of him, not the unreasonable, but what he is capable of attaining.

In this atmosphere, his achievements may be more than you hope for, and his aspirations for himself may exceed even those you hold for him.

Problems

1. Most child-training authorities agree with Father Flanagan's observation, "There is no such thing as a bad boy." Why then is discipline considered essential in training children?
2. In using the word "discipline," people often mean very different things. Give a definition and example of at least two different usages.
3. Hill Street is a busy thoroughfare lined with middle-class homes. In the nine-hundred block there are three houses on the north side of the street and in each there is a child under two years of age. These youngsters frequently play together on one of their lawns while their mothers sit together talking and watching them play. The children, of course, are too young to know about the dangers of the traffic on Hill Street so they frequently venture out toward the exciting highway. When this happens the mothers react in very different ways.

     Analyze the typical behavior of each mother described below, and discuss it in terms of:

   a. Effectiveness in controlling child's behavior.
   b. Effectiveness in controlling child's future behavior.
   c. Effect of behavior on child-mother relationship.
   d. Theory of behaviour on child-mother relationship.

   Mother A: Runs after child, screaming "Don't!" Grabs the child and spanks it. Repeats this if child goes out again.

   Mother B: Sees her child wandering in general direction of street and calls out in frightening voice, "Don't you go out there. If you do a big car will hit you and kill you." If child continues, mother pulls her back to middle of lawn. Repeats this ritual if child starts out again.

   Mother C: Sees her child wandering toward street and says nothing. When child reaches a certain point, mother calls pleasantly, "Mary," to get her attention. If child does not return, mother goes out and takes her hand and watches the cars. If child wants to go nearer street, mother picks her up and carries her back to center of lawn without saying anything. Repeats this action whenever necessary.
4. Read pages 253–260, entitled "Discipline," in Dr. Benjamin Spock's *Baby and Child Care*. What are Dr. Spock's views on punishment? Do you think he is correct in his evaluation of its effectiveness?
5. Two very healthy, high-spirited, inquisitive young boys are handled in two very different ways. Both are described by their parents as "difficult to manage."

     One is encouraged in his inquisitiveness, urged ahead in all physical activity, and given maximum freedom within the limits of health and safety. The other boy's parents try to curtail his excesses by discouraging his constant questions, and trying to channel his interests into reading. They do not punish him physically, but rebuke him frequently for his tactlessness and forwardness, and remind him that, "where choices are concerned, we know what is best." Which boy is most likely to:

   a. Be an unmanageable adult?
   b. Respect his parents most?
   c. Develop antisocial energy outlets?
   d. Develop a distaste for reading?

e. Be most successful as an adult in terms of leadership and achievement?

6. A well-meaning young mother has read that "permissiveness" is the best method in child rearing. She feels that she should do what the authorities say is best for the child, but secretly she feels that a good spanking is what her child needs most. What are the dangers of attempting to administer a system of discipline in which one does not sincerely believe? What course would you advise this parent to follow?

7. *Sociodrama:* The scene opens a moment after Mary's twelve-year-old daughter, Jean, has rushed out of the room screaming at her mother, "I hate you! I hate you! I hate you! You're the meanest person I know!"

Mary's mother-in-law, who has witnessed the scene, says, "Call that child back and punish her on the spot. She can't be allowed to talk to you that way. Why, when I was a child. . . ."

Mary interrupts, "I'll do nothing of the sort, Mother. You probably felt just as Jean does many times when you were young, and it would have been better if you hadn't been punished for expressing what you felt."

Let the drama picture the two philosophies of discipline held by the two women. Try to show both philosophies in a sympathetic light.

Selected References

Articles in Books of Readings

Cavan, Ruth S., *Marriage and the Family in the Modern World: A Book of Readings,* third edition (New York: Thomas Y. Crowell Co., 1969).

Halpern, Howard, "Children and Parents in the Kibbutz and America," Reading 59.

Christensen, Harold T., *Handbook of Marriage and the Family* (Chicago: Rand McNally & Co., 1964).

Dager, Edward Z., "Socialization and Personality Development," Ch. 18.

Haimowitz, Morris L. and Natalie (eds.), *Human Development: Selected Readings* (New York: Thomas Y. Crowell Co., 1966).

Haimowitz, Morris L., "What Price Virtue?" Reading 1.

Talmon-Garber, Yonina, "The Modern Family in Israel: The Kibbutz," Reading 13.

Davis, Clara M., "Results of Self-Selection of Diets by Young Children," Reading 29.

Landis, Judson T., and Mary G., *Readings in Marriage and the Family* (Englewood Cliffs, N.J.: Prentice-Hall, Inc., 1952).

Dale, Martha Ericson, "Child-Rearing and Social Status," pp. 260–263.

Rodman, Hyman, *Marriage, Family and Society* (New York: Random House, 1966)

Wolfenstein, Martha, "Trends in Infant Care," Reading 10.

Sussman, Marvin B., *Sourcebook in Marriage and the Family,* third edition (Boston: Houghton Mifflin Co., 1968).

Hoffman, Lois Wladis, "Effects of Maternal Employment on the Child," Reading 40.

Vincent, Clark E., *Readings in Marriage Counseling* (New York: Thomas Y. Crowell Co., 1957).

Kirkendall, Lester A., "Helping Parents Become Better Sex Educators," pp. 80–88.

Winch, Robert F., and Goodman, Louis Wolf, *Selected Studies in Marriage and the Family,* third edition (New York: Holt, Rinehart and Winston, Inc., 1968).

Kohn, Melvin, "Social Class and Parental Values," pp. 349–363.

Baumrind, Diana, "Effects of Authoritative Parental Control on Child Behavior," pp. 299–317.

Strodtbeck, Fred L., "Family Interaction, Values, and Achievement," pp. 364–380.

General References

Barnett, Larry D., "Opinion and Knowledge of Child-Rearing, Professionals and Nonprofessionals, Regarding Three Child-Rearing Systems, *The Family Life Coordinator,* 15:101–106, July, 1966.

Blanton, Smiley, *Love or Perish* (New York: Simon and Schuster, Inc., 1955).

Child Study Association of America, *What to Tell Your Child about Sex* (New York: Pocket Books, 1968).

Driver, Helen (editor), *Sex Guidance for Your Child* (Madison, Wis.: Monona Publications, 1960).

Eckert, Ralph, *Sex Attitudes in the Home* (New York: Association Press, 1956).

Gesell, Arnold, and Ilg, Frances L., *The Child from Five to Ten* (New York: Harper & Row, Publishers, 1946).

Ginot, Haim G., *Between Parent and Child* (New York: The Macmillan Co., 1965).

Hymes, James L., *How to Tell Your Child About Sex* (New York: Public Affairs Pamphlets), No. N.L. 149.

Kell, Leone, and Aldous, Joan, "Trends in Child Care over Three Generations," *Marriage and Family Living,* 22:176–177, May, 1960.

Landis, Judson T., "Experiences of 500 Children with Adult Sexual Deviation," *The Psychiatric Quarterly Supplement,* Part I, 30:91–109.

Landis, Judson T., "The Nondelinquent Child and the Sexual Deviant," *Research Studies of the State College of Washington,* 22:92–101, March, 1955.

Landis, Paul H., and Stone, Carol L., *The Relationship of Parental Authority Patterns to Teenage Adjustments* (Pullman, Wash: Washington Agricultural Experiment Station, September, 1952), Bulletin 538.

McCord, William, *Origins of Crime* (New York: Columbia University Press, 1959).

Maslow, A. H., *Motivation and Personality* (New York: Harper & Row, Publishers, 1954).

Mead, Margaret, *A Creative Life for Your Children* (Washington, D.C.: U.S. Department of Health, Education, and Welfare, 1962).

Neisser, Edith, *Brothers and Sisters* (New York: Harper & Bros., 1951).

Rabin, A. I., *Growing Up in the Kibbutz* (New York: Springer Verlag, 1965).

Sherman, Vivian S., "What Injures a Child's Self-Esteem?" *The PTA Magazine,* 61:23–25, March, 1967.

Spock, Benjamin, *Baby and Child Care* (New York: Pocket Books, Inc., revised edition, 1968).

Spock, Benjamin, "What a Father's Role Should Be," *Redbook,* 129, 202–215, February, 1967.

Spock, Benjamin, "How Parents Can Control Children's Quarrels," *Redbook,* 130:28–31, April, 1968.

Stephens, William N., *The Family in Cross-Cultural Perspective* (New York: Holt, Rinehart and Winston, Inc., 1963), Chs. 7–8.

U.S. Department of Labor, *Your Child from One to Six* (Washington, D.C.: U.S. Department of Labor), Children's Bureau Publication 30.

29

Family Discipline

Few areas in husband-and-wife relationships, as far as children are concerned, are likely to cause more disagreement and strife than that of discipline. This has been a focal point of dissension between the generations, too, with parents and grandparents viewing the developing child from the perspective of different disciplinary patterns.

In the college classroom and in student autobiographies, it becomes clear that male and female subcultures today lack a unified perspective. Girls are brought up on women's magazines, many have had courses in some aspects of child development, and some have had both training and experience in baby-sitting or in nursery-school management. They are more likely to have a developmental, democratic approach to child training than is the college male, who is confident about his opinions, which are more often derived from folklore or from his own parental home. Often as not, he seems quite as sure of his opinions as a child-rearing expert as the more informed college woman he is going to marry.

This too often means conflict ahead, or else the wife and mother is going to have to take charge and educate the husband along with the baby. As the child gets older, inconsistency and uncertainty make for insecurity in the child. He has difficulty knowing what is expected of him.

The transition from authoritarian methods to the developmental, democratic methods is the basis for much of the conflict. The one parent operates on the philosophy that responding to the child's need and making him an equal partner in the family relationship is important to the development of the young personality. The other assumes that such efforts amount to nothing more than pampering and spoiling the child. The one assumes, for example, that crying indicates discomfort and need and that the baby should be picked up and patted until he burps; the other believes he should be allowed to cry it out and not be pampered and petted lest he become a demanding tyrant, not realizing that the demanding, "spoiled" older child is one suffering from lack of loving care, not overattention. As the infant becomes a child, the father operates under the ordering-and-forbidding technique, which has come down from time immemorial; the mother believes in consideration for the child's wishes and approves of reasoning with him and attempting to understand him. The one believes in punishment; the other believes in correction by nonpunitive methods. The husband is more likely to tend toward a harsh extreme in the handling of the child, which the mother considers to be frightening and shocking. In such extreme cases, neither parent has any sympathy toward the approach of the other in child care.

In such families, the husband should visit nurseries and nursery schools to learn how children are properly handled, or he should read some of the better books on child development to know the outcome of different systems of discipline, or he should retire from the administrative situation, leaving it to the better-trained wife. Certainly, unless one or the other can change, the marriage is in for turmoil, as well as the children being in for a rough time during their critical years. A day's visit to the college nursery school can be an eye-opener for the average college man. There he can see democratic methods of child discipline in practice.

Young wives with just a smattering of information on permissive child rearing are often attracted to the method without understanding its full implications or recognizing the degree of thought and effort it requires. Above all it should be understood that this is not a "do-nothing" approach. It does not mean that the mother can stand aside and let the child rear itself, so to speak. Slapping a youngster's hands or shouting "No!" everytime he does something wrong is much easier than calmly and repeatedly restraining him until he understands and accepts certain limits. Patience, tact, and the ability to see the world as your child must see it are important prerequisites to success in developmental training. All parents ought to get down on their hands and knees occasionally and see how different the world looks to a child who cannot even see what's on the table.

There is much more to the theory behind modern practices than can be set forth in this chapter. All young couples owe it to themselves and to their unborn children to look into the literature before attempting parenthood. "Gentle discipline" can easily deteriorate into "no discipline at all," and a great deal of behavior which may be lastingly detrimental to the young person is often countenanced in the name of "progressive child training."

Parental Authority

All social control begins in the family. The pattern of family authority is shaped to fit the parent's conception of what the child must become to function in the adult society of his time. The parent is provided with a general framework of patterned behavior by which to be guided. In simple cultures, where each institution and where each group hold like conceptions, the task is an easy one. In complex cultures where institutional patterns are different in their emphasis and where many groups have different expectations of their members, the parent's task is a difficult one indeed.

No society has a place for the individual who ignores all authority. Those who fail to recognize the authority of the law find themselves outcasts or in institutions for the delinquent and criminal. Those who fail to accept the ethical or religious standards and customs of their group may find themselves in moral confusion. Those who fail to recognize that every game has to be played according to its rules find themselves maladjusted in many situations, at odds with their fellows, and in discord with the general tenor of social life.

The child who has never known authority is of all children most unhappy. Adulthood assumes a willingness to recognize the rights and wishes of others and to assume one's share of the load of human responsibilities. The child who grows up without ever having recognized that every human being has obligations to others is not ready to face the compulsory restrictions of an adult society happily.

Margaret Mead has described the experience of children of the Manus tribe, primitives on the island of New Guinea.[1] There, children are allowed to grow up with almost no restriction by parents or elders, carefree and with their every wish indulged by the adults of the group. In adolescence they are initiated into adulthood, a state in which men and women everywhere have to recognize social control and assume their share of the world's duties. These young people enter adulthood sorrowfully and always look back upon their childhood as the happy period of their lives.

Disciplinary failure brings much anguish to the parent and disaster to the child, for discipline is a necessary part of effective socialization. There is no place in society for the undisciplined. They must be banished, caged in prison, or otherwise removed for the safety of the group.

---

[1] Margaret Mead, *Growing Up in New Guinea* (New York: William Morrow & Co., Inc., 1935); also her *From the South Seas* (New York: William Morrow & Co., Inc, 1939).

There Is No Perfect Disciplinary Recipe

No society has developed the perfect disciplinary system. All produce their misfits. And all pay the price of dealing with the unsocialized portion of each generation. Ours has no perfect disciplinary system and no universal disciplinary techniques by which success in this step in socialization may be assured. Theories are not lacking, and new ones are always in the making. A part of the problem is that society now changes so rapidly that parents are often unsure of the kind of end product they want.

Most any kind of discipline is better than none at all. In the United States it differs markedly between the social classes. Kohn and Carroll found[2] that "to the middle-class parents, it is of primary importance that a child be able to decide for himself how to act, and that he have personal resources to act on these decisions—to working-class parents . . . it is of primary importance that the child act reputably, that he not transgress the proper rules."

A survey of over 400 mothers in Chicago gave a revealing picture of differences between the traditional and modern group's conceptions of their role as mothers and the goals to be achieved in child training.[3]

Those who held the traditional concept considered their functions to be those of (1) keeping house, (2) taking care of the child's physical needs, (3) training him to regularity, and (4) disciplining him and teaching him obedience and goodness.

Mothers with a modern concept of parenthood considered their function to be a developmental one. They felt that they should (1) train the child for self-reliance and citizenship, (2) see to his emotional well-being, (3) help him develop socially, (4) provide for his mental growth, (5) guide him with understanding, (6) give him love and affection, (7) be calm, cheerful, growing persons themselves.

The first group of mothers thought the child should be judged by whether or not he (1) was neat and clean, (2) was obedient and respectful of adults, (3) pleased adults, (4) respected property, (5) was religious, (6) worked well, (7) fitted into the family program.

The second group of mothers felt they were succeeding as mothers if the child (1) was healthy and well, (2) shared and cooperated with others, (3) was happy and contented, (4) loved and confided in his parents, (5) was eager to learn, (6) was growing as a person.

[2] Melvin L. Kohn and Eleanor E. Carroll, "Social Class and the Allocation of Parental Responsibilities," *Sociometry*, 23:372–392, December, 1960.
[3] Evelyn Millis Duval, "Conceptions of Parenthood," *American Journal of Sociology*, 52:193–203, 1946.

Obviously these concepts of motherhood are far apart in practice and basic philosophy, yet they are both part of the American scene. The first is more common among the lower classes; the second, among the middle and upper classes; the first, among the uneducated; the second, among the educated; the first, among large families; the second, among small families.[4]

The father's role is also changing. As shorter working hours provide for greater interaction between father and child, the role of fatherhood becomes an increasingly important one. He is no longer primarily the stern disciplinarian. Yet, many fathers today still conceive of their function in terms of the traditional pattern. Like their fathers before them, they willingly leave child rearing to their wives but consider themselves the final authority in any uncertain situation or in circumstances where the mother's methods prove inadequate. Traditionally the father's chief function was that of providing for the physical support of the family. He entered into the world of the children also as a disciplinarian when the mother asked for help. His attitude toward the children was likely to be one of impatient tolerance rather than understanding companionship. He did not pretend to understand the child or his special needs and did not feel that such understanding was his responsibility. He, like the old-fashioned mother, was inclined to judge children in terms of the children's effect upon his own life, reputation, and comfort. He believed that children have been properly handled if they are obedient, respectful, and useful.

The father with the modern concept of parenthood willingly accepts a much more complex and involved role for himself. He is likely to differentiate very little between the mother's duties in child training and those he himself accepts. He is concerned about each step in his child's development and assumes that he can and must play an important part in it. He considers himself less the disciplinarian and more the companion of his children. He is likely to plan his hours with them not around ritualized activities but around play, hobbies, and other enjoyable pursuits.

While the mother in most modern families must of necessity still take chief responsibility for the actual rearing of the children, present-day fathers generally desire to play as active a part as their time and energy permit. When working hours are long, this may mean that their chief influence over their children is an indirect one—the result of plans and policies agreed upon by husband and wife in late evening talks and put into practice by the wife. Whenever possible, however, most modern couples agree that every effort should be made to provide situations in which father and child can develop an intimate and companionable relationship. Some young men even consider the amount of leisure time for family life a major factor in the selection of a vocation or a particular job.

[4] For research on some of these points, see Paul H. Landis and Carol L. Stone, *The Relationship of Parental Authority Patterns to Teenage Adjustments* (Pullman, Wash.: Washington Agricultural Experiment Station, September, 1952), Bulletin 538.

Although the more favored socioeconomic classes have likely acquired an improved philosophy of child rearing and may more often practice a democratic type of family administration, some believe that during infancy and early childhood parents of the lower classes are more permissive than are parents of the middle classes. Dale's study shows that in the middle class (which social-class experts often refer to as the frustrated class), fewer children are breast-fed than in the other social classes.[5] In this class, too, three times as many children were thumb-suckers as in the other social classes. It was found that the middle class trains children in bowel and bladder control earlier than do the other classes. In general, the disciplinary pattern throughout childhood was found to be more rigid in the middle than in the lower classes. This study was conducted some time ago with small samples and by personal interviews in which 48 middle-class mothers and 52 lower-class mothers were studied. The middle-class group was selected from nursery schools and child-study groups. The families of both social classes had only normal children. The author expresses the belief that the disciplinary regime employed by the middle class tends to condition the child toward frustration and anxiety. The lower-class infant, by contrast, is permitted a more natural and spontaneous development.

While these results may be taken as suggestive, they should not be accepted as conclusive. The culture has shifted from the view that the infant and the child should be handled by the cold Watsonian techniques of an earlier generation to the view that warm "rooming-in," "self-demand" feeding, and a permissive pattern are the only safe ones. The new approach assumes that discomfort and denial lead to frustration and frustration to a neurotic condition. The new method, like the old, must be taken on faith and the outcome observed in the development of the child.

Parents who still cling tenaciously to yesterday's methods generally do so out of a certain distress at the new or because they have linked their child-training philosophy with religious convictions and justified their practices on moral grounds rather than by their practical results. Those who feel a strong attachment to the methods their own parents or grandparents used need to understand that, while suited to the world and values of yesterday, the authoritarian pattern does not adequately prepare young people for life in modern times.

The goal of yesterday's training system was to make of the child a working member of the household at as early an age as possible. This meant that he was taught to work. He began with simple chores and each year was given an increasing share of the household work load. With

[5] Martha Ericson Dale, "Child-Rearing and Social Status," *American Journal of Sociology*, 52:191–192, 1946.

work playing so important a part in the child's life, discipline was necessarily strong. A heavy hand was needed to channel energies away from play into routine duties.

Except on farms, and even there to a lesser extent than in the past, children are no longer valued in terms of their ability to make an immediate contribution to the family's economic well-being. Child-labor legislation has eliminated children from industry and greatly limited the number of jobs in which young teen-agers can be gainfully employed. Custom and school pressure further limit the work demands parents can make on their children. The type of discipline which was necessary when children were workers is pointless now that their chief activities are centered around school and play.

Other adults are skeptical of the newer disciplinary pattern because it seems to produce a more casual parent-child relationship. They remember the strong emphasis of the past upon the obligations of children to their parents and they fear that when these obligations are no longer stressed family loyalty and unity will vanish. It is true that the commandment, "Honor thy father and thy mother" was a basic one in generations past, often repeated to the child by parents, grandparents, aunt, and uncle, in fact by all of the elders. Honor and obedience were the criteria of good child training. Disobedience was looked upon as a cardinal sin.

Religious leaders as well as educators of the past lent their full support to the commandment. In orthodox theological terms, this philosophy took the form of an admonition to parents to "break the child's will," it being held that the child was almost worthless until his carnal nature was destroyed by discipline and punishment, his will broken, and submission to authority achieved. Only then could he attain to grace and become a submissive member of the church, community, and family.

Although the relationship between parent and child in the democratic family does tend to be more casual (less ritualistic and formalized), it is actually a closer and more mutually satisfying one than existed in the past.[6] The loyalty which young people give their families is much more likely to be given freely; their sense of obligation much more likely to grow out of real respect than parent-instilled fear. When the break with parents comes, as it inevitably must if the young person is to become a self-directing adult with a family of his own, it is less likely to be the cruel and complete break that it once was. In the old-fashioned American family, far too often father and so came to either physical or verbal blows, leading to an abrupt and unqualified break. This assertion of independence by the son was looked upon as a direct challenge to the father's position of supreme authority. The son was sometimes ordered

---

[6] Landis and Stone, *op. cit.;* also Stone and Landis, "An Approach to Authority Patterns in Parent-Teenage Relationships," *Rural Sociology,* 18:233–242, September, 1953.

out of the home and told never to return. The old revival song, "Oh, Where Is My Wandering Boy Tonight?" grew out of this characteristic break in family relations.

In the modern family, parents accept each new step the child takes toward independence as not only inevitable but also desirable. They visualize for their son or daughter not a life of submission but one of independence, self-respect, creativity, and ambition. To cultivate these qualities, greater rather than lesser freedom of thought, choice, and behavior are permitted.

The democratic system of child discipline has emerged with urban industrial development. It is in direct contrast to the older system of child training at almost every point, and the clash of the two explains the frequent conflict of values of young husbands and wives as they face the task of child training.

Child-Centered Discipline

Democratic discipline can best be differentiated from the authoritarian by recognizing its focal point. In almost every aspect of its pattern of living, the home is child-centered rather than adult-centered. It assumes that the needs of the child are paramount to those of the father and mother. Parents do not consider that their children "owe" them anything —either love, respect, gratitude, or repayment for their own work and worry in the child's behalf. They hope, however, that by their own attitude of unselfish devotion they can arouse and develop similar attitudes in their offspring.

Even legal statutes recognize the paramount obligation of parent to child, for the state is willing to investigate where there is evidence of neglect or mistreatment of the child, and even to remove the child from the parent. This is a striking contrast to early agrarian cultures, in some of which the child could be stoned to death for disobedience to parents. No question was ever raised then about the parents' right to demand obedience. Now it is assumed that the child has to become an independent and self-sufficient adult. It is taken for granted that some time during his youth he will become almost entirely weaned from the family and lose practically all sense of obligation to it.

This is true in the emotional sense to a degree; it is even more true in the economic sense. The Social Security Act provides through the state means of support for the old when they are no longer able to care for themselves. In a wage economy, it is enough for most young people to carry the support of their own children. The obligation is now to the new generation, not to the old.

Because democratic discipline is directed toward the development of independence and individualism, rather than conformity and submission, It tends to be guidance-centered rather than discipline-centered. This does not mean that discipline is absent in the family; it is rather a discipline achieved by cooperation and mutual understanding. It operates by discussion and explanation, by pointing out a better way when error is committed, by giving the child sufficient freedom to make mistakes and gain experience from them, to choose and, eventually, through trial and error, choose wisely. Punishment as such is disappearing as a disciplinary concept. Sharing and working together, rather than honor and obedience, have become the bonds.

With individualism rather than familism as the goal, it is the dream of most parents that their children will become creative, independent, self-sufficient persons, able to play a highly individuated, self-directed role in a specialized social order. For this reason a parent cannot stamp his own pattern and philosophy upon the child. He shares the training function with many other institutions. He encourages initiative in the child, smiles upon evidence of independence, even welcomes a certain amount of revolt, for he knows that only through such independence and originality can greatness be achieved.

The democratic parent does not expect a period of sowing wild oats and complete teen-age rebellion. He expects the child gradually to achieve independence and to be ready for the freedom that inevitably comes in the teens. With the recognition of increasing maturity, the parental hand is gradually withdrawn and the child is given greater opportunities to exercise his own judgment within the areas and limits which the parents consider safe. The way he behaves when not in the custody of parents is the final test of the disciplinary system employed.

The Democratic Family and Parental Patience

In a democracy, as Margaret Mead has stated, "A child is a person from the moment of his birth." As a person, his growth is encouraged from the beginning. In a sense he becomes the most important person in the family environment—the most needy, the most demanding, certainly, but also the one with the greatest potentialities for rapid development.

The home now becomes his environment and must be shaped to fit his needs. The routine of the family must be in response to his demands. Here is a little creature demanding an audience and needing a receptive and appreciative rather than a critical and hostile one. As his growth unfolds, he will gain a voice for words and need a sounding board against which to repeat over and over the same words, and new words, and a wide range of sounds. And as he becomes mobile and takes over his environment, he inspects it all by touch and taste and attempts to dismantle it to learn its parts and how they are put togeher. And to each thing he must attach a name, and later to each, feeling. He is a dwarf in a world of giants but, if given an appreciative adult audience, feels no inferiority, only a consuming desire to learn and conquer the environment about him.

The democratic family wants the child to be free, within established limits, to give him room for maximum development. The authoritarian family quickly tries to curb and restrain, to protect property and adult comforts and routines. This is the easier course. It makes life smoother for parents but curbs growth in the child. The democratic way from the very beginning requires more adaptability by the parents.

To many, the idea of handling young children democratically is overwhelming because of the tremendous drain on patience that such a system implies. To command obedience and to force it by virtue of greater physical strength seems to be much the easier course. Blood's[7] study of forty couples shows that the permissive pattern does disrupt parents' lives more. The children are inclined to be more noisy, to encroach on the parents' privacy from morning to night. The parents also need to be more alert in controlling the children's activities in order to protect them from harm and to protect the family possessions from damage.

In general, the living quarters of permissive parents were more cluttered by the activities of the children, and the parents had to supervise the picking up of toys or, more frequently, do it themselves. In homes where the pattern of discipline was strict, the children expected little freedom and conformed more or less to the rigid controls of their parents.

In the permissive homes, the ideal was to give the children a chance to grow and learn. In the authoritarian homes, the virtues of obedience, honesty, manners, and neatness were emphasized. The democratic parents were inclined to use the living room as a place to which the children had full access, making its use for guests secondary.

The developmental parent, as Blood states, works on the assumption that in the long run the independence he gives and the sacrifices he makes for his children in early childhood will make them more self-sufficient later on and perhaps more self-directive, requiring a total of less time and worry on his part.

We live in a time when reactionaries blame Dr. Spock and more

[7] Robert O. Blood, Jr., "Consequences of Permissiveness for Parents of Young Children," *Marriage and Family Living*, 15:209–212, August, 1953.

democratic methods of child rearing for the violence and rebellion of youth. Time will show they are quite wrong.

Olim has studied[8] "self-actualizing" young people. These are young people reared in democratic homes. They are people with a strong humanitarian outlook. They do challenge tradition in many areas, are particularly critical of judging life by primarily economic motives. They are strongly motivated toward the Peace Corps, the Teachers' Corps, VISTA, civil rights struggles, and student revolts. They may be questioning and nonconformist, but are not violent or destructive.

The violent and destructive are most likely to come from environments of frustration, authoritarianism, and despair. It is much too soon to write off the democratic ideal as a failure. Great masses of American youth have never had any experience with it in their homes.

Below are some principles for a positive approach to discipline developed by Washington State University Nursery School as a guide for baby-sitters. It is a list worth the attention of any young parent:

1. Give a child a choice only when you intend to accept his decision.
2. Redirect the child's interest or activity.
3. State suggestions or directions in a positive way. For example, instead of saying, "Don't throw the ball," say, "You can roll the ball on the floor."
4. Disregard some of his no's and assume he will conform.
5. Give only one direction at a time.
6. Remember that children tend to be slow and tend to dawdle.
7. Maintain necessary limits.
8. If one method doesn't work, wait a while and try another.
9. Always ask yourself why the child is behaving in this particular way.
10. Try to look at the situation through the child's eyes.

Discipline Without Punishment

Many parents cannot reconcile the idea of a need for discipline of children with the view that the child should be free of punishment. The late Ellsworth Faris, sociologist, differentiates the two and makes a strong case for discipline without punishment. He defines punishment as "the intentional inflicting of suffering administered by authority on one who has been guilty of offense.[9] He ably defends the thesis that discipline without punishment is feasible and more effective than discipline achieved by punishment.

He begins his defense by citing his early observations among natives

---

[8] Ellis G. Olim, "The Self-Actualizing Person in the Fully Functioning Family: A Humanistic Viewpoint," *The Family Coordinator,* 17:141–148, July, 1968.

[9] Ellsworth Faris, *Discipline Without Punishment* (Salt Lake City: University of Utah Press, 1952), (pamphlet).

of the Belgian Congo rain forest, who never punish children. He indicates that critics were inclined to look upon his observations as being inaccurate but reports that all anthropologists have come to recognize that punishment of children is unknown among preliterate people everywhere. The children are taught the taboos, inhibitions, rituals, and customs of tribal life. They are well disciplined, but they are not subjected to punishment.

Our logic for punishment, he believes, is to deter the offender from future transgression and to deter others by publicizing his punishment. This is particularly true in the field of penal practice with adults.

In applying his theory of discipline to the child, Faris indicated that the child must have its full measure of love. When language begins, discipline takes on new meaning for the child. If, for example, he picks up objects which he should not have, they should be taken away from him with "affectionate inflexibility accompanied by gentle tones." In this way he learns that some things are for grownups and not for him. Close bonds are maintained between child and parent which should never be broken.

Punishment in any form tends to weaken this bond. He should not begin his own way, but by "loving, gentle compulsion be required to do what he is expected to do and do it on time." There should be no violation of the intimacy and trust which exist between child and parent. In the childhood stage, when he is no longer a toddler, praise should be added to the love-and-fun relationship between child and parent. Expressions of approval soon become important factors in discipline. The parent, by rewarding certain conduct with approval, makes the child eager to repeat the conduct and thus win approval again. The never-ending thirst of children for affection and admiration is a parent's most valuable ally in drawing out the best in his child.

The later stage of boyhood or girlhood brings the need not only for love, fun, and praise but also for membership. There is a desire to belong to the group, to be accepted and appreciated by his age mates. Organized games become very important, and the child is eager for the first time to play by rules. Now is the time when abstract moral precepts can be taught "in cozy, intimate moments, when only two are present, the child and one parent." Faris believed that moral teaching should be divorced from particular offenses and that an offense should not be reproved until a day or two afterward, when there is no tendency on the part of the child to want to justify what he did.

The next stage is adolescence. All the teaching that the parent can effectively do has been done before this stage is reached. Those who have done the job well need have little anxiety about the future. Those who have failed can do very little at this time to undo the effects of their serious mistakes.

In concluding his statement of child-training theory, Faris indicated that discipline is essential and that any method of producing it is better than no discipline at all but reaffirms his thesis that discipline without punishment is possible and effective. In summarizing his views, Faris states:

> The rearing of children is not a science and can never be; it is rather an art, for no two situations are identical. But scientific principles must guide the method, whether these principles are learned systematically or transmitted by tradition.
>
> The young parent can lovingly overpower the runabout, define the objects for the child, give a due measure of love, fun, and praise, avoid producing a sense of guilt, never reprove what has been done accidentally, and, if it is thought important make disobedience impossible by substituting polite requests for arbitrary or semi-military commands. There is a strong close intimate bond between parent and child, given—not acquired—and this precious bond can be kept unbroken. The child's very conception of himself is wholly within the power of the parents in the early years.
>
> The subject here discussed is controversial, highly controversial. Many have argued the point with me and have contended that discipline without punishment is inferior to the method which visits every offense with its appropriate penalty. This can be argued and I have tried to argue it here. But when I am told that discipline without punishment is not possible, then I insist that there is no argument. It has been done and is being done, and successfully.
>
> Not only is the example of the millions of preliterate children in Africa and the islands of the sea before us but many of my own students have tried this better way and have been successful.
>
> And if I may be pardoned for a more personal reference I will say that I have fourteen (14) grandchildren, ages from two to thirteen, all of whom are, so far, well disciplined but none of whom have been punished in any manner.[10]

Recognize Growing Independence

Even though authority and discipline must enter into the child's world, it is equally important that discipline leave room for growing individuality. As the youngster passes from infancy into childhood, the parent must accept his growing need for independence. Each year the normal child develops new interests and an ever-increasing belief in himself and his own power and wisdom. He challenges his parents' opinions and authority, not because he is bad but because he is developing a normal confidence in his own opinions—a confidence which is necessary in adults but often resented in children. Parents who do not understand the genesis of this growing assertiveness are inclined to "clamp down" before the

---

[10] *Ibid.*

child gets completely out of hand. Clamping down is an open challenge and may mark the beginning of real disciplinary problems.

The Power of Example

In the disciplinary area, example is quite as important as teaching, in fact, much more so. What parents condone in themselves and in their children will become the behavior of the child. The parent's maturity, and lack of it, will form the patterns of the child's reactions to situations.

No such striking statement in concrete terms of this principle in child training has come to the writer's attention as that of Nolte. She says:[11]

If a child lives with criticism, he learns to condemn.
If a child lives with hostility, he learns to fight.
If a child lives with fear, he learns to be apprehensive.
If a child lives with pity, he learns to feel sorry for himself.
If a child lives with ridicule, he learns to be shy.
If a child lives with jealousy, he learns what envy is.
If a child lives with shame, he learns to feel guilty.

If a child lives with encouragement, he learns to be confident.
If a child lives with tolerance, he learns to be patient.
If a child lives with praise, he learns to be appreciative.
If a child lives with acceptance, he learns to love.
If a child lives with approval, he learns to like himself.
If a child lives with recognition, he learns that it is good to have a goal.
If a child lives with sharing, he learns about generosity.
If a child lives with honesty and fairness, he learns what truth and
    justice are.
If a child lives with security, he learns to have faith in himself and in
    those about him.
If a child lives with friendliness, he learns that the world is a nice place
    in which to live.
If you live with serenity, your child will live with peace of mind.
        With what is your child living?

The Ultimate Test of Effective Discipline

The way the child acts when the parent is absent is the true test of whether the parent's disciplinary patterns have been internalized. Until

[11]Written in 1954 by Dorothy Law Nolte for her column "Creative Family Living" in the *Torrance* (Calif.) *Herald*.

the child is self-disciplined, the goal of discipline remains unattained. It seems likely that in the authoritarian disciplinary system this goal is often unattainable.

In the early farm home, children were taught never to play with matches and were severely punished if ever caught with them. A not unusual consequence was that when parents were out doing the chores or visiting neighbors, the child set the lace curtains on fire, built a fire under the bed with wastepaper, or set fire to shavings in the woodshed or elsewhere.

In the democratic family, children are as fascinated by matches as children ever were. Parents let them start the fire when a picnic fire is being lighted or when kindling in the fireplace is ready to be ignited. They light the candles on the birthday cake. Since the children have not been taught never to play with matches and have had experience in the correct use of matches, child-started family fires no longer occur with regularity. The child internalizes mature standards with regard to matches.

Blind obedience is the lowest possible standard of discipline. It can be enforced because parents are physically stronger, but what does enforcement accomplish? If it succeeds, it destroys the child. Initiative, inventiveness, and experimentation are the way to learning. Curb these, and growth is curbed. Permit them to develop under an atmosphere of guidance, and unlimited growth is possible.

John Anderson, director of the University of Minnesota Child Welfare Research Station, in an address many years ago in Los Angeles made the point strikingly clear. "The world is always waiting for the executive in the $100,000 class. Positions are never filled. There are always plenty of people to fill the routine factory jobs where others make all the decisions. These masses are trained to obedience."

Democratic Patterns at the Launching Stage

As the child moves toward the teen years, his life becomes oriented outside the home to an increasing degree. This is when the last test of discipline comes, and results become apparent much too late for the parent to remodel his training patterns.[12]

Margaret Mead has likened the American family to a launching platform from which young people are cast to live independent and self-sufficient lives. It is this fact of modern life which makes the democratic family training pattern have significance in our mobile, urbanized social system.

[12] Helena Znaniecki Lopata, "The Life Cycle of the Social Role of the Housewife," *Sociology and Social Research*, 51:5–22, October, 1966.

FIGURE 29–1   RESPONSES OF TEEN-AGERS, BY FAMILY DISCIPLINARY PATTERN: Source: Paul H. Landis and Carol L. Stone, **The Relationship of Parental Authority Patterns to Teenage Adjustments** (Pullman, Wash.: Washington Agricultural Experiment Station, September, 1952), Bulletin No. 538.

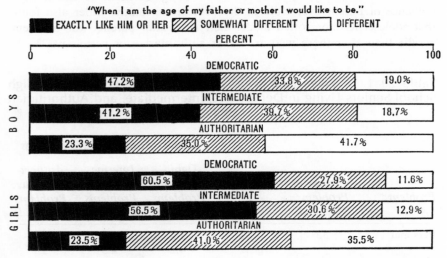

The democratic does not stress honor and obedience, but young people on the threshold of adulthood reared under the democratic pattern are more desirous of emulating parents than those reared in authoritarian homes.

The evidence is strongly in favor of the democratic family insofar as parent–teen-ager relationships and the adjustment of teen-agers to the peer group, church, community, and school and in social relations is concerned. Studies of more than 4,300 seniors in high school show that the teen-ager in the democratic family has fewer problems than the one reared in an authoritarian family.[13] He feels more ready to enter the world as an independent person, and yet he is more closely attached to his parents. He has less of a sense of rebellion against parents. The bond is one welded out of mutual respect and close emotional ties, rather than being one of honor and obedience.

One way to test the extent to which the child has internalized the values and standards of his parents is the extent to which he wishes to emulate the parents in their life patterns. Figure 29–1 shows in striking contrast, by type of authority, the compartive desires of 4,310 high school seniors to emulate their parents. Those under authoritarian discipline[14]

[13] Landis and Stone, *op. cit.;* also Stone and Landis, *op. cit.*

[14] Families were classified into the three administrative types on the basis of young people's responses to a lengthy questionnaire which dealt with all aspects of their adjustment. Relationships within the home as checked by teen-agers were used

in few cases considered their parents' lives as ones they wished to follow. Those under democratic discipline often wished to pattern after parents, and less than a fifth of the boys and little more than a tenth of the girls wished to be entirely different. This is striking testimony to the stronger influence of parent over child in the democratic family. Elder also found that adolescents more often model their roles after parents who are democratic than after those who are either authoritarian or permissive.[15]

Table 29–1   Average Number of Problems Checked by 4,310 High School Seniors Living in Democratic, Intermediate, and Authoritarian Families

			Family Administrative Patterns		
Problem Areas	Number of Problems Checked	Sex	Democratic (av. Problems Checked)	Intermediate (av. Problems Checked)	Authoritarian (av. Problems Checked)
Personal	33	boys	3.5	3.6	4.4
		girls	4.2	4.5	5.1
Family	63	boys	2.9	3.3	5.1
		girls	3.2	3.9	6.5
Social	30	boys	1.8	1.9	2.5
		girls	1.9	2.4	2.7
Boy-girl relations	34	boys	2.0	2.2	2.7
		girls	2.2	2.6	3.0
School	30	boys	2.2	2.4	3.0
		girls	2.2	2.5	3.0
Vocational	30	boys	2.9	2.9	3.4
		girls	2.6	3.1	3.2
Morals, religion	30	boys	2.2	2.4	2.5
		girls	2.4	2.9	3.0
All problems	250	boys	17.5	18.7	23.6
		girls	18.7	21.9	26.5

Source: Landis and Stone, op. cit.

---

in classifying families, a scale following the Guttman technique being employed in the classification. In other words, young people themselves were not asked to classify their homes into authority types by direct questions.

[15] Glen H. Elder, Jr., "Parental Power Legitimation and Its Effects on the Adolescent," Sociometry, 26:50–65, March, 1963.

A second index of comparative adjustment of the democratically disciplined and authoritarian by discipline child is shown in Table 29–1, which summarizes responses of 4,310 high school seniors to a check list of 250 adjustment problems. These problems are classified by area and sex. It will be seen that in all areas, and in total problems, the more democratic the family, the fewer the problems checked.

These are but a few aspects of the problem studied but they illustrate the kind of conclusions which were found in almost every aspect of teen-age adjustments and relationships.

Rose finds, from an analysis of 183 male and 206 female University of Minnesota students, that the transition of the adolescent to maturity seems to be made much more easily by those who have secure family relationships. He advances the hypothesis that difficult family relationships, particularly when their origin is in relationship to the mother, cause the adolescent to withdraw from the family before he is fully socialized and/or emotionally mature. He is, therefore, likely to be less able to accept adult roles than is the youth whose family relationships are more congenial.[16]

The home atmosphere—relationship of parents to each other, of father to child, and, above all, of mother to child—is the key factor in juvenile delinquency. A long-time study of delinquent children, begun in the 1930s and following them into adult life, indicates that where the home is a destructive environment, community efforts, social-work programs, and counseling show little results in improvement.[17] The absent father, or the cruel neglectful one, tends to produce criminality in the child. Mothers who are absent, passive, cruel, rejecting, or neglectful tend to produce criminal sons. A home marked by a great deal of quarreling, with or without affection, produces delinquents, as do also lack of discipline and erratic punitive discipline. A firm but kindly discipline is preventive. The treatment of the young delinquent is primarily a problem of working with the family, so McCord concludes in summarizing results of this study, which follows the group up through the year 1955.

The Glueck study of delinquency rated overstrict and erratic discipline high as the factor predictive of delinquency.[18]

[16] Arnold M. Rose, "Acceptance of Adult Roles and Separation from the Family," Marriage and Family Living, 21:120–126, May, 1959.

[17] William McCord, Origins of Crime (New York: Columbia University Press, 1959). This is a report of the Cambridge-Somerville Youth Study begun in the early 1930s with 650 boys—a group of 325 delinquents and a matched control group. The one was subject to all the reform efforts which money and social-work knowledge could provide. Reform for the most part failed utterly, yet it was probably the most extensive and costly project of this nature ever attempted in this country.

[18] Eleanor T. Glueck, "Spotting Potential Delinquents; It Can Be Done," Federal Probation, September, 1956, p. 9.

Problems

1. A young man leaves his home in a small town and moves into a dormitory of a large state university located in a metropolis. Describe the adjustments that face this young man and discuss the way he will react to them if he is:
   a. The product of a highly authoritarian training pattern.
   b. The product of a democratic training pattern.
2. What type of personality is best suited to parenthood in a democratic family? Describe common traits that would be assets to parents adhering to the democratic pattern. Describe traits that would handicap the practice of modern child-rearing techniques.
3. Describe several aspects of the childhood training patterns in typical middle-class and lower-class homes: Consider the differing degrees of emphasis put on toilet training and, a little later, on training in manners and early formal learning. Which training pattern do you consider superior? Why?
4. In what respects do the training patterns of rural America still differ from those common in urban centers?
5. When conscientious parents find themselves disagreeing on disciplinary philosophy and techniques, which course of action is best? Discuss advantages and disadvantages of:
   a. Leaving the discipline entirely in the hands of one parent.
   b. Getting an authoritative handbook on child rearing and doing exactly as it advises.
   c. Reading books on child discipline and consulting a specialist in the field.
   d. Leaving the discipline in the hands of one parent until an agreement on techniques and philosophy can be reached.
6. *Sociodrama:* Two young wives, both of whom consider themselves "modern" in their child-rearing practices, find that they disagree on some basic principles. One argues that modern theory "teaches you to keep your hands off and let nature take its course." The other feels that modern practices call for "greater thought, patience, and hard work for the parent than ever before."
7. Does the democratic pattern of family living require that young people have a voice equal to that of their parents in family matters?
8. List on the chalkboard several of the traits and characteristics which are admired and encouraged in young people in authoritarian homes. Make another list of youthful traits that are most admired by democratic parents. With these traits in mind, discuss the probable adult personality which would emerge from each training pattern.

Selected References

Articles in Books of Readings

Haimowitz, Morris L., and Natalie, eds., *Human Development: Selected Readings* (New York: Thomas Y. Crowell Co., 1966).
   Haimowitz and Haimowitz, "What Makes Them Creative?" Reading 6.
   Haimowitz, Morris L., "Criminals Are Made Not Born," Reading 44.

Terman, Lewis M., "The Discovery and Encouragement of Exceptional Talent," Reading 72.

Lewis, Drayton W., "Some Characteristics of Very Superior Children," Reading 73.

Rodman, Hyman, *Marriage, Family and Society* (New York: Random House, 1965).

Brim, Orville G., Jr., "Family Structure and Role Learning of Children," Reading 13.

Kohn, Melvin L., "Social Class and Parent-Child Relationships: An Interpretation," Reading 20.

General References

Baumrind, Diana, "Effects of Authoritarian Parent Control on Child Behavior," *Child Development*, 37:887–907, December, 1966.

Benson, Leonard, *Fatherhood: A Sociological Perspective* (New York: Random House, 1968).

Blood, Robert O., Jr., "Consequence of Permissiveness for Parents of Young Children," *Marriage and Family Living*, 15:209–212, August, 1953.

Bossard, James H. S., *The Sociology of Child Development*, third edition (New York: Harper & Row, Publishers, 1960).

Brothers, Joyce, "The His and Hers of Discipline," *Good Housekeeping*, 166:36 ff. January, 1968.

Dreikurs, Rudolph, with Soltz, Vickie, *Children the Challenge* (New York: Duell, Sloan and Pearce, 1964).

Gesell, Arnold, and Ilg, Frances L., *The Child from Five to Ten* (New York: Harper & Row, Publishers, 1946).

Ginot, Haim G., *Between Parent and Child* (New York: The Macmillan Co., 1965).

Landis, Paul H., and Stone, Carol L., *The Relationship of Parental Authority Patterns to Teenage Adjustments* (Pullman, Wash.: Washington Agricultural Experiment Station, September, 1952), Bulletin No. 538.

Maslow, A. H., *Motivation and Personality* (New York: Harper & Row, Publishers, 1954).

Mead, Margaret, "How Are Children Disciplined in Other Cultures?" *Redbook*, 129:10 ff., August, 1967.

Neisser, Edith, *Brothers and Sisters* (New York: Harper & Bros., 1951).

Neisser, Edith G., "The Goal of Discipline," *Parents' Magazine*, 42:66–67, October, 1967.

Olim, Ellis G., "The Self-Actualizing Person in the Fully Functioning Family: A Humanistic Viewpoint," *The Family Coordinator*, 17:141–148, July, 1968.

Slocum, Walter L., and Stone, Carol L., "Family Culture Patterns and Delinquent Type Behavior," *Marriage and Family Living*, 25:202–208, May, 1963.

Smith, Noel, "Psychology and Child Discipline," *Child and Family*, 6:29–41, 1967.

"What Every Parent Should Know—Advice From a Child Psychologist," (Interview with Dr. Joseph M. Babbitt), *U.S. News and World Report*, March 4, 1968, pp. 76–80.

7

MARRIAGE PROBLEMS

30

Divorce and Remarriage

Divorce is a part of all marriage and family systems. The requirements for marriage termination differ, but social systems universally recognize that there must be a means of termination other than the ultimate one of death.

Because divorce is not only a common, but in many cases, a necessary form of adjustment, both from the standpoint of the couple and of their children, it must be discussed in a book designed for helping young people develop a philosophy of marriage and parenthood that will lead to success. The fact that some will fail cannot be ignored. It is important that all understand the divorce process as it affects the couple involved as well as their children. Recent research and clinical experience provide insight into this very common phenomenon of our time.

The Changing Philosophy of Divorce

Divorce is no longer considered a sin, but is rather looked upon as a means of adjustment—a necessary one under our family philosophy. Divorce is the ultimate solution to be resorted to only if all other means of adjustment fail.

Consequently, the rigorous condemnation of divorce a few generations ago no longer exists. Many states have liberal divorce provisions. But regardless of state law, the general public, even including religious bodies, are more tolerant of divorce than in previous generations. They are more tolerant because there is at least a vague understanding of the social forces which make modern marriage quite a different institution from that of the past and give divorce a different meaning than it had previously.

There is general recognition that the bonds of love are the basic bonds of the modern family; that the ties of common property, common work, and a large family no longer exist for many couples. There is also a general recognition that the day when a woman was safe only in marriage has passed. She is often more secure economically, and more emotionally at ease, freed of an unsatisfactory marriage. There are even cases where, through divorce, she may assure her children a better future than within an unsatisfactory and tumultuous marriage. This fact is recognized in public policy under the Social Security Act, which makes no distinction between widowhood by death and widowhood by divorce where the welfare of dependent children is involved. Even before that act was passed many states had mothers' pension laws which similarly made no distinction.

The emerging philosophy also holds that a person who has failed to find happiness in marriage should be made free to seek it again in another marriage if he chooses to do so. While this philosophy is not accepted by all religious groups, or by all elements in the population, it is law and is a prevailing sentiment which is becoming increasingly accepted with each passing decade.

Extent of Divorce

General statistics are a very poor index of whether any given individual or couple are likely to end up in the divorce court. Studies by Judson T. Landis[1] indicate, however, that divorce, like permanence, runs in families. There are many families that have never had a divorce as far back as memory or geneologies carry them, and there are other family lines that are divorce-prone.

Landis studied the ancestors of 1,977 college students and found this to be strikingly so. Taking the students' own parents, and aunts and uncles, he related the divorces of this generation to whether or not the students' grandparents had been divorced. In the group of parents, and aunts and uncles, there were 13,255 persons. Where there had been no divorces in the grandparent generation, only 14.6 percent of parents, and aunts and uncles had been divorced; where one set of grandparents had been divorced, 23.7 percent had been divorced; where both sets of grandparents had divorced, 38 percent had been divorced.

To get a more accurate picture of divorce than that given by general rates, one must also know the racial group being referred to. Glick[2] has

[1] Judson T. Landis, "The Pattern of Divorce in Three Generations," *Social Forces*, 34:213–216, March, 1956.
[2] Paul C. Glick, "Marriage Instability: Variations by Size of Place and Religion," *The Milbank Memorial Fund Quarterly*, 41:43–55, January, 1963.

shown that disrupted marriages are three times as high among nonwhites as among whites. Two-thirds of disrupted white marriages are broken by divorce, whereas only one-third of disrupted nonwhite marriages are broken by divorce. Among nonwhites the separation ratio is very high. The disrupted marriages of the nonwhite are three times as likely to have dependent children as are the disrupted marriages of the white.

The long-term national trend of divorce has been upward. Of marriages taking place in 1900, only about one in twelve was ultimately terminated by divorce rather than death; of those taking place in 1922, about one in eight so ended. It is assumed that of current marriages almost one in four will eventually terminate in divorce (see Figure 30–1). Clearly the traditional goal of marriage, "until death do us part," is now held in less esteem than is the happiness of the marriage partners. When the choice is one of living unhappily together or of divorce, the second alternative is now more frequently chosen.

FIGURE 30–1   ONE OUT OF FOUR MARRIAGES ENDS IN DIVORCE.

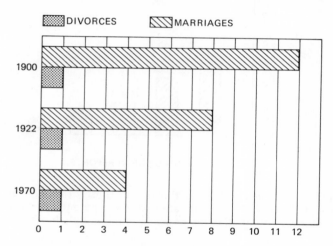

"Until death do us part," is the marriage vow taken by all, but in our nation the divorce court often does the parting.

In the United States now some 450,000 children are from homes broken by divorce, and the proportion of broken homes in which children are involved is increasing.[3] In 1960, 57 percent of homes broken by divorce had children under 18. The average number of children per family was 1.18.[4] Even large families are not immune to divorce and annulment. A

[3] U. S. Department of Health, Education and Welfare, "Trends in Divorce and Family Disruption," *Indicators*, Washington, D.C., September, 1963.
[4] *Ibid.*

special analysis of data gathered by the Census of 1965 shows the number of families of different sizes involved in divorce (see Figure 30–2). Only-child families are more exposed to divorce, but a substantial number of families of all sizes are affected.

FIGURE 30–2   DIVORCES AND ANNULMENTS BY NUMBER CHILDREN UNDER 18 REPORTED: DIVORCE-REGISTRATION AREA, 1965. Source: "Excerpts from Vital Statistics of the United States, 1965, Vol. III—Marriage and Divorce," U.S. Department of Health, Education, and Welfare, Table 2–18, p. 2–15.

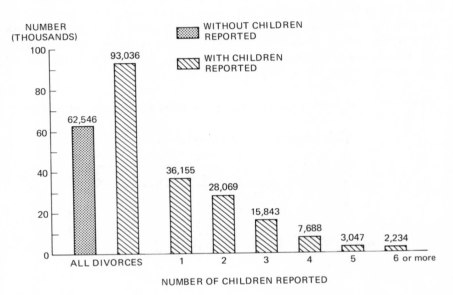

Almost half a million children in the nation under 18 years of age have lived through the divorce or separation of their parents. According to this sample, well over half of all divorces are in families with dependent children.

Burgess and Wallin, in their study of engagement, found that of 913 engaged men and 911 engaged women, approximately two-thirds thought that the couple should divorce if they ceased to be "in love." Over two-thirds of the group, however, felt that their attitude would be changed on this matter of divorce if there were children in the family.[5] Even when there are children involved there is increased public tolerance because divorce in many cases is the only means of removing the child from an environment of conflict.

[5] Ernest W. Burgess and Paul Wallin, *Engagement and Marriage* (Philadelphia: J. P. Lippincott Co., 1953), pp. 394–396.

Divorce by Occupation

Divorce is an escape device of the lower socioeconomic and lower educational classes more than of the more prosperous and better educated classes.[6] Desertion is even more so. Divorce is also an escape for those who marry too young, more than for others.[7]

Using occupational categories, Monahan studied couples involved in divorce in the state of Iowa.[8] Employing vital statistics data for the state, he found, as did Lang,[9] that marriage problems are very closely related to socioeconomic status. The divorce measure, like the happiness measure used by Lang, shows that generally the higher the occupational level the lower the divorce rate. His divorce data for the year 1953 show ratio to employed males in the various occupational categories. Although labor constituted less than ten percent of the population, they had almost one-third of the divorces. Professional people had less than half the divorces that would be expected on the basis of their ratio of population. Owners and officials had a few more than one-third of the expected divorces.

Divorce—A Legal Farce

Divorce is a legal action. Only the law can "put asunder" those whom the church or the law have joined together. Every divorce must, therefore, present to the court a legal cause. From a strictly legal standpoint, the court case is almost always a farce, not only because false reasons are given for the action, but because the couple usually agrees to the divorce in advance, rather than one party bringing grievance against the other as is presumed in divorce laws.

The usual legal grounds for divorce vary only slightly from year to year with proportions being about those shown in Figure 30–3.

There are marked variations among the states regarding legal grounds for divorces. The East and South are conservative with regard to permitting divorces and have low divorce rates. The West, acknowledging more grounds for divorce, has had a high divorce rate. This high rate was explained in part by the fact that Easterners went west to take advantage of

[6] Glick's study shows this, as have many others; see Paul C. Glick, *American Families* (New York: John Wiley & Sons, Inc., 1958), p. 147 ff.

[7] *Ibid.*, Table 72, p. 112.

[8] Thomas P. Monahan, "Divorce by Occupational Level," *Marriage and Family Living*, 17:322–324, November, 1955.

[9] See Figure 21–1, p. 438.

the ease of Western divorce laws, and also by the fact that residents of the West resort to divorce as a solution to marriage problems more often than those of other regions. The West lacks an established tradition; community pressures are weaker than in longer-settled areas where people have lived together for three or four generations. Its people are more mobile and are often far removed from the claims of kinship, many having left all relatives behind in moving west. Attitudes of the institutional family which persist more tenaciously in the deep South and the conservative East, matter less in this area.

FIGURE 30-3   REASONS GIVEN IN COURT FOR WANTING DIVORCE: DIVORCE REGISTATION AREA, 1965. Source: "Excerpts from Vital Statistics of the United States, 1965, Vol. III—Marriage and Divorce," U.S. Department of Health, Education, and Welfare, Table 2-21, p. 2-18.

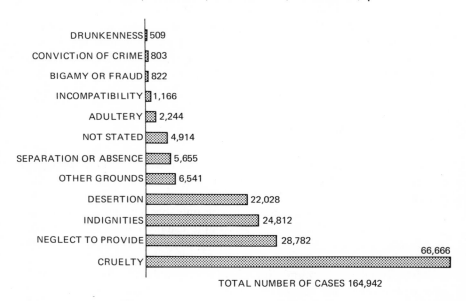

TOTAL NUMBER OF CASES 164,942

Divorce is considered a legal farce. Reasons given in court and the real motives for divorce may have little similarity.

Florida has since 1935 drawn part of the divorce trade by shortening its residence requirements, as has also Arkansas. And now, in a day of jetting between continents, Paris, Havana, Mexico, and the Virgin Islands offer easy escapes from marriage.

Ernest R. Mowrer, many years ago, studied broken families to get at the real reasons for divorce and desertion.[10] His studies make it strikingly

[10] Ernest R. Mowrer, "The Variance Between Legal and Natural Causes for Divorce," *Social Forces,* 2:388–392, March, 1924.

clear that a great deal of rationalization enters into the court reason for obtaining a divorce. For example, in 295 divorces where desertion was given as the legal grounds, he found that in 40.2 percent of the cases financial tension was the actual cause for the desertion. In 13.2 percent of the cases, the party forsook the mate for another. In 10.9 percent of the cases dissatisfaction with home or married life was the real reason. In 10.5 percent of the cases, infidelity was the real cause. In other cases, drink, cruelty, and irregular habits were found to be the cause.

In the case of 156 divorces granted on legal grounds of cruelty, he found that 45 percent were in reality brought on by financial tensions; 28.6 percent by drink; 14.6 percent by jealousy and infidelity. Divorce on the grounds of adultery seems to most nearly represent the facts. In ninety-six cases he found that all but 8 percent had actually been involved in illicit sexual intercourse.

Harmsworth and Minnis have made an extensive analysis, through contact with lawyers in the state of Idaho, of the statutory and the non-statutory causes of divorce. They find great contradiction between the real and the legal causes. Lawyers admit that they tend to substitute for the real cause broad categories which are least likely to be challenged by the court. Extreme cruelty seems to be one of those and is therefore extensively used. This means that even statutory causes are abused as far as integrity is concerned.[11]

Divorce—A Social Process

People abroad get the impression that divorce in the United States is a very casual experience. It is not so. There is a revival of hope and return to despair; a period of good adjustment and a glimpse of happiness, then a slipping back. Often this goes on until misery is so great that temporary separations are necessary. Love may revive only to be followed with disillusionment and near despair. For most couples there is a long time lapse between the first consideration of divorce and the decree (see Table 30–1).

Under the companionship-family social system, divorce is a social process which in outline is not unlike the process of dating, courtship, engagement, and marriage. It is, in fact, those processes in reverse. Instead of a series of experiences creating greater intimacy and involvement and culminating in marriage, divorce is a series of experiences beginning with the initial frictions and climaxing in emotional indifference or even violent hatred.

[11] Harry C. Harmsworth and Nhyra S. Minnis, "Non-Statutory Causes of Divorce: The Lawyer's Point of View," *Marriage and Family Living,* 17:316–321, November, 1955.

Table 30–1   Time From First Serious Consideration of Divorce to
Decree

Time (months)	Percentage	Cumulative Percentage
0–5	6	6
6–11	15	21
12–23	30	51
24–35	23	74
36–47	17	91
Not known	15	
Total	425	

Median = 23.8 months

Source: William J. Goode, *After Divorce* (New York: Free Press of Glencoe, Inc., 1956), p. 137.

The late Willard Waller once traced the various steps which lead to the divorce court.[12] The first stage is a disturbance in the love life of the pair. This eventually leads to the point where friction is so intense that the possibility of divorce is mentioned.

The next stage is that in which husband or wife tells some outside person or persons of their difficulty. This puts the marriage on a different basis, since the couple loses face with other people. Usually this does not end the marriage; discussions ensue concerning a course of action.

Finally, there comes the stage when the husband and wife definitely decide to make a break. This is followed by a separation, which is followed later by the divorce action itself. The divorce does not end the relationship. There is still the important period of mental conflict, during which both individuals are confronted with the problem of reconstructing their lives to fit the new situation.

There is also the problem of emotional readjustment. Waller has stated that, in his studies of divorce cases, he had yet to find a divorce which was not followed by a serious form of bereavement, along with problems of loneliness, sex tensions, and problems of lowered income and social standing among friends. In many cases the bereavement following divorce for one or sometimes for both parties is much more serious than bereavement (grief and shock) following the death of a mate. Death is always classed among the inevitable occurrences of life. The shock of death may be more sudden, but it can be charged to Providence, to accident, or

[12] Willard Waller and Reuben Hill, *The Family: A Dynamic Interpretation* (New York: Holt, Rinehart and Winston, Inc., 1951), p. 540.

to natural causes, and one can absolve himself of blame. But in the case of divorce, there is always the knowledge that it might have been avoided and awareness of disappointed happiness against which to project the divorce.

This early analysis of Waller's, based on the case history analysis of thirty-three couples involved in divorce, shows great insight. Much of it is still irrefutable. It does, however, need some modification and elaboration to suit current conditions.

First, it should be stressed that the divorce process may be arrested at any step, and adjustment turned toward better rather than worse relationships. This is particularly true today when more specialists are available for counsel and where many ministers, teachers, and others are sufficiently informed to help a couple in conflict gain insight into their problems, thus helping to solve them. Waller's basic thesis that marriage relationships are dynamic, always tending either to get better or worse at any stage of the relationship, is probably more true now than when he made the observation.

Second, bereavement and shock do not inevitably follow divorce. Some find in it genuine relief from tension. Greater public tolerance may be a factor here, although it is doubtful that the shock reaction was ever universal. Locke's case histories[13] show that in many instances there is no shock at all. He also suggests the probability that where there is emotional trauma, it may be eased by early remarriage. Goode[14] studied one hundred urban mothers who had been divorced. He found that there is no consistent traumatic pattern following divorce. Half of the subjects studied indicated an attitude of indifference toward the former spouse.

Divorce in the Marriage Cycle

Generally speaking, the longer the marriage survives, the less likelihood that it will end in divorce. The divorce rate is highest during the first few years of marriage, when major adjustments must be made or the marriage declared a failure. The peak in number of divorces comes in the third year of marriage and drops sharply after the seventh.[15] (see Figure 30–4)

In about three-fourth of all cases, the wife initiates the divorce action. In most cases, collusion is involved; the couple agreeing that she is most likely to succeed in obtaining a decree. Most divorce cases are uncontested, indicating that there has been prior agreement as to obtaining a divorce.

[13] Ernest W. Burgess and Harvey J. Locke, *The American Family,* third edition (New York: American Book Co., 1963), pp. 451–460.

[14] William J. Goode, "Problems in Postdivorce Adjustment," *American Sociological Review,* 14:394–400, June, 1949.

[15] Paul H. Jacobson, "Differentials in Divorce by Duration of Marriage and Size of Family," *American Sociological Review,* 15:238–239, April, 1950.

FIGURE 30–4   PERCENTAGE OF DIVORCES AND ANNULMENTS—BY DU-
RATION OF MARRIAGE: DIVORCE REGISTRATION AREA, 1965. Source:
"Excerpts from Vital Statistics of the United States, 1963, Vol. III—Marriage
and Divorce," U.S. Department of Health, Education, and Welfare, Table
2–5, p. 2–8.

Note the high rates during the early years of marriage.

It must, however, be granted that women use divorce as a solution to
marriage problems more often than men do. The wife's happiness, success,
mental health, and general well-being is much more identified with success
of the marriage than is that of the husband. He may use outside recreation,
work, an extramarital affair, or even desertion as an escape much more
readily than she. He becomes the overt offender against the marriage. She
requests the divorce on the grounds of his offense.

Remarriage as a Postdivorce Adjustment

Some churches try to discourage divorce by hindering remarriage or forbidding it altogether. Some states require a waiting period of months or
even years before a new marriage license will be granted. Yet most persons

separated from a spouse by divorce or death do remarry. Chances of remarriage after divorce are much higher than: (1) chances of eventual marriages for single persons of the same age group, and (2) the chances of remarriage after widowhood for given ages (see Figure 30–5). At age 30, the chances of remarriage for a divorced woman are 94 in 100; for the widowed woman, only 60 in 100; and marriage for the spinster, only 48 in 100. At age 30, the divorced man's chances of remarriage are 96 in 100; the widowed male's chances of remarriage, 92 in 100; and the bachelor's chances of marriage, only 67 in 100.[16]

FIGURE 30–5   CHANCES OF MARRIAGE FOR SINGLE, DIVORCED, .AND WIDOWED WOMEN. Source: Based on data from Metropolitan Life Insurance Company, **Statistical Bulletin.** Chart by Paul H. Landis, "Sequential Marriage," **Journal of Home Economics,** 42:625–628, October, 1950.

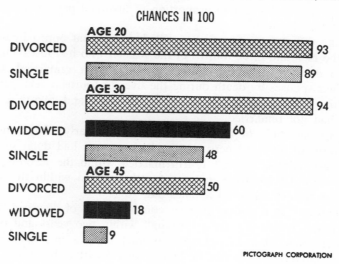

At all ages the divorced woman's chances of marriage are greatest. The divorced man is also more likely to marry than the single or widowed man.

Marriage rates drop with increased age for all groups and for both sexes, dropping faster for females than males, but throughout life the divorced person continues to have much better chances of marriage than the other groups. For example, at age 40, the divorced woman has 65

[16] Metropolitan Life Insurance Company, "The Chances of Remarriage for the Widowed and Divorced," *Statistical Bulletin,* May, 1945, pp. 1–3; data are from records in 22 states and the District of Columbia and are, therefore, extensive and conclusive; see also Paul H. Jacobson, *American Marriage and Divorce* (New York: Holt, Rinehart and Winston, Inc., 1959); Jacobson compares remarriage rates at age 25 and finds them higher for the divorced than the single or the widowed; see Ch. 6.

chances in 100 of remarriage; the widowed woman, only 29 chances in 100; and the single woman, only 16 chances in 100 of marriage. Or to approach it differently, a spinster of 30 has approximately a fifty-fifty chance of marriage; the widow of 33 has a similar chance; but the divorcee of 45 has a fifty-fifty chance of remarriage.

How soon does remarriage take place? There are as yet no specific and comprehensive data on this subject, but data for a five-year interval indicate that remarriage after divorce usually comes within the first five years. Glick[17] made estimates from large samples and concluded that of those divorced in the five years preceding the 1948 Bureau of the Census survey, all but one-fourth had remarried. Of those who had been divorced five to fourteen years, only about one-seventh had not remarried. While Glick advises caution in the acceptance of his data, he suspects that the estimates may be low in that unattached adults tend to be missed in sample Census surveys and a certain proportion of divorced persons fail to report themselves as divorced.

Using the same series of data, Glick found that approximately one-half of the men and three-fourths of the women who had lost their spouses by death during the preceding five years had not remarried. Of those losing their spouses by death during the five- to fourteen-year period preceding the survey, about one-third of the men and two-thirds of the women had not remarried.

A special study of remarriages during the early 1950s shows that over a third of divorced persons who had married had done so within a year or less. Almost another fourth married within the second year (see Table 30–2). Of widowed males a fourth married within the year, but less than a fifth of widowed females did.

Jacobson[18] in a similar analysis concludes that of divorced women, a third remarry within a year; almost half within two years and two-thirds within five years. Men are not quite so quick to take on new marriage responsibilities, but three in five, he finds, remarry within five years.

The above is clear evidence that divorced persons remarry much more quickly than the widowed. The fact that such a high proportion remarry so quickly makes one suspect that students of the family have discounted too heavily the notion of the man in the street that some divorces take place so that one or both parties may be free to marry a person already selected. Even behind such divorces there is often a long period of tension, in which one spouse or the other has attempted to escape by forming an extra-marital relationship. The male is most often the offender in such cases.

---

[17] P. C. Glick, "First Marriages and Remarriages," *American Sociological Review,* 14:726–734, December, 1949.

[18] Paul H. Jacobson, *American Marriage and Divorce* (New York: Holt, Rinehart and Winston, Inc., 1959), pp. 67–71.

Table 30–2   Period of Divorce or Widowhood Prior to Remarriage
              for Widowed Men and Women Who Remarried

Years Since Divorced	Males (percent)	Females (percent)
One year or less	34.4	34.3
2	18.4	19.4
3	10.7	12.7
4	10.4	6.1
5–9	12.2	14.5
10 and over	7.4	8.8
not reported	6.5	4.2
	100.0	100.0

Years Since Widowed	Males (percent)	Females (percent)
One year or less	25.7	19.0
2	17.1	23.2
3	10.5	7.0
4	7.6	4.9
5–9	22.9	23.2
10 and over	13.3	14.1
not reported	2.9	8.6
	100.0	100.0

Source: "Demographic Characteristics of Recently Married Persons, United States, April, 1953," *Vital Statistics-Special Reports*, Vol. 39, No. 3, October 12, 1954. Data are for persons in the United States who remarried between January, 1950 and April, 1953.

Success of Remarriage After Divorce or Widowhood

It is known that marriages now are about four times as likely to be broken by divorce as in 1890, but what of remarriages? Until recently little has been known, except from scattered studies of small samples, concerning the success of remarriage. Studies by Popenoe[19] and others[20] give the

[19] Paul Popenoe, "Divorce and Remarriage from a Eugenic Point of View," *Social Forces*, 12:48–51, October, 1933.

[20] H. Hart and E. B. Hart, *Personality and the Family* (Boston: D. C. Heath & Co., 1935), p. 109.

FIGURE 30–6   DIVORCES PER 100 MARRIAGES, IOWA 1953–1955—BY PRIOR MARITAL STATUS. Source: Thomas P. Monahan, "The Changing Nature and Instability of Remarriage," **Eugenics Quarterly,** June, 1958.

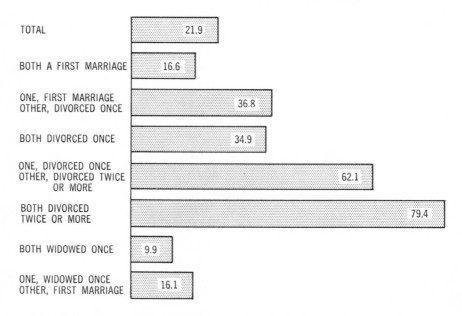

Note how divorce experience pyramids toward repeated divorce. The widowed are very stable in remarriage.

impression that remarriage is less often successful than original marriages. Locke's[21] comparison of a small sample of happily married and divorced persons led to the tentative hypothesis that divorced women are approximately as good a risk in remarriage as single women; divorced men are a poorer risk. These findings give an erroneous picture of the general situation.

Studies by the Bureau of the Census[22] with a sample practically nationwide in scope present for the first time convincing evidence that remarriages do not work out so well as first marriages. In 1948, 20 percent of the divorced and 18 percent of the married persons whose spouses were absent had been married before. Only 13 percent of widowed persons and of married persons living with their spouses had been previously married. For 19.2 percent of divorced men, this was at least the second break; for

[21] H. J. Locke and W. J. Klausner, "Prediction of Marital Adjustment of Divorced Persons in Subsequent Marriages," *Research Studies of the State College of Washington,* 16:30–32, March, 1948.

[22] U. S. Department of Commerce, Bureau of the Census, "Marital Status, Number of Times Married, and Duration of ‚Present Marital Status, April 1948," Series P-20. No. 23, March 4, 1949.

FIGURE 30–7   REMARRIAGES—BY AGE AND MARITAL STATUS OF BRIDE AND GROOM, 28 STATES, 1959. Source: U.S. Public Health Service, National Vital Statistics Division, "Trends in Divorce and Family Disruption," September, 1963, Chart 6.

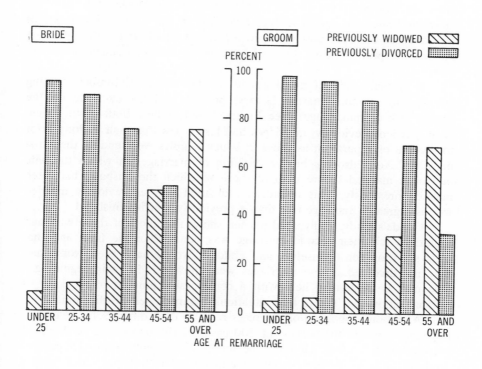

Those marrying someone who has previously been married will find that most in this category are divorced. Among older persons, most are widowed. Almost all the eligibles under 25 years of age are divorced.

21.2 percent of divorced women, the same. While there is no way of knowing what proportion of the first marriages were broken by death and what proportion by divorce, the evidence suggests that second marriages are about 50 percent more risky than first marriages, and the woman in her second or subsequent marriage is a somewhat poorer risk than the man. Specifically, the remarried woman is, according to these data, a 10 percent poorer risk than the remarried man.

Monahan's study of Iowa data, where statewide statistics are available, shows that not only are second marriages of shorter duration than first marriages but that the oftener the divorced person remarries, the shorter the average duration of the marriage is (see Figure 30–6). His data also prove conclusively that it is the remarried divorced person who accounts for the high divorce statistics among those with one or more previous marriages.[23]

Most younger persons who remarry are divorced; in the older years, most are widowed (see Figure 30–7). A high percentage of women remarrying under the age of 45 are divorced. In the 45 to 54 age group, the ratios of divorced and widowed are about equal. It is not until past 55 that the proportion of divorced men who remarry is smaller than the widowed.

A special study of marriages in the District of Columbia, relating duration to previous marital history, presents striking evidence on the greater risk of remarriages (see Figure 30–8). Where both partners had been married previously, marriages had lasted less than half as long prior to divorce or separation as those in which couples were ending their first marriage. Note also the briefer duration of marriages in which the wife had been married before than of those in which the husband had been married previously. This is further indication that a previously married wife is a greater marriage risk than a previously married husband.

Goode's study of divorced women shows that most of those who had remarried felt their second marriage was better than the first, and that their situation for themselves and children would have been worse had they not divorced. These marriages were, however, in their beginning.[24] One may be reckoning here with a considerable amount of the kind of rationalization that enters into situations requiring self-justification.

A certain proportion of divorcees remarry each other. Some years ago Popenoe[25] studied the success of 200 cases of the remarriage of divorced persons to each other. Of these, he found 48 percent happy, 15 percent doubtful, and 37 percent definitely unhappy. The unhappy ones usually resorted to divorce again very soon.

These data indicate that remarriage is for many a successful postdivorce adjustment. Some no doubt gain maturity and insight into their own personalities and into the nature of marriage itself from their first experience as well as from their period of widowhood following divorce. This makes it possible for them to find happiness in a new relationship. On the other hand, the facts also show clearly that those who have been through divorce once, more readily seek this solution to marriage problems than those who have not been previously married.

[23] Thomas P. Monahan, "The Duration of Marriage to Divorce: Second Marriages and Migratory Types," *Marriage and Family Living*, 21:134–138, May, 1959.

[24] William H. Goode, *After Divorce* (New York: Free Press of Glencoe, Inc., 1956).

[25] Paul Popenoe, "Remarriage of Divorcees to Each Other," *American Sociological Review*, 3:695–699, October, 1938.

Schlesinger's[26] in-depth study of eighty-four Canadian couples—middle class, somewhat superior in intelligence and schooling, and still fairly young—who had made a success of a second marriage suggests that they entered it cautiously, analytically, but with love the major motivation. These couples tended to seek mates different from their first. About half sought professional help regarding their decision to remarry. They considered that they had learned from their marriage failure, and that it had been a maturing experience.

FIGURE 30-8   MEDIAN DURATION OF MARRIAGE, DISTRICT OF COLUMBIA, 1957—BY FIRST MARRIAGE AND REMARRIAGE OF SPOUSE. Source: U.S. Public Health Service, National Vital Statistics Division, "Trends in Divorce and Family Disruption," September, 1963, Chart 4.

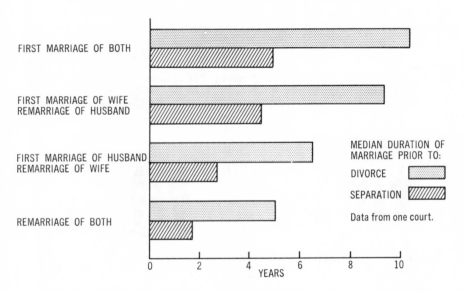

First marriages last longest. Remarriages of males are next while remarriages of females are of much shorter duration. When both are remarrying, the new marriage has a low median duration.

Dr. Schlesinger views remarriage as a testimony to "strength of character" and belief in "one's self." He believes that for the successful it means a "depth of self-understanding never before achieved." Deep and conscious rational involvement marked these successful marriages.

[26] Benjamin Schlesinger, "Successful Remarriage after Divorce," *Family Life*, 29:1–4, January, 1969.

Divorce and the Child

Society has ceased to be very greatly concerned about the divorce of man and wife but can not view lightly the effects on children. For statistics on the children of broken homes, see Figure 30–9. One cannot, however, ignore the evidence that perpetual marital conflict may be much worse for the child than divorce itself. There is in many cases great damage to children in continuing a marriage in which an established pattern of antagonistic relationship exists.

One of the most convincing analyses on this point is that by Plant.[27] Writing for judges involved in the legal processes of the divorce courts, he stated that in many cases divorce is the best possible solution for the child. He found that ten times as many children were sent to the Essex County, New York, Juvenile Clinic from separated parents as from di-

FIGURE 30–9   CHILDREN IN BROKEN FAMILIES. U.S. Department of Commerce, Bureau of the Census, **Current Population Reports: Population Characteristics,** Series P–20, No. 112, December 29, 1961, p. 13.

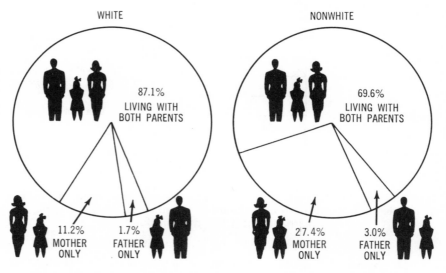

Distribution, by race, of children under 18 living with one parent.
See also Paul C. Glick, "Marriage Instability: Variations by Size of Place and Religion," **The Milbank Memorial Fund Quarterly,** 41:43–55, January, 1963.

[27] James S. Plant, "The Psychiatrist Views Children of Divorced Parents," *Law and Contemporary Problems*, 10:807–818, Summer, 1944.

vorced parents. Less disturbance was shown in the lives of children of divorced parents than in those of separated parents. He believed the divorce court, in granting the decree and in assigning the child to one parent, making whatever financial arrangements are necessary, is often doing the most that can be done to remedy the situation from the standpoint of the welfare of the child. Divorce is not an ideal solution, but is the only one possible in certain instances. In such cases, it comes as a great relief to the child.

There has been much publicity of the fact that children of divorced homes make up an undue proportion of delinquents. As a consequence of such reports, the public generally blames divorce for these problems. Actually, this kind of thinking is erroneous. Divorce itself is simply the legal incident in the conflict of marriage partners.

Far from being the cause for children's problems, divorce is often the solution. The damage to the child was done long before the divorce decree was sought and might have been avoided had the divorce come sooner. The damage to the child comes from perpetual conflict between parents; from his being used as a pawn in their conflict. Those who work with children's problems and with courts of domestic relations observe that parents in conflict are rarely fair to the child. Each parent will try to influence the child against the other parent. In some cases, one parent will use the child as an excuse for holding the marriage together. Without any regard for his feelings or interests, a parent may pour out his miseries and condemnations of the other parent into the innocent child's ears.

Judge Paul W. Alexander, of Toledo, Ohio, who presided over 30,000 divorces and who on alternate days presided over the juvenile court, observed that during some years as many as 40 percent of couples with children who come for divorces have been to the juvenile court previously with their children's problems.[28] Certainly this is striking evidence that problems of delinquency appear before the divorce.

There is an increasing body of evidence that divorce in and of itself is not seriously harmful to children. The aftereffects depend a great deal on the kind of relationship that preceded the breakup. There is the strong likelihood in many instances that the effects on the child might have been

---

[28] Paul W. Alexander, "A Therapeutic Approach," *Conference on Divorce* (Chicago: University of Chicago Law School, February 29, 1952). Numerous other recent studies have supported the view that it is the tension that precedes divorce rather than the divorce itself that does the damage. See such studies as F. Ivan Nye, "Child Adjustments in Broken and in Unhappy Unbroken Homes," *Marriage and Family Living,* 19:356–361, November, 1957; Judson T. Landis, "A Comparison of Children of Divorced Parents and Children of Happy or Unhappy Nondivorced Parents on Parent-Child Relationships, Dating, Maturation, and Sex and Marriage Attitudes," a paper read before the National Council on Family Relations, Minneapolis, Minn., August 27, 1955; Paul H. Landis, *The Broken Home in Teenage Adjustment* (Pullman, Wash.: Washington Agricultural Experiment Station, June, 1953), Bulletin No. 542.

more disastrous had the divorce not taken place. Burchinal,[29] in one of the most refined pieces of research to date, compared five types of family groups in their effects on some 1,500 young people in grades seven through eleven: unbroken families, mothers only, mother and stepfather, both parents remarried, and fathers and stepmothers.

For the most part, he finds no differences in personality and social relationship scores. He concludes that the broken family, and even the reconstituted family, where remarriage of a parent or parents takes place, "was not the overwhelming influential factor in the children's lives that many thought it to be."

Perhaps the social adjustment process is far different today, even for children, than it was in an earlier day when divorce was a more definite challenge to the mores. Greater tolerance has no doubt permeated both community and school.

Judson T. Landis has found that the effect of divorce on the child varies greatly with the age of the child at the time of divorce—it is less traumatic for younger children—and how the child viewed the parent relationship prior to the divorce—those who considered the home happy suffered more trauma.[30]

Bernard[31] studied attitudes of men and women toward children acquired through remarriage. Almost two-thirds of divorced men and 56 percent of divorced women were affectionate toward children acquired. Only about 5 percent of divorced men and 7 percent of divorced women rejected them. About a third neither rejected nor were affectionate.

Schlesinger's study[32] in depth of eighty-six Canadian couples, who had made a success of remarriage finds that couples are keenly aware of the dual adjustment the marriage requires, that to each other and to any children brought into the marriage.

The problem for the one who has no children, usually the male, is to learn to be a father, which involves loving children he did not sire, and learning to establish effective discipline. This study of successful marriages shows that there was a strong tendency on the part of both parents and step-children to want to adjust. About half of step-parents admitted some difficulty in adjusting.

Another unique problem of the remarried with step-children is equality

[29] Lee G. Burchinal, "Characteristics of Adolescents from Unbroken, Broken, and Reconstituted Families," *Marriage and Family Living,* 26:44–50, February, 1964; see also F. Ivan Nye, *op. cit.;* also Judson T. Landis, *op. cit.;* also Judson T. Landis, "A Comparison of Children from Divorced and Nondivorced Unhappy Marriages," *Coordinator,* 11:61–65, July, 1962.

[30] Judson T. Landis, "The Trauma of Children Where Parents Divorce," *Marriage and Family Living,* 22:7–13, February, 1960.

[31] Jessie Bernard, *Remarriage* (New York: Holt, Rinehart and Winston, Inc., 1956), p. 111.

[32] Benjamin Schlesinger, "Successful Remarriage after Divorce," *Family Life,* 29:1–4, January, 1969.

of treatment with any children born into the new marriage. Here couples have to rationalize and resolve in a way that is not done when siblings are being added to a first marriage. Schlesinger finds that parents do have the new children with a resolution to treat all children equal. In the successful marriage, they are apparently usually able to carry out the resolutions. It is probable that in marriages which fail, reasonableness cannot be carried over into emotional acceptance.

Margaret Mead expresses the view that the shock of divorce could be eased by bringing up children to realize that people today live a very long time and may not wish to spend their full lifetime together. She feels women should also be taught not to feel abandoned and hurt when a marriage ends after twenty years. She believes that we haven't even accepted the fact of divorce yet.

It will be quite a different world when children are brought up to believe that a parent may leave at his discretion for another mate, and when wives do not feel abandoned if their husband chooses to leave them for another.[33] It seems not to be in the making now.

A Therapeutic Approach to Divorce

There is much discussion today of a therapeutic approach to divorce. Pioneer of this approach has been Paul W. Alexander, Judge of the Court of Common Pleas in Lucas County, Ohio. For some time he held the chairmanship of an interprofessional commission on marriage and divorce laws which helped develop socialized procedures to terminate the divorce fraud perpetuated by law in most states. The commission recommended that a case-work approach to divorce be instituted, replacing the traditional adversary procedure which requires bringing charges against the mate.[34]

In his own court, Dr. Alexander maintained a staff of specialists to investigate cases and work out reasonable solutions to the marriage. Where there was a child of under fourteen, the family situation had to be investigated before being brought into the court. The aim of the divorce court proceedings was to be helpful rather than punitive.

Judge Alexander has advocated that we should try to do away with legal grounds for divorce. As long as there are legal grounds for divorce,

[33] "Margaret Mead's Sound Insights into the Furor over Shifting American Morals," *Life*, 65:30–34, August 25, 1968.

[34] See Thomas M. French, "Contributions to a Therapeutic Solution to the Divorce Problem: Psychiatry," in *Conference on Divorce* (Chicago: University of Chicago Law School, February 29, 1952); see also Aaron L. Rutledge, "Should the Marriage Counselor Ever Recommend Divorce?" *Marriage and Family Living*, 25:319–325, August, 1963.

courts will probably continue to pit one party against the other in a bitter emotional battle that may be largely of the court's making. Each divorce case, he believes, should be approached with the question, "What is best for the individuals concerned?" If a child is affected, "What is best for the child?" Divorce will then proceed without public trial in line with evidence presented. The judge, with the investigators' evidence at hand, is in a position to apply the greatest scientific insight into the problems involved.

Psychiatrist Lawrence S. Kubie recommends that custody of children be assigned to a committee. Parents would agree on custody arrangements, as is now usually the case, but would select a committee composed of a pediatrician, a child psychologist, an educator, and a lawyer or clergyman who would arbitrate disagreements between parents rather than have custody disputes thrown into court. Another child specialist would serve as an "adult ally" for the child, winning his confidence and keeping informed as to the child's feelings about the custody relationships. This ally would report to the committee.

Although this sounds like a cumbersome arrangement, a growing number of parents are using it and finding it better than a court for settling custody disputes and for holding down quarrels about custody. It also relieves the courts of a heavy burden.[35]

Postdivorce Adjustment

In 1969 California adopted a Family Law Act which may well set a pattern in humaneness. The judge alone hears the case, and without witnesses or adversary proceedings of any kind, may grant the divorce if it appears to him that there are irreconcilable differences. If he feels that there is a possibility of reconciliation, the couple is referred to the Domestic Relations Court. The Act even does away with the term *divorce*, using instead the term, *dissolution of marriage*. Child support and alimony may still be given, and community property division is equal between spouses.

It is believed that by eliminating the adversary situation, there will be less opening of old wounds. Private matters will not be aired in court, false testimony given by witnesses to bolster the claims of one or the other mate will no longer be necessary, and other damaging exposures will cease. There is more likelihood that both the couple and the children will suffer less damage and carry over less hostility as they take up their new life. There will be greater possibility of later reconciliation, too, or at least of genuine cooperation in sharing the child where children are involved.

[35] See "Domestic Relations: Custody by Committee?" *Time,* September 18, 1964, pp. 67–68.

There is likely to be a great deal of insecurity after divorce, particularly for the woman. She has had to acknowledge defeat in the relationship that means most to women. She is likely to feel abandoned, and she may feel bereaved. She faces a world in which she must accept both masculine and feminine roles, as far as business and managerial affairs are concerned and in supporting and disciplining the children.

When she begins to circulate among friends again, she is more suspect than is the widow in that insecure wives consider her a threat to their marriage and a competitor for the attentions of their husbands. Males are likely to consider her fair game, although for a time she may feel as though she never wants anything to do with men again.

Divorcées Anonymous[36] now exists nationwide for mutual help and understanding, and many churches have "divorcée clubs" to try to give support to the many who feel shame and stigma and yet who are religiously inclined.[37] Many divorced persons need the church to help them find new purpose in life. Parents Without Partners is a nationwide organization designed to help the divorced and the widowed with their special problems.[38]

In conclusion, while divorce is not to be condoned as an easy solution to superficial marriage problems, society has come to recognize it, legally and extralegally, as the ultimate solution where marriage difficulties arise from deep-seated psychological and emotional problems. When such difficulties are established by professional counsel, the quicker the divorce the better, even when children are involved. Divorce is looked upon by the social scientist as therapeutic when it is used in this connection. It can only be condemned when used casually. In such instances it solves no problems, but leads to a series of necessary new adjustments which place the unstable person in a more vulnerable situation than he was in before.

Problems

1. Which of these philosophies do you consider most desirable in a young bride or groom?
    a. "I said it and I meant it, 'until death do us part.' I shall never never consider divorce."
    b. "If things don't work out well, there is always the divorce court."
    c. "I believe in this marriage and I'll do my best to make it a happy one. If my best isn't good enough, however, I won't let pride or pressure frighten me of divorce."

[36] 188 West Randolph Street, Chicago, Illinois.

[37] See Thomas J. Fleming, "The Divorced Ones," *This Week* Magazine, January 26, 1964.

[38] 80 Fifth Avenue, New York, N. Y. 10011.

2. Dividing the class into two opposing groups, discuss divorce as: (*a*) an indication that marriage is taken less seriously than in the past, (*b*) an indication that marriage is taken more seriously than in the past.

3. Upon what legal grounds are most divorces obtained? Compare these reasons with the actual grounds as shown by special studies.

4. Divorce, unlike death, is a separation usually preceded by tension and antagonism. Why, then, are so many divorces accompanied by tears and a period similar to bereavement?

5. Charles and Hana have read about the undesirable effect divorce has on children. They no longer love one another; seldom ever speak, and Charles, who is deeply in love with another woman, spends most of his time in town to escape Hana's bitter tears. They have agreed, however, that until their children, five and seven, are fully grown, they will not consider separation.
   a. How wise do you consider their decision?
   b. What might the effect of their relationship be on the two children?
   c. Do you think their two children might profit if Charles and Hana obtained a divorce?

6. Compare the motives and justifications for divorce and remarriage among average people with the motives and justification in such cases as Tommy Manville's and certain Hollywood personalities'.

7. Considering the statistical evidence, would you say that a marriage ending in divorce tends to embitter most individuals against the institution of marriage?

8. Marriage is, after all, a relationship between two people that is capable of producing intense and lifelong misery as well as happiness. Do you think that it is justifiable for any individual judge to have the power to deny a divorce to an unhappy couple? Discuss.

9. Upon what grounds may divorces be obtained in your state? In what ways could divorce laws be improved?

10. *Sociodrama:* A young divorcée returns to her parents' home but receives a rather cool reception. The drama might open with the observation of one of her parents: 'Now, you've been bitten once, I hope you don't expect to try marriage again. You just aren't the type!"
    "Nonsense!" The girl might reply. "This has been sad, but it has also been the best thing that ever happened to me."
    Go on to picture the therapeutic results of the divorce.

Selected References

Articles in Books of Readings

Cavan, Ruth S., *Marriage and the Family in the Modern World: A Book of Readings*, third edition (New York: Thomas Y. Crowell Co., 1969).
   Goode, William J., "Divorce as an Escape Mechanism," Reading 49.
   LeMasters, E. E., "Holy Deadlock: A Study of Unsuccessful Marriages," Reading 48.
   Bernard, Jessie, "Remarriage of the Widowed and the Divorced," Reading 51.
   Plant, James S., "The Psychiatrist Views Children of Divorced Parents," Reading 74.
   Ploscowe, Morris, "Who Gets the Children?" Reading 60.

Bowerman, Charles E., and Irish, Donald P., "Some Relationships of Stepchildren to their Parents," Reading 6.

Landis, Judson T., and Landis, Mary G., *Readings in Marriage and the Family* (Englewood Cliffs, N.J.: Prentice-Hall, Inc., 1952).

Smith William C., "The Stepmother," pp. 306–310.

Smith, William C., "The Stepchild," pp. 310–313.

Davis, Kingsley, "Statistical Perspective on Divorce," pp. 333–338.

Jacobson, Paul H., "Divorce and Size of Family," pp. 339–341.

Davis, Kingsley, "Children of Divorce," pp. 351–360.

Alexander, Paul W., "A Therapeutic Approach to the Problem of Divorce," pp. 360–374.

Sussman, Marvin B., *Sourcebook in Marriage and the Family,* third edition (Boston: Houghton Mifflin Co., 1968).

Bernard, Jessie, "The Institutionalization of Remarriage," Reading 60.

Hill, Reuben, "Social Stresses of the Family," Reading 50.

Rheinstein, Max, "Trends in Marriage and Divorce Law of Western Countries," Reading 59.

Nye, F. Ivan, "Child Adjustment in Broken and in Unhappy Homes," Reading 49.

Vincent, Clark E., *Readings in Marriage Counseling* (New York: Thomas Y. Crowell Co., 1957).

Harper, Robert A., "Failure in Marriage Counseling," pp. 197–203.

Berkowitz, Sidney J., "An Approach to the Treatment of Marital Discord," pp. 203–213.

Winch, Robert F., and Goodman, Louis Wolf, third edition (New York: Holt Rinehart and Winston, Inc., 1968).

Carter, Hugh, and Plateris, Alexander, "Trends in Divorce and Family Disruption," pp. 564–571.

Levinger, George, "Marital Cohesiveness and Dissolution: An Integrative Review," pp. 579–592.

Scanzoni, John, "A Reinquiry into Marital Disorganization and Reorganization," pp. 593–604.

Goode, William J., "The Anomic Social Position of the Divorcee," pp. 605–608.

Monahan, Thomas P., "The Changing Nature and Instability of Remarriages," pp. 609–614.

General References

Allen, Anne, "Children of a Broken Marriage," *Mental Health,* 25:3–5, 1966.

Bernard, Jessie, *Remarriage* (New York: Holt,Rinehart and Winston, Inc., 1956).

Chen, Ronald, "The Dilemma of Divorce: Disaster or Remedy," *The Family Coordinator,* 17:251–254, October, 1968.

Christensen, Harold T., and Meissner, Hanna H., "Studies in Child Spacing: III—Premarital Pregnancy as a Factor in Divorce," *American Sociological Review,* 18:641–644, December, 1953.

Clements, William H., "Marital Interaction and Marital Stability: A Point of View and a Descriptive Comparison of Stable and Unstable Marriages," *Journal of Marriage and the Family,* 29:697–702, November, 1967.

Conference on Divorce, a symposium (Chicago: University of Chicago Law School, February 29, 1952).

Glick, Paul C., "First Marriages and Remarriages," *American Sociological Review*, 14:726–734, December, 1949.

Goode, William J., *After Divorce* (New York: The Free Press of Glencoe Inc., 1956).

Goode, William J., "Problems in Postdivorce Adjustment," *American Sociological Review*, 14:392–401, June, 1949.

Haussamen, Florence, and Guitar, Mary Anne, *The Divorce Handbook* (New York: G. P. Putnam's Sons, 1960).

Ilgenfritz, Marjorie P., "Mothers on Their Own—Widows and Divorcees," *Marriage and Family Living*, 23:38–41, February, 1961.

Jacobson, Paul H., *American Marriage and Divorce* (New York: Holt, Rinehart and Winson, Inc., 1959).

Kirkpatrick, Clifford, *The Family as Process and Institution*, revised edition (New York: The Ronald Press Co., 1963), Chs. 21, 22.

Landis, Judson T., "The Trauma of Children When Parents Divorce," *Marriage and Family Living*, 22:7–12, February, 1960.

Monahan, Thomas P., "Divorce by Occupational Level," *Marriage and Family Living*, 17:233–234, November, 1955.

Monahan, Thomas P., "The Duration of Marriage to Divorce: Second Marriages and Migratory Types," *Marriage and Family Living*, 21:134–138, May, 1959.

Pinard, Maurice, "Marriage and Divorce Decision and the Layer Social System: A Case Study in Social Change," *Social Forces*, 44:341–355, March, 1966.

Pollack, Jack Harrison, "Seven Mistakes Divorced Parents Make," *Parents*, 42:48, May, 1967.

Rutledge, Aaron L., "Should the Marriage Counselor Even Recommend Divorce?" *Marriage and Family Living*, 25:319–325, August, 1963.

Schlesinger, Benjamin, "Remarriage—An Inventory of Findings," *The Family Coordinator*, 17:248–250, October, 1968.

Simon, Anne W., *Stepchild in the Family: A View of Children in Remarriage* (New York: The Odyssey Press, 1964).

31

Better Marriages

American culture is especially optimistic about tomorrow, particularly with regard to the materialistic aspects of life. The new model has so often been demonstrated to be an improvement that technological change has come to be identified with improvement in level of living. The belief that man can improve himself has not been so readily accepted. It has, however, an increasing number of followers.

We take for granted that the family environment is going to improve almost beyond the scope of imagination and that a higher percentage of the population is going to share in the best that material improvements bring. Leisure will increase. Health will improve and life be made more safe.

It is in the quality of individuals and of marriages that the greatest improvement must come if we are to have better families and a better nation. Achievement in this area is less easily realized. Only part of this goal can be approached through plans and programs. Much of it must come through a revision of values and goals.

Three Approaches to Marriage Improvement

Improvements may be expected from (1) the legal and governmental policy-making, (2) the educational, and (3) the remedial directions. These are not mutually exclusive approaches; in fact, they overlap at points.

The legal and governmental has the advantage of quick and decisive action in that it can exercise the prohibitive function, "Thou shalt not." In areas of promotion, the legislative process is much slower in operation, but even that is fast compared with education, where one must often work a generation ahead for results. Urban industrial society has come to depend so much on governmental action for social improvement that it is often referred to as "the welfare state."

The educational has no power to compel change, rather it controls by internalizing values and goals, it guides and presents evidence and incentives. It shows that if better methods of living and doing are adopted, outcomes will be more satisfying. It selects from the culture, transmits the better parts of it to the young, and uses the lessons both of failure and success.

The remedial approach is the proverbial method of "locking the stable after the horse is stolen," but society is never without its need for cures, for there is no way of keeping all men from error, no way of educating for marriage or of restricting youth adequately by law, so as to prevent many making unwise marriage choices. And married people do encounter difficulties and must seek remedial measures.

In the area of marriage and that of children's problems, the remedial is so much in demand that neither sound techniques nor trained personnel are accessible in sufficient numbers to deal with them.

Legal Restriction of Marriage

States have jurisdiction over marriage and divorce. This may not soon change. Until it does, and there are uniform marriage and divorce laws—a highly desirable objective from a sociological point of view—the most to be hoped for is that the various states will adopt measures that have proved effective in states having them and that all states will improve on their best measures.

Age requirements   Age regulations have to do with: (1) age below which one cannot marry at all, (2) age below which parent's or guardian's consent is required, (3) age at which one is free to marry of his own choice. Most states require that girls be 16 before they can marry with parental consent and that boys be 18. The usual age for marriage without parental consent is 18 for girls and 21 for boys. Age restrictions may be waived when the girl is pregnant. A few states have no age restrictions at all. A few states recognize common-law marriages at age 12. A few states permit marriage of girls age 13 or 14 with parental consent.

In requiring the male to be older, the state recognizes the difficulty the young male is likely to have in supporting a wife and family.

A nationwide goal of a minimum age of 18 for girls and 21 for boys would seem to be a reasonable objective for every state. The problems of teen-agers are so many in urban society that this rule would be a quick way to cut the divorce rate and ease the social burden of dependent children.

Exceptions would have to be made in cases of pregnancy, but even in such cases, the right to marry might well be prefaced by a requirement of counseling and other guidance and help.

Waiting period   States with stricter laws purposely delay marriage, thus hindering hasty and ill-advised marriages. All states require a marriage license, common-law marriages being the exception. Except in divorce-mill cities a license usually can be bought only during working hours and on weekdays, when county officials have office hours. This fact alone hinders many marriages of couples who otherwise would marry without much forethought.

Some states require that the license be applied for a few days before it can be issued. Some require a lapse of time between acquiring the license and marriage. A medical certificate clearing the pair of venereal disease must have been obtained in advance in most states, and be presented to the clerk as part of the license application.

Research indicates that where people are compelled to wait many do change their minds and fail to follow through to marriage.[1] Others, of course, under present conditions cross the line into states which have no waiting period. Uniformity of law in the various states would require that all go through a period during which they could reconsider.

Lengthening the waiting period beyond that in effect in any state would undoubtedly cut down on ill-advised marriages further still. Few states have a waiting period of more than three days. Oregon has the longest waiting period, seven days. It is likely that the goal of a thirty-day waiting period nation wide would be a realistic one for legislation in this field.

Control of Divorce

In the area of restrictive legislation, a period of separation prior to divorce seems to offer some promise as a way of lowering divorce rates and thus avoiding the tangled web of relationships, emotional and financial, that the ill-considered divorce brings. The period of separation prior to divorce,

[1] Alexander Plateris, "The Impact of the Amendment of Marriage Laws in Mississippi," *Journal of Marriage and Family Living*, 28:206–212, May, 1966. Also Gordon Shipman and H. Yuan Tien, "Non-Marriage and the Waiting Period," *ibid.*, 27:277–280, May, 1965. Also *Divorce in California* (Sacramento: Bureau of Vital Statistics, October, 1967, pp. 64–65).

required in several states, gives the couple a chance to compare their marriage with return to single life, to sense to an extent what it will mean to them, and if there are children, to the children also. We know that some couples divorce and later remarry each other.[2] A waiting period could forestall some of this legal burden and family disruption.

A waiting period before remarriage, now in effect in some states, may be of value also. It may not deter divorce, but it can be a factor in a new marriage's being considered more carefully than in the case of two couples who divorce, then go to the other floor of the courthouse and remarry, as they now can, and sometimes do, in Reno.

Divorce reform   Courts of reconciliation have their place, but the remedy usually comes too late. By the time a couple goes to court, most bridges have already been burned behind them. Uniform divorce laws between the states would stop some divorces entered into too hastily. More readily available counseling services would be a better deterrent. In the court procedure of divorce itself, reform must be in the direction of eliminating the adversary approach and settling the case in the interest of the children and the couples with the fewest possible battles. The case-history approach has as the first objective the welfare and rehabilitation of the persons involved.

Governmental Social Policies

In the supportive area, numerous welfare programs and policies have built minimum security about the family. We look to government still as the action agency from which further help must come in urban industrial society. The broad areas of Social Security have given mothers with dependent children and the widowed a minimum of protection. Medicare has lifted another load from the young couple for the care of elderly parents. All these programs can be improved.

There are two important areas where our nation lags behind most industrial nations: (1) adequate medical care for the entire family and (2) family allowances to equalize in part the economic load of the couple with and the one without children.

Medical care   We are backward among Western industrial nations in medical care. Most of them have a lower infant and maternal death rate, and we lag in many other indices of health. We have some of the best medical facilities in the world but a poor system of medical administration. Millions have inadequate medical care.

[2] Paul Popenoe, "Remarriage of Divorcées to Each Other," *American Sociological Review*, 3:695–699, October, 1938.

Our medical system is very much profit-oriented. We are one of the few industrial nations without a salaried medical profession and a system of tax supported medical and dental care. It is in the nations with such care that health records exceed ours.

It is not likely that the family's health will be adequately protected until we adopt Medicare for all. Whether it should be by compulsory health insurance under the Social Security Act or directly tax-supported will be debated in the halls of Congress, but some such protection for all families is a must.[3]

Annual wage   The annual wage for industrial workers is full of promise for greater happiness in marriage. Research has shown that regularity of income is associated with successful marriage.[4] The industrial classes, which now show the greatest amount of unhappiness in marriage,[5] might well enjoy a higher level of marital happiness with a regularity of income that would provide for greater stability and permit more meaningful planning.

Family allowances   In the economic field, too, the family allowance systems now in effect in practically every other major industrial nation represent a means of bringing about greater equality between the sexes. This system is also conducive to a greater feeling of economic security and to greater marital stability. Family allowances, paid by taxation, usually are paid to the mother, giving her a new sense of independence and equality. The family allowance also gives her vocation a new dignity. By providing a regular guarantee for the minimum support of all children, it places marriage on a safer foundation.

In Canada, for example, all mothers receive a monthly allowance for each child from birth to age sixteen (provided the child remains in school). The average per family is $16.63 per month, $6.69 per child. Allowances are from taxation.[6] All political parties in Canada now agree on the value of this program, according to the Ministry of National Health and Welfare.[7] It provides children with better food, shelter, health, care, and education than would have been possible otherwise. The program is the best truant officer, too, since the child must attend school for the mother to get payment. This expenditure of funds, which is constantly turned over in the purchase of consumable goods, keeps the economy primed with spending power.

---

[3] For an analysis of American medical care as it exists today, see *Time*'s feature "What's Wrong with U.S. Medicine?", February 21, 1969.

[4] Ernest W. Burgess and Leonard S. Cottrell, *Predicting Success or Failure in Marriage* (Englewood Cliffs, N.J.: Prentice-Hall, Inc., 1939), p. 416 ff.

[5] Refer to Figure 21–1, p. 438.

[6] Bernice Madison, "Canadian Family Allowances and Their Major Social Implications," *Journal of Marriage and Family Living,* 26:134–141, May, 1964.

[7] Before allowances came into effect, a 1943 Gallup poll showed 49 percent favorable; in a 1955 poll, 90 percent favorable. *Ibid.*

In an agrarian society, security is in the land, and all members of the family, as workers, increase that security. In an industrial society, a man and wife's security is in their own earning power. The economic disadvantage of having children in an industrial society is clearly shown by data presented in Figure 8–2 (see p. 156). Democratic industrial society must, through such social policies as those suggested above, make life safer for marriage and the family.

Population control   The time has come when complete control of fertility is possible, yet we have many working-class families, particularly among the nonwhites, who are propagating themselves into the third generation on relief. There is little hope of successfully attacking poverty or raising the standard of living of this great dispossessed group in the city slums and rural poverty pockets except by bringing fertility under control.

Children in all families, the privileged and underprivileged alike, should be the voluntary issue of the family. This can be only as we develop a national policy of birth control which seeks aggressively to make parenthood voluntary. It will require a system of birth control clinics throughout underprivileged rural areas and slum sections where such programs can be promoted as an end toward raising the standard of living and economic and educational aspirations.

Planned Parenthood now has offices in many cities where advice and help is given. The American Association for Voluntary Sterilization has carried out experimental projects in selected areas. It is now possible to use "poverty" funds for birth control. Abortion laws are being liberalized, but slowly, but are not much used as yet for reasons of privation.

The time must come quickly when greater voluntary control will be exercised or compulsory limitations of families will be necessary. It is estimated that there are now 5,300,000 women 18–44 years of age in need of subsidized family limitation. This will require an expenditure of $90 million to $100 million annually.[8]

As long-term freedom from pregnancy becomes possible, such necessary programs will become more effective and more economical. For many sterilization is the economic answer, and state law needs to be so restated as to remove fears that doctors will be subject to penalty for sterility operations. Such operations are not illegal.

Quality control   Quality control is the goal of industry. Its practice in American agriculture through selective plant and animal breedings has doubled production and made our agriculture second to none. Quality control in human population is no less necessary and deserves attention in a world where numbers must be limited.

[8] Lynn Landman, "United States, Underdeveloped Land in Family Planning," *Journal of Marriage and Family Living,* 30:191–201, May, 1968.

The first step is registration of all families with known defective traits. A computerized national register is now possible to the point where each engaged pair could be compared for like recessive traits. It is time to begin controlling the quality of the next generation. Social policy must determine what degrees of risk society can tolerate. The too risky must not marry unless first sterilized.

There could be endless debate as to the rightness of such measures but few could face the evidence and make a case against the resulting improvement in the welfare of children, and in the happiness of married pairs.

The Educational Approach

America has great faith in education as a long-term means of social improvement. In the marriage field the most direct approaches are (1) courses in marriage preparation, (2) instruction in sex education of children and young people, and (3) premarital counseling.

Family-life education   Although marriage has always occupied an important place in the lives of most men and women, there has been little thought of any formal preparation for the roles of husband and wife and parent. The case for marriage education has never been adequately demonstrated, but certain studies suggest there is a definite benefit. Moses' study of students and married alumni shows that they do feel that they gain insight and learn to solve problems as a consequence of their training for marriage.[9]

One of the aims of family-life education is to help young people approach marriage and family living realistically. This requires providing information concerning those things which can make marriage a success. Family-life education helps to develop an understanding of interaction patterns which make for greater marriage competence. The fact that it helps young people to discard certain folklore conceptions can be of great value.

Most colleges now teach a general marriage course and a course in the history of the family, as well as various courses in child psychology and child development. Unfortunately, these courses are still taken primarily by women, even though men need them.

One of the interesting developments in this field has been the tendency for the content to become increasingly functional, that is, directed at the

[9] Virginia Musick Moses, "A Study of Learning Derived from a Functional Course in Marriage and Family Relationships," *Marriage and Family Living,* 18:204–208, August, 1956.

specific problems which young people face in their adjustments to the opposite sex during the premarital period and during the early years of marriage. The greatest handicap in the development of this approach to date is the lack of sufficient research material to provide an adequate guide, but an increasing amount of sociological and psychological research is in the making.

Family-life education needs to be extended in the high school to provide both boys and girls with opportunity to observe nursery schools in operation, to observe the care of small babies, and to learn more about parenthood and child training. One of the barriers to popular acceptance of broad courses in preparation for marriage, particularly on the elementary and high school level, is that they are frequently equated with sex education courses. Many parents are still frightened or suspicious of group teaching in this area. Sex education has an important place in these courses because of its importance in marriage, but it is not the only, not even the primary, purpose of the course. Combating folklore notions of mate finding and marriage adjustment and instilling some appreciation of the full possibilities of marriage and family life—these are more often the basic goals.

Sex education   High on the list of personal needs which marriage now seeks to satisfy are those of intimacy, companionship, and love. These needs, as has been observed, derive their fulfillment in large part from the sexual relations of man and wife. This elevates sex to a position of new importance in marriage. Most couples now consider satisfactory sex relations a necessary part of marriage and unsatisfactory relations as ample justification for divorce.

Sex education is gaining increased acceptance on the elementary and secondary level of the public school system. Were it practical to delay this formal education until later adolescence, the program would probably arouse much less opposition. Many parents feel that instruction in the lower grades is either unnecessary or dangerous. They argue that it may only raise questions and arouse curiosity. But, sex education does begin in a child's early years, see Figure 31–1). During the first six years of a child's life, he inevitably begins to wonder about such obvious and fascinating matters as "where babies come from." How this and similar questions are handled—the atmosphere in which they are discussed, the individual answering them, the facts or fictions that are passed along—can have a serious and lasting effect upon a young person's attitudes toward sex, marriage, and parenthood.

Sex education must begin at home, for there is where the child's questions begin. Parents need to be sufficiently prepared for these early questions to answer them honestly and without evasion or shame. Both fathers and mothers need to so respond when asked. This education is readily carried forward in the nursery school, where both sexes use the

FIGURE 31-1 COMPARISON OF MOTHERS AND DAUGHTERS WHO RE-
CEIVED FIRST SEX INFORMATION BEFORE AGE 13. Source: Paul H. Landis,
"Marriage Preparation in Two Generations," **Marriage and Family Living,**
November, 1951.

Sex information in the preadolescent period is important to sound emotional
development. This chart compares two generations of women—mothers and
daughters. Preadolescents today receive more sex education than did their
mothers a generation ago.

same toilets and have a chance to observe each other and to have questions
answered by trained personnel, who answer without undesirable emotional
overtones.

The older the child is, the less likely is the parent to give adequate
information, or even to guide at all. Many parents do not have the vocabulary, and some allow the communication gap to close before they get
around to the subject of sex in its various aspects. Perhaps even the well-
informed parent will not be able to handle the subject naturally and fully.
Mace suggests[10] that incest taboos may make parents reticent to discuss
sex subjects with their own children. This would be particularly true with
older sons and daughters. (See Figure 31-2 for source of sex information
for women of two generations.)

We know that appalling ignorance abounds. Poffenberger reports that
anonymous questions put in a question box by eighth-grade girls in a
marriage-and-family-life course indicate a shocking lack of information.
About half of the girls asked questions about sexual intercourse using
vulgar terms.[11]

[10] David R. Mace, "Some Reflections on the American Family," *Journal of
Marriage and Family Living,* 24:109–112, May, 1962.
[11] Thomas Poffenberger, "Family Life Education in a Scientific Age," *Marriage
and Family Living,* 21:150–154, May, 1959.

FIGURE 31–2 COMPARISON OF MOTHERS AND DAUGHTERS ON SOURCE OF SEX INFORMATION. Source: Paul H. Landis, "Marriage Preparation in Two Generations," **Marriage and Family Living,** November, 1951.

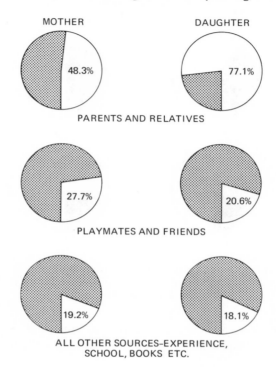

MOTHER   DAUGHTER

48.3%   77.1%

PARENTS AND RELATIVES

27.7%   20.6%

PLAYMATES AND FRIENDS

19.2%   18.1%

ALL OTHER SOURCES–EXPERIENCE,
SCHOOL, BOOKS ETC.

The generation of daughters more often received sex information from adult sources.

Hillman's study of letters to an advice column showed that more informational inquiries centered around sex than around any other single topic. Second were queries about birth control. This would seem to indicate a great deficiency in the sex education in the typical person writing to such a source for information.[12]

Judson T. Landis[13] finds no improvement in the number of parents giving sex education to their children among the thousands of college students studied, comparing 1967 students with 1952 students. This may in part reflect the fact that college enrollments now reach into lower status groups with the mass movement into college. But even allowing for this factor as a possible influence, there is much room for improvement.

[12] Christine H. Hillman, "An Advice Column's Challenge for Family-Life Education," *Marriage and Family Living,* 16:51–54, February, 1954.
[13] Reported in Judson and Mary Landis, *Successful Marriage,* fifth edition (Englewood Cliffs, N.J.: Prentice-Hall, Inc., 1968), pp. 516–519.

The most severe critics of sex education are to be found in communities where the training of youth in this field has not been tried. In communities where it has been tried, fears vanish, for the results are favorable. In Pittsburgh, for example, four years after a course in sex education had been instituted, pregnancies among 60,000 public and parochial school girls declined by more than one-half. In Wisconsin, where social hygiene courses have been given for twenty years, illegitimacy rates have fallen 18 percent, while they have risen 2 percent in surrounding states. Wisconsin also had the lowest syphilis rate of any state in the union among returning veterans of World War II. The divorce rate in that state, too, has shown less increase than in most other states (only three have a better record).[14] A statewide program of sex education in Oregon was introduced with favorable results.

The Oregon film experiment indicates how few are the critics of an adequate program of sex education, when community support is sought in advance. The Oregon film, developed by the Brown Trust Fund under the direction of Dr. Lester R. Beck, at the University of Oregon, deals frankly with the problem of sex in a movie aimed at school children on the sixth-grade level. This film has been shown in every kind of community in Oregon, was presented first to the parent-teacher group, where a questionnaire was handed out and reactions obtained. In communities of all kinds, less than 2 percent of the parent-teacher group criticized the film; more than 98 percent fully approved it. When the problem of sex education is approached in this manner, the superintendent or principal has evidence with which to combat the inevitable, though increasingly few, critics of innovation.

Sex education is best presented as part of a broader course in family-life education. This fits it into proper context and helps ward off community attack. Any sex education program, presented in isolation from such a context, tends to bring strong protest from a vocal minority in the community and risks causing principals and superintendents of schools to clamp down on the program.

A storm of controversy now rocks communities throughout the nation, centering about the Sex Information and Education Council of the United States (SIECUS). It is a nonprofit organization which encourages communities to institute sex education programs in schools from kindergarten to the twelfth grade. SIECUS provides study guides and resource material for professional leaders and does consultation work with teachers.

Under the name of family-life education, the program no doubt could have aroused less opposition and still attained its worthy goals, but with

---

[14] This summary of results of various programs is taken from "Effects of Education for Family Life," *Family Life*, 16:1-2, February 1, 1954. For a critical evaluation on a college marriage course, see Judson T. Landis, "An Evaluation of Marriage Education," *Marriage and Family Living*, 10:81 ff., 1948.

the label of sex education, the program has been called communistic, atheistic, and pornographic. Crusades against it even threaten family life education itself. To date, SIECUS work with medical, ministerial, and teacher groups has been highly effective.

Premarital counseling   One of the aims of professional counseling is to discover the unmarriageable person or incompatible pair before marriage. Research gives some clues here. In fact, tests of some reliability are now available for predicting the success or failure of a marriage.[15] Greater development can be expected in this field, but aside from this, counseling can be of great value in helping people understand themselves and each other prior to marriage. Objectivity at this stage, when change is easy, involves little personal and social damage.

Measurements of temperament and personality are becoming more dependable. Tests for predicting marriage outcome are based on more dependable norms. It is increasingly possible that the premarital counseling clinic can be helpful in the area of psychological and emotional relationships, in addition to the psychosexual.

Perhaps it is premature to expect that all contemplating marriage be required to submit to certain tests and examinations. Facilities are not adequate, nor is sufficient personnel available. But the goal is worth seeking. Perhaps even now all teen-age marriages for which pregnancy is the cause should have to undergo counseling and be assigned social service counsel for their beginning years. This would seem to be in the interest of protecting the child from too-immature parents.

The Remedial Approach

The remedial approach includes not only preparatory and marital counseling in clinics but also help from the minister or the family doctor, who actually do most of the counseling according to the study of Gurin, Veroff, and Field (See Table 31–1), going to relatives, and in serious cases seeking out the psychiatrist, psychologist, or lawyer for advice.

Now, when many have no close relative or friend in whom to confide, there is great need to confide and to shed burdens in the counseling situation. How many of these counseling sources are qualified to render assist-

---

[15] For a brief summary of traits found to be of predictive value in indicating the probable outcome of a marriage, see E. W. Burgess and Harvey J. Locke, *The Family*, second edition (New York: American Book Co., 1953), pp. 408–429. An earlier and more comprehensive summary is found in Clifford Kirkpatrick, *What Science Says About Happiness in Marriage* (Minneapolis: Burgess Publishing Co., 1947).

Table 31–1   Relationship of Source of Help Used to the Problem Area
(First-Mentioned Responses Only)

Source of Help

Problem Area	Clergy	Doctor	Psychia- trist	Coun- selor	Other Psycho- logical Agencies	Non- psycho- logical Agencies	Lawyer
Spouse; mar- riage							
frequency	60	32	16	11	9	1	8
percentage	43.8	23	12	8	6.5	.7	5

Source: Gerald Gurin, Joseph Veroff, and Sheila Field, *Americans View Their Mental Health* (New York: Basic Books, 1960), p. 309.

ance no one knows, and what their motive is in rendering the assistance varies with individual and by profession. But it is likely that just being able to talk with someone and to get problems out into the open brings relief.

Presumably the professional counselor is the ideal source in that he is not oriented toward a moral solution or a religious goal in his work, but toward a solution to the person's problem, but the fact remains that in most states the counseling profession is unlicensed and passes no qualifying tests. In these states anyone can put up his shingle. Those counselors belonging to the American Association of Marriage Counselors meet the standards of this professional group.[16] Most practicing marriage counselors are not members.

Psychiatrists, psychoanalysts, and clinical psychologists are trained but also highly individuated in theoretical perspective, conceptual premises, and methods of treatment. Their results are not submitted to scientific verification and are often suspect, even among more critical members of their own professions. Their services are high in cost, and there is great scarcity of personnel. For the most part they serve the affluent.

Various group methods of treatment are now in use, which helps spread the limited time available. Some methods of treating groups are also highly individualistic, being perhaps more a reflection of a particular man and his theoretical premises rather than of a proved sound method

[16] The following national agencies have information about legitimate marriage-counseling facilities in any community: American Association of Marriage Counselors, 27 Woodcliff Drive, Madison, N.J. 07940, Family Service Association of America, 44 East 23rd Street, New York, N.Y. 10010, National Council on Family Relations, 1219 University Avenue, S.E., Minneapolis, Minn. 55414. In most areas, information can also be obtained from your doctor or minister or from community organizations such as the United Fund, Community Chest, or Community Welfare Council.

of rendering permanent help to the couple in trouble. Whether they provide more than a place where one can relieve his frustrations by talking or acting is to be proven. In many instances, time may be the real healer, rather than the particular ritual through which one specialist or another leads the person or the pair in trouble. All approaches must be considered experimental.

The ministerial profession begins with a bias in the counseling approach. Ministers are apostles of the good life. This predisposes them to seek certain values in their guiding people in marital difficulties. Whether they are more inclined to save a marriage which cannot and should not be saved for sake of parents, and particularly for the sake of children, than other counselors is not known from research. Probably they lean in this direction more than, say, doctors or psychiatrists, or even bartenders, who no doubt listen to many marriage confessions and may also be generous with advice.

Doctors are more involved with physical and sexual problems of marriages, but these carry over into the psychosomatic; any doctor with experience and insight knows very often that he is dealing with problems that exceed those of the flesh. Perhaps the majority avoid giving advice beyond the physical, and provide for relief with placebos and the tranquilizers, but they do listen, even if briefly, and no doubt at times drop hints as to a wise alternative.

Dr. William M. Sheppe, Jr., Associate Professor of Psychiatry at the University of Virginia School of Medicine finds[17] doctors very inadequate in the field of sex counseling, owing to "the physician's own personality structure, his life experience, and inadequate medical curricula." He reports that in working with both doctors and clergy, the better-educated clergy are "far more knowledgeable and emotionally free in discussing human sexuality and marital problems than their medical peers."

More and better-trained marriage counselors and more strict licensing requirements are goals to be reached, but it is likely that most people are still going to the minister as the first source of help. He is a trusted source of sympathy, he is accessible, he is salaried and his services free to the parishoner, and in many instances to any who come, and there are more ministers than there can ever be professional counselors.

Ministers in the better seminaries are being given much more extensive training in counseling and related disciplines. There will continue to be the great mass without seminary training, whose qualifications for duty are "the call" and whose counseling will be authoritarian admonitions, "Thus saith the Lord."

The Ministerial Association of Prescott, Arizona, illustrates what

[17] An address before the Kentucky Medical Association reported in *Family Life*, 29:3, March, 1969.

united action in a community can do in putting bars in the way of unwise marriage and in making the pair consider the step they are taking. Here are their resolutions:[18]

1. Outright refusal to perform "doorbell" marriages (couples seeking immediate ceremony).
2. A minimum of three premarital counseling sessions with the engaged couple, reserving the right to refuse to perform the service if the first session indicates the wisdom of such a decision.
3. The minister shall secure from the engaged couple written permission to intervene voluntarily and at his own discretion if the marriage appears at some later date to be threatened with dissolution.
4. The minister shall exert the strongest possible persuasion to discourage marriage of girls under 18 and men under 21 years of age.
5. The minister shall consider with the couple and other interested parties the possibility that marriage is not necessarily the best solution to out-of-wedlock pregnancies.
   The association also agreed to arrange at least one annual school for engaged couples and to promote in every way the sanctity of marriage.

Medical training has been seriously deficient in sex education and in providing background for understanding psychosomatic complaints. It has not given a broad basic background such as is needed for either premarital counseling or remedial counseling. Conditions are improving, but the pressure for more and more technical training, and the growing body of medical knowledge, is likely to threaten this broader training. The doctor, by law, is the only professional person with whom persons must consult prior to marriage, and he is the one to whom they are certain to go after marriage.

In conclusion, the tendency of young people, particularly college-trained young people, to be more realistic about the whole matter of mate selection and marriage is a most hopeful sign for the future. The fact that young people today are interested in studying marriage, serious about its purpose, and concerned about its outcome, is salutary.

Those who enter marriage with serious purpose and who put the success of marriage above numerous petty difficulties and adjustments have already risen above the factors that defeat most marriages. One hope of marriage education is that it will help young people to defer marriage until they believe they are adult enough to assume its responsibilities and assume them finally and without question—that they will put the success of the marriage above everything else and, in so doing, not be detracted from its ultimate purpose by petty difficulties, emotional upsets, and temporary sexual tensions. When young people enter marriage with a determination to work out a way of life together, they are well on the road to success.

[18] *Family Life,* "Clergymen Act," 28:5, July, 1968.

Problems

1. List and discuss various attitudes and skills which might be taught to young people in courses in family-life education.
2. Which goals do you believe should be uppermost in such courses—teaching specific homemaking skills or developing specific homemaking and family-oriented attitudes?
3. At what grade level do you believe sex education should begin in school?
4. What are the chief arguments presented by some parents in opposition to sex education at any level in public schools? How might these arguments best be met?
5. Ideally, should sex education be handled chiefly by the home or the school? Why?
6. Discuss the views presented in the following conversation.

    One mother, "I'm opposed to sex education in or out of school. I believe that young men and women should be given the necessary facts when they're old enough to need them, not before." She adds, "All of this fuss about children being 'naturally curious' is just poppycock. Why my eleven-year-old daughter has never once asked a question having to do with sex, reproduction, or the like."

    Her companion answers, "If I had an eleven-year-old daughter who hadn't asked about anything associated with sex, I would not brag, I'd be alarmed."
7. A respected marriage counselor in a New York community was recently sued for a divorce. As a result he lost many of his clients who seemed to feel, as one woman put it, "If he can't make a success of his own marriage, how can others have faith in him?" Among those who remained with him was a young husband who answered this charge with, "My physician is often sick, but this does not reflect upon his professional skill."

    What would your reaction have been to this divorce had you been a client? Justify your position.
8. In the West Haven Marriage and Family Relations Clinic there are two marriage counselors using very different techniques in their counseling. Of the two, Dr. Robell is the more popular. He is generous with his advice and not at all reluctant to suggest specific action as a cure for a couple's problems.

    Dr. Murry seldom gives advice. His chief goal seems to be getting man and wife, or an engaged couple, into the clinic together. Once there, Dr. Murry speaks only enough to keep the two of them going in their conversation together about their differences.

    a. Upon what principle is Dr. Murry operating?
    b. Why is Dr. Robell more popular?
    c. Which counselor do you believe is the more successful in helping couples work out solutions to their problems?
9. Which of the areas of legal action do you think is the most promising as a way to improve marriage?
10. Debate: *Resolved:* That the United States should adopt the family allowance.

Selected References

Articles in Books of Readings

Cavan, Ruth S., *Marriage and the Family in the Modern World: A Book of Readings*, third edition (New York: Thomas Y. Crowell Co., 1969).
> Beck, Dorothy Fahs, "Marital Conflict: Its Course and Treatment as Seen by Caseworkers," Reading 62.
> Cavan, Ruth S., "Legal Regulation of Marriage," Reading 33.
> Women's Bureau of the U.S. Department of Labor, "Marriage and Divorce Laws," Reading 34.

Christensen, Harold T., *Handbook of Marriage and the Family* (Chicago: Rand McNally & Co., 1964).
> Brown, Muriel C., "Organizational Programs to Strengthen the Family," Ch. 20.
> Kerckhoff, Richard K., "Family Life Education in America," Ch. 21.
> Leslie, Gerald R., "The Field of Marriage Counseling," Ch. 22.
> Kephart, William M., "Legal and Procedural Aspects of Marriage and Divorce," Ch. 23.
> Christensen, Harold T., "The Intrusion of Values," Ch. 24.

Landis, Judson T., and Landis, Mary G., *Readings in Marriage and the Family* (Englewood Cliffs, N.J.: Prentice-Hall, Inc., 1952).
> Mudd, Emily Hartshorne, and Preston, Malcolm C., "The Contemporary Status of Marriage Counseling," pp. 439–445.
> Cottrell, Leonard S., "The Present Status and Future Orientation of Research on the Family," pp. 445–453.

Sussman, Marvin B., *Sourcebook in Marriage and the Family*, third edition (Boston: Houghton Mifflin Co., 1968).
> Cottrell, Leonard S., "New Directions for Research on the American Family," Reading 61.
> Pollak, Otto, "The Outlook for the American Family," Reading 62.

Vincent, Clark E., *Readings in Marriage Counseling* (New York: Thomas Y. Crowell Co., 1957).
> Stone, Abraham, "Marriage Education and Marriage Counseling in the United States," pp. 12–19.
> Bowman, Henry A., "Collegiate Education for Marriage and Family Living," pp. 19–29.
> Mace, David R., "What Is a Marriage Counselor?" pp. 29–35.

General References

Boyer, Clayton L., "Group Therapy with Married Couples," *Marriage and Family Living*, 22:21–24, February, 1960.

Burns, Evelin M., ed., *Children's Allowances and the Economic Welfare of Children* (New York: Citizens Committee for Children of New York, Inc., 1968).

Child Study Association of America, *What to Tell Your Child about Sex?* (New York: Pocket Books, Inc., 1968).

Cuber, John F., *Marriage Counseling Practice* (New York: Appleton-Century-Crofts, 1948).

Dager, Edward Z., Harper, Glenn A., and Whitehurst, Robert N., "Family Life Education in Public High Schools: A Survey in Indiana," *Marriage and Family Living*, 24:365–370, November, 1962.

Emery, Alan E. H., *Hereditary Disease and Man* (Berkeley: University of California Press, 1968).

Glazer, Nathan, "Housing Policy and the Family," *Journal of Marriage and the Family*, 29:1–17, February, 1967.

Heredity and Marriage Counseling (Los Angeles: American Institute of Family Relations), a pamphlet.

Hine, James R., *Religious Beliefs Inventory Kit* (Danville, Ill.: Interstate Printers, 1968).

Israel, S. Leon, and Nemser, Sondra, "Family-Counseling Role of the Physician," *Journal of Marriage and the Family,* 30:311–316, May, 1968.

Jaff, Frederick S., and Folgar, Stevan, "Family Planning and Public Policy: Is the Culture of Poverty the New Cop-Out?" *Journal of Marriage and the Family*, 30:228–235, May, 1968.

Johnson, Kathryn P., "Self-Concept Validation as a Focus of Marriage Counseling," *The Family Coordinator*, 17:174–180, July, 1968.

Kirkendall, Lester A., and Cox, Helen M., "Starting a Sex Education Program," *Children*, .14:136–140, August, 1967.

Kirkpatrick, Clifford, *The Family as Process and Institution*, revised edition (New York: The Ronald Press Co., 1963), Ch. 23.

Landman, Lynn, "United States, Underdeveloped Land in Family Planning," *Journal of Marriage and the Family,* 30:191–201, May, 1968.

Linner, Birgitta, *Sex and Society in Sweden* (New York: Pantheon Books, 1967).

Luckey, Elenore Braun, "Sex Education, and an In-Service Training Program," *The Family Coordinator*, 17:89–95, April, 1968.

Mace, David R., "What Is a Marriage Counselor?" *Marriage and Family Living*, 16:135–138, 1954.

Madison, B., "Canadian Family Allowances and Their Major Social Implications," *Journal of Marriage and the Family*, 26:134–141, May, 1964.

Malfettic, James L., and Rubin, Arline M., "Sex Education: Who Is Teaching the Teachers?" *The Family Coordinator*, 17:110–117, April, 1968.

Moses, Virginia Musick, "A Study of Learning Derived from a Functional Course in Marriage and Family Relationships," *Marriage and Family Living,* 18:204–208, August, 1956.

Myrdal, Alva, *Nation and Family* (New York: Harper and Bros., 1941).

Oliver, C. R., Jr., "Ministers and Marriage Counseling," *Family Life*, 28:1–2, July, 1968.

Olson, David H. and Cravatt, Arthur E., "Attitude Change in a Functional Marriage Course," *The Family Coordinator*, 17:99–104, April, 1968.

Peterson, James A., ed., *Marriage and Family Counseling: Perspective and Prospect* (New York: Association Press, 1968).

Phillips, Clinton E., *Marriage Counselors and Marriage Counseling* (Los Angeles: American Institute of Family Relations), a pamphlet.

Phillips, Clinton E., "Some Considerations for the Newlyweds," *Family Life,* 28:4–6, December, 1968.

Poffenberger, Thomas, "Family Life Education in a Scientific Age," *Marriage and Family Living*, 21:150–154, May, 1959.

Pollak, Otto, "The Outlook for the American Family," *Journal of Marriage and the Family*, 29:193–205, February, 1967.

Rosenberg, Bernard, and Bensman, Joseph, "Sexual Patterns in Three Ethnic Subcultures of an American Underclass," *The Annals*, 376:61–75, March, 1968.

Schwartzberg, Bernard, and Hammer, Edna, "Joint Interview Sessions With Adolescent Girls and Their Mothers as a Family Treatment Tool," *The Family Coordinator*, 17:75–77, April, 1968.

Shipman, Gordon, "Proposal for Revising Marriage License Procedures," *Journal of Marriage and the Family*, 27:281–284, May, 1965.

Shipman, Gordon, "The Psychodynamics of Sex Education," *The Family Coordinator*, 17:3–12, January, 1968.

Shipman, Gordon, and Tien, H. Yuan, "Nonmarriage and the Waiting Period," *Journal of Marriage and the Family*, 27:277–280, May, 1965.

Sparks, Geraldine M., "Parental Involvement in Family Therapy," *Journal of Marriage and the Family*, 30:112 ff., February, 1968.

Turner, Bernadette F., "Common Characteristics of Persons Seeking Professional Marriage Counseling," *Marriage and Family Living*, 16:143–144, 1954.

Vadakin, James C., *Children, Poverty, and Family Allowances* (New York: Basic Books, Inc., Publishers, 1968).

Vincent, Clarke E., "Mental Health and the Family," *Journal of Marriage and the Family*, 299:18–39, February, 1967.

APPENDIX

AUTOBIOGRAPHICAL TERM PAPER

On each topic trace your background, and show how each trait or characteristic is likely to affect you as a marriage partner and parent.

I. Love

A. Affection: Can you give and receive affection? Is love or hostility the dominant trait of your personality? Relate to family background. Relate to marriageability and parenthood.
B. Romantic love: (1) On separate sheets of paper, chart your completed love affairs; love, attraction, indifference, dislike (page 193 of text for pattern). . . .
(2) Chart course of your emotions after breakup of love affair using the same curve—love, attraction, indifference, dislike (text page 193). . . .

II. Work Duty Patterns

What is your balance between work and pleasure? Can you pursue goals to their conclusion? Are you willing to assume the obligations of caring for others, particularly children? Is your orientation primarily toward consumption or production; acquiring goods or display? Relate to the past and the future.

III. Psychological Patterns

A. Ego needs: Are you essentially ego-centered or love-centered? Why?
B. Basic emotions: What is your dominant emotion, love, hate, fear, anxiety, etc.? Completing statements like the following will be helpful, "I hate most deeply"; "I fear most deeply"; "I am most anxious about"; etc.
C. Approach: Is your approach to people and to life essentially negative or positive?
D. Psychosexual orientation: Here consider the physical, psychological, and moral orientation of your personality. Is your personality in this area primarily guilt-centered, pleasure-centered, love-centered? Are your attitudes those of disgust or wholesome anticipation?

IV.   Life Goals

Dominant aspirations: What do you want most in life? Wealth? Happiness? Learning? What influences built this goal? How will it affect your mate choice and the development of your family life?

V.   Role Orientation

Male and female grow up under different subcultures. Do you accept the role of your sex or protest it? What do you expect in the way of behavior of the person you marry? Do you anticipate a role of equality or the traditional male-female pattern of roles? Can you readily compromise your role expectations for a member of the opposite sex whom you expect to marry? If you are already engaged, what role changes do you expect of your future spouse?

VI.   Sibling Position

What is your place among brothers and sisters? How has this affected your personality as it relates to your marriageability? If an only child, how has this affected your adjustments to the opposite sex?

VII.   Conventionality

Are you a rebel or an easily institutionalized person? Do you regard conventions of marriage important? Does marriage make sense in the obligations and vows it imposes? Do you want children in marriage? Do you consider a similar religion important to your marriage? Were there family ceremonial occasions in your parental family you plan to reproduce in your family?

Specifications:

1. Paper should range between 2,000 and 5,000 words.
2. Place name on a face sheet, which will be keyed and removed before papers are read to assure anonymity.
3. Papers will be held in complete confidence for two years when the file will be available to marriage classes.

Author Index

Subject Index